W9-DFD-381

MODERN
Elementary Statistics

PRENTICE-HALL MATHEMATICS SERIES

MODERN
Elementary Statistics

third edition

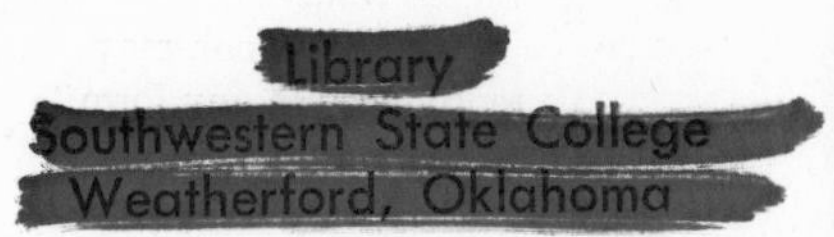

JOHN E. FREUND

Professor of Mathematics
Arizona State University

PRENTICE-HALL, INC., ENGLEWOOD CLIFFS, N.J

Library of Congress
Catalog Card Number: 66–29560

Current printing (last digit) 10 9 8 7 6 5 4 3 2 1

PRINTED IN THE UNITED STATES OF AMERICA

C–59340

PREFACE

Although *Modern Elementary Statistics* has been rewritten almost completely in this third edition, its objectives have remained the same: to acquaint beginning students in the biological, social, and physical sciences with the fundamentals of modern statistics. Most of the illustrations and exercises are new; as in previous editions, they are distributed over many different fields of application.

In line with current thought, there is increased emphasis on statistical inference. The material has been rearranged so that there are now separate chapters on inferences concerning means, inferences concerning proportions, etc., rather than separate chapters on problems of estimation and on tests of hypotheses. Also, there is added material on nonparametric tests, analysis of variance, regression analysis, and inferences concerning standard deviations.

The chapter on probability has been rewritten completely and it now presents the popular *set-oriented* approach. It also contains a discussion of *personal probability* (in Sections 5.4, 5.5, and also in Section 6.1). Generally speaking, there is more emphasis on decision making, including a brief introduction to the *theory of games* (Section 6.3) and *Bayesian decision making* (in Section 7.2); there is also new material on *simulation*. *Bayesian inference* is introduced in two places (Sections 9.4 and 11.2). In connection with these two sections, it should be observed that they serve to illustrate what is meant by the prior distribution of a parameter, and also to demonstrate one of the concrete things a Bayesian inference can accomplish, namely, combine direct sample evidence with collateral (objective or subjective) information. In more advanced terms, the estimators of these two sections may be referred to as *best linear Bayesian estimators for quadratic loss functions.*

In view of the increased emphasis on statistical inference, the material on purely descriptive methods has been diminished to some extent. In particular, the chapters on index numbers and time series have been omitted, although some material on these subjects is included among the exercises of Chapters 3 and 14.

Mathematical proofs and derivations are still keyed to the lowest level at which, in the opinion of the author, modern statistics can effectively be taught. Since the mathematical training assumed of the reader is a knowledge of arithmetic and some algebra, many theorems (for example, those relating to sampling distributions) are given without proof but with suitable references in annotated bibliographies.

The author would like to express his appreciation to his many colleagues and students whose helpful suggestions and criticisms contributed to previous editions of this text as well as to this third edition. In particular, he would like to thank his friend and colleague Professor Frank J. Williams for use of his bottomless bag of good exercise material, and Miss Pat McGrath for checking the answers to the exercises. The author would also like to express his appreciation to the editorial staff of Prentice-Hall, Inc., for their courteous cooperation in the production of this book and, above all, to his wife for her cheerful encouragement in spite of the demands made by this project on her husband's time.

Finally, the author is indebted to the Literary Executor of the late Sir Ronald Fisher, F.R.S., Cambridge, to Dr. Frank Yates, F.R.S., Rothamsted, and also to Oliver and Boyd, Edinburgh, for permission to reprint parts of Tables IV and VI, respectively, from their books *Statistical Methods for Research Workers* and *Statistical Tables for Biological, Agricultural, and Medical Research;* and to Professor E. S. Pearson and the Biometrika trustees for permission to reproduce Tables 8, 18, and 41 from their *Biometrika Tables for Statisticians.*

JOHN E. FREUND

CONTENTS

PART II. BASIC THEORY

PART III. STATISTICAL INFERENCE

FIFTEEN Correlation

Statistical Tables

Answers to Odd-Numbered Exercises

Index

MODERN
Elementary Statistics

ONE
Introduction

1.1 Modern Statistics

Students in the natural and social sciences often face the study of statistics with mixed emotions; they realize that advanced work in their fields requires some understanding of statistics, but they may also remember some of the difficulties they have experienced previously in the study of mathematics. They are correct on both counts: statistics *is* a branch of applied mathematics, and the claim that an understanding of statistics is needed in the study of science is not an exaggeration. In fact, the growth of statistics has been such in recent years that it has made itself felt in almost every phase of human activity. Statistics no longer consists merely of the collection and presentation of data in tables and charts; it encompasses—indeed, it constitutes—the science of decision making in the face of uncertainty, and we meet uncertainties when we toss a coin, when we experiment with a new drug, when we try to predict an election or the outcome of a game, when we dig for oil, when we decide which of two production processes is more efficient, and so on. It would be presumptuous to say that statistics, in its present state of development, can handle *all* situations involving uncertainties and risks, but new methods are constantly being developed and it can be said that modern statistics, at least, provides the framework for looking at these situations in a logical and systematic way.

There can be no doubt that it is virtually impossible to understand a good part of the work done in the natural and social sciences without having at least a speaking acquaintance with the subject of statistics. Numerical data derived from surveys and experiments constitute the raw material on which interpretations, analyses, and decisions are based, and it is essential to know how to squeeze usable information from such data. This, in fact, is the major objective of statistics.

Numerous textbooks have been written on educational statistics, business statistics, psychological statistics, medical statistics, and so forth, and it is true, of course, that these various fields of scientific inquiry demand somewhat different and specialized techniques. Nevertheless, the fundamental principles underlying these techniques are the same regardless of the field of application, and it is hoped that this will become apparent to the reader once he realizes that *statistical concepts and statistical methods are really nothing but a refinement of everyday thinking.*

The approach we shall use in this elementary text is, indeed, keynoted by the above statement. It is our goal to introduce the reader to the ideas and concepts that are basic to modern statistics, and we hope that this, in turn, will enable him to gain a better understanding of scientific principles in general and a clearer picture of the scope and limitations of scientific knowledge.

As we said earlier, the study of statistics may be directed toward applications in various fields of inquiry; furthermore, the subject may be presented in many different degrees of mathematical difficulty and in almost any balance between theory and application. As it is more important, in our opinion, to understand the meaning and implications of basic ideas than it is to memorize an impressive list of formulas, we shall sacrifice some of the details that are sometimes included in introductory courses in statistics. This may be unfortunate in some respects, but it will prevent us from getting lost in an excessive amount of detail which could easily obscure the more important issues. It is hoped that this will avoid some of the unfortunate consequences which often result from the indiscriminate application of so-called standard techniques without a thorough understanding of the basic ideas that are involved.

It cannot be denied that a limited amount of mathematics is a prerequisite for any course in statistics, and that a thorough study of the theoretical principles of statistics would require a knowledge of mathematical subjects taught ordinarily only on the graduate level. Since this book is designed for students with relatively little background in mathematics, our aims, and, therefore, also our prerequisites are considerably more modest. Actually, the mathematical background needed for this study of statistics is amply covered in a course in college algebra; in fact, even a good knowledge of high school algebra provides a sufficient foundation.

1.2 Descriptive Statistics

Everything dealing even remotely with the collection, processing, analysis, interpretation, and presentation of numerical data belongs to the domain of statistics. This includes such diversified tasks as calculating a baseball player's batting average, the collection and presentation of data on marriages and divorces, the evaluation of the reliability of missile components, and even the study of laws governing the behavior of neutrons and electrons. The word "statistics" itself is used in a variety of ways. In the plural it denotes a collection of numerical data such as those found in the financial pages of newspapers or, say, the *Statistical Abstract of the United States*, published each year by the Department of Commerce. A second meaning of "statistics," also in the plural, is that of the totality of methods employed in the collection, processing, analyzing, etc., of any kind of data; in this sense, statistics is a branch of applied mathematics, and it is this field of mathematics which is the subject matter of this book. To complete our linguistic analysis of "statistics," let us also mention that the word "statistic," in the singular, is used to denote a numerical description (such as an average, an index number, or a correlation coefficient) calculated on the basis of sample data.

The origin of statistics may be traced to two areas of interest which are very dissimilar: *games of chance* and what we now call *political science*. Mid-eighteenth century studies in probability (motivated in part by interest in games of chance) led to the mathematical treatment of errors of measurement and the theory which now forms the foundation of statistics. In the same century, interest in the description and analysis of political units led to the development of methods which nowadays come under the heading of *descriptive statistics*. This includes any treatment designed to summarize, or describe, important features of a set of data *without going any further;* that is, without attempting to infer anything that goes beyond the data, themselves. Thus, if someone compiles the necessary data and reports that 5.6 million persons visited Disneyland in 1963 and that they spent 33.0 million dollars, his work belongs to the domain of descriptive statistics. This is true also if he determines the average amount a person spent that year on a visit to Disneyland, namely, $5.89, but *not* if he uses the data to predict future attendance, to estimate future sales, or to make other kinds of predictions.

1.3 Statistical Inference

Although descriptive statistics is an important branch of statistics and it continues to be widely used, statistical information usually arises from samples (from observations made on only part of a large set of items), and this means that its analysis will require generalizations which go beyond the data. As a result, the most important feature of the recent growth of statistics has been a shift in emphasis from methods which merely describe to methods which serve to make generalizations; that is, a shift in emphasis from descriptive statistics to the methods of *statistical inference*, or *inductive statistics*. To mention but a few examples, the methods of statistical inference are required to predict the operating lifespan of an experimental rocket, to estimate the 1969–1970 assessed value of all property in Montgomery County, Virginia, to compare the effectiveness of two teaching machines, or to decide upon an appropriate dosage of an antibiotic.

To clarify the distinction between descriptive statistics and statistical inference by means of a numerical example, let us suppose that two students, Henry and George, have taken three tests in a certain subject and that Henry received grades of 63, 41, and 55, while George received 60, 58, and 59. On the basis of this information we can say that Henry had an *average* of $\frac{1}{3}(63 + 41 + 55) = 53$ and that George had an *average* of $\frac{1}{3}(60 + 58 + 59) = 59$. What we have done with these numbers belongs to the domain of *descriptive statistics;* we followed simple arithmetical rules in calculating the two averages which are, indeed, descriptive of the two sets of grades. However, if we now conclude on the basis of these averages that George is the better student, we are making a generalization, that is, a *statistical inference.* So long as we restricted ourselves to the calculation of the two averages, we did not add anything to the given information, we merely arranged it in a different and possibly more useful form. *This is characteristic of descriptive statistics.* However, as soon as we generalized by saying that George is the better student (which is more than saying that he had a higher average), we are making a statistical inference. It does not follow by any means that George is necessarily the better student. Henry might have had an off day when he took the second test, he might have been ill, or George might have been plain lucky in studying the right material for the test or in guessing some of the answers. Thus, we face uncertainties, and if we say that George is the better student we may or may not be correct. The careful evaluation, analysis, and control of the chances and risks that must be taken when making such generalizations (or decisions) is one of the main tasks of statistical inference.

Giving some more thought to this example, there are many questions that immediately come to one's mind. For instance, if the difference between the two averages had been very large, say, if Henry had averaged 23 and George 95, we might have been inclined to say that George is the better student without going through much of a statistical analysis. If the difference had been very small, say, if Henry had averaged 58 and George 59, we probably would have been extremely reluctant to say that George is actually a better student. *But what if the difference on which the decision has to be based is neither "very large" nor "very small"—where do we draw the line?* Also, how do we know that 3 test scores for each student provide enough information to reach any conclusion whatsoever? Would it not have been better, or necessary, to give them 5 tests or perhaps 10? These are important questions, the kind we shall be able to answer at least partially with the methods of statistical inference.

There is another point which is extremely important whenever we want to make generalizations like the one concerning the ability of the two students; *we must ask ourselves whether the data were obtained in such a way (the survey or experiment conducted in such a way) that generalizations are at all possible.* For instance, if George had been told what books to study for the tests and Henry had not, it is obvious that no reasonable, or meaningful, comparison can be made.

We mentioned this last point to stress the fact that in statistics we do not merely concern ourselves with looking at sets of data, performing certain calculations, and arriving at conclusions. The questions *how the data were collected* and *how the whole experiment or survey was planned* are of major importance. Indeed, unless proper care is taken in the planning of experiments, surveys, or other kinds of investigations, it may be impossible to arrive at any valid results whatsoever.

BIBLIOGRAPHY

A brief and informal discussion of *what statistics is* and *what statisticians do* may be found in a pamphlet titled *Careers in Statistics,* 2nd ed., published by the American Statistical Association in 1964.

PART ONE
Descriptive Methods

TWO
Frequency Distributions

2.1 Introduction

Grouping, classifying, and thus describing measurements and observations is as basic in statistics as it is in science and in many activities of everyday life. To illustrate its importance in statistics, let us consider the problem of an economist who wants to study before-tax income of families and unattached individuals in the United States. Not even giving a thought to the possibility of conducting a survey of his own—the expense would be staggering—he immediately turns to one of the many organizations that specialize in the gathering of statistical data, namely, the U.S. Department of Commerce. This department not only provides government agencies with statistical data needed for over-all planning and day-by-day operations, but it also makes this information available to businessmen and research workers in various fields. Like other organizations engaged in gathering statistical data, it thus faces the problem of *how to present* the results of its surveys in the most effective and the most usable form. With reference to the information needed by the above-mentioned economist, the Department of Commerce *could* print sheets containing millions of numbers, the actual incomes reported by individual families; it is needless to say, however, that this would not be very effective and, without some treatment, not very "usable."

When dealing with large sets of numbers, a good over-all picture and sufficient information can often be conveyed by grouping the data into a number of classes, and the Department of Commerce could, and in fact does, publish its data on family income in tables like the following for the year 1960:

Before-Tax Income (dollars)	*Number of Families and Unattached Individuals* (thousands)
under 2,000	7,213
2,000 – 2,999	5,083
3,000 – 3,999	5,926
4,000 – 4,999	6,327
5,000 – 5,999	6,005
6,000 – 7,499	8,007
7,500 – 9,999	8,238
10,000 – 14,999	5,833
15,000 and over	3,428
Total	56,060

This kind of table is called a *frequency distribution* (or simply a *distribution*): it shows the frequencies with which the various incomes are distributed among the chosen classes. Tables of this sort, in which the data are grouped according to numerical size, are called *numerical* or *quantitative* distributions. In contrast, tables like the one given below, in which the data are sorted according to certain categories, are called *categorical* or *qualitative* distributions:

	Number of Persons Employed by Domestic Air Carriers in 1961
Pilots and copilots	11,741
Other flight personnel	3,334
Pursers, stewards, stewardesses	9,926
Meteorologists and dispatchers	2,728
Mechanics	28,360
Other hangar and field personnel	36,120
Office employees	28,885
All others	15,893
Total	136,987

Although frequency distributions present data in a relatively compact form, give a good over-all picture, and contain information which is adequate for many purposes, there are evidently some things which can be obtained from the original data that cannot be obtained from a distribution. For instance, referring to the first of the above tables, we cannot find the exact size of the highest or lowest incomes, nor can we find the exact average income of the 7,213 families in the lowest group. Nevertheless, frequency distributions present *raw* (unprocessed) data on which they are based in a more usable form, and the price which we must pay, the loss of certain information, is usually a fair exchange.

Data are sometimes grouped solely to facilitate the calculation of further statistical descriptions. We shall go into this briefly in Chapters 3 and 4, but it is worth noting that this function of frequency distributions is diminishing in importance in view of the ever-increasing availability of high-speed computing equipment.

2.2 Frequency Distributions

The construction of a numerical distribution consists essentially of three steps: (1) we must choose the classes into which the data are to be grouped, (2) we must sort (or tally) the data into the appropriate classes, and (3) we must count the number of items in each class. Since the last two of these steps are purely mechanical, we shall concentrate on the first, namely, the problem of choosing suitable classifications. Note that if the data are recorded on punch-cards or tape, methods that are nowadays widely used, the sorting and counting can be done automatically in a single step.

The two things we shall have to consider in the first step are those of determining the *number of classes* into which the data are to be grouped and the *range of values* each class is to cover, that is, "from where to where" each class is to go. Both of these choices are largely arbitrary, but they depend to some extent on the nature of the data and on the ultimate purpose the distribution is to serve. The following are some rules which are generally observed:

(a) *We seldom use fewer than 6 or more than 15 classes.* This rule reflects sound practice based on experience; in any given example, the actual choice will have to depend on the number of observations we want to group (we would hardly group 5 observations into 12 classes), and on their range.

(b) *We always choose classes which will accommodate all the data.* To this end we must make sure that the smallest and largest values fall within the classification, and that none of the values can fall into possible gaps between successive classes.

(c) *We always make sure that each item goes into only one class.* In other words, we must avoid successive classes which overlap, that is, successive classes having one or more values in common.

(d) *Whenever possible, we make the class intervals of equal length, that is, we make them cover equal ranges of values.* It is generally desirable to make these ranges (intervals) multiples of 5, 10, 100, etc., or other numbers that are easy to work with, to facilitate the tally (perhaps, mechanically) and the ultimate use of the table.

Note that the first three, but not the fourth, of these rules were observed in the construction of the income distribution on page 10, assuming that the figures were rounded to the nearest dollar. (Had these figures been given to the nearest cent, an income of, say, $2,999.45 could not have been accommodated, as it would have fallen between the second class and the third.) The fourth rule was violated in two ways: first, the intervals from $6,000 to $7,499, from $7,500 to $9,999, and from $10,000 to $14,999 cover considerably wider ranges of values than those of the second, third, fourth, and fifth classes of the distribution. Secondly, the first and last classes are *open;* for all we know, the first class might include a negative value indicating a deficit or a loss, and the last class might include incomes of a million dollars or more. If a set of data contains a few values that are much greater (or much smaller) than the rest, open classes can help to simplify the overall picture by reducing the number of required classes; otherwise, open classes should be avoided as they can make it impossible (or at least difficult) to give further descriptions of the data.

As we have pointed out in the preceding paragraph, the appropriateness of a classification may depend on whether the data are rounded to the nearest dollar or to the nearest cent. Similarly, it may depend on whether data are given to the nearest inch, tenth of an inch, or hundredth of an inch, whether they are given to the nearest per cent or to the nearest tenth of a per cent, and so on. Thus, if we wanted to group heights measured to the nearest tenth of an inch, we might use the classification

Height (inches)
20.0 – 29.9
30.0 – 39.9
40.0 – 49.9
50.0 – 59.9
etc.

and if we wanted to group the sizes of orders received by a mail-order house, we might use the classification

Size of Order (dollars)
5.00 – 9.99
10.00 – 14.99
15.00 – 19.99
20.00 – 24.99
etc.

Similarly, for the number of empty seats on hourly flights between Los Angeles and San Francisco we might use the classification

Number of Empty Seats
0 – 4
5 – 9
10 – 14
15 – 19
etc.

Note that in each of these examples the nature of the data is such that a value can fall into one and only one class.

To give a concrete illustration of the construction of a frequency distribution, let us consider the following data representing the readings obtained with a Geiger counter of the number of particles emitted by a radioactive substance in 100 successive 40-second intervals:

23	20	16	18	30	22	26	15	13	18
14	17	11	37	21	16	10	20	22	25
19	19	19	20	12	23	24	17	18	16
27	16	28	26	15	29	19	28	20	17
12	24	21	22	20	15	18	16	23	24
15	24	28	19	24	22	17	19	8	18
17	18	23	21	25	19	20	22	21	21
16	20	19	11	23	17	23	13	17	26
26	14	15	16	27	18	21	24	33	20
21	27	18	22	17	20	14	21	22	19

Since the smallest of these values is 8 and the largest is 37, it would seem reasonable (for most practical purposes) to choose the *seven* classes going from 5 to 9, from 10 to 14, . . ., and from 35 to 39. Performing the actual tally and counting the number of values falling into each class, we obtain the results shown in the following table:

Number of Particles	*Tally*	*Frequency*
5 – 9	/	**1**
10 – 14	⫽⫽ ⫽⫽	**10**
15 – 19	⫽⫽ ⫽⫽ ⫽⫽ ⫽⫽ ⫽⫽ ⫽⫽ ⫽⫽ //	**37**
20 – 24	⫽⫽ ⫽⫽ ⫽⫽ ⫽⫽ ⫽⫽ ⫽⫽ ⫽⫽ /	**36**
25 – 29	⫽⫽ ⫽⫽ ///	**13**
30 – 34	//	**2**
35 – 39	/	**1**
	Total	**100**

The numbers shown in the right-hand column of this table are called the *class frequencies;* they give the number of items falling into each class. Also, the smallest and the largest values that can go into any given class are referred to as its *class limits;* thus, the class limits of the above table are 5 and 9, 10 and 14, 15 and 19, and so on. More specifically, 5, 10, 15, . . ., and 35 are referred to as the *lower class limits,* while 9, 14, 19, . . ., and 39 are referred to as the *upper class limits* of the respective classes.

If we are dealing with figures rounded to the nearest dollar, as in the income distribution on page 10, the class which has the limits $2,000 and $2,999 actually contains all values between $1,999.50 and $2,999.50. Similarly, if we are dealing with measurements rounded to the nearest tenth of an inch, as in the distribution on page 12, the class which has the limits 30.0 and 39.9 actually contains all values between 29.95 and 39.95. It is customary to refer to these dividing lines between successive classes as the *class boundaries,* although they have also been referred to as *"real" class limits.* We also speak of *upper and lower class boundaries,* but of course the upper boundary of one class is the lower boundary of the next. In order to make this concept apply also to the classes which are at the two extremes of a distribution, we simply act as if the table were continued in both directions. Thus, the first class of the radiation-count distribution has a lower boundary of 4.5, while the last class has an upper boundary of 39.5. Had there actually been radiation counts less than 5, we would have needed the class 0–4, and the boundaries of this class are -0.5 and 4.5.

It is important to remember that class boundaries should always be "impossible" values; that is, numbers which cannot occur among the values we want to group. We make sure of this by accounting for the extent to which the numbers are rounded when we choose the class limits of a distribution. For instance, the class boundaries of the size-of-order distribution on page 12 are $4.995, $9.995, $14.995, and so on. Similarly, the class boundaries of our radiation-count distribution are 4.5, 9.5, 14.5, . . ., whereas the figures, themselves, are of course whole numbers.

Two other terms used in connection with frequency distributions are "class mark" and "class interval." A *class mark* is simply the midpoint of a class, and it is obtained by averaging the class limits (or boundaries), that is, by adding the class limits (or boundaries) and dividing by 2. Thus, the class marks of the radiation-count distribution are 7, 12, 17, . . ., 32, and 37, while those of the size-of-order distribution on page 12 are 7.495, 12.495, 17.495, and so on. A *class interval* is merely the length of a class (the range of values it can contain), and it is given by the difference between the class boundaries. If the classes of a distribution are all equal in length, their common class interval is also given by the difference between any two successive class marks. Thus, the radiation-count distribution has class intervals of length 5, or as it is customary to say, it has a class interval of 5. Note that the class interval is *not* given by the difference between the respective upper and lower class limits, which in our example would equal 4, and not 5.

Suppose now that the person who collected the data used in our example is interested in showing how often the radiation count fell below various levels. To accomplish this he has only to convert the distribution on page 13 into what is called a *cumulative frequency distribution* or simply a *cumulative distribution.* Successively adding the frequencies in the table, this leads to the following *"less than" distribution:*

Number of Particles	*Cumulative Frequencies*
less than 5	0
less than 10	1
less than 15	11
less than 20	48
less than 25	84
less than 30	97
less than 35	99
less than 40	100

Note that in this table we could just as well have written "4 or less" instead of "less than 5," "9 or less" instead of "less than 10," . . . , and "39 or less" instead of "less than 40."

If we successively add the frequencies starting at the other end of the distribution, we can similarly construct a *cumulative "or more" distribution* (or a *cumulative "more than" distribution*), which shows how many of the counts were "5 or more" (or "more than 4"), "10 or more" (or "more than 9"), and so on.

Sometimes it is preferable to show what *percentage* of the items falls into each class, or what *percentage* of the items falls above or below various values. To convert a frequency distribution (or a cumulative distribution) into a corresponding *percentage distribution,* we have only to divide each class frequency (or each cumulative frequency) by the total number of items grouped and multiply by 100. This would be trivial in our radiation-count example where we actually grouped 100 items; however, referring to the income distribution on page 10, it might be preferable to indicate that the first class contains 7,213/56,060 = 0.129, or 12.9 per cent of the families, the second class contains 5,083/56,060 = 0.091, or 9.1 per cent of the families, and so on. *Percentage distributions are particularly useful when we want to compare two or more sets of data.* Thus, it may well be more informative to say that the percentage of students failing in two classes of size 50 and 400 is, respectively, 24 per cent and 9 per cent, than to say that the number of failures is, respectively, 12 and 36.

So far we have discussed only numerical distributions, but the general problem of constructing categorical (or qualitative) distributions is very much the same. Again we must decide how many classes (categories) to use and what kind of items each category is to contain, making sure that all of the items are accommodated and that there are no ambiguities. Since the categories must often be selected before any data are actually obtained, sound practice is to include a category labeled "others." This was done in the illustration on page 10.

When dealing with categorical distributions we do not have to worry about such mathematical details as class limits, class boundaries, class marks, etc.; on the other hand, we now have a more serious problem with ambiguities, and we must be careful and explicit in defining what each category is to contain. For instance, if we tried to classify items sold at a supermarket into "meats," "frozen foods," "baked goods," and so on, it would be difficult to decide where to put, for example, frozen hamburger steaks.

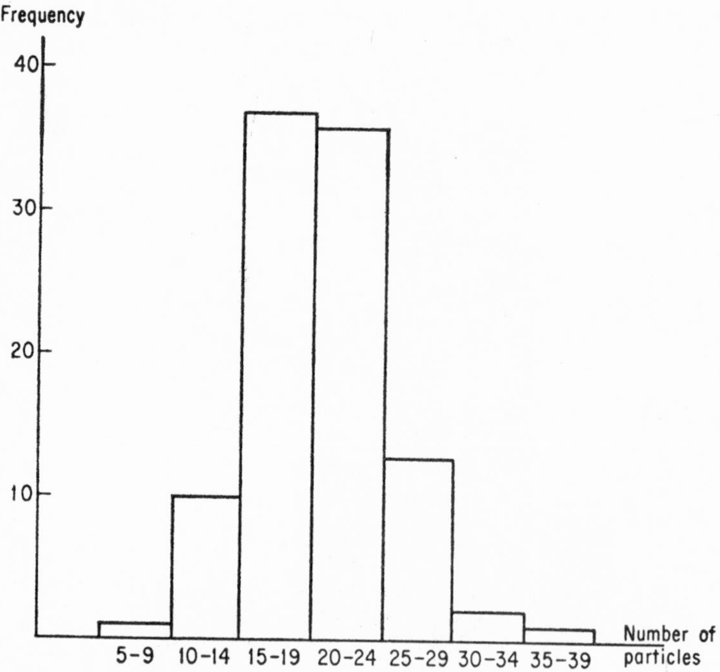

Fig. 2.1 Histogram of the radiation-count data.

Similarly, if we wanted to classify occupations, it would be difficult to decide where to put a farm manager, if our table contained (without qualification) the two categories "farmers" and "managers." For this reason, it is often advisable to use standard categories developed by the Bureau of the Census and other government agencies. (For references to such lists see the book by P. M. Hauser and W. R. Leonard in the Bibliography at the end of this chapter.)

2.3 Graphical Presentations

When frequency distributions are constructed primarily to condense large sets of data and display them in an "easy to digest" form, it is usually advisable to present them graphically, that is, in a form that appeals to the human power of visualization. The most common among all graphical presentations of statistical data is the *histogram*, an example of which is shown in Figure 2.1. A histogram is constructed by representing measurements or observations that are grouped (in Figure 2.1 the radiation counts) on a horizontal scale, the class frequencies on a vertical scale, and drawing rectangles whose bases equal the class interval and whose heights are deter-

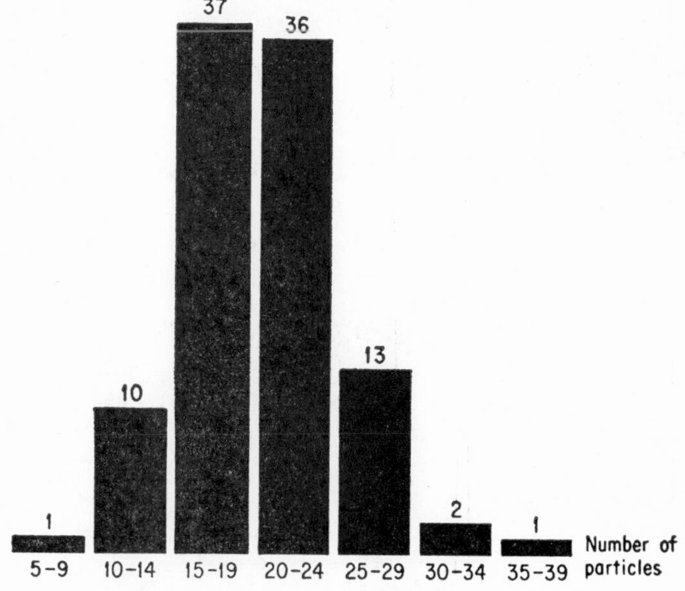

Fig. 2.2 Bar chart of the radiation-count data.

mined by the corresponding class frequencies. The markings on the horizontal scale can be the class limits as in Figure 2.1, the class boundaries, the class marks, or arbitrary key values. For easy readability it is generally preferable to indicate the class limits, although the bases of the rectangles actually go from one class boundary to the next.

Similar to histograms are *bar charts*, like the one of Figure 2.2; the lengths of the bars are proportional to the class frequencies, but there is no pretense of having a continuous (horizontal) scale.

There are several points that must be watched in the construction of histograms. First, it must be remembered that this kind of figure cannot be used for distributions with *open* classes. Second, it should be noted that the picture presented by a histogram can be very misleading if a distribution has unequal classes and no suitable adjustments are made. To illustrate this point, let us regroup the radiation-count data by combining all counts from 20 to 34 into one class. The distribution on page 13 thus becomes

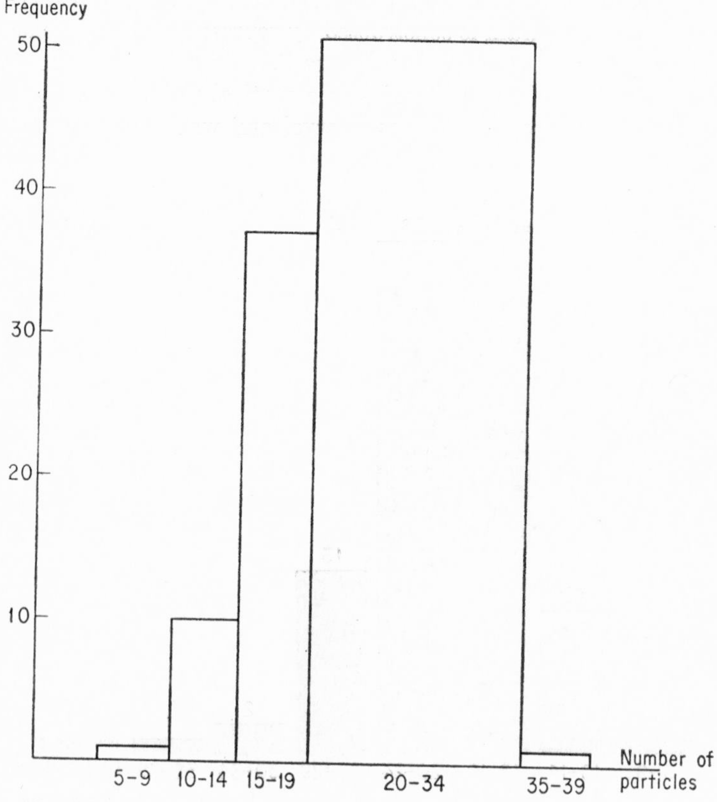

Fig. 2.3 Incorrectly modified histogram of the radiation-count data.

Number of Particles	*Frequency*
5 – 9	1
10 – 14	10
15 – 19	37
20 – 34	51
35 – 39	1
	100

and its histogram (with the class frequencies represented by the heights of the rectangles) is shown in Figure 2.3. This figure gives the impression that close to 3/4 of the radiation counts fall on the interval from 20 to 34, whereas the correct proportion is about 1/2. This error is due to the fact that when we compare the size of rectangles, triangles, and other plane figures, we instinctively compare their *areas* and not their sides. In order to correct for this, we simply draw the rectangles so that the class frequencies are

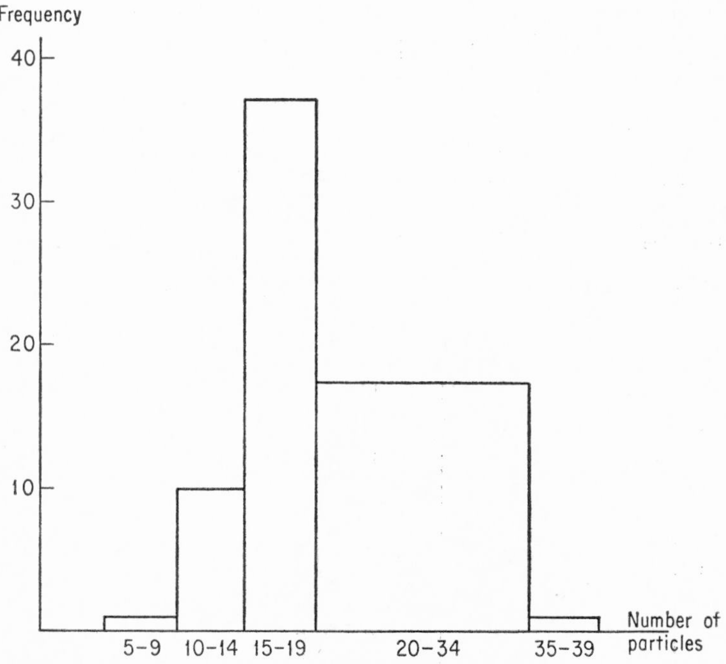

Fig. 2.4 Correctly modified histogram of the radiation-count data.

represented by their areas, not by their heights. In Figure 2.4 we accomplished this by reducing the height of the rectangle representing the class 20–34 to one-third of what it was in Figure 2.3.

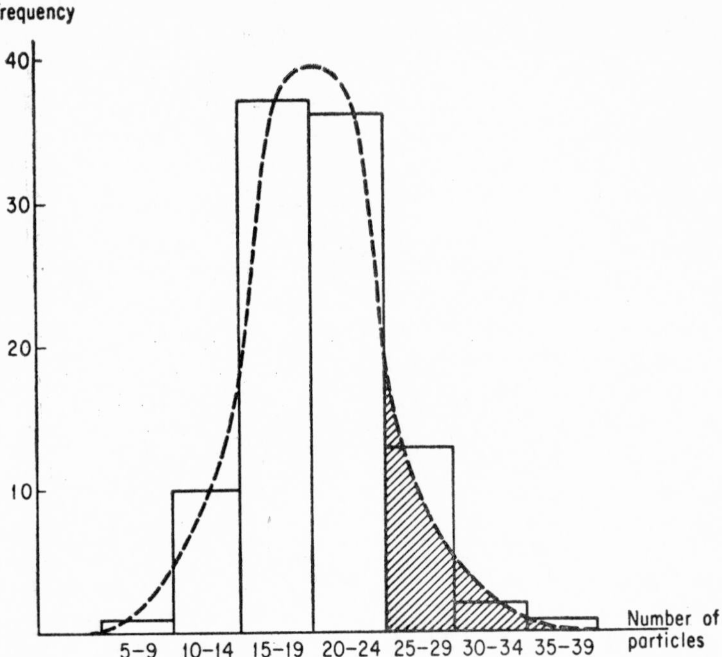

Fig. 2.5 Histogram of the radiation-count data approximated by means of a smooth curve.

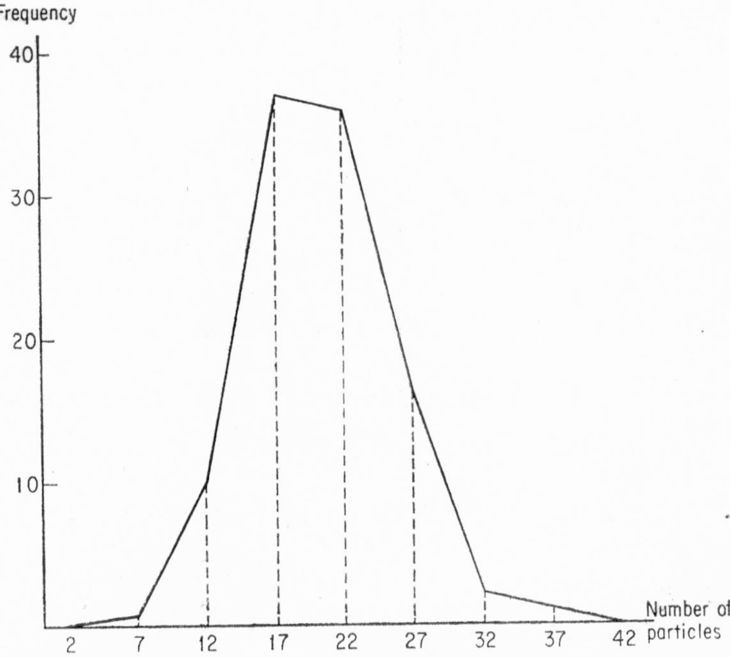

Fig. 2.6 Frequency polygon of the radiation-count data.

The practice of representing class frequencies by means of areas is especially important if histograms are to be approximated with smooth curves. For instance, if we wanted to approximate the histogram of Figure 2.1 with a smooth curve, we could say that the number of radiation counts exceeding 24 is given by the shaded area of Figure 2.5. Clearly, this area is approximately equal to the sum of the areas of the corresponding three rectangles.

An alternate, though less widely used, form of graphical presentation is the *frequency polygon* (see Figure 2.6). Here the class frequencies are plotted at the class marks and the successive points are connected by means of straight lines. Note that we added classes with zero frequencies at both ends of the distribution in order to "tie down" the graph to the horizontal scale.

If we apply the same technique to a cumulative distribution, we obtain what is called an *ogive*. Note, however, that now the cumulative frequencies are *not* plotted at the class marks—it stands to reason that the cumulative frequency corresponding, say, to "less than 20" in our example should be plotted at 20, or preferably at the class boundary of 19.5, since "less than 20" actually includes everything up to 19.5. Figure 2.7 shows an ogive representing the cumulative "less than" distribution of the radiation-count data.

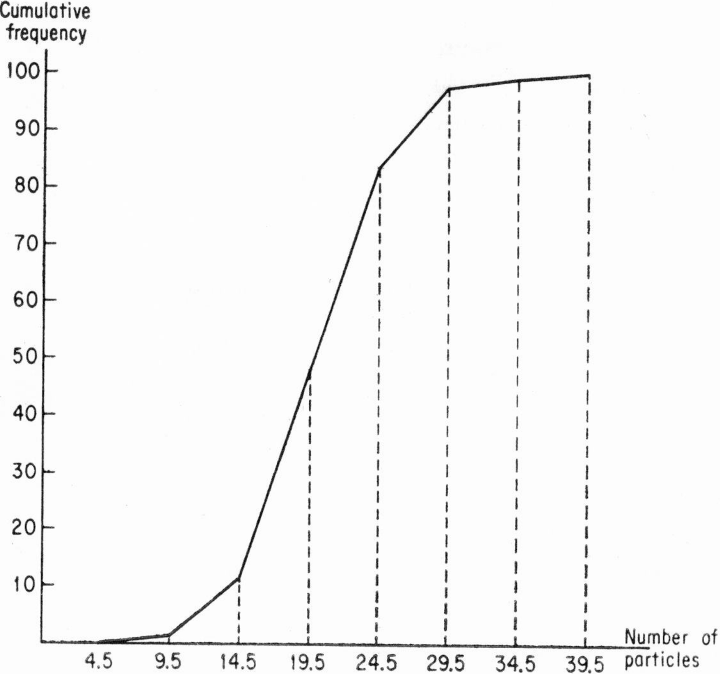

Fig. 2.7 Ogive of the radiation-count data.

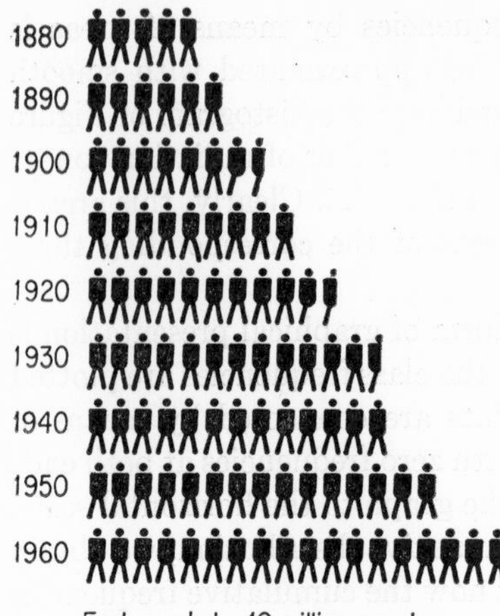

Fig. 2.8 Pictogram of the population of the United States.

Although the visual appeal of histograms, frequency polygons, and ogives exceeds that of frequency tables, there are ways in which distributions can be presented even more dramatically and probably also more effectively. We are referring here to the various kinds of pictorial presentations (see, for example, Figures 2.8 and 2.9) with which the reader must surely be familiar through newspapers, magazines, advertising, and other sources. The number of ways in which distributions (and other statistical data) can be displayed pictorially is almost unlimited, depending only on the imagination and artistic talent of the individual preparing the presentations.

EXERCISES

1. Decide for each of the following quantities whether it can be determined on the basis of the distribution on page 13 and, if possible, give a numerical answer:
(a) The number of times the radiation count was at least 20.
(b) The number of times the radiation count was at most 20.
(c) The number of times the radiation count was more than 20.
(d) The number of times the radiation count was 20 or more.

2. If hospital bills are grouped into a frequency table with the classes \$50.00–\$99.99, \$100.00–\$149.99, \$150.00–\$199.99, \$200.00–\$249.99, \$250.00–\$299.99, and \$300.00 or more, decide for each of the following quantities whether it can be determined on the basis of this distribution:
(a) How many of the bills amounted to less than \$150.00.
(b) How many of the bills amounted to \$150.00 or less.
(c) How many of the bills amounted to more than \$200.00.
(d) How many of the bills amounted to \$200.00 or more.
(e) How many of the bills amounted to \$500.00 or more.
(f) How many of the bills amounted to less than \$175.00.

3. If the electricity bills paid by the residents of a community during the month of September, 1965, varied from \$6.32 to \$34.76, construct a table with six classes into which these amounts might be grouped. Give the class limits as well as the class marks.

4. The weights of certain freight shipments are given to the nearest tenth of a pound, with the lowest being 32.4 and the highest being 104.9 pounds. Give the class limits of a table with eight classes into which these weights might be grouped.

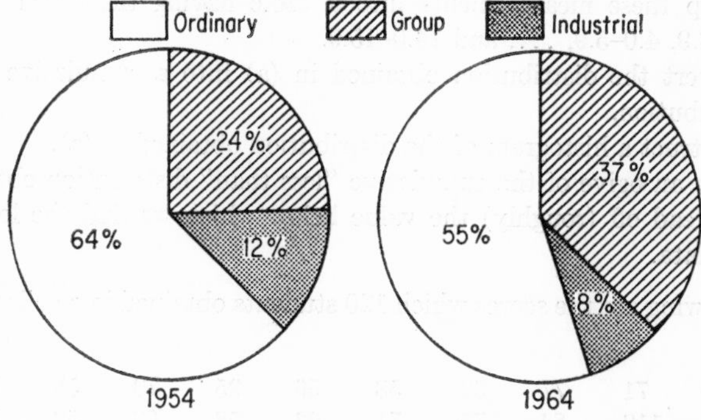

Fig. 2.9 Pie chart of insurance death benefit payments in the United States.

5. A set of temperature readings, given to the nearest hundredth of a degree Fahrenheit, are grouped into a table having the class boundaries 49.995, 74.995, 99.995, 124.995, and 149.995. What are the limits of the four classes of this distribution?

6. The class marks of a distribution of test scores (given in whole numbers) are 23, 38, 53, 68, and 83. Find the class limits of this distribution, and also the class boundaries.

7. The mileages obtained per gallon in test runs with a new automobile engine are rounded to the nearest mile and grouped into a table having the classes 10–13, 14–17, 18–21, 22–25, 26–29, and 30–33. Find the corresponding class boundaries, the class marks, and the class interval.

8. The methods discussed lead to some complications when applied to age distributions. For example, a person is considered to belong to the age group from 5 to 9 if he has passed his fifth birthday and has not yet reached his tenth. Taking this into account, what are the class boundaries and the class marks of the following distribution: 10–14, 15–19, 20–24, 25–29, and 30–34 years?

9. A survey conducted by a forestry service crew yielded the following measurements of the diameters of oak trees (in inches at breast height):

8.5	2.3	9.5	4.8	7.2	9.8	3.0	6.7
6.1	5.8	4.2	10.8	4.1	4.5	8.8	10.3
11.4	8.2	9.1	7.7	9.6	8.2	5.1	9.4
9.4	7.9	6.2	5.0	7.2	9.4	6.9	5.5
7.6	9.6	12.8	6.5	3.8	6.9	10.7	8.0
5.1	6.8	7.7	9.3	6.3	7.0	7.2	7.3
6.3	7.3	11.0	8.7	5.0	5.3	5.7	4.4
11.6	9.3	8.3	6.9	7.0	6.1	6.4	7.8
4.0	7.4	4.9	2.7	8.5	15.2	7.5	8.9
8.1	5.9	7.5	8.6	9.7	5.6	5.7	2.5

(a) Group these measurements into a table having the seven equal classes 2.0–3.9, 4.0–5.9, . . ., and 14.0–15.9.
(b) Convert the distribution obtained in (a) into a cumulative "less than" distribution.
(c) Construct a histogram of the distribution obtained in (a).
(d) Draw an ogive of the cumulative "less than" distribution obtained in (b) and read off (roughly) the value below which we find the lowest half of the data.

10. The following are the scores which 120 students obtained in a college placement test:

54	86	71	77	69	53	56	95	79	58	76	84
25	59	112	84	75	71	62	58	63	52	77	51
79	67	49	81	58	53	74	75	81	68	114	67
90	57	90	63	60	47	87	64	92	88	71	61
66	73	70	59	41	48	51	64	57	68	80	52
14	41	63	93	57	59	44	74	61	59	58	76
84	99	45	69	73	79	65	61	54	65	79	38
63	68	52	82	50	63	35	58	81	73	57	79
64	90	57	90	68	65	47	61	92	88	71	52
58	41	68	71	69	77	62	41	82	83	75	71

(a) Group these scores into a table with a class interval of 10 and draw a histogram of the resulting distribution.
(b) Group the distribution obtained in (a) into a cumulative "or more" distribution.
(c) Draw a frequency polygon of the distribution obtained in (a) and an ogive of the cumulative distribution obtained in (b).

11. A scientist obtained the following daily field estimates of radioactive fallout (in micro-microcuries per cubic meter of air) in Phoenix during the months of May through August, 1964:

9.3	6.8	9.8	6.6	4.3	6.7	6.4	10.1	8.9	3.7
5.3	6.5	7.4	8.3	4.6	7.9	6.5	5.1	7.2	8.7
7.9	6.3	2.7	5.3	8.8	7.3	9.0	7.7	8.4	7.8
5.8	6.4	6.2	5.8	6.5	6.0	7.7	5.0	4.4	4.7
5.4	2.9	4.0	4.1	4.1	5.5	3.1	3.5	5.4	4.1
4.7	6.2	3.2	2.7	4.8	2.6	3.4	6.2	5.1	4.0
5.0	3.3	2.4	4.6	2.8	1.7	0.9	7.2	9.9	4.0
2.0	2.0	1.0	3.2	5.6	3.4	5.7	7.0	4.3	3.4
3.0	4.4	2.0	5.8	1.5	5.1	5.0	8.8	4.0	6.1
5.6	5.4	8.3	8.8	10.0	4.8	3.6	2.5	5.3	2.2
4.1	5.0								

(a) Group these data into a distribution having the classes 0.0–0.9, 1.0–1.9, 2.0–2.9, . . ., and 10.0–10.9.
(b) Convert the distribution obtained in (a) into a cumulative "less than" distribution.
(c) Construct a histogram and a frequency polygon of the distribution obtained in (a).

(d) Draw an ogive of the cumulative distribution obtained in (b) and use it to read off (roughly) below which value we should find the lowest 25 per cent of the data. (*Hint:* First convert the vertical scale of the ogive into a percentage scale.)

12. The following are the number of steak dinners a restaurant served on 50 consecutive Sundays:

41	52	46	42	46	36	44	68	58	44
49	48	48	65	52	50	45	72	45	43
47	49	57	44	48	49	45	47	48	43
45	56	61	54	51	47	42	53	41	45
58	55	43	63	38	42	43	46	49	47

(a) Group these figures into a table having the classes 35–39, 40–44, 45–49, . . ., and 70–74.
(b) Convert the distribution obtained in (a) into a cumulative "or more" *percentage* distribution.
(c) If the manager of the restaurant decided to stock only 59 steaks on each Sunday, how often (what per cent of the time) could he expect to run short?
(d) Draw a histogram and a frequency polygon of the distribution obtained in (a).
(e) Draw a percentage ogive of the cumulative percentage distribution obtained in (b), and read off (roughly) below which value we can find the lowest half of the data.

13. The following are 80 measurements of the iron-solution index of tin-plate samples, designated to measure the corrosion resistance of tin-plated steel:

0.72	0.92	0.92	1.43	0.83	0.48	0.65	0.78
0.48	0.96	0.72	0.48	0.83	0.49	0.78	0.96
0.88	1.03	0.78	1.12	0.83	0.78	0.83	1.06
1.23	0.18	0.96	1.18	0.48	0.55	0.97	1.21
0.94	0.38	0.73	0.65	1.36	0.47	0.72	0.77
0.79	1.26	1.06	0.90	0.77	0.35	0.78	0.77
0.88	1.20	0.71	0.95	0.91	0.64	0.73	1.09
0.83	0.78	1.04	1.33	0.47	0.16	0.57	0.65
0.64	0.65	1.43	0.63	0.79	1.00	0.92	0.45
0.48	0.79	0.97	0.57	0.95	1.12	0.70	1.05

(a) Group these measurements into a table having a class interval of 0.20 and draw its histogram.
(b) Convert the distribution obtained in (a) into a cumulative "less than" percentage distribution and draw its ogive.
(c) Use the percentage ogive obtained in (b) to read off (roughly) below what values we can find the lowest 25 per cent, the lowest 50 per cent, and the lowest 75 per cent of the data.

14. The following are the number of years the 100 filing cabinets owned by a chain of drug stores have been in service:

4.2	5.8	6.1	9.1	4.7	5.8	6.9	4.0	6.4	7.7
6.9	8.6	8.2	4.0	5.5	5.6	9.4	7.2	2.5	6.3
8.2	8.1	5.2	8.8	9.2	6.6	7.8	6.9	5.8	7.5
5.3	5.6	5.7	3.5	6.0	5.4	2.6	9.3	5.2	2.3
6.1	5.3	2.0	5.4	9.8	6.0	5.2	8.6	5.1	9.2
5.6	4.3	3.8	6.5	7.5	4.5	4.2	3.7	6.1	5.4
6.2	6.3	10.4	6.7	7.8	3.9	7.1	5.6	3.3	6.7
5.0	6.5	5.0	5.8	5.7	4.8	8.5	6.3	7.5	3.1
7.5	3.7	10.6	5.8	6.8	7.4	3.0	9.7	8.4	5.9
2.6	5.9	6.8	5.1	5.0	5.8	5.5	5.2	4.1	6.8

(a) Group these figures, which are rounded to the nearest tenth of a year, into a distribution having the classes 2.0–2.9, 3.0–3.9, 4.0–4.9, . . ., and 10.0–10.9, and draw a histogram as well as a frequency polygon of this distribution.
(b) Convert the distribution obtained in (a) into a cumulative "less than" distribution and draw its ogive.
(c) Changing over to different equipment, the chain of drug stores is offered by one firm a trade-in of $60 for each filing cabinet which (rounded to the nearest tenth of a year) is less than 4 years old, $30 for each filing cabinet which (rounded to the nearest tenth of a year) is at least 4 years but less than 8 years old, and $5 each for those that are older. Use the cumulative distribution obtained in (b) to decide whether this firm offers a higher total trade-in than another firm which offers a flat $2,500 for the 100 filing cabinets.

15. The following are the daily figures on the midnight cloud cover (*rounded to the nearest 10 per cent*) at Sky Harbor Airport, Phoenix, during June and July, 1964: 0, 60, 30, 10, 70, 20, 0, 0, 0, 0, 0, 0, 0, 0, 0, 20, 0, 0, 0, 0, 0, 0, 20, 100, 90, 30, 0, 0, 0, 50, 0, 0, 20, 0, 0, 100, 60, 10, 0, 10, 100, 10, 100, 20, 0, 100, 100, 100, 20, 30, 100, 100, 100, 100, 100, 0, 30, 100, 100.
(a) Construct a table showing the frequencies with which the various figures occurred.
(b) What are the class boundaries of the distribution obtained in (a)?
(c) Draw a histogram of the distribution obtained in (a), being careful to adjust for the fact that the first and last class intervals are only half as long as the others.

16. Choose a local television station and construct a table showing how many of the half-hour periods between 6 P.M. and 10 P.M. it broadcasts during one week are situation comedies, serious dramas, educational programs, news, and so forth.

17. Take that part of the classified ads of a large daily newspaper where individuals (not dealers) advertise cars for sale, and construct a distribution showing how many of these cars are station wagons, how many are sedans, how many are convertibles, and so on.

18. Categorical distributions are often presented graphically as *pie charts* like the one of Figure 2.9, where a circle is divided into sectors which are proportional in size to the frequencies of the corresponding categories. Making use of the fact that 1 per cent of the data is represented by a central angle of 3.6 degrees, draw a pie chart of the following categorical distribution:

Military Reserve Personnel not on Active Duty in 1961 (thousands)

Army	2,294
Navy	891
Air Force	571
Total	3,756

19. Draw a pie chart (see Exercise 18) of the distribution of the employees of domestic air carriers shown on page 10.

20. The *pictogram* of Figure 2.10 is intended to illustrate the fact that the total value of industrial bonds held by U.S. life insurance companies has tripled from 1950 to 1960. Does this pictogram convey a "fair" impression of the actual change? If not, how should it be modified?

Fig. 2.10 Value of industrial bonds held by U.S. life insurance companies.

BIBLIOGRAPHY

More detailed treatments of the material in this chapter may be found in some of the older standard texts, for example, in

Croxton, F. E., and Cowden, D. J., *Applied General Statistics*, 2nd ed. Englewood Cliffs, N.J.: Prentice-Hall, Inc., 1955.

Waugh, A. E., *Elements of Statistical Method*, 3rd ed. New York: McGraw-Hill Book Company, 1952.

The question of *what not to do* in the presentation of statistical data is discussed in

Huff, D., *How to Lie with Statistics*. New York: W. W. Norton & Company, Inc., 1954.

Reichmann, W. J., *Use and Abuse of Statistics*. London: Methuen & Co., Ltd., 1961.

Useful references to lists of standard categories may be found in

Hauser, P. M., and Leonard, W. R., *Government Statistics for Business Use*. New York: John Wiley & Sons, Inc., 1956.

THREE
Measures of Location

3.1 Introduction

Descriptions of statistical data can be quite brief or quite elaborate, depending partly on the nature of the data themselves, and partly on the purpose for which they are to be used. Sometimes, we even describe the same set of data in several different ways. To draw an analogy, a large motel might describe itself to the public as having luxurious facilities, a heated swimming pool, and TV in every room; on the other hand, it might describe itself to the fire department by giving the floor space of each unit, the number of sprinklers, and the number of employees. Both of these descriptions may serve the purpose for which they are designed, but they would hardly satisfy the State Corporation Commission in passing on the owner's application for issuing stock. This would require detailed information on the management of the motel, various kinds of financial statements, and so on.

Whether we describe things statistically or whether we simply describe them verbally, it is always desirable to say neither too little nor too much. Thus, it may sometimes be satisfactory to present data simply as they are and let them "speak for themselves"; in other instances it may be satisfactory to group, classify, and present them using the methods of Chapter 2. However, most of the time it is necessary to summarize them further by means of one or more well-chosen descriptions. In this chapter and in Chapter 4 we shall concentrate mainly on two kinds of descriptions, called *measures of location* and *measures of variation;* some others are mentioned briefly in Section 4.4.

The measures of location we shall study in this chapter are also referred to at times as "measures of central tendencies," "measures of central values," and "measures of position." Except for some of the measures discussed in Section 3.4, they may also be referred to crudely as "averages" in the sense that they provide numbers that are indicative of the "center," "middle," or the "most typical" of a set of data.*

When we said that the choice of a statistical description depends partly on the nature of the data themselves, we were referring among other things to the following distinction: *if a set of data consists of all conceivably possible (or hypothetically possible) observations of a certain phenomenon, we refer to it as a population; if it contains only part of these observations, we refer to it as a sample.* The qualification "hypothetically possible" was added to take care of such clearly hypothetical situations where, say, twelve flips of a coin are looked upon as a sample from the population of all possible flips of the coin, or where we shall want to look upon the weights of eight 30-day-old calves as a sample of the weights of all (past, present, and future) 30-day-old calves. In fact, we often look upon the results obtained in an experiment as a sample of what we might obtain if the experiment were repeated over and over again.

In actual practice, whether a set of data is looked upon as a sample or as a population depends to some extent on what we intend to do with the data. Suppose, for example, that we are offered a lot of 5,000 ceramic tiles which we may or may not be interested in buying, depending on their strength. If we measure the breaking strength of ten of these tiles to estimate the average breaking strength of all the tiles, these ten measurements constitute a sample from the population which consists of the breaking strengths of all the tiles. We thus have a sample of *size* 10 from a population of *size* 5,000. In a different context, however, we might look upon the 5,000 tiles and their breaking strengths as only a sample of all the millions of tiles which the tile manufacturer produces throughout the years. To consider another illustration of this important distinction, suppose that we are interested in the monthly mileages of police cars, and that we have at our disposal complete figures on the mileages that police cars were driven in Orange County, California, during June 1964. If we do not generalize about corresponding mileages for other counties or other years (including the future), we are justified in saying that the data constitute a population; they contain all the information that is relevant to the phenomenon with which we are concerned. On the other hand, if we want to make generalizations about corresponding mileages for the whole year 1964, for the whole State of California, or for the entire United States, then the June 1964 figures for Orange County are only a sample.

As we have defined it here, the word "sample" is used in very much the same way as it is used in everyday language. An employer considers the opinions of 25 of his 600 employees a sample of all their opinions on a given

* Rigorously speaking, a measure of location may be defined as a statistical description having the following property: *if the same number is added to each observation, this number must also be added to the corresponding description.* (See Exercise 6 on page 57 and also Exercise 22 on page 42.)

matter, and a consumer considers a box of Blum's candy a sample of the firm's product. (Later, in Chapters 8 through 15, we shall interpret the term "sample" in a somewhat narrower fashion, limiting it to data that can reasonably serve for the making of generalizations about the population from which they are obtained. Thus, the above-mentioned sample of data pertaining to Orange County may not be acceptable as a sample if generalizations are to be made about police-car mileages in the entire United States.) The fact that the word "universe" is sometimes used instead of "population" makes it evident that neither term is used here in its colloquial sense. In statistics, both terms refer to the actual or hypothetical totality of measurements or observations with which we are concerned, and not necessarily (or directly) to human beings or animals.

In this chapter and the next we shall limit ourselves to methods of description without making generalizations, but it is important even here to distinguish between samples and populations. As we have said before, the kind of description we may want to use will depend on what we intend to do later on, whether we merely want to present facts about populations or whether we want to generalize from samples. We shall, thus, begin in this chapter with the practice of using different symbols depending on whether we are describing samples or populations; in Chapter 4 we shall carry this distinction one step further by even using different formulas.

3.2 The Mean

There are many problems in which we have to represent data by means of a single number which, in its way, is descriptive of the entire set. The most popular measure used for this purpose is what the layman calls an "average" and what, in statistics, is called an *arithmetic mean*, or simply a *mean*. We gave the word "average" in quotes because it generally has a loose connotation and different meanings—for example, when we speak of a batting average, an average housewife, a person with average taste, and so on. (Since there also exist *geometric means* and *harmonic means*, see Exercises 22 and 24 on pages 42 and 43, it must be kept in mind that when we speak of *the mean*, we refer to the arithmetic mean and not to the others.)

The arithmetic mean of a set of n numbers is defined simply as their sum divided by n. For instance, given that the number of paid admissions to Disneyland for the years 1959 through 1962 totaled, respectively, 4.9, 4.7, 5.1, and 5.6 million, we find that the *mean*, namely, the "average" annual number of paid admissions, is

$$\frac{4.9 + 4.7 + 5.1 + 5.6}{4} = 5.075$$

or approximately 5.1 million a year.

In order to develop a simple formula for the mean that is applicable to any set of data, it will be necessary to respresent the figures (measurements or observations) to which the formula is to be applied with some general symbols such as x, y, or z. In the above example, we could have represented the annual paid admissions with the letter x and referred to the four values as x_1 (*x sub-one*), x_2 (*x sub-two*), x_3, and x_4. More generally, if we have n measurements which we designate $x_1, x_2, x_3, \ldots$, and x_n, we can write

$$\text{mean} = \frac{x_1 + x_2 + \ldots + x_n}{n}$$

This formula is perfectly general and it will take care of any set of data, but it is still somewhat cumbersome. To make it more compact, we introduce the symbol Σ (capital *sigma*, the Greek letter for S), which is simply a mathematical shorthand notation indicating the process of summation or addition. If we write $\Sigma\, x$, this represents the "sum of the x's," and we now have

$$\text{mean} = \frac{\Sigma\, x}{n}$$

Using the sigma notation in this form, the number of terms to be added is not stated explicitly; it is tacitly understood, however, to refer to all the x's with which we happen to be concerned. If we wanted to use a more explicit notation, we could write the sum $x_1 + x_2 + \ldots + x_n$ as $\sum_{i=1}^{n} x_i$ instead of $\Sigma\, x$; this would indicate explicitly that we are adding the x's with subscripts from 1 to n. For a further discussion of the use of subscripts and the Σ notation, see Section 3.6.

To go one step further, we shall finish simplifying our notation by assigning a special symbol to the mean itself. If we look upon the x's as a sample, we write their mean as $\bar{x}$(*x-bar*); if we look upon them as a population, we write their mean as μ (*mu*, the Greek letter for m). If we refer to sample data as y's or z's, we correspondingly write their means as $\bar{y}$ or $\bar{z}$. To further emphasize the distinction between samples and populations, we denote the number of values in a sample, the *sample size*, with the letter n and the number of values in a population, the *population size*, with the letter N. We thus have the formulas*

$$\blacktriangle \qquad \bar{x} = \frac{\Sigma\, x}{n} \quad \text{or} \quad \mu = \frac{\Sigma\, x}{N} \qquad \blacktriangle$$

depending on whether we are dealing with a sample or a population. In

* Formulas marked ▲ are actually used for practical computations. This will make it easier for the reader to distinguish between formulas needed for calculations and those given primarily as part of definitions or derivations.

order to distinguish between descriptions of samples and descriptions of populations, statisticians not only use different symbols, but they refer to the first as *statistics* and the second as *parameters*. Hence, we say that $\bar{x}$ is a statistic and that μ is a parameter.

To illustrate this usage, let us consider the problem of a consumer testing service which wants to investigate a manufacturer's claim that in a large shipment of paint a gallon can will on the average cover 400 square feet. As it is obviously impossible to test all of the paint (the manufacturer would have none left to sell), five cans are selected and the corresponding areas covered are recorded as 409, 383, 400, 394, and 404 square feet. These measurements constitute a sample, since the testing service is interested in all the paint in the large shipment; in other words, they are interested in μ, the mean for all the paint, but they have only enough information to calculate $\bar{x}$. The value they get is

$$\bar{x} = \frac{409 + 383 + 400 + 394 + 404}{5} = 398$$

and they can use this figure to *estimate* the parameter μ (the true mean for the entire shipment), provided that sufficient care was taken in obtaining the sample. Note how our notation eliminates such confusing language as "we use a mean to estimate a mean"; the statement "we use $\bar{x}$ as an estimate of μ" makes it clear that we are using a statistic to estimate a parameter, namely, a sample mean to estimate the mean of a population.

The popularity of the mean as a measure describing the "middle" or "center" of a set of data is not just accidental. Anytime we use a single number to describe a set of data, there are certain desirable properties we must keep in mind. Thus, some of the noteworthy properties of the mean are: (1) it is familiar to most persons, although they may not call it by this name; (2) it always exists, that is, it can be calculated for any kind of numerical data; (3) it is always unique, or in other words, a set of data has one and only one mean; (4) it takes into account each individual item; (5) it lends itself to further statistical manipulation (as we shall see on page 38, it is possible to combine the means of several sets of data into an over-all mean without having to refer back to the original raw data); and (6) it is relatively *reliable* in the sense that it does not vary too much when repeated samples are taken from one and the same population, at least not as much as some other kinds of statistical descriptions. This question of reliability is of fundamental importance when it comes to problems of estimation, hypothesis testing, and making predictions, and we shall have a good deal more to say about it in later parts of this book.

Whether the fourth property of the mean listed above is actually desirable is open to some doubt; a single extreme (very large or very small) value can affect the mean to such an extent that it is debatable whether it is really "representative" or "typical" of the data. To illustrate, let us consider the matter of changes in automobile insurance rates, which are established statistically to assure fair indemnification. In general, rates have been rising, and data from Creek County, Oklahoma, for instance, show that the average size of claims paid by insurance companies has recently increased by 3,500 per cent. However, closer inspection of the data shows that this figure is distorted by one unusually large claim of $650,000, which affected the mean as well as the percentage change. Omitting this one atypical value, the Insurance Information Institute showed that the increase reduced to 573 per cent, a figure which it considers much more representative of the data as a whole.

To give another illustration, suppose that in the example concerning the paint the last figure was recorded *incorrectly* as 204 instead of 404. They would thus have obtained a mean of

$$\frac{409 + 383 + 400 + 394 + 204}{5} = 358$$

instead of the correct value of $\bar{x} = 398$ square feet. This shows how one careless mistake can have a pronounced effect on the mean. There could have been serious consequences if the testing service had accepted the result and estimated μ, the actual mean for the entire shipment of paint, as 358 square feet instead of 398. Note that in Section 3.4 we shall meet another kind of "average," called the *median*, which has the important feature that it is not so readily affected by a very large or a very small value.

Since the computation of means is quite easy, involving only addition and one division, there is usually no need to look for short-cuts or simplifications. However, if the numbers are unwieldy, that is, if each number has many digits, or if the sample (or population) size is very large, it may be advantageous to group the data first and then compute the mean from the resulting distribution. Another reason why we shall investigate the problem of obtaining means from grouped data is that published data are very often available only in the form of distributions.

Earlier, on page 10, we observed that the grouping of data entails some loss of information. Each item, so to speak, loses its identity (we know only how many items fall into each class), and the *actual* mean of the data can no longer be calculated. However, a good approximation can be obtained by assigning the value of the class mark to each item falling into a given class, and this is how we *define* the mean of a distribution. Thus, the 10 values which fall into the second class of the radiation-count distribution on page 13 are treated as if they all equaled 12, the midpoint of the class going from 10 to 14. Similarly, the value which falls into the first class is treated as if it equaled 7, the 37 values which fall into the third class are treated as if they all equaled 17, and so forth. This procedure is generally very satisfactory, since the errors we introduce will more or less "average out."

To obtain a formula for the mean of a distribution, let us write the successive class marks as $x_1, x_2, \ldots, x_k$ (assuming that there are k classes) and the corresponding class frequencies as $f_1, f_2, \ldots, f_k$. The total that goes into the numerator of the formula for the mean is thus obtained by adding f_1 times the value x_1, f_2 times the value x_2, ..., and f_k times the value x_k; in other words, it is equal to $x_1f_1 + x_2f_2 + \ldots + x_kf_k$. Using the Σ notation introduced on page 32, we can now write the formula for the mean of a distribution as

$$\blacktriangle \qquad \bar{x} = \frac{\Sigma\, x \cdot f}{n} \qquad \blacktriangle$$

where $\Sigma\, x \cdot f$ represents, in words, the sum of the products obtained by multiplying each class mark by the corresponding class frequency, and n equals the sum of the class frequencies, or $\Sigma\, f$. (When dealing with a population instead of a sample, we have only to substitute μ for $\bar{x}$ in this formula and N for n.)

To illustrate the calculation of the mean of a distribution, let us refer again to the radiation-count distribution on page 13. Writing the class marks in the second column, we get

Number of Particles	*Class Marks* x	*Frequencies* f	*Products* $x \cdot f$
5 – 9	7	1	7
10 – 14	12	10	120
15 – 19	17	37	629
20 – 24	22	36	792
25 – 29	27	13	351
30 – 34	32	2	64
35 – 39	37	1	37
		Total	2,000

and the mean of the distribution is

$$\bar{x} = \frac{2{,}000}{100} = 20$$

It is interesting to note that the mean of the raw data on page 13 is 2002/100 = 20.02 and, hence, that the difference between the two means is extremely small.

The calculation of the mean of the radiation-count distribution was especially easy because the frequencies were small and the class marks were easy-to-work-with two-digit numbers. When necessary, we can simplify the calculations by performing a change of scale; that is, we replace the class marks with numbers that are easier to handle. Referring to this process as "coding," we might replace the class marks of the radiation-count distribution with the consecutive integers -3, -2, -1, 0, 1, 2, and 3. Of course, when we do something like this, we also have to account for it in the formula we use to calculate the mean. Referring to the new (coded) class marks as u's, it can easily be shown (see Exercise 7 on page 57) that the formula for the mean of a distribution becomes

$$\bar{x} = x_0 + \frac{\Sigma\, u \cdot f}{n} \cdot c$$

where x_0 is the class mark (in the original scale) to which we assign 0 in the new scale, c is the class interval, n is the number of items grouped, and $\Sigma u \cdot f$ is the sum of the products obtained by multiplying each of the coded class marks by the corresponding frequency.

Illustrating this short-cut technique by recalculating the mean of the radiation-count distribution, we obtain

x	u	f	$u \cdot f$
7	-3	1	-3
12	-2	10	-20
17	-1	37	-37
22	0	36	0
27	1	13	13
32	2	2	4
37	3	1	3
			-40

and

$$\bar{x} = 22 + \frac{(-40)}{100} \cdot 5 = 22 - 2 = 20$$

It should be noted that this agrees with the result obtained earlier; the short-cut formula does *not* entail any further approximation, and it should always yield the same result as the formula on page 35.

Unless one can use an automatic computer, the short-cut method will generally save a good deal of time; about the only time that the short-cut method does not provide appreciable savings in time and energy is when the original class marks are already easy-to-use numbers, such as those in our example. In order to reduce the work to a minimum, it is generally advisable to put the zero of the u-scale near the middle of the distribution, preferably at a class mark having one of the highest frequencies.

A fact worth noting is that the short-cut method cannot be used for distributions with *unequal* classes, although there exists a modification which makes it applicable also in that case. Neither the short-cut formula nor the formula on page 35 is applicable to distributions with *open classes;* the means of such distributions cannot be found without going back to the raw data or making special assumptions about the values which fall into an open class.

3.3 The Weighted Mean

In some situations it would be very misleading to average quantities without accounting in some way for their relative importance in the over-all picture we are trying to describe. For instance, if an investor bought American Airlines stock at \$12.50 in 1954, at \$17.75 in 1958, and at \$20.00 in 1962, we cannot calculate his average cost per share unless we know how many shares he actually bought in each case. Similarly, we cannot combine (or average) the batting averages of several baseball players without accounting for their respective times at bat, and we would probably get a very misleading picture if we averaged the prices several service stations charge for a gallon of gasoline, without paying proper attention to their volume of sales.

Returning to the first example, let us suppose that the investor bought 200 shares of American Airlines in 1954, 250 in 1958, and 100 in 1962. Simple calculations show that he thus spent a total of

$$200(12.50) + 250(17.75) + 100(20.00) = \$8,937.50$$

for $200 + 250 + 100 = 550$ shares, and $8937.50/550 = \$16.25$ per share. The average we have calculated here is called a *weighted mean;* we averaged the prices giving due weight to their relative importance.

In general, the *weighted mean* of a set of n numbers $x_1, x_2, \ldots,$ and x_n, whose relative importance is expressed numerically by a corresponding set of numbers $w_1, w_2, \ldots,$ and w_n, called the *weights,* is given by the formula

▲ $$\bar{x}_w = \frac{\Sigma\, w \cdot x}{\Sigma\, w}$$ ▲

Here $\Sigma\, w \cdot x$, written more fully as $\sum_{i=1}^{n} w_i \cdot x_i$, represents the sum of the products obtained by multiplying each of the x's by the corresponding weight, while $\Sigma\, w$, or $\sum_{i=1}^{n} w_i$, represents the sum of the weights. Note that when the weights are all equal, the formula for the weighted mean reduces to that of the ordinary (arithmetic) mean.

To give another example, suppose that on a certain trip a motorist bought 12 gallons of gasoline at 28 cents per gallon, 18 gallons at 31 cents per gallon, and 48 gallons at 34 cents per gallon. Substituting $x_1 = 28$, $x_2 = 31$, $x_3 = 34$, $w_1 = 12$, $w_2 = 18$, and $w_3 = 48$ into the above formula for the weighted mean, we find that on the average he paid

$$\bar{x} = \frac{12(28) + 18(31) + 48(34)}{12 + 18 + 48} = 32.4 \text{ cents per gallon}$$

The choice of the weights did not pose any problems in this and in the preceding examples, but there are situations in which their selection is not quite so obvious. For instance, if we wanted to compare figures representing the cost of living in different locations or at different times, we would face the difficult task of having to account for the relative importance in the average person's budget of such items as food, rent, entertainment, medical care, and so on.

A special form of the weighted mean arises when we want to determine the over-all mean of several sets of data on the basis of their individual means and the number of items in each. Given n_1 numbers whose mean is $\bar{x}_1$, n_2 numbers whose mean is $\bar{x}_2$, . . ., and n_k numbers whose mean is $\bar{x}_k$, the over-all mean of all these numbers is given by

▲ $$\frac{\Sigma\, n \cdot \bar{x}}{\Sigma\, n}$$ ▲

Note that the numerator, written more fully as $\sum_{i=1}^{k} n_i\bar{x}_i$, represents the sum of the products obtained by multiplying each individual mean by the size of the corresponding set of data and, hence, it represents *the actual total of all the data;* the denominator, $\sum_{i=1}^{k} n_i$, stands for the total number of items in the combined data.

To illustrate, suppose that 26 students in one section had an average (mean) grade of 74.7 in a final examination in American History, while 32 in another section had a mean grade of 85.2, 35 students in a third section had a mean grade of 71.5, and 21 students in a fourth section had a mean grade of 86.4. Substituting these values into the above formula, we find that the over-all mean of the grades received by these $26 + 32 + 35 + 21 = 114$ students is

$$\frac{26(74.7) + 32(85.2) + 35(71.5) + 21(86.4)}{26 + 32 + 35 + 21} = 78.8$$

This illustrates what we meant on page 33 when we said that the mean lends itself readily to further statistical manipulation.

EXERCISES

1. Suppose we are given complete information about the refunds residents of Arizona obtained on the federal income tax which was withheld from their paychecks in 1965. Give one illustration each of situations where we would consider this set of data to be (a) a population and (b) a sample.

2. Suppose that the final election returns from a given county show that two candidates for a certain office received 14,856 votes and 12,915 votes, respectively. What office might these candidates be running for so that we can look upon these figures (a) as a sample and (b) as a population?

3. In planning appropriations for new school buses, a school board is conducting a survey on the distances pupils live from their schools. Given complete data for the pupils attending a particular elementary school indicate (a) under what circumstances this information might be looked upon as a population, and (b) under what circumstances it might be looked upon as a sample.

4. Find the mean of the following grades 30 students received in a final examination in Chemistry: 63, 70, 55, 58, 67, 60, 92, 44, 63, 75, 82, 54, 69, 78, 81, 85, 33, 76, 64, 48, 75, 57, 41, 98, 62, 73, 52, 66, 81, and 65.

5. The following are 12 temperature readings taken at various locations in a large kiln (in degrees Fahrenheit): 432, 440, 412, 405, 427, 415, 409, 422, 417, 439, 411, and 411.
   (a) Calculate the mean of these 12 readings.
   (b) Recalculate the mean of these 12 readings by first subtracting 400 from each value, finding the mean of the numbers thus obtained, and then adding 400. (What general simplification does this suggest for the calculation of means?)

6. In its *Scientific Manpower Bulletin* the National Science Foundation reported the following figures on the number of psychologists employed in 1962 in the Mountain States and in the Pacific States:

Mountain States		*Pacific States*	
Montana	22	Washington	273
Idaho	15	Oregon	155
Wyoming	26	California	2,238
Colorado	222	Alaska	4
New Mexico	66	Hawaii	55
Arizona	113		
Utah	88		
Nevada	24		

   (a) Calculate the mean number of psychologists employed in the Mountain States. Would this mean be of much value to someone who is planning a professional meeting to which all psychologists in the Mountain States are to be invited?

(b) Calculate the mean number of psychologists employed in the Pacific States. Indicate under what conditions this mean might be extremely misleading.

7. The following are figures on the monthly number of passengers arriving at and departing from the Seattle-Tacoma International Airport during 1963:

Arrivals (in thousands): 61,134, 54,300, 62,204, 66,670, 71,809, 89,784, 90,360, 104,312, 81,268, 74,253, 66,843, 70,965

Departures (in thousands): 59,483, 54,933, 60,217, 64,143, 72,244, 91,510, 87,408, 97,695, 84,225, 75,598, 63,649, 75,521

Find the mean of the monthly arrivals and also that of the monthly departures. Would these means be of much value to a committee investigating the adequacy of parking facilities at the airport?

8. Twenty-four bottles of liquid detergent are randomly selected from a very large production lot and their net weights (in ounces) determined with the following results: 14.0, 13.9, 14.0, 14.0, 14.1, 13.9, 13.9, 14.0, 14.1, 14.2, 13.9, 13.9, 14.1, 14.0, 14.0, 13.8, 14.1, 14.0, 14.0, 13.9, 14.0, 14.2, 13.9, 14.0. What is the mean weight of these bottles?

9. Fifteen general practitioners interviewed in a certain city stated that they charge the following fees for making house calls: $8.00, $7.50, $6.00, $12.00, $6.00, $8.00, $10.00, $7.50, $9.00, $6.00, $7.50, $8.00, $9.00, $7.00, and $8.00. Calculate the mean.

10. An elevator is designed to carry a maximum load of 3,500 pounds. If it is loaded with 20 passengers having a mean weight of 156 pounds, is there any danger that it might be overloaded?

11. A student took six readings on the direction from which the wind was blowing at a certain place, obtaining 9, 349, 350, 4, 18, and 350 degrees. (These angles are measured clockwise with 0° being due North.) Averaging these figures he obtains a mean of 180°, which means that the wind blew from the South. Find the fallacy of this argument and a more appropriate way of averaging these readings.

12. Find the mean of the tree diameters of Exercise 9 on page 23.
(a) on the basis of the raw (ungrouped) data;
(b) on the basis of the distribution obtained in that exercise.

13. Referring to Exercise 10 on page 24, calculate the mean of the ungrouped as well as the grouped data and compare the results.

14. Using the distribution obtained in Exercise 11 on page 24, calculate the mean of the daily field estimates of radioactive fallout (a) without coding, and (b) with coding.

15. Referring to the data of Exercise 12 on page 25, calculate the mean number of steak dinners served by the restaurant

(a) on the basis of the ungrouped data;
(b) on the basis of the distribution obtained in that exercise.

16. Calculate the mean of the iron-solution indices of Exercise 13 on page 25 on the basis of the distribution obtained in that exercise.

17. Calculate the mean of the ages of the filing cabinets of Exercise 14 on page 25 on the basis of the distribution obtained in that exercise.

18. In business and economics, there are many problems in which we are interested in *index numbers*, that is, in measures of the changes that have taken place in the prices (quantities, or values) of various commodities. In general, the year or period we want to compare by means of an index number is called the *given year* or *given period*, while the year or period relative to which the comparison is made is called the *base year* or *base period*. Furthermore, given-year prices are denoted p_n, base-year prices are denoted p_0, and the ratio p_n/p_0 for a given commodity is called the corresponding *price relative*. A very simple kind of index number is given by the *mean of the price relatives* of the commodities with which we are concerned, multiplying the result by 100 to express the index as a percentage.

(a) Find the mean of the price relatives comparing the following 1961 prices with those of 1950, where all prices are in cents per pound:

	1950	*1961*
Round steak	93.6	103.6
Chuck roast	61.6	59.4
Hamburger	56.6	51.2
Bacon, sliced	63.7	71.2
Lamb, leg	74.4	70.1

(b) Find the mean of the price relatives comparing the following 1961 prices with those of 1955, where all prices are in cents per pound:

	1955	*1961*
Copper	37.4	30.3
Lead	14.9	10.7
Zinc	12.3	11.5

19. If we substitute q's for p's in the index number of Exercise 18, where given-year quantities (produced, sold, or consumed) are denoted q_n and base-year quantities are denoted q_0, we obtain a corresponding *quantity index*. Given the following data in thousands of short tons, find the mean of the quantity relatives comparing the 1961 production figures with those of 1955:

	1955	*1961*
Copper	1,107	1,200
Lead	479	480
Zinc	964	844

20. Another way of obtaining an index comparing given-year prices with a corresponding set of base-year prices (see Exercise 18) is to average the two sets of prices separately, take the ratio of the two means, and then multiply by 100 to express the index as a percentage. Canceling denominators, the formula for such a *simple aggregative index* is thus given by $\frac{\Sigma\, p_n}{\Sigma\, p_0} \cdot 100$, where $\Sigma\, p_n$ is the sum of the given-year prices and $\Sigma\, p_0$ is the sum of the base-year prices.
(a) Referring to part (a) of Exercise 18, calculate a simple aggregative index comparing the 1961 prices of the five kinds of meat with those of 1950.
(b) Referring to part (b) of Exercise 18, calculate a simple aggregative index comparing the 1961 prices of the metals with those of 1955.

21. In actual practice, simple aggregative indexes are seldom used because they fail the so-called *units test*. This means that the value of the index depends on the units for which the different prices are quoted. To illustrate this, change the prices of round steak in part (a) of Exercise 18 to cents per 1,000 pounds (while leaving the other prices unchanged), and compare the resulting simple aggregative index with the one obtained in part (a) of Exercise 20.

22. The *geometric mean* of a set of n numbers is given by the nth root of their product, namely, by $\sqrt[n]{x_1 \cdot x_2 \cdot \ldots \cdot x_n}$, and it is used mainly to average ratios, rates of change, index numbers, and the like.
(a) Find the geometric mean of 8 and 32.
(b) Find the geometric mean of 4, 6, and 9.
(c) Find the geometric mean of 1, 1, 3, and 27.
(d) In a French vocabulary test consisting of 280 words a student answered 81 correctly on the first try, 108 on the second try a week later, and 256 on the third try a week after that. Find the "average improvement ratio" between successive tries by calculating the geometric mean of 108/81 and 256/108.
(e) Does the geometric mean satisfy the strict definition of a measure of location given on page 30? (*Hint:* Check with reference to part (a), adding 2 to each number and verifying whether or not this adds 2 to the geometric mean.)

23. In actual practice, the *geometric mean* is often obtained by making use of the fact that the logarithm of the geometric mean of a set of numbers equals the (arithmetic) mean of the logarithms of the numbers.
(a) Using logarithms (Table IX at the end of the book) verify that the geometric mean of 114, 145, 133, 154, 146, and 123, the 1960 values of the Wholesale Price Index for six major commodity groups, is approximately 135.

(b) Referring to part (b) of Exercise 18, use logarithms to find the geometric mean of the price relatives comparing the 1961 prices of the three metals with those of 1955. Multiply by 100 to express the resulting index as a percentage and compare with the mean of the price relatives obtained in that exercise.

24. The *harmonic mean* of n numbers is given by n divided by the sum of the reciprocals of the n numbers, namely, by $\frac{n}{\Sigma\, 1/x}$, and it is used only in very special situations. For instance, if $12 is spent on pills costing 40 cents a dozen and another $12 is spent on pills costing 60 cents a dozen, the average price is not $\frac{40 + 60}{2} = 50$ cents a dozen; it is 48 cents, since a total of $24 is spent on a total of 50 dozen pills.
(a) Verify that 48 is, in fact, the harmonic mean of 40 and 60.
(b) If a motorist travels the first 10 miles of a trip at 30 miles per hour and the next 10 miles at 60 miles per hour, what is his average speed for these 20 miles? Does the harmonic mean give the correct answer?

25. If someone invests $5,000 at 3 per cent, $10,000 at 4 per cent, and $10,000 at 4.5 per cent, use the formula for the weighted mean to determine the average interest he receives on these investments.

26. In 1950, 1955, and 1960 the passenger fatalities per 100 million passenger miles flown by domestic scheduled air carriers were 2.1, 0.04, and 0.10, respectively. Given that the passenger miles flown by such carriers in these years were, respectively, 8,003, 19,582, and 30,557 million passenger miles, find the average fatality rate for the three years.

27. The average price paid for a pound of aluminum in 1930, 1940, 1950, and 1960 was 23.8, 18.7, 17.7, and 26.0 cents. Given that in these same years the production of aluminum was 115, 206, 719, and 2,014 thousands of short tons, what is the average price paid for a pound of aluminum in these four years?

28. The following table shows a baseball player's batting average and the number of times he was at bat in four consecutive seasons:

Year	*Batting Average*	*Times at Bat*
1962	0.285	408
1963	0.266	320
1964	0.294	402
1965	0.302	470

What is his over-all batting average for these four seasons?

29. In 1962 the average hourly wages paid to production workers in Arizona was $4.05 in contract construction, $2.57 in manufacturing, $2.92 in mining, and

\$2.60 in transportation and utilities. Given that the corresponding 1962 employment totals were 32,300, 55,900, 15,800, and 24,700, find the average hourly wages paid to these workers.

30. In an experiment designed to test the effectiveness of a new reducing diet, 5 persons in the age group from 20 to 29 lost on the average 7.7 pounds, 12 persons in the age group from 30 to 39 lost on the average 8.3 pounds, 20 persons in the age group from 40 to 49 lost on the average 11.2 pounds, while 8 persons older than 49 lost on the average 4.6 pounds. Combine these four means into an overall mean.

31. Aggregative index numbers (see Exercise 20) can be improved by weighting the various prices by the corresponding quantities (produced, sold, or consumed) in the given year, the base year, or some other fixed period of time. Using the given-year quantities as weights we obtain the *weighted aggregative index* $\frac{\Sigma\, q_n p_n}{\Sigma\, q_n p_0}\cdot 100$, and using the base-year quantities as weights we obtain the *weighted aggregative index* $\frac{\Sigma\, q_0 p_n}{\Sigma\, q_0 p_0}\cdot 100$, where the notation is the same as in Exercises 18 and 19. Note that these index numbers are essentially ratios of weighted means with the sum of the weights canceled.

(a) Using the data of Exercises 18 and 19 and the 1961 quantities as weights, calculate a weighted aggregative index comparing the 1961 prices of the three metals with those of 1955.

(b) Repeat part (a) using the 1955 quantities instead of the 1961 quantities as weights.

(c) The following are data on the prices of four major crops in dollars per bushel and their production in millions of bushels:

	1957 Prices	*1960 Prices*	*1960 Quantities*
Wheat	1.93	1.75	1,357
Corn	1.11	1.00	3,908
Oats	0.61	0.60	1,155
Barley	0.89	0.84	431

Using the 1960 quantities as weights, calculate a weighted aggregative index comparing the 1960 prices of these crops with those of 1957.

32. When averaging price relatives, we often use as weights the given-year *values* of the corresponding commodities, namely, the products $p_n q_n$, where the notation is the same as in Exercises 18 and 19.

(a) Use the data of Exercises 18 and 19 to calculate such a weighted mean of price relatives comparing the 1961 prices of the metals with those of 1955.

(b) Use the data of part (c) of Exercise 31 to calculate such a weighted mean of price relatives comparing the 1960 prices with those of 1957.

3.4 The Median and Other Fractiles

To avoid the difficulty met on page 34, where we showed that an extreme value (perhaps, a gross error) can have a pronounced effect on the mean, we sometimes describe the "middle" or "center" of a set of data with other kinds of statistical descriptions. One of these is the *median,* which is defined simply as *the value of the middle item* (*or the mean of the values of the two middle items*) *when the data are arranged in an increasing or decreasing order of magnitude.*

If we have an *odd* number of items, there is always a middle item whose value is the median. For example, the median of the five numbers 5, 10, 2, 7, and 8 is 7, as can easily be verified by first arranging these numbers according to size, and the median of the nine numbers 3, 5, 6, 9, 9, 10, 10, 12, and 13 is 9. Note that there are two 9's in this last example and that we do not refer to either of them as *the* median. The median is a number and not an item, namely, the value of the middle item. Generally speaking, if there are n items and n is *odd*, the median is the value of the $\frac{n+1}{2}$th largest item. Thus, the median of 25 numbers is given by the value of the $\frac{25+1}{2} =$ 13th largest, the median of 49 numbers is given by the value of the $\frac{49+1}{2}$ $=$ 25th largest, and the median of 81 numbers is given by the value of the $\frac{81+1}{2} =$ 41st largest.

If we have an *even* number of items, there is never a middle item, and the median is defined as the mean of the values of the two middle items. For instance, the median of the six numbers 3, 6, 8, 10, 13, and 15 (which are already ordered according to size) is $\frac{8+10}{2} = 9$. It is halfway between the two middle values (here the 3rd and the 4th) and, if we interpret it correctly, the formula $\frac{n+1}{2}$ again gives the *position* of the median. For the six given numbers the median is, thus, the value of the $\frac{6+1}{2} =$ 3.5th largest, and we interpret this as "halfway between the values of the third and the fourth." Similarly, the median of 100 numbers is given by the value of the $\frac{100+1}{2} =$ 50.5th largest item, or halfway between the values of the 50th and the 51st.

It is important to remember that the formula $\frac{n+1}{2}$ is *not* a formula for the median, itself; it merely tells us the position of the median, namely, the number of items we have to count until we reach the item whose value is the median (or the two items whose values have to be averaged to obtain the median).

It should not be surprising that the median and the mean of a set of data do not always coincide. Both of these measures describe the "middle" of a set of data, but they describe it in different ways. The median is central in the sense that it divides the data so that the values of half the items are less than or equal to the median while the values of the other half are greater than or equal to the median. The mean is central in a different sense, namely, in the sense of a *center of gravity*. (If we were to cut the histogram of a distribution out of cardboard, its center of gravity would lie on a vertical line through the point on the horizontal scale which corresponds to the mean.) Sometimes the median and the mean do coincide, though, and we interpret this as indicative of the *symmetry* of the data, a further property we shall discuss in Chapter 4.

The median has certain desirable properties, some of which it shares with the mean. Like the mean it always exists—that is, it can be calculated for any kind of numerical data—and it is always unique. Once the data are arranged according to size, the median is simple enough to find, but (unless the work is done with automatic equipment) ordering large sets of data can be a very tedious job. Unlike the mean, the median is *not* easily affected by extreme values, as is illustrated in Exercise 7 on page 52. Also unlike the mean, the median can be used to define the middle of a number of objects, properties, or qualities, which do not permit a quantitative description. It is possible, for instance, to rank a number of tasks according to their difficulty and then describe the middle one as being of "average" difficulty; also we might rank samples of chocolate sauce according to their consistency and then describe the middle one as having "average" consistency. Perhaps the most important distinction between the median and the mean is that in problems of inference (estimation, prediction, and so on) the mean is usually *more reliable* than the median. In other words, the median is usually subject to greater chance fluctuations than the mean, as is illustrated in Exercise 8 on page 52 and in Exercise 6 on page 214.

So far as symbolism is concerned, we shall write the median of a set of x's (looked upon as a sample) as $\tilde{x}$. Some statisticians correspondingly represent population medians with the symbol $\tilde{\mu}$, but there is no real need to introduce this notation. In most problems of estimation we assume that the population mean and median coincide; in fact, we shall be interested in the median mainly in connection with problems where *sample medians* are used to estimate *population means*.

If we want to determine the median of a set of data that has already been grouped, we find ourselves in a position similar to the one in which we found ourselves on page 34; we can no longer determine the *actual* value of the median, although we can find the class into which the median must fall. What we do then is most easily understood with the aid of a diagram like that of Figure 3.1, showing again the histogram of the radiation-count distribution. The median of a distribution is defined as a number, a point, which is such that *half the total area of the rectangles of the histogram lies to its left and half lies to its right.* This means that the sum of the areas of the rectangles to the left of the dotted line of Figure 3.1 equals the sum of the

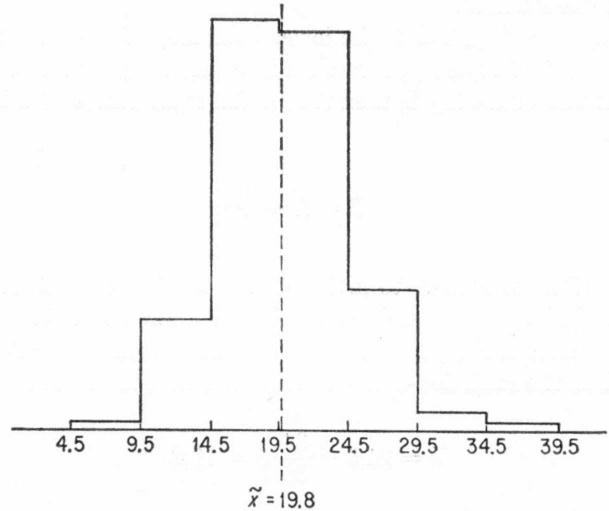

Fig. 3.1 Median of the radiation-count distribution.

areas of the rectangles to its right. Note that this definition is equivalent to the assumption that, within each class, the items are distributed (or spread out) evenly throughout the class interval.

In contrast to the problem of finding the median of ungrouped data, where we looked for the middle item (or items) and counted off $\frac{n+1}{2}$, we are now looking for a number, a dividing line, that divides the total area of the histogram into two equal parts, each representing a frequency of $n/2$. *Hence, to find the median of a distribution with a total frequency of n, we must, so to speak, count $n/2$ items starting at either end.*

To illustrate this procedure, let us again refer to the radiation-count distribution on page 13. Since $n = 100$ in this example, we will have to count $n/2 = 50$ items from either end. Beginning at the bottom of the distribution, we find that 48 of the values are less than 20 while 84 are less than 25, and it follows that the median must fall into the class whose limits are 20–24. Now we must count another 2 items in addition to the 48 items falling below this class, and we accomplish this by adding 2/36 of the class interval of 5 to 19.5, the lower boundary of the class. (We add 2/36 of the class interval because we want to count 2 of the 36 values contained in this class.) We thus get

$$\tilde{x} = 19.5 + \frac{2}{36}\cdot 5 = 19.8$$

rounded to one decimal.

Generally speaking, if L is the lower boundary of the class containing the median, f is its frequency, c the class interval, and j the number of items we still lack when reaching L, then the *median of the distribution* is given by the formula

▲ $$\tilde{x} = L + \frac{j}{f}\cdot c$$ ▲

It is possible, of course, to arrive at the median of a distribution by starting at the other end and *subtracting* an appropriate fraction of the class interval from the upper boundary U of the class into which the median must fall. For the radiation-count distribution we thus obtain

$$\tilde{x} = 24.5 - \frac{34}{36}\cdot 5 = 19.8$$

and the two answers are identical, as they should be. A general formula for the case where we start counting from the top of a distribution is given by

▲ $$\tilde{x} = U - \frac{j'}{f}\cdot c$$ ▲

where j' is the number of items we still lack when reaching U.

The median belongs to a general class of statistical descriptions called *fractiles*, and we shall study them briefly at this time because the method we have just described can be used to determine any fractile of a distribution. Generally speaking, *a fractile is a value below which lies a given fraction of a set of data;* for the median this fraction is 1/2. Similarly, the three *quartiles* Q_1, Q_2, and Q_3 are such that 25 per cent of the data fall below Q_1, 25 per cent fall between Q_1 and Q_2, 25 per cent fall between Q_2 and Q_3, and 25 per cent fall above Q_3. To find the first and third quartiles of a distribution (Q_2 actually *is* the median), we can use either of the two formulas given above. For Q_1 we count 25 per cent of the items starting at the bottom of the distribution, and for Q_3 we count 75 per cent of the items starting at the bottom or 25 per cent starting at the top. Referring again to the radiation-count distribution, we obtain

$$Q_1 = 14.5 + \frac{14}{37}\cdot 5 = 16.4$$

and

$$Q_3 = 24.5 - \frac{9}{36}\cdot 5 = 23.25$$

The *deciles* $D_1, D_2, \ldots,$ and D_9 are such that 10 per cent of the data fall below D_1, 10 per cent fall between D_1 and D_2, 10 per cent fall between D_2 and $D_3, \ldots,$ and 10 per cent fall above D_9. For example, counting 40 per cent of the items starting at the bottom of the radiation-count distribution, we find that

$$D_4 = 14.5 + \frac{29}{37}\cdot 5 = 18.4$$

and counting 10 per cent of the items starting at the other end, we find that

$$D_9 = 29.5 - \frac{7}{13}\cdot 5 = 26.8$$

The *percentiles* of a distribution, $P_1, P_2, \ldots,$ and P_{99} are such that 1 per cent of the data falls below P_1, 1 per cent falls between P_1 and $P_2, \ldots,$ and 1 per cent falls above P_{99}. (Note that the fifth decile and the fiftieth percentile are both equal to the median, and that the twenty-fifth and seventy-fifth percentiles equal Q_1 and Q_3, respectively.)

Directly, fractiles serve to indicate above or below what values we can find certain percentages of a set of data; indirectly, they can also provide short-cut estimates of other kinds of statistical descriptions. For instance, either the median or the *mid-quartile*, $\frac{1}{2}(Q_1 + Q_3)$, can be used to estimate the mean of a population, and in Chapter 10 we shall see that a certain measure based on fractiles can be used to estimate the so-called standard deviation (which measures the variability of a population). For this purpose it may be necessary to determine fractiles on the basis of ungrouped data, and how this can be done is explained in Exercise 24 on page 54. Note also that fractiles can be read directly off the ogive of a distribution without much loss of accuracy; in fact, we already used this method in the exercises on pages 24 and 25 to determine the median and the quartiles of some of the distributions.

3.5 Further Measures of Central Location

Besides the mean and the median, there are numerous other ways of describing the "middle," "center," or "average" of a set of data. Among these, the *geometric* and *harmonic means* were introduced earlier in Exercises 22 and 24 on pages 42 and 43, and the *mid-quartile* was mentioned briefly on page 49. Two other measures of central location worth mentioning are the *mid-range* and the *mode:* The *mid-range* of a set of data is given by the mean of the smallest value and the largest, and it sometimes serves as a quick estimate of the mean of the population from which the data were obtained; the *mode* is simply the value which occurs with the highest frequency. Thus, if more applicants for a job are 26 years old than any other age, we say that 26 is their *modal age* (that is, the mode is 26); similarly, in the radiation-count distribution the class which has the limits 15–19 is the *modal class* (it has the highest frequency.) An obvious advantage of the mode is that it requires no calculations, and its principal value lies in the fact that it can be used with qualitative as well as quantitative data. For instance, if we wanted to study consumers' preferences for different kinds of food, different kinds of packaging, or different kinds of advertising, we could in each case determine the modal choice; in some problems we might even compare the modal preferences expressed by several different groups. In situations like these we could not have used the median or the mean; although the median can sometimes be used to describe the "middle" of qualitative data, it is not applicable unless the objects or items can be *ordered* in some way.

When dealing with quantitative data, the disadvantages of the mode outweigh its desirable features, and it is, in fact, rarely used. A definite disadvantage of the mode is that it need not be unique, as is illustrated by the following data:

$$3 \quad 5 \quad 8 \quad 3 \quad 6 \quad 3 \quad 4 \quad 9 \quad 8 \quad 5 \quad 8$$

Here 3 and 8 both occur with the highest frequency of three. (The fact that there is more than one mode is sometimes an indication that the data are not homogeneous, that is, they constitute a combination of several sets of data.) Another disadvantage of the mode is that if no two values are alike, the mode does not exist.

So far as the mode of grouped data is concerned, we have already pointed out that the class with the highest frequency is called the *modal class.* If one wants to be more specific, one can define the mode of a distribution as the class mark of the modal class or in some other way (see Bibliography on page 57). We shall not go into this any further since there are very few occasions where it is necessary, or desirable, to use the mode of a distribution.

The question of what particular "average" should be used in a given problem is not always easily answered. As we saw in Exercises 22 and 24 on pages 42 and 43, there are problems in which the nature of the data dictates the use of such averages as the geometric and harmonic means. The nature of the data may also dictate the use of a weighted mean, perhaps even a *weighted* geometric mean. We also saw that when dealing with qualitative data, we may have no choice but to use the mode or in some special instances the median.

A very interesting distinction between the mean, median, and mode will be brought out in Section 6.6, where we shall discuss their use in a problem of *decision making*. At that time we shall see that the choice between these three measures of central location (and others) may well depend on the risks, penalties, and rewards that are involved.

Generally speaking, the mean is by far the most widely used measure of central location, and we shall use it almost exclusively in the third part of this book. In problems of inference the mean has generally such definite advantages that other measures—for instance, the median—are used mainly because of their computational ease.

The fact that there is a certain amount of arbitrariness in the selection of statistical descriptions has led some persons to believe that they can take a set of data, apply the magic of statistics, and prove almost anything they want. In fact, a nineteenth century British statesman once said that there are three kinds of lies: lies, damned lies, and statistics. To give an example where such a criticism might be justified, suppose that a paint manufacturer asks his research department to "prove" that on the average a gallon of his paint covers more square feet than that of his two principal competitors. Suppose, furthermore, that the research department tests five cans of each brand, getting the following results (in square feet per gallon can):

Brand A: 488, 513, 515, 523, 526
Brand B: 521, 496, 522, 496, 520
Brand C: 495, 500, 494, 530, 506

If the manufacturer's own brand is Brand A, the person who is analyzing the data will find to his delight that the means of the three samples are, respectively, 513, 511, and 505. Hence, he can claim that in actual tests a can of his employer's product covered on the average more square feet than those of his competitors.

Now suppose, for the sake of argument, that the manufacturer's own brand is Brand B. Clearly, the person doing the analysis can no longer base the comparison on the sample means—this would not prove his point. Trying instead the sample medians, he finds that they are, respectively, 515, 520, and 500, and this provides him with exactly the kind of "proof" he wants. The median is a perfectly respectable measure of the "average" or "middle" of a set of data, and using the medians he can claim that his employer's product came out best in the test.

Finally, suppose the manufacturer's own brand is Brand C. After trying various measures of central location, the person doing the analysis finally comes upon one that does the trick: the *mid-range*, which we defined on page 50. Since the mid-ranges of the three samples are, respectively, 507, 509, and 512, he can claim that "on the average" his employer's product scored highest in the test. The moral of this example is that *if data are to be compared, the method of comparison should be decided on beforehand, or at least without looking at the actual data.* All this is aside from the fact that comparisons based on samples are often far from conclusive. It is quite possible that whatever differences there may be among the three means (or other descriptions) can be attributed entirely to chance (see Exercise 5 on page 309).

EXERCISES

1. The following are the numbers of students absent from an elementary school on fifteen consecutive school days: 39, 55, 46, 38, 41, 40, 33, 49, 42, 37, 49, 44, 51, 48, 44. Calculate the mean, the median, and the mid-range.

2. Find the median of the following figures on the average monthly percentage of possible sunshine in Pittsburgh, Pa., as reported by the U.S. Weather Bureau: 38, 40, 53, 53, 57, 65, 66, 63, 68, 59, 50, and 40 per cent.

3. Find the median of the grades of Exercise 4 on page 39.

4. Find the median and the mid-range of the 12 temperature readings of Exercise 5 on page 39.

5. Referring to Exercise 6 on page 39, determine the median number of psychologists employed (a) in the Mountain States, and (b) in the Pacific States.

6. Referring to Exercise 9 on page 40, find the median of the fees charged by the 15 doctors for making house calls.

7. Each of 12 women taking part in a drive to raise money for an addition to the community hospital was assigned a certain quota, and the following are the percentages of their respective quotas which they actually collected: 94, 110, 80, 98, 95, 108, 101, 460, 75, 105, 110, and 85. Calculate the median and the mean of these percentages, and indicate which of these measures is a better indication of the "average" performance of these 12 women.

8. To verify the claim that the mean is generally *more reliable* than the median (namely, that it is subject to smaller chance fluctuations), a student conducted an experiment consisting of 10 tosses of three dice. The following are his results: 4, 3, and 5; 2, 6, and 5; 4, 6, and 2; 2, 3, and 5; 6, 1, and 5; 2, 5, and 2; 3, 1, and 4; 5, 5, and 2; 3, 4, and 3; 2, 1, and 6.

(a) Calculate the ten medians and the ten means.

(b) Group the means and the medians into separate distributions having the class limits 1.5, 2.5, 3.5, 4.5, and 5.5.

(c) Draw histograms of the two distributions obtained in (b) and explain how they illustrate the claim concerning the relative reliability of the median and the mean.

9. Repeat Exercise 8 with your own data obtained by actually rolling three dice ten times. (In case the reader does not have any dice, he might read ahead in Section 8.3, where it is explained how an experiment like this can be simulated with the use of random numbers.)

10. Find the median of the tree diameters of Exercise 9 on page 23
(a) without grouping the data;
(b) using the distribution obtained in that exercise.

11. Referring to the distribution of tree diameters obtained in Exercise 9 on page 23, find
(a) Q_1, Q_3, and the mid-quartile;
(b) the deciles D_1 and D_9;
(c) the percentiles P_{30} and P_{70}.

12. Referring to the distribution of test scores obtained in Exercise 10 on page 24, find
(a) the median;
(b) Q_1, Q_3, and the mid-quartile;
(c) the deciles D_2 and D_8;
(d) the percentiles P_5 and P_{95}.

13. Find the median as well as the quartiles Q_1 and Q_3 of the radioactive-fallout distribution obtained in Exercise 11 on page 24. Also compare these results with the corresponding values read off the ogive constructed in part (d) of that exercise.

14. Find the median of the distribution of the number of steak dinners obtained in Exercise 12 on page 25
(a) without grouping the data;
(b) using the distribution obtained in that exercise.

15. Referring to the distribution of the number of steak dinners obtained in Exercise 12 on page 25,
(a) how many steaks should the manager stock so that he can expect to run short only 10 per cent of the time?
(b) How many steaks should the manager stock so that he can expect to have 40 or more steaks left over only 25 per cent of the time?

16. Use the distribution obtained in Exercise 13 on page 25 to determine the median as well as the first and third quartiles of the iron-solution indices. Compare these results with the corresponding values read off the ogive in part (c) of that exercise.

17. Find the median of the ages of the filing cabinets given in Exercise 14 on page 25
(a) using the ungrouped data;

(b) using the distribution obtained in that exercise;
(c) reading the value off the ogive constructed in part (b) of that exercise.

18. Referring to the distribution obtained in Exercise 14 on page 25, find
(a) Q_1, Q_3, and the mid-quartile;
(b) the deciles D_4 and D_6;
(c) the percentiles P_{15} and P_{85}.
Also determine how wide a range of values is covered by the middle 70 per cent of the data.

19. Find the mode and the mid-range of the ungrouped radiation counts on page 13.

20. Find the mode (if it exists) of each of the following sets of numbers:
(a) 14, 15, 16, 16, 18, 16, 16, 15, 17, 15, 14, 17, 13;
(b) 32, 36, 39, 35, 33, 36, 31, 36, 39, 37, 36, 39, 39;
(c) 57, 41, 65, 50, 68, 34, 42, 38, 46, 59, 33.

21. Referring to Exercise 9 on page 40, find the mode of the fees charged by the 15 doctors for making house calls.

22. Referring to the ungrouped data of Exercise 10 on page 24, find the mode of the grades obtained by the 120 students.

23. Thirty school children who had just returned from a visit to Disneyland were asked what ride they liked best. Their replies were: Submarine, Circus Train, Jungle Cruise, Monorail, Pirate Ship, Jungle Cruise, Submarine, Mine Train, Matterhorn, Submarine, Jungle Cruise, Monorail, Circus Train, Mr. Toad's Wild Ride, Submarine, Tree House, Pirate Ship, Tiki Room, Jungle Cruise, Monorail, Monorail, Submarine, Jungle Cruise, Circus Train, Matterhorn, Jungle Cruise, Tiki Room, River Boat, Tree House, and Jungle Cruise. What is their modal choice?

24. In general, we define the jth k-tile, $F_{j/k}$, to be such that j/k is the fraction of the data falling below $F_{j/k}$. For grouped data, we calculate $F_{j/k}$ by the method indicated in the text; for ungrouped data, we arrange the n observations according to size and let $F_{j/k}$ be given by the value of the $\dfrac{j(n+1)}{k}$ th largest observation.
(a) Is this rule consistent with the definition of the median for ungrouped data?
(b) Find the two quartiles $F_{1/4}$ and $F_{3/4}$ of the data on absenteeism given in Exercise 1.
(c) Find the two quartiles $F_{1/4}$ and $F_{3/4}$ of the chemistry grades of Exercise 4 on page 39. Note that if $\dfrac{j(n+1)}{k}$ is not a whole number, we have to interpolate between successive observations. For instance, to find the $5\frac{1}{4}$th largest value in an ordered array of numbers, we must go 1/4 of the way from the fifth to the sixth. Thus, if the fifth largest number is 17 and sixth largest number is 19, then the "$5\frac{1}{4}$th largest" is 17.5.
(d) Find the two deciles $F_{1/10}$ and $F_{9/10}$ of the chemistry grades of Exercise 4 on page 39. (See comment to part (c).)

(e) Find $F_{1/16}$ and $F_{15/16}$ of the chemistry grades of Exercise 4 on page 39. (See comment to part (c).)

(f) Find the two quartiles of the ungrouped radiation counts on page 13, and compare the results with the corresponding values obtained for the grouped data on page 49.

3.6 Technical Note (Subscripts and Summations)

In order to make the formulas of statistics applicable to any kind of data, it is customary to represent measurements or observations by means of letters such as x, y, and z. Furthermore, to make it easy to refer to individual measurements within a set of data we use *subscripts*, writing, for example, x_1, x_2, and x_3 for the weights of three guinea pigs. Thus, n measurements may be referred to as $x_1, x_2, \ldots,$ and x_n, and if we want to refer to one of these measurements in general, we write x_i, where i can assume any one of the values from 1 to n.

Instead of writing the subscript as i we could just as well have used j, k, or some other letter, and instead of x we could have used y, z, or some other letter. Generally speaking, *it is customary to use different letters for different kinds of measurements and the same letter with different subscripts for different measurements of the same kind.* Thus, we might write x_{31} and x_{57} for the heights of the thirty-first and fifty-seventh persons on a list, and we might write x_{24}, y_{24}, and z_{24} for the I.Q., age, and income of the twenty-fourth person in a certain sample.

In connection with this notation we must be careful not to confuse, say, the subscript 24 appearing in x_{24} with the double subscript "2 and 4" used, for example, to indicate that x_{24} is the morning temperature of the 2nd patient on the 4th day after an operation. In advanced work in statistics we frequently use two or more subscripts to indicate, for example, that x_{ijk} is the cost of operating the ith washing machine with the jth kind of detergent and the kth kind of load. Except for Chapter 12, we shall use only single subscripts in the remainder of this book.

When we introduced the Σ notation on page 32, we referred to it as a kind of mathematical shorthand; in fact, we pointed out that it is an abbreviated sort of shorthand, as it does not tell us explicitly what x's, or how many of them, we are supposed to add. This is taken care of in the more explicit notation

$$\sum_{i=1}^{n} x_i = x_1 + x_2 + \ldots + x_n$$

where it is made clear that we are adding the x's whose subscript i is 1, 2, . . ., and n. Generally, we shall not use this explicit notation in the text, in order to simplify the over-all appearance of the formulas, assuming that it is clear in each case what x's we are referring to and how many there are.

Using the Σ notation, we shall also have the occasion to write such expressions as Σx^2, Σxy, $\Sigma x^2 f$, ..., which (more explicitly) represent the sums

$$\sum_{i=1}^{n} x_i^2 = x_1^2 + x_2^2 + x_3^2 + \ldots + x_n^2$$

$$\sum_{j=1}^{m} x_j y_j = x_1 y_1 + x_2 y_2 + \ldots + x_m y_m$$

$$\sum_{i=1}^{n} x_i^2 f_i = x_1^2 f_1 + x_2^2 f_2 + \ldots + x_n^2 f_n$$

Working with several subscripts, we may have to evaluate a *double summation* such as

$$\sum_{j=1}^{3} \sum_{i=1}^{4} x_{ij} = \sum_{j=1}^{3} (x_{1j} + x_{2j} + x_{3j} + x_{4j})$$

$$= x_{11} + x_{21} + x_{31} + x_{41} + x_{12} + x_{22}$$

$$+ x_{32} + x_{42} + x_{13} + x_{23} + x_{33} + x_{43}$$

To verify some of the formulas involving summations that are stated, but not proved, in the text, the reader will find it convenient to use the following rules:

Rule A: $$\sum_{i=1}^{n} (x_i \pm y_i) = \sum_{i=1}^{n} x_i \pm \sum_{i=1}^{n} y_i$$

Rule B: $$\sum_{i=1}^{n} k \cdot x_i = k \cdot \sum_{i=1}^{n} x_i$$

Rule C: $$\sum_{i=1}^{n} k = k \cdot n$$

The first of these rules states that the summation of the sum (or difference) of two terms equals the sum (or difference) of the individual summations, and it can be extended to the sum or difference of more than two terms. The second rule states that we can, so to speak, factor a constant out of a summation, and the third rule states that the summation of a constant is simply n times that constant. All of these rules can be proved by actually writing out in full what each of the summations represents.

EXERCISES

1. Write each of the following in full, that is, without summation signs:

(a) $\sum_{i=1}^{4} x_i$

(b) $\sum_{i=1}^{3} x_i^2$

(c) $\sum_{i=1}^{5} (x_i + y_i)$

(d) $\sum_{j=1}^{5} (x_j + 4)$

(e) $\sum_{i=1}^{8} x_i y_i$

(f) $\sum_{j=1}^{4} x_j f_j$

2. Write each of the following expressions as summations, showing the subscripts and the limits of summation:
(a) $x_1 + x_2 + x_3 + x_4 + x_5 + x_6$;
(b) $x_1y_1 + x_2y_2 + \ldots + x_7y_7$;
(c) $x_1^2 + x_2^2 + x_3^2 + \ldots + x_9^2$;
(d) $(x_1 - 3) + (x_2 - 3) + \ldots + (x_8 - 3)$.

3. Given $x_1 = 2$, $x_2 = 7$, $x_3 = -3$, $x_4 = 2$, $x_5 = -1$, and $x_6 = 1$, find $\sum_{i=1}^{6} x_i$ and $\sum_{i=1}^{6} x_i^2$.

4. Given $x_1 = 4$, $x_2 = -1$, $x_3 = 5$, $f_1 = 4$, $f_2 = 6$, $f_3 = 2$, $y_1 = -3$, $y_2 = 5$, and $y_3 = 2$, find (a) $\Sigma\, x \cdot f$, (b) $\Sigma\, x^2 \cdot f$, (c) $\Sigma\, xy$, and (d) $\Sigma\, (x - y)$.

5. Prove that $\sum_{i=1}^{n} (x_i - \bar{x}) = 0$, where $\bar{x}$ is the mean of the given x's.

6. Referring to the definition on page 30, give a formal proof that the (arithmetic) mean is a measure of location.

7. If the class marks of a distribution are coded so that $x_i = c \cdot u_i + x_0$, where the x_i are the class marks in the original scale, the u_i are the class marks in the coded scale, c is the class interval, and x_0 is the class mark (in the original scale) which is the origin of the coded scale, prove that $\bar{x} = c \cdot \bar{u} + x_0$, where $\bar{x}$ is the mean of the distribution in the original scale and $\bar{u}$ is its mean in the coded scale.

8. Given $x_{11} = 2$, $x_{12} = -1$, $x_{13} = 2$, $x_{14} = 3$, $x_{21} = 1$, $x_{22} = 5$, $x_{23} = -1$, $x_{24} = -4$, $x_{31} = 5$, $x_{32} = 14$, $x_{33} = -2$, and $x_{34} = 6$, find
(a) $\sum_{i=1}^{3} x_{ij}$ separately for $j = 1, 2, 3$, and 4;
(b) $\sum_{j=1}^{4} x_{ij}$ separately for $i = 1, 2$, and 3.

9. With reference to the data of Exercise 8, evaluate the double summation $\sum_{i=1}^{3} \sum_{j=1}^{4} x_{ij}$ using
(a) the results obtained in part (a) of Exercise 8;
(b) the results obtained in part (b) of Exercise 8.

10 Using the values of Exercise 8, find

(a) $\sum_{i=1}^{3} \sum_{j=1}^{4} x_{ij}^2$ (b) $\sum_{i=1}^{3} \left[\sum_{j=1}^{4} x_{ij} \right]^2$ (c) $\sum_{j=1}^{4} \left[\sum_{i=1}^{3} x_{ij} \right]^2$

BIBLIOGRAPHY

More detailed treatments of the various measures of location, including more elaborate ways of defining the mode of a distribution, may be found in the book by A. E. Waugh and in the book by F. E. Croxton and D. J. Cowden mentioned on page 28, and in other introductory tests. Further material on index numbers is given in

Freund, J. E., and Williams, F. J., *Modern Business Statistics.* Englewood Cliffs, N.J.: Prentice-Hall, Inc., 1958

and in most other texts dealing specifically with problems of business statistics. With regard to the ethics involved in the selection of a measure of location, see also the book by D. Huff listed on page 28.

FOUR
Measures of Variation and Further Descriptions

4.1 Introduction

An important characteristic of most sets of data is that the values are generally *not all alike;* indeed, the extent to which they are unalike, or vary among themselves, is of fundamental importance in statistics. Since the measures discussed in Chapter 3 do not tell us anything about this characteristic, we shall now investigate other measures, so-called *measures of variation,* which tell us something about the extent to which data are dispersed, spread out, or bunched. (For a rigorous definition of such measures see Exercise 33 on page 73.)

First, let us give a few examples to illustrate the importance of measuring variability. Suppose, for instance, that we are interested in buying stock in a certain company and we find that the most recent price quoted at the New York Stock Exchange is $42\frac{5}{8}$ (dollars per share). In order to decide whether this is a good buy, many factors will have to be taken into account; among other things we may want to know how much the price of the stock *fluctuates,* and we thus look for the year's High and Low. If these figures are 61 and $39\frac{1}{2}$, respectively, we now have some information about the *variation* in the price of the stock, and this may be critical in deciding whether or not to buy the stock. Of course, an intelligent investor would want to compare the fluctuations of this stock with those of other stocks and also with those of the market as a whole.

To consider another example, suppose that an executive has to choose one of two applicants for a secretarial position and that, to be objective, he asks each of them to copy five rather lengthy reports. If the results of this test show that each made on the average 8 mistakes per report, it might be inferred that the two are equally good. However, if the first applicant made 7, 10, 8, 9, and 6 errors in typing the five reports and the second applicant made 5, 14, 2, 2, and 17, this shows that even though they averaged the same number of mistakes, the first was fairly consistent while the second was highly erratic. This may influence the executive's choice and it illustrates the importance of considering, and in some way measuring, the variability of a set of data (even if it is only by inspection).

The concept of variability is of special importance in statistical inference, because it is here that we have to cope with questions of *chance variation.* To illustrate the meaning of this term, suppose that a balanced coin is flipped 100 times. Although we may expect 50 heads and 50 tails, we would certainly not be surprised if we got, say, 54 heads and 46 tails, 49 heads and 51 tails, or 53 heads and 47 tails. Most likely, we would ascribe the occurrence of a few extra heads or a few extra tails to chance. In order to study this phenomenon called chance, suppose we repeatedly flip a balanced coin 100 times and that in 10 such "experiments" we obtain 48, 56, 50, 53, 49, 46, 51, 48, 44, and 56 heads. This gives us some idea about the magnitude of the fluctuations (variations) produced by chance in an experiment of this kind, and knowledge like this would be important, for example, if we had to decide whether there was anything "phony" about a coin (or the person by whom it is tossed), if 100 tosses yield 28 heads and 72 tails. Judging by the above data, it would seem that most of the time we should get anywhere from 40 to 60 heads (in the experiment the number of heads ranged from 44 to 56); hence, we conclude that probably there is something wrong with the coin or the way in which it was flipped. We have presented this argument on an intuitive basis to demonstrate the importance of measuring variability; it will be treated more formally in Chapter 7.

As a final example, let us consider a problem in which the *variability of the population* plays an important role. Suppose we want to estimate the average I.Q. of two groups of individuals. The first group consists of the high school seniors in a fairly large community, and the second group consists of all the graduate students enrolled in a state university. So far as intelligence is concerned, the first group is not very homogeneous, and the I.Q.'s of the high school students may well vary anywhere from 85 to 140. The graduate students, on the other hand, must all have pretty high I.Q.'s, most of which will probably fall on the interval from 115 to 135. Thus, it stands to reason that if we take the same number of measurements for each group (say, we measure the I.Q.'s of 10 of the high school students and 10 of the graduate students), the information for the graduate students is apt to be *more reliable.* In other words, the sample mean obtained for the graduate students is apt to be closer than that of the high school seniors to the respective *true* average I.Q.'s. This illustrates the fact that *in order to evaluate the "closenesss" of an estimate or the "goodness" of a generalization one must know something about the variability of the population from which the sample is obtained.* There is not much variability among the I.Q.'s of the graduate students, and a sample mean cannot help but be fairly close; so far as the high school seniors are concerned, their I.Q.'s vary considerably and a sample mean may well be off by a large amount.

We have given these four examples to show that the concept of variability plays a fundamental role in the analysis of statistical data. In what follows, we shall learn how to measure variability statistically. The first example on page 59 already introduced one way of indicating (or measuring) variability, namely, by giving the two extreme (largest and smallest) values of a sample. More or less the same is accomplished by giving the *difference between the two extreme values*, which we refer to as the *sample range*. Thus, for the example on page 59, the range of the prices paid for a share of the given stock is $61 - 39\frac{1}{2} = \$21.50$.

In spite of the obvious advantage of the range that it is *easy to calculate* and *easy to understand*, it is generally not looked upon as a very useful measure of variation. As it is based only on the two extreme values, its main shortcoming is that it does not tell us anything about the actual *dispersion* of the data which fall in between. Each of the following three sets of data

8	20	20	20	20	20	20	20	20	20
8	8	8	8	8	20	20	20	20	20
8	9	11	12	13	15	15	18	19	20

has a range of $20 - 8 = 12$, but the dispersions of the data are by no means the same. As a result, the range is used mainly in situations where it is desired to get a quick, though not necessarily very accurate, picture of the variability of a set of data. When the sample size is very small, the range is quite adequate, and it is, thus, used widely in *quality control*, where it is important to keep a continuous check on the variability of raw materials, machines, or manufactured products (see also Section 10.1).

4.2 The Standard Deviation

Since the dispersion of a set of numbers is *small* if they are bunched closely about their mean and it is *large* if they are spread over considerable distances away from their mean, it would seem reasonable to define variation in terms of the distances (deviations) by which numbers depart from their mean. If we have a set of numbers $x_1, x_2, \ldots,$ and x_n, whose mean is $\bar{x}$, we can write the amounts by which they differ from their mean as $x_1 - \bar{x}$, $x_2 - \bar{x}, \ldots,$ and $x_n - \bar{x}$. These quantities are called the *deviations from the mean* and it suggests itself that we might use their average, namely, their *mean*, as a measure of the variation of the n numbers. This would not be a bad idea, if it were not for the fact that we would always get 0 for an answer, no matter how widely dispersed the data might be. As the reader was asked to show in Exercise 5 on page 57, $\Sigma\,(x - \bar{x})$ is always equal to zero—some of the deviations are positive, some are negative, and their sum as well as their mean is equal to zero.

Since we are really interested in the *magnitude* of the deviations and not in their signs, we might simply "ignore" the signs and, thus, define a measure of variation in terms of the *absolute values* of the deviations from the mean. Indeed, if we added the values of the deviations from the mean as if they were all positive and divided by n, we would obtain a measure of variation called the *mean deviation* (see Exercises 5 and 6 on page 70). Unfortunately, this measure of variation has the drawback that, owing to the absolute values, it is difficult to subject it to any sort of theoretical treatment; for instance, it is difficult to study mathematically how *in problems of sampling*, mean deviations are affected by chance. However, there exists another way of eliminating the signs of the deviations from the mean, which is preferable on theoretical grounds: The *squares* of the deviations from the mean cannot be negative; in fact, they are positive unless a value happens to coincide with the mean, in which case both $x - \bar{x}$ and $(x - \bar{x})^2$ are equal to zero. Thus, if we average the squared deviations from the mean and then take the square root to compenstate for the fact that the deviations were squared, we obtain the formula

$$\sqrt{\frac{\Sigma\,(x - \bar{x})^2}{n}}$$

and this is how, traditionally, the *standard deviation* has been defined. Expressing literally what we have done here mathematically, it has also been called the *root-mean-square deviation*.

In recent years there has been a growing tendency among statisticians and research workers to make a slight modification in this definition. It consists of dividing the sum of the squared deviations from the mean by $n - 1$ instead of n. Following this practice, let us formally define s, the *standard deviation of a sample*, as

$$\blacktriangle \qquad s = \sqrt{\frac{\Sigma\,(x - \bar{x})^2}{n - 1}} \qquad \blacktriangle$$

and its square, the *sample variance*, as

$$\blacktriangle \qquad s^2 = \frac{\Sigma\,(x - \bar{x})^2}{n - 1} \qquad \blacktriangle$$

By using the symbol $\bar{x}$ we tacitly assumed that the x's constitute a sample; however, substituting μ for $\bar{x}$ we could define an analogous measure for populations (see also page 65). Note that to facilitate the calculation of standard deviations a table of square roots is given at the end of the book; the use of this table is explained in the Technical Note on page 78.

The following explains why we divided by $n - 1$ instead of n in the definition of the standard deviation: if a sample variance were used to estimate a population variance, we would obtain a value which *on the average* is too small if we divide by n rather than $n - 1$. As a matter of fact, it would be too small *on the average* by the factor $(n - 1)/n$. We cannot prove this theoretical fact at the level of this book, but since we shall frequently use sample variances and sample standard deviations as estimates of the corresponding population parameters, we prefer the above definition of s and s^2. Note, however, that this modification is significant only when n is small; its effect becomes negligible when n is large, say, 100 or more.

To illustrate the calculation of a sample standard deviation, let us find s for the following figures on the number of microorganisms found in six cultures: 13, 17, 7, 10, 16, and 9. First calculating $\bar{x}$, we obtain

x	$(x - \bar{x})$	$(x - \bar{x})^2$
13	1	1
17	5	25
7	−5	25
10	−2	4
16	4	16
9	−3	9
72	0	80

$$\bar{x} = \frac{72}{6} = 12$$

$$s = \sqrt{\frac{80}{5}} = \sqrt{16} = 4$$

This provides us with an estimate of the standard deviation of the number of microorganisms in cultures of the given kind; later on this figure will be of aid in judging how close $\bar{x}$ might be to μ, the true mean of the number of microorganism in cultures of this kind (see Exercise 17 on page 235).

The calculation of s was very easy in this example, and this was due largely to the fact that the x's, their mean, and hence also the deviations from the mean were all whole numbers. Had this not been the case, it might have been profitable to use the following *short-cut formula for s:*

$$\blacktriangle \qquad s = \sqrt{\frac{n(\Sigma\, x^2) - (\Sigma\, x)^2}{n(n - 1)}} \qquad \blacktriangle$$

This formula does not involve any approximations and it can be derived from the other formula for s by using the rules for summations given on page 56 (see Exercise 32 on page 73). The advantage of this short-cut formula is that we do not have to go through the process of actually finding the deviations from the mean; instead we calculate Σx, the sum of the x's, Σx^2, the sum of their squares, and substitute directly into the formula. Referring again to the microorganism data, we now have

x	x^2
13	169
17	289
7	49
10	100
16	256
9	81
72	944

$$s = \sqrt{\frac{6(944) - (72)^2}{6 \cdot 5}} = 4$$

It appears that in this particular example the "short-cut" method is actually more involved; this may be the case, but in actual practice, when we are dealing with realistically complex data, the short-cut formula usually provides considerable simplifications.

To demonstrate the advantages of the short-cut formula, let us determine the sample variance of the numbers 12, 7, 9, 5, 4, 8, 17, 2, 11, 14, 13, and 9, using first the formula on page 62 and then the short-cut formula on page 63. Without using the short-cut formula we get

x	$(x - \bar{x})$	$(x - \bar{x})^2$
12	2.75	7.5625
7	−2.25	5.0625
9	−0.25	0.0625
5	−4.25	18.0625
4	−5.25	27.5625
8	−1.25	1.5625
17	7.75	60.0625
2	−7.25	52.5625
11	1.75	3.0625
14	4.75	22.5625
13	3.75	14.0625
9	−0.25	0.0625
111	0	212.2500

$$\bar{x} = \frac{111}{12} = 9.25, \qquad s^2 = \frac{212.2500}{11} = 19.3$$

and working with the short-cut formula we get

x	x^2
12	144
7	49
9	81
5	25
4	16
8	64
17	289
2	4
11	121
14	196
13	169
9	81
111	1,239

$$s^2 = \frac{12(1{,}239) - (111)^2}{12 \cdot 11} = 19.3$$

Here the mean was 9.25, not a whole number, and the short-cut formula provided considerable simplifications.

A further simplification in the calculation of s or s^2 consists of adding an arbitrary positive or negative number to each measurement. It is easy to prove that this would have no effect on the final result, and had we used this trick in the last example, we might have subtracted 10 (added -10) from each number, getting 2, -3, -1, -5, -6, -2, 7, -8, 1, 4, 3, and -1 instead of the original numbers. The sum of these numbers is -9, the sum of their squares is 219, and substitution into the formula for s^2 yields

$$s^2 = \frac{12(219) - (-9)^2}{12 \cdot 11} = 19.3$$

which is exactly what we had before. Since the purpose of this trick is to reduce the size of the numbers with which we have to work, it is usually desirable to subtract a number that is close to the mean. In our example the mean was 9.25, and the calculations might have been even simpler if we had subtracted 9 instead of 10.

The formulas given so far in this section apply essentially to samples, but if we substitute μ for $\bar{x}$ and N for n we obtain analogous formulas for the standard deviation and the variance of a *population*. It has become fairly general practice to write population standard deviations as σ (small Greek *sigma*) when dividing by N, as in the first formula on page 62, and as S when dividing by $N - 1$. So far as actual calculations are concerned, we can still use the short-cut formulas, although for σ the $n - 1$ in the denominator must be replaced with an N and for S it must be replaced with $N - 1$. It cannot be too strongly emphasized that the difference between the two formulas (that is, those for σ and S) is negligible unless N is very small.

If we want to calculate the standard deviation of data which have already been grouped, we are faced with the same problem as on page 34. Proceeding as we did in connection with the mean, and assigning the value of the class mark to each value falling into a given class, we obtain the formula

$$s = \sqrt{\frac{\Sigma\,(x - \bar{x})^2 \cdot f}{n - 1}}$$

and, if we substitute μ for $\bar{x}$ and N or $N - 1$ for $n - 1$, we obtain analogous formulas for σ and S. Note that in this formula the x's are now the class marks and the f's are the corresponding class frequencies.

The above formula serves to *define* s for grouped data, but it is seldom used in actual practice. Either we use a *computing formula* analogous to the one on page 63, namely,

▲ $$s = \sqrt{\frac{n(\Sigma\,x^2 f) - (\Sigma\,xf)^2}{n(n - 1)}}$$ ▲

where the x's are the class marks and the f's the corresponding class frequencies, or we use the same kind of *coding* as in the calculation of the mean of grouped data. Following the notation on page 36, we obtain

▲ $$s = c\sqrt{\frac{n(\Sigma\,u^2 f) - (\Sigma\,uf)^2}{n(n - 1)}}$$ ▲

This is the *short-cut formula for computing the standard deviation of grouped data*. Note that this formula can be used only when the class intervals are all equal.

Although the short-cut formula may look fairly complicated, it makes the calculation of s very easy. Instead of having to work with the actual class marks and the deviations from the mean, we have only to find the sum of the products obtained by multiplying each u by the corresponding f, the sum of the products obtained by multiplying the square of each u by the corresponding f, and substitute into the formula.

To illustrate the use of the short-cut formula for s, let us calculate the standard deviation of the radiation-count distribution on page 13. Using the same u-scale as on page 36, we get

x	u	f	uf	u^2f
7	−3	1	−3	9
12	−2	10	−20	40
17	−1	37	−37	37
22	0	36	0	0
27	1	13	13	13
32	2	2	4	8
37	3	1	3	9
			−40	116

$$s = 5\sqrt{\frac{100(116) - (-40)^2}{100 \cdot 99}} = 5.025$$

The variation of the radiation-count data is, thus, measured by a standard deviation of, roughly, 5 particles per 40-second interval.

We have computed the standard deviation of grouped data under the assumption that all measurements falling into a class are located at its class mark. The error introduced by this assumption, which is appropriately called a *grouping error,* can be appreciable when the class interval c is very large. A correction which compensates for this error, called *Sheppard's correction,* is mentioned in the Bibliography on page 79.

In the argument which led to the definition of the standard deviation we observed that the dispersion of a set of data is small if the values are bunched closely about their mean and that it is large if the values are spread over considerable distances away from the mean. Correspondingly, we can now say that if the standard deviation of a set of data is small, the values are concentrated near the mean, and if the standard deviation is large, the values are scattered widely about the mean. To present this argument on a less intuitive basis (after all, *what is small and what is large?*), let us mention an important theorem, called *Chebyshev's Theorem* after the Russian mathematician P. L. Chebyshev (1821–1894). According to this theorem we can be *certain* for any kind of data (populations as well as samples) that *the proportion of the data falling within k standard deviations of their mean is at least* $1 - 1/k^2$. Thus, at least 75 per cent of any set of data must fall within 2 standard deviations of its mean, and if a distribution has the mean $\bar{x} = 127$ and the standard deviation $s = 18$, we can be *certain* that at least 75 per cent of the data fall between $127 - 2(18) = 91$ and $127 + 2(18) = 163$. Also, at least 96 per cent of any set of data must fall within 5 standard deviations of its mean, and if two sets of data have the same mean $\bar{x} = 210$ while their standard deviations are, respectively, $s = 50$ and $s = 20$, we can assert for the first set of data that at least 75 per cent of the values must fall between 110 and 310, while for the second set of data we can make the much stronger statement that at least 96 per cent of the data must fall on the same interval. This illustrates how the magnitude of the standard deviation "controls" the concentration of a set of data about its mean.

An important feature of Chebyshev's Theorem is that it holds for any kind of data; this generality is also a shortcoming, however, for if we do have some information about the over-all shape of a set of data, that is, the over-all shape of their distribution, we can often make much *stronger* statements. For instance, if a distribution is *bell-shaped* (like the one shown in Figure 4.1), we can expect roughly 95 per cent, instead of *at least* 75 per cent, of the data to fall within two standard deviations of the mean. Under the same conditions we can also expect over 99 per cent, instead of *at least* 88.8 per cent) of the values to fall within three standard deviations of the mean. The percentages given here pertain to so-called *normal distributions*, which we shall discuss later in Chapter 7.

In the beginning of this section we demonstrated that there are many ways in which knowledge of the variability of a set of data can be important. Another interesting application arises in the comparison of numbers belonging to two or more *different* sets of data. To illustrate, let us suppose that Tom and George, who attend *different* universities, received grades of 72 and 76, respectively, in final examinations in Freshman Sociology. If their respective classes averaged 54 and 52, we can conclude that they both scored above average, but we could say more if we also knew the corresponding standard deviations. Thus, let us suppose that the Freshman Sociology grades of students in the two universities had standard deviations of 20 and 12 points, respectively. With this information we can now say that Tom was $\frac{72 - 54}{20} = 0.9$ standard deviations above average in his class, while George was $\frac{76 - 52}{12} = 2.0$ standard deviations above average in his. This indicates that George's performance was, relatively speaking, much better than Tom's, and this was not apparent by looking only at the grades and the means.

What we have done here consisted of converting the grades into so-called *standard units*. Generally speaking, if x is a measurement belonging to a set of data having the mean $\bar{x}$ (or μ) and the standard deviation s (or σ), then its value in *standard units* is

$$\frac{x - \bar{x}}{s} \quad \text{or} \quad \frac{x - \mu}{\sigma}$$

Standard units, *standard scores*, or *z-scores*, as they are also called, tell us how many standard deviations an item is above or below the mean of the set of data to which it belongs. Their use is particularly important in the comparison of different *kinds* of measurements; for instance, the information that a man's weight is 20 pounds above average, his blood pressure is 12 mm above average, and his pulse rate is 5 beats per minute below average, might contribute much more to a doctor's ability to diagnose the man's troubles if these quantities were all expressed in terms of standard units.

4.3 Measures of Relative Variation

The standard deviation of a set of measurements is often used as an indication of their inherent precision. If we repeatedly measure the *same* quantity, for example, a person's I.Q., the circumference of a tree, or the horsepower of an experimental engine, we would hardly expect always to get the same result. Consequently, the amount of variation we do find in repeated measurements of the same kind provides us with information about their precision. To give an example, suppose that 5 measurements of the length of a certain object have a standard deviation of 0.20 in. Although this information may be important, it does not allow us to judge the relative precision of these measurements; for this purpose we would also have to know something about the actual size of the quantity we are trying to measure. Clearly, a standard deviation of 0.20 in. would indicate that the measurements are very precise if we measured the span of a bridge; on the other hand, they would be far from precise if we measured the diameter of a small ball bearing.

This illustrates the need for measures of *relative variation*, that is, measures which express the magnitude of the variation relative to the size of whatever is being measured. The most widely used measure of relative variation is the *coefficient of variation*, V, which is defined as

$$V = \frac{s}{\bar{x}} \cdot 100$$

This simply expresses the standard deviation of a set of data (or distribution) as a percentage of its mean. When dealing with populations, we analogously define the coefficient of variation as $\frac{\sigma}{\mu} \cdot 100$ or $\frac{S}{\mu} \cdot 100$.

If in the above example the standard deviation $s = 0.20$ in. had referred to 5 measurements of the length of a room and if the mean of the measurements had been 240 in., we would have had

$$V = \frac{0.2}{240} \cdot 100$$

or approximately *eight hundredths of one per cent.* For most practical purposes this would be regarded as very precise.

By using the coefficient of variation, it is also possible to compare the dispersions of two or more sets of data that are given in different units of measurement. Instead of having to compare, say, the variability of weights in pounds, lengths in inches, ages in years, and prices in dollars, we can instead compare the respective coefficients of variation—they are all percentages. Another measure of relative variation, the *coefficient of quartile variation*, is referred to in Exercise 26 below.

EXERCISES

1. Find the range of the temperature readings of Exercise 5 on page 39.

2. Find the range of the scores of Exercise 10 on page 24.

3. Find the range of the number of years the filing cabinets of Exercise 14 on page 25 have been in service.

4. Find the ranges of the arrivals as well as the departures of Exercise 7 on page 40.

5. Find the *mean deviation* (the mean of the absolute values of the deviations from the mean) of the six microorganism counts on page 63.*

6. Find the *mean deviation* (the mean of the absolute values of the deviations from the mean) of the temperature readings of Exercise 5 on page 39.*

7. On page 33 we gave the areas covered by five cans of a certain kind of paint as 409, 383, 400, 394, and 404.
(a) Calculate s using the formula on page 62.
(b) Calculate s using the short-cut formula on page 63.
(c) Repeat part (b) after subtracting 400 from each measurement.

8. Calculate the range and the variance of the 15 doctor fees of Exercise 9 on page 40.

9. Find s for the number of heads obtained in the ten series of 100 flips of a coin referred to in the text on page 60.

10. Find s for the ungrouped radiation counts given in the text on page 13 and compare with the result obtained on page 67.

11. Find σ for the ungrouped tree diameters of Exercise 9 on page 23.

12. Find s for the chemistry grades obtained by the 30 students referred to in Exercise 4 on page 39.

13. Calculate s^2 for the 10 means as well as for the 10 medians obtained in Exercise 8 on page 52. What is demonstrated by the comparison of these two variances?

* The absolute value of a *positive* number is the number itself, whereas the absolute value of a *negative number* is the number without its minus sign.

14. Suppose we are planning to select a sample from among the filing cabinets of Exercise 14 on page 25, so that the data given in that Exercise can be looked upon as a population. Calculate σ as well as S for the ungrouped data (the ages of the filing cabinets) and compare your results.

15. The following is the distribution of relative humidity readings taken each day at noon at Sky Harbor Airport, Phoenix, during June of 1964:

Relative Humidity (per cent)	*Frequency*
5 – 9	1
10 – 14	5
15 – 19	14
20 – 24	6
25 – 29	3
30 – 34	0
35 – 39	1
	30

(a) Calculate s for this distribution without coding.
(b) Calculate s for this distribution using an appropriate coding.
(c) Calculate the *mean deviation* of this distribution using the formula

$$\frac{\Sigma\, |x - \bar{x}| \cdot f}{n}$$

where the x's are the class marks, the f's are the class frequencies, and $|x - \bar{x}|$ represents the *absolute value* of the difference between x and $\bar{x}$.

16. Calculate σ for the distribution of tree diameters obtained in Exercise 9 on page 23 and compare with the result obtained in Exercise 11.

17. Calculate s for whichever data you grouped among those of Exercises 10, 11, and 12 on pages 24 and 25.

18. Calculate S for the distribution obtained for the ages of the filing cabinets in Exercise 14 on page 25 and compare with the result obtained in Exercise 14 above.

19. Calculate s for the distribution obtained in Exercise 13 on page 25 for the 80 iron-solution indices.

20. Having kept records for several months, Mr. Hughes knows that it takes him on the average 47.7 minutes to mow his front lawn; the standard deviation is 2.46 minutes. If he always starts exactly one hour before it is time for dinner, *at most* what percentage of the time was he unable to finish mowing the lawn before dinner?

21. In a final examination in a first course in philosophy 800 students averaged 72.5 with a standard deviation of 8.2. *At least* how many of students must have received grades from 55 to 90, inclusive?

22. The manager of a movie theater knows that his average attendence is 322 with a standard deviation of 20.5. If his beak-even point is a paid attendance of 240, at most how often (what per cent of the time) does he lose money?

23. An investment service reports for each stock that it lists the price at which it is currently selling, its average price over a certain period of time, and a measure of its variability. Stock A, it reports, has a normal (average) price of \$56 with a standard deviation of \$11 and it is currently selling at \$74.50; Stock B sells normally for \$35, has a standard deviation of \$4, and is currently selling at \$47. If an investor owns both kinds of stock and wants to dispose of one, which one might he sell and why?

24. Mr. Evans belongs to an age group for which the average weight is 156 pounds with a standard deviation of 15 pounds, and Mr. Finch belongs to an age group for which the average weight is 171 pounds with a standard deviation of 18 pounds. If Mr. Evans weighs 191 pounds and Mr. Finch weighs 202 pounds, which of the two is more seriously overweight compared to his group?

25. In a large Western city the average cost of an appendectomy is \$237.50 (with a standard deviation of \$24.60), the average cost of a tonsilectomy is \$112.50 (with a standard deviation of \$16.25), and the average cost of having a tooth filled is \$8.67 (with a standard deviation of \$1.80). Among two surgeons and a dentist practicing in this city, Dr. A charges \$275.00 for an appendectomy, Dr. B charges \$135.00 for a tonsilectomy, and Dr. C charges \$10.00 for filling a tooth. Which of the three doctors is relatively most expensive?

26. An alternate measure of variation is given by the *interquartile range* $Q_3 - Q_1$; it represents the length of the interval which contains the middle 50 per cent of a set of data. Some research workers prefer to use the *semi-interquartile range* (also called the *quartile deviation*) which, as its name implies, is given by the formula $(Q_3 - Q_1)/2$. Also, when working with the quartiles, a corresponding measure of *relative* variation is the so-called *coefficient of quartile variation*, which is given by the ratio of the semi-interquartile range to the *mid-quartile* $\frac{Q_1 + Q_3}{2}$ multiplied by 100.

(a) Use the results obtained in the text on page 49 to calculate the interquartile range as well as the coefficient of quartile variation for the radiation-count data.

(b) Use the results obtained in part (a) of Exercise 11 on page 53 to calculate the semi-interquartile range and the coefficient of quartile variation for the distribution of the tree diameters.

(c) Use the quartiles obtained in part (a) of Exercise 18 on page 54 to calculate the semi-interquartile range and the coefficient of quartile variation for the distribution of the ages of the filing cabinets.

27. Use the values of $\bar{x}$ and s obtained, respectively, on pages 35 and 67 to calculate the coefficient of variation for the radiation-count data.

28. Find the coefficient of variation of the temperature readings of Exercise 5 on page 39.

29. Use the result of Exercise 8 above to calculate the coefficient of variation for the fees charged by the 15 doctors for making house calls.

30. In order to compare the precision of two micrometers, a laboratory technician studies recent measurements made with both instruments. The first micrometer was recently used to measure the diameter of a ball bearing and the measurements had a mean of 4.73 mm and a standard deviation of 0.015 mm; the second was recently used to measure the unstretched length of a spring and the measurements had a mean of 1.56 in. with a standard deviation of 0.006 in. Which of the two micrometers is relatively more precise?

31. Calculate $\bar{x}$ and s for each of the three paint samples given on page 51 and compare their respective coefficients of variation.

32. Use the rules of summation of Section 3.6 to prove that the formulas for s given on pages 62 and 63 are equivalent. [*Hint:* Make use of the binomial expansion $(a + b)^2 = a^2 + 2ab + b^2$.]

33. Rigorously speaking, a measure of variation may be defined as a statistical description having the following two properties: (1) *if the same number is added to each observation, the description remains unchanged;* (2) *if each observation is multiplied by the same number, the corresponding description is also multiplied by that number.* Check whether these conditions are satisfied by
(a) the standard deviation;
(b) the range;
(c) the mean;
(d) the interquartile range;
(e) the coefficient of variation.
This definition is often extended to include also statistical descriptions which are *powers* of measures of variation. Would this qualify the variance as a measure of variation?

4.4 Some Further Descriptions

So far we have discussed statistical descriptions coming under the general heading of "measures of location" and "measures of variation." Actually, there is no limit to the number of ways in which statistical data can be described, and statisticians are continually developing new methods of describing characteristics of numerical data that are of interest in particular problems. In this section we shall briefly study the problem of describing the *over-all shape* of a distribution.

Although frequency distribution can assume almost any shape or form, there are certain standard types which fit most distributions we meet in actual practice. Foremost among these is the aptly described *bell-shaped* distribution, which is illustrated by the histogram of Figure 4.1. One often

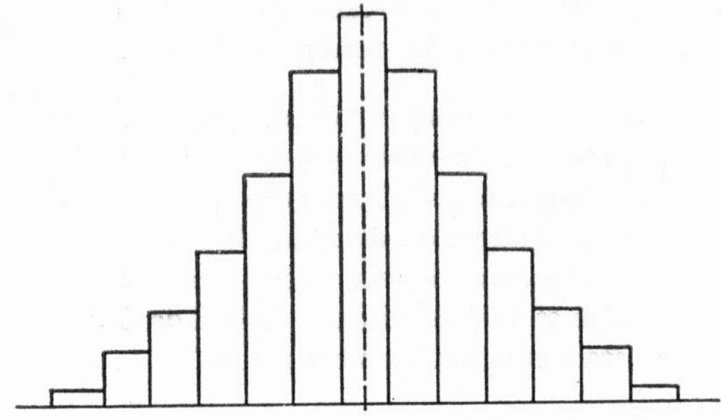

Fig. 4.1 A bell-shaped distribution.

runs into this kind of distribution when dealing with actual data, and there are certain theoretical reasons why, in many problems, one can actually *expect* to get bell-shaped distributions. Although the distribution of Figure 4.2 is also more or less bell-shaped, it differs from the one of Figure 4.1 in-

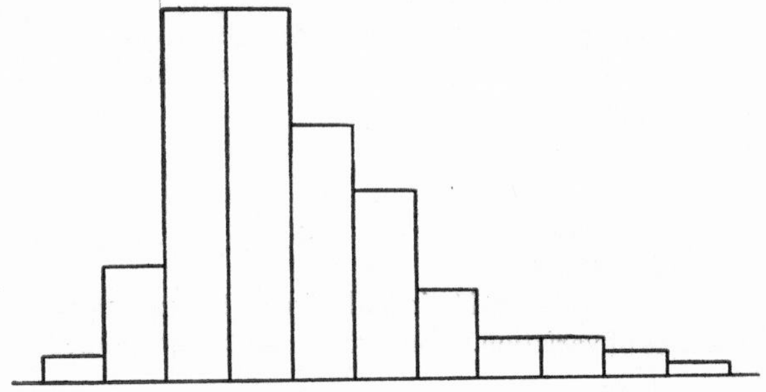

Fig. 4.2 A skewed distribution.

asmuch as the latter is *symmetrical* while the former is *skewed*. Generally speaking, a distribution is said to be *symmetrical* if we can picture the histogram folded (say, along the dotted line of Figure 4.1) so that the two halves will more or less coincide. If a distribution has a more pronounced "tail" on one side, such as the distribution of Figure 4.2, we say that the distribution is *skewed*. Note that the income distribution on page 10 is skewed with a "tail" on the right—we say that it has *positive skewness* or that it is *positively skewed*. Correspondingly, if a distribution has a pronounced "tail" on the left, we say that the distribution has *negative skewness* or that it is *negatively skewed.*

There are several ways of measuring the extent to which a distribution is skewed. A relatively easy one is based on the fact illustrated in Figure 4.3, namely, that if a distribution has a "tail" on the right, its median will

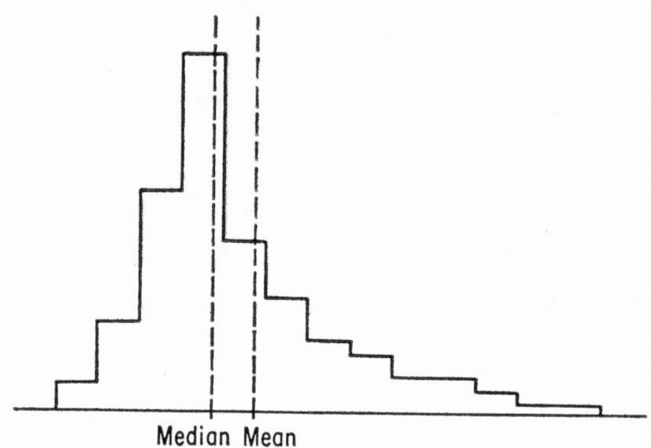

Fig. 4.3 The median and the mean of a positively skewed distribution.

generally be exceeded by its mean. (If the "tail" is on the left, this order will be reversed, and the median will generally exceed the mean.) Based on this difference, the so-called *Pearsonian coefficient of skewness* measures the skewness of a distribution by means of the formula

▲ $$\frac{3(\text{mean} - \text{median})}{\text{standard deviation}}$$ ▲

Here the difference between the mean and the median is divided by the standard deviation, to make this description of the shape of the distribution independent of the units of measurement we may happen to use.

If we substitute into this formula the values obtained for the mean, median, and standard deviation of the radiation-count distribution on pages 35, 48, and 67, we find that the Pearsonian coefficient of skewness equals

$$\frac{3(20 - 19.8)}{5} = 0.12$$

This value is positive, but so small that we can reasonably describe the radiation-count distribution as symmetrical.

Besides bell-shaped distributions, two other kinds—*J-shaped* and *U-shaped* distributions—are sometimes, though less frequently, met in actual practice. As is illustrated by means of the histograms of Figure 4.4, the names of these distributions literally describe their shapes; examples of J-shaped and U-shaped distributions may be found in Exercises 7 and 8 below.

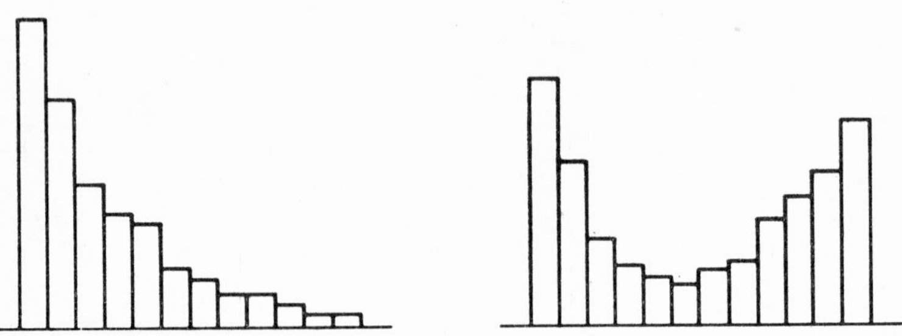

Fig. 4.4 A J-shaped distribution and a U-shaped distribution.

EXERCISES

1. Use the values of the mean, median, and standard deviation of the distribution of tree diameters obtained in Exercise 12 on page 40, Exercise 10 on page 53, and Exercise 16 on page 71, to find the Pearsonian coefficient of skewness of this distribution.

2. Calculate the Pearsonian coefficient of skewness for the radioactive-fallout data of Exercise 11 on page 24. The mean and the median were previously determined in Exercises 14 on page 40 and 13 on page 53.

3. Using the results of Exercises 17 on page 41, 17(b) on page 54, and 14 on page 71, find the Pearsonian coefficient of skewness for the distribution of the ages of the filing cabinets.

4. An alternate measure of skewness, α_3 (*alpha-three*), is defined in terms of so-called *moments about the mean*. For grouped data the kth moment about the mean is given by

$$m_k = \frac{\Sigma\,(x - \bar{x})^k \cdot f}{n}$$

where the x's are the class marks of the distribution and the f's are the corresponding frequencies.* Note that if the divisor were $n - 1$ instead of n, the second moment about the mean, m_2, would be the variance of the distribution. Using these moments, alpha-three is defined by the ratio

▲ $$\alpha_3 = \frac{m_3}{(\sqrt{m_2})^3}$$ ▲

* The calculation of moments about the mean can be greatly simplified by using the same kind of coding as was used on page 66 in calculating the standard deviation of a distribution.

and it is easy to show that for a symmetrical distribution $\alpha_3 = 0$. Calculate α_3 for the following distribution, which, judging by its histogram, is negatively skewed:

x	f
2	5
4	20
6	15
8	45
10	10
12	5

5. Using moments about the mean (see Exercise 4) the peakedness (or *kurtosis*) of a distribution is often measured by the statistic α_4 (*alpha-four*), which is defined by the formula

$$\alpha_4 = \frac{m_4}{(m_2)^2}$$

Draw a histogram and calculate α_4 for each of the following distributions, of which the first is relatively peaked while the other is relatively flat:

(a)

x	f
−3	6
−2	9
−1	10
0	50
1	10
2	9
3	6

(b)

x	f
−3	4
−2	11
−1	20
0	30
1	20
2	11
3	4

Also verify that in spite of their differences in shape, the two distributions have the same standard deviation.

6. Give one example each of actual data whose distribution might reasonably be expected to be
(a) bell-shaped and symmetrical;
(b) bell-shaped but not symmetrical;
(c) positively skewed;
(d) negatively skewed;
(e) J-shaped;
(f) U-shaped.

7. Roll a pair of dice 100 times and construct a distribution showing the number of times 0, 1, and 2 sixes were obtained. Draw a histogram of this distribution, which should be J-shaped, and calculate α_3 (see Exercise 4).

8. If a coin is flipped five times, the result may be represented by means of a sequence of H's and T's (for example, HHTTH), where H stands for *heads* and T for *tails*. Having obtained such a sequence of H's and T's, we can then check after each successive flip whether the number of heads exceeds the number of tails. For example, for the sequence HHTTH, heads is ahead after the first flip, after the second flip, after the third flip, *not* after the fourth flip, but again after the fifth flip; altogether, it is ahead *four times*. Repeating this experiment 50 times, construct a histogram showing in how many cases heads was ahead altogether 0 times, 1 time, 2 times, . . ., and 5 times. Explain why the resulting distribution should be U-shaped.

4.5 Technical Note (The Use of Square Root Tables)

Although square root tables are relatively easy to use, most beginners seem to have some difficulty in choosing the right column and in placing the decimal point correctly in the answer. Table XII, in addition to containing the *squares* of the numbers from 1.00 to 9.99 spaced at intervals of 0.01, gives the *square roots* of these numbers rounded to 6 decimals. To find the square root of any positive number rounded to 3 significant digits, we have only to use the following rule in deciding whether to take the entry of the $\sqrt{n}$ or the $\sqrt{10n}$ column:

> *Move the decimal point an even number of places to the right or to the left until a number greater than or equal to 1 but less than 100 is reached. If the resulting number is less than 10 go to the* $\sqrt{n}$ *column; if it is 10 or more go to the* $\sqrt{10n}$ *column.*

Thus, to find the square root of 14,600, 459, or 0.0315 we go to the $\sqrt{n}$ column since the decimal point has to be moved, respectively, 4 places to the left, 2 places to the left, or 2 places to the right, to give 1.46, 4.59, or 3.15. Similarly, to find the square root of 2,163, 0.192, or 0.0000158 we go to the $\sqrt{10n}$ column since the decimal point has to be moved, respectively, 2 places to the left, 2 places to the right, and 6 places to the right, to give 21.63, 19.2, 15.8.

Having found the entry in the appropriate column of Table XII, the only thing that remains to be done is to put the decimal point in the right position in the answer. Here it will help to use the following rule:

> *Having previously moved the decimal point an even number of places to the left or right to get a number greater than or equal to 1 but less than 100, the decimal point of the entry of the appropriate column in Table XII is moved half as many places in the opposite direction.*

For example, to determine the square root of 14,600 we first note that the decimal point has to be moved *four places to the left* to give 1.46. We thus take the entry of the $\sqrt{n}$ column corresponding to 1.46, move its decimal point *two places to the right*, and get $\sqrt{14{,}600} = 120.8305$. Similarly, to find the square root of 0.0000158, we note that the decimal point has to be moved *six places to the right* to give 15.8. We thus take the entry of the $\sqrt{10n}$ column corresponding to 1.58, move the decimal point *three places to the left*, and get $\sqrt{0.0000158} = 0.003974921$. In actual practice, if a number whose square root we want to find is *rounded*, the square root should be rounded to as many significant digits as the original number.

BIBLIOGRAPHY

Sheppard's correction for the grouping error introduced when calculating the standard deviation of grouped data is discussed in

Mills, F. C., *Introduction to Statistics*. New York: Holt, Rinehart & Winston, Inc., 1956.

A formal discussion of why one divides by $n - 1$ rather than n in the formula for the sample variance may be found in most textbooks on mathematical statistics, for example, in

Freund, J. E., *Mathematical Statistics*. Englewood Cliffs, N.J.: Prentice-Hall, Inc., 1962.

PART TWO
Basic Theory

FIVE Probability

5.1 Introduction

Directly or indirectly, the concept of probability plays an important role in all problems of science, business, and everyday life which in any way involve an element of uncertainty. Hence, if we identify statistics with the art, or science, of making decisions in the face of uncertainty—as we did in Chapter 1—it follows that questions concerning probabilities, their meaning, their determination, and their mathematical manipulation are basic to any treatment of statistics. Thus, the study of statistics requires the study of probability, and in order to present this subject in its modern form, we shall first have to investigate certain simple, yet interesting, mathematical preliminaries. These are covered in the next two sections, dealing with some "sophisticated" methods of counting and some elementary mathematical ideas concerning sets.

5.2 Mathematical Preliminary: Counting

In contrast to the complexity of most of the methods used in modern science, the simple process of counting should not be overlooked. One still has to count 1, 2, 3, 4, . . ., say, when determining the number of cars passing a checkpoint, the number of guinea pigs surviving a given dosage of a poison, the number of rainy days in the month of July, the number of students passing an examination, and so on. Sometimes the process of counting can be simplified by the use of mechanical devices (for instance, when counting spectators passing through a turnstile) or by performing the count indirectly (for instance, when determining the total number of sales from the serial numbers of invoices.) At other times the process can be simplified by the use of special mathematical theory, some of which will be introduced below.

In order to perform an actual count, it is necessary to list, align, or otherwise arrange the objects to be counted in some way. Although this may sound easy, the following example illustrates that this is not always the case. Suppose, for instance, that in an investigation of the process of learning, students are asked to study a list of French words for a fixed period of time, after which they are given a test. If a student fails, the whole process of studying and being tested is repeated, if necessary more than once. The persons conducting the experiment record only the number of students passing at each stage, and they are interested in knowing the total number of possible outcomes for the special case where they work with two students and allow a maximum of three repetitions of the study-testing cycle. Clearly, there are many possibilities: Both students might pass on the first try; they might both fail every time; one might pass on the first try while the other fails every time; one might pass on the second try and the other on the third try. Being very careful, we may thus be able to continue and list

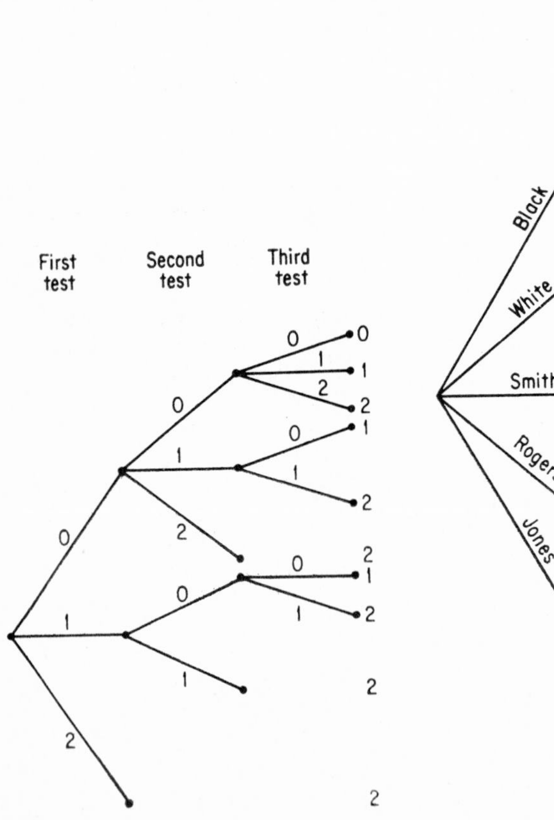

Fig. 5.1 A tree diagram.

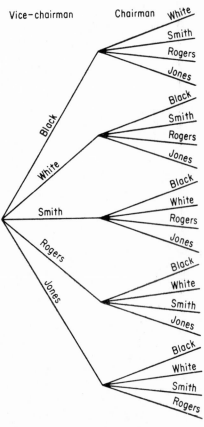

Fig. 5.2 A tree diagram.

all possibilities; however, to handle this kind of problem systematically, it is helpful to refer to a *tree diagram* like that of Figure 5.1. This diagram shows that there are three possibilities (three branches) for the first test corresponding to 0, 1, or 2 students passing the test; for the second test there are three branches growing out of the top branch, two out of the middle branch, and none out of the bottom branch. Clearly, there are three possibilities when none of the students passed the first test, but only two possibilities when one of them passed the first test, and the experiment ends when both pass the first test. The same sort of reasoning applies to the third test, and we thus find that (going from left to right) there are altogether 10 different *paths* along the branches of the tree corresponding to the 10 possible outcomes of the experiment. It can also be seen from this diagram that among the 10 possible outcomes there are 6 where both students pass sooner or later, 3 where only one student passes, and 1 where none of the students passes. Furthermore, it can be seen that in one case the experiment ends after the first test, in two cases it ends after the second test, and in seven cases it ends after the third test.

To consider another example where a tree diagram can be of some aid, suppose that the Board of Directors of a company consists of Mr. Black, Mrs. White, Mr. Smith, Mrs. Rogers, and Mr. Jones. One of them is to be elected chairman, one is to be elected vice-chairman, and we would like to know in how many ways this might come to pass. Looking at the tree diagram of Figure 5.2, it is apparent that the selection can be made in 20 different ways, corresponding to the 20 distinct paths along the branches of the tree. Starting at the top, the first path represents the election of Mr. Black as vice-chairman and Mrs. White as chairman, the second path represents the election of Mr. Black as vice-chairman and Mr. Smith as chairman, . . ., and the bottom path represents the election of Mr. Jones as vice-chairman and Mrs. Rogers as chairman. Note that our answer is the *product* of the number of ways in which they can first elect a vice-chairman and the number of ways in which they can then elect a chairman from among the four board members who remain after the vice-chairman has been elected. Generalizing from this example, we have the following theorem:

> *If an operation consists of two separate steps, of which the first can be performed in m ways and the second can be performed in n ways, then the whole operation can be performed in $m \cdot n$ ways.*

Thus, if a person has to buy one of six items on a list at one of three different department stores, he can do his shopping in $6 \cdot 3 = 18$ different ways; if a menu provides the choice of 12 different sandwiches and 5 kinds of drinks, there are altogether $12 \cdot 5 = 60$ different ways in which one can order a sandwich and a drink.

Using appropriate tree diagrams, it is easy to generalize the above theorem so that it will apply to operations involving more than two steps. If there are k steps, we have the following theorem:

If an operation consists of k separate steps, of which the first can be performed in n_1 ways, the second can be performed in n_2 ways, . . ., and the kth can be performed in n_k ways, then the whole operation can be performed in $n_1 \cdot n_2 \cdot \ldots \cdot n_k$ ways.

Thus, if a building contractor offers 2-, 3-, and 4-bedroom houses, which may be had in 4 different exterior finishes and with or without garage, there are $3 \cdot 4 \cdot 2 = 24$ possible selections a homebuyer can make. Also, if a teacher has to rate four students as being below average, average, or above average, there are $3 \cdot 3 \cdot 3 \cdot 3 = 81$ possibilities; and if a tire manufacturer wants to test 5 different tread designs on 2 different kinds of road surfaces and at 4 different speeds, there are altogether $5 \cdot 2 \cdot 4 = 40$ tests he will have to perform. The methods discussed in this section come under the general heading of "Combinatorial Analysis"; some further problems of this kind will be taken up when needed in Section 7.2.

5.3 Mathematical Preliminary: Sets and Events

In statistics one often refers to any process of observation or measurement as an *experiment*. Thus, using the term in a very wide sense, an experiment may consist of the simple process of noting whether a light is on or off; it may consist of determining the number of imperfections in a piece of cloth; or it may consist of the very complicated process of finding the mass of an electron. The results one obtains from an experiment, whether they be simple "yes" or "no" answers, instrument readings, or whatever, are called the *outcomes* of the experiment.

In most problems in which uncertainties are connected with the various outcomes of an experiment, it is convenient to represent the outcomes by means of points. This has the advantage that we can treat such problems mathematically, where we would otherwise have to verbalize about the various outcomes. For example, if an experiment consists of determining whether a person interviewed in a poll favors Candidate P, is undecided, or favors Candidate Q, we might represent these three outcomes by means of the three points of Figure 5.3, to which we arbitrarily assigned the code numbers 1, 2, and 3. Note that we could just as well have used any other configuration of points, and that we could have assigned to them any other arbitrary set of numbers (or letters).

Had we been interested in the reactions of two persons interviewed in the poll, we could have presented the outcomes by means of the points of Figure

5.4, where 1, 2, and 3 stand again for a response favoring Candidate P, indecision, and a response favoring Candidate Q. Thus, the point (1, 2) represents the outcome where the first person interviewed is for Candidate

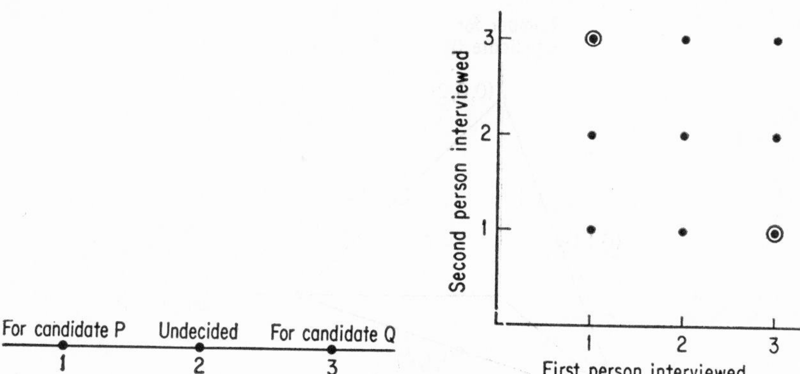

Fig. 5.3 Outcomes of interview of one person.

Fig. 5.4 Outcomes of interview of two persons.

P while the second is undecided, and the point (3, 1) represents the outcome where the first person interviewed is for Candidate Q while the second is for Candidate P. Had we been interested in the reactions of n persons in this experiment, there would have been 3^n possible outcomes and as many points. For instance, for 4 persons there would have been $3 \cdot 3 \cdot 3 \cdot 3 = 81$ points, among which (2, 1, 1, 3), for example, represents the outcome where the first person interviewed is undecided, the second and third are for Candidate P, while the fourth is for Candidate Q. (Since each point is now determined by 4 numbers, we cannot picture these points as readily as those of Figures 5.3 and 5.4; in fact, this would require a space of four dimensions.)

It is customary to refer to the set (totality) of points representing all possible outcomes of an experiment as the *sample space* of the experiment and to denote it by the letter S. Thus, the three points of Figure 5.3 constitute the sample space for interviewing one person, and the nine points of Figure 5.4 constitute the sample space for interviewing two. In any discussion of an experiment, no matter how simple, it is always important to specify the sample space with which we are concerned; as we shall see, this may depend partly on what we look upon as an individual outcome. For example, if in the two-person-interview case we had been interested only in the total number of persons favoring Candidate P, undecided, or favoring Candidate Q, we could have used the *three-dimensional* sample space of Figure 5.5 instead of the *two-dimensional* sample space of Figure 5.4. Here the first coordinate gives the number of persons favoring Candidate P, the second coordinate gives the number of persons who are undecided, while the third coordinate gives the number of persons favoring Candidate Q. Thus, the point (2, 0, 0) represents the outcome where both

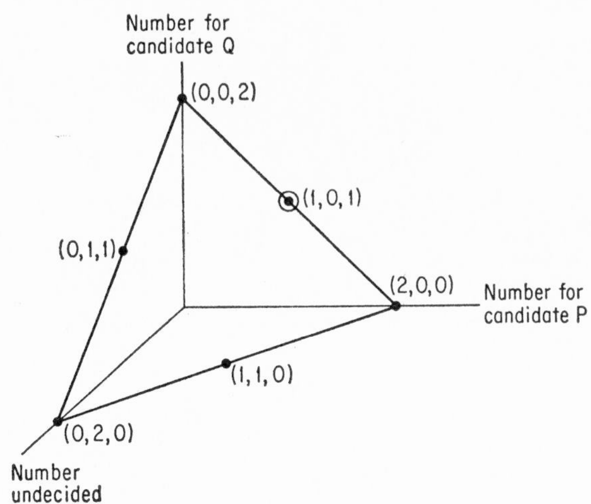

Fig. 5.5 A three-dimensional sample space.

persons interviewed are for Candidate P, while (0, 1, 1) represents the case where one is undecided and one favors Candidate Q. Note that the two points circled in Figure 5.4 correspond to the single point circled in Figure 5.5, and that the sample spaces of Figures 5.4 and 5.5 consist of 9 points and 6 points, respectively, even though they pertain to the same experiment. Generally speaking, it is desirable to use sample spaces whose points represent outcomes which cannot be further "subdivided"; that is, each individual point should not represent two or more possibilities which are distinguishable in some fashion. Unless there is a special reason for not following this rule, we would thus prefer the sample space of Figure 5.4 to that of Figure 5.5.

Earlier we described the sample spaces of Figures 5.4 and 5.5 as two-dimensional and three-dimensional, and we could similarly describe the sample space of Figure 5.3 as one-dimensional. Although it may be useful to know the number of dimensions in which we happen to picture the points of a sample space, it is more common to classify sample spaces according to the number of points which they contain. All the sample spaces mentioned so far have been *finite;* that is, they consisted of a finite, or fixed, number of points. Other examples of finite, though much larger, sample spaces are the one representing all possible 5-card poker hands one can deal with an ordinary deck of 52 playing cards (there are 2,598,960 possibilities), and the one representing all the possible ways in which the 10 National

League baseball teams can finish the season (there are 3,628,800 possibilities, not counting ties). In the remainder of this chapter we shall consider only finite sample spaces, although in later chapters we shall consider also sample spaces that are *infinite* (for instance, when dealing with measurements assuming values on a continuous scale).

Having explained what we mean by a sample space, let us now state what we mean by an *event*. This is important because probabilities always refer to the occurrence or nonoccurrence of events. For instance, we may assign a probability to the event that there will be anywhere from 24 to 30 drop-outs among 85 high school students, the event that a 60-year-old person will live to be 70, the event that there will be at least 6 heads in 10 flips of a coin, the event that a tire will last at least 18,000 miles before it has to be recapped, and so forth. Generally speaking, *all events with which we are concerned in probability theory are represented by subsets of appropriate sample spaces* (by *subset* we mean any part of a set including the set as a whole and, trivially, the empty set which has no elements at all). In other words, "event" is the nontechnical term and "subset of a sample space" is the corresponding mathematical counterpart. Thus, in Figure 5.4 the subset which consists of the point (2, 2) represents the event that both persons interviewed are undecided; the subset which consists of the two points circled in Figure 5.4 represents the event that one of the persons interviewed is for Candidate P while the other is for Candidate Q; and the subset which consists of the five points (3, 1), (3, 2), (3, 3), (1, 3), and (2, 3) represents the event that at least one of the two persons interviewed is for Candidate Q.

Still referring to the two-person-interview example, let us now suppose that X stands for the event that at least one of the persons interviewed is undecided, Y stands for the event that both persons interviewed respond in the same way, while Z stands for the event that one of the persons interviewed is for Candidate P and the other is for Candidate Q. Referring to Figure 5.6, which shows the same sample space as Figure 5.4, we find that event X is represented by the five points inside the dotted line, event Y is represented by the three points inside the dashed line, and event Z is represented by the two points which are circled. Note that the subsets which represent events X *and* Z (or Y *and* Z, but not X *and* Y) have no points in common; they are referred to as *mutually exclusive* events, which means that they cannot both occur in the same experiment.

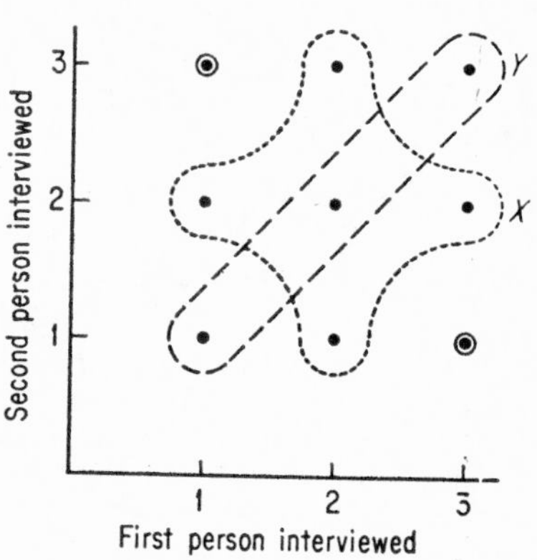

Fig. 5.6 Sample space for interview of two persons.

In many situations we are interested in events which are actually combinations of two or more simpler kinds of events. For instance, in our example we might be interested in the event that *either both persons interviewed respond in the same way or there is one vote for each candidate*, or we might be interested in the event that *both persons interviewed respond in the same way and at least one of them is undecided*. In the first case we are interested in the event that *either* Y *or* Z *occurs*, which is represented by the subset consisting of the points (1, 1), (2, 2), (3, 3), (1, 3), and (3, 1); in the second case we are interested in the event that Y *and* X *both occur*, which is represented by the single point (2, 2).

In general, if A and B are any two events we define their *union* $A \cup B$ as the event which consists of all the individual outcomes contained either in A, in B, or in both. It is customary to read $A \cup B$ as "A *cup* B" or simply as "A *or* B." Referring again to the example of the preceding paragraph, we can now say that we found that $Y \cup Z$ consists of the points (1, 1), (2, 2), (3, 3), (1, 3), and (3, 1), and it will be left to the reader to check that $X \cup Z$ consists of all of the points of the sample space except (1, 1) and (3, 3).

If A and B are any two events we define their *intersection* $A \cap B$ as the event which consists of all the individual outcomes contained in both A and B. Here $A \cap B$ reads "A *cap* B" or simply "A *and* B." Again referring to the same example, we can now say that we found that $Y \cap X$ consists of the single point (2, 2); earlier we saw that $X \cap Z$ has no elements at all, and if we use the symbol $\emptyset$ to denote the *empty set*, we can now write $X \cap Z = \emptyset$.

To complete our notation, let us define A', the *complement* of event A with respect to a given sample space S, as the subset which consists of all the individual outcomes of S that are *not* contained in A. Thus, with reference to our example X' represents the event that neither person is undecided, and Y' represents the event that the two persons interviewed did not respond the same way. It will be left to the reader to verify that Z' is, in fact, identical with $X \cup Y$.

Sample spaces and events, particularly relationships among events, are often depicted by means of *Venn diagrams* like those of Figures 5.7, 5.8, and 5.9. In each case the sample space is represented by a rectangle, while subsets (or events) are represented by regions within the rectangles, usually circles or parts of circles. Thus, the shaded regions of the three Venn diagrams of Figure 5.7 represent, respectively, the complement of event A, the union of events A and B, and the intersection of A and B. When dealing with three events, it is customary to draw the respective circles as in Figure 5.8. Note that the shaded region represents the event $A \cap (B \cup C)$, namely, the event which consists of all outcomes belonging to A and also to either B or C (or both).

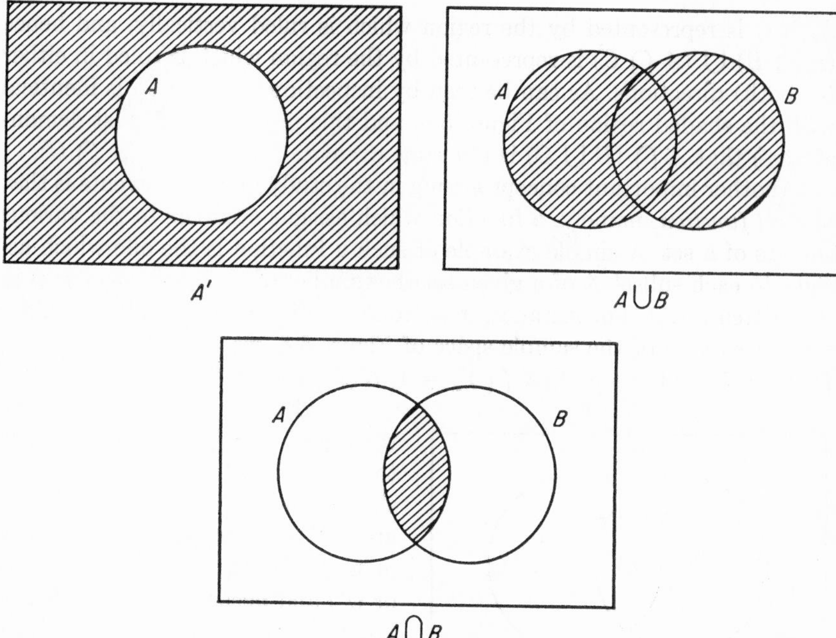

Fig. 5.7 Venn diagrams.

Venn diagrams are often used to verify relationships among sets, thus making it unnecessary to give formal proofs based on the Algebra of Sets. To illustrate, let us verify that $A \cap (B \cup C) = (A \cap B) \cup (A \cap C)$, one of the so-called *distributive laws*. As we already pointed out, the event $A \cap (B \cup C)$ is represented by the shaded region of Figure 5.8. Now, $A \cap B$ is represented by the region of Figure 5.9 which is ruled horizontally,

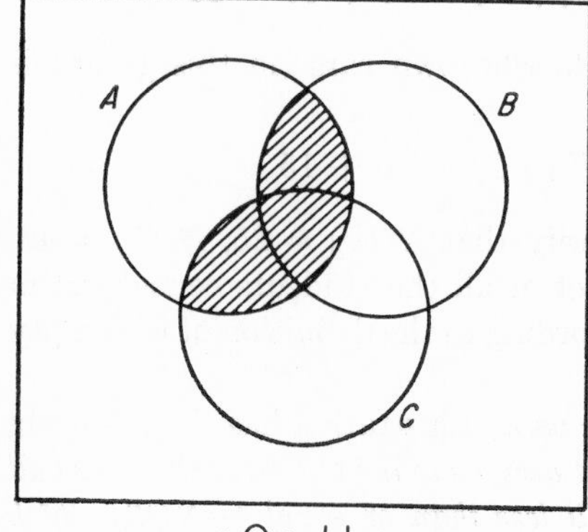

Fig. 5.8 Venn diagram.

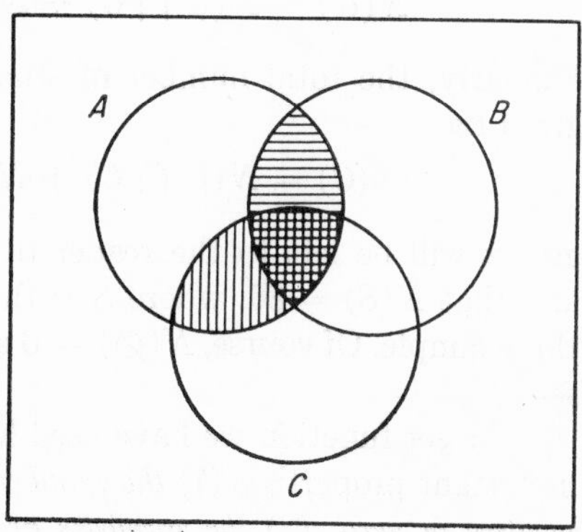

Fig. 5.9 Venn diagram.

$A \cap C$ is represented by the region which is ruled vertically, and hence $(A \cap B) \cup (A \cap C)$ is represented by the region which is ruled in either (or both) directions. As can be seen by inspection, this region is identical with the shaded region of Figure 5.8, and this proves (or at least demonstrates) that $A \cap (B \cup C)$ is the same event as $(A \cap B) \cup (A \cap C)$.

Another important concept arising in the study of sets or events is that of a *set function,* namely, a function which assigns numbers to the various subsets of a set. A simple example of such a function is the one which assigns to each subset A of a given set the number of *elements* (members) in A, written $N(A)$. For instance, if we count the individual outcomes in the various subsets of the sample space of Figure 5.6, we find that $N(S) = 9$, $N(X) = 5$, $N(Y) = 3$, $N(X \cap Y) = 1$, $N(X \cap Z) = 0$, and so on.

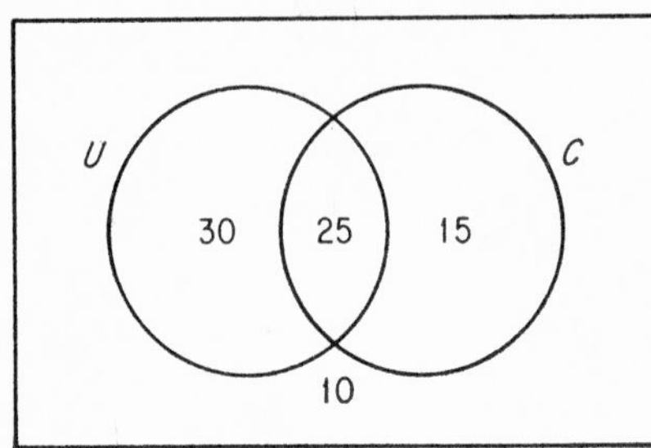

Fig. 5.10 Venn diagram.

To give another illustration of this special set function, let us refer to Figure 5.10. This Venn diagram shows how certain college students are classified according to whether or not they are undergraduates (U or U') and according to whether or not they own cars (C or C'). Note that the four numbers are assigned, respectively, to the subsets $U \cap C'$, $U \cap C$, $U' \cap C$, and $U' \cap C'$. Using these numbers, we can determine what numbers must be assigned to any other subset. For instance, to obtain $N(U)$, the number of undergraduates in this group, we have only to add the number of undergraduates who own cars to the number of undergraduates who do not own cars, and we obtain

$$N(U) = N(U \cap C) + N(U \cap C') = 25 + 30 = 55$$

Similarly, the total number of students who own cars (in this group) is given by

$$N(C) = N(U \cap C) + N(U' \cap C) = 25 + 15 = 40$$

and it will be left to the reader to verify that $N(U') = 25$, $N(C') = 40$, and that $N(S) = 80$, where S is the set of all the students considered in this example. Of course, $N(\emptyset) = 0$ according to the definition of the empty set.

The set function we have used here as an illustration has the following important properties: (1) *the numbers it assigns to the various subsets are all positive or zero;* (2) *the numbers are all less than or equal to* $N(S)$, *which equaled 9 in the first example and 80 in the second;* (3) *if two subsets have no elements in common, the number assigned to their union equals the sum of the numbers assigned to the individual subsets.* It was this last property which enabled us to calculate the number of undergraduates by adding the number of undergraduates having cars to the number of undergraduates who do not have cars.

The properties we have listed here are useful to know in special applications (see Exercises 22, 23, and 24 on page 96), but what is more important, they are common to all *measure functions*, that is, functions which assign physical weights to objects, areas to geometrical regions, volumes to solids, and so on. We have mentioned them here because of the role they play in the definition of probability as a special kind of *measure* which we assign to events.

EXERCISES

1. Coming to work on a Wednesday morning, a laboratory technician finds that he has to perform two chemical analyses before the end of the week, that is, on Wednesday, Thursday, or Friday. If each analysis has to be completed on the day it is begun and he could perform both analyses on the same day, draw a tree diagram to verify that he can schedule his work in 6 different ways.

2. At a roadblock, cars are classified according to whether they have faulty brakes, according to whether they have 0, 1, or 2 or more bad tires, and according to whether they have defective headlights.

(a) Construct a tree diagram showing the 12 different ways in which a car can thus be classified.

(b) If there are 40 cars in each of the 12 categories obtained in (a) and a courteous warning is issued to the owners of cars having defective headlights and (or) one bad tire, how many of the owners will receive a courteous warning?

(c) If tickets are issued to the owners of cars having faulty brakes and (or) two or more bad tires, how many of the owners will receive tickets [assuming again that there are 40 in each of the 12 categories obtained in (a)]?

(d) Referring to (b) and (c), how many of the car owners received a courteous warning as well as a ticket?

3. The manager of an appliance store stocks *one each* of two different models of an automatic washer, reordering at the end of each day (for delivery early the next morning) if and only if both machines have been sold. Construct a tree diagram to show that if he starts on a Monday with both machines, there are altogether 12 ways in which he can make sales on Monday and Tuesday of that week. In how many ways can he make sales on Monday, Tuesday, and Wednesday of that week?

4. On the faculty of a college there are three professors named Jones. In how many ways can the payroll department distribute their paychecks so that each one receives a check made out to Professor Jones, but none gets the right check?

5. If a chain of drug stores has 4 warehouses and 15 retail outlets, in how many different ways can an item be shipped from one of the warehouses to one of the stores?

6. Given that 5 different steamship lines provide service between Southampton and New York, in how many distinct ways can a person plan a boat trip from New York to Southampton and back if
(a) he must travel both ways by the same line;
(b) he can but need not travel both ways by the same line;
(c) he cannot travel both ways by the same line.

7. An agency classifies airplane accidents as being due to structural failure, weather conditions, or human failure, and it classifies the injury to the pilot as fatal, serious but not fatal, not serious but requiring hospitalization, or negligible.
(a) In how many ways can they classify an airplane accident and the injury to the pilot?
(b) In how many of these categories is the accident not due to human failure and the injury to the pilot not negligible?
(c) In how many of these categories is the accident due to weather conditions and the injury to the pilot not fatal?

8. At a certain lunchcounter a person can order a hamburger with or without onion, with or without relish, with or without mustard, and have the meat broiled rare, medium rare, medium, or well done. In how many ways can a person thus order a hamburger?

9. Among 30 families chosen for a sociological study there are 21 where the head of the family is salaried, 6 where he is self-employed, and 3 where he is unemployed. In how many ways can one select one family of each kind?

10. Suppose that in the example on page 85 a chairman, a vice-chairman, and a treasurer are to be selected from among the five members of the Board of Directors.
(a) In how many ways can the selection be made?
(b) In how many of these is Mrs. White elected treasurer?
(c) In how many of the cases is a man elected chairman?

11. A psychologist is preparing four-letter nonsense words for use in a memory experiment. If he chooses the first letter from among the consonants w, t, z, r, the second letter from among the vowels a, e, i, o, u, the third letter from among the consonants k, x, v, and the fourth letter from among the vowels e, o, u, how many such nonsense words can he construct? Also, how many of these nonsense words will begin with the letter w and how many words will have the vowel o for the second and fourth letters?

12. A multiple-choice test consists of 5 questions, each permitting a choice of four alternatives. In how many ways can a student answer all five questions?

13. An experiment consists of rolling a pair of dice, one green and one red. If the point (2, 3) represents the outcome where the green die comes up 2 and the red die comes up 3, the point (6, 6) represents the outcome where both dice come up

6, etc., draw a figure showing the 36 points of the sample space and list the points which represent each of the following:
(a) the event that both dice come up 2 or less;
(b) the event that both dice come up with the same number;
(c) the event that at least one of the dice comes up 1;
(d) the event that the sum obtained with the dice is 2, 3, or 12.

14. Among six applicants for an executive job Mr. A is a college graduate, foreign born, and single; Mr. B is not a college graduate, foreign born, and married; Mr. C is a college graduate, native born, and married; Mr. D is not a college graduate, native born, and single; Mr. E is a college graduate, native born, and married; and Mr. F is not a college graduate, native born, and married. One of these applicants is to get the job and the event that the job is given to a college graduate, for example, is denoted $\{A, C, E\}$. Indicate in a similar manner
(a) the event that the job is given to a married person;
(b) the event that the job is given to a native-born college graduate;
(c) the event that the job is given to a single person who is foreign born;
(d) the position is given to a person who is either a college graduate or married and foreign born.

15. A small taxicab company has two cabs, of which the larger can carry 5 passengers and the smaller can carry 4 passengers. Using the point (0, 2) to indicate that at a given moment the larger cab is empty while the smaller one has 2 passengers, the point (4, 3) to indicate that the larger cab has 4 passengers while the smaller one has 3 passengers, and so on, draw a figure showing the 30 points which correspond to the different ways in which the cabs can be occupied. Also, if D stands for the event that at least one of the cabs is empty, E stands for the event that together they carry 2, 4, or 6 passengers, and F stands for the event that there is the same number of passengers in each cab, list the points of the sample space belonging to
(a) D;
(b) E;
(c) F:
(d) $D \cup E$;
(e) $D \cap E$;
(f) $E \cup F$;
(g) $D \cup F$;
(h) $D \cap F'$;
(i) $E' \cap D'$.

16. The guidance mechanism of a rocket consists of two subassemblies, with the first containing 4 components and the second containing 2 components. We are concerned only with the number of defective components in each subassembly and we let the point (x, y) represent the case where the first subassembly has x defective components while the second subassembly has y defective components. (Note that $x = 0, 1, 2, 3$, or 4, and $y = 0, 1$, or 2.) Draw a figure showing the 15 possible outcomes. Also, if U stands for the event that the first subassembly has one defective component, V stands for the event that the second subassembly has more defective components than the first, and W stands for the event that the two subassemblies together have either 3 or 4 defective components, list the sample points (outcomes) belonging to
(a) U;
(b) V;
(c) W;
(d) $U \cap V$;
(e) $U \cap V'$;
(f) V';
(g) $U \cup W$;
(h) $V \cup W$;
(i) $U \cap (V \cap W)$.

17. In a survey of houses advertised for sale, each house is classified according to whether it has 1, 2, 3, or 4 bedrooms and according to whether it has 1, 2, or 3 baths. Letting (3, 1) represent a house with 3 bedrooms and 1 bath, (4, 2) a house with 4 bedrooms and 2 baths, and so on, draw a figure showing the 9 points which correspond to the different ways in which a house can be classified, assuming that none of the houses has fewer bedrooms than baths. Also, if K is the event that the sum of the number of bedrooms and baths is 5, L is the event that there are more bedrooms than baths, and M is the event that there are at least 2 bedrooms, list the points (possibilities) belonging to

(a) K;
(b) L';
(c) M;
(d) $L \cap M$;
(e) $K \cup L$;
(f) $K \cap L'$;
(g) $L \cup (K \cap M)$;
(h) $(L \cup K) \cap (L \cup M)$.

18. Which of the following pairs of events are mutually exclusive:
(a) having rain and sunshine on a given day;
(b) wearing green sox and black shoes;
(c) being intoxicated and being sober (at the same time);
(d) obtaining a king or a queen when drawing one card from an ordinary deck of 52 playing cards;
(e) obtaining a king or a black card when drawing one card from an ordinary deck of 52 playing cards;
(f) owning a Chevrolet and owning a Ford (at the same time);
(g) driving a Chevrolet or a Ford;
(h) being under 25 years of age and being President of the United States?

19. Use Venn diagrams to verify that $(A \cup B)' = A' \cap B'$.

20. Use Venn diagrams to verify that $A \cup (A \cap B) = A$.

21. Use Venn diagrams to verify that $A \cup (B \cap C) = (A \cup B) \cap (A \cup C)$.

22. A market research organization claims that among 100 housewives interviewed 62 regularly buy Product X, 53 regularly buy Product Y, 18 regularly buy both, and 13 buy neither product regularly. Using a Venn diagram and entering figures corresponding to the number of housewives belonging to the various regions, check whether the results of this survey should be questioned.

23. In a group of 200 college students 85 are enrolled in a course in Philosophy, 69 are enrolled in a course in English Literature, and 73 are not taking either course. How many of these students must be enrolled in both courses?

24. Among 50 new cars shipped to a dealer there are 5 with airconditioning, bucket seats, and automatic transmission; 4 with airconditioning, automatic transmission, but no bucket seats; 3 with airconditioning, bucket seats, but no automatic transmission; 8 with airconditioning, but neither bucket seats nor automatic transmission; 19 with automatic transmission, but neither airconditioning nor bucket seats; 2 with automatic transmission, bucket seats, but no airconditioning; 3 with bucket seats, but neither airconditioning nor automatic transmission; and 6 without any of these features.

(a) How many of these cars have airconditioning?
(b) How many of these cars have bucket seats?
(c) How many of these cars have automatic transmissions as well as airconditioning?
(d) How many of these cars have neither automatic transmission nor bucket seats?

5.4 The Concept of Probability

Probabilities are numbers we assign to events—a patient's recovering from malaria, rolling 7 with a pair of dice, catching a fish at a certain time of the day, getting an A in a final examination, drawing a red ball out of an urn, having rain spoil one's vacation, making a profit on the sale of stocks, and so on. Obviously, probabilities cannot be just any numbers if they are to be indicative in some way of the "chances" or "likelihood" that the respective events will actually take place, and this is why we shall impose some restrictions on their choice. The reasons for these restrictions, called the *postulates of probability*, will become apparent later; for the moment let us merely point out that, for all practical purposes, they are identical with the properties (of measure functions) listed on page 92. (In case the reader finds it difficult to rid himself of some of the preconceptions attached to the term "probability" in everyday language, he may find it profitable to go along with some authors who use instead the terms "measure" or "weight".)

POSTULATE 1: *A probability is a positive real number or zero.*

POSTULATE 2: *If S is the sample space of an experiment, its probability equals 1.*

The first postulate simply states that we do not want the probability of an event (namely, the degree of "credibility" or the degree of "certainty" we attach to it) to be negative. The second postulate states that *certainty* is identified with a probability of 1; after all, it is always assumed that one of the individual outcomes of an experiment must occur, and it is to this certain event that we assign a probability of 1. Postulate 2 is very similar to the second property listed on page 92; the only difference is that now the maximum value is not 9 or 80, but 1. (Later, we shall demonstrate that the probability of an event can never exceed 1.)

POSTULATE 3: *If A and B are mutually exclusive events, then the probability of $A \cup B$ equals the sum of the individual probabilities of events A and B.**

* As formulated here, the postulates of probability apply only when the sample space S is *finite*. When the sample space is *countably infinite* (namely, when there are as many outcomes as there are whole numbers), the third postulate will have to be modified so that for any sequence of mutually exclusive events $A_1, A_2, A_3, \ldots,$

$$P(A_1 \cup A_2 \cup A_3 \cup \ldots) = P(A_1) + P(A_2) + P(A_3) + \ldots$$

Thus, if the probability that a football team will win a certain game is 0.68 and the probability that it will tie is 0.05, then the probability that it will win or tie *must* be $0.68 + 0.05 = 0.73$; if the probability that a person who applies for a job was born in the State of New York is 0.22 and the probability that he was born in Pennsylvania is 0.13, then the probability that he was born in either state *must* equal $0.22 + 0.13 = 0.35$. Note that this rule for assigning a probability to the union of two mutually exclusive events agrees with the third property listed on page 92.

So far we have assigned a meaning to a probability of 1, but we have not yet decided how to interpret probabilities of, say, 0.07, 0.30, or 0.85. To this end let us introduce a remarkable result, called the *Law of Large Numbers*, which can be derived formally as a mathematical consequence of the three postulates of probability. Informally, this law reads as follows:

> *If the number of times an experiment is repeated grows larger and larger, the proportion of the time a given outcome occurs will tend to come closer and closer to the probability of the outcome for each individual experiment.*

To illustrate how this works, let us refer to the following example, with which everyone must surely be familiar: A coin is flipped again and again, and we observe the accumulated proportion of heads, say, after every fifth flip as in Figure 5.11. As can be seen, the accumulated proportion of heads

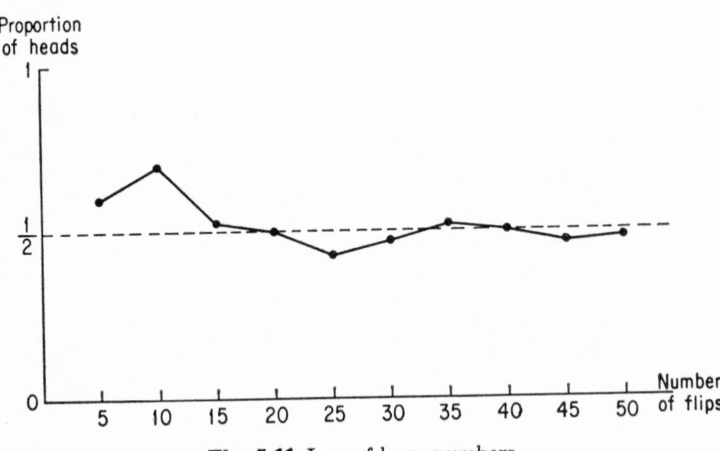

Fig. 5.11 Law of large numbers.

fluctuates, but it comes closer and closer to a value of 1/2, *the probability of heads for each flip of the coin*. We shall not be able to prove the law of large numbers in this text, but the reader should be able to get a good understanding of how it works by actually performing some of the experiments suggested in Exercises 1 and 5 on page 203. Also, we shall formulate the law of large numbers more rigorously in Chapter 7.

As a result of this discussion, we can now interpret the probability of an event as *the proportion of the time it will occur in the long run.* If we say that an event has a probability of 0.30, we mean that if the experiment is repeated a great many times the event will occur about 30 per cent of the time. The more often the experiment is repeated, the "more certain" we can be that the proportion of "successes"—that is, the proportion of the time the event will occur—will be very close to 0.30. Note that we do not claim that the event *must* occur 3 times out of 10, 30 times out of 100, or 300 times out of 1,000; we can only claim that *if the experiment is repeated a sufficient number of times* the proportion of "successes" will practically always (say, 99.99 per cent of the time) be very close to 0.30.

Another consequence of the law of large numbers is that we now have a way of determining, or *estimating*, the values of probabilities. If an experiment is repeated n times, n is large, and event A has occurred x times out of n, we have good reason to assert that the *relative frequency* x/n is very close to the probability that event A will occur in any one of the experiments. Thus, if in the past 624 of 800 flights from Los Angeles to San Francisco arrived within 5 minutes of their scheduled arrival, we can say that there is a probability of (about) $624/800 = 0.78$ that such a flight will arrive within 5 minutes of its scheduled arrival. Also, if 278 of 500 housewives interviewed in a market study favored Brand Y over Brand X, we can estimate as $278/500 = 0.556$ the probability that any one housewife (in the area studied) favors Brand Y over Brand X. The general question of how close we can expect such an estimate to be to the correct value of the probability is a matter we shall discuss in detail in Chapter 10.

It can now be seen why we chose the three postulates as we did. Clearly, the proportion of the time an event occurs cannot be negative, and one of the possible outcomes must occur—of this we are certain 100 per cent of the time. Furthermore, if events A and B are mutually exclusive, A occurs 10 per cent of the time and B occurs 20 per cent of the time, then one or the other will occur 30 per cent of the time. The meaning we have assigned here to the word "probability" is called the *frequency interpretation;* as we have just seen, the frequency interpretation is *consistent* with the three postulates of probability.

Having defined probabilities in terms of repeated experiments and what will happen "in the long run," let us now see whether it is at all meaningful to talk about such things as the probability that Mr. Jones' broken knee will heal within a month's time, the probability that the University of Minnesota's football team will win its season opener in 1970, or the probability that the candidate of a given major party will receive at least 52 per cent of the popular vote in an upcoming presidential election. Since none of these events can happen more than once, it would seem that the frequency concept of probability does not apply. In a sense this is true, but in an indirect sense the frequency interpretation of probability can nevertheless be employed. To explain, let us put ourselves in the position of the doctor who is asked whether Mr. Jones' knee will heal within a month's time. He can refer to hundreds of similar cases of broken knees, and if 34 per cent of these were healed within a month's time he can apply this figure to Mr. Jones' knee. This may not be very comforting to Mr. Jones, but it does provide a meaning to the probability statement concerning his knee, namely, to the statement that the probability of his recovery within a month's time is 0.34. Similarly, with reference to the Minnesota football team we might consider the outcomes of previous season openers, the outcomes of previous games played against the same team scheduled for the season opener in 1970, and so forth. *Thus, if we want to make a probability statement about a specific (nonrepeatable) event, we consider it reasonable and meaningful to refer to a set of similar events.* This can lead to complications, since the choice of such a set of similar events may be neither obvious nor easy. For instance, with reference to Mr. Jones' knee we might consider only similar cases where the patients were of the same age as Mr. Jones; or we might limit ourselves further to cases where the patients had the same weight and blood pressure as Mr. Jones. Although we can thus narrow things down more and more, we will also have less and less information on which an estimate of a suitable probability can be based.

Returning now to the third example on page 99, suppose that a polling organization takes a sample of the electorate and arrives at the conclusion that the given candidate will receive at least 52 per cent of the vote. Suppose, furthermore, that we ask them "how sure" they are of this result, and they reply that they are "95 per cent sure"; in other words, they assign to the event that the candidate will receive at least 52 per cent of the total vote a probability of 0.95. To explain what this means, let us emphasize the fact that they *are* referring to a specific election; the 0.95 probability is not meant to imply that the candidate would receive the estimated vote 95 per cent of the time, if he ran for office a great number of times. No, if the persons conducting the poll assign their estimate a probability of 0.95, this means that *they used a method of estimation which in the long run will be successful 95 per cent of the time.* In other words, *the estimate is either right or wrong, and the probability assigned to it is really a measure of the "goodness" of the method of estimation which they employed.* As we shall explain in more detail later, all probabilities used in statistics to express the merits of estimates, predictions, and decisions are really indications of the "goodness" or reliability, namely, the "success ratio" of the methods employed.

A point of view that is currently gaining in favor among some statisticians is to interpret probabilities (particularly those relating to single, nonrepetitive events) as *personal*, or *subjective*, probabilities. Such probabilities are measures of the strength of a person's belief concerning the occurrence or nonoccurrence of events, and they are arrived at by mental processes which are generally difficult to reconstruct or evaluate. Nevertheless, the concept is a useful one when dealing with situations where there is otherwise very little direct evidence. In that case there may be no choice but to consider pertinent collateral information, educated guesses, and perhaps intuition or other factors. Thus, a businessman may determine the probability for the success of a new venture as 0.60 (or more loosely as better than an even chance) on the basis of an analysis of business conditions in general, the opinions of experts, and his own subjective evaluation of the whole situation.

The problem of actually *determining* subjective probabilities is a very interesting one, and we shall suggest possible solutions in Sections 5.5 and 6.1. It is not an easy problem, and it is complicated by the fact that subjective probabilities must satisfy the three postulates of probability, particularly the third which (in this connection) is sometimes referred to as the "consistency requirement."

In most parts of this book we shall assume that there is either enough direct evidence available to interpret probabilities in the frequency sense, or that there are theoretical grounds on the basis of which we can interpret probabilities as the "success ratios" of the methods which we employ. Whenever we do interpret probabilities as subjective, or personal, probabilities, we shall mention this specifically in the text.

5.5 Probabilities and Odds

Starting with the postulates of probability, it is possible to derive many further rules (or theorems) which play important roles in applications. In order to state some of these rules, it will be convenient to denote the probability of event A by $P(A)$, in which case we can express the three postulates of probability by writing

$$P(A) \geqslant 0 \qquad \textit{for any event } A$$
$$P(S) = 1 \qquad \textit{where } S \textit{ is the whole sample space}$$
$$P(A \cup B) = P(A) + P(B) \qquad \textit{when } A \textit{ and } B \textit{ are mutually exclusive events}$$

Two immediate consequences of the three postulates are expressed by the fact that *a probability can never exceed 1* and that *the empty set* $\varnothing$ *has a probability of 0*. Symbolically,

▲
$$P(A) \leqslant 1 \qquad \textit{for any event } A$$
$$P(\varnothing) = 0$$
▲

The first of these results expresses the fact that an event cannot possibly occur more than 100 per cent of the time; the second expresses the fact that we assign a zero probability to an event which cannot possibly occur. In Exercise 15 on page 106 the reader will be asked to prove both of these theorems in a rigorous fashion.

Another simple rule which follows directly from the three postulates states that if the probability of event A is $P(A)$, then the probability that event A will *not* occur is

$$P(A') = 1 - P(A)$$

Thus, if the probability that it will rain on a given day is 0.15, then the probability that it will not rain on that day is $1 - 0.15 = 0.85$. This agrees with *both* the frequency and the subjective interpretation (and, for that matter, any other interpretation which satisfies the three postulates). So far as the frequency interpretation is concerned, it is obvious that if it rains on days like that 15 per cent of the time, it does not rain 85 per cent of the time. Similarly, if the probability that a student will pass a test is 0.75, then the probability that he will not pass is 0.25; and if the probability that a seed will germinate is 0.44, then the probability that it will not germinate is 0.56.

If the probability of an event is 3/4, we say that the odds are 3 to 1 in its favor; if the probability of an event is 0.95, we say that the odds are 19 to 1 in its favor; and if the probability of an event is 0.10, we say that the odds are 9 to 1 against it. Generally speaking, *the odds for the occurrence of an event are given by the ratio of the probability that the event will occur to the probability that it will not occur.* (Equivalently, the odds *against* the occurrence of an event are given by the ratio of the probability that the event will not occur to the probability that it will occur.) It is customary, though not necessary, to express odds in terms of whole numbers having no common factors. For instance, if the probability of an event is 5/7, we say that the odds in its favor are 5 to 2, rather than $2\frac{1}{2}$ to 1 or 10 to 4.

In gambling, the term "odds" is used in a somewhat different sense. If someone is willing to give us 2 to 1 odds on a certain event, this means that if we take his bet *the amount we may win is twice the amount we stand to lose*. Similarly, if someone is willing to give 3 to 1 odds on the outcome of a football game, this means that he would be willing to bet, say, \$30 against our \$10 that his team will win. Gambling odds, or money odds, are regarded as *fair* if they actually equal the odds that the corresponding event will occur. Thus, if we wanted to bet on an event which has a probability of 0.80, the bet would be *fair* if we had to risk, say, \$4.00 to our opponent's \$1.00; that is, we would have to give him odds of 4 to 1.

In a curious way, the use of gambling odds makes it possible to evaluate personal, or subjective, probabilities. Suppose, for instance, that we want to determine how strongly a friend feels about his football team's chances of winning a particular game, and that we propose a bet of a small sum of money, giving him 2 to 1 odds. These odds would be fair so far as our friend is concerned, if he considered his team's chances to be given by a probability of $\frac{1}{1+2} = 1/3$. Hence, if he accepts the bet, we can conclude that the subjective probability he associates with his team's winning is *at least* 1/3; if he does not accept the bet (unless we offer him better odds), we can conclude that his subjective probability concerning the event (his team's winning) is *less than* 1/3.

To consider another example, suppose that an archeologist is starting out on an expedition to look for Aztec ruins and that he feels pretty optimistic about his potential success. Asked at what odds he would be willing to make a small wager on the success of the expedition, he replies that he would be willing to give odds of 3 to 1 (say, bet \$3.00 against \$1.00), but that he would not be willing to give odds of 4 to 1. This means that he considers the probability of success to be *at least* $\frac{3}{3+1} = 0.75$, but *less than* $\frac{4}{4+1} = 0.80$.

Although we can thus evaluate subjective probabilities, it should be pointed out that this method leaves a good deal to be desired. If the amount of money involved is very small, a person may be very careless in judging the odds; also, we assumed in our examples that the *utility* (or *desirability*) of, say, \$40 is actually four times that of \$10, thus ignoring such things as the law of diminishing returns. Other complications arise when a person objects to any form of gambling on moral grounds, or if he is unwilling to risk any of his capital regardless of the odds. In the latter case there exists a way of avoiding this difficulty, and we shall go into this briefly in Section 6.1.

Another reason why the method of the preceding paragraphs may fail is that throughout history the human mind has proven itself singularly inept at estimating odds. This is true particularly in situations where there is very little or no direct evidence, thus making it necessary to rely on one's common sense or intuition. The following is a classical example: There are 40 persons at a party and someone offers even money (odds of 1 to 1) that at least two of the 40 persons have the same birthday. Since there are 365 days and only 40 persons, common sense suggests that it is quite unlikely that any two of them have the same birthday and, hence, that we should take the bet. If we did, we would be at a great disadvantage; in fact, it can be shown mathematically (see Bibliography on page 124) that the correct odds are better than 8 to 1 that at least two of the 40 persons have the same birthday. Had there been 50 persons at the party, the odds would have been better than 32 to 1. Incidentally, in calculating these odds we assumed that the party is not attended by twins.

Further illustrations which show how misleading common sense or intuition can be in the estimation of odds are given in Exercise 14 on page 105 and in Exercise 19 on page 130. To make a case for subjective probabilities (and their use in statistics), we shall thus have to make sure that such probabilities are not based on "common sense" and intuition alone; to be of any value, they must be arrived at by some mental process on the basis of pertinent direct and/or collateral information.

EXERCISES

1. If D represents a drop in barometric pressure and R represents a rise in temperature, state in words what probabilities are expressed by each of the following:
(a) $P(D')$; (c) $P(D \cap R)$; (e) $P(D' \cap R')$;
(b) $P(R)$; (d) $P(D \cup R')$; (f) $P(D' \cup R)$.

2. If M stands for the event that the person who is elected mayor of a given town is married, W stands for the event that he is wealthy, and H stands for the event that he is honest, write each of the following probabilities in symbolic form:
(a) the probability that the mayor is wealthy and honest;
(b) the probability that the mayor is honest but not wealthy;
(c) the probability that the mayor is neither wealthy nor married;
(d) the probability that the mayor is honest and married;
(e) the probability that the mayor is wealthy but neither honest nor married.

3. Mr. Smith flipped a coin 100 times and obtained 30 heads; then he flipped the coin another 100 times and obtained 42 heads. Looking at these results he complains that the *law of averages*, as he calls the law of large numbers, is letting him down. After all, he claims, things are worse after the 200 flips than they were after the first 100. Explain the fallacy of this argument; that is, explain how Mr. Smith misinterprets the law of large numbers.

4. A gambler claims that if one flips a coin 400 times it is "reasonable" to expect anywhere from 170 to 230 heads, and if one flips a coin 4,000,000 times it is "reasonable" to expect anywhere from 1,997,000 and 2,003,000 heads. Does this argument conflict or agree with the law of large numbers?

5. Given the mutually exclusive events A and B for which $P(A) = 0.25$ and $P(B) = 0.60$, find
(a) $P(A')$; (c) $P(A \cup B)$; (e) $P(A' \cup B')$;
(b) $P(B')$; (d) $P(A \cap B)$; (f) $P(A' \cap B')$.
(*Hint:* Draw a Venn diagram and fill in the probabilities associated with the various regions.)

6. What are the odds for the occurrence of event X, if its probability is (a) 11/13, (b) 5/7, and (c) 1/5?

7. If someone is willing to bet \$15.00 against \$6.00 that event X of Exercise 6 will occur, state in each case whether this would be to his advantage, would be to his disadvantage, or would be fair.

8. What are the odds *against* the occurrence of event Y, if its probability is (a) 0.15, (b) 0.30, and (c) 0.40?

9. If someone is willing to bet \$3.00 against \$2.00 that event Y of Exercise 8 will *not* occur, in which of the three cases would this bet be fair? In which of the three cases would this bet be to his greatest advantage?

10. In order to determine how the manager of a new restaurant feels about his chances of suceess, someone offers him a bet of \$50 against his \$30 that the venture will not succeed. What can we say about the manager's personal probability concerning the restaurant's success if (a) he accepts the bet, and (b) he wants better odds?

11. In order to determine how a scientist feels about the possible truth of a hypothesis which is going to be subjected to experimental verification, we offer him a bet of \$16 to his \$4 that the experiment *will not* substantiate the hypothesis. What can we say about the scientist's personal probability concerning the experiment's success if (a) he accepts the bet, and (b) he wants better odds?

12. Suppose that in Exercise 11 the scientist turns down the bet of \$16 against his \$4, but he is willing to accept a corresponding bet of \$26 against his \$4. What does this tell us about the scientist's personal probability concerning the experiment's success?

13. A friend is going on an ocean cruise and we propose to him a bet of \$22.50 to his \$2.50 that he will not get seasick. What can we say about his feelings concerning the matter if he is willing to accept the bet?

14. The following is a good example of the difficulties in which we may find ourselves if we use only "common sense," or intuition, in judgments concerning probabilities:

> "Among three indistinguishable boxes one contains 2 pennies, one contains a penny and a dime, and one contains 2 dimes. Selecting one of these boxes at random (each box has a probability of 1/3), one coin is taken out at random (each coin has a probability of 1/2) without looking at the other. The coin that is taken out of the box is a penny, and without giving the matter too much thought, we may well be inclined to say that there is a probability of 1/2 that the other coin in the box is also a penny. After all, the penny must have come either from the box with the penny and the dime or from the box with two pennies. In the first case the other coin is a dime, in the second case it is a penny, and it would seem reasonable to say that these two possibilities are equally likely."

Actually, the correct value of the probability that the other coin is also a penny is 2/3, and it will be left to the reader to verify this result by mentally labeling the two pennies in the first box P_1 and P_2, the two dimes in the third box D_1 and D_2, and drawing a tree diagram showing the six possible (and equally likely) outcomes of the experiment.

15. (a) Prove that $P(A) \leqslant 1$ for any event A, making use of the fact that $A \cup A' = S$, and that A and A' are mutually exclusive. [*Hint:* Assume that $P(A)$ is greater than 1, and show that this leads to a contradiction; that is, to a violation of one of the postulates of probability.]
(b) Prove that $P(\varnothing) = 0$, making use of the fact that $S \cup \varnothing = S$, and that S and $\varnothing$ are mutually exclusive.

5.6 Some Rules of Probability

In the study of probability there are essentially three kinds of questions: the question of what we mean when we say that a probability is 0.15, 0.32,. . ., the question of how numerical values of probabilities can actually be obtained, and the question of how to use known probabilities of simple events to calculate those of more complicated kinds of events. Having discussed the first two kinds of questions in the preceding sections, we shall devote the remainder of this chapter mainly to the third.

To begin with, let us extend the third postulate of probability so that it can apply to more than two mutually exclusive events, that is, to k events which are *pairwise* mutually exclusive. Repeatedly applying Postulate 3, we obtain

GENERALIZATION OF POSTULATE 3: *If A_1, A_2, . . ., and A_k are mutually exclusive events, then*

$$P(A_1 \cup A_2 \cup \ldots \cup A_k) = P(A_1) + P(A_2) + \ldots + P(A_k)$$

With this formula we can now calculate the probability that one of a set of mutually exclusive events will occur. For instance, if the probability that a graduate of a certain prep school will enroll at Harvard is 0.12, the probability that he will enroll at M.I.T. is 0.08, and the probability that he will enroll at Boston College is 0.10, then the probability that he will enroll at one of these schools is $0.12 + 0.08 + 0.10 = 0.30$. Also, if the probabilities that a person eating at a given restaurant will order steak, chicken, turkey, or lobster are, respectively, 0.34, 0.22, 0.15, and 0.12, then the probability that he will order one of these main courses is $0.34 + 0.22 + 0.15 + 0.12 = 0.83$; the probability that he will order something else is $1 - 0.83 = 0.17$.

The problem of determining the probabilities of various events relating to an experiment can be quite complicated (or very tedious); for a sample space with as few as 20 individual outcomes there are already over a million different subsets or events, 1,048,576 to be exact. To simplify this problem, we often use the following theorem:

The probability of any event A equals the sum of the probabilities of the individual outcomes comprising A.

To illustrate the use of this theorem, let us refer again to the two-person-interview example on page 87, and let us suppose that the nine possible outcomes have the probabilities shown in Figure 5.12. If we are interested in the probability that the first person interviewed is undecided, we find that it is given by the sum of the probabilities assigned to the points (2, 1), (2, 2), and (2, 3), and that it equals $8/16 = 1/2$. Similarly, the probability that at least one of the two persons interviewed will be for Candidate P is given by the sum of the probabilities assigned to the points (1, 1), (1, 2), (1, 3), (2, 1), and (3, 1), and it equals 7/16.

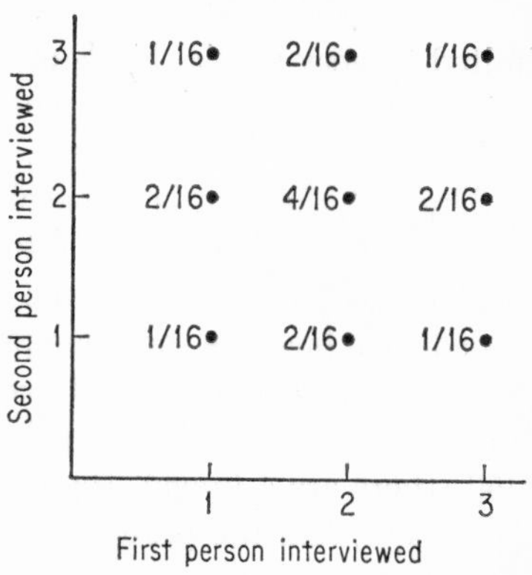

Fig. 5.12 Sample space for interview of two persons.

To consider another illustration, let us refer again to the example on page 92 and let us suppose that one of the 80 students is to be elected by lot to serve on a committee. Assuming that each of the students thus has a probability of 1/80 of being selected, the probability that the one chosen is *an undergraduate who does not own a car* is given by

$$\underbrace{\frac{1}{80} + \frac{1}{80} + \cdots + \frac{1}{80}}_{30 \text{ terms}} = \frac{30}{80}$$

and the probability that he is a *graduate student* is given by

$$\underbrace{\frac{1}{80} + \frac{1}{80} + \cdots + \frac{1}{80}}_{25 \text{ terms}} = \frac{25}{80}$$

Observe that in this example, where the 80 possible outcomes have equal probabilities, the probability of any particular event is given by 1/80 *times* the number of individual outcomes comprising the event. In general, when dealing with experiments in which the individual outcomes are all *equiprobable,* we can use the following theorem, sometimes called the SPECIAL RULE FOR EQUIPROBABLE EVENTS, to considerable advantage:

> *If an experiment has n equiprobable outcomes and if s of these constitute event A, then* $P(A) = s/n$.

This theorem follows immediately from the preceding one on page 106. It is sometimes given as a *definition* of probability, although this definition is limited to very special kinds of experiments (with equiprobable outcomes) and there is an obvious circularity in defining probability in terms of equiprobable, or equally likely, events.

The last theorem is of special value in problems relating to games of chance, where it is reasonable to assume that if a deck of cards is properly shuffled each card has the same chance of being drawn, if a coin is properly flipped each face has the same probability of coming up, if a die is properly rolled each face is as likely to come up as any other, and so on. Thus, the probability of drawing a king from an ordinary deck of 52 playing cards is 4/52 (there are 4 kings), the probability of getting heads with a balanced coin is 1/2, and the probability of rolling an even number with one die is 3/6. The special rule also applies, say, when each animal in a litter has the same chance of being selected for an experiment, when each family in a town has the same chance of being selected as part of a survey, or when each ball-bearing in a lot has the same chance of being chosen for inspection.

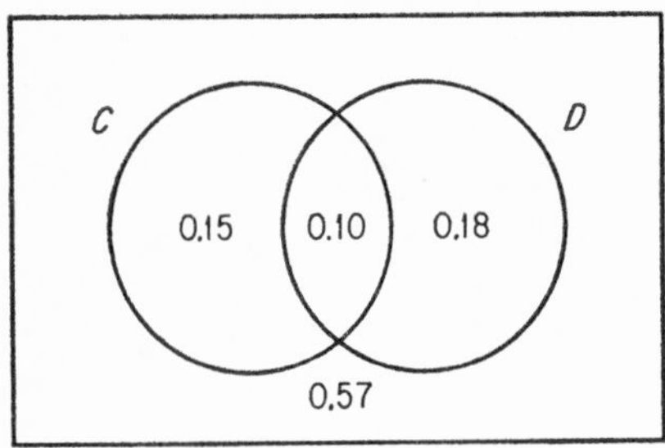

Fig. 5.13 Venn diagram.

Since Postulate 3 applies only to mutually exclusive events, let us now look for a formula for $P(A \cup B)$ which holds also when A and B are not mutually exclusive. To this end, let us consider the example illustrated by the Venn diagram of Figure 5.13, where C stands for the event that a delinquent child's father is unemployed, D stands for the event that his parents are separated or divorced, and the figures are the probabilities assigned to the corresponding events. It can be seen from this diagram that $P(C) = 0.15 + 0.10 = 0.25$, $P(D) = 0.10 + 0.18 = 0.28$, and $P(C \cup D) = 0.15 + 0.10 + 0.18 = 0.43$. (We are able to add the respective probabilities since they evidently refer to mutually exclusive events.) Had we erroneously used Postulate 3 to calculate $P(C \cup D)$, we would have obtained $0.25 + 0.28 = 0.53$, which exceeds the correct value by 0.10, since $P(C \cap D) = 0.10$ was added in *twice*—once in $P(C) = 0.25$ and once in $P(D) = 0.28$. Thus, we could also have obtained the correct result by subtracting $P(C \cap D)$ from $P(C) + P(D)$, namely, by writing

$$P(C \cup D) = 0.25 + 0.28 - 0.10 = 0.43$$

Accounting in this way for the outcomes which are included *twice* when we add the probabilities of the two individual events, we arrive at the following result which holds regardless of whether the two events are mutually exclusive:

GENERAL RULE OF ADDITION: *Given any two events A and B,*

$$P(A \cup B) = P(A) + P(B) - P(A \cap B)$$

To illustrate this rule, let us refer again to the two-person-interview example and Figure 5.12. If, as before, X is the event that at least one of the persons interviewed is undecided while Y is the event that both persons respond in the same way, it can be seen that $P(X) = 12/16$, $P(Y) = 6/16$, and $P(X \cap Y) = 4/16$. Hence,

$$P(X \cup Y) = \frac{12}{16} + \frac{6}{16} - \frac{4}{16} = \frac{14}{16}$$

This result can be verified by calculating $P(X \cup Y)$ directly, that is, by adding the probabilities assigned to the seven points comprising $X \cup Y$ in Figure 5.12. Note that if we had erroneously used Postulate 3 in this example, we would have obtained the *impossible* value of 18/16.

To consider another example, suppose we want to determine the probability of getting either a black card (event A) or a king (event B) when drawing a card from an ordinary deck of 52 playing cards. Assuming that each card has a probability of 1/52, we get

$$P(A \cup B) = \frac{26}{52} + \frac{4}{52} - \frac{2}{52} = \frac{28}{52}$$

since there are 26 black cards, 4 kings, and 2 black kings. This result can be verified by observing that the total number of outcomes comprising $A \cup B$ is 28; there are 26 black cards and 2 red kings.

EXERCISES

1. Analyzing business conditions in general, three economists made the following claims: The first economist claims that the probabilities for the cost of living to go up, remain unchanged, or go down are, respectively, 0.64, 0.23, and 0.09; the second economist claims that the respective probabilities are 0.53, 0.36, and 0.11; and the third economist claims that the probabilities are 0.55, 0.39, and 0.08. Comment on these claims.

2. Explain why there must be a mistake in each of the following statements:
(a) An inspector claims that the probabilities for a large shipment of machine parts to contain 0, 1, 2, 3, 4, or 5 defectives are, respectively, 0.10, 0.25, 0.37, 0.15, 0.09, and 0.06.
(b) The probabilities that there will be 0, 1, 2, or 3 or more accidents at a certain intersection during 1968 are, respectively, 0.52, 0.21, 0.12, and 0.05.
(c) The probability that a laboratory technician will make exactly one mistake during a chemical analysis is 0.04, and the probability that he will make at least one mistake is 0.02.

(d) The probability that Mr. Jones' income tax return will be audited in detail by the Internal Revenue Service is 0.25, and the probability that Mr. Jones' return as well as that of his father will both be audited in detail by the Internal Revenue Service is 0.40.

3. An experiment has the four possible (mutually exclusive) outcomes A, B, C, and D. Check whether the following assignments of probability are permissible:
(a) $P(A) = 0.34$, $P(B) = 0.29$, $P(C) = 0.17$, $P(D) = 0.30$;
(b) $P(A) = 0.17$, $P(B) = 0.59$, $P(C) = 0.21$, $P(D) = 0.03$;
(c) $P(A) = 0.24$, $P(B) = -0.05$, $P(C) = 0.48$, $P(D) = 0.33$;
(d) $P(A) = 13/80$, $P(B) = 1/2$, $P(C) = 11/40$, $P(D) = 3/80$.

4. The probability that Mr. Brown will play poker on a Saturday night is 0.23, the probability that he will watch television is 0.38, the probability that he will go to the movies is 0.06, the probability that he will go bowling is 0.15, and the probability that he will work around the house or go to bed early is 0.18.
(a) What is the probability that he will watch television, go to the movies, or go bowling?
(b) What is the probability that he will play poker, go bowling, or watch television?
(c) What is the probability that he will neither go bowling nor go to the movies?

5. The probabilities that a student will receive an A, B, C, D, or F in a final examination in a course in statistics are, respectively, 0.12, 0.24, 0.45, 0.12, and 0.07.
(a) What is the probability that he will receive at least a C?
(b) What is the probability that he will receive neither an A nor an F?
(c) What is the probability that he will get at most a C?

6. If the two teams are evenly matched for each game, the probabilities that a World Series lasts 4, 5, 6, or 7 games are, respectively, 1/8, 1/4, 5/16, and 5/16.
(a) What is the probability that a World Series will not require the sixth game?
(b) If the players share only in the receipts of the first four games, what is the probability that there will be at least two games for which the players do not share in the receipts?
(c) What is the probability that each team will win at least one game?

7. Sometimes Mr. Morris has lunch at his company's cafeteria, sometimes he goes to a privately owned restaurant in the building where he works, sometimes he brings his own lunch, sometimes he takes a customer to the country club for lunch, and sometimes he skips lunch altogether to lose weight. If the probabilities of these alternatives are, respectively, 0.24, 0.15, 0.33, 0.12, and 0.16, find
(a) the probability that he will have lunch at the cafeteria, the privately owned restaurant in the building where he works, or at the country club;
(b) the probability that he will not bring his own lunch nor skip lunch to lose weight;
(c) the probability that he will either have lunch in the building where he works (the cafeteria or the restaurant) or bring his own lunch.

8. Assuming that each point of the sample space of Exercise 15 on page 95 is assigned a probability of 1/30, evaluate each of the following:
(a) $P(D)$; (b) $P(E)$; (c) $P(F)$; (d) $P(E \cap F)$; (e) $P(D \cup E)$; (f) $P(D \cap F)$; (g) $P(E \cup F)$.

9. Referring to Exercise 17 on page 96, suppose that the 9 possible outcomes are assigned probabilities in the following way: Each outcome in which there are as many bedrooms as baths is assigned a probability of 1/10, each outcome where there is one more bedroom than there are baths is assigned a probability of 3/20, each outcome in which there are two more bedrooms than there are baths is assigned a probability of 1/10, and each outcome where there are three more bedrooms than there are baths is assigned a probability of 1/20. Verify that this is a permissible way of assigning probabilities to the 9 possible outcomes. Also, if the events K, L, and M are defined as in Exercise 17 on page 96, find each of the following probabilities:
(a) $P(K)$; (b) $P(L)$; (c) $P(M)$; (d) $P(K \cup L)$; (e) $P(K \cap M)$; (f) $P(L \cup M)$; (g) $P(K \cap L')$; (h) $P(L' \cap M')$.

10. A student is chosen at random from a class of 40 students, of whom 25 are English majors, 9 are on the Dean's list, and among those on the Dean's list 4 are also English majors.
(a) What is the probability that the student chosen is either an English major or not on the Dean's list?
(b) What is the probability that the student chosen is not an English major but on the Dean's list?
(c) What is the probability that the student chosen is neither an English major nor on the Dean's list?

11. Referring to Exercise 24 on page 96, suppose that one of the cars in the shipment is damaged. Assuming equal probabilities, find the probability that
(a) the damaged car has airconditioning;
(b) the damaged car has bucket seats;
(c) the damaged car has airconditioning but no automatic transmission;
(d) the damaged car has no bucket seats, but airconditioning and an automatic transmission.

12. Assuming that each of the 52 cards of an ordinary deck of playing cards has a probability of 1/52 of being drawn, what is the probability of drawing
(a) a red queen;
(b) a jack, queen, king, or ace;
(c) a card which is neither an ace nor a spade;
(d) a 2, 3, 4, 5, 6, or 7;
(e) a diamond or a heart?

13. Playing with balanced dice, what is the probability of rolling
(a) a six with one die;
(b) less than 5 with one die;
(c) a total of 6 with a pair of dice;
(d) a total of 7 or 11 with a pair of dice?
[*Hint:* For (c) and (d) refer to the sample space of Exercise 13 on page 94 and assign each of the sample points a probability of 1/36.]

14. An urn contains 12 red balls, 10 white balls, 15 blue balls, and 3 black balls. If one ball is drawn at random (each ball has a probability of 1/40), find the probability that the ball is (a) red, white or blue; (b) neither white nor black; and (c) black or blue.

15. Given $P(A) = 0.63$, $P(B) = 0.28$, and $P(A \cap B) = 0.11$, find

(a) $P(A')$; (c) $P(A \cup B)$; (e) $P(A \cup B')$;

(b) $P(B')$; (d) $P(A \cap B')$; (f) $P(A' \cap B')$.

(*Hint:* Draw a Venn diagram and fill in the probabilities associated with its four regions.)

16. To raise money for a worthy cause, an organization sells raffle tickets numbered from 1 to 300. What is the probability that the number drawn is (a) divisible by 5, (b) divisible by 6, (c) divisible by 30, and (d) divisible by either 5 or 6?

17. The probability that a car entering the Grand Canyon National Park has California license plates is 0.14, the probability that it is a station wagon is 0.36, and the probability that it is a station wagon with California license plates is 0.08.

(a) What is the probability that such a car is either a station wagon or has California plates?

(b) What is the probability that such a car does not have California plates or is not a station wagon? (*Hint:* Draw a Venn diagram and fill in the probabilities associated with its four regions.)

18. The probability that a patient visiting his dentist will have a tooth extracted is 0.07, the probability that he will have a cavity filled is 0.19, and the probability that he will have a tooth extracted as well as a cavity filled is 0.02. What is the probability that a patient visits his dentist but has neither a tooth extracted nor a cavity filled?

5.7 Conditional Probability

As we have defined probability, it is meaningless to speak of the probability of an event unless we specify the sample space to which it belongs. To ask for the probability that a psychologist has an annual income of $12,000 or more is meaningful only if we specify whether we are referring to all psychologists in the United States, all those employed in industry, all those holding advanced college degrees, or perhaps all those who belong to a certain professional organization.

Since the choice of a sample space is by no means always self-evident, it is often helpful to use the symbol $P(A \mid S)$, denoting the *conditional probability of event A relative to S*, to indicate that we are referring to the specific sample space S. In this sense, every probability is a conditional probability, and we use the abbreviated notation only when the tacit choice of S is clearly understood.

To investigate some of the ideas connected with conditional probabilities, let us consider the following problem: The first stage of an agricultural experiment consists of planting corn on 100 test plots, some with and some without fertilizer, and observing whether the yield is high or low; then in the second stage one plot is selected at random (each plot has a probability of 0.01) for further investigation. Given that the results of the first stage are as shown in the following table

	High Yield	*Low Yield*
With Fertilizer	66	14
Without Fertilizer	12	8

let us first determine the probabilities that the plot selected for the second stage has a high yield and that it was fertilized. Referring to these events as H and F, we have

$$P(H) = \frac{66 + 12}{100} = 0.78 \quad \text{and} \quad P(F) = \frac{66 + 14}{100} = 0.80$$

by virtue of the assumption that the 100 possible selections are equiprobable. [Had we *misread* the statement and looked for the probability that the plot selected for the second stage has a high yield and was fertilized as well, we would have obtained $P(H \cap F) = 66/100 = 0.66$.]

Now suppose that for some reason the selection of the plot for the second stage is to be restricted to those that were fertilized. Instead of $P(H)$, we are now interested in the probability $P(H \mid F)$, namely, the probability of obtaining a lot with a high yield *given that it was fertilized.* The reduced sample space with which we are now concerned has 80 possible outcomes and, assuming that these 80 outcomes are still equally likely, we obtain

$$P(H \mid F) = \frac{66}{80} = 0.825$$

Note that this conditional probability can also be written as

$$P(H \mid F) = \frac{66/100}{80/100} \quad \text{or as} \quad P(H \mid F) = \frac{P(H \cap F)}{P(F)}$$

namely, as the *ratio* of the probability that the chosen lot has a high yield and was fertilized to the probability that it was fertilized.

Had the selection been restricted to lots with a low yield and had we been interested in $P(F' \mid H')$, the probability that the chosen lot was not fertilized *given that it had a low yield,* we would similarly have obtained $P(F' \mid H') = 8/22$, assuming that the 22 possible outcomes in the reduced sample space H' are still equally probable. This result can also be written in the form

$$P(F' \mid H') = \frac{P(F' \cap H')}{P(H')}$$

namely, as the *ratio* of the probability that the chosen lot was not fertilized and had a low yield to the probability that it had a low yield. Following these observations, let us now make the following definition of a *conditional probability:*

If A and B are events belonging to some sample space S and if $P(B) \neq 0$, then the conditional probability of A relative to B is given by

$$P(A \mid B) = \frac{P(A \cap B)}{P(B)}$$

Note that this definition is quite general; it does not depend on the assumption of equal probabilities made in our illustration.

To give another example, suppose it is known to the U.S. Forest Service that the probability for a thunderstorm in Pleasant Valley on an August day is 0.40 and that the probability for a fire caused by lightning is 0.32. What we would like to know is the probability that there will be a fire caused by lightning *given that there is a thunderstorm.* Letting T stand for the event that there will be a thunderstorm and L for the event that there will be a fire caused by lightning, we have $P(T) = 0.40$, $P(L) = 0.32$, and since there can be no lightning without a thunderstrom, $P(L \cap T) = P(L)$. Hence,

$$P(L \mid T) = \frac{P(L \cap T)}{P(T)} = \frac{0.32}{0.40} = 0.80$$

Observe how the probability for a fire caused by lightning has increased once it is known that there is a thunderstorm.

An immediate consequence of our definition of conditional probability is expressed by the following theorem, called the GENERAL RULE OF MULTIPLICATION:

Given any events A and B

$$P(A \cap B) = P(B) \cdot P(A \mid B) \qquad \textit{provided } P(B) \neq 0$$
$$P(A \cap B) = P(A) \cdot P(B \mid A) \qquad \textit{provided } P(A) \neq 0$$

In words, this theorem states that the probability that events A and B *both* occur is given by the product of the probability that one of them will occur and the probability that the other will occur *given* that the first has occurred (occurs, or will occur.) The first part of this theorem can be proved by simply multiplying $P(A \mid B)$, as it is defined above, by $P(B)$; the second part can be proved by interchanging A and B in the first part and making use of the fact that $A \cap B = B \cap A$. As an immediate consequence of this theorem we find that $P(B) \cdot P(A \mid B) = P(A) \cdot P(B \mid A)$, and we shall make use of this important relationship between $P(A \mid B)$ and $P(B \mid A)$ in Section 5.8, where it forms the basis for Bayes' Theorem.

To illustrate the general rule of multiplication, suppose we want to determine the probability of choosing two defective TV sets in succession from a shipment of 12 TV sets among which 4 are defective. Assuming equal probabilities for each selection, the probability that the first one is defective is 4/12, and the probability that the second is defective *given that the first was defective* is 3/11. (There are only 3 defectives among the 11 sets which remain after the first selection has been made.) Hence, the probability of choosing two defective sets in a row is $(4/12)(3/11) = 1/11$.

The general rule of multiplication can easily be extended to the occurrence of more than two events. In fact, the probability of the occurrence of several successive events can be obtained by multiplying the probabilities of the individual events, assuming in each case that all previous events have occurred. For instance, the probability of drawing 3 kings in a row from an ordinary deck of 52 playing cards is given by $(4/52)(3/51)(2/50) = 1/5{,}525$. It is assumed here that we do not replace each card before the next one is drawn; had each card been immediately replaced, the probabilities of getting a king on the second and third draw would both have equaled 4/52. In that case, the correct answer would have been $(4/52)(4/52)(4/52) = 1/2{,}197$. Since the probability of getting a king on the second draw is now 4/52 regardless of what happened on the first draw, we say that the second draw is *independent* of the first; similarly, the third draw is now *independent* of the second as well as the first. In general, we use the following definition:

Event A is independent of event B if and only if

$$P(A \mid B) = P(A)$$

In words, event A is independent of event B when the occurrence of A is not affected by the occurrence of B. An immediate consequence of event A's independence of event B is that A is also independent of B', namely, the occurrence of A is not affected either by the *nonoccurrence* of B. Another important consequence (which follows directly from the rule on page 114) is that *if A is independent of B, then B is also independent of A*. Thus, we say that *A and B are independent*, whenever A is independent of B (or B is independent of A.) Otherwise, we say that A and B are *dependent*.

In the special case where A and B are independent, the formula for $P(A \cap B)$ assumes the form given in the following theorem, called the SPECIAL RULE OF MULTIPLICATION:

If A and B are independent events, then

$$P(A \cap B) = P(A) \cdot P(B)$$

Thus, the probability of getting a 6 in each of two successive rolls of a die is $(1/6)(1/6) = 1/36$; also, if the probability that a person examined for induction into the army has bad eyes is 0.08 and the probability that he has flat feet is 0.05, then the probability that he has bad eyes as well as flat feet is $(0.08)(0.05) = 0.004$.

The above rule can easily be extended to apply to more than two independent events. Following the suggestion on page 115, we have only to multiply the individual probabilities of the independent events. For instance, the probability of getting 4 heads in a row with a balanced coin is $(1/2)(1/2)(1/2)(1/2) = 1/16$.

In actual practice, we are apt to meet more *dependent* events than independent ones. For instance, if A and B represent, respectively, a husband and his wife's having completed 4 years of college, these events are dependent; A and B would also be dependent if they represented a person's being a school teacher and his having an annual income of over $6,000, or if they represented the success of a Broadway play and the happiness of its backers.

5.8 The Rule of Bayes

There are many experiments in which the ultimate outcome depends on what happens in various intermediate stages. For instance, a person's recovery from a disease depends on the diagnosis as well as the treatment; the success of a space flight depends on preliminary calculations, the performance of all systems, and the competence of the pilot; the success of a sales campaign depends not only on how it is planned, but also on how it is carried out; and so on.

To illustrate the general technique used in problems of this kind, suppose that a soap manufacturer is auditioning several television programs to advertise his product, and he wants to know what the chances are that his program will ultimately receive a high rating. It is known that he generally favors situation comedies over panel shows and panel shows over Westerns; in fact, the probabilities that he will choose one of these three kinds of shows are, respectively, 0.60, 0.30, and 0.10. If it is also known that the probabilities of getting a high rating with such shows are, respectively, 0.10, 0.30, and 0.20, we are now in the position to calculate the probability that the soap manufacturer's show will ultimately get a high rating.

Referring to the tree diagram of Figure 5.14, we find that the probability that the soap manufacturer will choose a situation comedy and subsequently get a high rating is $(0.60)(0.10) = 0.06$, where we multiplied the two probabilities in accordance with the rule on page 114. Similarly, the probabilities for the other two branches are $(0.30)(0.30) = 0.09$ and

$(0.10)(0.20) = 0.02$. Now, since the three possibilities are mutually exclusive, the desired probability of getting a high rating is $0.06 + 0.09 + 0.02 = 0.17$. Note that the tree diagram of Figure 5.14 does not represent *all* possible outcomes, but only those leading to high ratings.

Symbolically, if A stands for the event that the program will get a high rating, while B_1, B_2, and B_3 stand, respectively, for the soap manufacturer's choice of a situation comedy, a panel show, or a Western, the proba-

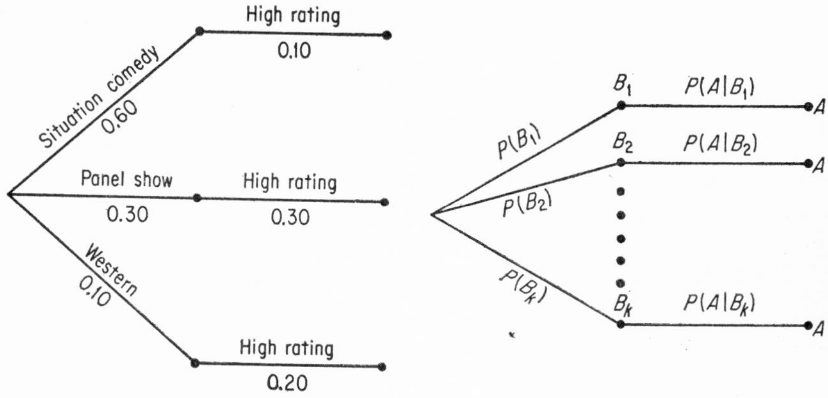

Fig. 5.14 Tree diagram.

Fig. 5.15 Rule of elimination.

bilities we were originally given are $P(B_1) = 0.60$, $P(B_2) = 0.30$, $P(B_3) = 0.10$, $P(A \mid B_1) = 0.10$, $P(A \mid B_2) = 0.30$, and $P(A \mid B_3) = 0.20$. Our subsequent calculations can now be written as

$$
\begin{aligned}
P(A) &= P(B_1) \cdot P(A \mid B_1) + P(B_2) \cdot P(A \mid B_2) + P(B_3) \cdot P(A \mid B_3) \\
&= (0.60)(0.10) + (0.30)(0.30) + (0.10)(0.20) \\
&= 0.17
\end{aligned}
$$

and if we generalize the argument used as the basis for these calculations, we obtain the following theorem, called the RULE OF ELIMINATION:

If $B_1, B_2, \ldots,$ and B_k are mutually exclusive events, of which none has zero probability and one must occur, then for any event A

$$
▲ \qquad P(A) = \sum_{i=1}^{k} P(B_i) \cdot P(A \mid B_i) \qquad ▲
$$

Note that in this sum each term represents a path (along the branches of a tree diagram) which leads to event A. As shown in Figure 5.15, the first leads to A via B_1, the second leads to A via B_2, . . ., and the last leads to A via B_k.

To give another example, suppose that if a person with tuberculosis is given a chest X-ray, the probability that his condition will be detected is 0.98; if a person without tuberculosis is given a chest X-ray, the probability that he will erroneously be diagnosed as having tuberculosis is 0.0001. If 0.3 per cent of the residents of a county have tuberculosis, what is the probability that one of them, selected at random (with equal probabilities), will be diagnosed as having tuberculosis? Symbolically, we have $P(B_1) = 0.003$ and $P(B_2) = 1 - 0.003 = 0.997$, where B_1 and B_2 stand, respectively, for the events that the person selected does or does not have tuberculosis; furthermore, if A represents the event that a person is diagnosed as having tuberculosis, then $P(A \mid B_1) = 0.98$ and $P(A \mid B_2) = 0.0001$. Substituting these figures into the formula for the rule of elimination, we obtain

$$\begin{aligned} P(A) &= (0.003)(0.98) + (0.997)(0.0001) \\ &= 0.00294 + 0.0000997 \\ &= 0.00304 \end{aligned}$$

and this is the probability that a person will be diagnosed as having tuberculosis.

Still referring to this same example, suppose now that we are interested in an entirely different question: We want to know the probability that *a person diagnosed as having tuberculosis actually has the disease.* To answer this kind of question, we need the following theorem, called the RULE OF BAYES:

If $B_1, B_2, \ldots,$ and B_k are mutually exclusive events, of which none has zero probability and one must occur, then for any event A

▲ $$P(B_i \mid A) = \frac{P(B_i) \cdot P(A \mid B_i)}{\sum_{j=1}^{k} P(B_j) \cdot P(A \mid B_j)}$$ ▲

for $i = 1, 2, \ldots,$ or k.

This theorem (which the reader will be asked to prove in Exercise 30 on page 124) gives the probability that an event is reached along a *particular* path of a tree diagram like those of Figures 5.14 and 5.15, given that it is reached along one of these paths. In words, the Rule of Bayes states that the probability $P(B_i \mid A)$ is given by the *ratio* of the probability of the path leading to A via B_i to the *sum* of the probabilities of all the paths leading to A.

Returning now to the question asked in the preceding paragraph, we find that if one of the persons in the given county is diagnosed as having tuberculosis, the probability that he actually has the disease is given by

$$\begin{aligned} P(B_1 \mid A) &= \frac{(0.003)(0.98)}{(0.003)(0.98) + (0.997)(0.0001)} = \frac{0.00294}{0.00304} \\ &= 0.97 \text{ (approximately)} \end{aligned}$$

Note that the denominator in the formula for $P(B_i \mid A)$ actually equals $P(A)$, as it is given by the Rule of Elimination, and that for our example we already found that this quantity equals approximately 0.00304.

Although the Rule of Bayes has been subjected to extensive criticism, it follows directly from the postulates of probability and the definition of conditional probability; *thus, its validity cannot be assailed.* A good deal of the mysticism and controversy surrounding this theorem is due to the fact that it entails a "backward" or "inverse" sort of reasoning, that is, *reasoning from effect to cause.* In our numerical example we thus asked for the probability that the diagnosis of tuberculosis was "caused" by the person's actually having the disease. To illustrate this idea further, let us return to the example on page 116 and let us suppose that we heard later that the soap manufacturer's program turned out to be a success, namely, that it received a high rating. Suppose, furthermore, that we were unable to find out what kind of program he finally decided to sponsor, and we would like to know the probability that the success of his show was "caused" by the fact that he sponsored a panel show. Substituting the appropriate probabilities into the formula for the Rule of Bayes, we obtain

$$P(B_2 \mid A) = \frac{(0.30)(0.30)}{(0.60)(0.10) + (0.30)(0.30) + (0.10)(0.20)}$$
$$= 0.53 \text{ (approximately)}$$

Knowing that the show turned out to be a success, we can thus say that there is better than an even chance that the soap manufacturer sponsored a panel show. Further applications of the Rule of Bayes will be given in Section 7.2 and in Chapters 9 and 11; they deal with so-called *Bayesian inference*, that is, a form of statistical reasoning based on the Rule of Bayes (and generalizations of this theorem).

EXERCISES

1. If K is the event that a person discharged from the armed forces will return to his home town, L is the event that he will immediately find work, and M is the event that he will get married within a year, state in words what probability is expressed by each of the following:
(a) $P(M \mid K)$; (c) $P(M \mid L)$; (e) $P(M \mid K \cap L)$;
(b) $P(L \mid K')$; (d) $P(L \cap M \mid K)$; (f) $P(M' \cap L' \mid K')$.

2. Referring to Exercise 1, express each of the following symbolically:
(a) the probability that a person discharged from the armed forces will not find work immediately, given that he does not return to his home town;
(b) the probability that a person discharged from the armed forces who is not going to get married within a year will immediately find work;

(c) the probability that a person discharged from the armed forces who returns to his home town will get married within a year but will not immediately find work;
(d) the probability that a person discharged from the armed forces will not get married within a year, given that he either will not return to his home town or not immediately find work.

3. Referring to Exercise 1 on page 104, write in words what probability is represented by each of the following:
(a) $P(D \mid R)$;
(b) $P(R \mid D)$;
(c) $P(R \mid D')$;
(d) $P(D' \mid R')$.

4. Referring to Exercise 2 on page 104, write each of the following in symbolic form:
(a) the probability that the mayor will be honest, given that he is married;
(b) the probability that the mayor will be neither married nor wealthy, given that he is honest;
(c) the probability that the mayor will be honest, given that he is not wealthy;
(d) the probability that the mayor will be married, given that he is honest as well as wealthy.

5. If A and B are mutually exclusive events, $P(A) = 0.40$, and $P(B) = 0.50$, find each of the following probabilities:
(a) $P(A \mid B)$;
(b) $P(A \cup B)$;
(c) $P(B \mid A)$;
(d) $P(A \cap B)$;
(e) $P(A')$;
(f) $P(A' \cup B')$.

6. In giving away a door prize, the owner of a gas station randomly (with equal probabilities) selects one of 2,000 slips filled in by his customers. There is only one slip per customer and their breakdown into those who paid cash and those who used their credit card, and also into those who are regular customers and those who are not, is as follows:

	Credit-card Customers	*Cash Customers*
Regular Customers	270	530
Not Regular Customers	210	990

Letting R represent the event that the prize is won by a regular customer and C the event that the prize is won by a credit-card customer, find each of the following probabilities:
(a) $P(R)$;
(b) $P(C)$;
(c) $P(R \cap C')$;
(d) $P(R \cap C)$;
(e) $P(R' \cap C')$;
(f) $P(R \mid C')$;
(g) $P(C \mid R)$;
(h) $P(C' \mid R')$;
(i) $P(C' \mid R)$.

7. Suppose that in Exercise 6 the owner of the gas station arranges things so that each of his regular customers has a probability of 3/3,600 while each of the other customers has a probability of 1/3,600 of winning the prize. Recalculate the nine probabilities asked for in Exercise 6.

8. Referring to Exercise 10 on page 111, what is the probability that the student chosen is on the Dean's list given that he is an English major, and what is the probability that he is an English major given that he is on the Dean's list?

9. Referring to Exercise 11 on page 111 and Exercise 24 on page 96, find each of the following:
(a) The probability that the damaged car has airconditioning, given that it has an automatic transmission.
(b) The probability that the damaged car has bucket seats, given that it has airconditioning as well as an automatic transmission.
(c) The probability that the damaged car has no airconditioning, given that it has neither bucket seats nor an automatic transmission.
(d) The probability that the damaged car has an automatic transmission, given that it has airconditioning, bucket seats, or both.

10. The director of a research laboratory has the following information: The probability that all of the equipment needed for a project will be delivered on time is 0.75, and the probability that all the equipment will be delivered on time *and* the project will be completed on time is 0.60.
(a) What is the conditional probability that the project will be completed on time, given that all of the necessary equipment was delivered on time?
(b) If the probability that the project will be completed on time is 0.72, what is the probability that it will be completed on time given that all the necessary equipment was not delivered on time? (*Hint:* The probability that the project will be completed in time is the *sum* of the probability that the project will be completed in time and all the equipment arrived in time and the probability that the project will be completed in time and all the equipment did not arrive in time.)

11. Referring to Exercise 17 on page 112, what is the probability that a station wagon entering the Grand Canyon National Park has California license plates?

12. What is the probability of drawing 2 white balls in succession from an urn containing 18 red balls and 12 white balls
(a) if the first ball is replaced before the second is drawn;
(b) if the first ball is not replaced before the second is drawn?

13. An interviewer working for a public opinion poll randomly selects 2 persons in succession from a group of 20, including 12 favoring Candidate X, 6 favoring Candidate Y, and 2 who are undecided.
(a) What is the probability that both favor Candidate X?
(b) What is the probability that both favor Candidate Y?
(c) What is the probability that one favors Candidate X and the other favors Candidate Y?
(d) What is the probability that one favors Candidate Y and the other is undecided?

[*Hint:* In parts (c) and (d) the desired probability is given by the sum of the probabilities corresponding to the different ways of obtaining the required event.]

14. Referring to Exercise 13, what is the probability that if 3 of the 20 persons are interviewed
(a) they all favor Candidate X;
(b) two favor Candidate X and one favors Candidate Y? (*Hint:* Take the sum of the probabilities corresponding to the cases where the person favoring Candidate Y is interviewed first, second, and third.)

15. Given $P(A) = 0.40$, $P(B) = 0.50$, and $P(A \cap B) = 0.20$, verify that
(a) $P(A) = P(A \mid B)$;
(b) $P(A) = P(A \mid B')$;
(c) $P(B) = P(B \mid A)$;
(d) $P(B) = P(B \mid A')$.

16. If A and B are independent events, $P(A) = 0.30$, and $P(B) = 0.50$, find each of the following probabilities:
(a) $P(A \mid B)$;
(b) $P(B \mid A)$;
(c) $P(A \cup B)$;
(d) $P(A \cap B)$;
(e) $P(A' \cap B')$;
(f) $P(B' \mid A')$.

17. Which of the following pairs of events are independent?
(a) Getting fives in two successive rolls of a die.
(b) Being intoxicated and having an accident.
(c) Being a teacher and having green eyes.
(d) Being on time for the theater and there being a blizzard.
(e) Wearing grey slacks and wearing brown slacks.
(f) Being a building contractor and being a good musician.

18. What are the probabilities of drawing (a) two aces in succession, and (b) three aces in succession from an ordinary deck of 52 playing cards, if each card is replaced before the next one is drawn? What are the corresponding probabilities if the cards are not replaced?

19. In a bottling plant, machines A, B, and C account, respectively, for 50 per cent, 35 per cent, and 15 per cent of the plant's output. If 0.4 per cent of the bottles from machine A are improperly sealed, while the corresponding percentages for machines B and C are, respectively, 0.8 per cent and 1.0 per cent, what is the over-all percentage of bottles that are improperly sealed?

20. Referring to Exercise 19, suppose that a bottle is selected at random from a day's production and that it is found to be improperly sealed. What is the probability that it came from machine A? What are the corresponding probabilities for machines B and C?

21. There is a fifty-fifty chance that Firm A will bid for the construction of a new laboratory. Firm B submits a bid and the probability is 3/4 that it will get the job provided Firm A does not bid; if Firm A submits a bid, the probability that Firm B will get the job is only 1/3.
(a) What is the probability that Firm B will get the job?
(b) If Firm B gets the job, what is the probability that Firm A did not bid?

22. In a T-maze, a rat is given food if it turns left and an electric shock if it turns right. On the first trial there is an equal chance that a rat will turn either way. If a rat receives food on a given trial, the probability that it will turn left again on the next trial is 0.66; if it receives a shock on a given trial, the probability that it will turn left on the next trial is 0.84. What is the probability that a rat will turn left on the second trial?

23. Referring to Exercise 22, what is the probability that a rat will turn left on the third trial? (*Hint:* Draw a tree diagram, multiply the probabilities corresponding to the three steps of each path, and add the probabilities corresponding to the cases where the rat turns left on the third trial.)

24. Referring to Exercise 22, what is the probability that a rat turned left on the first trial, given that it turned right on the second trial?

25. Three candidates are running for the office of governor of a certain state. The probability that Mr. Arnold will be elected is 0.25, the probability that Mr. Bowman will be elected is 0.55, and the probability that Mr. Carlson will be elected is 0.20. Should Mr. Arnold be elected, the probability for an increase in sales tax is 0.70; should Mr. Bowman or Mr. Carlson be elected, the corresponding probabilities for an increase in sales tax are 0.10, and 0.40.
(a) What is the probability that there will be an increase in sales tax?
(b) If someone reads months later in a newspaper that there has been an increase in sales tax, what is the probability that Mr. Bowman was elected?

26. The probability that an airplane accident which is due to structural failure is diagnosed correctly is 0.82 and the probability that an airplane accident which is *not* due to structural failure is diagnosed incorrectly as being due to structural failure is 0.38. If 40 per cent of all airplane accidents are due to structural failure, find the probability that an airplane accident which is diagnosed as being due to structural failure is actually due to this cause.

27. (From Hans Reichenbach's *The Theory of Probability*, University of California Press, 1949.) Mr. Smith's gardener is not dependable; the probability that he will forget to water the rosebush during Smith's absence is 2/3. The rosebush is in questionable condition anyhow; if watered, the probability for its withering is 1/2; if it is not watered, the probability for its withering is 3/4. Upon returning Smith finds that the rosebush has withered. What is the probability that the gardener did not water the rosebush?

28. A statistics instructor knows from past experience that a student who does his homework consistently has a probability of 0.95 of getting a passing grade, while a student who does not do his homework consistently has a probability of 0.30 of getting a passing grade.
(a) If 25 per cent of the students in a large statistics class do their homework consistently, what percentage can one expect to get passing grades?
(b) If one student randomly selected from the class referred to in (a) gets a passing grade, what is the probability that he did his homework consistently?

29. Three giftwrappers are employed in a toy store at Christmas time. Mary, who wraps 40 per cent of all toys wrapped, fails to remove the price tag before wrapping 1 time in 50; Joan, who wraps 30 per cent of all toys wrapped, fails to remove the price tag before wrapping 1 time in 10; and Helen, who wraps the remaining toys, fails to remove the price tag before wrapping 1 time in 20.

(a) Given that a customer complains that a price tag was not removed from a toy before it was wrapped, what is the probability that the toy was wrapped by Mary?

(b) What would be the answer to (a) if it were known that Joan was sick on the day the particular gift was wrapped and nobody was hired to take her place?

30. Prove the Rule of Bayes by substituting into $P(A) \cdot P(B_i \mid A) = P(A \cap B_i)$ the expression given for $P(A)$ by the rule of elimination.

BIBLIOGRAPHY

More detailed, though still elementary, treatments of the theory of probability may be found in

Goldberg, S., *Probability—An Introduction*. Englewood Cliffs, N.J.: Prentice-Hall, Inc., 1960.

Mosteller, F., Rourke, R. E. K., and Thomas, G. B., *Probability with Statistical Applications*. Reading, Mass.: Addison-Wesley Publishing Co., Inc., 1961.

An interesting discussion of various philosophical questions concerning probabilities is given in

Nagel, E., *Principles of the Theory of Probability*. Chicago: University of Chicago Press, 1939,

and subjective probabilities, in particular, are discussed in

Borel, E., *Elements of the Theory of Probability* (translated by John E. Freund). Englewood Cliffs, N.J.: Prentice-Hall, Inc., 1965.

Kyburg, H. E. Jr., and Smokler, H. E., *Studies in Subjective Probability*. New York: John Wiley & Sons, Inc., 1964.

Lindley, D. V., *Introduction to Probability and Statistics from a Bayesian Viewpoint. Part 1, Probability*. Cambridge: Cambridge University Press, 1965.

Savage, L. J., *The Foundations of Statistics*. New York: John Wiley & Sons, Inc., 1954.

Savage, L. J., and other contributors, *The Foundations of Statistical Inference*. New York: John Wiley & Sons, Inc., 1962.

Schlaifer, R., *Probability and Statistics for Business Decisions*. New York: McGraw-Hill Book Company, 1959.

Informal introductions to the theory of probability, written essentially for the layman, may be found in

Levinson, H. C., *Chance, Luck, and Statistics*. New York: Dover Publications, Inc., 1963.

Weaver, W., *Lady Luck—The Theory of Probability*. Garden City, N.Y.: Doubleday & Company, Inc., 1963.

The birthday problem referred to on page 103 is discussed in the above-mentioned book by S. Goldberg.

SIX
Expectations, Games, and Decisions

6.1 Mathematical Expectation

If we say that in California a married couple can *expect* to have 1.51 children, that a person living in the United States can *expect* to eat 85.2 pounds of beef and 334.6 eggs per year, or that an insurance company can *expect* losses of \$37.65 for a certain type of accident policy, it must be clear that we are not using the word "expect" in its colloquial sense. Some of these expected events cannot possibly occur, and it would certainly be very surprising if a person actually did eat 85.2 pounds of beef during a calendar year. So far as the insurance example is concerned, the expected losses do not reflect predictions based on an actuary's horoscope; they represent an average, or as we shall call it here, a *mathematical expectation.* On some of the policies the insurance company will pay no claims at all, on some it will pay the full face value of, say, \$5,000, and on the average it will pay about \$37.65 per policy.

Originally, the concept of a mathematical expectation was designed for games of chance, and in its simplest form a mathematical expectation is given by *the product of a player's possible gains and the probability that these gains will be realized.* Thus, if we are to get \$10.00 if a balanced coin comes up heads, our mathematical expectation is $10(1/2) = \$5.00$. Similarly, if someone holds 1 of 1,000 raffle tickets for which the prize is \$450.00, his mathematical expectation is $450(0.001) = \$0.45$; 999 of the tickets will not pay anything, one ticket will pay \$450.00, and *on the average* they will pay \$0.45 per ticket.

To generalize the concept of a mathematical expectation, let us change the raffle referred to in the preceding paragraph, so that there is also a second prize of \$100.00 and a third prize of \$50.00. Now we can argue that 997 tickets will not pay anything at all, one ticket will win \$450.00, one ticket will win \$100.00, one ticket will win \$50.00, and on the average they will win \$0.60 per ticket. Looking at the problem in a different way, we could also argue that if the raffle were repeated again and again, we would win nothing about 99.7 per cent of the time and each of the three prizes about 0.1 per cent of the time. On the average we would thus win

$$0(0.997) + 450(0.001) + 100(0.001) + 50(0.001) = \$0.60$$

Note that this value is the sum of the products obtained by multiplying each amount by the corresponding probability. Hence, let us make the following definition:

If $A_1, A_2, \ldots,$ and A_k represent the k mutually exclusive events of obtaining the amounts $a_1, a_2, \ldots,$ and a_k, then the mathematical expectation is

▲ $$a_1P(A_1) + a_2P(A_2) + \ldots + a_kP(A_k)$$ ▲

Each amount is multiplied by the corresponding probability, and the mathematical expectation is the sum of the products thus obtained. For instance, if we played "heads or tails," won \$10 on each head and lost \$10 on each tail, we would have $a_1 = 10$, $a_2 = -10$, $P(A_1) = 1/2$, $P(A_2) = 1/2$, and a mathematical expectation of $10(1/2) + (-10)(1/2) = 0$. Note that this defines what we mean by an *equitable game:* each player has a mathematical expectation of zero and he expects neither to win nor lose. *Observe also that the amounts $a_1, a_2, \ldots,$ and a_k are positive or negative depending on whether they are won or lost, spent or received.*

To consider another example, suppose that an importer is offered a shipment of coffee for \$40,000 and that the probabilities that he will be able to sell it for \$48,000, \$44,000, \$40,000, or \$36,000 are, respectively, 0.28, 0.43, 0.17, and 0.12. Whether this transaction is worthwhile will depend among other things on the amount of money the importer can *expect* to receive. Substituting into the formula for a mathematical expectation, we get

$$48{,}000(0.28) + 44{,}000(0.43) + 40{,}000(0.17) + 36{,}000(0.12) = \$43{,}480$$

so that the *expected gross profit* is \$3,480. Whether this makes the transaction worthwhile is another matter; it would have to depend on the importer's overhead, the length of time his money will be tied up, and other factors.

Although we referred to the quantities $a_1, a_2, \ldots,$ and a_k as "amounts," they need not be *cash* winnings, losses, penalties, or rewards. When we said that in California a couple can *expect* 1.51 children, we obtained this result by multiplying 0, 1, 2, ..., by the respective probabilities of a California couple's having that many children and then adding these products. Similarly, if we say that a person over 65 can expect to visit a doctor 6.8 times per year, the a's in the formula for the mathematical expectation are 0, 1, 2, 3, ..., and they represent the corresponding number of visits.

It has been suggested that a person's behavior is *rational* if in situations involving uncertainties and risks he always chooses the alternative having the highest mathematical expectation. Although this may look like a reasonable criterion for rational behavior, it involves a number of difficulties which we shall discuss later in this chapter. For the moment, let us merely point out that we actually used this criterion in our discussion of subjective probabilities, where we assumed that it is rational to accept a bet when the odds are in one's favor, that is, when the mathematical expectation is *positive*. Similarly, it would seem rational to reject a bet when the odds are against us, namely, when the mathematical expectation is *negative*. (When the mathematical expectation is zero, there is no definite advantage or disadvantage to accepting the bet, leaving aside all considerations of the pleasure one might possibly get from making a bet.) Thus, if we feel that Candidate X has a probability of 0.30 of winning an election and someone offers us odds of 4 to 1 (say, \$4.00 to \$1.00) that he will not win, it would be "rational" for us to accept the bet since our expectation would be

$$4(0.30) + (-1)(0.70) = \$0.50$$

On the other hand, had we been offered odds of only 2 to 1 (say, \$2.00 to \$1.00), our expectation would have been

$$2(0.30) + (-1)(0.70) = -\$0.10$$

and it would not have been rational to accept the bet. Had we been offered odds of 7 to 3, our expectation would have been 0, and the bet would have been fair.

As we pointed out on page 103, the problem of evaluating subjective probabilities runs into some difficulties when a person is unwilling to risk any part of his capital, that is, when he is unwilling to gamble with his own money regardless of the odds. Of course, one cannot force a person to risk part of his capital, but there is another approach; it is based on the assumption that few persons would refuse an outright gift in exchange for a small mental effort. To illustrate, let us return to the example on page 103, and let us suppose that we make the archeologist the following offer: *He has the choice of accepting a gift of \$30.00 now with no strings attached, or to wait till after his return from the expedition, in which case he is to receive a gift of \$40.00 if the expedition was a success and nothing if it failed.*

If he decides to wait, presumably because this gives him a higher expectation, we can now argue as follows: if he assigns the subjective probability for the success of the expedition the value p, his mathematical expectation for the second alternative is $40p + 0(1 - p) = 40p$; since he prefers this to an outright gift of \$30.00, we have $40p > 30$ or $p > 30/40$, and we can say that the probability he assigns to the success of the expedition is greater than 0.75.

By varying the amounts, we can arrive at various other results concerning this personal probability. For instance, if he prefers \$30.00 now to the alternative where he is to receive \$35.00 if the expedition is a success and \$10.00 if it fails, we can argue that he prefers \$30.00 to a mathematical expectation of $35p + 10(1 - p) = 25p + 10$, and hence that $25p + 10 < 30$ and $p < 20/25$. If we combine the two results, we can conclude that the subjective probability he assigns to the success of the expedition is greater than 0.75 but less than 0.80. Note that if he had been unable to make up his mind in the first case, we could have argued that the mathematical expectation of $40p$ actually *equals* \$30.00, and we could thus have pinpointed his subjective probability for the success of the expedition at 0.75.

There is another way of pinpointing the subjective probability a person assigns to an event. Suppose we offer the archeologist the following deal: *he is to receive \$40 if the expectation turns out to be successful, nothing if it fails, and for the privilege of playing this "game" he is to pay us now what he considers a fair amount of money.* If he feels that \$31.20 would be just about right, we can argue that this amount equals his mathematical expectation for the gamble, namely, $40p + 0(1 - p)$, where p is again his subjective probability for the success of the expedition. Thus, we have

$$31.20 = 40p + 0(1 - p)$$

and $p = 31.20/40 = 0.78$. Of course, this method of determining a subjective probability has the same disadvantage as the one used in Section 5.5; our subject has to be willing to risk some of his own capital.

It should be observed that these methods of determining subjective probabilities (as well as the method of Section 5.5) are based on the premise that a person will be relatively consistent in making decisions concerning risk-taking situations, that he will take such gambles seriously, and that he will act (at least intuitively or subconsciously) according to the principle of maximizing his expectations. Although these points are all open to discussion, it is important that ways of assigning numerical values to subjective probabilities do exist.

EXERCISES

1. Two prizes are awarded in a lottery: a first prize of \$10,000 and a second prize of \$5,000. What is the "value" of each ticket, if altogether 25,000 tickets are sold?

2. An urn contains 20 white balls and 10 red balls. If we are to receive \$12.00 when a white ball is drawn and \$6.00 when a red ball is drawn, what should we have to pay for the privilege of playing this game, which is assumed to be equitable?

3. If someone were to give us \$1.00 each time we roll a 1 with a balanced die, \$2.00 each time we roll a 2, \$3.00 each time we roll a 3, and \$4.00 each time we roll a 4, how much should we pay him when we roll a 5 or 6 to make the game equitable?

4. Two finalists in a bowling tournament play a game in which the winner will receive \$5,000 and the loser \$2,500. What is each player's expectation (a) if they are evenly matched, and (b) if one player is four times more likely to win than the other?

5. A builder is bidding on a construction job which promises a profit of \$20,000 with a probability of 4/5, or a loss (from rework, strikes, late performance penalties, etc.) of \$14,000 with a probability of 1/5. What is the builder's expectation?

6. A lot containing 12 parts among which 3 are defective is put on sale "as is" at \$10.00 per part with no inspection possible. If a defective part represents a complete loss of the \$10.00 to the buyer and good parts can be resold at \$14.50 each, is it worthwhile to buy one of these parts and select it at random?

7. A grab-bag contains 10 packages worth 25 cents apiece, 10 packages worth 50 cents apiece, and 2 packages worth \$1.00 apiece. Is it worthwhile to pay 45 cents for the privilege of selecting one of these packages at random?

8. The probability that Mr. Adams will sell his house at a profit of \$2,000 is 3/20, the probability that he will sell it at a profit of \$1,000 is 8/20, the probability that he will break even is 7/20, and the probability that he will lose \$1,000 is 2/20. What is his expected profit?

9. If the two teams are evenly matched, the probabilities that a World Series will end in 4, 5, 6, or 7 games are, respectively, 1/8, 1/4, 5/16, and 5/16. Under these conditions, how many games can we expect a World Series to last? Also, if Mr. Jones has tickets only for the fourth and fifth games, how many games can he expect to see?

10. Jimmy's parents promise him a dollar if he gets a 1 in mathematics on his next report card, 50 cents if he gets a 2, and otherwise no reward. What is his expectation if the probability for a 1 is 0.35 and the probability for a 2 is 0.44?

11. The probabilities that there will be 1, 2, 3, 4, 5, or 6 persons in a car stopped at a roadblock near Flagstaff are, respectively, 0.11, 0.48, 0.20, 0.13, 0.05, and 0.03. What is the expected number of persons per car?

12. Mr. Jones has the option of accepting a gift of \$5.00 or of gambling on the outcome of a basketball game, where he is to receive \$15.00 if the home team wins, nothing if it loses. What can we say about the subjective probability he assigns to the outcome of the game if he prefers to accept the \$5.00?

13. Mr. Smith is a music lover who claims that he "would give his right arm" to hear a famous violinist whose concert has been sold out. Given the choice of \$5.00 cash or drawing a slip of paper from a box among which 18 are blanks and 2 are actually concert tickets, what can we say about the value he attaches to such a ticket if he prefers to risk the gamble?

14. Mr. Brown feels that it is about a toss-up whether to accept \$10.00 cash or to gamble on drawing a bead from an urn containing 20 white beads and 80 red beads, where he is to receive \$2.00 if he draws a white bead and a new fishing reel if he draws a red bead. What value, or utility, does he attach to the new fishing reel?

15. Mr. Smith has the option of accepting \$200 outright, or to gamble on the success of a new Broadway play, where he is to receive \$1,000 if the play turns out to be a hit, nothing if it fails. What can we say about the personal probability he assigns to the success of the play if he finds it impossible to make up his mind?

16. Mr. Green has the choice of staying home and reading a good book, to which he assigns a utility of 10 units, or going to a party. If he goes to the party he might have a terrible time, to which he assigns a utility of 0 units, or he might have a wonderful time, to which he assigns a utility of 50 units. What does he think of his chances of having a wonderful time at the party if he decides to stay home and read a good book?

17. An insurance company agrees to pay the promoter of a rodeo \$5,000 in case the event has to be canceled because of rain. If the company's actuary figures that their expected loss for this risk is \$640, what probability does he assign to the possibility that the event will have to be canceled because of rain?

18. Referring to Exercise 12, suppose that Mr. Jones considers \$4.80 a fair price to pay for the gamble of receiving \$15.00 if the home team wins, and nothing if it loses. What probability does he assign to the event that the home team will win?

19. A box contains 100 marbles, some red and some white. One marble will be drawn at random, and you are asked beforehand to choose between "red" and "white." For the correct choice there is a reward of \$10.00, otherwise nothing. How much would you be willing to pay for this gamble if

(a) you do not know how many red marbles and how many white marbles there are in the box;

(b) you know that the box contains 50 red marbles and 50 white marbles?

[It is a curious fact that most people seem to be much more willing to gamble under condition (b) than under condition (a); also, they are generally willing to pay more for playing under condition (b). This strange kind of behavior in risk-taking situations has been referred to jokingly as the "Ellsberg Syndrome"; the example is due to Daniel Ellsberg.]

6.2 A Decision Problem

To illustrate some of the difficulties involved in basing decisions on mathematical expectations, let us consider a numerical example. Suppose that a group of college students wants to raise money by selling pennants outside the stadium after a big football game. They can buy the pennants from a supplier in either of two batches: Batch 1, which contains more of the home team's pennants and less of the visiting team's pennants, or Batch 2, which contains just the reverse. Previous experience shows that if they buy Batch 1 and the home team wins they will make a profit of \$150.00, but if the home team loses or ties they will make only \$50.00. On the other hand, if they buy Batch 2 and the home team wins they will make a profit of \$110.00, but if the home team loses or ties they will make \$130.00. Schematically, this information can be arranged as follows:

	Home Team Wins	*Home Team Loses or Ties*
Batch 1	\$150	\$50
Batch 2	\$110	\$130

It is apparent that they will be better off with Batch 1 if the home team wins, and that they will be better off with Batch 2 if the home team loses or ties. *To make an intelligent choice, it will thus help them to know something about the probability that the home team will win.* First let us suppose that they figure (on the basis of past experience or sound subjective judgment) that there is a fifty-fifty chance that their team will win. They might then argue as follows: if they buy Batch 1 their *expected profit* is

$$150(1/2) + 50(1/2) = \$100$$

and if they buy Batch 2 their *expected profit* is

$$110(1/2) + 130(1/2) = \$120$$

Being rational, in the sense of choosing the alternative having the higher expectation, they will thus take Batch 2.

If mathematical expectations are to serve as criteria for making rational decisions, it is essential to know the correct values of all relevant probabilities. Had the probability been 3/4 that the home team will win in our example, the *expected profit* for Batch 1 would have been

$$150(3/4) + 50(1/4) = \$125$$

the *expected profit* for Batch 2 would have been

$$110(3/4) + 130(1/4) = \$115$$

and it would have been smarter to choose Batch 1.

Having shown in this example how mathematical expectations can be used as a basis for rational decisions, let us examine briefly what the students might have done if they had no idea whatsoever about the home team's chances of winning the game. To suggest one possible approach, suppose they are *confirmed optimists;* looking at the situation through rose-colored glasses, they note that with Batch 1 they might make as much as \$150, whereas Batch 2 would at best yield \$130. Always expecting the best (in the sense of wishful thinking), they would thus decide to order Batch 1. On the other hand, if they were *confirmed pessimists,* they would note that Batch 1 might yield only \$50, whereas the corresponding minimum for Batch 2 is \$110. Always expecting the worst (in the sense of resignation or fear), they would thus order Batch 2. (Note that this analysis ignores whatever loyalties they might have for their team, and whatever it might be worth to them *indirectly* to see their team win.)

Since decisions based on optimism or pessimism alone can hardly be called rational, let us consider another way in which the problem might be solved. Suppose that in desperation they agree to leave the ultimate choice to chance by writing "Batch 1" on a number of slips of paper, "Batch 2" on a number of others, mixing them thoroughly, and then making their decision according to which kind is drawn. Suppose furthermore that the numbers of slips marked "Batch 1" and "Batch 2" are such that the probability for drawing one of the first kind is p, the probability of drawing one of the second kind is $1 - p$, and that *the purpose of this whole procedure is to fix the odds in such a way that the expected profit is the same regardless of the outcome of the game.* Letting E represent the expected profit, we now have

$$E = 150p + 110(1 - p)$$

if the home team wins, and

$$E = 50p + 130(1 - p)$$

if the home team loses or ties. Putting these two expected profits equal to one another and solving for p, we get

$$150p + 110(1 - p) = 50p + 130(1 - p)$$

and

$$p = 1/6$$

By labeling one slip of paper "Batch 1" and five slips "Batch 2" (or equivalently basing the decision on the roll of a die), they can thus make sure that the expected profit does not depend on the outcome of the game. In fact, substituting $p = 1/6$ into either of the above equations for E, we find that this expected profit is \$$116\frac{2}{3}$, or \$116.67 rounded to the nearest cent. *Note that this expectation is higher than the minimum guaranteed by directly choosing Batch 1 or Batch 2.*

This kind of decision procedure, in which the ultimate decision is left to chance, is called *randomized* or *mixed.* Although it may seem strange that a "rational" decision should be left even partially to chance, there are situations in which randomized decision procedures actually provide the most desirable results. This is true, particularly, in games of strategy, such as the ones we shall discuss in the next section. In such games two or more players try to outwit one another, and on page 140 we shall reanalyze the above problem as a game between the students and Nature—the students have the choice between Batches 1 and 2, while Nature "controls" the outcome of the football game.

Earlier in this section, we pointed out that optimism or pessimism *alone* can hardly be looked upon as rational criteria for making decisions. Nevertheless, there are situations in which questions of optimism or pessimism might outweigh all other factors. Suppose, for example, that in our illustration the students have to pay off a debt of $100, and all they really care about is making at least $100. In that case it would be sensible that they protect themselves against the worst that can happen and order Batch 2. A parallel example, where questions of optimism outweigh other factors, is given in Exercise 2 on page 140. It is hoped that examples like these will serve to stress the point that there is no universal rule or criterion which will invariably lead to the "best" decision.

6.3 Games of Strategy

The idea of treating the decision problem of the preceding section as a game is not at all farfetched; in fact, the problem we have discussed is typical of the kind of situation studied in the *Theory of Games*, a branch of mathematics which has become increasingly important in recent years. Although we are using here the word "game," this theory is not limited to parlor games or sports; it is applied to any kind of competitive situation such as one might find in the conduct of a war, in the study of social behavior, in business management, and in many other areas.

To introduce some of the basic concepts of the Theory of Games, let us first consider what is called a *2-by-2 zero-sum two-person game*. The "two-person" means that there are two players, or more generally two sets of conflicting interests; the "2-by-2" means that each player has the choice of two possible strategies (or moves); and the "zero-sum" means that whatever amount is won by one player is lost by the other. In other words, there is no "cut for the house" as in professional gambling, and no capital is created or destroyed during the course of play.

Thus, suppose that there are two players A and B, with the strategies of Player A labeled I and II and those of Player B labeled 1 and 2. Depending on the strategies chosen by the two players, the *payoff* to Player B, namely, the amount Player A has to pay Player B, is a, b, c, or d, as shown in the following table:

		Player A I	*Player A* II
Player B	1	a	b
	2	c	d

Although it does not really matter, we shall assume that these payoff amounts are in terms of money (dollars); in actual practice, they could be in terms of any goods or services, units of satisfaction or utility, or even life or death. It should also be observed that in all of the games described in this section each player has to choose his strategy *without* knowledge of the choice made by his opponent.

Thus, if Player A chooses Strategy I and Player B chooses Strategy 1, Player A pays Player B the amount a; if Player A chooses Strategy I and Player B chooses Strategy 2, Player A pays Player B the amount c, and so on. Since most games require payments from Player A to Player B as well as payments from Player B to Player A, we shall adopt the following convention: if a payoff amount a, b, c, or d is *positive*, this means that it is paid by Player A to Player B; if it is *negative*, this means that it is paid by Player B to Player A. For example, if $a = 3$, Player A has to pay Player B \$3.00 when their respective strategies are I and 1; if $c = -5$, Player B has to pay Player A \$5.00 when their respective strategies are I and 2.

In actual practice, we ordinarily describe games by listing the various rules according to which they are played; we describe the pieces or other kinds of equipment that are being used, and we might state what prizes, penalties, or rewards there are involved. All this is important if we actually want to play a game, but its analysis in the Theory of Games requires only that we list the moves (strategies) available to each player and the corresponding payoff amounts. This information is all that is needed to determine what choices of strategies or moves are most profitable for each player, and this is the main objective of the Theory of Games. In the examples which follow we shall thus ignore the question of whether a game is played with cards, dice, or basketballs, whether it involves physical activity, whether it pertains to combat with missiles and rockets, or whether it pertains to the competition between two stores.

To illustrate some of the problems involved in selecting a "best" strategy for each player, let us consider a few examples. First, let us study the game which is represented by the following scheme, where the notation is as indicated above:

		Player A	
		I	II
Player B	1	3	−4
	2	4	6

As can be seen by inspection, it would be foolish of Player B to choose Strategy 1; regardless of the choice made by his opponent, Player B will be better off if he chooses Strategy 2, and this strategy is thus said to *dominate* Strategy 1. Having eliminated the first line of the above table of payoff values, also called the *payoff matrix*, the best strategy for Player A becomes immediately apparent. Since he would rather lose \$4.00 than \$6.00, his best choice is obviously Strategy I. The payoff of \$4.00 corresponding to Strategies I and 2 is said to be the *value* of the game. The fact that it is positive means that the game favors Player B; had it been *negative* the game would have favored Player A, and had it been zero the game would have been equitable (see also Exercise 18 on page 144).

To introduce another concept which is important in the Theory of Games, let us consider the following 3-by-3 zero-sum two-person game, where the amounts are, as before, the payment made by Player A to Player B:

		Player A		
		I	II	III
	1	−1	6	−2
Player B	2	2	4	6
	3	−2	−6	12

Looking at this table, it can be seen that there are no dominances among the strategies of either player, and we will, therefore, have to find some other way of obtaining the best strategies. Considering first the strategies of Player A, we find that if he uses Strategy I the most he can lose is \$2.00, if he uses Strategy II the most he can lose is \$6.00, and if he uses Strategy III the most he can lose is \$12.00. Looking at it from this point of view, it would seem advantageous for Player A to choose Strategy I, since this would *minimize his maximum losses*. Considering now the strategies of Player B, we find that if he uses Strategy 1 the most he can lose is \$2.00, if he uses Strategy 2 the least he can win is \$2.00, and if he uses Strategy 3 the most he can lose is \$6.00. Looking at it from this point of view, it would seem advantageous for Player B to choose Strategy 2, since this would *maximize the minimum amount he stands to win.*

The selection of Strategies I and 2, called *minimax strategies,* is really very reasonable. By playing Strategy I, Player A makes sure that his opponent can win at most \$2.00, and by choosing Strategy 2, Player B makes sure that he actually does win this amount. The *value* of this game is the payoff corresponding to the minimax strategies, and it is equal to \$2.00. This means that the game favors Player B, but Player A could make it equitable by charging Player B \$2.00 for the privilege of playing the game. This would amount to subtracting 2 from each of the payoffs in the above table which characterized the game. Another important aspect of minimax strategies is that they are completely "spyproof" in the sense that neither player can profit from knowledge of the other's choice of strategies. Even if Player B announced publicly that he would use Strategy 2, Player A would still choose Strategy I; similarly, the information that Player A intends to use Strategy I would be of no value to Player B, since changing to either of his other strategies would hurt rather than help.

Strategies I and 2, for which the payoff gives the value of the game in this last example, define what is called a *saddle point.* In practice, if a saddle point exists, it can easily be found by making use of the fact that, by definition, the corresponding payoff must be *the smallest value of its row* and *the largest value of its column.* To facilitate finding saddle points, we write the row minima and the column maxima, respectively, alongside and at the bottom of the payoff table. Then, if the largest among the row minima (indicated below by means of an arrow) *equals* the smallest among the column maxima (also indicated by means of an arrow), they correspond to a saddle point. For the game discussed directly above, we can show this as follows:

		Player A			*Row*
		I	II	III	*Minima*
	1	−1	6	−2	−2
Player B	2	2	4	6	2 ←
	3	−2	−6	12	−6
Column Maxima		2 ↑	6	12	

and it can be seen that the saddle point corresponds to Strategies I and 2.

Note that in the first example of this section the solution of the game (optimum strategies and the value of the game) was also given by a saddle point, since 4 is less than 6 but greater than 3. It is also of interest to observe that if a game has more than one saddle point, the corresponding payoffs must all be equal and it does not matter which of the saddle points is used to determine the best strategies for the two players (see also Exercise 12 on page 143).

Games which have a saddle point are said to be *strictly determined*, and if every game were strictly determined, the above analysis would provide a satisfactory solution to the problem of finding optimum strategies. Unfortunately, this is not the case, as is illustrated by the following example:

		Player A		*Row*
		I	II	*Minima*
Player B	1	6	10	6 ←
	2	17	4	4
Column Maxima		17	10 ↑	

As can be seen by inspection, the largest of the row minima is 6, the smallest of the column maxima is 10, the two are *not equal*, and there is no saddle point. However, if we analyze the game like the last one, we find that if Player A uses Strategy I the worst that can happen is that he will lose \$17.00, and if he uses Strategy II the worst that can happen is that he will lose \$10.00. Player B, on the other hand, will win at least \$6.00 if he chooses Strategy 1 and at least \$4.00 if he chooses Strategy 2. By playing Strategy II, Player A can thus make sure that he will not lose more than \$10.00, and by playing Strategy 1, Player B can make sure that he will win at least \$6.00.

If A and B actually used these strategies, the payoff would be \$10.00, and this should be a pleasant surprise to Player B; it is more than the \$6.00 minimum he tried to assure for himself by choosing Strategy 1. On the other hand, this situation is not very satisfactory so far as Player A is concerned, and he might try to improve things by reasoning as follows: if Player B is the kind of player who always tries to make the minimum he stands to win as large as possible, he will choose Strategy 1; hence, Player A can hold his losses down to \$6.00 by playing Strategy I. This would work nicely, unless Player B reasons that this is precisely what Player A intends to do and that it would, therefore, be smart for him to play Strategy 2 and win \$17.00. *This argument can be continued ad infinitum.* If Player A thinks that Player B will try to outsmart him by playing Strategy 2, he can in turn try to outsmart Player B by choosing Strategy II, thus holding his losses down to \$4.00. If Player B thinks that this is what Player A intends to do, he has only to switch to Strategy 1 to assure for himself a payoff of \$10.00, and so on, and so on.

An important aspect of this situation is that one player can outsmart the other if he knows how his opponent will react under given conditions. For instance, if Player A knows that Player B is an *incurable optimist,* he can figure that Player B will select Strategy 2 hoping to make \$17.00, and he can take advantage of this by playing Strategy II. In view of all this, it would seem reasonable to suggest that each player should somehow *mix up* his strategies, so that he cannot be outsmarted by his opponent's use of psychology or outside information arrived at in any way. Since each player must always choose one strategy or another, this can only be accomplished by somehow leaving the ultimate choice to chance. Proceeding as in the example on page 132, let us now determine what probabilities each player should use in the selection of his strategy. On page 132 we based this selection on the criterion that the expected profit should not depend on the outcome of the football game; in the Theory of Games it is usually based on the criterion of *maximizing the least a player can expect to win,* or which is the same, *minimizing the most he can expect to lose.* The word "expect" is, of course, used here in the sense of a mathematical expectation.

Referring again to the last example, suppose thus that Player B chooses between his two strategies with the respective probabilities of p and $1 - p$. He can then expect to win

$$E = 6p + 17(1 - p)$$

if Player A selects Strategy I, and he can expect to win

$$E = 10p + 4(1 - p)$$

if Player A selects Strategy II. Graphically, this situation is described by Figure 6.1, where we have plotted the two lines whose equations are $E = 6p + 17(1 - p)$ and $E = 10p + 4(1 - p)$ for values of p from 0 to 1. (Actually, these lines were obtained by connecting the respective values of E obtained for $p = 0$ and $p = 1$, namely, 17 and 6 for the line which corresponds to the case where Player A chooses Strategy I, and 4 and 10 for the line which corresponds to the case where Player A selects Strategy II.)

Analyzing Figure 6.1, we find that the least Player B can expect to win, that is, the smaller of the two values of E for any given value of p, is *greatest* where the two lines intersect and the two values of E are, in fact, the same. To find the corresponding value of p we have only to put $6p + 17(1 - p)$ equal to $10p + 4(1 - p)$, and we get

$$6p + 17(1 - p) = 10p + 4(1 - p)$$

and

$$p = 13/17$$

Labeling 13 slips of paper "Strategy 1," 4 slips of paper "Strategy 2," shuffling them thoroughly and drawing one, Player B can thus assure for himself *expected winnings* of

$$6(13/17) + 17(4/17) = 8\tfrac{10}{17}$$

or $8.59 rounded to the nearest cent. If the ultimate choice is thus left to chance, the over-all strategy of Player B is referred to as a *randomized* or *mixed strategy*. Note that this *optimum mixed strategy* assured Player B expected winnings of $8.59, whereas the direct choice of one of his *pure strategies* (Strategy 1 or Strategy 2) could guarantee him only minimum winnings of $6.00. So far as Player A is concerned, the analysis is very much the same, and the reader will be asked to show in Exercise 17 on page 144 that Player A can hold his expected losses to $8.59 by choosing between his two strategies with probabilities of 6/17 and 11/17. Incidentally, the amount of $8.59 to which Player A can hold down his expected losses and to which Player B can raise his expected winnings is called the *value* of this game.

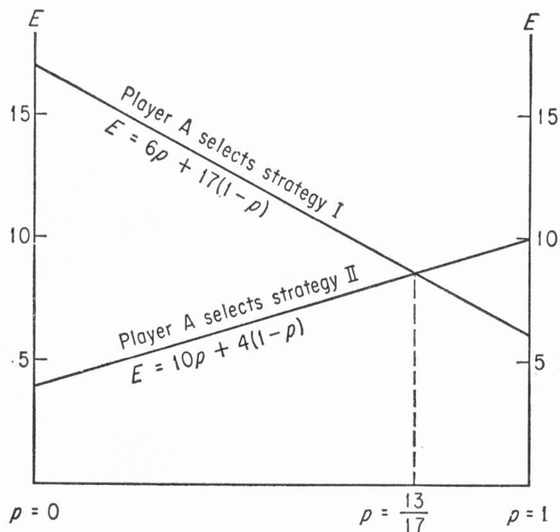

Fig. 6.1 Expected winnings of player B.

The examples of this section were designed to introduce the reader to some of the basic concepts of the Theory of Games, such as dominating strategies, saddle points, and randomized strategies which served to minimize the most a player can expect to lose or to maximize the least he can expect to win. These same concepts are also used in the analysis of more complicated kinds of games, although the mathematical detail may then get quite involved. Most of the games that are of any real practical significance have to allow for more than two strategies for each player; also there are often more than two players, and many important applications are not even *zero-sum* (that is, they involve the creation or destruction of capital during the course of play).

The numerical examples of this section were all given without any "real" physical interpretation, since we were interested mainly in the mathematical structure of the problems. Had we interpreted the decision problem of Section 6.2 as a two-person game, we could have argued that the students *maximized* the *minimum* expected profit by choosing between Batches 1 and 2 with the respective probabilities of 1/6 and 5/6. Note that their corresponding *expected profit* is \$116.67, which is more than they could have assured for themselves by either of their two *pure* strategies, namely, by choosing Batch 1 or Batch 2 directly. It must be remembered, though, that this analysis assumes that Nature (which determines the outcome of the football game) is a malevolent opponent, and that the students must thus protect themselves against an opponent who tries to make their life as difficult and unprofitable as possible. Whether or not such an assumption is reasonable, or justifiable, can only be judged individually for each problem. As we shall see in Section 6.4, this does raise some obstacles to the application of game theory, especially the *minimax criterion* (that is, the criterion of minimizing maximum expected profits), to realistic problems of statistics. Nevertheless, it is important to note how, as an important by-product, the game-theoretical approach forces one to formulate problems clearly, to anticipate the various consequences of one's actions, to retain the relevant and eliminate the irrelevant, to place "cash values" on the different consequences, and so on.

EXERCISES

1. At one point in a generally bad growing season it is very cold, and Mr. Brown is considering whether to accept a firm offer for his crop which will yield him a profit of \$15,000. If he does not sell now but waits until harvesting time, he figures that he can make a profit of \$20,000 provided there is no frost within the next few weeks; if there is a frost within the next few weeks, however, Mr. Brown will suffer a loss of \$10,000 for labor, fertilizers, etc.

(a) What action should he take if he wants to maximize his expected profit and feels that the probability for a frost within the next few weeks is 1/2?

(b) What action should he take if he wants to maximize his expected profit and feels that the probability for a frost within the next few weeks is 1/10?

(c) Show that so long as the probability for a frost is greater than 1/6, he will maximize his expected profit by selling now.

(d) What action would Mr. Brown take if he were the kind of person who always visualizes the worst?

2. A contractor has to choose between two jobs. The first promises a profit of

\$120,000 with a probability of 3/4 or a loss of \$30,000 (due to strikes and other delays) with a probability of 1/4; the second promises a profit of \$180,000 with a probability of 1/2 or a loss of \$45,000 with a probability of 1/2.

(a) Which job should the contractor choose so as to maximize his expected profit?

(b) What job might the contractor choose if his business is in fairly bad shape and he will go broke unless he can make a profit of at least \$150,000 on his next job?

3. Dr. Green is planning to attend a medical convention in Chicago, and he must send in his hotel reservations immediately. The convention is so large that it is held in part at Hotel A and in part at Hotel B, and Dr. Green does not know whether the particular sessions he wants to attend will be scheduled for Hotel A or Hotel B. He is planning to stay only one day, which would cost him \$21.00 at Hotel A and \$18.00 at Hotel B. If he stays at the wrong hotel, he will have to pay an additional \$5.00 for cab fare.

(a) Where should he make his reservation if he wants to minimize his expected expenses and feels that the odds are 5 to 1 that the session he wants to attend will be held at Hotel A?

(b) What if he felt that the odds are 2 to 1 rather than 5 to 1?

4. The director of a large research laboratory is faced with the decision of either terminating a certain research project or authorizing funds for its continuation. If the project is continued and turns out to be successful, this will be worth \$100,000 to the laboratory; if it is continued but proves to be unsuccessful, this will entail a loss of \$15,000. If the project is not continued but later performed successfully by another research laboratory, this will entail a loss of \$5,000 (largely, to allow for the bad publicity of having abandoned a good project); if it is not continued but later shown to be unsuccessful by another research laboratory, there is no loss or gain so far as the first laboratory is concerned.

(a) What should the director decide to do if he wants to maximize the expected profit and he feels that the probability for success is 1/10?

(b) What if he felt that the probability for success is 1/5?

(c) For what success probability would his decision have the same expected profit either way?

(d) What action would the director take if he were a confirmed pessimist?

(e) What action would the director take if he were a confirmed optimist?

5. A catering company intends to prepare a number of box lunches to sell at a dog show. They pay \$0.80 per box and sell them for \$1.50, so that the profit per box sold is \$0.70. On the basis of past experience the company feels that it can sell 2,000 boxes if the crowd is small and 3,000 if it is large. All unsold boxes are destroyed (at no extra cost to the company) because of the danger of spoilage.

(a) Should the company plan on 2,000 boxes or 3,000 boxes, if they want to maximize expected profits and feel that the probability for a large crowd is 0.40?

(b) What should they plan to do if they feel that the probability for a large crowd is 0.60?

6. A pastry shop has refrigerator space for 3 highly perishable cakes, which are given away free at the end of the day if they are not sold. The unit cost of these cakes is \$3.00, their selling price is \$6.00, and the profit is thus \$3.00 per cake sold. It is known from past experience that the probabilities of a demand for 0, 1, 2, or 3 of these cakes are, respectively, 0.10, 0.30, 0.50, and 0.10.
(a) What is their expected profit if they stock only 1 of these cakes?
(b) What is their expected profit if they stock 2 of these cakes?
(c) What is their expected profit if they stock 3 of these cakes?
(d) What should they do to maximize their expected profit?

7. Suppose that the students referred to in the example in the text are the kind of persons who always worry about "what might have happened if." Looking at the table on page 131, they find that if they decide on Batch 1 and the home team does not win, they will lose out on \$80.00 (the difference between what they could have made with Batch 2 and what they will make with Batch 1). Referring to this difference as the *regret* associated with this situation, they also find that the regret associated with their choosing Batch 2 when the home team wins is \$40.00, and that in the other two cases the regret is 0. What action should they take to *minimize the maximum regret?*

8. Using the concept of *regret* introduced in the preceding exercise, what action should the director of the research laboratory of Exercise 4 take so as to minimize the greatest regret associated with his two options?

9. Each of the following is the payoff matrix (the payments Player A makes to player B) for a zero-sum two-person game. Eliminate all dominated strategies and determine the best strategy for each player as well as the value of the game:

(a)

4	−1
6	8

(b)

11	8
13	−5

(c)

−1	4	7
−2	1	1
−8	3	5

(d)

1	4	2
2	2	5
1	−1	3

10. Find the saddle point of each of the games of Exercise 9.

11. Each of the following is the payoff matrix (the payments Player A makes to Player B) for a zero-sum two-person game. Find the saddle point (or saddle points) as well as the value of each game.

(a)

5	−2	−1
3	1	0
−4	5	−2

(b)

8	2	1	3
2	3	3	3
5	4	5	4
8	4	6	4

12. If a game has a saddle point corresponding to Strategies I and 3 and another corresponding to Strategies III and 1, prove that there must also be saddle points corresponding to Strategies I and 1 and corresponding to Strategies III and 3, and that all four of these saddle points must have the same value.

13. The following is the payoff matrix of a zero-sum two-person game:

5	−2
−1	3

(a) What randomized strategy should Player A use so as to minimize his maximum expected losses?
(b) What randomized strategy should Player B use so as to maximize his minimum expected gain?
(c) What is the value of this game?

14. First eliminate all dominated strategies and then determine the best strategies and the value of each of the following games:

(a)

−1	−3	7
7	4	−1
4	0	10

(b)

0	−1	4	9
7	6	2	7

15. The following is the payoff matrix of a zero-sum two-person game:

14	8
8	20
10	12

(a) Show that the third strategy of Player B is dominated by a strategy which consists of choosing between the first two strategies by flipping a coin.
(b) Using the result of part (a), that is, eliminating the third strategy of Player B, find optimum strategies for both players and the value of the game.

16. The following is the payoff matrix (the amounts Player A has to pay Player B) of a zero-sum two-person game:

2	6	5
−3	−6	−5
4	2	3

(a) Show that the third strategy of Player A can be eliminated because it is dominated by a strategy which consists of randomly choosing between his first two strategies with respective probabilities of 1/3 and 2/3.
(b) Complete the solution of the game by finding optimum strategies for both players and the value of the game.

17. Referring to the example on page 139, verify that Player A can hold his expected losses down to \$8.59 by assigning his two strategies the respective probabilities of 6/17 and 11/17.

18. Referring to the 2-by-2 game on page 135, show that nothing is changed insofar as the choice of optimum strategies is concerned, if we subtract 4 from each entry in the payoff matrix. What will this do to the value of the game?

19. A country has two airfields with installations worth \$200,000 and \$1,000,000, respectively. Of these airfields it can defend only one against an attack by its enemy. The enemy, on the other hand, can attack only one of these airfields and take it successfully only if it is left undefended. Considering the "payoff" to the country to be the total value of the installations it holds after the attack, find the optimum strategies for both countries and the value of this "game." Explain why it would not be best for the country simply to defend the airfield with the more valuable installations.

20. Two people agree to play the following game: the first writes either 9 or 4 on a slip of paper, and at the same time the second writes either 5 or 6 on another slip of paper. If S, the sum of the two numbers, is *even*, the first player wins $\frac{S}{2} - 5$ dollars; if S is *odd*, the second player wins $8 - \frac{S}{3}$ dollars.
(a) Find the best strategy for each player.
(b) How much should the second player pay the first for the "privilege" of playing the game, so as to make the game equitable?

21. Referring to Exercise 3, how should Dr. Green randomize his choice between the two hotels, so as to minimize his maximum expected expenses?

22. Referring to Exercise 4, how should the director of the research laboratory randomize his decision, so as to minimize his maximum expected losses (or, which is the same, maximize his minimum expected profit)?

23. Referring to Exercise 5, how should the catering company make its choice so as to maximize its minimum expected profit?

24. Referring to Exercise 7, how should the students randomize their choice, if they wanted to minimize the maximum *expected regret?*

25. Because of various difficulties, the supplier of glue used in the manufacture of a laminated fiberboard product can guarantee the manufacturer only that he will deliver on schedule the required quantity of Glue F, Glue G, or Glue H. Because of time requirements, however, the manufacturer must set up his production process prior to knowing which glue will be available if he is to meet contractual obligations. All three glues can be used with either of two production methods open to the manufacturer, but for technical reasons the profit per piece differs substantially from one method to the other for the same glue. Using Glue F, the unit profits (in cents) are 160 and 80 for the two methods of production; using Glue G the corresponding figures are 90 and 110; and using Glue H they are 70 and 150. How should the manufacturer decide which production method to use so as to maximize his minimum expected unit profit? (*Hint:* Let p be the probability that he chooses the first production method and $1 - p$ the probability that he chooses the second production method; then draw three lines like those of Figure 6.1 giving the expected unit profit using, respectively, Glue F, Glue G, and Glue H; finally, find the value of p for which the smallest of the corresponding values on the lines is as large as possible.)

26. There are two gas stations at a busy intersection. The owner of the first station knows that if neither station lowers its prices, he can expect a net profit of \$200.00 on any given day. If he lowers his prices while the other station does not, he can expect a net profit of \$280.00; if he does not lower his prices but the other station does, he can expect a net profit of \$140.00; and if both stations participate in this "price war," he can expect a net profit of \$160.00. The owners of the two gas stations decide independently what prices to charge on any given day, and it is assumed that they cannot change their prices after they discover those charged by the other.

(a) Should the owner of the first gas station charge his regular prices or should he lower them, if he wants to maximize his minimum net profit?

(b) Assuming that the identical profit figures apply also to the second gas station, how might the owners of the two gas stations *collude* so that each could expect a net profit of \$210.00? (Note that this "game" is not zero-sum, so that the possibility of collusion opens entirely new possibilities.)

6.4 Statistical Decision Problems

The purpose of the minimax criterion, as it was used in Section 6.3, was to protect us against the worst thing that can possibly happen. This may be desirable in games against rational opponents, but it becomes questionable in most problems of statistical inference, where generalizations and decisions are based on samples. Suppose, for example, that a manufacturer is ready to ship a lot of 40,000 electric light bulbs, and that the department in charge of controlling outgoing quality tested a sample of 25 of these bulbs, all of which met specifications. The manufacturer is faced with a typical problem of statistical inference—he must make a decision about the quality (acceptability) of the whole lot on the basis of a sample. Now then, the worst that can possibly happen is that the 39,975 light bulbs which were not tested are all defective, and if this is what the manufacturer wants to protect himself against, he has no choice but to junk the whole lot.

Since this example is typical of many problems of statistics, it is clear that we must look for alternate criteria on which to base decisions, estimates, and predictions. To examine some possibilities, let us consider the following example, which also serves to bring out some interesting properties of the mean, the median, and some of the other measures of location discussed in Chapter 3: Suppose that the numbers 11, 15, 19, 20, and 20 are written on five slips of paper which are thoroughly mixed in a bowl; one slip is drawn at random, and *we are to predict the number that is on this slip.* Thus, we are faced with making a decision, and before we go any further, we shall have to know something about the consequences to which we are exposed. After all, if there are no penalties for being wrong, no rewards for being right or close, *there is nothing at stake* and we might just as well predict that the number drawn will be 137 or 55.1 even though we know that there are no such numbers in the bowl. Thus, let us investigate what decision we might reach in each of the following situations:

1. *We are given a reward of $10.00 if the number drawn is exactly the one we predict, and we are fined $3.00 if a different number is drawn.*
2. *We are paid a fee of $5.00 for making the prediction, but fined an amount of money equal in dollars to the size of our error.*
3. *We are paid a fee of $15.00 for making the prediction, but fined an amount of money equal in dollars to the square of our error.*

To select in each case a "best possible" decision, we shall use the criterion of maximizing one's expected profit.

Investigating the first case, we find that if we decide on the number 20, the *mode* of the five numbers, we stand to make $10.00 with a probability of 2/5, we stand to lose $3.00 with a probability of 3/5, and our expected profit is $10(2/5) + (-3)(3/5) = \$2.20$. It can easily be verified that this is the best prediction; if we predicted 11, 15, or 19, the expected profit would be -0.40, or a *loss* of $0.40, while any other prediction, say, 8 or 13, would entail a *sure* loss of $3.00. This demonstrates that in a situation where we have to pick the exact value on the nose (that is, where there is no reward for being close), the best decision is to use the mode.

In the second case it is the *median* which yields the most profitable predictions. If we predict that the number drawn will be 19, the *median* of the five numbers, the fine will be \$8.00, \$4.00, \$0.00, or \$1.00, depending on whether the number drawn is 11, 15, 19, or 20, and hence the *expected fine* is $8(1/5) + 4(1/5) + 0(1/5) + 1(2/5) =$ \$2.80. A proof of the fact that the expected fine would be greater if we used a number other than the median may be found in the first edition of *Elements of Statistics* by E. B. Mode, published by Prentice-Hall, Inc., in 1941. For instance, had we used 17, the mean of the five numbers, the fine would have been \$6,00, \$2.00, \$2.00, or \$3.00, depending on the number drawn, and the *expected fine* would have been $6(1/5) + 2(1/5) + 2(1/5) + 3(2/5) =$ \$3.20.

The mean comes into its own right in the third case, where the fine goes up very rapidly with the size of the error. Predicting that the number drawn will by 17, the *mean* of the five numbers, we find that the fine will be \$36.00, \$4.00, \$4.00, or \$9.00, depending on whether the number drawn is 11, 15, 19, or 20, and hence the *expected fine* is $36(1/5) + 4(1/5) + 4(1/5) + 9(2/5) =$ \$12.40. It can easily be shown that the expected fine would be greater for any other prediction, and it will be left to the reader to verify in Exercise 2 on page 148 that it would have been \$16.40 if we had used the median, that is, if we had predicted the number 19. A general proof may be found on page 110 of the book by A. E. Waugh mentioned in the Bibliography on page 28.

The third case, where we are concerned with the *squares* of the errors, plays a very important role in the theory of statistics; it ties in closely with the *method of least squares* which we shall study in Chapter 14. The idea of trying to minimize the squared errors is justifiable on the grounds that in actual practice the seriousness of an error often increases very rapidly with the size of the error, *more* rapidly than the magnitude of the error itself.

One of the greatest difficulties in applying the methods of this chapter to realistic problems in statistics is that we seldom know the exact values of all the risks that are involved; that is, we seldom know the exact values of the "payoff" corresponding to the various eventualities. If a medical research group has to decide whether or not to recommend the general release of a new experimental drug, how can they put a cash value on the damage that might be done by not waiting for a more thorough analysis of possible side effects, or on the lives that might be lost by not making the drug available to the public right away? Similarly, if a committee of professors has to decide which of several applicants should be admitted to medical school or, perhaps, receive a scholarship, how can they possibly foresee all the consequences that might be involved?

The fact that we seldom have adequate information about relevant probabilities also provides obstacles to finding suitable decision criteria. Without them, is it "reasonable" to base decisions on optimism, pessimism, or the assumption that we are "playing" against a malevolent opponent? Questions like these are difficult to answer, but their analysis serves the purpose of revealing some of the logic behind statistical reasoning. Indeed, the reader will find that many of the methods of statistical inference are easier to grasp if we formulate them (at least tacitly) as games in which all sorts of things can happen, in which interested parties including Nature have various moves, and in which there are all kinds of consequences on which one may or may not be able to put appropriate cash values.

EXERCISES

1. Referring to the pastry shop of Exercise 6 on page 142, suppose that the owner of the shop has no idea at all about the probabilities concerning the demand for the cakes. How many of the cakes should he stock if he wants to minimize his maximum losses? Discuss the reasonableness of this criterion in a problem of this kind.

2. Verify that in the third case listed on page 147, the expected fine would be \$16.40 if we used the median of the five numbers to make our prediction.

3. To consider a variation of the example of this section, suppose that there are several slips of paper marked 11, several marked 15, several marked 19, several marked 20, and we do not know how many there are of each kind. If the payoff is as in the second case on page 146, what prediction would *minimize the maximum possible fine?* What name did we give to this statistic in Chapter 3?

4. Suppose we are asked to predict what proportion of the seniors of a very large high school will fail a college admission test, and all the information we have is that the proportion is not less than 0.08 and not greater than 0.20. What prediction would be "best" if we wanted to *minimize the maximum error?*

5. The ages of seven finalists in a beauty contest are 17, 17, 17, 18, 19, 22, and 23, and we are to predict the age of the winner.

(a) If we assign each finalist the same probability and there is a reward for being exactly right, none for being close, what prediction maximizes the expected reward?

(b) If we assign each finalist the same probability and there is a penalty proportional to the magnitude of the error, what prediction minimizes the expected penalty?

(c) Repeat part (b) for the case where the penalty is proportional to the square of the size of the error.

(d) What prediction would we make if we had no idea about the finalists' chances and we wanted to minimize the greatest possible error?

BIBLIOGRAPHY

The material discussed in this chapter is treated more thoroughly in many books devoted exclusively to Decision Theory and the Theory of Games; some of the more elementary treatments may be found in

Bross, I. D. J., *Design for Decision.* New York: The Macmillan Company, 1953.

Chernoff, H., and Moses, L. E., *Elementary Decision Theory.* New York: John Wiley & Sons, Inc., 1959.

Dresher, M., *Games of Strategy: Theory and Applications.* Englewood Cliffs, N.J.: Prentice-Hall, Inc., 1961.

Luce, R. D., and Raiffa, H., *Games and Decisions.* New York: John Wiley & Sons, Inc., 1958.

McKinsey, J. C. C., *Introduction to the Theory of Games.* New York: McGraw-Hill Book Company, 1952.

Williams, J. D., *The Compleat Strategyst.* New York: McGraw-Hill Book Company, 1954.

SEVEN
Probability Distributions

7.1 Probability Functions

The two tables shown below give some of the probabilities associated with two simple experiments; one consists of the roll of a die and the other of three flips of a balanced coin. Their purpose is to illustrate what we mean by a *probability function*, namely, *a correspondence which assigns probabilities to numerical descriptions of the outcome of an experiment.* The first of these tables was easily obtained on the basis of the assumption that each face of the die has a probability of 1/6; the second was obtained by considering as equally likely the eight possible outcomes TTT, HTT, THT, TTH, HHT, HTH, THH, and HHH, where H stands for "head" and T for "tail."

Number of Points Rolled with a Die	*Probability*
1	1/6
2	1/6
3	1/6
4	1/6
5	1/6
6	1/6

Number of Heads Obtained in Three Flips of a Coin	*Probability*
0	1/8
1	3/8
2	3/8
3	1/8

Whenever possible, we try to express probability functions by means of formulas which enable us to calculate the probabilities associated with the various numerical descriptions of the outcomes. With the usual functional notation we can thus write

$$f(x) = 1/6 \qquad \text{for } x = 1, 2, 3, 4, 5, 6$$

for the first of the above examples; $f(1)$ represents the probability of rolling a 1, $f(2)$ represents the probability of rolling a 2, and so on.

Using the *factorial notation* where $n!$ (called "*n-factorial*") equals $n(n - 1)(n - 2) \cdot \ldots \cdot 3 \cdot 2 \cdot 1$ for any positive integer n (hence, $2! = 2$, $3! = 6$, $4! = 24$, $5! = 120$, and so forth) and by definition $0! = 1$, we can similarly write for the second example

$$f(x) = \frac{3/4}{x!(3 - x)!} \qquad \text{for } x = 0, 1, 2, 3$$

As can easily be verified, this will, indeed, give the probabilities listed in the right-hand column of the second table.

It is customary to refer to the number of points rolled with the die in the first example, the number of heads obtained in the second example, and numerical descriptions of experiments in general, as *random variables*. The value a random variable assumes in a given experiment is controlled by chance; that is, the probability that a random variable takes on a particular value is given by an appropriate probability function. To be rigorous, let us say that *a random variable (actually a misnomer) is a function defined over the sample space of an experiment*, and the probability that any one of its values will occur is given by a suitable probability function. Note also that since a random variable has to assume one of its values, the sum of the probabilities in a probability function must always equal 1. Of course, the values of a probability function, being probabilities, must be positive or zero.

7.2 The Binomial Distribution

There are many applied problems in which we are interested in the probability that an event will take place x times in n "trials," or in other words, x times out of n, while the probability that it will take place in any one trial is some fixed number p and the trials are independent. We may thus be interested in the probability of getting 24 responses to 80 mail questionnaires, the probability that in a sample of 50 voters 32 will favor Candidate A, the probability that 3 of 10 laboratory mice react positively to a new drug, and so on. Referring to the occurrence of any one of the individual events as a "success" (which is a holdover from the days when probability theory was applied mainly to games of chance), we are thus interested in the probabilitity of getting x *successes in* n *trials*. To handle problems of this kind, which incidentally include the second example on page 150, we use a special probability function, that of the *binomial distribution*.

To obtain a formula for this probability function, we shall first have to investigate some mathematical preliminaries pertaining to the number of *permutations* and the number of *combinations* of n objects taken r at a time. Generally speaking, if r objects are selected from a set of n objects, any particular arrangement of these r objects is referred to as a *permutation*. Thus, 41253 is a permutation of the first five positive integers, and ACE

might be looked upon as a permutation of three letters chosen from among the first five letters of the alphabet. The following theorem is an immediate consequence of the one on page 86:

The number of permutations of r objects selected from a set of n objects is $n(n-1)\cdot\ldots\cdot(n-r+1)$.

To prove this result we have only to observe that in the application of the theorem on page 86 (with $k = r$) we now have $n_1 = n$, $n_2 = n - 1, \ldots,$ and $n_r = n - r + 1$. [The rth, and final, selection is made from the $n - (r-1) = n - r + 1$ objects which remain after the first $r - 1$ selections have been made.] Thus, the number of ways in which each of 3 drivers can be assigned one of 5 trucks is $5\cdot4\cdot3 = 60$, and the number of ways in which 4 guinea pigs can be put into 4 of 8 cages is $8\cdot7\cdot6\cdot5 = 1{,}680$. Note also that in the special case where $r = n$ we have

The number of permutations of n objects taken all together is

$$n(n-1)\cdot\ldots\cdot2\cdot1 \quad \textit{or} \quad n!$$

Thus, the number of ways in which 5 teachers can be assigned to 5 classrooms is $5\cdot4\cdot3\cdot2\cdot1 = 120$, and the number of ways in which 6 different books can be arranged on a shelf is $6\cdot5\cdot4\cdot3\cdot2\cdot1 = 720$.

Suppose now that in the two earlier examples we had been interested only in which trucks and which cages are being used, without caring which driver gets which truck and which guinea pig goes into which cage. We would thus have been interested in the number of *combinations* of n objects taken r at a time, namely, the number of ways in which r objects can be selected from a set of n objects without paying attention to the order in which the selection is made. To obtain a formula, let us note that there are always $r!$ permutations of r specific objects selected from a set of n objects which count only as 1 combination. Hence, the $n(n-1)\cdot\ldots\cdot(n-r+1)$ permutations of r objects selected from a set of n objects contain each set of r objects $r!$ times. For example, among the 12 permutations of 2 of the first four letters of the alphabet, namely, *ab*, *ac*, *ad*, *bc*, *bd*, *cd*, *ba*, *ca*, *da*, *cb*, *db*, and *dc*, each pair of letters occurs together twice. Thus, if we divide $n(n-1)\cdot\ldots\cdot(n-r+1)$ by $r!$, we have

The number of ways in which r objects can be selected from a set of n objects is

$$\frac{n(n-1)\cdot\ldots\cdot(n-r+1)}{r!}$$

Symbolically, we write the number of ways in which r objects can be selected from a set of n objects as $\binom{n}{r}$ and we refer to it as the number of *combinations* of n objects taken r at a time. In Exercise 15 on page 159, the reader will be asked to verify that in the factorial notation

$$\binom{n}{r} = \frac{n!}{(n-r)!r!}$$

for $r = 0, 1, 2, \ldots,$ and n.

An easy way of calculating the quantities $\binom{n}{r}$, also called *binomial coefficients*, is indicated in Exercise 7 on page 157; otherwise, their values up to $n = 20$ can be obtained from Table VII at the end of the book. The reason why these quantities are called "binomial coefficients" is explained in Exercise 14 on page 158.

Applying the result just obtained, we find, for example, that a person can invite 4 of his 9 friends to a party in $\frac{9\cdot 8\cdot 7\cdot 6}{4\cdot 3\cdot 2\cdot 1} = 126$ ways, and that a light fixture with 10 bulbs can have 2 bulbs burn out in $\binom{10}{2} = \frac{10\cdot 9}{2\cdot 1} =$ 45 different ways.

We are now ready to derive the formula for the *binomial* probability function. Since p is the probability of getting a success on any one trial, the probability of getting x successes in n trials and, hence, x successes and $n - x$ failures, in some *specific order* is $p^x(1-p)^{n-x}$. There is one factor p for each success, one factor $1 - p$ for each failure, and the x factors p and $n - x$ factors $1 - p$ are all multiplied together by virtue of the assumption that the n trials are independent. Since this probability is the same for each point of the sample space where there are x successes and $n - x$ failures (it does not depend on the order in which the successes and failures are obtained), the desired probability for x successes in n trials *in any order* is obtained by multiplying $p^x(1-p)^{n-x}$ by the number of points of the sample space (that is, individual outcomes) where there are x successes and $n - x$ failures. In other words, $p^x(1-p)^{n-x}$ is multiplied by the number of ways in which the x successes can be distributed among the n trials, namely, by $\binom{n}{x}$. We have thus arrived at the following result:

The probability of getting x successes in n independent trials is given by

$$f(x) = \binom{n}{x}p^x(1-p)^{n-x} \qquad \text{for } x = 0, 1, 2, \ldots, n$$

where p is the constant probability of a success for each individual trial.

It is customary to say that the number of successes in n trials is a random variable having the *binomial probability distribution*, or simply the *binomial distribution.* The terms "probability distribution" and "probability function" are often used interchangeably, although some persons make the distinction that the term "probability distribution" refers to *all* the probabilities associated with a random variable, and not only those given directly by its probability function. [The following illustrates this rather technical distinction: The probabilities of getting, say, "1 *or* 2 successes" or "at least 3 successes" are part of the *probability distribution* of the number of successes; although these probabilities are easily obtained by adding some of the value of the corresponding *probability function,* strictly speaking, they are not part of it.]

To illustrate the use of the above formula let us first calculate the probability of getting 4 heads and 8 tails in 12 flips of a balanced coin. Substituting $x = 4$, $n = 12$, $p = 1/2$, and $\binom{12}{4} = 495$ (see Table VII), we get

$$f(4) = 495\left(\frac{1}{2}\right)^4\left(1 - \frac{1}{2}\right)^8 = \frac{495}{4{,}096}$$

or approximately 0.12. Similarly, to find the probability that 3 of 10 mice used in an experiment will react positively to a drug, when the probability that any one of them will react positively is 0.20, we substitute $x = 3$, $n = 10$, $p = 0.20$, $\binom{10}{3} = 120$, and get

$$f(3) = 120(0.20)^3(0.80)^7 = 0.20 \qquad \text{(approximately)}$$

In actual practice, problems involving the binomial distribution are usually solved by referring to special tables (see Bibliography on page 188) or by using approximations, among others the ones described in Exercise 29 on page 160 and in Section 7.6. The direct application of the formula would be much too involved, for instance, to calculate the probability that 3 of 10,000 patients will have an undesirable side-effect from a new drug, the probability that at least 350 of 750 seeds will germinate, or the probability that fewer than 180 of 1,000 persons drafted by the army have an I.Q. of over 105.

Before we discuss another example involving the binomial distribution, let us remind the reader that this distribution applies only when the probability of a "success" remains constant from trial to trial and the trials are, furthermore, independent. The formula on page 153 cannot be used, therefore, to find the probability that it will rain, say, on 25 of 100 consecutive days (at a certain weather station). Not only does the probability for rain vary over such a lengthy period of time, but the "trials" are not even independent. Clearly, the probability that it will rain on any given day will depend to some extent on whether it did or did not rain on the day before.

The following is an interesting example involving the binomial distribution as well as the Rule of Bayes: The landscaping plans for the entrance to a new building call for a row of pyracantha bushes to flank the entry sign. Mr. Higgins, the landscaper, claims that 20 per cent of the bushes will fail to survive the first frost while Mr. Peters, the developer, feels that the loss will be 40 per cent. In the past, Mr. Higgins has been about three times as reliable as Mr. Peters in matters like this, so that (in the absence of any further knowledge and assuming that *one of them must be correct*) we assign to their "educated guesses" the respective probabilities of 3/4 and 1/4. What we would like to know is *how these probabilities would be affected if they found that among 10 pyracantha bushes planted as an experiment only 1 fails to survive the first frost.* Letting B_1 represent the event that Mr. Higgins is correct, B_2 the event that Mr. Peters is correct, and A the event that exactly 1 of 10 pyracantha bushes does not survive the first frost, we have $P(B_1) = 3/4$, $P(B_2) = 1/4$,

$$P(A \mid B_1) = \binom{10}{1}(0.20)^1(0.80)^9 = 0.2684$$

and

$$P(A \mid B_2) = \binom{10}{1}(0.40)^1(0.60)^9 = 0.0403$$

If we now substitute all these probabilities into the formula for the Rule of Bayes (see page 118), we obtain

$$P(B_1 \mid A) = \frac{(3/4)(0.2684)}{(3/4)(0.2684) + (1/4)(0.0403)} = 0.95$$

and it follows that $P(B_2 \mid A) = 1 - 0.95 = 0.05$. It is interesting to observe how we have thus combined the direct evidence (only 1 of the 10 bushes failed to survive the first frost) with the "educated guesses," and how the weight of the direct evidence has given increasing credibility to Mr. Higgins' claim.

To continue this example, let us suppose now that Mr. Peters must decide whether the correct proportion is, in fact, 0.20 or 0.40. If the correct value is $p = 0.20$ and he accepts $p = 0.40$, this will entail a loss of \$20.00 (accounted for by the fact that he will probably end up with too many bushes); if the correct value is $p = 0.40$ and he accepts $p = 0.20$, this will entail a loss of \$100.00 (accounted for by the fact that another order will probably have to be placed and a gardener will have to be hired to get them planted); if he accepts the correct value, there will be no loss in either case. Schematically, this situation is described by the following table:

	Correct Value	
	$p = 0.20$	$p = 0.40$
Accept $p = 0.20$	no loss	\$100
Accept $p = 0.40$	\$20	no loss

Using all this information, let us now see what decision Mr. Peters should reach, whether to accept $p = 0.20$ or $p = 0.40$, if he wants to *minimize his expected losses*. Proceeding as in Chapter 6, we find that if he accepts $p = 0.20$ his *expected losses* are

$$0(0.95) + 100(0.05) = \$5.00$$

and if he accepts $p = 0.40$ his *expected losses* are

$$20(0.95) + 0(0.05) = \$19.00$$

Observe that we calculated these expected losses in accordance with the definition of a *mathematical expectation* (see page 126), namely, as the sum of the products obtained by multiplying each possible loss by the corresponding probability. It follows that if he wants to minimize his expected losses, Mr. Peters should accept $p = 0.20$, namely, that 20 per cent of the pyracantha bushes will fail to survive the first frost. It is of interest to note that if Mr. Peters had no knowledge of the experiment in which only 1 of 10 bushes failed to survive the first frost, he would have minimized his expected losses by accepting $p = 0.40$. As the reader will be asked to verify in Exercise 36 on page 163, the expected losses corresponding to his accepting $p = 0.20$ and accepting $p = 0.40$ would thus have been \$25.00 and \$15.00, respectively.

An analysis of this kind is referred to as *Bayesian;* although it has a certain appeal, it also presents some serious problems. Not only is it generally difficult, perhaps even impossible, to put cash values on the consequences of various decisions, but we must ask what credibility, if any, can be assigned to the collateral information, especially when this information consists of the personal judgment of one or two persons.

EXERCISES

1. The probability that a random variable assumes the values 1, 2, 3, 4, or 5 is given by $f(x) = x/15$.

(a) Verify that this is a probability function, namely, that none of the values of $f(x)$ are negative and that the sum of the probabilities for all x equals 1.

(b) Find the probability that this random variable assumes a value less than 4.
(c) Find the probability that this random variable assumes a value greater than 2.

2. The probability function for the number of points rolled with a pair of balanced dice can be written as

$$f(x) = \frac{6 - |x - 7|}{36} \qquad \text{for } x = 2, 3, \ldots, 11, 12$$

where the absolute value $|x - 7|$ equals $x - 7$ or $7 - x$, whichever is positive or zero.

(a) Use this formula to find the probability of rolling a total of 6 with a pair of balanced dice, and compare with the result obtained in part (c) of Exercise 13 on page 111.
(b) Use this formula to find the probability of rolling a total of either 7 or 11 with a pair of balanced dice, and compare with the result obtained in part (d) of Exercise 13 on page 111.
(c) What is the probability of rolling a total of either 2, 3, or 12 with a pair of balanced dice?

3. In how many different ways can six persons be seated in a row?

4. In how many ways can 5 executives each choose a car from a pool of 8 cars?

5. The price of a European tour includes three stop-overs to be selected from among 10 cities. In how many ways can one plan such a tour if (a) the order of the stop-overs does not matter, and (b) the order does matter?

6. How many 5-man basketball teams can be chosen from a squad of 12 if one disregards the positions played by the members of the squad?

7. The number of combinations of n objects taken r at a time can easily be determined by means of the following arrangement called *Pascal's triangle:*

$$\begin{array}{ccccccccccc}
 & & & & 1 & & 1 & & & & \\
 & & & 1 & & 2 & & 1 & & & \\
 & & 1 & & 3 & & 3 & & 1 & & \\
 & 1 & & 4 & & 6 & & 4 & & 1 & \\
1 & & 5 & & 10 & & 10 & & 5 & & 1 \\
\end{array}$$

. . . .

where each row begins with a 1, ends with a 1, and each other entry is given by the sum of the nearest two entries in the row immediately above.

(a) Verify that the third row of the triangle contains the values of $\binom{3}{r}$ for $r = 0, 1, 2$, and 3.
(b) Verify that the fourth row of the triangle contains the values of $\binom{4}{r}$ for $r = 0, 1, 2, 3$, and 4.

(c) In general the nth row of Pascal's triangle contains the values of $\binom{n}{r}$ for $r = 0, 1, 2, \ldots,$ and n. Use this fact to calculate the values of $\binom{6}{r}$ for $r = 0, 1, 2, 3, 4, 5,$ and 6.

8. Find the number of ways in which 3 of 6 mice can be selected for an experiment
(a) using the method suggested in Exercise 7;
(b) using the formula on page 152.

9. Find the number of ways in which a social worker can select 5 of 8 families living in an apartment house
(a) using the method suggested in Exercise 7;
(b) using the formula on page 152.

10. Mr. Jones has 7 suits and 8 pairs of shoes. In how many ways can he select 3 suits and 2 pairs of shoes to take along on a business trip? (*Hint:* Use the theorem on page 85.)

11. In hiring his staff, the director of a research laboratory has to choose 3 chemists from among 7 applicants, 2 physicists from among 4 applicants, 5 laboratory technicians from among 10 applicants, and 6 secretaries from among 14 applicants. Use Table VII and the theorem on page 86 to find the total number of ways in which the director can hire his staff.

12. If among n objects r are alike while the others are all distinct, the number of permutations of these n objects taken all together is $n!/r!$.
(a) Use this formula to find the number of permutations of the letters in the word "roof."
(b) Use this formula to find the number of ways in which five cars can place in a race by *makes* if three are Thunderbirds, one is a Corvette, and one is a Jaguar.

13. If among n objects r_1 are identical and another r_2 are identical, while the others are all distinct, the number of permutations of these n objects taken all together is $\frac{n!}{r_1!r_2!}$.
(a) Use this formula to find the number of permutations of the letters in the word "success."
(b) In its "How to Play Golf" section, a bookstore has 3 copies of a book by Arnold Palmer, 4 copies of a book by Sam Sneed, and 1 copy each of books by five other golfers. If these books are sold one at a time, in how many different ways (orders) can they be sold?

14. The quantity $\binom{n}{r}$ defined on page 152 is referred to as a *binomial coefficient* because it is, in fact, the coefficient of a^r in the binomial expansion of $(a + b)^n$. Verify that this is true for $n = 2, 3,$ and 4, by expanding $(a + b)^2$, $(a + b)^3$, and $(a + b)^4$, and comparing the coefficients with the corresponding values of $\binom{n}{r}$ given in Table VII.

15. Multiplying and dividing by $(n - r)!$, verify symbolically that the number of *permutations* of n objects taken r at a time can be written $n!/(n - r)!$ and, hence, that the number of *combinations* of n objects taken r at a time can be written $\dfrac{n!}{(n - r)!r!}$.

16. Use the formula for the binomial distributions to find (a) the probability of rolling exactly 2 threes in 5 rolls of a balanced die; (b) the probability of rolling at most 2 threes in 5 rolls of a balanced die; (c) the probability of getting exactly 5 heads in 7 flips of a balanced coin; and (d) the probability of getting at least 5 heads in 7 flips of a balanced coin.

17. A multiple-choice test consists of 10 questions and 4 answers to each question. Each question is answered by drawing a card from an ordinary deck of 52 playing cards and marking answer 1, 2, 3, or 4 depending on whether the card drawn (with replacement) is a spade, heart, diamond, or club.
(a) What is the probability of getting exactly 4 correct answers?
(b) What is the probability of answering each question incorrectly?
(c) If it takes at least 7 correct answers to pass, what is the probability of passing the test by this method?

18. In a certain country 30 per cent of all losses due to fraudulent, dishonest, or criminal acts are indemnified by insurance. What is the probability that among 8 cases (randomly selected from court files) only 1 was indemnified by insurance?

19. It is claimed that among all drivers whose cars are equipped with seat-belts, 75 per cent use them on long trips. What is the probability that among 5 cars (equipped with seat-belts) which pass through a toll station on a turnpike all of the drivers are using their seat-belts?

20. An owner of 6 overnight cabins has 4 television sets which he installs upon request at an extra charge. If there is a fifty-fifty chance that any one of his guests wants a television set installed in his cabin, find the probability that on a night when all the cabins are occupied there will be more requests for sets than there are sets.

21. It is known that 40 per cent of the rats used in an experiment will die after being administered a given dose of an experimental drug. Should the experimenter be very surprised if among 10 rats none died after having received the given dose of the drug?

22. If incompatibility is the legal reason given for 9 out 10 divorce cases, find the respective probabilities that among 4 divorce cases 0, 1, 2, 3, and 4 are attributed to incompatibility. Also draw a histogram (or a bar chart) representing this probability function.

23. The probability that a freshman entering a large state university will not survive the first year is 0.35. What is the probability that fewer than 3 of 5 freshmen (randomly selected from the registrar's files) will *survive* the first year?

24. If n elements are selected from a set containing a (distinguishable) elements of one kind and b (distinguishable) elements of another kind,

(a) find an expression for the total number of ways in which n elements can be selected from this set;

(b) find an expression for the total number of ways in which x elements of the first kind and also $n - x$ elements of the second kind can be selected from this set;

(c) use the results of parts (a) and (b) to show that the probability that n elements (randomly) selected from this set contain x elements of the first kind and $n - x$ elements of the second kind is given by

$$f(x) = \frac{\binom{a}{x}\binom{b}{n-x}}{\binom{a+b}{n}} \qquad \text{for } x = 0, 1, 2, \ldots, a$$

(d) This probability function defines the *hypergeometric distribution,* and it applies to what is called *sampling without replacement;* use it to find the probability that a 5-card poker hand dealt from an ordinary deck of 52 playing cards contains exactly one ace.

(e) How big an error would we make in part (d) if we calculated the probability using the binomial distribution with $p = 1/13$? Would this answer be correct if we were dealt one card each from 5 different decks?

25. Certain machine parts are shipped in lots of 20. Three parts are selected from each lot, and the lot is accepted if none of the parts is defective. What is the probability that a lot will be accepted if it contains (a) 4 defectives, (b) 8 defectives, and (c) 12 defectives?

26. A toy store receives a shipment of 25 model airplane kits among which 3 have one or more components missing. If a customer (randomly) selects 2 kits from this shipment, what is the probability that neither kit lacks any components?

27. Among 25 income tax forms filed with the Internal Revenue Service 6 contain errors favoring the taxpayer. What is the probability that among 5 of these forms selected for audit, 2 contain such an error?

28. Mrs. Brown selects three 60-watt lightbulbs from a carton containing 30 of these bulbs including 2 defectives. Find the probability that none of the bulbs she selects is defective.

29. If n is large and p is small, the binomial distribution is often approximated by means of the *Poisson distribution,* given by the probability function

$$f(x) = \frac{(np)^x \cdot e^{-np}}{x!} \qquad \text{for } x = 0, 1, 2, \ldots$$

Here e is the number 2.71828... used in connection with natural logarithms; values of e^{-np} may be obtained from Table X at the end of the book. Note that for a random variable having the Poisson distribution the set of values assumed by x is *infinite;* this is a matter of mathematical convenience and in actual practice the probabilities become negligible (very close to 0) after a fairly small set of values of x.*

(a) Use the Poisson distribution to find an approximation for the probability of getting 3 successes in 100 independent trials when $p = 0.05$.

(b) A very large shipment of textbooks contains 2 per cent with imperfect bindings. What is the probability that among 400 textbooks taken from this shipment exactly 5 have imperfect bindings?

(c) To meet specifications, each can of fruit cocktail must contain at least one cherry. If the fruit cocktail coming from a certain cannery is such that 1.5 per cent of the cans are actually without cherries, what is the probability that among 400 cans delivered from this cannery to a supermarket exactly 2 are without cherries?

30. The Poisson distribution (see Exercise 29) has many important applications which have no direct connection with the binomial distribution. In that case np is replaced in its formula by the parameter λ (*lambda*) and we calculate the probability for getting x successes by means of the formula

$$f(x) = \frac{\lambda^x \cdot e^{-\lambda}}{x!} \qquad \text{for } x = 0, 1, 2, \ldots$$

(As we shall see in Exercise 7 on page 168, λ can be interpreted as the *expected,* or *average,* number of successes.) Use the above formula to solve each of the following problems:

(a) The probability that there will be x accidents at a busy intersection during a week can be calculated by means of the formula for the Poisson distribution with $\lambda = 2.4$. What is the probability that there will be exactly 3 accidents at this intersection during a given week?

(b) In the inspection of sheet metal produced in continuous rolls, the probability of spotting x defects in 5 minutes may be calculated by means of the formula for the Poisson distribution with $\lambda = 1.2$. What is the probability that an inspector will not find any defects during 5 minutes of inspection?

(c) Assuming that the number of telephone calls arriving at a company's switchboard during a 3-minute span has a Poisson distribution with $\lambda = 2.8$, what is the probability that there will be exactly 4 incoming calls during such a 3-minute span?

(d) A hotel manager knows from past experience that during any week in June there will be on the average 6 honeymoon couples among his guests. Find the probability that during any given week in June there will be fewer than 3 honeymoon couples among his guests.

31. Mr. Butler and Mr. Daniels intend to go pheasant hunting using Mr. Butler's dog. According to Mr. Butler the probability that his dog will find a downed

* When the sample space is *countably infinite* (that is, when there are as many possible outcomes as there are whole numbers), the third postulate of probability must be modified as indicated in the footnote to page 97.

bird is 0.90 and according to Mr. Daniels this probability is only 0.60. In the absence of any further information we would judge that, since it is Mr. Butler's dog, he is 4 times as likely to be right as Mr. Daniels. Assuming that one or the other must be right, how would this judgment be affected if on the hunting trip the dog actually finds only 3 of the 9 pheasants they downed? (*Hint:* Use the Rule of Bayes.)

32. In planning the operations of a new insurance agency, one expert claims that only 1 out of 4 salesmen can be expected to stay with the agency for more than a year, while a second expert claims that it would be more correct to say 1 out of 3. In the past, the two experts have been about equally reliable, so that in the absence of any direct information we would assign their judgments equal weight. Assuming that one or the other must be right, what probabilities would we assign to their claims if it were found that among 3 salesmen actually hired by the agency only 1 stayed for more than a year? (*Hint:* Use the Rule of Bayes.)

33. Three scientists (who are otherwise considered about equally reliable in their claims) make the conflicting statements that the number of gamma rays emitted per second by a certain radioactive substance have an average of 1.4, 2.0, and 3.1. If one of these values has to be correct, what probabilities would we assign to the claims of the three scientists after observing that the substance actually yielded a count of 4 gamma rays during an interval of one second? Assume that the number of gamma rays emitted is a random variable having the Poisson distribution described in Exercise 30. (*Hint:* Use the Rule of Bayes.)

34. (*Continuation of Exercise 33*) Suppose that the losses associated with the various possible decisions concerning the average number of gamma rays emitted per second are as shown in the following table:

	True Value		
	1.4	2.0	3.1
Accept 1.4	0	\$60	\$170
Accept 2.0	\$60	0	\$110
Accept 3.1	\$170	\$110	0

(a) If one's decision is based only on the collateral information that in the past the three scientists have been equally reliable, which decision will minimize one's expected losses?

(b) If one considers also the direct sample evidence that 4 gamma rays were emitted, which decision will minimize one's expected losses?

35. A paperboy claims that only 1 in 5 customers will report a wet paper on a rainy day, while the boy's circulation manager feels that the proportion is 0.15. In the past the paperboy has been about twice as reliable as his manager in matters of this kind. How is this judgment of their reliability affected, if on a given rainy day 4 wet papers are delivered and only 1 is reported?

36. Verify for the example in the text that, without considering the direct sample data, Mr. Peters' expected losses are \$25.00 and \$15.00 depending on whether he accepts $p = 0.20$ or $p = 0.40$.

37. A quality control engineer must decide whether the true proportion of defectives in a large shipment of optical equipment is $p = 0.01$, $p = 0.02$, or $p = 0.03$; no other values are possible. The losses associated with making the various possible correct and incorrect decisions are as shown in the following table:

	True Value		
	0.01	0.02	0.03
Accept 0.01	0	\$100	\$200
Accept 0.02	\$100	0	\$100
Accept 0.03	\$200	\$100	0

(a) If, on the basis of collateral information, the quality control engineer assigns $p = 0.01$, 0.02, and 0.03 (subjective) probabilities of 0.30, 0.40, and 0.30, respectively, which decision will minimize his expected losses?

(b) If a random sample of size 10 from this shipment includes 2 defective pieces, use the Rule of Bayes to calculate the revised probabilities the quality control engineer can now assign to the three values of p. Make use of the fact that the binomial probabilities for 2 successes in 10 trials are 0.004, 0.015, and 0.032, respectively, for $p = 0.01$, $p = 0.02$, and $p = 0.03$.

(c) Use the results of part (b) to determine which decision (based on the direct evidence as well as the collateral information) will minimize his expected losses.

7.3 The Mean and the Variance of a Probability Distribution

Let us now apply the concept of a mathematical expectation to the two examples on page 150. The first dealt with the number of points rolled with a balanced die, and if we multiply 1, 2, 3, 4, 5, and 6 by their respective probabilities, which all equaled 1/6, we find that the *expected* number of points is

$$1(1/6) + 2(1/6) + 3(1/6) + 4(1/6) + 5(1/6) + 6(1/6) = 3\tfrac{1}{2}$$

Of course, we cannot roll $3\frac{1}{2}$ with a die, but this is the *average* we should get if we rolled the die a great many times. Considering the second example on page 150, the one which dealt with the number of heads obtained in 3 flips of a balanced coin, we find that the *expected* number of heads is $1\frac{1}{2}$. This value, which must also be interpreted as an *average*, is the sum of the products obtained by multiplying 0, 1, 2, and 3 by their respective probabilities of 1/8, 3/8, 3/8, and 1/8.

The expected values we have calculated in these two examples are referred to as the *means* of the respective probability distributions. In general, if we are given a probability function, that is, the probabilities $f(x)$ which are associated with the various values of a random variable, we define the *mean of the distribution of this random variable*, or simply, the *mean of its probability distribution*, as

▲ $$\mu = \Sigma\, x \cdot f(x)$$ ▲

where the summation extends over all values assumed by the random variable.

To study another example, let us consider the probability function whose histogram is shown in Figure 7.1; it gives the probabilities (rounded

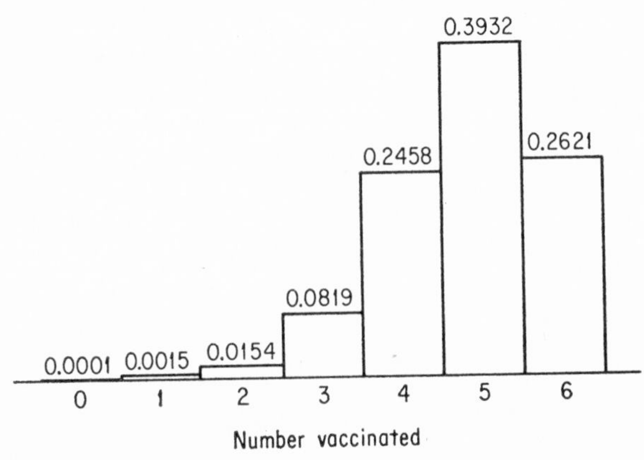

Fig. 7.1 Histogram of a binomial distribution.

to four decimals) that among 6 patients admitted to a hospital, 0, 1, 2, 3, 4, 5, or 6 have had an anti-polio vaccine, when the probability that any one of them has had such a vaccine is 0.80. Multiplying 0, 1, 2, ..., and 6 by the corresponding probabilities and adding the products thus obtained, one can easily verify that the mean of the distribution is $\mu = 4.7998$ or approximately 4.8.

When a random variable assumes a very large set of values, the calculation of μ can be quite laborious. For instance, if we wanted to know how many among 800 customers entering a store can be expected to make a purchase, and the probability that any one of them will make a purchase is 0.40, we would first have to calculate the 801 probabilities corresponding to 0, 1, 2, . . ., and 800 of them making a purchase. However, if we think for a moment, we might argue that in the long run 40 per cent of the customers make a purchase, 40 per cent of 800 is 320, and, hence, we can *expect* 320 of the 800 customers to make a purchase. (We are assuming here that the customers are shopping individually and not in parties of two or more.) Similarly, if a balanced coin is flipped 1,000 times, we can argue that we will get heads about 50 per cent of the time and, hence, that we can *expect* 1,000(0.50) = 500 heads. These two values are, indeed, correct, and we were able to find them so easily because there exists the special formula

$$\mu = np$$

for the *mean of a binomial distribution.* In words, the mean of a binomial distribution is simply the product of the number of trials and the probability of success on an individual trial. A proof of this important result is referred to in the Bibliography on page 188.

Using this special formula, we can now verify the value obtained for the mean of the distribution of Figure 7.1 and the value obtained for the mean of the second distribution on page 150. For the probability function of Figure 7.1 we have $n = 6$, $p = 0.80$, $\mu = 6(0.80) = 4.80$, and the difference between this result and the one obtained before is the small rounding error of 0.0002; for the distribution of the number of heads obtained in 3 flips of a balanced coin we have $n = 3$, $p = 1/2$, $\mu = 3(1/2) = 1\frac{1}{2}$, and this agrees with the value obtained before. It is important to remember that the special formula $\mu = np$ applies only to binomial distributions; special formulas for other probability distributions are given in Exercises 6 and 7 on page 168.

In Chapter 4 we saw that there are many problems in which we must describe the variability of a distribution (that is, its spread or dispersion) as well as its mean or some other measure of central location. This applies also to probability distributions, whose variability we describe in very much the same way in which we describe the variability of actual data. Instead of *averaging* the squared deviations from the mean, as we did in the definition of σ^2 for a set of data looked upon as a population, we take their *expected value.* If x is a value of some random variable and the mean of its probability distribution is equal to μ, then the deviation from the mean is $x - \mu$ and we define the *variance of the probability distribution* as the value we can expect for the squared deviation from the mean, namely, as

$$\sigma^2 = \Sigma\, (x - \mu)^2 \cdot f(x)$$

The summation extends over all values assumed by the random variable and, as in Chapter 4, the square root of the variance defines the *standard deviation* σ of the probability distribution.

To illustrate the calculation of the variance of a probability distribution, let us refer again to the second of the two examples on page 150, namely, the one concerning the number of heads obtained in 3 flips of a balanced coin. Since the mean of this distribution was shown to equal $\mu = 3(1/2) = 1.50$, we can arrange the required calculations as in the following table:

Number of Heads x	*Probability*	*Deviation from Mean*	*Square of Deviation from Mean*	$(x - \mu)^2 f(x)$
0	1/8	−1.50	2.25	0.28125
1	3/8	−0.50	0.25	0.09375
2	3/8	0.50	0.25	0.09375
3	1/8	1.50	2.25	0.28125
				$\sigma^2 = 0.7500$

The values in the last column are obtained by multiplying each squared deviation from the mean by the corresponding probability, and their sum gives the variance of the distribution. Thus, the standard deviation of this probability distribution is $\sigma = \sqrt{0.75}$, which equals approximately 0.87. Following these same steps, the reader will be asked to show in Exercise 3 on page 168 that the variance of the first probability distribution on page 150 is $\sigma^2 = 35/12$, and that the one for the probability distribution of Figure 7.1 equals approximately 0.96.

As in the case of the mean, the calculation of the standard deviation or the variance can generally be simplified when we deal with special kinds of probability distributions. For instance, for the *binomial distribution* we have the formula

$$\blacktriangle \qquad \sigma^2 = np(1 - p) \qquad \blacktriangle$$

which we shall not prove, but which can easily be verified for our various examples. For the distribution of the number of heads obtained in 3 flips of a balanced coin we have $n = 3$, $p = 0.50$, and

$$\sigma^2 = 3(0.50)(0.50) = 0.75$$

which agrees with the result obtained above. Similarly, for the probability distribution of Figure 7.1 we have $n = 6$, $p = 0.80$, and

$$\sigma^2 = 6(0.80)(0.20) = 0.96$$

namely, the value the reader is asked to verify by the long method in Exercise 3 on page 168.

Intuitively speaking, the variance or the standard deviation of a probability distribution measure its spread or its dispersion: when σ is small the probability is high that we will get a value close to the mean, and when σ is large we are more likely to get a value far away from the mean. This important idea is expressed rigorously in *Chebyshev's Theorem,* which we introduced on page 67 in connection with distributions of observed data. For probability distributions, the theorem reads as follows:

> *Given a probability distribution with the mean μ and the standard deviation σ, the probability of obtaining a value within k standard deviations of the mean is at least $1 - 1/k^2$.*

Thus, the probability of getting a value within two standard deviations of the mean (a value on the interval from $\mu - 2\sigma$ to $\mu + 2\sigma$) is at least 3/4, the probability of getting a value within five standard deviations of the mean is at least 24/25, and the probability of getting a value within ten standard deviations of the mean is at least 99/100. The quantity k in Chebyshev's Theorem can be any positive number, although the theorem becomes trivial when k is 1 or less.

Changing around the argument, we can also say that *the probability of getting a value which differs from the mean by more than k standard deviations is less than $1/k^2$.* We thus have a probability less than 0.25 of getting a value which differs from the mean by more than two standard deviations, a probability less than 0.04 of getting a value which differs from the mean by more than five standard deviations, and so on.

To give a concrete application, suppose we obtained 148 heads and 252 tails in 400 flips of a coin and we are wondering whether this is sufficient evidence to raise the question whether the coin is really balanced. If the coin is balanced we are dealing with a binomial distribution having $n = 400$ and $p = 1/2$, and substitution into the special formulas on pages 165 and 166 yields

$$\mu = np = 400(1/2) = 200$$

and

$$\sigma = \sqrt{np(1-p)} = \sqrt{400(1/2)(1/2)} = 10$$

For $k = 5$, Chebyshev's Theorem asserts that the probability of getting anywhere from 150 to 250 heads is at least 0.96, *or* that the probability of getting fewer than 150 or more than 250 heads is less than 0.04. Since this probability is quite small, it would seem reasonable to question the balance of the coin.

EXERCISES

1. Find the mean of the probability distribution of Exercise 1 on page 156.

2. The probabilities of getting 0, 1, 2, 3, or 4 heads in 4 tosses of a balanced coin are, respectively, 1/16, 4/16, 6/16, 4/16, and 1/16. Use the formulas defining μ and

σ^2 to compute the mean and the variance of this probability distribution and verify the results using the special formulas for the mean and the variance of the binomial distribution.

3. Use the formula defining the variance on page 165 to show that (a) the variance of the first probability distribution on page 150 equals 35/12, and (b) the variance of the probability distribution of Figure 7.1 equals 0.96.

4. In actual practice, the variance of a probability distribution is usually calculated by means of the formula

$$\sigma^2 = \Sigma\, x^2 f(x) - \mu^2$$

which has the advantage that we do not have to work with the deviations from the mean.
   (a) Use this short-cut formula to calculate the variance of the probability distribution of Exercise 1 on page 156.
   (b) Use this short-cut formula to verify the results obtained in Exercise 3.

5. Find the mean and the standard deviation of the distribution of each of the following (binomial) random variables:
   (a) the number of heads obtained in 900 tosses of a balanced coin;
   (b) the number of cars with faulty headlights among 625 cars stopped at a road-block, if the probability that any one of the cars has faulty headlights is 0.20;
   (c) the number of seeds which will germinate among those contained in a package of 200, if the probability that any one of the seeds will germinate is 0.60;
   (d) the number of persons (among 80 visiting a dealer's showroom) who prefer to have a stick-shift in their car, if the probability that any one of them has this preference is 0.25.

6. The mean of the *hypergeometric distribution* (see Exercise 24 on page 160) is given by the formula

$$\mu = \frac{na}{a+b}$$

   (a) Find the probabilities of getting 0, 1, or 2 red beads when 2 beads are drawn (without replacement) from an urn containing 6 red beads and 4 white beads.
   (b) Calculate the mean of the probability distribution obtained in part (a) using the formula defining μ on page 164.
   (c) Use the special formula to determine the mean of the hypergeometric distribution of part (a) and compare with the result obtained in part (b).

7. Referring to part (b) of Exercise 30 on page 161, it can be shown that the probabilities of spotting 0, 1, 2, 3, 4, 5, or 6 defects are, respectively, 0.301, 0.361, 0.217, 0.087, 0.026, 0.006, 0.001, and that the probability of spotting more than 6 defects is negligible. Calculate the mean and the variance of this probability distribution and use the results to verify the fact that the mean and the variance of a *Poisson distribution* are given by $\mu = \lambda$ and $\sigma^2 = \lambda$.

8. Referring to part (a) of Exercise 5, what can we say (according to Chebyshev's Theorem) about the probability of getting anywhere from 400 to 500 heads in 900 flips of the coin?

9. Referring to part (b) of Exercise 5, what can we assert (according to Chebyshev's Theorem) about the probability that fewer than 100 of the 625 cars have faulty headlights?

10. Referring to part (c) of Exercise 5, what can we assert (according to Chebyshev's Theorem) with a probability of at least 15/16 about the number of seeds which will germinate among those in a package of 200 seeds?

11. Referring to Exercise 7, what can we say (according to Chebyshev's Theorem) about the probability of spotting more than 4 defectives? Compare this value with the actual probability of spotting more than 4 defectives as given in that exercise.

7.4 Continuous Distributions

Random variables are usually classified according to the sets of values they can assume. We speak of *discrete* random variables when they can assume only a finite set of values or as many values as there are whole numbers. The number of heads obtained in 12 flips of a coin is a discrete random variable as it cannot assume values other than 0, 1, 2, . . ., and 12; if a coin is flipped until heads appears for the first time, the number of the flip on which this occurs is also a discrete random variable, but this time the random variable can assume as many values as there are whole numbers. This is true also for a random variable having the Poisson distribution which we introduced in Exercises 29 and 30 on pages 160 and 161.

In contrast to discrete random variables, we shall say that a random variable is *continuous* if it can assume values on a continuous scale. Such quantities as time, length, and temperature are measured on continuous scales and their measurements are referred to as values of continuous random variables. In order to associate probabilities with continuous random variables, we shall now introduce the concept of a *continuous distribution*, or *probability density*.

When we first discussed histograms in Chapter 2, we pointed out that the frequencies, percentages, and proportions (and we might now add probabilities) which are associated with the various classes are represented by the *areas* of the rectangles. For example, the areas of the rectangles of Figure 7.2 represent the probabilities of getting 0, 1, 2, . . ., and 10 heads in 10 flips of a balanced coin or, better, they are equal to or proportional to these probabilities. If we now look carefully at Figure 7.3, which is an enlargement of a portion of Figure 7.2, it is apparent that the area of rectangle $ABCD$ is nearly equal to the shaded area under the continuous curve which we have drawn to approximate the histogram. Since the area of rectangle $ABCD$ is equal to (or proportional to) the probability of getting 3 heads in 10 tosses

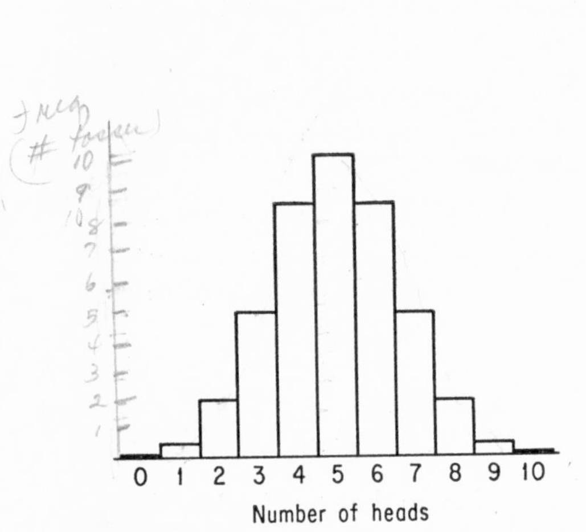

Fig. 7.2 Distribution of the number of heads in 10 flips of a coin.

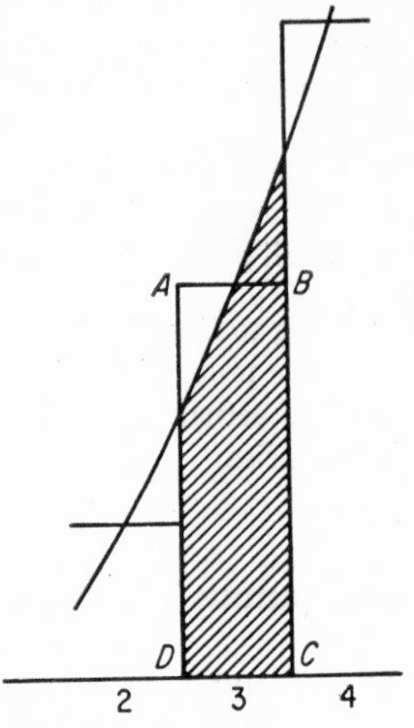

Fig. 7.3 Enlargement of part of figure 7.2.

of a balanced coin, we can say that this probability is also given by the shaded area under the continuous curve. More generally, *if a histogram is approximated by means of a smooth curve, the frequency, percentage, or probability associated with any given class (or interval) is represented by the corresponding area under the curve.*

If we approximate the income distribution on page 10 with a smooth curve, as we did in Figure 7.4, we can determine what proportion of the incomes falls into any given interval by dividing the corresponding area under the curve by the total area under the curve (which represents 100 per cent

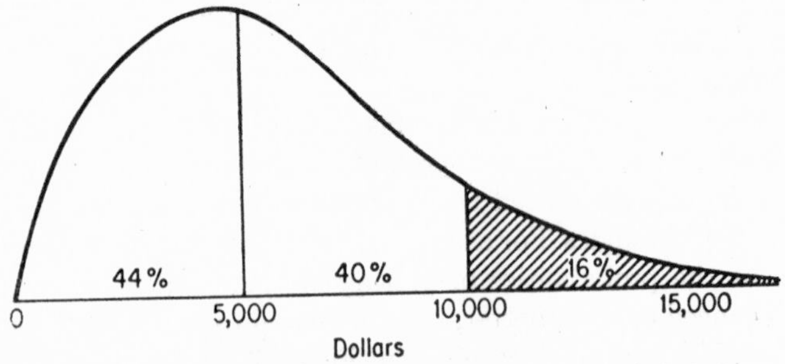

Fig. 7.4 An income distribution.

of the incomes). Thus, it can be seen that roughly 16 or 17 per cent of the incomes were $10,000 or more and that about 44 per cent of the incomes were below $5,000. We obtained these percentages by (mentally) dividing the corresponding areas under the curve by the total area under the curve.

Had we drawn Figure 7.4 so that the total area under the curve actually equaled 1, the proportion of the families belonging to any income group would have been given directly by the corresponding area under the curve. Speaking in terms of probabilities rather than proportions, we refer to a function whose graph is like that of Figure 7.4 (with the area under the curve equal to 1) as a *probability density*, and sometimes informally as a *continuous distribution.** What characterizes a probability density is the fact that *the area under the curve between two values a and b (see Figure 7.5)*

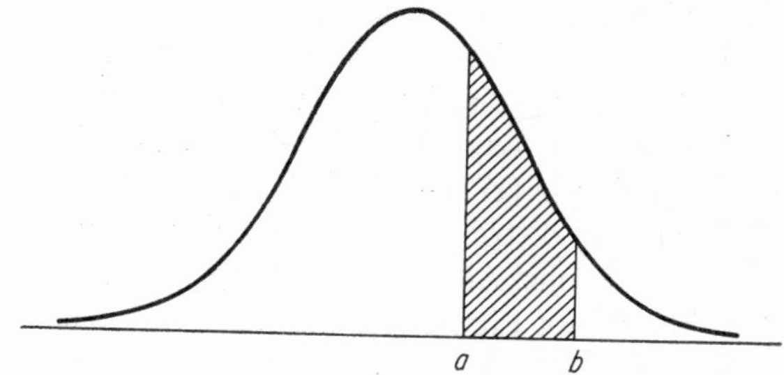

Fig. 7.5 A probability density.

is equal to the probability that a random variable having this "continuous distribution" will assume a value between a and b. Thus, when dealing with continuous random variables, probabilities are given by areas under appropriate curves.

Since continuous distributions can always be looked upon as close approximations to histograms, we can define the mean and the standard deviation of continuous distributions in the following informal way: if a continuous distribution is approximated with a sequence of histograms having narrower and narrower classes, the means of the distributions represented by these histograms will approach a value which defines the mean of the continuous distribution. Similarly, the standard deviations of these distributions will approach a value which defines the standard deviation of the continuous distribution. Intuitively speaking, the mean and the standard deviation of a continuous distribution measure the identical features as the mean and the standard deviation of a probability distribution or a

* This terminology is borrowed from physics, where usage of the terms "weight" and "density" parallels usage of the terms "probability" and "probability density" in statistics.

distribution of observed data, namely, its center and its spread. More rigorous definitions of these concepts cannot be given without the use of integral calculus.

7.5 The Normal Distribution

Among the many continuous distributions used in statistics, the *normal distribution* is by far the most important. Its study dates back to the eighteenth century and investigations into the nature of experimental errors. It was observed that discrepancies between repeated measurements of the same physical quantity displayed a surprising degree of regularity; their patterns (distribution), it was found, could be closely approximated by a certain kind of continuous distribution, referred to as the "normal curve of errors" and attributed to the laws of chance. The mathematical properties of this continuous distribution and its theoretical basis were first investigated by Pierre Laplace (1749–1827), Abraham de Moivre (1667–1745), and Carl Gauss (1777–1855).

The graph of a normal distribution is a bell-shaped curve that extends indefinitely in both directions. Although this may not be apparent from a small drawing like the one of Figure 7.6, the curve comes closer and closer

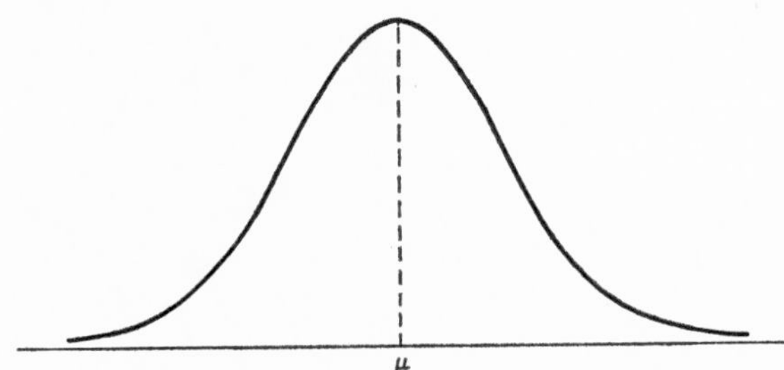

Fig. 7.6 Graph of normal distribution.

to the horizontal axis without ever reaching it, no matter how far we might go in either direction away from the mean. Fortunately, it is seldom necessary to extend the tails of a normal distribution very far because the area under that part of the curve lying more than 4 or 5 standard deviations away from the mean is for most practical purposes negligible.

An important feature of a normal distribution is that it is completely determined by its mean and its standard deviation. In other words, the mathematical equation for the normal distribution is such that we can determine the area under the curve between any two points on the horizontal scale if we are given its mean and its standard deviation. In practice, we obtain areas under the graph of a normal distribution, or simply a normal curve, by means of special tables, such as Table I at the end of the book. To be able to use this table, we shall first have to explain what is meant by the normal distribution in its *standard form* or, as it is also called, the *standard normal distribution.* Since the equation of the normal distribution depends on μ and σ, we get different curves and, hence, different areas for different values of μ and σ. For instance, Figure 7.7 shows the superimposed

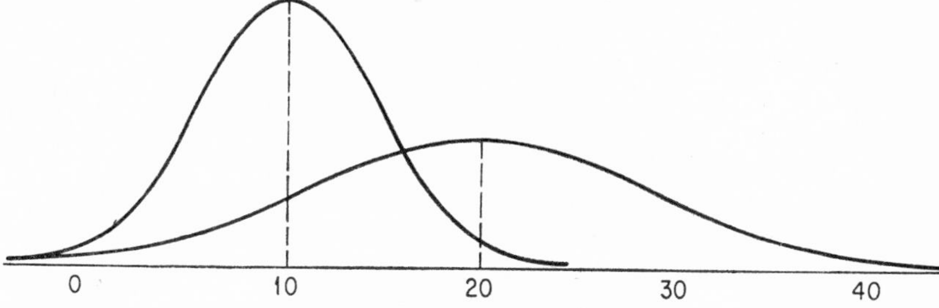

Fig. 7.7 Two normal distributions.

graphs of two normal distributions, one having $\mu = 10$ and $\sigma = 5$, and the other having $\mu = 20$ and $\sigma = 10$. As can be seen from this diagram, the area under the curve, say, between 10 and 12, is *not* the same for the two distributions.

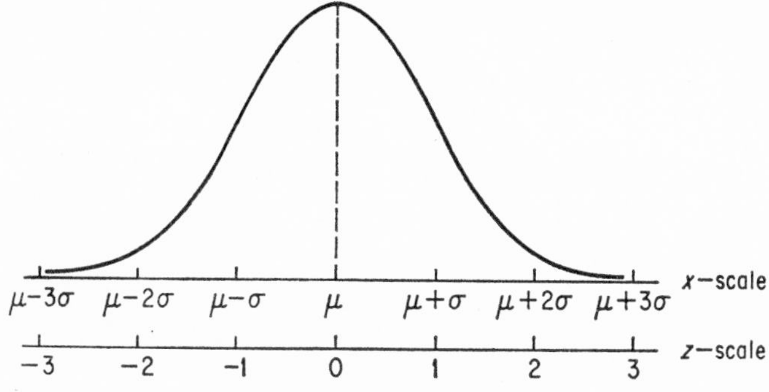

Fig. 7.8 Change of scale.

As it would be physically impossible to construct separate tables of normal curve areas for each conceivable pair of values of μ and σ, we tabulate these areas only for the so-called *standard normal distribution* which has $\mu = 0$ and $\sigma = 1$. Then, we obtain areas under *any* normal distribution by performing the change of scale shown in Figure 7.8. All we really do here is to convert the units of measurement into *standard units* (see page 68) by means of the formula

▲ $$z = \frac{x - \mu}{\sigma}$$ ▲

To find areas under normal curves whose mean and standard deviation are not 0 and 1, we have only to convert the x's (the values to the left of which, to the right of which, or between which we want to determine areas under the curve) into z's and then use Table I. *The entries in this table are the areas under the standard normal distribution between the mean* ($z = 0$) *and* $z = 0.00, 0.01, 0.02, \ldots, 3.08,$ *and* 3.09. In other words, the entries in Table I are areas under the standard normal distribution like the one shaded in Figure 7.9. Note that Table I has no entries corresponding to

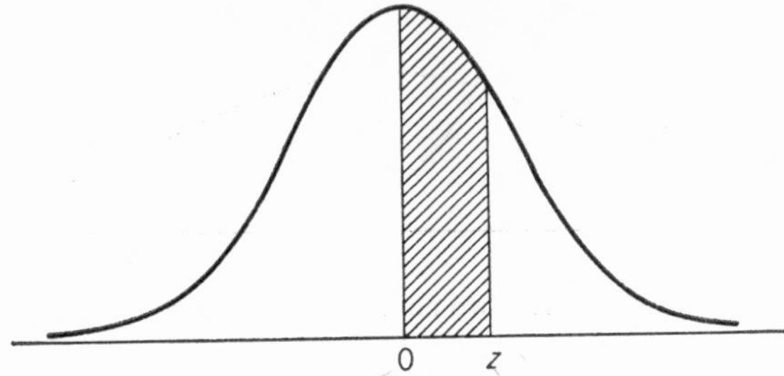

Fig. 7.9 Tabulated areas under graph of standard normal distribution.

negative values of z, but these are not needed by virtue of the *symmetry* of a normal curve about its mean. We can find the area under the standard normal distribution, say, between $z = -1.33$ and $z = 0$, by looking up instead the area between $z = 0$ and $z = 1.33$. As can be checked in Table I, the answer is 0.4082.

Questions concerning areas under normal distributions arise in various ways, and the ability to find any desired area quickly can be a big help. For instance, although the table gives only areas between the mean $z = 0$ and selected positive values of z, we often have to find areas to the right of a given value of z, to the right or left of $-z$, between two given values of z, and so forth. Finding any one of these areas is easy, provided we remember exactly what area corresponds to an entry in the table and we make use of the fact that the normal curve is symmetrical, so that the area to the left of $z = 0$ as well as the area to the right of $z = 0$ is equal to 0.5000. With this knowledge we find, for example, that the probability of getting a z less than 0.94 (the area under the curve to the left of $z = 0.94$) is $0.5000 + 0.3264 = 0.8264$, and that the probability of getting a z greater than -0.65 (the area under the curve to the right of $z = -0.65$) is $0.5000 + 0.2422$ (see also Figure 7.10). Similarly, we find that the probability of getting a z greater than 1.76 is $0.5000 - 0.4608 = 0.0392$, and that the probability of getting a z less than -0.85 is $0.5000 - 0.3023 = 0.1977$ (see Figure 7.10). The probability of getting a z between 0.87 and 1.28 is $0.3997 - 0.3078 =$

0.0919, and the probability of getting a z between -0.34 and 0.62 is 0.1331 + 0.2324 = 0.3655 (see Figure 7.10).

There are also problems in which we are given areas under the normal

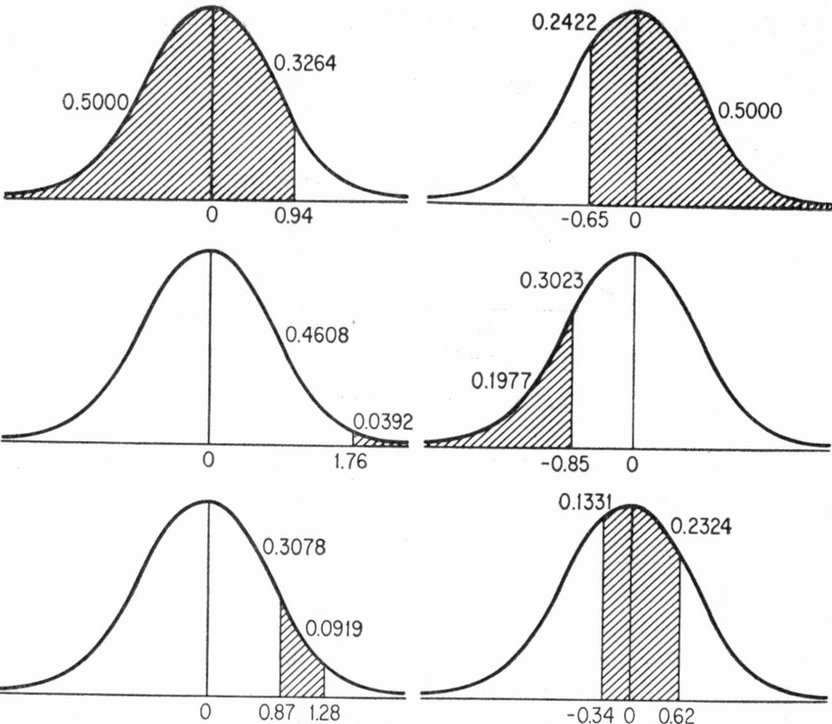

Fig. 7.10 Areas under the standard normal distribution.

curve and we are asked to find corresponding values of z. For instance, if we want to find a z which is such that the area to its right equals 0.1000, it is apparent from Figure 7.11 that this z will have to correspond to an entry

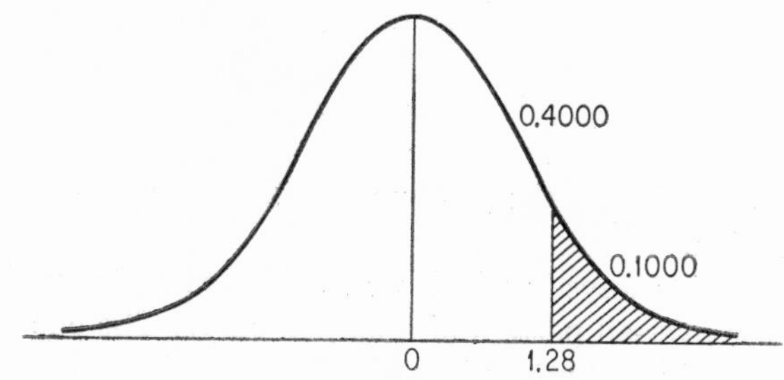

Fig.7. 11 Area under normal curve.

of 0.4000 in Table I. Referring to this table, we find that the closest value is $z = 1.28$.

To give an example in which we must first convert to standard units, let us suppose that a random variable has a normal distribution with $\mu = 24$ and $\sigma = 12$, and that we want to find the probability that it will assume

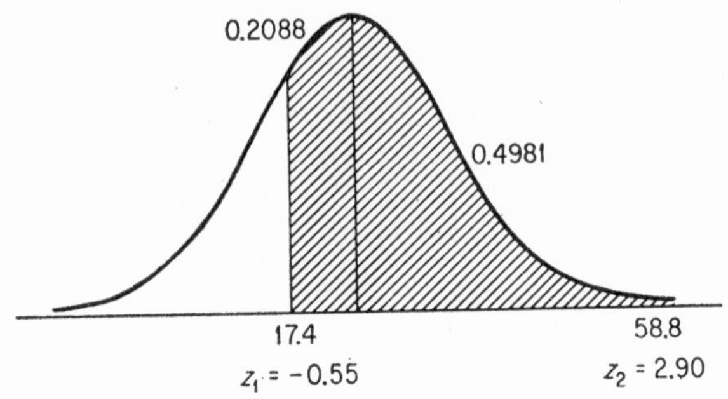

Fig. 7.12 Area under normal curve.

a value between 17.4 and 58.8 (see Figure 7.12). Converting to standard units we obtain

$$z_1 = \frac{17.4 - 24}{12} = -0.55 \quad \text{and} \quad z_2 = \frac{58.8 - 24}{12} = 2.90$$

and since the areas corresponding to these z's are 0.2088 and 0.4981, respectively, the answer is $0.2088 + 0.4981 = 0.7069$.

In many of the applications we shall discuss in this and in later chapters it will be assumed that we are dealing with data whose distribution can be approximated closely with a normal curve. This requires some elaboration, because the area under a normal curve is by definition equal to 1, and this may not be the case for the histogram of a distribution which the normal curve is to approximate. To avoid this difficulty we can either modify the histogram of the observed distribution so that the area of each rectangle actually equals the *proportion* of the items falling into the corresponding class, or we can "enlarge" the normal curve, that is, change the vertical scale, so that the area under the curve equals the total area of the rectangles of the histogram. Actually, this is a technicality we shall not have to worry about in this chapter; we shall refer to it again briefly in Exercise 12 on page 300, where we shall discuss the problem of fitting a normal curve to an observed distribution.

There are various ways in which we can test whether an observed distribution fits the over-all pattern of a normal curve. The one we shall discuss here is not the best; it is largely subjective, but it has the decided advantage that it is very easy to perform. To illustrate this technique, let us refer again to the radiation-count distribution of Chapter 2; converting this distribution into a "less than" percentage distribution, we have

Number of Particles	*Cumulative Percentages*
less than 4.5	0
less than 9.5	1
less than 14.5	11
less than 19.5	48
less than 24.5	84
less than 29.5	97
less than 34.5	99
less than 39.5	100

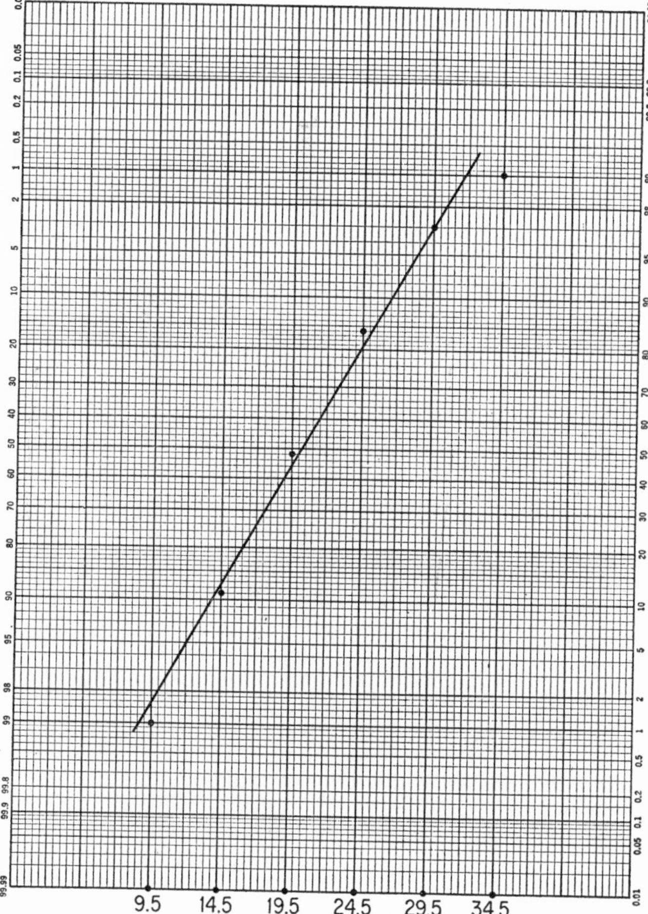

Fig. 7.13 Arithmetic probability paper.

where we indicated the class boundaries (rather than the class limits) in the left-hand column.

Before we actually plot this cumulative percentage distribution on the special graph paper illustrated in Figure 7.13, let us briefly investigate its scales. As can be seen from Figure 7.13, the cumulative percentage scale is already marked off in the rather unusual pattern which makes the paper suitable for our special purpose. The other scale consists of equal subdivisions that are not labeled; in our problem they will be used to indicate the class boundaries 9.5, 14.5, 19.5, 24.5, 29.5, and 34.5. The graph paper shown in Figure 7.13 (which is commercially available) is called *arithmetic probability paper*.

If we now plot the cumulative "less than" percentages corresponding to 9.5, 14.5, 19.5, 24.5, 29.5, and 34.5, we obtain the six points shown in Figure 7.13. *If such points lie very close to a straight line, we consider this as evidence that the distribution follows the general pattern of a normal distribution.* In our example, the six points lie fairly close to the solid line, and we conclude that the over-all shape of the radiation-count distribution follows quite closely the pattern of a normal distribution. (Actually, in a graph like that of Figure 7.13 only large and obvious departures from a line are real evidence that the data do not follow the pattern of a normal curve.) Note that in Figure 7.13 we did not plot points corresponding to 0 and 100 per cent of the data; as we pointed out earlier, the normal curve never quite reaches the horizontal axis no matter how far we go away from the mean in either direction.

It must be understood that the use of arithmetic probability paper, which should really be called *normal probability paper*, is only an approximate (and highly subjective) device for checking whether a distribution follows the pattern of a normal curve. A more objective way will be introduced later in Exercise 12 on page 300. Let us also point out that the special graph paper shown in Figure 7.13 can be used to get quick estimates of the mean and the standard deviation of a distribution having, roughly, the shape of a normal distribution. How this is done is explained in Exercise 9 below.

EXERCISES

1. The *exponential distribution* is another continuous distribution which has many applications in problems of statistical inference. If a random variable has an exponential distribution with the mean μ, the probability that it assumes a value between 0 and a given *positive* value x (see shaded area of Figure 7.14) is $1 - e^{-x/\mu}$. Here e is the constant 2.71828... which also appears in the formula for the Poisson distribution; values of $e^{-x/\mu}$ can be obtained directly from Table X.

(a) Find the probabilities that a random variable having an exponential distribution with $\mu = 10$ assumes a value between 0 and 3, a value greater than 8, and a value between 9 and 11.

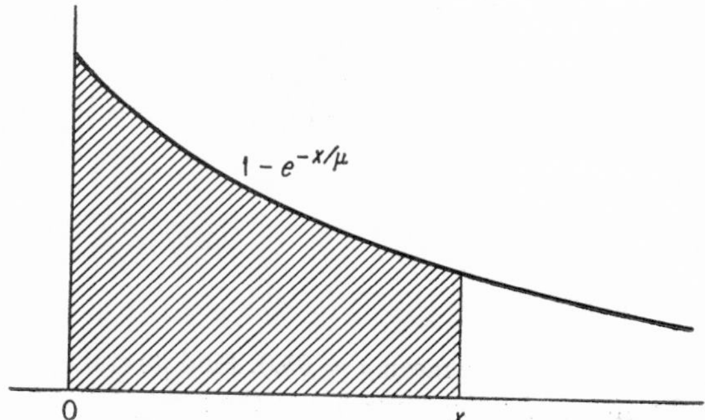

Fig. 7.14 Exponential distribution.

(b) The lifetime of a certain kind of battery is a random variable which has an exponential distribution with a mean of 250 hours. What is the probability that such a battery will last at most 200 hours? Also find the probability that such a battery will last anywhere from 300 to 400 hours.

(c) Medical research has shown that the interval between successive reports of a rare contagious disease is a random variable having an exponential distribution with a mean of 120 days. What is the probability of not getting a report on an incidence of the disease for at least 180 days from the day the last case was reported?

2. Find the area under the standard normal distribution which lies
(a) between $z = 0$ and $z = 1.50$;
(b) between $z = -0.63$ and $z = 0$;
(c) to the right of $z = 2.37$;
(d) to the left of $z = 1.06$;
(e) to the right of $z = -0.92$;
(f) to the left of $z = -1.54$;
(g) between $z = 1.27$ and $z = 1.73$;
(h) between $z = -0.80$ and $z = -1.75$;
(i) between $z = -1.35$ and $z = 1.42$.

3. Find z if
(a) the normal curve area between 0 and z is 0.3729;
(b) the normal curve area to the right of z is 0.2946;
(c) the normal curve area to the right of z is 0.5948;
(d) the normal curve area to the left of z is 0.0075;
(e) the normal curve area between $-z$ and z is 0.8324.

4. Find the probability that a random variable having a standard normal distribution assumes a value between $-z$ and z if
(a) $z = 1$; (b) $z = 2$; (c) $z = 3$.

5. In later chapters we shall use the symbol z_α to denote the value for which the area under the standard normal distribution *to its right* is equal to α. Find

(a) $z_{0.10}$; (c) $z_{0.025}$; (e) $z_{0.01}$;
(b) $z_{0.05}$; (d) $z_{0.02}$; (f) $z_{0.005}$.

6. A random variable has a normal distribution with the mean $\mu = 121.8$ and the standard deviation $\sigma = 5.9$. What is the probability that this random variable assumes a value
(a) less than 127.6;
(b) greater than 113.4;
(c) between 124.6 and 125.9;
(d) between 118.5 and 123.5?

7. A normal distribution has the mean $\mu = 95.0$. Find its standard deviation if 20 per cent of the area under the curve lies to the right of 103.4.

8. A random variable has a normal distribution with a standard deviation of 24.5. Find its mean if the probability that the random variable assumes a value less than 60.0 equals 0.3745.

9. Arithmetic probability paper can be used to obtain crude estimates of the mean and the standard deviation of a distribution, provided that this distribution follows fairly closely the pattern of a normal curve. To find the mean, we have only to observe that since the normal distribution is symmetrical, 50 per cent of the area under the curve lies to the left of the mean. Hence, if we check the 50 per cent mark on the vertical scale and go horizontally to the line we fit to the points, then the corresponding point on the horizontal scale provides an estimate of the mean of the distribution. To obtain an estimate of the standard deviation, let us observe that the area under the standard normal distribution to the left of $z = -1$ is roughly 0.16 and that the area to the left of $z = +1$ is roughly 0.84. Hence, if we check 16 and 84 per cent on the vertical scale, we can judge by the straight line we have fitted to the points (representing the cumulative distribution of the data) what values on the horizontal scale correspond to $z = -1$ and $z = +1$; their difference divided by 2 provides an estimate of the standard deviation. Use this method to estimate the mean and the standard deviation of the radiation-count distribution from Figure 7.13 and compare with the results obtained in Chapters 3 and 4.

10. Plot the cumulative "less than" percentages of whichever data you grouped among those of the exercises on pages 23 through 26 on arithmetic probability paper and judge whether a normal curve provides a reasonably good fit. If the fit is good, use the method of Exercise 9 to estimate the mean and the standard deviation of the distribution and compare with the exact values previously obtained.

11. Convert the frequency distribution of Exercise 15 on page 71 into a cumulative "less than" percentage distribution and use arithmetic probability paper to judge whether the shape of this distribution is roughly that of a normal curve.

12. The following is a distribution of the weights of 200 freshmen entering a Western college:

Weight (pounds)	*Number of Freshmen*
120.0 – 129.9	4
130.0 – 139.9	16
140.0 – 149.9	35
150.0 – 159.9	44
160.0 – 169.9	50
170.0 – 179.9	31
180.0 – 189.9	15
190.0 – 199.9	5
	200

(a) Convert this distribution into a cumulative "less than" percentage distribution and use arithmetic probability paper to judge whether the distribution has roughly the shape of a normal curve.

(b) Use the method explained in Exercise 9 to estimate the mean and the standard deviation of this distribution.

7.6 Applications of the Normal Distribution

When we discussed the standard deviation in Chapter 4, we mentioned that in practice we often meet distributions for which certain fixed proportions of the items fall within one standard deviation of the mean, within two standard deviations of the mean, and so on. Actually, we were referring to distributions that can be approximated closely with normal curves, and we can now verify these proportions with the use of Table I. Since the tabular values corresponding to $z = 1$, $z = 2$, and $z = 3$ are 0.3413, 0.4772, and 0.4987, respectively, we find that, roughly, 68 per cent of the area under a normal curve falls between $z = -1$ and $z = 1$, about 95 per cent of the area falls between $z = -2$ and $z = 2$, while 99.7 per cent of the area falls between $z = -3$ and $z = 3$. In other words, *if a distribution can be approximated closely with a normal curve, the proportions of the cases falling within one, two, or three standard deviations of the mean are, respectively, 0.68, 0.95, and 0.997.*

Let us now consider some applied problems in which we shall assume that the distribution of the data with which we are dealing can be approximated closely with a normal curve. Suppose, for instance, that the number of telephone calls made daily in a certain community between 3 P.M. and 5 P.M. is a random variable having a normal distribution with a mean of

584 and a standard deviation of 26. What we would like to know is the probability that there will be more than 600 calls between 3 P.M. and 5 P.M. on a given day. Note, first of all, that the number of telephone calls made in the community during the given period of time is a *discrete* random variable and that we shall, therefore, have to make what is called a *continuity correction.* This consists of representing each integer k (each value the random variable can assume) by the interval from $k - \frac{1}{2}$ to $k + \frac{1}{2}$. Thus 600 is represented by the interval from 599.5 to 600.5, and the occurrence of more than 600 calls is represented by the interval to the right of

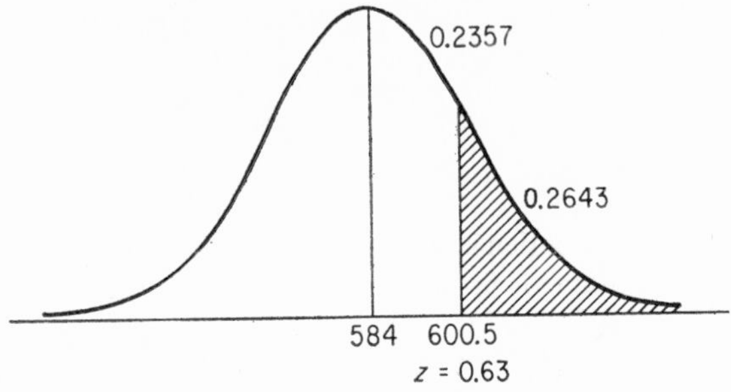

Fig. 7.15 Distribution of number of telephone calls.

600.5, namely, the shaded area of Figure 7.15. Changing 600.5 into standard units, we obtain

$$z = \frac{600.5 - 584}{26} = 0.63$$

and the corresponding entry in Table I is 0.2357. Hence, the shaded area of Figure 7.15 is $0.5000 - 0.2357 = 0.2643$ and we find that the desired probability for more than 600 calls is approximately 0.26; the odds against it are slightly less than 3 to 1.

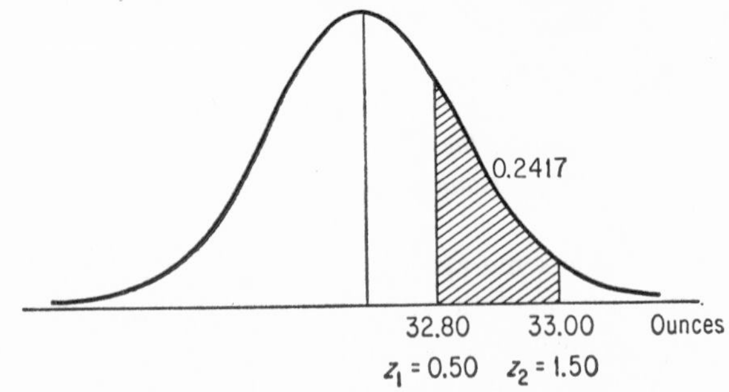

Fig. 7.16 Distribution of weight of milk cartons.

To consider another example, suppose that the weights of all quart cartons of milk from a certain dairy have a mean of 32.70 ounces and a standard deviation of 0.20 ounces. Assuming that the weights can be measured to any degree of accuracy and that the distribution of the weights can be approximated closely with a normal curve, we want to know what percentage of the cartons weigh between 32.80 and 33.00 ounces. Since the weights are values of a continuous random variable there is no need for a continuity correction, and we must look for the area under the normal curve between 32.80 and 33.00, namely, the shaded area of Figure 7.16. Converting 32.80 and 33.00 into standard units, we obtain

$$z_1 = \frac{32.80 - 32.70}{0.20} = 0.50 \quad \text{and} \quad z_2 = \frac{33.00 - 32.70}{0.20} = 1.50$$

and the corresponding entries in Table I are 0.1915 and 0.4332. It follows that the desired percentage is $0.4332 - 0.1915 = 0.2417$; that is, roughly 24 per cent of the cartons weigh between 32.80 and 33.00 ounces.

To consider a somewhat different problem, suppose that a very large set of final examination grades has a mean of 66.3 and a standard deviation of 13.7. What we would like to know is what grade is the lowest possible A, if the top 10 per cent of the students are to receive A's and it can be assumed that the distribution of the grades follows the over-all pattern of a normal curve. This problem differs from the preceding ones inasmuch as we are now given the percentage and we are asked to find the corresponding z and x. As is apparent from Figure 7.17, we must first find the z which

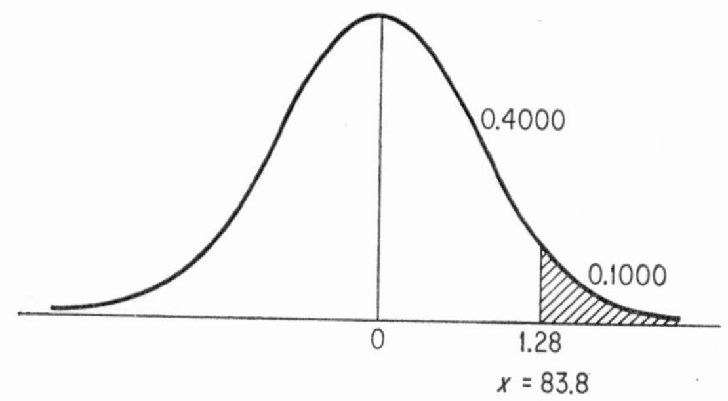

Fig. 7.17 Distribution of final examination grades.

corresponds to an area of $0.5000 - 0.1000 = 0.4000$, and Table I shows that the nearest value is $z = 1.28$. Substituting into the formula for converting measurements into standard units, we get

$$1.28 = \frac{x - 66.3}{13.7}$$

and upon solving for x we obtain $x = 1.28(13.7) + 66.3 = 83.8$; thus, the lowest A is a grade of 84.

The normal distribution is sometimes introduced as a continuous distribution which provides a very close approximation to the binomial distribution when n, the number of trials, is very large and p, the probability of a success on an individual trial, is close to 0.50. Figure 7.18 contains

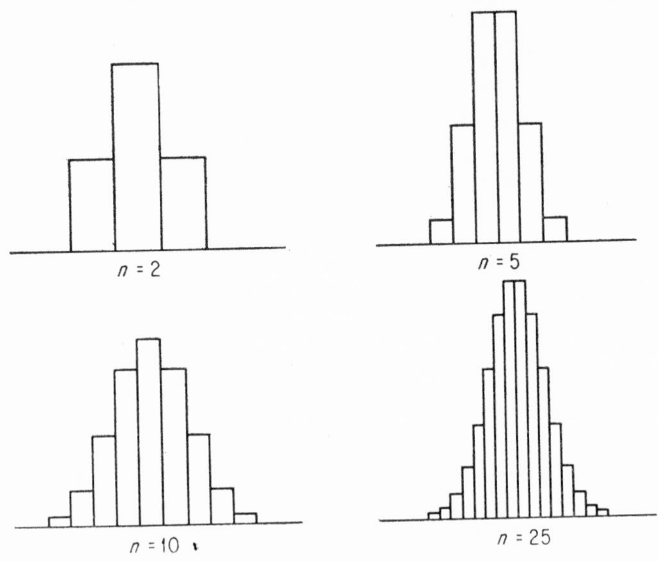

Fig. 7.18 Binomial distributions with $p = 0.50$.

the histograms of binomial distributions having $p = 0.50$ and $n = 2, 5, 10$, and 25, and it can be seen that with increasing n these distributions approach the symmetrical bell-shaped pattern of the normal distribution. In fact, a normal curve with the mean $\mu = np$ and the standard deviation $\sigma = \sqrt{np(1-p)}$ can often be used to approximate a binomial distribution even when n is "not too large" and p differs from 0.50, but is not too close to either 0 or 1. A good rule of thumb is to use this approximation only when np as well as $n(1-p)$ are both greater than 5.

To illustrate this normal curve approximation of the binomial distribution, let us first consider the probability of getting 4 heads in 12 tosses of a balanced coin. Substituting $n = 12$, $x = 4$, $p = 1/2$, and $\binom{12}{4} = 495$ into the formula on page 153, we get

$$495\left(\frac{1}{2}\right)^4\left(1 - \frac{1}{2}\right)^8 = \frac{495}{4{,}096}$$

or approximately 0.12. To find the normal curve approximation to this probability, we shall again have to use the *continuity correction* mentioned on page 182, namely, represent 4 (heads) by the interval from 3.5 to 4.5 (see Figure 7.19). Since $\mu = 12(1/2) = 6$ and $\sigma = \sqrt{12(1/2)(1/2)} = 1.732$, it

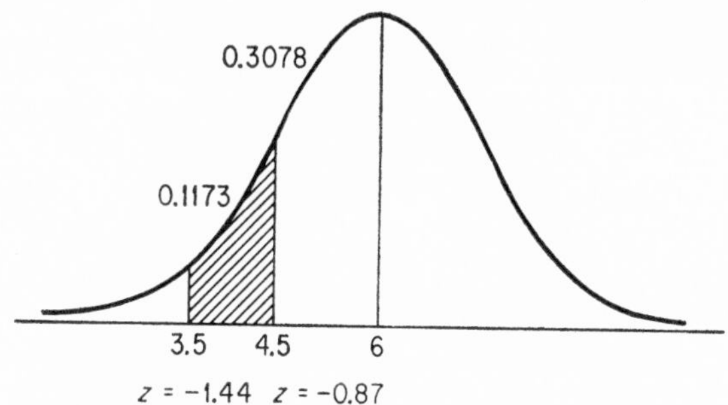

Fig. 7.19 Distribution of number of heads ($n = 12$).

follows that the values between which we want to determine the area under the normal curve are, in standard units,

$$\frac{3.5 - 6}{1.732} = -1.44 \quad \text{and} \quad \frac{4.5 - 6}{1.732} = -0.87$$

The corresponding entries in Table I are 0.4251 and 0.3078, and the required probability is $0.4251 - 0.3078 = 0.1173$. Note that the difference between this value and the one obtained with the formula for the binomial distribution is negligible for most practical purposes.

The normal curve approximation of the binomial distribution is particularly useful in problems where we would otherwise have to use the formula for the binomial distribution repeatedly to obtain the values of many different terms. Suppose, for example, we want to know the probability of getting at least 12 replies to mail-questionnaires sent to 100 persons, when the probability that any one of them will reply is 0.18. In other words, we want to know the probability of getting at least 12 successes in 100 trials when the probability of a success on an individual trial is 0.18. In we tried to solve this problem by using the formula for the binomial distribution, we would have to find the sum of the probabilities corresponding to 12, 13, 14, . . ., and 100 successes (or those corresponding to 0, 1, 2, . . ., and 11). Evidently, this would involve a tremendous amount of work. On the other hand, using the normal curve approximation we have only to find the shaded area of Figure 7.20, namely, the area to the right of 11.5. Note that we are again using the continuity correction according to which 12 is represented by the interval from 11.5 to 12.5, 13 is represented by the interval from 12.5 to 13.5, and so on.

Since $\mu = 100(0.18) = 18$ and $\sigma = \sqrt{100(0.18)(0.82)} = 3.84$, we find that in standard units 11.5 becomes

$$\frac{11.5 - 18}{3.84} = -1.69$$

and that the desired probability is $0.4545 + 0.5000 = 0.9545$. This means that we can expect to get at least 12 replies to 100 of these questionnaires *about 95 per cent of the time*, provided that 0.18 is the correct figure for the probability that any one person will reply. It is interesting to note that, rounded to two decimals, the *actual* value of this probability (obtained from an appropriate table) is 0.96.

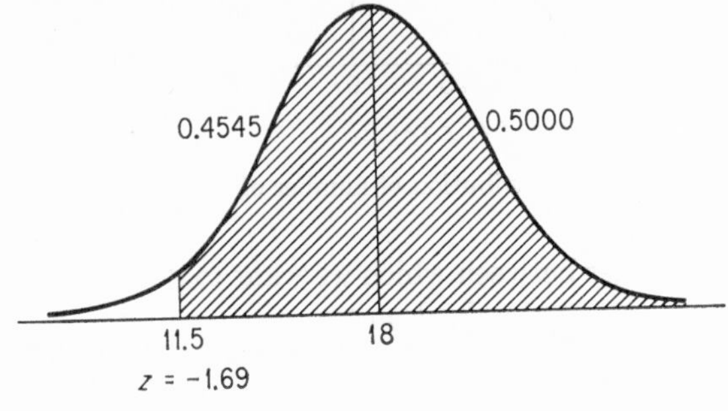

Fig. 7.20 Distribution of number of replies.

The fact that the normal distribution is the only continuous distribution discussed so far in this text (except for the distribution of Exercise 1 on page 178) may have given the erroneous impression that it is the only one that matters in the study of statistics. Although it is true that the normal distribution plays an important role in many applications, its indiscriminate use can yield very misleading results. In later chapters we shall meet several other continuous distributions, among them the *t distribution*, the *chi-square distribution*, and the *F distribution*, which play important roles in problems of statistical inference.

EXERCISES

1. The burning time of a rocket is a random variable having a normal distribution with $\mu = 3.685$ seconds and $\sigma = 0.036$ seconds.

(a) What is the probability that such a rocket will burn for less than 3.600 seconds?

(b) What is the probability that such a rocket will burn for more than 3.700 seconds?

(c) What is the probability that such a rocket will burn anywhere from 3.650 to 3.750 seconds?

2. In a large suburban area, the monthly food expenditures of families with annual incomes between \$8,000 and \$10,000 are approximately normally distributed with a mean of \$124.72 and a standard deviation of \$21.55.

(a) What proportion of these families have monthly food expenditures less than \$100.00?

(b) What proportion of these families have monthly food expenditures greater than \$130.00?

(c) Above what value does one find the highest 25 per cent of these monthly food expenditures?

3. Among the 4,000 employees of a large company, I.Q. is approximately normally distributed with a mean of 104 and a standard deviation of 15. If it is known that a particular job requires a minimum I.Q. of 98 while it bores those with an I.Q. over 110, how many of the employees are suitable for this job on the basis of I.Q. alone? (Use continuity correction.)

4. A machine is set to fill "eight-ounce net" cans of instant coffee with 8.1 ounces on the average. If it is known from experience that the distribution of the weights is approximately normal with a standard deviation of 0.08 ounces, how many of a lot of 100,000 cans may be expected to contain less than the desired eight-ounce net?

5. The average time required to perform Job A is 75 minutes with a standard deviation of 15 minutes, and the average time required to perform Job B is 100 minutes with a standard deviation of 10 minutes. Assuming normal distributions, what proportion of the time will Job A take longer than the average Job B, and what proportion of the time will Job B take less time than the average Job A?

6. In 1945, after World War II, all servicemen were given point scores based on length of service, number of purple hearts, number of decorations, campaigns, etc. Assuming that the distribution of these point scores can be approximated closely with a normal curve whose mean and standard deviation are 63 and 20, respectively, how many men from an army of 8,000,000 would be discharged if the army discharged all men with more than 79 points? (Courtesy, Department of Mathematics, U.S. Military Academy.)

7. Find the probability of getting 4 heads in 14 tosses of a balanced coin using (a) the formula for the binomial distribution, and (b) the normal curve approximation.

8. Use the normal curve approximation to find the probability of getting more than 325 heads in 600 flips of a balanced coin.

9. Use the normal curve approximation to find the probability of getting anywhere from 50 to 70 ones in 360 rolls of a balanced die.

10. A multiple-choice test consists of 200 questions, each with four possible answers. What is the probability of getting more than 60 correct answers, if one were to answer each question by drawing (with replacement) a card from an ordinary deck of 52 playing cards and basing one's decision on the card's suit?

11. If 40 per cent of the customers of a service station use their credit cards, what is the probability that among 300 customers more than 200 *pay cash?*

12. If 60 per cent of the voters in a large school district are for a new bond issue while 40 per cent are against it, what is the probability that the bond issue will nevertheless be defeated if a random sample of only 160 of the voters actually goes to the polls?

13. It is known that on the average 1 per cent of the fuzes delivered to an army arsenal are duds. What is the probability that among 800 of these fuzes there are 10 or more duds?

14. Television Network A claims that 20 per cent of the viewers will be tuned to its stations during the coverage of a Presidential news conference. If this figure is correct, what is the probability that among 500 viewers reached by telephone during this telecast fewer than 80 will be tuned to Network A?

15. It is known that 30 per cent of the mice used in an experiment can be expected to die after being administered a given dosage of an experimental drug. What is the probability that among 150 mice which received the drug more than 50 will die?

BIBLIOGRAPHY

The following are two widely used tables of binomial probabilities.

Tables of the Binomial Probability Distribution, National Bureau of Standards Applied Mathematics Series No. 6. Washington, D.C.: U.S. Government Printing Office, 1950.

Romig, H. G., *50–100 Binomial Tables*. New York: John Wiley & Sons, Inc., 1953.

Derivations of the formulas for the mean and the standard deviation of the binomial distribution may be found in

Freund, J. E., *Mathematical Statistics*. Englewood Cliffs, N.J.: Prentice-Hall, Inc., 1962.

and in many other textbooks on mathematical statistics.

EIGHT
Sampling and Sampling Distributions

8.1 Random Sampling

In Chapter 3 we made the following distinction between populations and samples: a population consists of all conceivably or hypothetically possible instances (or observations) of a given phenomenon, while a sample is simply a part (subset) of a population. Now let us distinguish further between populations that are *finite* and those that are *infinite*. A population is said to be *finite* if it consists of a finite, or fixed number, of elements (items, objects, measurements, or observations). In statistics, we are concerned mainly with populations whose elements are numbers, such as the finite population which consists of the I.Q.'s of all the students enrolled at Cornell University or the finite population which consists of the relative humidity readings taken at all official weather stations throughout the United States at noon on January 1, 1968.

In contrast to finite populations, a population is said to be *infinite* if there is (at least hypothetically) no limit to the number of elements it can contain. For instance, the population consisting of the results of all hypothetically possible rolls of a pair of dice is an infinite population, and so is the one consisting of all the hypothetically possible multiplications that could be performed by a digital computer. Also, we may want to look at the weights of 5 mice as a sample from the hypothetically infinite population consisting of the weights of all past, present, and future mice, and we may want to look at the number of mistakes three secretaries made in copying a technical report as a sample from the hypothetically infinite population consisting of the number of mistakes these secretaries (and, perhaps, other secretaries) might make while copying similar reports.

The purpose of most statistical investigations is to generalize from samples about both finite and infinite populations, and there are certain rules that must be observed to avoid getting results which are obviously poor, irrelevant, or invalid. Suppose, for instance, that we want to determine how much money the average person spends on his vacation. It seems unlikely that we would arrive at anything even remotely accurate, if we based our conclusions only on information supplied by Deluxe Class passengers on a two-week ocean cruise. Similarly, we can hardly expect to obtain reasonable generalizations about personal income in the United States from data reporting only the incomes of doctors, and we can hardly expect to infer much about wholesale prices of farm products in general on the basis of figures pertaining only to wholesale prices of fresh asparagus. These examples are, of course, extreme, but they serve to emphasize the point that sound generalizations (that is, sound inferences) do not come easily.

The whole problem of when and under what conditions samples permit reasonable generalizations is not easily answered. In most of the theory we shall develop in this book it will be assumed that we are dealing with a particular kind of sample called a *random sample*. (Other kinds of sampling procedures will be discussed very briefly in Section 8.2.) To illustrate the notion of a *random sample from a finite population*, let us consider first a finite population consisting of 5 elements which we shall label a, b, c, d, and e. (These might be the incomes of 5 professors, the weights of 5 students, the prices of 5 kinds of tires, and so on.) To begin with, let us see how many different samples of, say, size 3 can be taken from this finite population. To answer this question, we have only to refer to the theorem on page 152, according to which there are $\binom{n}{r}$ ways in which r objects can be selected from a set of n objects. For our example, we have $n = 5$, $r = 3$, and there are therefore $\binom{5}{3} = 10$ different samples; one of these contains the elements a, b, c, another contains the elements a, c, e, a third contains the elements b, d, e, and so forth.

If we select one of the 10 possible samples in such a way that each has the same probability of being chosen, we say that we have a *simple random sample*, or more briefly, a *random sample*. One way in which this might be done is by writing each combination on a slip of paper, mixing the slips thoroughly, and then drawing one without looking. It would seem reasonable to say that with this method of selection each sample has a probability of 1/10 of being drawn. *More generally, a sample of size n taken from a population of size N is referred to as random if each of the $\binom{N}{n}$ possible samples has the same chance, namely, a probability of $1/\binom{N}{n}$, of being chosen.* This clearly conveys the idea that the selection of a random sample must, in some way, be left to chance; in fact, it is common practice to use various kinds of gambling devices as sampling aids.

In most realistic problems it is impossible, or at least impractical, to proceed as in our example; if a random sample of size 3 had to be drawn from a finite population of size 100, we would require 161,700 slips of paper to list all possible samples. Fortunately, such an elaborate and tedious procedure is unnecessary, since we can achieve the identical results by choosing the sample values one at a time, making sure that in each successive drawing each of the remaining elements of the population has the same chance of being selected. To obtain a random sample of size 3 from a population of size 100, we might thus list each element on a slip of paper, mix the 100 slips of paper thoroughly, and then draw 3 in succession. Similarly, if we wanted to investigate the attitudes of the 220 members of a county's Medical Association toward a proposed piece of legislation, we could select a random sample of, say, 10 by writing each name on a slip of paper, mixing them thoroughly, and drawing 10 without looking.

As we have indicated earlier, the use of a gambling device can become impractical, but there exists a device which does most of the work for us. It is a table of *random numbers* (or *random digits*) which consists of many pages on which the digits 0, 1, 2, 3, . . . , and 9 are recorded in "random" fashion, much as they would appear if they had been generated by a gambling device giving each digit an equal probability of being selected. In fact, we could construct such a table ourselves by using a perfectly constructed spinner like the one shown in Figure 8.1. In actual practice, most tables of random numbers like Table VIII at the end of the book are generated by means of electronic computers; several commercially published tables of random numbers are listed in the Bibliography at the end of this chapter.

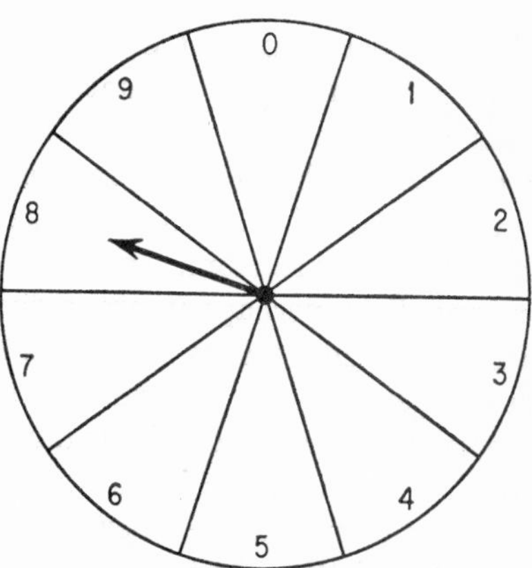

Fig. 8.1 Spinner.

Working with prepared tables of random numbers, it is quite simple to select a random sample from a finite population. Referring again to the problem of selecting 10 of the 220 members of a Medical Association, we might number the doctors 000, 001, 002, 003, . . . , and 219, arbitrarily pick a page in a table of random numbers, a row and three columns from which to start, and then move down the page reading off 3-digit numbers. For instance, if we arbitrarily use the table on page 393 and the 6th, 7th, and 8th columns starting with the 5th row, our sample will consist of the Association's members whose numbers are

018 154 216 136 063 081 178 184 049 055

Note that in this selection we ignored numbers exceeding 219 and we also ignored (or would have ignored) each number after it has occurred for the first time. Incidentally, if we had wanted to be "even more random" in this example, we could have left the selection of the page, columns, and row to chance by using some gambling device or, perhaps, another page of random numbers.

Having defined random sampling from finite populations and having indicated how random samples can be obtained with the use of gambling devices or random numbers, we should add that in actual practice this is often easier said than done. For example, if we wanted to estimate (on the basis of a sample) the average outside diameter of a lot of 100,000 ball bearings packed in large cases, it would hardly be practical to number the bearings 000,001, 000,002, 000,003, ..., 100,000, choose 6-digit numbers from a table of random numbers, and locate the corresponding bearings as their numbers appeared. Similarly, it would be virtually impossible to sample trees in the Rocky Mountains by assigning a number to each tree or to sample housewives in Chicago by assigning each one a number and then proceeding with the use of random numbers. In situations like these there is really little choice but to proceed according to the dictionary definition of the word "random," namely, "haphazardly without definite aim or purpose," or perhaps improve the situation by using one of the special sample designs treated in Section 8.2. In the first case we might well keep our fingers crossed that the samples we get will be such that statistical theory otherwise reserved for random samples can nevertheless be applied. This is true, particularly, in situations where we have little control over the selection of our data—for example, in medical studies where we often have to be satisfied with whatever cases happen to be available.

To this point we have been discussing only random sampling from finite populations. The concept of a random sample from an *infinite* population is somewhat more difficult to explain. To give a simple illustration, let us consider 10 flips of a balanced coin as a sample from the (hypothetically) infinite population which consists of all possible flips of the coin. We shall consider these 10 flips as a random sample provided the probability of getting heads was the same for each flip and if, furthermore, the 10 flips were independent. In general, we shall assert that *the selection of each item in a random sample from an infinite population must be controlled by the same probabilities, and successive selections must be independent of one another.* When we refer to measurements or observations (say, the weights of 10 persons, the diameters of 15 skulls, or the speeds of 50 cars) as random samples from infinite populations, it is thus implied that the above conditions are satisfied, or at least approximated, in obtaining the data.

8.2 Sample Designs

If we cannot take a simple random sample from a given population, it may nevertheless be possible to preserve some of the essential features of randomness by using one of the many *sample designs* developed for this purpose. *A sample design is a definite plan, completely determined before any data are collected, for obtaining a sample from a given population.* Thus, the plan to take a simple random sample of size 10 from among the 220 members of a Medical Association by using a table of random numbers in a prescribed way constitutes a sample design. Generally speaking, there are always many ways in which a sample can be taken from a given population; some of these are quite simple, while others are relatively involved. Sometimes two or more procedures are combined in sampling different parts of the same population. In the remainder of this section, we shall briefly mention some of the most important kinds of sample designs; detailed treatments of this subject are referred to in the Bibliography at the end of the chapter.

Systematic Sampling. There are many situations where the most practical way of sampling is to select, say, every 20th voucher in a file, every 10th name on a list, every 50th piece coming off an assembly line, and so on. Sampling of this sort is referred to as *systematic sampling,* and an element of randomness can be introduced into this kind of sampling by using random numbers or some gambling device to pick the unit with which to start. Although a systematic sample may not be a (simple) random sample in accordance with our definition, it is often reasonable to treat systematic samples as if they were random samples. Whether or not this is justified depends entirely on the structure (order) of the list, or arrangement, from which the sample is obtained. In some instances, systematic sampling actually provides an improvement over simple random sampling inasmuch as the sample is "spread more evenly" over the entire population.

The danger in systematic sampling lies in the possible presence of *hidden periodicities.* For instance, if we inspect every 50th piece made by a machine, our result would be quite biased if (owing to a regularly recurring failure) it so happened that every 25th piece had blemishes. Also, a systematic sample might yield biased results if we interviewed the residents of every 12th house along a certain route and it so happened that each of these houses was a corner house on a double lot.

Stratified Sampling. In this kind of sampling we divide the population into a number of nonoverlapping subpopulations, *strata,* to which we then allocate certain portions of the total sample. If the items selected from each of the strata constitute a simple random sample, the entire procedure (first stratification and then simple random sampling) is called *stratified (simple) random sampling*. Although the concept of this kind of sampling is simple, a number of problems immediately arise: How many strata should be formed? What should be the sample size for the different strata? How are the samples within the strata to be selected? Stratification does not guarantee good results, but if properly executed, stratified sampling generally leads to a higher degree of precision, that is, to improved generalizations about the whole population.

To illustrate the general idea behind stratified sampling, let us consider the following oversimplified, though concrete, example. Suppose we want to estimate the mean weight of 4 persons on the basis of a sample of size 2; the (supposedly unknown) weights of the 4 persons are, respectively, 115, 135, 185, and 205 pounds, so that the population mean we are trying to estimate is 160 pounds. If we take a simple random sample of size 2 from this population, it can easily be seen that the sample mean can be as small as 125 pounds or as large as 195 pounds. In fact, the 6 possible samples of size 2 that can be taken from this population have means of 125, 150, 160, 160, 170, and 195 pounds.

Now suppose that we make use of the fact that among the four persons there are 2 men and 2 women and that we *stratify* our sample by randomly selecting one of the two women and one of the two men. Assuming that the two smaller weights are those of the two women, we now find that the sample mean varies on the much smaller interval from 150 to 170. In fact, the four possible stratified samples have means of 150, 160, 160, and 170. *This illustrates how we improved our chances of getting a close estimate of the mean of the population by stratifying according to sex* (see also Exercise 3 on page 213).

Essentially, the goal of stratification is to form strata in such a way that there is some relationship between being in a particular stratum and the answer sought in the statistical study, and that within the individual strata there is as much homogeneity (uniformity) as possible. Note that in our example there was such a connection between sex and weight and that there was much less variability in weight within the two strata than there was within the entire population.

In the above example, we stratified the sample only with respect to one characteristic. A further refinement consists of stratifying with respect to *several* characteristics, say, with respect to income, nationality background, age, and geographic location, in a survey designed to determine public opinion concerning a political issue. We would thus allocate part of the total sample to persons with low incomes, who belong to nationality group A, are in the 25–45 year age bracket, and live in the Southwest; another portion to persons with high incomes, who belong to nationality group B, are in the over-65 years age bracket, and live in New England; and so forth. This process is called *cross-stratification,* and it is quite widely used, particularly in public opinion polls and market surveys.

Quota Sampling. In many applications of stratified sampling the selection of individuals within the various strata has traditionally been *nonrandom.* Instead, interviewers have been given quotas to be filled from the various strata, without too many restrictions as to *how* they are to be filled. For instance, in determining attitude toward increased foreign aid expenditures, an interviewer working a certain area for an opinion research organization might be told to interview 5 retail merchants of German origin who own homes, 12 wage-earners of Anglo-Saxon origin who live in rented apartments, 2 retired persons who live in trailers, etc., with the actual selection of the individuals being left to the interviewer's discretion. This is a convenient, relatively inexpensive, and often necessary procedure, but as it is usually executed, the resulting quota samples do not have the essential features of random samples. Interviewers naturally tend to select individuals who are most readily available, that is, persons who work in the same building, shop in the same store, or perhaps reside in the same general area. Quota samples are, thus, essentially *judgment samples,* and they generally do not lend themselves to any sort of formal statistical evaluation.

Cluster Sampling. To illustrate another important kind of sampling, suppose that a large foundation wants to study the changing patterns of family expenditures for recreation in the Detroit area. In attempting to complete schedules for a sample of 800 families, the foundation runs into a number of difficulties; simple random sampling is practically impossible since suitable lists are not available and the cost of contacting families scattered over a wide area (sometimes with 2 or 3 call-backs for the not-at-homes) can be very high. One way in which a sample can be taken in this example is to divide the total area of interest into a number of smaller, nonoverlapping areas, say, city blocks. A number of these blocks can then be chosen with the use of random numbers, and all (or samples of) the families residing in these blocks are included in the sample. This kind of sampling is referred to as *cluster sampling;* that is, the total population is divided into a number of relatively small subdivisions (which are themselves *clusters* of still smaller units) and then some of these subdivisions, or clusters, are randomly selected for inclusion in the over-all sample. If the clusters are geographic subdivisions, as in our example, this kind of sampling is also called *area sampling.*

Although estimates based on cluster samples are generally not as reliable as estimates based on simple random samples of the same size [see Exercise 11(c) on page 198], they are usually more reliable *per unit cost.* Referring again to the survey of family expenditures for recreation in the Detroit area, it is easy to see that it may well be possible to obtain a cluster sample several times the size of a simple random sample at the same expense. (It is much cheaper to visit and interview families living close together in clusters than families selected at random over a wide area.)

In practice, several of the methods we have discussed may well be used in the same survey. For instance, if government statisticians wanted to study the attitude of elementary school teachers toward certain federal programs, they might first stratify the country by states or some other geographic subdivision. To obtain a sample from each stratum they might then use cluster sampling, subdividing each stratum, say, into school districts, and finally they might use simple random sampling or systematic sampling within each cluster.

EXERCISES

1. How many different samples of size 2 can be selected
   (a) from a finite population of size 5?
   (b) from a finite population of size 20?
   (c) from a finite population of size 50?

2. How many different samples of size 3 can be selected
   (a) from a finite population of size 6?
   (b) from a finite population of size 20?
   (c) from a finite population of size 100?

3. Referring to the example on page 190, list the 10 possible samples of size 3 which can be drawn from the finite population consisting of the elements a, b, c, d, and e. Then assigning each of the 10 possible samples a probability of 1/10, show that the probability that element b will be included in a sample is 3/5. Does the same probability apply to elements a, c, d, and e?

4. Referring to Exercise 3, what is the probability that any specific pair, say, elements c and d, are included in the sample? Does the same probability apply to each possible pair?

5. List all possible samples of size 2 that can be drawn from the finite population whose elements are the numbers 1, 2, 3, 4, 5, 6, 7, and 8. How many of these samples contain a specific element of the population, say, the number 7? If we assign each sample of size 2 the same probability, what are the odds that it will contain the number 7?

6. Suppose you were involved in an automobile accident and you need three estimates of the extent of the damage to submit to your insurance company. Use random numbers to select three automobile repair shops from among those listed in the yellow pages of your telephone directory (or that of a neighboring city).

7. When registering at a certain university, the 1,200 incoming freshmen are assigned numbers serially from 0001 to 1200. Use random numbers to select a random sample of 25 of these freshmen to be assigned to a particular faculty advisor.

8. Use random numbers to select a restaurant from among those listed in the yellow pages of your telephone directory (or that of a neighboring city).

9. In all studies based on samples, great care must be exercised to ensure that the samples will lend themselves to valid generalizations, and every precaution must be taken to avoid *biases* of one kind or another. This includes the unfortunate tendency of samples not to be representative of whatever populations they are supposed to represent and, thus, to lead away from, rather than toward, the truth. Explain why each of the following samples does not qualify as a random sample from the required population or might fail to give the desired information:

(a) In order to predict a city election, a public opinion poll telephones persons randomly selected from the city's telephone directory.
(b) To estimate the average length of logs fed into a mill by a constant-speed conveyor belt, measurements are made of the length of the logs which pass a given point exactly every five minutes.
(c) To estimate the average annual income of Yale graduates ten years after graduation, questionnaires were sent in 1966 to all members of the class of '56, and the estimate was based on the ones returned.
(d) To ascertain facts about bathing habits, a random sample of the residents of a community are asked whether they take a bath each day.
(e) In a study of consumer reaction to its product, the manufacturer of Frigidaire refrigerators (that is, interviewers hired by its research department) ask people the question, "How do you like your Frigidaire?"
(f) To study the religious affiliation of its subscribers, a magazine sends a questionnaire to each 25th subscriber on its alphabetically arranged mailing list.

10. The following are the scores obtained by 16 students on a college admission test: 63, 90, 75, 81, 93, 55, 79, 84, 76, 80, 91, 72, 83, 75, 88, and 98.

(a) List the four possible systematic samples of size 4 that can be taken from this list by starting with one of the first four scores and then taking each fourth score on the list.
(b) Calculate the mean of each of the four samples obtained in part (a) and verify that *their* mean equals that of the 16 scores.

11. To generalize the example given in the text, suppose that in a group of 6 persons there are 3 women whose weights are 115 lb, 125 lb, and 135 lb, and 3 men whose weights are 185 lb, 195 lb, and 205 lb.

(a) List the 15 possible random samples of size 2 from this population and calculate their means.
(b) List the 9 stratified random samples of size 2 obtained by selecting one man and one woman and calculate their means.

(c) Suppose that the 6 persons are divided into clusters according to sex, each cluster is assigned a probability of 1/2, and a random sample of size 2 is taken from the chosen cluster. List the 6 possible samples and calculate their means.

(d) Compare the scattering of the sample means in parts (a), (b), and (c), and thus judge the relative merits of the three kinds of sampling (see also Exercise 4 on page 214).

12. On the basis of their total deposits, 120 banks in New York are classified into 60 that are small, 40 that are medium-sized, and 20 that are large.

(a) How would one allocate a 15 per cent sample to the three strata if one-third of the total sample is to be assigned to each stratum?

(b) How would one allocate a 15 per cent sample to the three strata if the portion of the total sample allocated to each stratum is to be proportional to its size?

8.3 Simulation

Although we introduced random numbers originally to select random samples from finite populations, they are used for many other purposes. They serve to *simulate* almost any kind of gambling device; in fact, they can be used to simulate any situation involving an element of uncertainty or chance. For example, we can play the game of "Heads or Tails" without ever flipping a coin by letting the digits 0, 2, 4, 6, and 8 represent *heads* while the digits 1, 3, 5, 7, and 9 represent *tails*. Thus, using the 5th column of the table on page 394 starting at the top, we get 1, 2, 2, 6, 6, 7, 0, 4, 5, . . ., and we interpret this as *tail, head, head, head, head, tail, head, head, tail*, ...

In recent years, techniques based on random numbers have been applied to a great variety of problems in the physical, social, and biological sciences. Referred to under the name of *Monte Carlo Methods*, they have been used to *simulate* such things as the spread of cholera epidemics, the collision of photons with electrons, the scattering of neutrons in a nuclear reactor, traffic congestion on freeways, air turbulence and its effect on airplane wings, to mention but a few. In this way, methods based on random numbers (and often high-speed computers) make it possible to simulate experiments which either cannot be performed in the laboratory (such as the spreading of an epidemic) or which would otherwise require prohibitively expensive equipment. Monte Carlo methods have also found wide application in business research, where they are used for solving inventory problems, or questions arising in connection with the allocation of resources, advertising, competition, and over-all planning and organization.

In this section we shall concern ourselves mainly with the problem of *simulating sampling experiments;* that is, we shall use random numbers to simulate the observation of random variables having given discrete or continuous distributions. To illustrate, let us consider a very simple experiment which consists of repeated flips of 3 balanced coins. There are many different ways in which this experiment can be simulated: one possibility is to proceed as in the first paragraph of this section, letting 0, 2, 4, 6, and 8 represent *heads* while 1, 3, 5, 7, and 9 represent *tails,* and using three random digits to represent the results obtained with three coins. Thus, if we used the first three columns of page 395 starting at the top, we would obtain 244, 574, 776, 683, 644, 882, 984, . . ., and we would interpret this as 3, 1, 1, 2, 3, 3, 2, . . ., heads.

Whenever possible, it is preferable to get values of random variables directly from random numbers, that is, without having to worry about the interpretation of each individual digit. Thus, remembering from Chapter 6 that the probabilities of getting 0, 1, 2, or 3 heads with 3 balanced coins (or in 3 flips of one balanced coin) are, respectively, 1/8, 3/8, 3/8, and 1/8, we might use the following scheme:*

Number of Heads	*Random Numbers*
0	000 – 124
1	125 – 499
2	500 – 874
3	875 – 999

Note that with this scheme 125 of the three-digit random numbers from 000 to 999 (or one-eighth) represent 0 heads, 375 of the random numbers (or three-eighths) represent 1 head, and so on. If we got 095, 632, 715, 309, and 897, for example, we would interpret this as representing 0, 2, 2, 1, and 3 heads.

Proceeding as in this last example, we can simulate any kind of probability distribution, and this is generally much more satisfactory than tossing coins, drawing numbered slips out of a hat, rolling dice, or gambling with other kinds of physical objects. To give another example, let us refer to part (b) of Exercise 30 on page 161, and let us actually simulate the inspection of the sheet metal. Calculating the required probabilities (rounded to three decimals) by using the formula for the Poisson distribution with

* Observe that we are using three-digit random numbers rather than, say, two-digit numbers, because 1,000 is divisible by 8 while 100 is not; in other words, we can allocate 1/8 of the 1,000 three-digit numbers from 000 to 999 to "0 heads" whereas we could not have done this with the 100 two-digit numbers from 00 to 99 without leaving some of them out.

$\lambda = 1.2$, we obtain the values shown in the middle column of the following table:

Number of Defects Observed in Five Minutes of Inspection	*Probability*	*Random Numbers*
0	0.301	000 – 300
1	0.361	301 – 661
2	0.217	662 – 878
3	0.088	879 – 966
4	0.026	967 – 992
5	0.006	993 – 998
6	0.001	999

Note that the 1,000 random numbers from 000 to 999 in the right-hand column are allocated to the values of the random variable so that the first 301 represent 0 defects, the next 361 represent 1 defect, the next 217 represent 2 defects, and so on. To perform the actual simulation of the inspection of the sheet metal, let us now turn to the random numbers on page 396, using the 11th, 12th, and 13th columns starting with the 11th row. We thus get 729, 012, 505, 031, 986, 625, 497, 135, 369, 889, . . . , and we interpret this as representing 2, 0, 1, 0, 4, 1, 1, 0, 1, 3, . . . , defects.

Very often it is convenient to use a graph rather than a table to check what value of a random variable corresponds to a given random number. If we wanted to do this in the experiment where we simulated tossing 3 coins, we would first have to convert the distribution for the member of

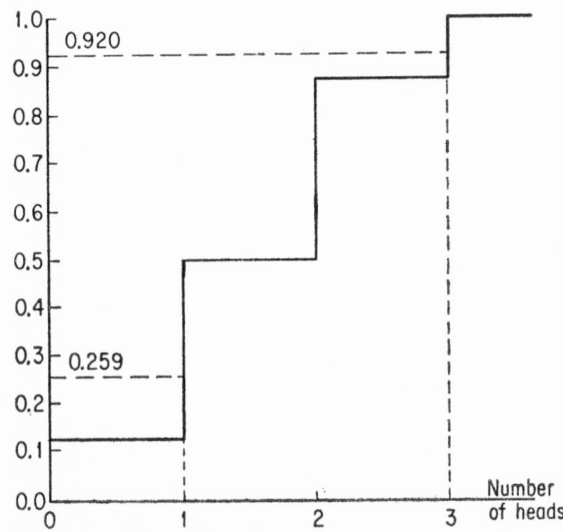

Fig. 8.2 Cumulative distribution of number of heads ($n = 3$).

heads into a cumulative "less than" distribution and draw its graph as in Figure 8.2. Then we would select two-digit or three-digit random numbers, place a decimal point to the left of the first digit, mark these values on the vertical scale, and read off the number of heads as is indicated in Figure 8.2. For instance, the diagram shows that the random number 920 (marked on the vertical scale as 0.920) corresponds to 3 heads on the horizontal scale, and that the random number 259 (marked on the vertical scale as 0.259) corresponds to 1 head on the horizontal scale.

Proceeding in the same manner in the second example, the one dealing with the inspection of the sheets of steel, we obtain the graph shown in Figure 8.3. Using this graph and two-digit random numbers, we find that

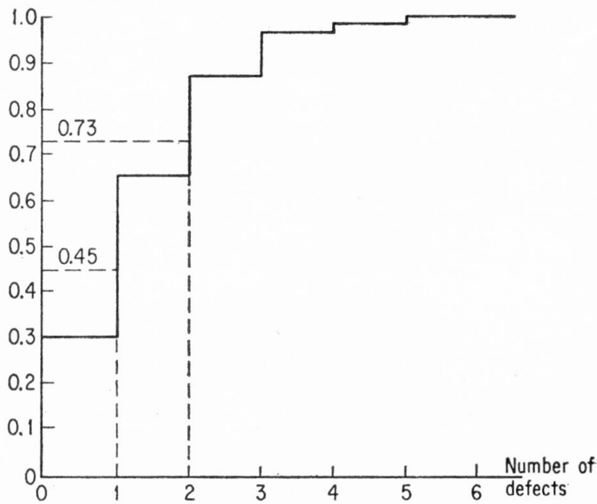

Fig. 8.3 Cumulative distribution of number of defects.

the random number 73 (marked on the vertical scale as 0.73) corresponds to 2 defects and that the random number 45 (marked on the vertical scale as 0.45) corresponds to 1 defect. Note that if we happen to get a random number which actually corresponds to one of the steps of the graph (for example, if we get the random number 125 in connection with Figure 8.2), we assign it the *larger* of the two values of the random variable. The reason for this is that we use the random numbers from 000 to 999 rather than those from 001 to 1000.

A great advantage of the graphical method is that it carries over directly to problems in which we simulate the sampling of random variables having *continuous distributions*. For instance, Figure 8.4 contains the "less than" ogive of the standard normal distribution, namely, the graph of the corresponding cumulative "less than" distribution. (This graph was easily obtained with the use of Table I by plotting the probabilities of getting values less than z for various values of z.) If we want to use this graph to simulate drawing, say, a random sample of size 5 from a population having

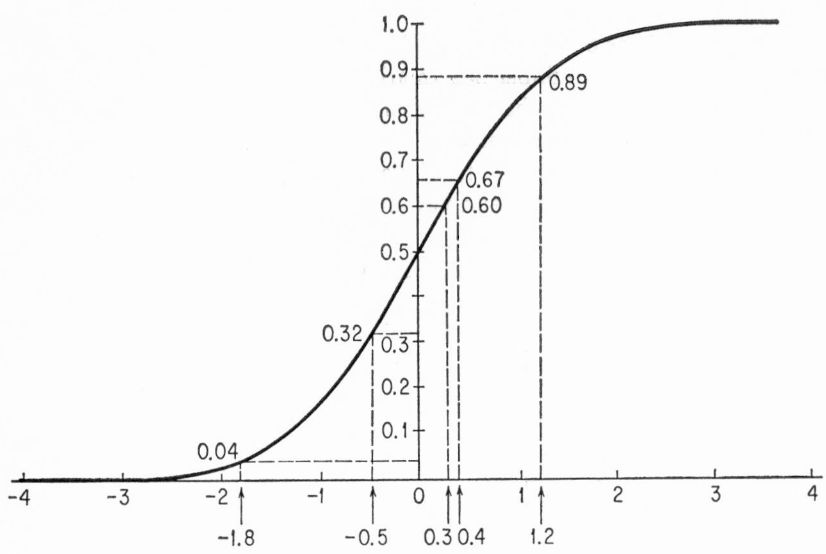

Fig. 8.4 Cumulative standard normal distribution.

a normal distribution with $\mu = 50$ and $\sigma = 12$, we proceed as follows: deciding (arbitrarily) to use two-digit random numbers, we go to page 393 and, using the first two columns starting at the top, we obtain 04, 60, 67, 89, and 32. Marking 0.04, 0.60, 0.67, 0.89, and 0.32 on the vertical scale of Figure 8.4, we read off $z = -1.8$, $z = 0.3$, $z = 0.4$, $z = 1.2$, $z = -0.5$. The only thing that remains to be done is to convert these values into the desired scale of measurement; to do this, we make use of the relation $z = \frac{x - \mu}{\sigma}$ or

$$x = \mu + \sigma \cdot z$$

which in our particular example becomes $x = 50 + 12z$. It follows that the values of the random variable obtained in this simulated sampling experiment are 28.4, 53.6, 54.8, 64.4, and 44.0. The reason we used only two-digit numbers in this example is that it would have been difficult to mark numbers to three decimals on the very small vertical scale. For the same reason, we might just as well have used two-digit random numbers in connection with Figure 8.2.

EXERCISES

1. Use random numbers to simulate 100 tosses of a balanced coin. Calculate the accumulated proportion of heads after each fifth flip and plot your results as in Figure 5.11 on page 98.

2. Using four random digits (with 0, 2, 4, 6, and 8 representing *heads* and 1, 3, 5, 7, and 9 representing *tails*) to represent the result obtained when tossing four balanced coins, simulate an experiment consisting of 80 tosses of four coins. Compare the observed frequencies for 0, 1, 2, 3, and 4 heads with the corresponding *expected* frequencies which are 5, 20, 30, 20, and 5.

3. Repeat Exercise 2, letting 0, 1, 2, 3, and 4 heads be represented by the four-digit random numbers 0000–0624, 0625–3124, 3125–6874, 6875–9374, and 9375–9999, respectively.

4. Repeat Exercise 2, letting 0, 1, 2, 3, and 4 heads be represented by the two-digit random numbers 00–05, 06–29, 30–65, 66–89, and 90–95, respectively. (The random numbers 96, 97, 98, and 99 are simply ignored in this scheme whenever they may occur.)

5. Using one-digit random numbers (omitting 7, 8, 9, and 0), simulate 120 tosses of a balanced die. Calculate the accumulated proportion of threes after each tenth toss and plot the results as in Figure 5.11.

6. The probabilities that a person who spends a morning fishing at a certain spot on the East Verde river catches 0, 1, 2, 3, . . ., or 8 trout are, respectively, 0.05, 0.15, 0.22, 0.22, 0.17, 0.10, 0.05, 0.03, and 0.01. Use two-digit random numbers with 00–04 corresponding to 0 trout, 05–19 corresponding to 1 trout, 20–41 corresponding to 2 trout, etc., to simulate the number of fish caught at this spot by a fisherman on 14 consecutive days. What was his average catch per day?

7. Figure 7.1 on page 164 gives the probabilities of 0, 1, . . ., or 6 successes in 6 trials when the probability of a success on any one trial is 0.80. Use four-digit random numbers with 0000 representing 0 successes, 0001–0015 representing 1 success, 0016–0169 representing 2 successes, etc., to simulate 100 such series of 6 trials. Compare the distribution thus obtained with the corresponding expected frequencies, that is, the corresponding probabilities multiplied by 100 (see also Exercise 11 on page 299).

8. Using the scheme on page 200, simulate an experiment which consists of observing (and recording) the number of defects in the sheet metal during 100 five-minute intervals.

9. In a certain town, the probabilities of an adult passing his driving test on the first, second, third, fourth, or fifth try are, respectively, 0.44, 0.32, 0.16, 0.05, and 0.03. Using two-digit random numbers, simulate the experience of 50 adults in trying to get their driving license. If a person has to pay $2.50 the first time he takes the test and after that $1.00 for each additional try, what is the average amount paid by these 50 persons?

10. Repeat Exercise 9 using the graphical method discussed on pages 200 and 201.

11. Using Figure 8.4, simulate an experiment which consists of obtaining 12 values of a random variable having the standard normal distribution.

12. Use Figure 8.4 to simulate an experiment which consists of making 10 observations of a random variable having a normal distribution with the mean 12.0 and the standard deviation 2.0.

13. Use Figure 8.4 to simulate an experiment in which a sample of size 15 is taken from a population having a normal distribution with the mean 100 and the standard deviation 15.

14. The time between the arrival of successive customers at a bakery is a random variable having a continuous distribution about which we have the following information:

Time Between Arrivals (minutes) t	*Probability that Time Between Arrivals is Less than* t
0	0.00
2	0.39
4	0.63
6	0.78
8	0.86
10	0.92
12	0.98
14	1.00

Draw a graph of this cumulative distribution (measuring time on the horizontal scale and the cumulative probabilities on the vertical scale), by connecting the 8 points representing the given values by means of a smooth curve. Use two-digit random numbers and this graph to simulate an experiment which consists of determining the time intervals (rounded to the nearest tenth of a minute) between the arrival of 25 successive customers. Supposing that the first customer arrives at 9 A.M., at what times did the other 24 customers arrive? If each customer spends exactly 8 minutes in the bakery, were there ever 5 or more customers in the bakery at the same time (during the course of the experiment)?

8.4 Sampling Distributions

Let us now introduce what is probably the most fundamental concept of statistical inference, that of the *sampling distribution* of a statistic. This concept ties in closely with the idea of chance variation, which we discussed earlier to emphasize the need for measuring the variability of a set of data. Suppose, for instance, that a highway traffic engineer wants to determine the average number of north-bound cars reaching a busy intersection during rush hours while the light is red for a period of 40 seconds. He needs this information to determine the adequacy of the present system of traffic control, possibly to improve the flow of traffic, and so on. Suppose, furthermore, that the number of north-bound cars arriving at the intersection is observed for 5 such 40-second intervals (while the light is red) and that the figures obtained are 12, 7, 9, 11, and 13 cars. The mean of these sample values is $\frac{1}{5}(12 + 7 + 9 + 11 + 13) = 10.4$, and in the absence of any further information it would seem reasonable to use this figure as an *estimate* of the true average number of north-bound cars arriving at the intersection under the given conditions. *In making such a generalization it must be recognized, however, that if the experiment were repeated, the mean of the sample values would probably be some number other than 10.4.* Indeed, it would be surprising if we again obtained 10.4, and if the experiment were repeated over and over again, we might well get such divergent values as 8.6, 11.2, 9.0, 10.6, 9.4, 8.8, 9.8, . . ., for the means of the respective samples. It will be assumed that these differences are due to chance (and not due to differences in the time of day or other possible factors), so that by studying the distribution of the $\bar{x}$'s we can learn something about the actual size of the chance fluctuations to which we are exposed in this problem. In other words, we can learn how the $\bar{x}$'s are scattered about the true mean they are intended to estimate, and, hence, we can learn something about the *error* to which we might be exposed in this example when basing an estimate on the mean of a sample. It is customary to refer to such a distribution of $\bar{x}$'s as a *sampling distribution of the mean.* If it is based on values obtained from repeated random samples as indicated above, we call it an *experimental sampling distribution;* if it is based on appropriate mathematical theory, we call it a *theoretical sampling distribution.* In what follows, we shall first consider a theoretical sampling distribution of the mean for random samples from a very small finite population; after that we shall actually construct an experimental sampling distribution of the mean with reference to the above example concerning the flow of traffic.

For our first example, let us suppose that we draw numbered slips of paper out of a hat containing five slips numbered 0, 3, 6, 9, and 12. Using the formulas of Chapters 3 and 4, it can easily be verified that the mean of the finite population which consists of these 5 numbers is $\mu = 6$, and that its variance is $\sigma^2 = 18$. If we now draw (without replacement) a random sample of 3 of these slips, we know from page 190 that there are 10 possibilities—we might draw the numbers 0, 3, and 6, the numbers 0, 3, and 9, the numbers 3, 6, and 12, the numbers 6, 9, and 12, and so forth. If we actually listed these 10 samples and calculated their means, we would find that these means are 3, 4, 5, 5, 6, 7, 6, 7, 8, and 9 (not necessarily in this order).

Since we assumed that sampling is random, each of the 10 possible samples has a probability of 1/10, each of the corresponding means has a probability of 1/10, and we arrive at the following *theoretical sampling distribution of the mean:*

$\bar{x}$	*Probability*
3	1/10
4	1/10
5	2/10
6	2/10
7	2/10
8	1/10
9	1/10

A histogram of this sampling distribution is shown in Figure 8.5, and it gives us some idea about the (chance) fluctuations of means of random samples of size 3 taken from the given population. It tells us that if we use

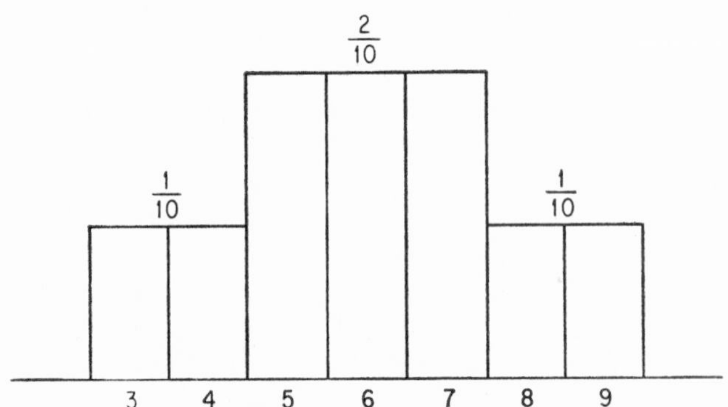

Fig. 8.5 Theoretical sampling distribution of the mean.

the mean of a random sample of size 3 to estimate the mean of the population (which is $\mu = 6$), the probability of being "off" by as much as 3 is 2/10, the probability of being "off" by 2 is 2/10, the probability of being "off" by 1 is 4/10, and the probability of exactly getting the correct value is 2/10.

In the study of sampling distributions it is generally useful to calculate their respective means and standard deviations. When dealing with the sampling distribution of $\bar{x}$ we denote its mean by $\mu_{\bar{x}}$ and its standard deviation by $\sigma_{\bar{x}}$, in order to distinguish these measures from μ and σ, the corresponding descriptions of the population. Referring to the definitions of the mean and the variance of a probability distribution in Section 7.3, we obtain for our example

$$\mu_{\bar{x}} = 3(1/10) + 4(1/10) + 5(2/10) + 6(2/10) + 7(2/10) + 8(1/10) + 9(1/10) = 6$$

and

$$\sigma_{\bar{x}}^2 = (3-6)^2(1/10) + (4-6)^2(1/10) + (5-6)^2(2/10) + (6-6)^2(2/10) + (7-6)^2(2/10) + (8-6)^2(1/10) + (9-6)^2(1/10) = 3$$

so that $\sigma_{\bar{x}}$ equals approximately 1.73. Note that the mean of this sampling distribution *equals* the mean of the population; the significance of the value obtained for $\sigma_{\bar{x}}$ will be discussed later on page 209.

To illustrate the concept of an *experimental sampling distribution of the mean,* let us return to the problem on page 205, namely, that of estimating the true average number of north-bound cars arriving at the given intersection during a 40-second interval when the light is red, and let us suppose that 40 repetitions of the experiment yielded the results shown in the following table:

Sample	*Number of Cars*	*Sample*	*Number of Cars*
1	11, 12, 9, 10, 12	21	6, 7, 10, 10, 9
2	9, 6, 8, 8, 8	22	8, 13, 10, 11, 9
3	12, 4, 7, 13, 11	23	14, 6, 5, 8, 13
4	7, 9, 12, 7, 8	24	9, 9, 9, 7, 17
5	8, 11, 10, 8, 6	25	17, 7, 13, 7, 9
6	6, 14, 9, 15, 10	26	13, 13, 7, 10, 11
7	15, 12, 6, 5, 12	27	15, 10, 11, 9, 12
8	17, 10, 7, 12, 15	28	10, 5, 8, 14, 4
9	6, 10, 7, 12, 11	29	16, 13, 9, 10, 13
10	8, 12, 6, 13, 12	30	8, 9, 10, 15, 5
11	10, 5, 10, 7, 10	31	8, 11, 9, 11, 12
12	10, 11, 7, 11, 10	32	10, 12, 5, 9, 11
13	5, 10, 11, 10, 4	33	7, 7, 9, 7, 5
14	7, 10, 8, 14, 8	34	8, 11, 11, 17, 9
15	8, 7, 11, 12, 8	35	4, 8, 9, 12, 8
16	4, 7, 11, 9, 9	36	20, 9, 8, 5, 12
17	5, 5, 9, 11, 4	37	9, 8, 6, 6, 8
18	11, 6, 9, 8, 13	38	12, 9, 9, 12, 6
19	13, 7, 9, 11, 8	39	8, 13, 10, 10, 4
20	15, 6, 8, 11, 10	40	8, 7, 11, 9, 14

Each of these samples contains five values, namely, the number of north-bound cars which arrived at the intersection during five 40-second intervals when the light was red. Calculating the means of these 40 samples, we obtain

10.8	7.8	9.4	8.6	8.6	10.8	10.0	12.2	9.2	10.2
8.4	9.8	8.0	9.4	9.2	8.0	6.8	9.4	9.6	10.0
8.4	10.2	9.2	10.2	10.6	10.8	11.4	8.2	12.2	9.4
10.2	9.4	7.0	11.2	8.2	10.8	7.4	9.6	9.0	9.8

and an over-all picture of their distribution is given by the histogram of Figure 8.6. Inspection of this distribution provides us with important information about the scattering (that is, the chance fluctuations) of these

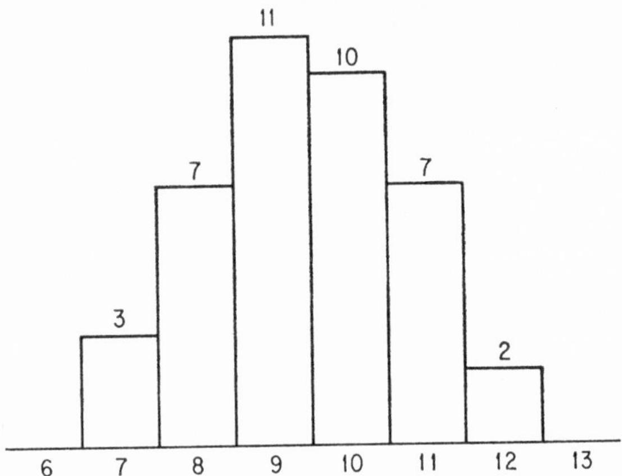

Fig. 8.6 Experimental sampling distribution of the mean.

means. For instance, we find that 28 out of 40 (or 70 per cent) of the means fall on the interval from 7.5 to 10.5, and that 38 out of 40 (or 95 per cent) of the means fall on the interval from 6.5 to 11.5.

These results will become more meaningful if we reveal the fact that the 40 samples were obtained with the use of random numbers, *simulating* a population for which the probabilities of getting 0, 1, 2, 3, . . ., cars are given by a Poisson distribution with $\lambda = 9$ and, hence, $\mu = 9$ and $\sigma = 3$. Using the fact that the mean of the population is equal to 9, we can now restate our description of the distribution of Figure 8.6 by saying that *70 per cent of the means were "off" by at most 1.5*, and that *95 per cent of the means were "off" by at most 2.5*. This kind of information is important, inasmuch as it tells us how close we can expect a sample mean to be to the mean of the population, namely, the quantity it is supposed to estimate.

The purpose of the two examples of this section was to introduce the concept of a sampling distribution, and it must be remembered that in actual practice we usually have *only one mean*, not 40, and we seldom can afford to go to the extreme of enumerating all possible samples from a finite population and, thus, construct a theoretical sampling distribution. In most practical situations we have no choice but to use special theorems, and so far as the sampling distribution of the mean is concerned, there are two theorems which generally provide all the information we need.

The first of these theorems expresses the fact which we discovered in connection with the example on page 207, namely, that $\mu_{\bar{x}} = \mu$ (the mean of the sampling distribution of $\bar{x}$ equals the mean of the population); it also provides formulas for the standard deviation $\sigma_{\bar{x}}$ of the sampling distribution of the mean. Formally,

> *For random samples of size n from a population having the mean μ and the standard deviation σ, the (theoretical) sampling distribution of $\bar{x}$ has the mean $\mu_{\bar{x}} = \mu$, and its standard deviation is given by*
>
> ▲ $$\sigma_{\bar{x}} = \frac{\sigma}{\sqrt{n}} \quad \text{or} \quad \sigma_{\bar{x}} = \frac{\sigma}{\sqrt{n}} \cdot \sqrt{\frac{N-n}{N-1}}$$ ▲
>
> *depending on whether the population is infinite or finite of size N.*

It is customary to refer to $\sigma_{\bar{x}}$, the standard deviation of the sampling distribution of the mean, as the *standard error of the mean.* Its role in statistics is fundamental, as it measures the extent to which means fluctuate, or vary, due to chance. Regarding the two formulas for $\sigma_{\bar{x}}$, note that the first consists of the quotient $\sigma/\sqrt{n}$, while in the second this quotient is multiplied by the "*finite population correction factor*" $\sqrt{\frac{N-n}{N-1}}$. The quotient $\sigma/\sqrt{n}$ exhibits the following important information: (1) *If σ is large and there is considerable variation in the population from which the sample is obtained, we can expect proportionately large fluctuations in the distribution of the means;* (2) *The larger the sample size n, the smaller is the variation among the means and the closer we can expect a sample mean to be to the mean of the population.* Both of these arguments should seem plausible on intuitive grounds; after all, if there is considerable variability in the values from which the sample is obtained, this is apt to reflect also in the sample. So far as the second point is concerned, it stands to reason that if we have more information, we should also get better, that is, more reliable, estimates.

The factor $\sqrt{\frac{N-n}{N-1}}$ in the second formula for $\sigma_{\bar{x}}$ is generally omitted unless the sample constitutes a substantial portion (5 per cent or more) of the population. For instance, when $n = 100$ and $N = 10{,}000$ (and the sample constitutes but 1 per cent of the population),

$$\sqrt{\frac{N-n}{N-1}} = \sqrt{\frac{10{,}000 - 100}{10{,}000 - 1}} = 0.995$$

and this is so close to 1 that the correction factor can be omitted for most practical purposes.

To verify the second formula for $\sigma_{\bar{x}}$, let us return for a moment to the example where we constructed the theoretical sampling distribution of the mean for random samples of size 3 from the finite population which consists of the numbers 0, 3, 6, 9, and 12. As we pointed out on page 205, $\sigma = \sqrt{18}$ for this finite population, and if we now substitute this value together with $n = 3$ and $N = 5$ into the second formula for $\sigma_{\bar{x}}$, we obtain

$$\sigma_{\bar{x}} = \frac{\sqrt{18}}{\sqrt{3}} \cdot \sqrt{\frac{5-3}{5-1}} = \sqrt{3}$$

This agrees with the result on page 207, where we showed directly that the variance of the theoretical sampling distribution of the mean equals 3 and, hence, the standard deviation equals $\sqrt{3}$ in this example. In Exercises 1 and 2 on page 213, the reader will be asked to verify the formula for $\sigma_{\bar{x}}$ for random samples from two other finite populations.

Now let us take another look at the experimental sampling distribution which we constructed for the traffic-count example, namely, the one where we took 40 random samples of size 5 and grouped their means into the distribution shown in Figure 8.6. As we pointed out on page 208, the mean and the standard deviation of the infinite population from which these samples were obtained are $\mu = 9$ and $\sigma = 3$, so that according to our theorem we would expect the mean and the standard deviation of the sampling distribution of $\bar{x}$ to be equal to 9 and $3/\sqrt{5} = 1.34$, respectively. If we actually calculated the mean and the standard deviation of the experimental sampling distribution whose histogram is shown in Figure 8.6, we would obtain 9.4 and 1.32, respectively; although these values are not identical with the ones we might expect according to the theorem they are sufficiently close to be regarded as an experimental verification of the formulas for $\mu_{\bar{x}}$ and $\sigma_{\bar{x}}$.

To show how the theorem on page 209 is actually applied in practice, we require another theorem, called the *Central Limit Theorem*, which provides us with information about the over-all shape of a sampling distribution of the mean. However, even without it we can get some idea by applying *Chebyshev's Theorem* (see page 167), according to which we can now assert that *the probability of getting a sample mean which differs from the population mean* μ *by more than* k *standard deviations, namely, by more than* $k \cdot \sigma_{\bar{x}}$, *is less than* $1/k^2$. For instance, if we take a random sample of size $n = 64$ from an infinite population with $\sigma = 20$, then the probability of getting a sample mean which differs from the population mean by more than $2 \cdot \sigma_{\bar{x}} = 2 \cdot \frac{20}{\sqrt{64}} = 5$ is less than $1/2^2 = 0.25$. Similarly, if we take a random sample of size $n = 100$ from an infinite population with $\sigma = 4$, then the probability of getting a sample mean which differs from the mean of the population by more than $5 \cdot \frac{4}{\sqrt{100}} = 2$ is less than $1/5^2 = 0.04$. Note that we can thus make probability statements concerning the difference between

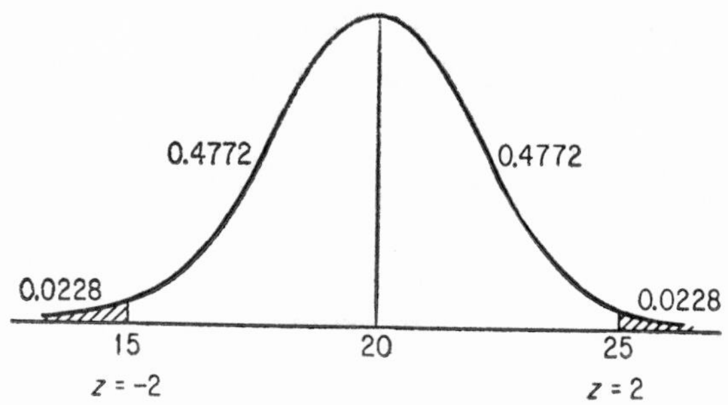

Fig. 8.7 Sampling distribution of the mean.

the mean of a random sample and the mean of the population without having to go through the tedious process of constructing the complete sampling distribution (as we did in the example on page 206).

The *Central Limit Theorem* is of fundamental importance in statistics, as it justifies the use of normal curve methods in a great variety of problems. In words, the theorem can be stated as follows:

> *If n is large, the (theoretical) sampling distribution of the mean can be approximated closely with a normal distribution.*

In other words, if n is large, the sampling distribution of the statistic

$$z = \frac{\bar{x} - \mu}{\sigma_{\bar{x}}}$$

can be approximated closely with the *standard* normal distribution. It is difficult to state precisely how large n must be so that this theorem applies; unless the distribution of the population has a very unusual shape, however, the approximation will be good even if n is relatively small—certainly, if n is 30 or more. Note that the distribution of Figure 8.6 is fairly symmetrical and bell-shaped even though the sample size on which each mean was based is only $n = 5$.

To illustrate the use of the Central Limit Theorem, let us refer to the first of the examples on page 210 to which we applied Chebyshev's Theorem. We found that if a random sample of size 64 is taken from a population having $\sigma = 20$, then the probability of getting a sample mean which differs from the mean of the population by more than 5 is less than 0.25. According to the Central Limit Theorem, this probability is given by the shaded area of Figure 8.7, and it can easily be verified that it is equal to 0.0456. Note that *without* the Central Limit Theorem we were only able to assert that this probability is "less than 0.25."

A sample of size $n = 5$ is ordinarily too small for application of the Central Limit Theorem unless the distribution of the population, itself, follows closely the pattern of a normal curve. Nevertheless, let us check briefly how the experimental sampling distribution on page 208, the one based on the 40 means, agrees with what we might expect according to the theorem. On page 208 we pointed out that 28 of the 40 means (or 70 per cent) fell on the interval from 7.5 to 10.5, namely, within 1.5 of the population mean $\mu = 9$.

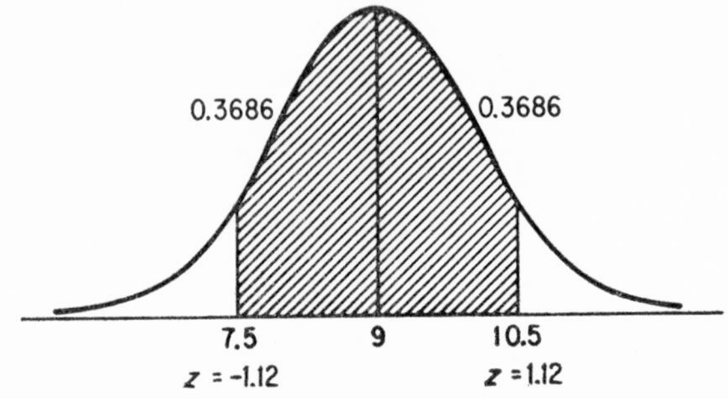

Fig. 8.8 Sampling distribution of the mean.

Since the population standard deviation equaled $\sigma = 3$, we have $\sigma_{\bar{x}} = 3/\sqrt{5} = 1.34$, and the probability of getting a sample mean on the interval from 7.5 to 10.5 is given by the normal curve area between $z = \frac{7.5 - 9}{1.34} = -1.12$ and $z = \frac{10.5 - 9}{1.34} = 1.12$ (see also Figure 8.8). It follows from Table I that the desired probability is $0.3686 + 0.3686 = 0.7372$, or in other words that we can expect about 74 per cent of the sample means to fall on the interval from 7.5 to 10.5. This agrees quite well with the actual 70 per cent we obtained in our sampling experiment. In Exercise 16 below, the reader will be asked to verify that for this sampling experiment the Central Limit Theorem would lead us to expect that about 94 per cent of the means should fall on the interval from 6.5 to 11.5; this is very close to the 95 per cent we actually obtained.

The main purpose of this section has been to introduce the concept of a sampling distribution, and we chose for this purpose the sampling distribution of the mean. We could continue our study of sampling distributions by calculating the medians, the ranges, the standard deviations, or other statistics of the 40 samples on page 207 and group them into corresponding (experimental) sampling distributions (see Exercises 6 and 8 below). Then we could check how closely the standard deviations of these sampling distributions agree with the corresponding *standard errors* (obtained according to appropriate statistical theory), or otherwise compare the shape or other features of these sampling distributions with theoretical expectations. As we shall see in our examples, many of these sampling distributions can be approximated closely with normal distributions.

EXERCISES

1. Random samples of size 2 are taken from the finite population which consists of the numbers 0, 2, 4, 6, 8, and 10.

(a) Show that the mean and the standard deviation of this population are $\mu = 5$ and $\sigma = \sqrt{35/3}$.

(b) List the 15 possible samples of size 2 that can be taken from this finite population and calculate their respective means.

(c) Using the results of part (b) and assigning each of the possible samples a probability of 1/15, construct the sampling distribution of the mean for random samples of size 2 from the given population.

(d) Calculate the mean and the standard deviation of the probability distribution obtained in part (c) and compare with the corresponding values expected in accordance with the theorem on page 209.

2. The finite population of Exercise 1 can be converted into an *infinite* population if we sample *with replacement*, that is, if we obtain the random sample of size 2 by first drawing one value and replacing it before drawing the second value.

(a) List the 36 possible samples of size 2 that can be drawn with replacement from the given population.

(b) Calculate the mean of each of the 36 samples obtained in part (a), and assigning each of the samples a probability of 1/36, construct the sampling distribution of the mean for random samples of size 2 obtained with replacement from the given population.

(c) Calculate the mean and the standard deviation of the probability distribution obtained in part (b) and compare with the corresponding values expected in accordance with the theorem on page 209; σ is given in part (a) of Exercise 1.

3. In Section 8.2 we showed that under certain conditions the variation of *stratified* samples can be much less than that of ordinary random samples of the same size.

(a) Assigning each of the random samples on page 194 a probability of 1/6, show that the mean and the standard deviation of this sampling distribution are $\mu_{\bar{x}} = 160$ lb and $\sigma_{\bar{x}} = 21.0$ lb.

(b) Assigning each of the stratified samples on page 194 a probability of 1/4, show that the mean and the standard deviation of this sampling distribution are $\mu_{\bar{x}} = 160$ lb and $\sigma_{\bar{x}} = 7.1$ lb.

(c) Discuss the results obtained in parts (a) and (b).

4. Referring to Exercise 11 on page 197, calculate $\sigma_{\bar{x}}$ for the 15 random samples of part (a), the 9 stratified samples of part (b), and the 6 cluster samples of part (c). Assume that sampling within each stratum and within each cluster is random, namely, that the samples have equal probabilities of 1/15, 1/9, and 1/6, respectively. Discuss the results.

5. Convert the 40 samples on page 207 into 20 samples of size 10 by combining Samples 1 and 21, Samples 2 and 22, . . . , and Samples 20 and 40. Calculate the mean of each of these samples of size 10 and determine their mean and their standard deviation. Compare the value obtained for the standard deviation of these 20 means with that expected in accordance with the theorem on page 209.

6. Find the *medians* of the 40 samples on page 207 and calculate their mean and their standard deviation. Comparing the standard deviation of this *experimental sampling distribution of the median* with that of the corresponding *experimental sampling distribution of the mean* (which was 1.32), what can we say about the relative "reliability" of the median and the mean in estimating the mean of the given population?

7. For random samples of size n from a population having the shape of a normal distribution, the *standard error of the median* (namely, the standard deviation of the sampling distribution of the median) is given by $\sqrt{\frac{\pi}{2}}\cdot\frac{\sigma}{\sqrt{n}}$ or approximately $1.25\cdot\frac{\sigma}{\sqrt{n}}$. How close is the value obtained for the standard deviation of the medians of Exercise 6 to the value expected according to this formula with $\sigma = 3$ and $n = 5$?

8. Calculating the standard deviations of the 40 samples on page 207, we obtain the following *experimental sampling distributions of s:*

Sample Standard Deviation	*Frequency*
0.5 – 1.5	4
1.5 – 2.5	11
2.5 – 3.5	15
3.5 – 4.5	9
4.5 – 5.5	0
5.5 – 6.5	1

(a) Calculate the mean and the standard deviation of this sampling distribution.

(b) For large samples, the formula $\frac{\sigma}{\sqrt{2n}}$ is often used for the *standard error of a sample standard deviation*. Substituting $\sigma = 3$ and $n = 5$, calculate the value of this standard error for the given example and compare it with the value of the standard deviation obtained for the experimental sampling distribution in part (a).

9. What happens to the standard error of the mean for random samples from an infinite population when
(a) the sample size is changed from 60 to 240;
(b) the sample size is changed from 128 to 1,152;
(c) the sample size is changed from 100 to 10,000?

10. Show that if the sampling distribution of a statistic W can be approximated closely with a normal distribution having the mean μ and the standard deviation σ_W, and the value of W obtained in a random sample is used as an estimate of μ, then there is a *fifty-fifty chance* that the error will be less than $0.6745 \cdot \sigma_W$. (*Hint:* Interpolate to find the value of z which corresponds to an area of 0.2500 in Table I.) It is customary to refer to 0.6745 *times* the standard error of a statistic as its *probable error*.

11. If random samples of size 100 are taken from a normal population with $\sigma = 12.5$, calculate the size of the *probable error* (see Exercise 10) and explain its significance.

12. The infinite population for which $x = 1, 2, 3, \ldots, 10$, and 11 with respective probabilities of 0.01, 0.03, 0.07, 0.12, 0.17, 0.20, 0.17, 0.12, 0.07, 0.03, and 0.01, has the mean $\mu = 6$ and the standard deviation $\sigma = 2$.
(a) Use two-digit random numbers to simulate a sampling experiment in which 50 samples of size 10 are taken from the given population.
(b) Calculate the mean of each of the 50 samples obtained in part (a).
(c) Calculate the mean and the standard deviation of the 50 $\bar{x}$'s obtained in part (b), and compare with the corresponding values expected in accordance with the theorem on page 209.

13. Referring to Exercise 12, determine the median of each of the 50 samples obtained in part (a), calculate their standard deviation, and compare it with the value obtained with the standard error formula of Exercise 7.

14. The mean of a random sample of size $n = 36$ is used to estimate the mean of a population having a normal distribution with the standard deviation $\sigma = 15$. What can we assert about the probability that the error will be less than 7.5
(a) using Chebyshev's Theorem;
(b) using the Central Limit Theorem?

15. The mean of a random sample of size $n = 144$ is used to estimate the mean of a population having the standard deviation $\sigma = 2.4$ in. What can we assert about the probability that the error will be less than 0.25
(a) using Chebyshev's Theorem;
(b) using the Central Limit Theorem?

16. Show that if the Central Limit Theorem is applied to the example on page 208 (even though n is only 5), we can expect 94 per cent of the sample means to fall on the interval from 6.5 to 11.5. Compare this figure with the percentage actually obtained.

17. If the distribution of the weights of all men traveling by air between Los Angeles and San Francisco has a mean of 158 lb and a standard deviation of 19 lb, what is the probability that the combined gross weight of 40 men on a plane between these two cities is more than 6,480 lb?

BIBLIOGRAPHY

The following are some of the most widely used tables of random numbers.

Interstate Commerce Commission, Bureau of Transport Economics and Statistics, *Table of 105,000 Random Decimal Digits.* Washington, D.C.: U.S. Government Printing Office, 1949.

Kendall, M. G., and Smith, B. B., *Tables of Random Numbers, Tracts for Computers No. XXIV.* Cambridge: Cambridge University Press, 1939.

Owen, D. B., *Handbook of Statistical Tables.* Reading, Mass.: Addison-Wesley Publishing Co., Inc., 1962.

RAND Corporation, *A Million Random Digits with 100,000 Normal Deviates.* New York: Free Press of Glencoe, Inc., 1954.

Detailed descriptions of various kinds of sample designs may be found in

Cochran, W. G., *Sampling Techniques.* New York: John Wiley & Sons, Inc., 1953.

Deming, W. E., *Sample Design in Business Research.* New York: John Wiley & Sons, Inc., 1960.

Stuart, A., *Basic Ideas of Scientific Sampling.* New York: Hafner Publishing Co., Inc., 1962.

Yates, F. A., *Sampling Methods for Censuses and Surveys.* London: Charles Griffin & Co., Ltd., 1960.

PART THREE
Statistical Inference

NINE
Inferences Concerning Means

9.1 Introduction

In recent years attempts have been made to treat all problems of statistical inference (that is, all problems concerning generalizations based on samples) within the framework of a unified theory. Although this theory, called *decision theory*, has many conceptual and theoretical advantages, its application poses problems which are difficult to overcome. To understand these problems, one must appreciate the fact that no matter how objectively an experiment or an investigation may be planned, it is impossible to eliminate all elements of subjectivity. It is at least partially a subjective decision whether to base an experiment (say, the determination of an index of diffraction) on 3 measurements, on 5 measurements, or on 10 or more. Also, subjective factors invariably enter the design of equipment, the hiring of personnel, and even the precise formulation of a problem one wants to investigate. An element of subjectivity enters even when we define such terms as "good" or "best" in connection with the choice between different decision criteria (say, when deciding between a sample mean and a sample median in a problem of estimation), or when looking for the straight line which "best" fits a set of paired data. Above all, subjective judgments are practically unavoidable when one is asked to put "cash values" on the risks to which one is exposed. In contrast to the examples which we used in our discussion of *game theory* in Chapter 6, it is generally impossible in statistics to be completely objective in specifying rewards for being right (or close) and penalties for being wrong (or not close enough). After all, if a scientist is asked to judge the safety of a piece of equipment, how can he put a cash value on the consequences of a possible error on his part, if such an error may result in the loss of human lives?

The general approach we shall use in this book to problems of statistical inference may be called the *classical approach*, insofar as it does not *formally* take into account the various subjective factors we have mentioned.

In other words, the subjective elements will not appear as part of the formulas, themselves; rather, they will appear in the choice among formulas to be used in a given situation, in decisions concerning the size of a sample, in specifying the probabilities with which we are willing to incur certain risks, in specifying the maximum errors we consider acceptable, and so forth. The *Bayesian approach,* which can account for some of these subjective factors, is introduced briefly in Sections 9.4 and 11.2.

9.2 Problems of Estimation

According to some dictionaries, an estimate is a valuation based on opinion or roughly made from imperfect or incomplete data. Although this definition may apply to a parent's opinionated estimate of the ability of his child, or a politician's wishful thinking based on incomplete returns from his own precinct, this is *not* how the term "estimate" is used in statistics. In statistics we allow estimates based on opinions or incomplete information only if such opinions are based on sound judgment or experience and if the samples are scientifically selected.

Statistical methods of estimation find applications almost anywhere, in science, in business, as well as in everyday life. *In science,* a biologist may wish to estimate what proportion of a certain kind of insect is born physically defective, a psychologist may wish to estimate the average (mean) time it takes an adult to react to a given stimulus, and an engineer may wish to estimate how much variability there is in the strength of a new alloy. *In business,* a finance company may wish to estimate what proportion of its customers plan to buy a new car within the next year, a contractor may wish to estimate the average monthly rent paid for two-room apartments in a suburb where he is planning to erect some new units, and a manufacturer of television tubes may wish to estimate how much variation there is in the lifetimes of his product. Finally, *in everyday life,* we may want to estimate what percentage of car accidents are due to faulty brakes, we may be interested in estimating the average time it takes to iron a pair of pajamas, and we may wish to know how much variation one can expect in a child's performance in school. Note that in each case we gave three examples: one dealing with the estimation of a percentage or proportion, one dealing with the estimation of a mean, and one dealing with an appropriate measure of variation. These (and particularly the first two) are the parameters with which we are concerned in most problems of estimation.

Referring again to the science examples, the biologist may estimate the proportion of physically defective insects as 0.08, the psychologist may estimate the average time it takes to react to the given stimulus as 0.32 seconds, and the engineer may estimate the standard deviation of measurements of the strength of different specimens of the new alloy as 240 pounds per square inch. Estimates like these are called *point estimates*, since each one consists of a single number, namely, a single point on the real number scale. Although this may be the most common way of expressing an estimate, point estimates have the serious shortcoming that they do not tell us anything about their relative merits; that is, they do not tell us how close we can expect them to be to the quantities they are supposed to estimate. In other words, *point estimates do not tell us anything about the intrinsic reliability or precision of the method of estimation which is being used.* For instance, if an advertisement claims on the basis of "scientific" evidence that 80 per cent of all doctors prefer Brand X cigarets, this would *not* be very meaningful if the claim were based on interviews with only 5 doctors, among whom 4 happen to prefer Brand X. However, the claim would become more and more meaningful if it were based on interviews with 100 doctors, 400 doctors, or perhaps even 1,000 doctors. This illustrates why point estimates should always be accompanied by some information which makes it possible to judge their merits. How this is done will be explained in the next section.

In most of the methods discussed in this chapter we shall assume that our estimates are to be based only on *direct* observations or measurements. If this kind of information is to be supplemented with collateral information based on *indirect data* or a person's *subjective judgment*, it may be necessary to use some form of *Bayesian inference;* perhaps, the method described in Section 9.4.

9.3 The Estimation of Means

To illustrate some of the problems we face in the estimation of means, let us consider a study in which a biologist wants to estimate the average (mean) length of young-of-the-year fresh-water drumfish, as can be found in a certain part of Lake Erie. The following are the sample data (in millimeters) which he has at his disposal:

92	88	85	82	89	86	81	66	75	61
78	76	91	82	82	78	82	86	96	61
62	59	80	65	70	86	78	78	71	71
95	86	84	84	88	72	81	64	71	58
60	81	73	67	85	89	75	79	77	65

The mean of this sample is $\bar{x} = 77.4$ mm, and in the absence of any other information this figure will serve as an estimate of μ, the *true* average length of this kind of fish.

In order to comply with the suggestion that point estimates should always be accompanied by information which makes it possible to judge their merits, we might add that the size of the sample on which the estimate is based is $n = 50$ and that the sample standard deviation is $s = 10.0$ mm. Unfortunately, this kind of information is meaningful only to someone who has some knowledge of statistics; to make it more meaningful to the layman, let us go back briefly to the discussion of the preceding chapter, in particular to that dealing with the sampling distribution of the mean. Of course, we know that sample means (of data describing the same phenomenon) will fluctuate from sample to sample, but we also know that the mean and the standard deviation of the sampling distribution which describes these fluctuations are μ and $\sigma/\sqrt{n}$. Here μ and σ are the mean and the standard deviation of the (supposedly infinite) population from which the sample was obtained. Also making use of the Central Limit Theorem (see page 211) according to which this samp'ing distribution can be approximated closely with a normal curve, we can now assert with a probability of $1 - \alpha$ that $\bar{x}$ will differ from μ by less than $z_{\alpha/2}$ standard deviations. As defined in Exercise 5 on page 180, $z_{\alpha/2}$ denotes the value for which the area

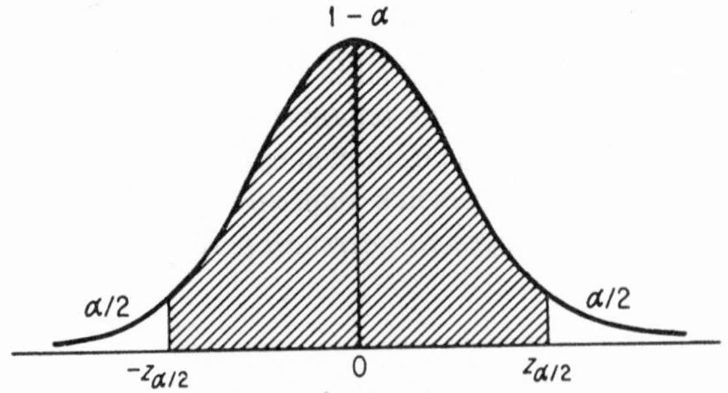

Fig. 9.1 Area under normal curve.

to its right under the standard normal distribution is equal to $\alpha/2$, and, hence, the area under the curve between $-z_{\alpha/2}$ and $+z_{\alpha/2}$ is equal to $1 - \alpha$ (see also Figure 9.1). In other words, *we can say that $\bar{x}$ will differ from μ by less than $z_{\alpha/2}\frac{\sigma}{\sqrt{n}}$, and since $\bar{x} - \mu$ is the error we make when we use $\bar{x}$ as an estimate of μ, we can assert with a probability of $1 - \alpha$ that the size of this error will be less than $z_{\alpha/2}\frac{\sigma}{\sqrt{n}}$.* Using the numerical results obtained in Exercise 5 on page 180, namely, that $z_{0.025} = 1.96$, $z_{0.010} = 2.33$, and $z_{0.005} = 2.58$, we find that we can assert with a probability of 0.95 that the error will be less than $1.96\frac{\sigma}{\sqrt{n}}$, with a probability of 0.98 that the error will be less than $2.33\frac{\sigma}{\sqrt{n}}$, and with a probability of 0.99 that the error will be less than $2.58\frac{\sigma}{\sqrt{n}}$.

The result we have obtained involves one complication: to judge the size of the error we might make when using $\bar{x}$ as an estimate of μ, we must know σ, the standard deviation of the population. Since this is seldom the case in practical situations, we have no choice but to replace σ with an estimate, usually the sample standard deviation s. Generally speaking, this is reasonable provided the sample size is sufficiently large, and by "sufficiently large" we mean $n = 30$ or more.

Returning now to our numerical example, we can assert with a probability of 0.95 that if we estimate the *true* average length of the given kind of fish as 77.4 mm, the error of this estimate is less than $1.96s/\sqrt{n} = 1.96(10.0)/\sqrt{50} = 2.8$ mm. Of course, the error of our estimate is either less than 2.8 mm or it is not (and we really do not know which), but *if we had to bet*, 95 to 5 (or 19 to 1) would be fair odds that the error *is* less than 2.8 mm. Similarly, 98 to 2 (or 49 to 1) would be fair odds that the error is less than $2.33s/\sqrt{n} = 2.33(10.0)/\sqrt{50} = 3.3$ mm, and 99 to 1 would be fair odds that it is less than $2.58s/\sqrt{n} = 2.58(10.0)/\sqrt{50} = 3.65$ mm. Note that these odds are based on the *success-ratio* of the method we have used, namely, the per cent of the time it can be expected to work. When σ is unknown and n is less than 30, the method we have just discussed cannot be used, but there exists a modification which applies also to small samples (n less than 30), provided we can assume that we are sampling from a population having roughly the shape of a normal distribution. We shall discuss this method later, on page 225.

An interesting feature of the formula for the maximum error is that it can also be used to determine the sample size that is required to attain a desired degree of precision. Suppose we want to use the mean of a random sample to estimate the mean of a population and we want to be able to assert with a probability of $1 - \alpha$ that the error of this estimate will be less than some quantity E. In accordance with the theory on page 222, we can thus write

▲ $$E = z_{\alpha/2} \frac{\sigma}{\sqrt{n}}$$ ▲

and upon solving this equation for n we get

▲ $$n = \left[\frac{z_{\alpha/2} \cdot \sigma}{E}\right]^2$$ ▲

Note that this formula cannot be used unless we know (or can approximate) the standard deviation of the population whose mean we want to estimate.

To illustrate this technique, suppose we want to estimate the average mechanical aptitude of a large group of people (as measured by a certain standard test) and that we want this estimate to be off by at most 2.0 with a probability of 0.98. Suppose also that (on the basis of experience with similar data) it is reasonable to let σ be 15.0. Substituting these values together with $z_{0.010} = 2.33$ into the formula for n, we obtain

$$n = \left[\frac{2.33(15.0)}{2.0}\right]^2 = 305 \text{ (approximately)}$$

and it follows that a sample of size $n = 305$ will suffice for the stated purpose. In other words, if we base our estimate on a random sample of size 305 we can assert with a probability of 0.98 that our estimate, namely, the sample mean, is within 2.0 of the true mean.

The error we make when using a sample mean to estimate the mean of a population is given by the difference $\bar{x} - \mu$, and the fact that the *magnitude* of this error is less than $z_{\alpha/2}\frac{\sigma}{\sqrt{n}}$ can be expressed by means of the inequality

$$-z_{\alpha/2}\frac{\sigma}{\sqrt{n}} < \bar{x} - \mu < z_{\alpha/2}\frac{\sigma}{\sqrt{n}}$$

(In case the reader is not familiar with inequality signs, let us point out that $a < b$ means "a is less than b," while $a > b$ means that "a is greater than b." Also, $a \leqslant b$ means "a is less than or equal to b," while $a \geqslant b$ means "a is greater than or equal to b.") Applying some simple algebra, we can rewrite the above inequality as

▲ $$\bar{x} - z_{\alpha/2}\frac{\sigma}{\sqrt{n}} < \mu < \bar{x} + z_{\alpha/2}\frac{\sigma}{\sqrt{n}}$$ ▲

and we can now assert with a probability of $1 - \alpha$ that the inequality is satisfied for any given sample, namely, that the interval from $\bar{x} - z_{\alpha/2}\frac{\sigma}{\sqrt{n}}$ to $\bar{x} + z_{\alpha/2}\frac{\sigma}{\sqrt{n}}$ actually contains the mean we are trying to estimate. An interval like this is called a *confidence interval,* its endpoints are called *confidence limits,* and the probability $1 - \alpha$ with which we can assert that such an interval will "do its job," namely, that it will contain the quantity we are trying to estimate, is called the *degree of confidence.* The values most commonly used for the degree of confidence are $1 - \alpha = 0.95$, 0.98, or 0.99, and, as we pointed out earlier, the corresponding values of $z_{\alpha/2}$ are 1.96, 2.33, and 2.58.

When σ is unknown and n is 30 or more, we proceed as before and estimate σ with the sample standard deviation s. The resulting $1 - \alpha$ *large-sample confidence interval* for μ becomes

▲ $$\bar{x} - z_{\alpha/2}\frac{s}{\sqrt{n}} < \mu < \bar{x} + z_{\alpha/2}\frac{s}{\sqrt{n}}$$ ▲

If we apply this technique to the numerical example on page 221, where we had $n = 50$, $\bar{x} = 77.4$, and $s = 10.0$, we obtain the following 0.95 confidence interval for the true average length of the given kind of fish:

$$77.4 - 1.96 \frac{10.0}{\sqrt{50}} < \mu < 77.4 + 1.96 \frac{10.0}{\sqrt{50}}$$

$$74.6 < \mu < 80.2$$

Had we wanted to calculate a 0.99 confidence interval for this example, we would have obtained

$$73.75 < \mu < 81.05$$

and this illustrates the interesting fact that *the surer we want to be in connection with a confidence interval, the less we have to be sure of.* In other words, if we increase the degree of certainty (the degree of confidence), the confidence interval becomes wider and thus tells us less about the quantity we want to estimate.

When we estimate the mean of a population with the use of a confidence interval, we refer to this kind of estimate as an *interval estimate*. In contrast to a point estimate, an interval estimate requires no further elaboration about its relative merits; this is taken care of indirectly by the degree of confidence and its actual width.

So far we have assumed that the sample size was large enough to treat the sampling distribution of the mean as if it were a normal distribution, and to replace σ with s in the formula for the standard error. In order to develop corresponding theory which applies also to *small samples*, let us now assume that the population from which we are sampling can be approximated closely with a normal curve. We can then base our methods on the statistic

▲ $$t = \frac{\bar{x} - \mu}{s/\sqrt{n}}$$ ▲

whose sampling distribution is called the *t distribution*. (More specifically, it is called the *Student-t distribution*, as it was first investigated by W. S. Gosset, who published his writings under the pen name of "Student.") The shape of this distribution is very much like that of the normal curve; it is symmetrical with zero mean, but there is a slightly higher probability of getting values falling into the two tails (see Figure 9.2). Actually, the shape of the t distribution depends on the size of the sample or, better, on the quantity $n - 1$, which in this connection is called the *number of degrees of freedom.**

* In other applications of the t distribution, for example, on page 256, the number of degrees of freedom may be given by a different expression.

For the standard normal distribution, we defined $z_{\alpha/2}$ in such a way that the area *to its right* under the normal curve equals $\alpha/2$ and, hence, the area

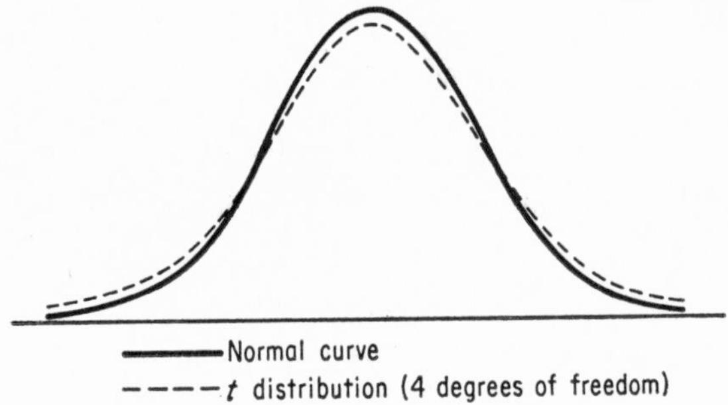

Fig. 9.2 Normal curve and t distribution.

under the curve between $-z_{\alpha/2}$ and $z_{\alpha/2}$ equals $1 - \alpha$. As is shown in Figure 9.3, the corresponding values for the t distribution are $-t_{\alpha/2}$ and $t_{\alpha/2}$; the main difference is that these values depend on $n - 1$ (the number of degrees of freedom) and, hence, must be looked up in each case in a special table.

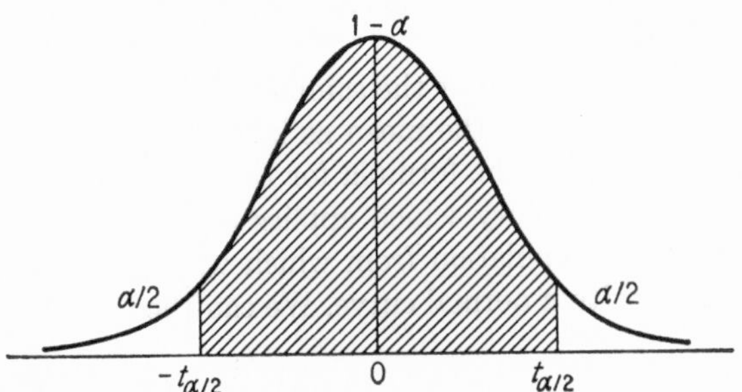

Fig. 9.3 t distribution.

Table II at the end of the book contains (among others) the values of $t_{0.025}$, $t_{0.010}$, and $t_{0.005}$, with the number of degrees of freedom going from 1 to 29. Observe that as the number of degrees of freedom increases, $t_{0.025}$ approaches 1.96, $t_{0.010}$ approaches 2.33, and $t_{0.005}$ approaches 2.58, the corresponding values for the normal distribution.

Duplicating the argument on page 224, we now find that a $1 - \alpha$ *small-sample confidence interval for* μ is given by

$$\bar{x} - t_{\alpha/2}\frac{s}{\sqrt{n}} < \mu < \bar{x} + t_{\alpha/2}\frac{s}{\sqrt{n}}$$

The only difference between this confidence-interval and the second one on page 224 is that $t_{\alpha/2}$ takes the place of $z_{\alpha/2}$; of course, the formula for t

did not contain the population standard deviation σ, so that we did not have to make the substitution (s for σ) which restricted the confidence interval on page 224 to large samples.

To illustrate the calculation of a small-sample confidence interval for μ, let us consider the following measurements of the length of the skulls (in centimeters) of fossil skeletons of an extinct species of birds:

5.82 6.10 5.63 5.95 6.24 5.51 6.06 6.63 6.19 5.67

The mean and the standard deviation of these measurements are $\bar{x} = 5.98$ cm and $s = 0.336$ cm, and since $t_{0.025}$ for $10 - 1 = 9$ degrees of freedom equals 2.262, substitution into the formula yields

$$5.98 - (2.262)\frac{0.336}{\sqrt{10}} < \mu < 5.98 + (2.262)\frac{0.336}{\sqrt{10}}$$

or

$$5.74 < \mu < 6.22$$

An estimate like this may be important in the identification of the species or, perhaps, in making comparisons with other species.

The method we used on page 223 to indicate the possible size of the error we make when using a sample mean to estimate the mean of a population can easily be adapted to small samples. All we have to do is substitute s for σ and $t_{\alpha/2}$ for $z_{\alpha/2}$ in the formula for E. To give an example, let us consider the following measurements of compressive strength obtained for a random sample of the steel beams produced by a certain mill (figures in pounds per square inch):

43,500 82,850 46,750 72,500 71,900

The mean and the standard deviation of this sample are $\bar{x} = 63{,}500$ and $s = 17{,}350$, respectively, and since $t_{0.025}$ for $5 - 1 = 4$ degrees of freedom equals 2.776 ,we find that

$$E = t_{0.025}\frac{s}{\sqrt{n}} = (2.776)\frac{17{,}350}{\sqrt{5}}$$

$$= 21{,}540 \text{ (rounded up to the nearest dollar)}$$

Thus, if we estimate the mean compressive strength of all the steel beams from which this sample was obtained as being $\bar{x} = 63{,}500$, we can assert with a probability of 0.95 that our error is less than 21,540 pounds per square inch. This illustrates the fact that *although we can make logically correct inferences on the basis of very small samples, our results are apt to involve considerable errors and our confidence intervals are apt to be very wide.*

9.4 A Bayesian Estimate*

In recent years there has been mounting interest in methods of inference which look upon parameters (for example, a population mean μ) as random variables. The whole idea is not really new, but these *Bayesian methods*, as they are called, have received a considerable impetus and much wider applicability through the concept of personal, or subjective, probability. In fact, this is why supporters of the personal concept of probability refer to themselves as *Bayesians*, or *Bayesian statisticians.*

In this section we shall illustrate a method of Bayesian inference with reference to two problems of estimation; one of these does not require subjective probabilities, while the other one does. The first is a problem of insurance rate making, to which the author was introduced by the late Arthur L. Bailey, while working for the Mutual Casualty Insurance Rating Bureau in New York City. To simplify this example, we shall consider only an insurance company's *expected losses*, ignoring sales commissions and other factors which enter into the calculation of an insurance premium.

When a new risk is first insured, the expected losses are based entirely on *collateral information.* For instance, when a company writes a fire insurance policy for a large new office building, their estimate of the expected losses is based entirely on previous experience with similar risks; that is, other office buildings of a similar kind. Also, when a company writes a liability policy to cover the delivery trucks of a brand new department store, their estimate of the expected losses is based entirely on data gathered for other, but similar, stores. After a number of years, when some *direct* information has become available, the company may *experience rate* the risk (the office building or the fleet of trucks) and modify the premium accordingly. When this is being done, the company's actuaries base their estimate of the expected losses partly on the direct information that has become available (that is, actual loss figures that have been observed for the given risk) and partly on the original collateral information based on other risks belonging to the same classification.

To present a formula which may be used for estimates of this kind, we shall first have to explain the notation we intend to use, and it will be convenient to do this with reference to the example where an insurance company writes a liability policy on the 5 delivery trucks of a new department store. If we consider this *particular risk*, namely, the delivery trucks of this *particular* department store, it is clear that the liability losses will vary from year to year, depending on the damage done in each accident involving the trucks. The annual losses will, thus, have a certain distribution, whose mean and standard deviation we shall denote μ and σ. Now, if we consider *different*

* See comment on this section in the Preface.

risks, that is, fleets of 5 delivery trucks operated by other stores, it stands to reason that the average annual losses will vary from fleet to fleet. There will be variations among the μ's due to differences in the size of the delivery area, differences in equipment, differences in driver training and ability, and so on. Considering various fleets of trucks which are similar to those of the new department store, we can thus say that μ, itself, has a distribution, and we shall denote the mean and the standard deviation of this distribution by $\bar{\mu}$ and σ_μ. Observe that $\bar{\mu}$, the average losses for various similar fleets of trucks, provides the original estimate of the expected losses, the one which was based entirely on collateral information.

To estimate the expected losses for the given fleet of delivery trucks on the basis of direct as well as collateral information, we shall want to compromise between the average losses that have actually been incurred over a number of years, $\bar{x}$, and the original estimate, $\bar{\mu}$, based on collateral data. One possibility is to use a *weighted mean* (see Section 3.3), and to write

▲ $$\text{Estimate} = w \cdot \bar{x} + (1 - w) \cdot \bar{\mu}$$ ▲

where w is a *percentage weight*, or *relative importance weight*, which must assume a value on the interval from 0 to 1. If $w = 0.14$, for example, this means that 14 per cent of the total weight is given to $\bar{x}$ and 86 per cent to $\bar{\mu}$; if $w = 0.68$, then 68 per cent of the total weight is given to $\bar{x}$ and 32 per cent to $\bar{\mu}$. Naturally, whatever value we use for w will have to depend on *how much*, and *what kind of*, direct as well as collateral information we have available.

If we now impose the condition that *on the average* the square of the error of this kind of estimate be as small as possible, it can be shown that

▲ $$w = \frac{n}{n + \dfrac{\sigma^2}{\sigma_\mu^2}}$$ ▲

where, as indicated above, σ measures the variation among the annual losses of a particular fleet of trucks, σ_μ measures the variation among the *average* annual losses for different (though similar) fleets of trucks, and n is the number of years for which the liability losses for the particular fleet of trucks have been observed.

Before we apply this formula, let us briefly examine some of its most important features. First, when no direct information is available and $n = 0$, the weight w equals 0 and the estimate is based entirely on the collateral information. When more and more direct evidence becomes available, that is, when n becomes larger and larger, w increases and comes closer and closer to 1. Thus, when more and more direct information becomes available, the estimate is based to a greater and greater extent on the direct information, namely, on $\bar{x}$. There are two other points that should be observed. First, when there are large differences among the average annual losses of different fleets of trucks, σ_μ will be large and the collateral information is relatively unreliable. As can be seen from the formula for w, if we increase σ_μ^2 while keeping σ^2 fixed, this will make σ^2/σ_μ^2 small and, hence, w large. *This is exactly as it should be, because most of the weight would then go to the direct information.* Now, when σ is very large, which means that the annual losses for a particular fleet of trucks vary considerably from year to year, this has the tendency to make σ^2/σ_μ^2 large and, hence, w relatively small. *This is also as it should be, because more weight would then go to the collateral information.*

As the reader will be asked to verify in Exercise 31 on page 237, the estimation formula for the expected losses may also be described as the weighted mean of $\bar{x}$ and $\bar{\mu}$, with the weights being n/σ^2 and $1/\sigma_\mu^2$. In connection with this, n/σ^2 has been referred to as the (amount of) *information* summarized by $\bar{x}$, and $1/\sigma_\mu^2$ as the (amount of) *information* summarized by $\bar{\mu}$. (This agrees with standard practice in sampling theory, where data are often weighted in inverse proportion to their variances.)

To illustrate the use of the estimation formula, let us suppose that data collected over a long period of time for the delivery trucks of many different department stores show that with a fleet of 5 trucks one can expect annual liability losses of about \$1,568 with a standard deviation of \$240. Suppose also that it is known from past data that for any particular fleet of 5 delivery trucks the year-to-year variations of the annual losses are measured by a standard deviation of \$385. Substituting $\bar{\mu} = 1{,}568$, $\sigma_\mu = 240$, and $\sigma = 385$ into the formula for w, we obtain

$$w = \frac{n}{n + \frac{385^2}{240^2}} = \frac{n}{n + 2.57}$$

and the formula for estimating the expected annual losses becomes

$$\frac{n}{n + 2.57} \cdot \bar{x} + \left(1 - \frac{n}{n + 2.57}\right) \cdot 1{,}568$$

Note that for $n = 3$ the weight w becomes $\dfrac{3}{3 + 2.57} = 0.54$, and that for $n = 10$ it becomes $\dfrac{10}{10 + 2.57} = 0.80$; this means that after 3 years 54 per cent of the weight is shifted to the direct information, and that after 10 years 80 per cent of the weight is shifted to the direct information. For instance, if during the first 3 years the liability policy is in effect the annual liability losses equaled \$1,500, \$1,950, and \$750, we have $\bar{x} = \$1{,}400$, and the expected annual losses are estimated as

$$(0.54)1400 + (0.46)1568 = \$1{,}477$$

Of course, this method of estimation is not limited to our insurance example; it applies to any kind of situation where meaningful values of $\bar{\mu}$, σ, and σ_μ can be obtained. It does not require any further assumptions; in particular, it does not require any assumptions about the population from which we are sampling or the distribution of μ.* This situation changes, however, if we want to judge the merits of this kind of estimate. In that case we may want to assume, or have to assume, that the population from which we are sampling as well as the distribution of μ can be approximated closely with normal distributions having the means μ and $\bar{\mu}$, and the standard deviations σ and σ_μ (see Exercise 29 on page 237). Some theory pertaining to this case, including a derivation of the estimation formula, itself, may be found in the books by R. Schlaifer and by D. V. Lindley listed in the Bibliography at the end of this chapter. Their arguments are based on a generalization of the Rule of Bayes introduced in Section 5.8; hence, the name "Bayesian inference."

As we pointed out at the beginning of this section, proponents of the concept of subjective, or personal, probability can apply Bayesian inferences on a much wider scale; they look upon the distribution of the parameter μ as an indication of how strongly a person feels about the various values μ can assume. In other words, they suggest that in a situation like this a person will feel most strongly that some particular value of μ is the correct one; his enthusiasm will diminish for values of the parameter μ which are further and further away from the one he likes the most. In the continuous case, the subjective probability associated with any interval of values of μ is, thus given by an area under a curve which, itself, is descriptive of the relative strength of a person's belief.

To illustrate this subjective approach, suppose that someone is planning to open a new donut shop, and that a business consultant feels that he should net on the average \$1,200 a month; well, in any case, the consultant is willing to give 3 to 1 odds that the average monthly net profit will be somewhere between \$1,050 and \$1,350. If no other information is available, one would probably accept the consultant's estimate of the average monthly profit. The problem is how to modify this figure if during the first 9 months of operation the donut shop nets, say, \$1,410, \$1,290, \$950, \$1,000, \$920, \$850, \$1,030, \$1,200, and \$1,270. The mean of these monthly net profits is \$1,102, their standard deviation is \$195, and so far as the formula on page 229 is concerned we have $\bar{x} = \$1{,}102$ and we can *estimate* σ as \$195. So far as $\bar{\mu}$ is concerned, we have the consultant's figure of \$1,200, and the only other quantity we need is an estimate of σ_μ. If we assume that the consul-

* In this connection, it is customary to refer to the distribution of μ as its *prior* or *a priori* distribution; it describes the situation prior to the consideration of specific sample evidence.

tant's feelings concerning μ (the average monthly net profit) can be described by a normal distribution, we can make use of his 3 to 1 odds and argue that 75 per cent of the area under this normal distribution must lie between

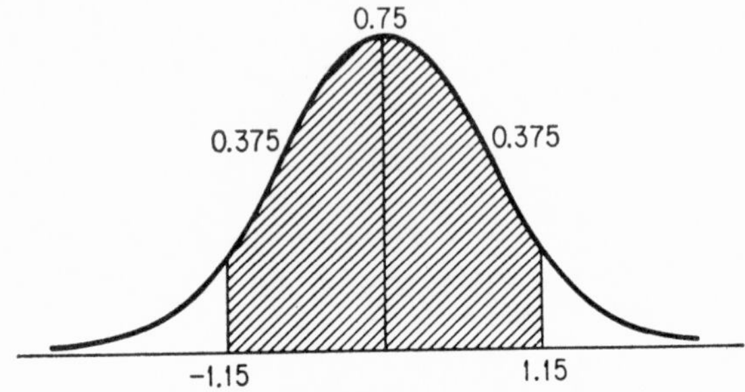

Fig. 9.4 Normal distribution.

1,050 and 1,350 (see Figure 9.4). Since 75 per cent of the area under the standard normal distribution falls between $z = -1.15$ and $z = 1.15$, it follows that

$$\frac{1350 - 1200}{\sigma_\mu} = 1.15 \quad \text{and} \quad \sigma_\mu = 130$$

If we now substitute $\sigma = 195$, $\sigma_\mu = 130$, and $n = 9$ into the formula for w on page 229, we get

$$w = \frac{9}{9 + \frac{195^2}{130^2}} = \frac{9}{9 + 2.25} = 0.80$$

and our *Bayesian estimate* of the shop's average monthly net profits becomes

$$(0.80)1{,}102 + (0.20)1{,}200 = \$1{,}122$$

to the nearest dollar. One way of judging the "goodness" of this kind of estimate is illustrated in Exercise 30 on page 237. It must be understood, of course, that any such evaluation would have to be largely subjective; among other things, it would have to depend on how one feels, personally, about the credibility of the consultant who supplied the prior, or collateral, information.

In conclusion, let us stress that we have illustrated the Bayesian approach only with regard to a very special method of estimation. Although this can hardly do justice to a general way of thought, practically a philosophy, it served to bring out the following important features: (1) *in Bayesian inference, the parameter about which the inference is to be made is looked upon as having a distribution of its own, and (2) this kind of inference permits the use of direct as well as collateral information—for example, the combination of objective information with subjective judgments.*

EXERCISES

1. A random sample taken as part of a study in nutrition showed that 400 young adults in an Australian city had an average protein intake of 1.274 gm (per kilogram of body weight) with a standard deviation of 0.62 gm. What can one say with a probability of 0.95 about the possible size of the error if $\bar{x} = 1.274$ gm is used to estimate the mean protein intake (per Kilogram of body weight) of all the young adults in this city?

2. Use the data of Exercise 1 to construct a 0.99 confidence interval for the mean protein intake (per kilogram of body weight) of all the young adults in the given city.

3. In order to determine the durability of a certain kind of airplane luggage, a random sample of 100 identical pieces of luggage were put to normal use until they started showing serious defects. If they lasted on the average 42,500 miles with a standard deviation of 2,850 miles, construct a 0.95 confidence interval for the true average "lifetime" of this kind of luggage.

4. Referring to Exercise 3, what can one assert with a probability of 0.98 about the possible size of the error, if the sample mean of 42,500 miles is used as an estimate of the true mean lifetime of the given kind of luggage?

5. A sample of 50 fuses is randomly selected from a very large shipment and subjected to tests under prescribed conditions. The mean blowing time of the fuses was found to be 11.75 seconds with a standard deviation of 0.14 second.

(a) What can be said with a probability of 0.95 about the possible size of the error, if this mean of 11.75 seconds is used as an estimate of the mean blowing time of all the fuses in the large shipment?

(b) Use the data to construct a 0.98 confidence interval for the mean blowing time of all the fuses in the shipment.

6. Taking a random sample from its very extensive files, a water company finds that the amounts owed in 150 delinquent accounts have a mean of \$16.35 and a standard deviation of \$4.55.

(a) Use these figures to construct a 0.95 confidence interval for the average amount owed on all of their delinquent accounts.

(b) What can they say with a probability of 0.99 about the possible size of their error, if they use \$16.35 as an estimate of the average amount owed on all their delinquent accounts?

7. A random sample of 64 scores on an achievement test given to thousands of college students has a mean of 218 and a standard deviation of 35. If this mean of 218 is used as an estimate of the average score obtained by all of the students who took the test, with what probability can one assert that the error of this estimate is less than 10.0? (*Hint:* Substitute z for $z_{\alpha/2}$ in the formula for E on page 223, solve for z, and find the area under the standard normal distribution between $-z$ and z.)

8. In order to price a new product, a manufacturer has to have an estimate of the time it takes to assemble the product. If 40 workers took on the average 20.4 minutes with a standard deviation of 3.5 minutes, with what probability can the manufacturer claim that his error will be less than 1 minute, if he takes 20.4 minutes as an estimate of the true average time it takes to assemble the new product? (*Hint:* Substitute z for $z_{\alpha/2}$ in the formula for E on page 223, solve for z, and find the normal curve area between $-z$ and z.)

9. It is known from experience that the standard deviation of the drained weights of all the number $2\frac{1}{2}$ cans of fruit salad in a large production lot is 0.60 ounce. How large a sample of these cans would have to be weighed so that one can assert with a probability of 0.95 that the error made in using the sample mean to estimate the true average weight is less than 0.15 ounce?

10. An efficiency expert wants to determine the average time it takes a housewife to iron a shirt. How large a sample will he need to be able to assert with a probability of 0.98 that his sample mean will not differ from the true mean by more than 20 seconds? Assume that it is known from other studies that measurements of this kind have a standard deviation of 72 seconds.

11. In a study of the reading habits of elected government officials it is desired to estimate the average number of newspapers they read per week. How large a sample would be required if one wants to be able to assert with a probability of 0.99 that the sample mean will not be "off" by more than 1.2? Assume that it is reasonable to use a standard deviation of 5.3.

12. If a sample constitutes an appreciable portion of a finite population (say, 5 per cent or more), the various formulas of Section 9.3 must be modified by basing them on the second standard-error formula of the theorem on page 209 instead of the first. For instance, the formula for E becomes

$$E = z_{\alpha/2}\frac{\sigma}{\sqrt{n}}\sqrt{\frac{N-n}{N-1}}$$

Repeat Exercise 1 assuming that there are 5,000 young adults in the given city.

13. Repeat part (b) of Exercise 6 assuming that there are altogether 750 delinquent accounts in the company's files and, hence, using the formula for E given in the preceding exercise.

14. Use the "finite population correction factor" $\sqrt{\frac{N-n}{N-1}}$ to modify the confidence-interval formula on page 224 and, thus, make it applicable to problems in which a sample constitutes an appreciable portion of a finite population. Assuming that there are altogether 750 delinquent accounts in the company's files, rework part (a) of Exercise 6.

15. If the population from which a sample is obtained has roughly the shape of a normal distribution, the first confidence-interval on page 224 applies also when n is small. Using this formula in connection with the samples obtained in Exercise 12 on page 215, the 0.95 confidence limits can be written as $\bar{x} \pm 1.96 \frac{2}{\sqrt{10}}$ or as $\bar{x} \pm 1.24$, since $\sigma = 2$ and $n = 10$. Calculate a corresponding 0.95 confidence interval for each of the 50 samples obtained in that exercise and check what proportion contains the population mean $\mu = 6$. How does this proportion compare with expectations?

16. The 40 samples used on page 207 to construct an experimental sampling distribution of the mean came from a bell-shaped distribution having a mean of 9 and a standard deviation of 3. As was pointed out in the preceding exercise, the confidence limits $\bar{x} \pm z_{\alpha/2} \frac{\sigma}{\sqrt{n}}$ can be used also when n is small provided that the population has roughly the shape of a normal distribution. Assuming that this is the case in this example, use the formula $\bar{x} \pm 1.96 \frac{3}{\sqrt{5}}$, namely, $\bar{x} \pm 2.63$, to calculate a 0.95 confidence interval for μ for each of the 40 samples and check what proportion contains the population mean $\mu = 9$.

17. In the example on page 63 we gave the number of microorganisms found in six cultures as 13, 17, 7, 10, 16, and 9. Assuming that the conditions underlying the t distribution are met (at least approximately), construct a 0.95 confidence interval for the true mean.

18. A chemist who took 12 measurements of the percentage of manganese in ferromanganese, an alloy or manganese and iron, obtained a mean of 81.27 per cent and a standard deviation of 0.38 per cent. Construct a 0.99 confidence interval for the true average per cent of manganese in the alloy.

19. In 8 test runs an experimental engine consumed, respectively, 14, 12, 11, 13, 15, 12, 16, and 13 gallons of gasoline per minute (under specified conditions). What can one assert with a probability of 0.95 about the possible size of the error, if the mean of this sample is used to estimate the engine's true average consumption of gasoline per minute?

20. Referring to Exercise 19, construct a 0.99 confidence interval for the engine's true average consumption of gasoline per minute.

21. A paint manufacturer wants to determine the average drying time of a new interior wall paint. Painting 10 test areas of equal size, he obtains a mean drying time of 68.5 minutes and a standard deviation of 9.4 minutes.

(a) Construct a 0.95 confidence interval for the true average drying time of the new paint.

(b) If the manufacturer uses 68.5 minutes as an estimate of the true average drying time of the new paint, what can he assert with a probability of 0.98 about the possible size of the error?

22. A metallurgist made four determinations of the melting point of a certain metal, getting 1258, 1261, 1260, and 1261 degrees centigrade. If he estimates the true melting point of the metal as 1260, what can he say with a probability of 0.90 about the possible size of his error?

23. A random sample of 20 delegates attending a national political convention showed that they spent on the average \$247.69 (with a standard deviation of \$21.73) while at the convention. Assuming that the small-sample method of Section 9.3 can be used, construct a 0.98 confidence interval for the actual average amount of money spent by delegates attending this convention.

24. Referring to the insurance example on page 230, obtain an estimate of the expected annual liability losses of the five-car fleet of trucks if the average liability losses for the first 5 years are \$843.25.

25. When using the weighted estimation formula of Section 9.4, it is important to know $\bar{\mu}$ to a high degree of precision (at least, when there is little direct information), but a lack of precision in the values of σ_μ and σ is not so critical.

(a) Calculate w for $n = 3$, $\sigma_\mu = 200$, and $\sigma = 400$.

(b) Calculate w for $n = 3$, $\sigma_\mu = 250$, and $\sigma = 350$.

(c) Using the value of w obtained in part (a) and the values of $\bar{x}$ and μ used in the text, namely, 1,400 and 1,568, estimate the expected annual losses for the given risk.

(d) Using the value of w obtained in part (b) and the values of $\bar{x}$ and μ used in the text, namely, 1,400 and 1,568, estimate the expected annual losses for the given risk.

(e) Compare the results of parts (c) and (d) with the estimate of \$1,477 obtained in the text.

26. Referring to the donut-shop example on page 231, construct a table showing the values of the weight w for $n = 2$, $n = 5$, $n = 10$, $n = 20$, and $n = 50$. This will give some idea of the speed with which the weight is shifted toward the direct evidence (in this example) when more and more direct data become available.

27. A distributor of soft-drink vending machines knows that in a supermarket one of his machines will sell on the average 738 drinks per week. Of course, this *mean* will vary somewhat from market to market, and this variation is measured by a standard deviation of 13.4. So far as a machine placed in a particular market is concerned, the number of drinks sold will vary from week to week, and this variation is measured by a standard deviation of 42.5.

(a) If this distributor plans to put one of his soft-drink vending machines into a brand new supermarket, what estimate would he use for the number of drinks he can expect to sell per week?

(b) How would he modify his estimate if during 10 weeks the machine sells on the average 692 drinks per week?

(c) How would he modify his original estimate if during 50 weeks the machine sells on the average 716 drinks per week?

28. A college professor is making up a final examination in history which is to be given to thousands of freshmen attending a very large school. Looking over the questions, he feels that the students should be able to average 72 points; at least, he feels that the odds are 4 to 1 that they should average anywhere from 68 to 76 points. Based on his experience, he also feels that the distribution of the grades for all the students should be close to a normal curve with the middle 95 per cent of the grades falling on the interval from 47 to 97.

(a) Obtain values for $\bar{\mu}$, σ_μ, and σ, stating in each case what assumptions may have to be made. (*Hint:* To find σ_μ assume that the distribution of μ is normal and make use of the fact that the normal curve area between 68 and 76 is given as 0.80; to find σ make use of the fact that for a normal distribution 95 per cent of the cases fall within 1.96 standard deviations on either side of the mean.)

(b) Suppose that after the test has been given he randomly selects and grades the tests of 25 students, obtaining a mean grade of 62.4. How would this affect his original estimate of 72 for the average grade all the students are expected to get on the test?

(c) Suppose that, subsequently, he randomly selects and grades the tests of another 75 students, getting a mean grade of 64.8. Find the over-all mean of the 100 tests and show how it affects his original estimate of 72 for the average grade all the students are expected to get on the test.

29. If the population from which we are sampling has a normal distribution with the mean μ and the standard deviation σ, and the prior distribution of μ is a normal distribution with the mean $\bar{\mu}$ and the standard deviation σ_μ, we can assert with the probability $1 - \alpha$ that μ lies between the limits

▲
$$w \cdot \bar{x} + (1 - w) \cdot \bar{\mu} \pm z_{\alpha/2} \cdot \frac{\sigma \cdot \sigma_\mu}{\sqrt{\sigma^2 + n \cdot \sigma_\mu^2}}$$
▲

where w is given by the formula on page 229 and $z_{\alpha/2}$ is as defined on page 222. *Note that these limits are not confidence limits for μ; we are actually making a probability statement about μ, itself. This is characteristic of a Bayesian inference.*

(a) Referring to the insurance example in the text, where the estimate of the expected losses was based on the collateral information as well as the losses actually observed for 3 years (page 230), what can we assert about μ with a probability of 0.95?

(b) Referring to part (c) of Exercise 27, what can the distributor assert with a probability of 0.99 about μ, the true average weekly sales for a machine put into the given supermarket?

(c) Referring to part (c) of Exercise 28, what can the professor assert with a probability of 0.95 about μ, the true mean grade for all the students taking the examination?

30. Referring to the donut-shop example on page 231, use the method and the assumptions of Exercise 29 to show that one can assert with a probability of 0.95 that his average monthly net profit will fall between \$1,008 and \$1,236.

31. Verify that the estimation formula of Section 9.4 may be described as the weighted mean of $\bar{x}$ and $\bar{\mu}$, with the weights being n/σ^2 and $1/\sigma_\mu^2$.

9.5 Hypothesis Testing: Two Kinds of Errors

So far, the problems we have treated in this chapter have all been problems of *estimation;* in each case we had to determine the actual value of the mean of a population, such as the "true" average length of a certain kind of fish, the "true" mean compressive strength of certain steel beams, the expected annual liability losses of an insurance risk, and so on. In the remainder of this chapter we shall study problems of a somewhat different nature; we shall have to decide, for example, whether it is reasonable to maintain that certain workers take on the average 49.6 minutes to get to work, whether one method of teaching computer programming is more effective than another, whether a typesetter averages 8 mistakes per galley, and so on. In each of these problems we must *test a hypothesis* concerning a mean; that is, we must decide whether to accept or reject a hypothesis (an assumption, or claim) concerning the mean of a population. In later chapters we shall also investigate tests concerning other parameters. For instance, we shall be asked to decide whether a new chemical will actually remove 85 per cent of all spots, or whether the variability of a child's reaction to a visual stimulus is within certain limits. It is important to keep in mind, however, that although such tests may concern a "true" percentage or a "true" standard deviation rather than a "true" mean, the general approach is very much the same.

To give an example that is typical of the kind of situation we face when testing a statistical hypothesis, suppose that a large-scale sociological study conducted several years ago in a metropolitan area showed that a worker takes on the average 49.6 minutes to get to his job (with a standard deviation of 8.1 minutes). These figures were determined as part of a depth study of American leisure, and it is desired to determine whether the same figures apply today. In particular, we shall discuss here a test concerning the mean travel time; a corresponding test concerning the standard deviation will be taken up in Chapter 10. Let us suppose, therefore, that the sociologists who are conducting the study take a random sample of 250 workers in the given metropolitan area, and that they want to decide on the basis of this sample whether, on the average, it still takes workers in this area 49.6 minutes to get to work. *Specifically, they decide to accept the hypothesis that the mean travel time is $\mu = 49.6$ minutes if the sample mean obtained for the travel times of the 250 workers falls between 48.4 and 50.8 minutes; otherwise, the hypothesis is to be rejected (and a further study may have to be initiated in order to discover exactly what changes have taken place).*

This provides a clear-cut criterion for deciding whether the mean is still 49.6 minutes, but unfortunately it is not infallible. Since we are dealing with a sample, it could happen *purely by chance* that the sample mean exceeds 50.8 or is less than 48.4 even though the true mean is still 49.6 minutes. If this happened, the sociologists would be wasting time and money on their continued investigation. Of course, they could reduce the chances of this happening by changing the decision criterion, say, by choosing wider limits and accepting the hypothesis $\mu = 49.6$ minutes so long as the sample mean falls between 47.2 and 52.0 minutes, but this would have the undesirable effect of increasing another risk to which they are exposed. This is the risk of obtaining a sample mean between 47.2 and 52.0 minutes (or whatever other wider limits are being used) even though there has been a change. In other words, it is the risk of deciding that the mean travel time is still $\mu = 49.6$ minutes, while actually it has changed, say, to 47.6 or 51.6 minutes. In either case, they would commit the error of *not* recognizing the change that has actually taken place.

Before adopting the above criterion (or, for that matter, any criterion), it would be wise for the sociologists to investigate what the chances are that the criterion will lead to a wrong decision. Thus, let us first investigate the possibility of getting a sample mean less than 48.4 or greater than 50.8 minutes even though the true mean travel time is still $\mu = 49.6$ minutes. In the language of statistics (especially that of Chapter 8), this means that we are interested in the probability of getting a sample mean less than 48.4 or greater than 50.8 when a random sample of size $n = 250$ is taken from a population whose mean and standard deviation are $\mu = 49.6$ and $\sigma = 8.1$, respectively. This probability is represented by the shaded area of Figure 9.5, and it can easily be found by approximating the sampling distribution

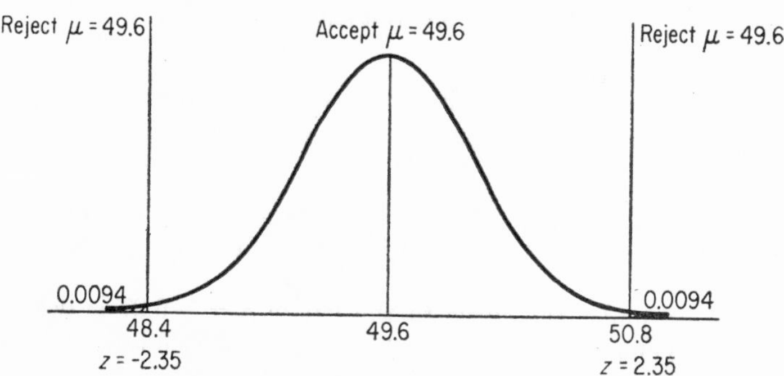

Fig. 9.5 Test criterion.

of the mean with a normal curve. According to the first theorem of Section 8.4, the standard deviation of this sampling distribution (namely, the standard error of the mean) is given by the expression $\sigma/\sqrt{n}$, and for our example we thus have $8.1/\sqrt{250} = 0.51$. Consequently, the dividing lines of the criterion are in standard units

$$\frac{50.8 - 49.6}{0.51} = 2.35 \quad \text{and} \quad \frac{48.4 - 49.6}{0.51} = -2.35$$

and it follows from Table I that the area in each tail of the sampling distribution of Figure 9.5 is $0.5000 - 0.4906 = 0.0094$. Hence, the probability of getting a value in either tail of this sampling distribution, namely, *the probability of erroneously rejecting the hypothesis that the mean travel time is* $\mu = 49.6$ *minutes* is $2(0.0094) = 0.0184$. Whether this is an acceptable risk is for the sociologists to decide; it would have to depend on the "cash values" they put on the consequences of making such an error.

Let us now look at the other kind of situation, where the test fails to detect a change in the average travel time μ. Suppose, for instance, that the average travel time has shifted to 51.6 minutes. The probability of *not* detecting this shift with the original criterion is represented by the shaded area of Figure 9.6, namely, the area under the curve between 48.4 and 50.8.

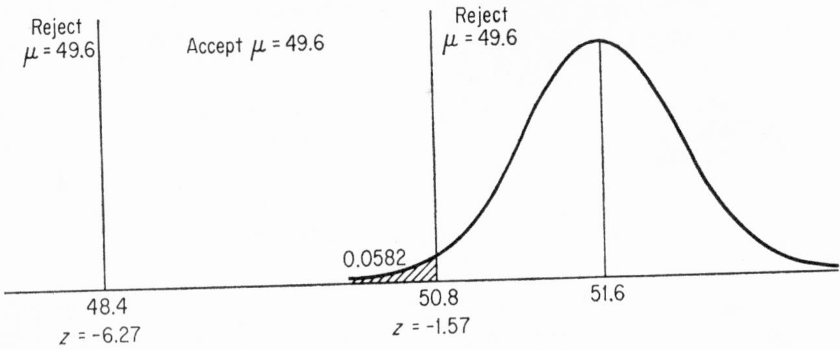

Fig. 9.6 Test criterion.

The mean of the sampling distribution is now $\mu = 51.6$, its standard deviation is as before $\sigma/\sqrt{n} = 8.1/\sqrt{250} = 0.51$, and the dividing lines of the criterion are in standard units

$$\frac{48.4 - 51.6}{0.51} = -6.27 \quad \text{and} \quad \frac{50.8 - 51.6}{0.51} = -1.57$$

Since the area under the curve to the left of $z = -6.27$ is negligible, it follows from Table I that the shaded area of Figure 9.6 is $0.5000 - 0.4418 = 0.0582$. We have thus shown that if the average travel time has changed to 51.6 minutes, the probability of *not* detecting this change with the given criterion is approximately 0.058. It is again up to the sociologists to decide whether this represents an acceptable risk.

To summarize what we have discussed, let us refer to the hypothesis that the mean travel time has remained unchanged (the hypothesis $\mu = 49.6$ minutes) as hypothesis H. Evidently, this hypothesis is either true or false, it is either accepted or rejected, and the sociologists are faced with the situation described in the following table:

	H is True	*H is False*
Accept H	*Correct decision*	*Type II error*
Reject H	*Type I error*	*Correct decision*

If the hypothesis is *true and accepted* or *false and rejected,* they are in either case making a correct decision; if the hypothesis is *true but rejected,* they are committing an error called a *Type I error* (the error of rejecting a true hypothesis); if the hypothesis is *false but accepted,* they are committing an error called a *Type II error* (the error of accepting a false hypothesis). Whether an error is a Type I error or a Type II error really depends on how we formulate whatever hypothesis we want to test. For example, if H is the hypothesis that the Republican candidate will win a certain gubernatorial election, we would be committing a Type I error if we *erroneously* predicted that his opponent will win the election. However, this same error would be a Type II error if we formulated H as the hypothesis that the Republican candidate will lose. In the first case we erroneously reject H and in the second case we erroneously accept it.

The scheme outlined above is reminiscent of what we did in Chapter 6, when we looked upon decision problems as games between two or more players, with each having the choice of several moves (or strategies). Analogous to the decision the students had to make concerning the two batches of pennants in Chapter 6, we now have to decide whether to accept or reject hypothesis H; analogous to Nature's control over the outcome of the football game, it now has control over the truth or falsity of hypothesis H. In the travel-time example, Nature has control over the value of μ, namely, whether it has changed or remained equal to 49.6. We can, thus, look upon a statistical decision problem as a game, where one player is the individual (or group of individuals) who has to make the decision, while the other player, Nature, has control over the value of the statistical parameter with which the test is concerned. The main difficulty in carrying this analogy much further is that in actual practice we can seldom put "cash values" on the various outcomes, as we did in Chapter 6. Of course, the seriousness of such consequences will determine, to some extent, whether a decision criterion presents an acceptable risk. For instance, in the travel-time example the seriousness of the consequences will determine whether 0.0184 (the probability of committing a Type I error) is acceptable, too high, or maybe too low. Also, the seriousness of the consequences of *not* detecting a change in the mean travel time from 49.6 to 51.6 minutes will determine whether 0.058 (the probability of committing a Type II error) is acceptable, too high, or too low. In case the reader is curious to know under what conditions a risk might be described as *too low*, we have only to point out that it might be possible to reduce the cost of the whole procedure, say, by interviewing fewer than 250 workers, and still keep the risks within reasonable bounds.

On page 240 we arbitrarily chose $\mu = 51.6$ minutes as the alternative value for which we calculated the probability of committing a Type II error, namely, the probability of not detecting a change in the mean travel time μ. Had the change been small (say, from 49.6 minutes to 49.55 or 49.65 minutes) the consequences would probably have been trivial; on the other hand, it may be of interest to know the probabilities of not detecting a change of 1, 2, or 3 minutes. Duplicating the method used on page 240, namely, approximating the sampling distribution of the mean with a normal curve, the reader will be asked to verify in Exercise 6 on page 248 the values shown in the following table:

Value of μ	*Probability of Type II error*	*Probability of Accepting H*
47.1	0.005	0.005
47.6	0.058	0.058
48.1	0.28	0.28
48.6	0.65	0.65
49.1	0.91	0.91
49.6	—	0.98
50.1	0.91	0.91
50.6	0.65	0.65
51.1	0.28	0.28
51.6	0.058	0.058
52.1	0.005	0.005

Since a Type II error is committed when hypothesis H is accepted and μ does not equal 49.6 in our example, the entries in the right-hand column of the table are identical with those of the middle column, except for the value which corresponds to $\mu = 49.6$ minutes. If $\mu = 49.6$ and, hence, hypothesis H is *true*, the probability of accepting H is the probability of *not* committing a Type I error, namely, $1 - 0.0184 = 0.9816$.

If we plot the probabilities of accepting H as we did in Figure 9.7 and fit a smooth curve, we obtain the *operating characteristic curve* of the given test criterion, or simply its *OC-curve*. An operating characteristic curve provides a good over-all picture of the advantages and disadvantages of a test criterion. For all values of the parameter except the one assumed under hypothesis H it gives the probability of committing a Type II error; for the value assumed under hypothesis H (in our case $\mu = 49.6$), it gives the probability of *not* committing a Type I error. A visual inspection of an operating characteristic curve thus enables us to decide whether the risks connected with a particular decision criterion are acceptable, too high, or too low; at least, it aids in the decision. Of course, it must be remembered that the OC-curve of Figure 9.7 applies only to the special test where the hypothesis $\mu = 49.6$ minutes is accepted if the mean of a random sample of size 250 falls between 48.4 and 50.8, and where σ is known to equal 8.1 minutes. Changes in the test criterion or the sample size will automatically change the shape of the operating characteristic curve (see Exercises 7 and 8 on page 249); in fact, an OC-curve can often be made to assume a particular desired shape by a suitable choice of the sample size and (or) the dividing lines of the test criterion.

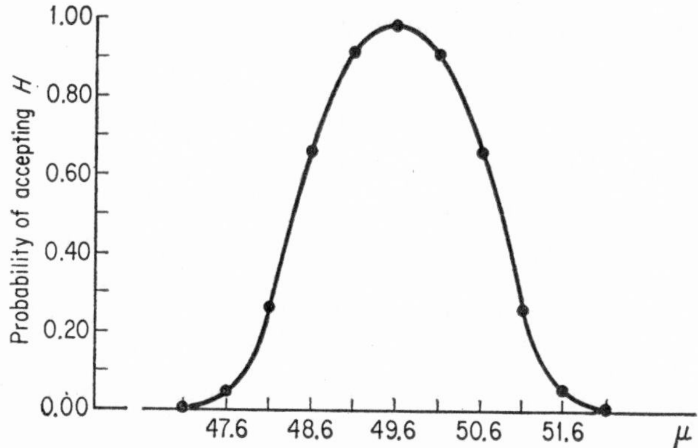

Fig. 9.7 Operating characteristic curve.

If we had plotted the probabilities of *rejecting H* instead of those of *accepting H*, we would have obtained the graph of the *power function* of the test criterion rather than its OC-curve. The concept of an OC-curve is used more widely in applications, especially in industrial applications, while the concept of a power function is used more widely in matters that are of theoretical interest. Either curve serves (or better, aids) in the evaluation of the risks to which one is exposed by a test criterion; of course, the general idea of an OC-curve or a power function is not limited to the particular test concerning the average time a worker takes to get to his job. Hypothesis H could have been the hypothesis that one fertilizer is better than another, the hypothesis that a new antibiotic is effective, the hypothesis that one teaching method is more effective than another—to mention but a few of countless possibilities.

9.6 Hypothesis Testing: Null Hypotheses and Significance Tests

In the travel-time example of the preceding section we had more difficulties with Type II errors than with Type I errors, because we formulated our hypothesis in such a way that the probability of a Type I error could actually be calculated. Had we formulated instead the hypothesis $\mu \neq 49.6$ minutes, namely, the hypothesis that the mean travel time *has* changed, we would not have been able to calculate this probability; at least we could not have done so without specifying the actual nature and extent of the change.

In choosing the hypothesis which we referred to as hypothesis H in our example, we followed the general rule of *formulating hypotheses in such a way that we know what to expect if they are true.* As it was known that $\sigma =$ 8.1 minutes, the hypothesis $\mu = 49.6$ minutes (and the theory of Chapter 8) enabled us to calculate probabilities concerning the sampling distribution of the mean; in particular, we were able to calculate the probability that the mean of a random sample of size 250 is less than 48.4 or greater than 50.8 minutes, namely, the probability of committing a Type I error.

In order to follow the rule given in italics in the preceding paragraph, we often have to assume (hypothesize) the exact opposite of what we may want to prove. If we wanted to show that one psychological test is more reliable than another, we would have to formulate the hypothesis that there is *no difference* in their reliability; if we wanted to show that a new medicine is more effective than an old one, we would have to formulate the hypothesis that there is *no difference*, namely, that the two medicines are equally effective; and if we wanted to show that one kind of ore has a higher uranium content than another, we would have to formulate the hypothesis that their uranium contents are *the same*. Since we assumed, respectively, that there is no difference in reliability, no difference in effectiveness, and no difference in uranium content, we refer to each of these hypotheses as a *null hypothesis* and denote it H_0. This explains how the term "null hypothesis" arose, although nowadays it is used for any hypothesis set up primarily to see whether it can be rejected. Note that the idea of setting up a null hypothesis is not uncommon even in nonstatistical thinking. It is precisely what is done in criminal court proceedings, where an accused is assumed to be innocent unless his guilt is proven beyond a reasonable doubt. The assumption that the accused is not guilty is a null hypothesis.

Although we avoid one kind of difficulty by formulating hypotheses so that the probability of a Type I error can be calculated, this will not help insofar as Type II errors are concerned. The only time there is no difficulty in finding the probabilities of either kind of error is when we test a *specific* hypothesis against a *specific* alternative. This would have been the case in our example if we had been interested *only* in the specific alternative that the mean travel time has changed to 51.6 minutes.

A possible escape from the difficulties connected with Type II errors is to avoid this kind of error altogether. To illustrate how this might be done, suppose we want to test the suspicion that one secretary (belonging to the typing pool of a large research organization) makes on the average more mistakes than the others. We are interested in particular in the typing of technical reports, where the other typists are known to average 2.1 mistakes per page with a standard deviation of 0.80. To test our suspicion we decide to count the mistakes on 40 randomly selected pages of the secretary's work and then base our final decision on the following criterion: *we reject the null hypothesis $\mu = 2.1$ errors per page, namely, the hypothesis that this secretary is as good as the others, if she averages more than 2.3 mistakes per page; otherwise we reserve judgment.* Note that with this criterion there is no need to calculate the probability of committing a Type II error; we never really accept the null hypothesis and, hence, we cannot possibly make the mistake of accepting a false null hypothesis.

The procedure we have just outlined is referred to as a *test of significance.* If the difference between what we expect and what we get is so large that it cannot reasonably be attributed to chance, we reject the null hypothesis on which our expectation is based. If the difference between what we expect and what we get is so small that it can well be attributed to chance, we say that the result is *not (statistically) significant.* We then reserve judgment or accept the null hypothesis depending on whether a definite decision, a definite action one way or the other, is required. In the above example, our suspicion that the secretary is not as good as the others is confirmed if she averages more than 2.3 mistakes; in that case it is felt that the difference between the sample mean and $\mu = 2.1$ is too large to be attributed to chance. [The reader will be asked to verify in Exercise 9 on page 249 that the probability of getting a sample mean greater than 2.3 when μ equals 2.1 (and $\sigma = 0.80$) is, in fact, equal to 0.06.] If the secretary averages 2.3 mistakes or fewer, we simply state that *the test did not confirm our suspicion.* Note that this is *not* a positive statement in her support; in fact, it is a negative sort of statement which merely says that we were unable to prove anything wrong. We may still be suspicious about the quality of her work.

Referring again to the travel-time example, we could convert the criterion on page 238 into that of a significance test by rewriting it as follows: *reject the null hypothesis H_0 (that $\mu = 49.6$ minutes) if the mean of the 250 sample values is less than 48.4 or greater than 50.8 minutes; reserve judgment if it falls anywhere from 48.4 to 50.8 minutes.* So far as the rejection of the null hypothesis is concerned, the criterion has remained unchanged and, hence, the probability of a Type I error is still 0.0184. However, so far as its acceptance is concerned, we are now playing it safe by reserving judgment. Of course, this raises the question whether we can really afford to reserve judgment in this example—if a decision one way or the other is required (say, for initiating further studies), we would have to return to the criterion on page 238. Reserving judgment in a situation like this is similar to what happens in court proceedings where the prosecution does not have sufficient evidence to get a conviction, but where in one's mind it would be going too far to say that the defendant is definitely not responsible for the crime. Thus, whether we can afford to reserve judgment in any given situation will have to depend on the nature of the circumstances and the objectives of the problem.

Since the general problem of testing hypotheses and constructing statistical decision criteria often presents some difficulties to beginners, it will help to proceed systematically as outlined in the following five steps:

(a) *We formulate a (null) hypothesis in such a way that the probability of a Type I error can be calculated.*

(b) *We formulate an alternative hypothesis so that the rejection of the null hypothesis is equivalent to the acceptance of the alternative hypothesis.*

In the travel-time example the null hypothesis was $\mu = 49.6$ minutes and, even though we did not say so specifically, the alternative hypothesis was $\mu \neq 49.6$ minutes. (After all, we were interested in determining whether the mean travel time might have shifted in either direction.) We refer to this kind of alternative as a *two-sided alternative.* since we want to reject the null hypothesis if the mean travel time has become less than 49.6 minutes and also if it has become greater than 49.6 minutes. An illustration of where we use a *one-sided alternative* is provided by the report-typing example. Here the null hypothesis is $\mu = 2.1$ mistakes per page and the alternative hypothesis is $\mu > 2.1$, since we are interested in confirming our suspicion that the given secretary makes on the average more mistakes than the others. Had we been interested in showing that she is actually *better* than the other secretaries, we would have used the alternative $\mu < 2.1$, and if we had been interested in showing that her performance is different, better or worse, than that of the others, we would have used the alternative $\mu \neq 2.1$. Beginners often find it difficult to decide upon an appropriate one-sided or two-sided alternative, and we want to stress the fact that there is no general rule—how one proceeds in a given example depends entirely on the nature of the problem.

Having formulated a null hypothesis and a suitable alternative, we then proceed with the following steps:

(c) *We specify the probability with which we are willing to risk a Type I error; if possible, desired, or necessary, we may also make some specifications about the probabilities of Type II errors for given alternate values of the parameter with which we are concerned.*

(d) *Using appropriate statistical theory we construct the test criterion.*

It is here that we depart from the travel-time illustration, where we first specified the criterion and then calculated the probabilities of committing

Type I and Type II errors. In general, we reverse this procedure, specifying the probability of committing a Type I error (and, perhaps, Type II errors) and then choosing an appropriate test criterion.

The probability of committing a Type I error is generally referred to as the *level of significance* at which the test is being conducted, and it is denoted by the Greek letter α (*alpha*). Thus, if we write $\alpha = 0.05$ in connection with a decision criterion, this means that we risk a Type I error with a probability of 0.05. Of course, the decision whether to use $\alpha = 0.05$, $\alpha = 0.01$, or some other value, will have to depend on whatever consequences there may be to committing a Type I error in a particular problem. Generally speaking, the more serious the consequences of an error of this kind, the smaller the risk of committing it one is willing to take. Note that with reference to the courtroom procedures mentioned earlier, the level of significance expresses formally what we mean by the phrase "beyond a reasonable doubt."

In the travel-time example, we based the test criterion on the normal curve approximation to the sampling distribution of the mean; in general, this will have to depend on the particular *statistic* on which we want to base the decision and on its sampling distribution. As we saw in our numerical examples, the construction of a test criterion depends also on the alternative hypothesis we happen to choose; a *two-sided test criterion* (or *two-tail test*) went with the two-sided alternative $\mu \neq 49.6$ in the travel-time example, and in the report-typing example we used a *one-sided test criterion* (or *one-tail test*) in conjunction with the one-sided alternative $\mu > 2.1$. In general, a test is said to be *one-sided* or *two-sided* (*one-tailed* or *two-tailed*), depending on whether the null hypothesis is rejected for values of the test statistic falling into *either* or *both* tails of its sampling distribution.

(e) *Finally, we specify whether the alternative to rejecting the hypothesis formulated in* (a) *is to accept it or to reserve judgment.*

As we saw in our examples, this will have to depend on the nature of the problem, possible consequences and risks, and whether a decision one way or the other must be reached. Quite often we accept a null hypothesis with the tacit hope that we are not exposing ourselves to excessively high risks of committing *serious* Type II errors.

The purpose of this discussion has been to present some of the basic problems connected with the testing of statistical hypotheses. Although the methods we have mentioned are *objective*, that is, two research workers analyzing the same data under the same conditions should arrive at identical results, their use does entail some arbitrary, or subjective, considerations. For instance, in the report-typing example it was partly a subjective decision to use a sample of size 40 and to "draw the line" at 2.3 mistakes per page. More generally, the choice of α, the probability of a Type I error, and perhaps also the probability of a Type II error, often denoted β (*beta*), must depend to some extent on the consequences of making wrong decisions. Although it may be very difficult to put exact "cash values" on all such eventualities, they must nevertheless be considered, at least indirectly or tacitly, in choosing suitable test criteria.

Before we go into the various special tests treated in the remainder of this chapter, let us point out that the preceding discussion is not limited to tests concerning means. The concepts we have introduced apply equally well to tests of hypotheses concerning proportions, population standard deviations, the randomness of samples, relationships among several variables, and so on.

EXERCISES

1. Suppose that a psychological testing service is asked to check whether an executive is emotionally fit to assume the presidency of a large company. What type of error is committed if the hypothesis that he is fit for the job is erroneously accepted? What type of error is committed if this hypothesis is erroneously rejected?

2. Suppose we want to test the hypothesis that during the tourist season the average price charged for a motel room in Palm Springs, California, is somewhere between \$9.50 and \$11.50. Explain under what conditions we would be committing a Type I error under what conditions we would be committing a Type II error.

3. An airline wants to test the hypothesis that at least 70 per cent of its passengers like to watch a movie on a transcontinental flight. What type of error is committed when this hypothesis is erroneously rejected? What type of error is committed when this hypothesis is erroneously accepted?

4. Whether an error is a Type I error or a Type II error depends on how we formulate the hypothesis we want to test. To illustrate this, rephrase the hypothesis of Exercise 3 so that the Type I error becomes a Type II error, and vice versa.

5. The director of an advertising agency is concerned with the effectiveness of a certain kind of television commercial.

(a) What hypothesis is he testing, if he is committing a Type I error when he says erroneously that the commercial is effective?

(b) What hypothesis is he testing, if he is committing a Type II error when he says erroneously that the commercial is effective?

6. Verify the values in the table on page 242 by duplicating the method used in the text to calculate the probability of a Type II error for $\mu = 51.6$.

7. Suppose that in the travel-time example the criterion is changed so that the hypothesis $\mu = 49.6$ is accepted if the mean of a random sample of size 250 falls between 48.8 and 50.4; otherwise the hypothesis is rejected.

(a) Calculate the probability of committing a Type I error with this new criterion.

(b) Calculate the probabilities of committing Type II errors with this new criterion for $\mu = 47.6, 48.1, 48.6, 49.1, 50.1, 50.6, 51.1$, and 51.6. Note that due to the symmetry of the criterion only 4 of these values have to be calculated.

(c) Draw a graph of the OC-curve of this criterion.

8. Suppose that in the travel-time example in the text the sample size is reduced from 250 to 150, while the criterion remains as stated on page 238.

(a) Calculate the probability of erroneously rejecting the hypothesis $\mu = 49.6$ minutes with this procedure.

(b) Calculate the probabilities of committing Type II errors with this modified test when $\mu = 47.6, 48.1, 48.6, 49.1, 50.1, 50.6, 51.1$, and 51.6. Note that due to the symmetry of the problem only 4 of these values have to be calculated.

(c) Draw a graph of the OC-curve of this testing procedure.

9. Verify for the report-typing example on page 245 that the probability of commiting a Type I error is approximately 0.06.

10. Using standard medical treatment, the mortality rate of a certain disease is known to be 0.08. Investigating the effectiveness of a new drug in the treatment of this disease, the manufacturer of the drug wants to test the null hypothesis $r = 0.08$ against a suitable alternative, where r is the mortality rate of the disease when treated with the new drug.

(a) What alternative hypothesis should the manufacturer use if he is very careful and does not want to introduce the new drug unless it is definitely proven superior?

(b) What alternative hypothesis should the manufacturer use if he is very anxious to put the drug on the market? That is, he does not want to put the burden of proof on the new drug; he wants to market it unless it is definitely proven inferior to the standard treatment of the disease.

11. A shirt manufacturer is considering the purchase of new sewing machines. If μ_1 is the average number of shirts made per hour by his old machines and μ_2 is the corresponding average for the new machines, he wants to test the null hypothesis $\mu_1 = \mu_2$ against a suitable alternative.

(a) What alternative hypothesis should he use if he does not want to buy the new machines unless they are definitely proven superior? In other words, the burden of proof is put on the new machines and the manufacturer will keep the old ones unless the null hypothesis can be rejected.

(b) What alternative hypothesis should the manufacturer use if he wants to buy the new machines (which have some other nice features) unless the old machines are actually superior? Note that now the burden of proof is on the old machines and the new ones will be bought unless the null hypothesis can be rejected.

12. According to the rules set down by a consumer testing service, a mattress is considered *acceptable* if it can outlast a "torture test" consisting of continuous pounding for at least 100 hours; otherwise the mattress is considered to be *non-acceptable.*
   (a) What alternative hypothesis should they use in conjunction with the null hypothesis $\mu = 100$ hours, if they do not want to rate a mattress *acceptable* unless it is actually shown to be superior? In other words, the burden of proof is on the mattress, and it will not be rated *acceptable* unless the null hypothesis can be rejected.
   (b) What alternative hypothesis should they use in conjunction with the null hypothesis $\mu = 100$ hours, if they do not want to put the burden of proof on the mattress? That is, a mattress is rated *acceptable* unless the null hypothesis can be rejected.

9.7 Tests Concerning Means

In Sections 9.5 and 9.6 we used tests concerning means to illustrate the basic principles of hypothesis testing; now we shall consider more generally the problem of testing the null hypothesis that the mean of a population equals some specified value μ_0 against an appropriate alternative. Usually, the alternative hypothesis is of the form $\mu < \mu_0$, $\mu > \mu_0$, or $\mu \neq \mu_0$; that is, it specifies that the population mean is less than, greater than, or not equal to the value assumed under the null hypothesis. Thus, if we wanted to test the hypothesis that the mean distance required to stop a car going 20 miles per hour is 25 feet against the alternative hypothesis that it takes more than 25 feet, we would begin by writing

Null Hypothesis: $\mu = 25$ feet

Alternative Hypothesis: $\mu > 25$ feet

To abbreviate our notation, we often use the symbols H_0 and H_A (or H_1) to denote the null hypothesis and the alternative.

Next, we specify the level of significance as $\alpha = 0.01$, $\alpha = 0.05$, or some other value as the case may be, and after that we depart slightly from the procedure used in the examples of the preceding section. In both the travel-time and the report-typing examples, we formulated the test criterion in terms of possible values of $\bar{x}$; now we shall base it on the statistic

▲ $$z = \frac{\bar{x} - \mu_0}{\sigma/\sqrt{n}}$$ ▲

which simply means that we work in *standard units*. The reason for this is easy to explain: *using standard units, we can formulate criteria which are applicable to a great variety of problems, and not just one*. Note that in the above formula for z the population standard deviation is assumed to be known while μ_0 is the value of the population mean assumed under the null hypothesis.

If we approximate the sampling distribution of the mean, as before, with a normal distribution, we can now use the test criteria shown in Figure 9.8; depending on the choice of the alternative hypothesis, the dividing line

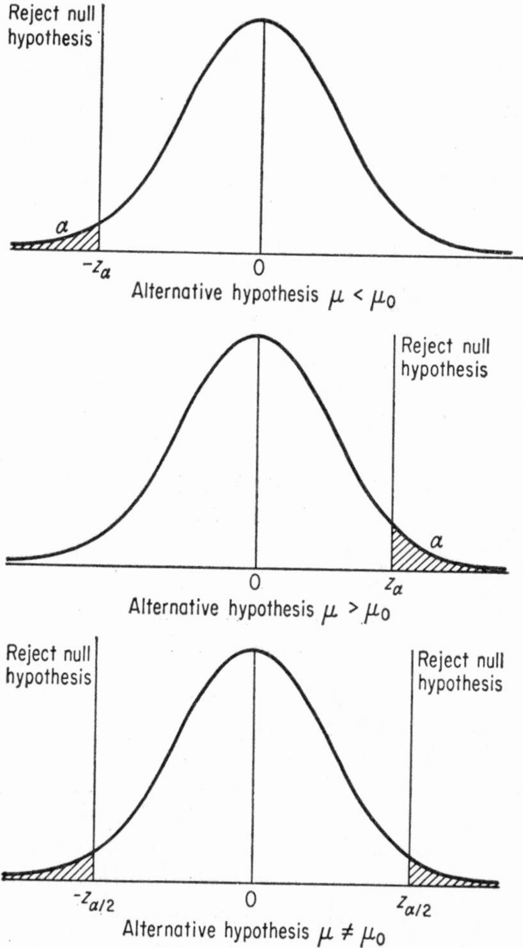

Fig. 9.8 Test criteria.

(or lines) of the criterion is $-z_\alpha$ or $+z_\alpha$ for the *one-sided* alternatives, and $-z_{\alpha/2}$ and $z_{\alpha/2}$ for the *two-sided* alternative. As we explained on page 222, z_α and $z_{\alpha/2}$ are values for which the area *to their right* under the standard normal distribution is α and $\alpha/2$, respectively. Symbolically, we can formulate these criteria as follows:

Alternative Hypothesis	*Reject the Null Hypothesis if*	*Accept the Null Hypothesis or Reserve Judgment if*
$\mu < \mu_0$	$z < -z_\alpha$	$z \geq -z_\alpha$
$\mu > \mu_0$	$z > z_\alpha$	$z \leq z_\alpha$
$\mu \neq \mu_0$	$z < -z_{\alpha/2}$ or $z > z_{\alpha/2}$	$-z_{\alpha/2} \leq z \leq z_{\alpha/2}$

The most commonly used values of the level of significance are 0.05 and 0.01. If $\alpha = 0.05$, the dividing lines of the criteria are -1.64 or 1.64 for the one-sided alternatives, and -1.96 and 1.96 for the two-sided alternative; if $\alpha = 0.01$, the dividing lines of the criteria are -2.33 or 2.33 for the one-sided alternatives, and -2.58 and 2.58 for the two-sided alternative. All these values were obtained earlier when we discussed confidence intervals for μ.

A serious shortcoming of the tests just described is that they require knowledge of σ, the standard deviation of the population from which the sample is obtained. Since σ is unknown in most practical applications, we usually have no choice but to replace it with an estimate in the formula for z. If n is large (30 or more), we usually substitute for σ the sample standard deviation s, base the tests on the statistic

$$z = \frac{\bar{x} - \mu_0}{s/\sqrt{n}}$$

and refer to them as *large-sample tests* for μ.

To illustrate such tests, let us investigate a leading car manufacturer's claim that the average weekly income of owners of his compact station wagon is \$180.00. More specifically, it is desired to test the null hypothesis $\mu = \$180.00$ against the alternative hypothesis $\mu \neq \$180.00$ at a level of significance of 0.05. Suppose, thus, that an investigator takes a random sample of 200 such car-owners and finds that they have an average weekly income of $\bar{x} = \$184.26$ with a standard deviation of $s = \$24.12$. Substituting all these values into the above formula for z, we obtain

$$z = \frac{184.26 - 180.00}{24.12/\sqrt{200}} = 2.50$$

and since this exceeds $z_{0.025} = 1.96$ the hypothesis must be rejected. *We conclude, in fact, that the car manufacturer's figure is too low.* It is of interest to observe that if we had used a level of significance of 0.01, the null hypothesis $\mu = \$180.00$ could *not* have been rejected; the value which we obtained for z lies between $-z_{0.005} = -2.58$ and $z_{0.005} = 2.58$. *This illustrates the very important point that the level of significance should always be specified before any statistical tests are actually performed. This will spare us the temptation of later choosing a level of significance which may happen to suit our purpose.*

To give an example of a one-tail test, let us consider a study of alleged unfair trade practices performed by the Federal Trade Commission. To check on the weight of so-called "9-ounce" candy bars (at a level of significance of 0.01), the Commission's investigators take a random sample of 50 of these candy bars and obtain a mean of $\bar{x} = 8.87$ ounces and a standard deviation of $s = 0.21$ ounces. Their null hypothesis is $\mu = 9.00$ ounces and their alternative hypothesis is $\mu < 9.00$ ounces, since they are only interested in the alternative that the candy bars might weigh less than claimed. Substituting the given values of $\bar{x}$, μ_0, s, and n into the formula for z, they obtain

$$z = \frac{8.87 - 9.00}{0.21/\sqrt{50}} = -4.38$$

and since this value is less than $-z_{0.01} = -2.33$, the null hypothesis can be rejected. Whether the result of this test justifies legal action against the manufacturer or, perhaps, only a warning, is another matter; this would have to depend largely on the consequences of the different actions.

If n is small (less than 30), we can proceed as on page 225, where we based small-sample confidence intervals for μ on the t distribution. Assuming again that the population from which we are sampling has roughly the shape of a normal distribution, we now base our decision on the statistic

▲ $$t = \frac{\bar{x} - \mu_0}{s/\sqrt{n}}$$ ▲

where μ_0 is the value of the population mean specified under the null hypothesis. Observe that this formula for t is identical with the one for z on page 252, where we substituted s for σ and, hence, restricted the method based on normal curve theory to large samples.

To perform tests based on the t statistic, we have only to refer to Figure 9.8 or the table on page 252 with z replaced by t, and z_α and $z_{\alpha/2}$ replaced by t_α and $t_{\alpha/2}$, respectively. As we explained on page 226, t_α and $t_{\alpha/2}$ are values for which the area *to their right* under the t distribution is equal to α and $\alpha/2$, respectively. All these dividing lines of the test criteria may be obtained from Table II, *with the number of degrees of freedom equaling $n - 1$.*

To illustrate this kind of *small-sample test* for μ, suppose that we want to investigate the claim that the average gasoline consumption of a certain type of aircraft engine is 14.0 gallons per minute, and that we have at our disposal the results of one-minute test runs performed with 16 of these engines. Suppose, furthermore, that we are interested in particular in the alternative that the engine's average consumption of gasoline might be greater than 14.0 gallons, and that we want to perform the test at a level of significance of 0.05. The figures obtained for the 16 test runs have a mean of 14.6 gallons and a standard deviation of 2.2 gallons. Substituting these numbers together with $\mu_0 = 14.0$ into the formula for t, we obtain

$$t = \frac{14.6 - 14.0}{2.2/\sqrt{16}} = 1.09$$

and since this is less than 1.753, the value of $t_{.050}$ for 15 degrees of freedom, the null hypothesis cannot be rejected. If we had to make a decision one way or the other, we would accept the claim that the average gasoline consumption of the engine is 14.0 gallons per minute; we might also observe, however, that a standard deviation of 2.2 gallons suggests that there is a considerable amount of variation in the performance of the engine, and that this might warrant further investigation.

9.8 Differences between Means

There are many applied problems in which we must decide whether an observed difference between two sample means can be attributed to chance or whether it is an indication of the fact that the samples came from populations with unequal means. We may want to decide, for instance, whether there is really a difference in the performance of two kinds of batteries, if a sample of one kind lasted on the average for 65.3 hours while a sample of another kind lasted on the average for 67.9 hours. Similarly, we may want to decide on the basis of samples whether men can perform a given task faster than women, whether the students in one school have a higher average I.Q. than those of another, whether one ceramic product is more brittle than another, and so on.

The method we shall employ to test whether an observed difference between two sample means can be attributed to chance is based on the following theory: *If $\bar{x}_1$ and $\bar{x}_2$ are the means of two large independent random samples of size n_1 and n_2, the sampling distribution of the statistic $\bar{x}_1 - \bar{x}_2$ can be approximated closely with a normal curve having the mean $\mu_1 - \mu_2$ and the standard deviation*

$$\sqrt{\frac{\sigma_1^2}{n_1} + \frac{\sigma_2^2}{n_2}}$$

where μ_1 and μ_2 are the means of the populations from which the two samples were obtained and σ_1 and σ_2 are their standard deviations. The above formula is also referred to as the standard error of the difference between two means.

By "independent" samples we mean that the selection of one sample is in no way affected by the selection of the other. Thus, the theory does not apply to "before and after" kinds of comparisons, nor does it apply, say, to the comparison of the I.Q.'s of husbands and wives. A special method for handling this kind of problem is given in Exercise 22 on page 260.

One difficulty in applying the above theory is that in most practical situations σ_1 and σ_2 are unknown. However, if we limit ourselves to *large samples* (neither n_1 nor n_2 should be less than 30), it is reasonable to substitute the sample standard deviations s_1 and s_2 for σ_1 and σ_2, and base the test of the null hypothesis $\mu_1 = \mu_2$ on the statistic

▲ $$z = \frac{\bar{x}_1 - \bar{x}_2}{\sqrt{\frac{s_1^2}{n_1} + \frac{s_2^2}{n_2}}}$$ ▲

Note that this formula for z is obtained by subtracting from $\bar{x}_1 - \bar{x}_2$ the mean of its sampling distribution, which under the null hypothesis is $\mu_1 - \mu_2 = 0$, and then dividing by the standard deviation of its sampling distribution with s_1 and s_2 substituted for $\sigma_1$and σ_2.

Depending on whether the alternative hypothesis is $\mu_1 < \mu_2$, $\mu_1 > \mu_2$, or $\mu_1 \neq \mu_2$, the criteria on which we base the actual tests are again the ones shown in Figure 9.8 and also in the table on page 252, with μ_1 and μ_2 substituted for μ and μ_0. Suppose, for example, that someone wants to investigate the claim that women are better than men at a certain job and that an appropriate aptitude test yielded the following results: $\bar{x}_1 = 79.5$, $s_1 = 9.8$, $\bar{x}_2 = 85.6$, and $s_2 = 10.6$, where the first sample consists of $n_1 = 40$ men and the second sample consists of $n_2 = 50$ women. To test the null hypothesis $\mu_1 = \mu_2$ against the alternative hypothesis $\mu_1 < \mu_2$ at a level of significance of 0.01, we have only to substitute all these values into the formula for z, getting

$$z = \frac{79.5 - 85.6}{\sqrt{\frac{(9.8)^2}{40} + \frac{(10.6)^2}{50}}} = -2.82$$

Since this value is less than $-z_{0.01} = -2.33$, the null hypothesis must be rejected; in other words, the sample data confirm the claim that women are better than men at the given job. Note that we chose the hypotheses as we did, so that by rejecting the null hypothesis we substantiated the claim.

The Student-t distribution also provides criteria for *small-sample tests* concerning differences between two means. To use these criteria, we have to assume that the two samples come from populations which can be approximated closely with normal distributions and which, furthermore, have *equal variances*. Specifically, we base the test of the null hupothesis $\mu_1 = \mu_2$ on the statistic

$$t = \frac{\bar{x}_1 - \bar{x}_2}{\sqrt{\frac{\Sigma\,(x_1 - \bar{x}_1)^2 + \Sigma\,(x_2 - \bar{x}_2)^2}{n_1 + n_2 - 2} \cdot \left(\frac{1}{n_1} + \frac{1}{n_2}\right)}}$$

where $\Sigma\,(x_1 - \bar{x}_1)^2$ is the sum of the squared deviations from the mean for the first sample while $\Sigma\,(x_2 - \bar{x}_2)^2$ is the sum of the squared deviations from the mean for the second sample. Note that since, by definition, $\Sigma\,(x_1 - \bar{x}_1)^2 = (n_1 - 1)s_1^2$ and $\Sigma\,(x_2 - \bar{x}_2)^2 = (n_2 - 1)s_2^2$, the above formula for t can be simplified somewhat when the two sample variances (or standard deviations) have already been calculated from the data.

Under the given assumptions, it can be shown that the sampling distribution of this t statistic is the Student-t distribution with $n_1 + n_2 - 2$ degrees of freedom. Depending on whether the alternative hypothesis is $\mu_1 < \mu_2$, $\mu_1 > \mu_2$, or $\mu_1 \neq \mu_2$, the criteria on which we base the *small-sample tests for the significance of the difference between two means* are again the ones shown in Figure 9.8 and also in the table on page 252, with t substituted throughout for z, and μ_1 and μ_2 substituted for μ and μ_0.

To illustrate this kind of test, suppose someone wants to compare the action of two different types of phosphorescent coatings of airplane instrument dials. He coats 5 dials with Type A, 5 others with Type B, excites them with an ultraviolet light, and records the number of minutes each dial glows after the light source has been turned off. His results are as shown in the following table:

Type A: 52, 60, 49, 55, and 54 minutes

Type B: 55, 54, 61, 65, and 60 minutes

The means of these two samples are 54 and 59 minutes, and it is desired to test the null hypothesis $\mu_1 = \mu_2$ (where the subscripts 1 and 2 refer to Types A and B, respectively) against the alternative $\mu_1 \neq \mu_2$ at a level of significance of 0.05. In order to calculate t in accordance with the above formula, one must first determine

$$\Sigma\,(x_1 - \bar{x}_1)^2 = (-2)^2 + 6^2 + (-5)^2 + 1^2 + 0^2 = 66$$

$$\Sigma\,(x_2 - \bar{x}_2)^2 = (-4)^2 + (-5)^2 + 2^2 + 6^2 + 1^2 = 82$$

Substituting these values together with $n_1 = 5$, $n_2 = 5$, $\bar{x}_1 = 54$, and $\bar{x}_2 = 59$ into the formula for t, one obtains

$$t = \frac{54 - 59}{\sqrt{\frac{66 + 82}{5 + 5 - 2} \cdot \left(\frac{1}{5} + \frac{1}{5}\right)}} = -1.84$$

Since -1.84 falls between -2.306 and 2.306, where 2.306 is the value of $t_{0.025}$ for $5 + 5 - 2 = 8$ degrees of freedom, it follows that the null hypothesis cannot be rejected on the basis of the given data. If the person conducting the experiment suspects nevertheless that the second kind of coating is better, he would be wise to repeat the experiment, preferably with larger samples. Note also that if the experimenter had wanted to compare three or four means rather than two, he could have used a somewhat more general method, which we shall treat later in Chapter 12.

EXERCISES

1. The police chief of a large city claims that the mean age of bicycle thieves is 10.5 years. A sociologist who feels that this figure is too high takes a random sample of 120 cases of bicycle theft from the police chief's files, getting a mean age of 8.9 years and a standard deviation of 5.2 years. What can he conclude from these figures at a level of significance of 0.01?
2. According to the norms established for a test designed to measure a person's ability to think logically, college sophomores should average 72.6 points with a standard deviation of 10.8. This test is given to a group of 60 college sophomores who have just completed a required course in mathematics which is supposed to sharpen their general powers of reasoning. What can one conclude about the effectiveness of the course if these students averaged 77.3 on the test? Use $\alpha = 0.01$.
3. A retail credit association wants to test the hypothesis that for all department stores in a certain city the average size of a delinquent charge account is \$108.65. To be specific, it wants to test this hypothesis against the alternative that the average is not \$108.65 at a level of significance of 0.05. What can they conclude if 100 delinquent accounts (selected at random) have a mean of \$114.27 and a standard deviation of \$8.30?
4. A bowler who has averaged 196 pins over hundreds of games is asked to experiment with a ball made of a new kind of material. If he rolls 50 lines with the new ball, averaging 188 pins with a standard deviation of 24.9, can one conclude at a level of significance of 0.01 that the new ball has adversely affected his score?
5. According to specifications, the mean blowing time of a certain kind of fuse is to be 10 seconds. What can one conclude (at $\alpha = 0.01$) about a large shipment of these fuses, if a random sample of size 30 had a mean blowing time of 9.8 seconds and a standard deviation of 0.60 second?
6. A real estate broker who is trying to sell a piece of property to a motel chain assures them that during the summer months *on the average* 1,850 cars pass by the property each day. Making their own investigation, the management of the motel chain obtains a mean of 1,739 cars and a standard deviation of 224 cars for 35 days. What can they say about the real estate broker's claim at a level of significance of 0.01?

7. A production process is considered to be under control if the machine parts it makes have a mean length of 35.50 mm with a standard deviation of 0.45 mm. Whether or not the process is under control is decided each morning by a quality control engineer who bases his decision on a random sample of size 40. Should he ask for an adjustment of the machine on a day when he obtains a mean of 35.62 mm? Use a level of significance of 0.05.

8. Specifications for a certain kind of 2-inch cotton ribbon call for a mean breaking strength of 150 pounds. Test at a level of significance of 0.01 whether this requirement is met by a large shipment, if 5 pieces of ribbon (randomly selected from different rolls) have a mean breaking strength of 147.2 pounds and a standard deviation of 8.6 pounds.

9. In an experiment concerning the process of learning, the average time required by 10 adults to memorize a list of French verbs was 5.2 minutes with a standard deviation of 1.3 minutes. Does this support the claim (at $\alpha = 0.05$) that the average adult should be able to memorize this list of French verbs in not more than 4 minutes?

10. A new drug given to 8 patients with heart trouble lowered their blood pressure by 12, 7, 15, 9, 8, 16, 10, and 11. Use a level of significance of 0.05 to test the claim that, on the average, this drug will lower such a patient's blood pressure by 15 or more. Formulate the hypotheses in such a way that the burden of proof is on the new drug.

11. A testing laboratory wants to check whether the average lifetime of a multi-toothed cutting tool is 2,500 pieces against the alternative that it is less than 2,500 pieces. What conclusion will they reach at a level of significance of 0.01 if 6 tests showed tool lives of 2,470, 2,520, 2,425, 2,505, 2,400, and 2,440 pieces?

12. A food buyer for a large restaurant chain invites packers to submit samples for grading; among other things, he checks the drained weight of canned fruits and vegetables. If a submitted sample of four No. 10 cans of carrots has drained weights of 71.3, 71.6, 72.4, and 71.9 ounces, will he conclude at the 0.05 level of significance that the shipment from which this sample is obtained violates the requirement that the average weight must be at least 72 ounces?

13. The yields of alfalfa from six test plots are 1.2, 1.6, 0.9, 1.1, 2.0, and 1.0 tons per acre. Test at a level of significance of 0.05 whether this supports the contention that the true average yield for this kind of alfalfa is 1.5 tons per acre.

14. In order to evaluate the clinical effects of a new steroid in treating chronically underweight persons, 50 such persons were given 25-mg dosages of the drug over a 12-week period, while another 50 such persons were given 50-mg dosages of the drug over the same period. After 6 months, it was observed that the persons in the first group had gained on the average 7 pounds with a standard deviation of 6 pounds, while those in the second group had gained on the average 10 pounds with a standard deviation of 7 pounds. Treating the two samples as random samples, test at the 0.05 level of significance whether there is a real difference in the average weight gains of persons receiving the two dosages.

15. The same achievement test was given to soldiers selected at random from two different units. The scores they obtained are summarized by the following results:

$$n_1 = 80, \quad \bar{x}_1 = 73.2, \quad s_1 = 6.3$$

$$n_2 = 100, \quad \bar{x}_2 = 70.5, \quad s_2 = 5.9$$

Use a level of significance of 0.01 to test whether the difference between the two sample means is significant.

16. In a study of television viewing habits, an investigator obtained the following data on the weekly number of hours a family's television set is turned on between 6 P.M. and 10 P.M.: $n_1 = 50$ families, where the head of the household is *not* a college graduate, averaged 19.5 hours with a standard deviation of 4.8 hours; $n_2 = 60$ families, where the head of the household is a college graduate, averaged 17.2 hours with a standard deviation of 3.6 hours. What can the investigator conclude from these data at a level of significance of 0.05?

17. Suppose that in Exercise 16 the investigator wants to test the hypothesis that if the head of the household is a college graduate, the family's television set is turned on (on the average) at least two and a half hours less each week between 6 P.M. and 10 P.M. Formulate precisely what null hypothesis and what alternative hypothesis he would have to use, and perform the test at a level of significance of 0.05. (*Hint:* substitute $\bar{x}_1 - \bar{x}_2 - 2.5$ for $\bar{x}_1 - \bar{x}_2$ in the numerator of the formula for z.)

18. Measurements performed on random samples of two kinds of cigarettes yielded the following results on their nicotine content (in milligrams):

Brand A: 26.4, 22.5, 24.9, 23.7, 21.5

Brand B: 25.7, 29.0, 23.4, 27.6, 22.3

Use a level of significance of 0.05 to check on the claim that Brand B has a higher average nicotine content than Brand A. (See also Exercise 6 on page 270.)

19. In order to decide whether the inhabitants of two South Pacific islands may be regarded as having the same racial ancestry, an anthropologist performs the necessary skull measurements and compares their cephalic indices. The values he obtains for six inhabitants of the first island are 72.4, 78.9, 75.4, 73.5, 74.7, and 81.1; for six inhabitants of the second island he obtains 71.8, 74.6, 72.0, 73.5, 70.2, and 75.9. Test at a level of significance of 0.05 whether the difference between the two sample means is significant. (See also Exercise 7 on page 271.)

20. In order to compare the merits of two short-range rockets, 8 of the first kind and 10 of the second kind are fired at a target. If those of the first kind have a mean target error of 36 feet with a standard deviation of 15 feet, while those of the second kind have a mean target error of 52 feet with a standard deviation of 18 feet, check on the claim that the second kind of rocket is worse than the first. Use a level of significance of 0.05. (See also Exercise 8 on page 271.)

21. A random sample of 12 manufacturing corporations with assets under \$1,000,000 showed an average profit (after taxes) of 1.8 per cent of sales with a standard deviation of 0.4 per cent; a random sample of 10 manufacturing corporations with assets between \$1,000,000 and \$5,000,000 showed an average profit (after taxes) of 2.4 per cent of sales with a standard deviation of 0.6 per cent. Is it reasonable to attribute the difference between the two average profits to the fact that we are only dealing with samples? Use a level of significance of 0.05.

22. If we want to study the effectiveness of a diet on the basis of weights "before and after," or if we want to study whatever differences there may be between the I.Q.'s of husbands and wives, the methods of Section 9.8 cannot be used. The samples are not independent; in fact, in each case the data are *paired*. To handle problems of this kind, we work with the differences of the paired data (retaining their signs), and test whether these differences may be looked upon as a sample from a population for which $\mu = 0$. If the sample is small, we use the t test on page 253, and if the sample is large, we use the test on page 252. Apply this technique to the following data designed to test whether there is a systematic difference in the blood-pressure readings obtained with two different instruments:

	Instrument A	*Instrument B*
Patient 1	144	147
Patient 2	165	167
Patient 3	125	124
Patient 4	149	152
Patient 5	141	146
Patient 6	118	120
Patient 7	131	135
Patient 8	126	126
Patient 9	147	149

Use a level of significance of 0.01 to investigate the claim that on the average Instrument *B* will give a higher reading than Instrument A.

23. In a study of the effectiveness of a reducing diet the following "before and after" figures were obtained for a random sample of 10 adult married women in the age group from 30 to 40 (data in pounds):

134 and 131, 147 and 140, 165 and 164, 152 and 153, 122 and 122

138 and 135, 147 and 148, 153 and 147, 178 and 165, 139 and 133

Use the method explained in Exercise 22 and $\alpha = 0.01$ to test the null hypothesis that the diet is not effective.

24. (*A Bayesian decision problem concerning means*) Having had some experience with similar situations, three equally reliable statisticians estimate subjectively that the average daily demand for a new product will be, respectively, $\mu = 116$, $\mu = 120$, and $\mu = 124$ units. It is assumed that one of these three figures must be correct and that the standard deviation of the daily demand for the new product is $\sigma = 25$.

(a) If the losses associated with the various possible decisions are as shown in the following table

	True Value		
	116	120	124
Accept 116	0	\$100	\$200
Accept 120	\$50	0	\$100
Accept 124	\$100	\$100	0

which decision would minimize one's expected losses, considering only the given collateral information?

(b) If figures obtained for the daily demand for the product on 100 days have a mean *greater than* 122.5, find the probabilities of this happening when $\mu = 116$, 120, and 124, respectively. (*Hint:* Use the normal curve approximation to the sampling distribution of the mean.)

(c) Use Bayes' Rule and the results of part (b) to calculate the revised probabilities one can assign $\mu = 116$, 120, and 124, on the basis of the collateral information as well as the direct evidence.

(d) Use the results of part (c) and the table of part (a) to determine which decision concerning the true average daily demand will minimize the expected losses.

BIBLIOGRAPHY

An informal introduction to interval estimation is given under the heading of "How to be precise though vague," in

Moroney, M. J., *Facts from Figures.* London: Penguin Books, 1951.

A discussion of the theoretical foundation of the *t* distribution, and its use in small-sample tests concerning means and differences between means, may be found in

Freund, J. E., *Mathematical Statistics.* Englewood Cliffs, N.J.: Prentice-Hall, Inc., 1962

and in most other texts on mathematical statistics. The above-mentioned book also contains a derivation of the formula for the standard error of the difference between two means. Some of the theory related to the Bayesian estimation formula of Section 9.4 is discussed on pages 441–442 of

Schlaifer, R., *Probability and Statistics for Business Decisions.* New York: McGraw-Hill Book Company, 1959

and in Section 5.1 of

Lindley, D. V., *Introduction to Probability and Statistics from a Bayesian Viewpoint, Part 2.* Cambridge: Cambridge University Press, 1965.

TEN
Inferences Concerning Standard Deviations

10.1 The Estimation of σ

Many of the methods described in Chapter 9 required knowledge of the population standard deviation σ, a quantity which, unfortunately, is often unknown. We got around this difficulty in the large-sample confidence interval for μ on page 224 and in the large-sample tests concerning μ on page 252 by substituting for σ the sample standard deviation s. Of course, this raises the question whether it is at all reasonable to make such a substitution, and to answer this question even in part, we shall have to investigate the general problem of estimating population standard deviations.

Although the sample standard deviation is by far the most popular estimate of the standard deviation of a population, there are other methods, other statistics, which are sometimes used to get quick estimates of σ. We already saw in Exercise 9 on page 180 that an estimate of σ can be obtained from the graph of a distribution on arithmetic probability paper, provided the distribution has roughly the shape of a normal curve. Other short-cut estimates based, respectively, on the sample range and on certain fractiles of a distribution are mentioned in Exercises 8 and 9 on page 266.

In the remainder of this section we shall limit our discussion to problems which arise when we use s as an estimate of σ (or s^2 as an estimate of σ^2); in particular, we shall establish confidence intervals for σ based on sample standard deviations. The theory on which these confidence intervals are based assumes that the population from which we are sampling has roughly the shape of a normal distribution. It can then be shown that the statistic

▲ $$\chi^2 = \frac{(n-1)s^2}{\sigma^2}$$ ▲

called "chi-square," has as its sampling distribution a well-known continuous distribution, the *chi-square distribution*. The mean of this distribution is $n - 1$ and, as in connection with the t distribution, we refer to this quantity as the *number of degrees of freedom*, or simply the *degrees of freedom*. An example of a chi-square distribution is shown in Figure 10.1; in contrast to

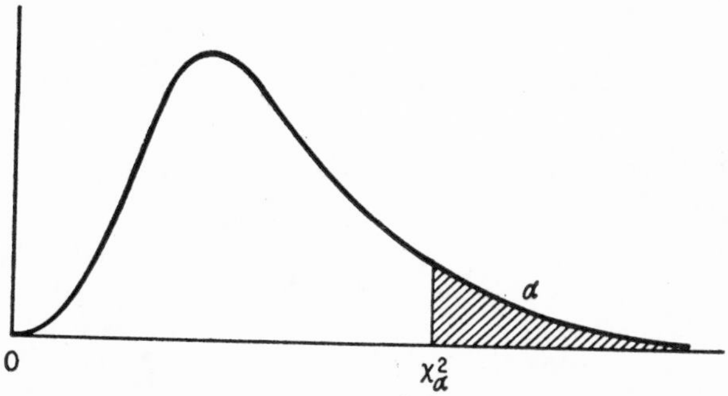

Fig. 10.1 Chi-square distribution.

the normal and t distributions, its domain is restricted to the nonnegative real numbers.

Analogous to z_α and t_α, we define χ^2_α as the value for which the area *to its right* under the chi-square distribution is equal to α. Thus, $\chi^2_{\alpha/2}$ is such that the area *to its right* under the curve is $\alpha/2$, while $\chi^2_{1-\alpha/2}$ is such that the area *to its left* under the curve is $\alpha/2$ (see also Figure 10.2). We made this dis-

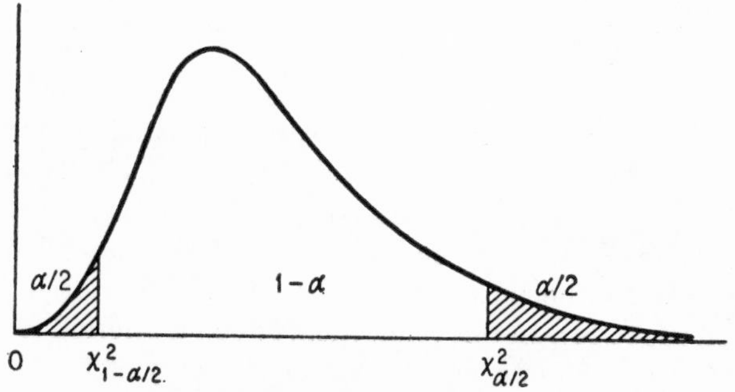

Fig. 10.2 Chi-square distribution.

tinction because the chi-square distribution is *not* symmetrical, and we shall need values corresponding to areas in either tail of the distribution. Among others, values of $\chi^2_{0.995}$, $\chi^2_{0.975}$, $\chi^2_{0.025}$, and $\chi^2_{0.005}$ are given in Table III at the end of the book for 1, 2, 3, . . . , and 30 degrees of freedom.

Referring to Figure 10.2, it is apparent that we can assert with a probability of $1 - \alpha$ that a random variable having the chi-square distribution will assume a value between $\chi^2_{1-\alpha/2}$ and $\chi^2_{\alpha/2}$. Making use of this fact in connection with the χ^2 statistic given on page 262, we can assert with a probability of $1 - \alpha$ that

$$\chi^2_{1-\alpha/2} < \frac{(n-1)s^2}{\sigma^2} < \chi^2_{\alpha/2}$$

Applying straightforward algebra, we can rewrite this inequality as

▲ $$\sqrt{\frac{(n-1)s^2}{\chi^2_{\alpha/2}}} < \sigma < \sqrt{\frac{(n-1)s^2}{\chi^2_{1-\alpha/2}}}$$ ▲

and we have thus obtained a $1 - \alpha$ *confidence interval for* σ. Omitting the square root signs, we obtain a corresponding confidence interval for the population variance σ^2.

To illustrate the use of this confidence-interval formula, let us return to the example on page 254, where we pointed out that there appears to be a considerable amount of variation in the performance of an experimental engine. We had $s = 2.2$ gallons for the 16 test runs, and since $\chi^2_{0.0975}$ and $\chi^2_{0.025}$ for 15 degrees of freedom equal 6.262 and 27.488, respectively, substitution into the formula yields

$$\sqrt{\frac{15(2.2)^2}{27.488}} < \sigma < \sqrt{\frac{15(2.2)^2}{6.262}}$$

or

$$1.6 < \sigma < 3.4$$

This is a 0.95 confidence interval for the population standard deviation, and it should help the engineer who designed the engine to judge whether or not it meets specifications.

The confidence interval we have just described is often referred to as a *small-sample* confidence interval; it is used mainly when n is small and, of course, only when one can assume that the shape of the population is close to that of a normal curve. Otherwise, we make use of the fact that *for large samples* the sampling distribution of s can be approximated with a normal distribution having the mean σ and the standard deviation $\sigma/\sqrt{2n}$ (see Exercise 8 on page 214). In this connection, $\sigma/\sqrt{2n}$ is referred to as the *standard error* of s. We can now assert with a probability of $1 - \alpha$ that

$$s - z_{\alpha/2}\frac{\sigma}{\sqrt{2n}} < \sigma < s + z_{\alpha/2}\frac{\sigma}{\sqrt{2n}}$$

and simple algebra leads to the following $1 - \alpha$ *large-sample confidence interval for the population standard deviation* σ:

▲ $$\frac{s}{1 + \dfrac{z_{\alpha/2}}{\sqrt{2n}}} < \sigma < \frac{s}{1 - \dfrac{z_{\alpha/2}}{\sqrt{2n}}}$$ ▲

Referring to the example on page 221, where we were interested in the length of young-of-the-year fresh-water drumfish, and substituting $n = 50$ and $s = 10.0$, we obtain

$$\frac{10.0}{1 + \frac{1.96}{\sqrt{100}}} < \sigma < \frac{10.0}{1 - \frac{1.96}{\sqrt{100}}}$$

or

$$8.36 < \sigma < 12.44$$

We can thus assert with a probability of 0.95 that the interval from 8.36 to 12.44 contains σ, the true standard deviation of the lengths of the fish.

EXERCISES

1. Ten measurements of the time required to kill a centipede with a given insecticide have a standard deviation of 4.5 seconds. Construct a 0.95 confidence interval for the true standard deviation of the time required by the insecticide to take effect.

2. Investigating the consistency of a new kind of processed yeast which has recently been put on the market, a home economist observed the time it took 6 batches of dough to double in size (under specified laboratory conditions). Given that the home economist obtained a sample *variance* of 7.35 minutes for the six observations, calculate a 0.99 confidence interval for σ, which is, in fact, a measure of the consistency of the action produced by the yeast.

3. Given that 8 temperature readings taken at various places inside a large kiln (when an outside dial indicated a temperature of 300 degrees) had a standard deviation of 0.45 degrees Fahrenheit, construct a 0.95 confidence interval for σ, which in this case is a measure of the consistency with which the kiln can maintain a given temperature.

4. Referring to Exercise 12 on page 258, construct a 0.99 confidence interval for σ, the standard deviation of the weights of all the cans of carrots from which the sample was obtained.

5. In an experiment designed to investigate the effects of a new drug, it was found that the increase in pulse rate of 25 patients (immediately after injection of a fixed dose of the drug) had a standard deviation of 2.8.

(a) Use the small-sample technique to construct a 0.95 confidence interval for σ, measuring the true variability in the drug's effect on the pulse rate.

(b) Repeat part (a) using the large-sample method, and compare the two results.

6. As part of a study designed to provide norms for a mechanical aptitude test, psychologists gave the test to a random sample of 300 eighth graders in a very large school system. Given that the standard deviation they obtained for the scores was 12.9, construct a 0.95 confidence interval for the corresponding population standard deviation.

7. Referring to Exercise 1 on page 233, construct a 0.99 confidence interval for the true standard deviation of the protein intake (per kilogram of body weight) of young adults in the given Australian city.

8. When dealing with very small samples, good estimates of the population standard deviation can often be obtained on the basis of the sample range (the largest sample value minus the smallest). Such quick estimates of σ are given by the sample range divided by the divisor d, which depends on the size of the sample; for samples from populations having roughly the shape of a normal distribution, its values are as shown in the following table:

n	2	3	4	5	6	7	8	9	10
d	1.13	1.69	2.06	2.33	2.53	2.70	2.85	2.97	3.08

(a) Referring to Exercise 7 on page 70, use this method to estimate σ, a measure of the true consistency of the paint, and compare the result with the value of s obtained in that exercise.

(b) Referring to Exercise 11 on page 258, use this method to estimate σ, the true standard deviation of the lifetimes of the given kind of cutting tool, and compare with the value obtained for the sample standard deviation.

(c) Referring to Exercise 13 on page 258, use this method to estimate the true standard deviation of the per-acre yield of the given kind of alfalfa.

9. Quick estimates of the standard deviation of a distribution (and, hence, of the population from which the data were obtained) can also be found by means of the formula $\frac{1}{3}(F_{15/16} - F_{1/16})$, where the two fractiles $F_{15/16}$ and $F_{1/16}$ are as defined in Exercise 24 on page 54. Use the results of part (e) of that exercise to estimate σ for the population from which the sample of chemistry grades was obtained.

10.2 Tests Concerning Standard Deviations

In this section we shall discuss two kinds of tests concerning population standard deviations—the first concerns the null hypothesis that a population standard deviation equals a specified constant σ_0, and the second concerns the equality of the standard deviations of two populations. The first kind of test is required whenever we want to check on the uniformity of a product, process, or operation. For instance, we may want to test whether a given kind of glass is sufficiently homogeneous for making delicate optical equipment, whether a group of trainees is sufficiently uniform to be taught in one class, whether the variation in the potency of a medicine is within permissible limits, and so on. The second kind of test is often used in conjunction with the two-sample t test described in Section 9.8, since this test requires that the standard deviations of the two populations are equal. For instance, in the airplane-instrument-dial example on page 256 the two samples had standard deviations of $s_1 = \sqrt{66/4} = 4.06$ and $s_2 = \sqrt{82/4} = 4.53$, and this may cast some doubt on the assumption that the corresponding population standard deviations are actually equal. In any case, this question should always be put to a test *before* the t test for differences between means is actually performed.

The test of the null hypothesis $\sigma = \sigma_0$, namely, the hypothesis that a population standard deviation equals a specified constant, is based on the same assumptions, the same statistic, and the same sampling theory as the small-sample confidence interval of Section 10.1. Assuming that our sample comes from a population having roughly the shape of a normal distribution, we base our decision on the statistic

▲ $$\chi^2 = \frac{(n-1)s^2}{\sigma_0^2}$$ ▲

where n and s^2 are the sample size and the sample variance, while σ_0 is the value of the population standard deviation assumed under the null hypothesis. As we pointed out on page 262, the sampling distribution of this statistic is the chi-square distribution with $n - 1$ degrees of freedom; hence, the criteria for testing the null hypothesis $\sigma = \sigma_0$ against the alternative hypothesis $\sigma < \sigma_0$, $\sigma > \sigma_0$, or $\sigma \neq \sigma_0$ are as shown in Figure 10.3. For the one-sided alternative $\sigma < \sigma_0$ we reject the null hypothesis for values of χ^2 falling into the left-hand tail of its sampling distribution; for the one-sided alternative $\sigma > \sigma_0$ we reject the null hypothesis for values of χ^2 falling into the right-hand tail of its sampling distribution; and for the two-sided alternative $\sigma \neq \sigma_0$ we reject the null hypothesis for values of χ^2 falling into either tail of its sampling distribution. The quantities χ^2_α, $\chi^2_{\alpha/2}$, and $\chi^2_{1-\alpha/2}$ are defined on page 263, and in practice they are obtained from Table III.

To illustrate this kind of test, suppose that the thickness of a part used in a semiconductor is its critical dimension and that measurements of the thickness of a random sample of 18 such parts have a standard deviation of $s = 0.82$ thousandth of an inch. The process is considered to be under control if the variation of these thicknesses is given by a standard deviation not larger than $\sigma = 0.60$ thousandth of an inch. In order to test the null hypothesis $\sigma = 0.60$ against the alternative hypothesis $\sigma > 0.60$ at a level of significance of, say, 0.05, we first calculate the value of the chi-square statistic, getting

$$\chi^2 = \frac{17(0.82)^2}{(0.60)^2} = 31.75$$

Since this exceeds 27.587, the value of $\chi^2_{0.05}$ for 17 degrees of freedom, the null hypothesis must be rejected (and the process used in the manufacture of the parts will have to be adjusted).

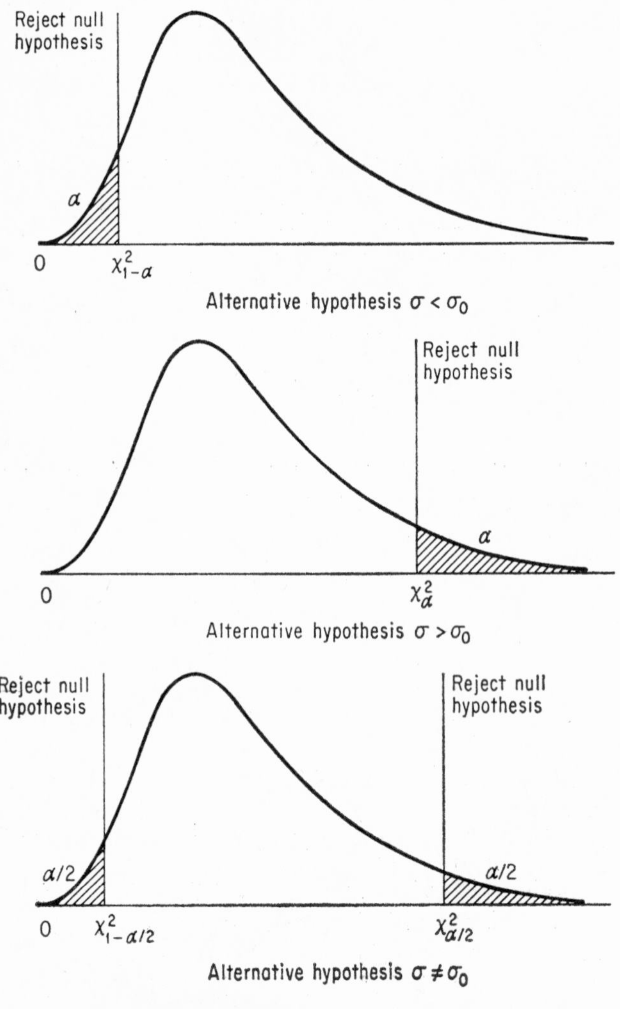

Fig. 10.3 Test criteria.

Given independent random samples from two populations, we usually base tests of the *equality* of the two population variances on the ratios s_1^2/s_2^2 or s_2^2/s_1^2, where s_1 and s_2 are the two sample standard deviations. Assuming that the populations from which the two samples were obtained have roughly the shape of normal distributions, it can be shown that the sampling distribution of such a ratio (appropriately called a *variance ratio*) is a continuous distribution called the *F distribution.* This distribution depends on the sample sizes n_1 and n_2, or better on the two parameters $n_1 - 1$ and $n_2 - 1$, referred to as the respective *degrees of freedom.* One difficulty connected with this distribution is that most tables give only values of $F_{0.05}$ (defined in the same way as $z_{0.05}$, $t_{0.05}$, and $\chi^2_{0.05}$) and $F_{0.01}$, so that we can work only with the right-hand tail of the distribution. It is for this reason that we base our decision concerning the equality of the two population standard deviations σ_1 and σ_2 on the statistic

$$F = \frac{s_1^2}{s_2^2} \quad \textit{or} \quad \frac{s_2^2}{s_1^2} \quad \textit{whichever is larger}$$

With this statistic we reject the null hypothesis $\sigma_1 = \sigma_2$ and accept the alternative $\sigma_1 \neq \sigma_2$ when the observed value of F exceeds $F_{\alpha/2}$, where α is the level of significance (see also Figure 10.4). Note that by using a right-

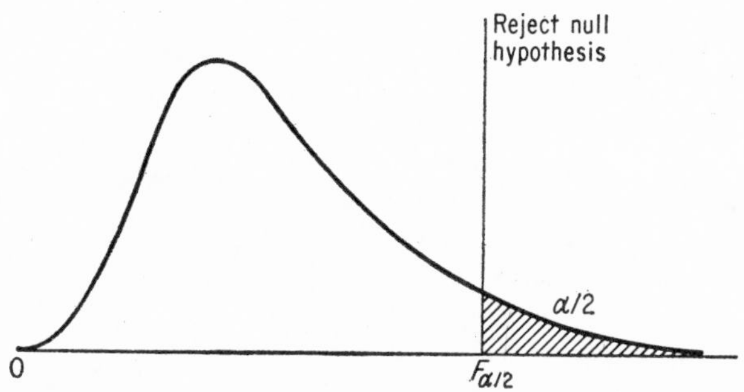

Fig. 10.4 *F* distribution.

hand tail area of $\alpha/2$ instead of α, we compensate for the fact that we always use the larger of the two variance ratios. The necessary values of $F_{\alpha/2}$ for $\alpha = 0.02$ or 0.10, namely, $F_{0.01}$ and $F_{0.05}$, are given in Table IV at the end of the book, where the number of degrees of freedom for the numerator is $n_1 - 1$ or $n_2 - 1$ depending on whether we are using the ratio s_1^2/s_2^2 or the ratio s_2^2/s_1^2; correspondingly, the number of degrees of freedom for the denominator is $n_2 - 1$ or $n_1 - 1$.

To illustrate this kind of test, let us return to the second example of Section 9.8, where we used a t test to check on the significance of the difference between two means. As we pointed out on page 267, this test requires that the standard deviations of the populations from which the two samples are obtained are equal, a fact which should really have been examined at the time. Since we had 5 observations for each of the two kinds of phosphorescent coatings and the two sample variances were $s_1^2 = 66/4 = 16.5$ and $s_2^2 = 82/4 = 20.5$, we now get

$$F = \frac{s_2^2}{s_1^2} = 1.24$$

This value is less than 16.00, the value of $F_{0.01}$ for 4 and 4 degrees of freedom, and the null hypothesis cannot be rejected at a level of significance of 0.02. In fact, since the value obtained for F is close to 1, there would seem to be very little risk in making the assumption that the two population standard deviations are equal.

EXERCISES

1. Test the null hypothesis that $\sigma = 0.02$ in. for the unstretched lengths of certain springs, if in a random sample of size 10 the lengths of the springs had a standard deviation of $s = 0.034$ in. Use a level of significance of 0.05.

2. Referring to the experiment of Exercise 9 on page 258, investigate the claim that the true standard deviation of the time it takes an adult to memorize the list of French verbs is less than 2 minutes. Use a level of significance of 0.01.

3. Referring to Exercise 8 on page 258, suppose that the specifications also require that the standard deviation of the breaking strength is at most 7.5 pounds. Use the data given in that exercise to test the null hypothesis $\sigma = 7.5$ against an appropriate alternative at a level of significance of 0.05.

4. Large-sample tests concerning population standard deviations are usually based on the fact that, *for large n*, the sampling distribution of

▲ $$z = \sqrt{2\chi^2} - \sqrt{2(n-1)}$$ ▲

is approximately the standard normal distribution, where χ^2 is the statistic given on page 267. One can thus test the null hypothesis $\sigma = \sigma_0$ against the alternatives $\sigma < \sigma_0$, $\sigma > \sigma_0$, or $\sigma \neq \sigma_0$ with the use of the criteria shown in Figure 9.8. Supposing that in the travel-time example discussed extensively in the text (mainly in Chapter 9) the 250 sample values have a standard deviation of 10.3 minutes, use a two-sided alternative and a level of significance of 0.05 to test the null hypothesis that σ is still equal to 8.1 minutes.

5. In a random sample, the weights of 50 Black Angus steers of a certain age have a standard deviation of 240 pounds. Use the method of Exercise 4 to test the null hypothesis that the true standard deviation of such weights is 225 pounds (at $\alpha = 0.01$).

6. Referring to Exercise 18 on page 259, test (at a level of significance of 0.02) whether it is reasonable to make the assumption that the two samples come from populations having the same standard deviation.

7. Referring to Exercise 19 on page 259, test the assumption that the variances of the two populations from which the samples were obtained are, in fact, equal. Use $\alpha = 0.02$.

8. Referring to Exercise 20 on page 259, check at a level of significance of 0.10 whether it is reasonable to assume that the populations from which the two samples came have the same standard deviation.

BIBLIOGRAPHY

Discussions of theory pertaining to the chi-square and F distributions may be found in mose textbooks on mathematical statistics; for example, in the author's book listed on page 301 and in

Hoel, P. G., *Introduction to Mathematical Statistics*, 3rd ed. New York: John Wiley & Sons, Inc., 1962.

ELEVEN
Inferences Concerning Proportions

11.1 The Estimation of Proportions

The information that is usually available for the estimation of a proportion (percentage, or probability) is the relative frequency with which an event has occurred. If an event occurs x times out of n, the relative frequency of its occurrence is x/n, and we generally use this *sample proportion* to estimate the corresponding true proportion p. For example, if 322 of 400 housewives prefer built-in dishwashers to the freestanding kind, then $x/n = 322/400 = 0.805$, and (provided the sample is random) we can use this figure as an estimate of the true proportion of housewives having this preference. Similarly, a company writing industrial accident insurance might estimate as 0.71 the proportion of its policyholders who file at least one claim per year, if a sample check of 200 policies shows that 142 had at least one claim filed during 1965.

In the remainder of this section we shall assume that the situations with which we are dealing satisfy (at least approximately) the conditions of the binomial distribution (see page 153). Our information will consist of how many successes there are in a given number of trials, and it will be assumed that the trials are independent and that the probability of a success is p for each trial. Thus, the sampling distribution with which we are concerned is the binomial distribution, for which we indicated on pages 165 and 166 that its mean is $\mu = np$ and the standard deviation is $\sigma = \sqrt{np(1-p)}$. An important feature of this formula for σ is that it involves the "true" proportion p, and this leads to some difficulties since p is the quantity we shall want to estimate. In order to avoid this complication, at least for the moment, we shall begin by constructing confidence intervals for p with the use of tables designed especially for this purpose.

Tables V(a) and V(b) at the end of the book provide 0.95 and 0.99 confidence intervals for proportions in situations where the conditions underlying the binomial distribution are met (at least approximately). These tables are easy to use and require practically no calculations. If a sample proportion is less than or equal to 0.50, we begin by marking the value obtained for x/n on the *bottom scale;* we then go up vertically until we reach the two contour lines (curves) which correspond to the size of the sample,

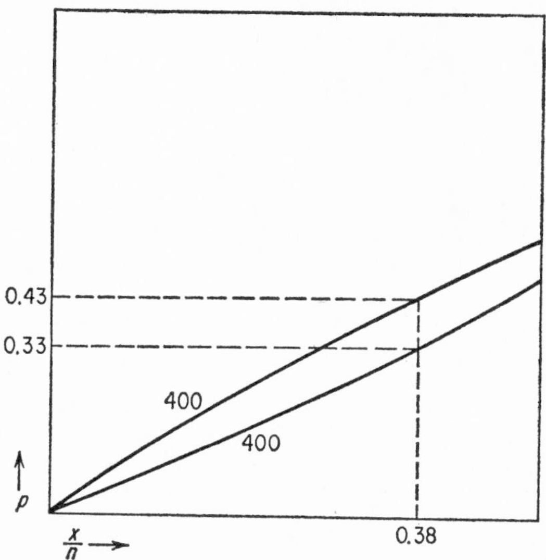

Fig. 11.1 Confidence limits for p.

and read the confidence limits for p off the *left-hand scale,* as indicated in Figure 11.1. If the sample proportion is greater than 0.50, we mark the value obtained for x/n on the *top scale,* go down vertically until we reach the two contour lines (curves) which correspond to the size of the sample, and read the confidence limits for p off the *right-hand scale,* as indicated in Figure 11.2.

To illustrate the use of Tables V(a) and V(b) when the sample proportion is less than or equal to 0.50, suppose that in a random sample of 400 college students 152 favored the quarter system to the semester system while 248 favored the semester system to the quarter system. Marking $x/n = 152/400 = 0.38$ on the bottom scale of Table V(a) and proceeding as in Figure 11.1, we find that a 0.95 confidence interval for the true proportion of students who favor the quarter system to the semester system (in the population from which the sample was obtained) is given by

$$0.33 < p < 0.43$$

Had we wanted to use a degree of confidence of 0.99, Table V(b) would have yielded the interval

$$0.32 < p < 0.44$$

As before, the confidence interval gets wider when the degree of confidence is increased.

To illustrate the use of Tables V(a) and V(b) when the sample proportion exceeds 0.50, let us return to the insurance example on page 272, where

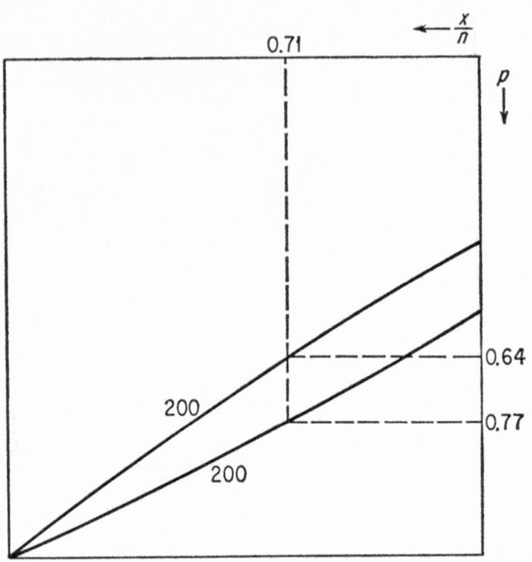

Fig. 11.2 Confidence limits for p.

142 of 200 policyholders filed at least one claim during 1965. Marking $x/n = 142/200 = 0.71$ on the *top scale* of Table V(a), halfway between 0.70 and 0.72, and proceeding as in Figure 11.2, we find that the desired 0.95 confidence interval for the true proportion is

$$0.64 < p < 0.77$$

Using Table V(b) we similarly find that

$$0.62 < p < 0.79$$

is a 0.99 confidence interval for the true proportion of policyholders of the given company who file at least one claim per year. Assuming that our sample is random (for the policyholders of the given company), we can thus assert with a probability of 0.95 that the interval from 0.64 to 0.77 contains the actual proportion of policyholders filing at least one claim per year, or with a probability of 0.99 that the interval from 0.62 to 0.79 contains this "true" proportion.

Note that in both of our examples Tables V(a) and V(b) had contour lines (curves) corresponding to the size of the samples; for values of n other than 8, 10, 12, 16, 20, 24, 30, 40, 60, 100, 200, 400, and 1,000, we literally have to read between the lines. For instance, the reader may wish to verify that for $x = 20$ and $n = 50$, Table V(a) yields the 0.95 confidence interval $0.26 < p < 0.55$.

When n is large and p is not close to either 0 or 1, large-sample confidence intervals for p can be based on the normal curve approximation to the binomial distribution. Using the results of Section 7.3, we can treat

$$z = \frac{x - np}{\sqrt{np(1 - p)}}$$

as a value of a random variable having the standard normal distribution and, duplicating the work on page 224, we obtain the following $1 - \alpha$ *large-sample confidence interval for p:*

$$\frac{x}{n} - z_{\alpha/2}\sqrt{\frac{p(1-p)}{n}} < p < \frac{x}{n} + z_{\alpha/2}\sqrt{\frac{p(1-p)}{n}}$$

This formula cannot be used *as is,* since the confidence limits, themselves, involve the parameter p we are trying to estimate. [$\sqrt{\frac{p(1-p)}{n}}$, the quantity which appears in these confidence limits, is generally called the *standard error of a proportion;* it *is* the standard deviation of the sampling distribution of a sample proportion.] We could manipulate the above inequality so that the middle term is p and the other two terms consist of expressions which can be calculated without knowledge of p (see Exercise 11 on page 281), but it is more common to use the $1 - \alpha$ *large-sample confidence interval*

$$\blacktriangle \qquad \frac{x}{n} - z_{\alpha/2}\sqrt{\frac{\frac{x}{n}\left(1 - \frac{x}{n}\right)}{n}} < p < \frac{x}{n} + z_{\alpha/2}\sqrt{\frac{\frac{x}{n}\left(1 - \frac{x}{n}\right)}{n}} \qquad \blacktriangle$$

which is obtained by substituting the sample proportion x/n for p in the standard error formula $\sqrt{\frac{p(1-p)}{n}}$. Here $z_{\alpha/2}$ is as defined on page 222, and the values most often used are $z_{0.025} = 1.96$, $z_{0.01} = 2.33$, and $z_{0.005} = 2.58$.

To illustrate this technique, let us return to the second of the examples on page 272, where 142 of the 200 policyholders filed at least one claim during 1965. Substituting $x = 142$, $n = 200$, and $z_{0.025} = 1.96$ (for a degree of confidence of 0.05), we obtain

$$\frac{142}{200} - 1.96\sqrt{\frac{(0.71)(0.29)}{200}} < p < \frac{142}{200} + 1.96\sqrt{\frac{(0.71)(0.29)}{200}}$$

or

$$0.647 < p < 0.773$$

Note that this is very close to the interval 0.64 − 0.77 obtained previously with the use of Table V(a).

The theory presented here can also be used to judge the possible size of the error one makes when using a sample proportion x/n as a point estimate of p. *In fact, we can assert with a probability of* $1 - \alpha$ *that the size of this error, that is, its magnitude, will be less than*

$$z_{\alpha/2}\sqrt{\frac{p(1-p)}{n}} \quad \textit{or approximately} \quad z_{\alpha/2}\sqrt{\frac{\frac{x}{n}\left(1-\frac{x}{n}\right)}{n}}$$

The first of these two formulas cannot be used in actual practice since p is always unknown in problems of this kind; the second formula should be used only when n is large.

To illustrate this technique, let us return to the first of the two examples on page 272, namely, the one where 322 of 400 housewives preferred built-in dishwashers to the freestanding kind. If we use $322/400 = 0.805$ as an estimate of the true proportion of housewives preferring built-in dishwashers to freestanding ones, we can assert with a probability of 0.99 that the error of this estimate is less than

$$2.58\sqrt{\frac{(0.805)(0.195)}{400}} = 0.051$$

As in the estimation of means, we can use the expression for the maximum error to determine how large a sample is needed to attain a desired degree of precision. If we want to be able to assert with a probability of $1 - \alpha$ that our sample proportion will differ from the "true" proportion p by less than some quantity E, we can write

$$E = z_{\alpha/2}\sqrt{\frac{p(1-p)}{n}}$$

and upon solving for n, we get

$$n = p(1-p)\left[\frac{z_{\alpha/2}}{E}\right]^2$$

Since this formula requires knowledge of p, the quantity we are trying to estimate, it cannot be used exactly as it stands. However, it can be shown that $p(1-p)$ is at most equal to 1/4, and that it assumes this maximum value only when $p = 1/2$. *It follows that it is always safe to use the above formula with* $p = 1/2$, *although the resulting sample size may be unnecessarily large.* In case we do have some preliminary information about the possible range of values on which p might fall, we can take this into account in determining n. For instance, if it is reasonable to suppose that a proportion we are trying to estimate lies on the interval from 0.60 to 0.80, we substitute into the above formula for n whichever value is closest to 0.50; in this particular case we would substitute $p = 0.60$.

To illustrate this technique, suppose we want to estimate what proportion of heavy smokers will get lung cancer, and we want to be "95 per cent sure" that the error of our estimate will be less than 0.03. If we have no idea what the true proportion might be, we substitute $E = 0.03$, $p = 1/2$, $z_{0.025} = 1.96$, and we get

$$n = (1/2)(1/2)\left[\frac{1.96}{0.03}\right]^2 = 1{,}067$$

Hence, if we base our estimate on a random sample of size $n = 1{,}067$, we can assert with a probability of (at least) 0.95 that the sample proportion will *not* be "off" by more than 0.03. (We added the words "at least" because the sample size of 1,067 may actually be larger than necessary because we used $p = 1/2$.)

Had we known in this example that the proportion we are trying to estimate is in the neighborhood of, say, 0.25, the formula for n would have yielded

$$n = (0.25)(0.75)\left[\frac{1.96}{0.03}\right]^2 = 800$$

This illustrates the fact that if we do have some information about the possible size of the proportion we are trying to estimate, this can appreciably reduce the size of the required sample.

11.2 A Bayesian Estimate*

The estimation procedures of Section 11.1 utilized only direct evidence, namely, the proportion of successes observed in n trials. Although there are many instances where this is entirely satisfactory, there are also situations in which it would be foolish and wasteful to ignore pertinent collateral information. Suppose, for instance, that the output of a certain transistor production line is checked daily by inspecting a sample of 200 units. Over a long period of time, the process has maintained a yield of 80 per cent, that is, a proportion defective of 20 per cent, and the variation of the proportion defective (from day to day) is measured by a standard deviation of 0.04. Now suppose that on a given day the sample (of size 200) contains 82 defectives. *Would it be reasonable to estimate the proportion defective for the whole day's production as* $x/n = 82/200 = 0.41$? Clearly, if we did this we would be ignoring all the information we have about the performance of the process over weeks, months, or perhaps even years. What we really need here is an estimation formula like that of Section 9.4, which assigns the weight

* See comment on this section in the Preface.

w to the *direct information,* in this case the sample proportion 0.41, and the weight $1 - w$ to the *collateral information,* in this case the average proportion defective observed over a long period of time, namely, 0.20.

If we denote by $\bar{p}$ the average proportion defective (observed over a long period of time) and by σ_p the standard deviation which measures the changes in the true proportion defective from day to day, we can, indeed, estimate the true proportion defective for any given day by means of the formula

▲ $$\text{Estimate} = w \cdot \frac{x}{n} + (1 - w) \cdot \bar{p}$$ ▲

where x is the observed number of successes in n trials and the weight w is given by

▲ $$w = \frac{n}{n + \dfrac{\bar{p}(1 - \bar{p})}{\sigma_p^2} - 1}$$ ▲

As in Section 9.4, we arrived at this formula for w by imposing the condition that *on the average* the square of the error of this kind of estimate be as small as possible. A discussion of this *Bayesian* estimation procedure may be found in Appendix A.2 and Chapter 7, respectively, of the books by R. Schlaifer and D. V. Lindley listed on page 261. (Actually, these authors base their results on the more specialized assumption that the distribution of p is a so-called *Beta* distribution.)

Before we return to our numerical example, let us point out some of the most important features of this Bayesian estimation formula. First, when no direct information is available and $n = 0$, the weight w equals 0 and the estimate is based entirely on the collateral information, namely, $\bar{p}$. When more and more direct information becomes available, that is, when n becomes increasingly large, w increases too and comes closer and closer to 1; thus, when more direct information becomes available, the estimate is based to a greater and greater extent on the sample proportion x/n. Another important point is that when the process varies considerably from day to day and σ_p is large, this tends to make w large; if the process is very consistent, however, and σ_p is small, this tends to make w small. *In other words, if the process varies considerably from day to day, we do not give much weight to the collateral information; if the process is very consistent, however, we tend to give most of the weight to the (extensive) information about itspast performance.*

To illustrate the use of the formula, let us return to the numerical example where we had $x = 82$, $n = 200$, $\bar{p} = 0.20$, and $\sigma_p = 0.04$. Substituting $n = 200$ and $\sigma_p = 0.04$ into the formula for w, we obtain

$$w = \frac{200}{200 + \dfrac{(0.20)(0.80)}{(0.04)^2} - 1} = 0.67$$

and the estimate of the proportion defective of the day's production becomes

$$(0.67)\frac{82}{200} + (1 - 0.67)(0.20) = 0.34$$

Note that this estimate is more *conservative* than the one based only on the direct evidence, in the sense that it gives about one-third of the total weight to information concerning the past performance of the process.

The method we have presented here is, of course, not limited to problems of industrial sampling inspection. It applies to any problem of estimating a proportion (percentage, or probability) in which meaningful values of $\bar{p}$ and σ_p can be obtained on the basis of collateral data and (or) subjective evaluations. If, prior to the collection of any data, any value of p is as likely as any other, or more correctly if the probability that p lies, say, on the interval from 0.1 to 0.2 equals the probabilities that it lies on the interval from 0.25 to 0.35, the interval from 0.67 to 0.77, or for that matter *any* interval of length 0.10, it can be shown that $\bar{p}$ and σ_p must equal 1/2 and $1/\sqrt{12}$, respectively. In that case $w = \dfrac{n}{n+2}$ and the estimate of the true proportion p can be written in the form $\dfrac{x+1}{n+2}$ (see Exercise 18 on page 282). This formula has a famous history; known as *Laplace's Rule of Succession*, it led to the claim that if an event has occurred n times out of n, the probability that it will happen *the next time* is $\dfrac{n+1}{n+2}$. It must be remembered, of course, that this result (which has been used to calculate, for example, the probability that the sun will rise the next day) is based on a very special, and also rather questionable, assumption about the *prior* distribution of the parameter p. (As we pointed out in the footnote to page 231, it is customary to refer to the distribution of a parameter as *prior* or "*a priori*" because it generally reflects prior, or collateral, information.)

EXERCISES

1. In a sample survey, 88 of 400 persons who had bought a new foreign-made sports car during 1965 stated that its performance exceeded their expectations. Use Table V to construct a 0.95 confidence interval for the corresponding true proportion.

2. In a random sample of 200 insurance claims against homeowners' policies, 128 were filed for \$800.00 or more. Use Table V to construct a 0.99 confidence interval for the actual proportion of claims for \$800.00 or more against policies of this kind.

3. In a group of 30 patients, 21 reported immediate improvement upon the injection of a new drug. Use Table V to construct a 0.95 confidence interval for the proportion of patients one can expect to show immediate improvement upon the injection of the drug.

4. Checking a sample of 50 electronic components prior to their shipment, it was found that 12 were assembled improperly. Use Table V to construct a 0.99 confidence interval for the true proportion of improperly assembled components in the (large) shipment from which the sample was obtained.

5. In a random sample of 1,000 persons who checked books out of a large library during the fall of 1966, 650 checked out fictional material and 350 checked out nonfictional material.

(a) Use Table V to construct a 0.95 confidence interval for the true proportion of persons who checked out fictional material during the fall of 1966.

(b) If we estimate the true proportion of persons (who checked out fictional material from the library during the fall of 1966) as 0.65, what can we assert with a probability of 0.95 about the possible size of the error of this estimate?

6. In a random sample of 100 cans of mixed nuts (taken from a very large shipment), 76 cans contained 200 or more peanuts.

(a) Use Table V to construct a 0.99 confidence interval for the actual proportion of cans of mixed nuts with 200 or more peanuts in the given shipment.

(b) Repeat part (a) using the large-sample confidence-interval formula on page 275 and compare results.

7. In a random sample of 300 students attending a large Western university, 180 stated that they held full or part-time jobs while 120 stated that they were not employed.

(a) Use Table V to construct a 0.95 confidence interval for the true proportion of students at that university who hold full or part-time jobs.

(b) Repeat part (a) using the large-sample confidence-interval formula on page 275 and compare the results.

8. In a random sample of 250 television viewers living in a certain area, 164 stated that they were satisfied with the programs supplied by the local station, while 86 had complaints of various kinds.

(a) Use Table V to construct a 0.99 confidence interval for the true proportion of television viewers in this area who are satisfied with the programs presented by the local station.

(b) If we estimate this true proportion as $164/250 = 0.656$, what can we assert with a probability of 0.99 about the possible size of the error of this estimate?

9. In a random sample of the members of a large regional teachers' association, it was found that of 400 high school English teachers only 212 majored in English in college.

(a) Use Table V to construct a 0.95 confidence interval for the true proportion of high school English teachers belonging to this association who majored in English in college.

(b) Repeat part (a) using the large-sample confidence-interval formula on page 275, and compare the results.

10. In a random sample of 2,000 consumers, 1,640 expressed a preference for Product A while the remaining 360 expressed a preference for Product B.

(a) Construct a 0.95 large-sample confidence interval for the true proportion of consumers preferring Product A to Product B.

(b) What can we assert with a probability of 0.99 about the possible size of our error, if we estimate this true proportion as $1{,}640/2{,}000 = 0.82$?

11. Solving the double inequality on page 275 for p, we obtain the confidence limits

$$\frac{x + \frac{1}{2}z_{\alpha/2}^2 \pm z_{\alpha/2}\sqrt{\frac{x(n-x)}{n} + \frac{1}{4}z_{\alpha/2}^2}}{n + z_{\alpha/2}^2}$$

(a) Referring to Exercise 1, use this formula to calculate 0.95 confidence limits for the true proportion of buyers of new sports cars who made the given statement, and compare results.

(b) Referring to Exercise 4, use this formula to calculate a 0.99 confidence interval for the actual proportion of improperly assembled components, and compare with the result obtained in that exercise.

12. If a sample constitutes a substantial portion (say, 5 per cent or more) of a population, the methods of this section should not be used without making an appropriate modification. If the sample itself is large, we can use the same *correction factor* as in the estimation of means, and write approximate large-sample $1 - \alpha$ confidence limits for p as

$$\frac{x}{n} \pm z_{\alpha/2}\sqrt{\frac{\frac{x}{n}\left(1 - \frac{x}{n}\right)}{n}} \cdot \sqrt{\frac{N-n}{N-1}}$$

where N is, as before, the size of the population.

(a) Rework part (b) of Exercise 6 assuming that the shipment contained 1,000 cans of these nuts.

(b) Rework part (b) of Exercise 7 assuming that the total enrollment at the given university is 2,000 students.

13. If we want to estimate the proportion of adults who prefer traveling by plane to all other modes of transportation, how large a random sample will we need to be able to assert with a probability of 0.95 that the error we make by using the sample proportion will be less than 0.04?

14. If we want to estimate the proportion of doctors who recommend a buffered aspirin rather than a plain aspirin, how large a random sample will we need to be able to assert with a probability of 0.99 that our sample proportion will differ from the true proportion by less than 0.05?

15. Suppose we want to estimate on the basis of a sample what proportion of a large shipment of radio tubes is defective, and we know from past experience that this proportion can be expected to be in the neighborhood of 0.05. How large a sample will we need to be able to assert with a probability of 0.95 that our sample proportion will not be "off" by more than 0.02?

16. A private opinion poll is hired by a political leader to estimate what proportion of the voters favor a certain piece of legislation. If it is known that the true proportion is in the neighborhood of 0.60, how large a sample will they have to take to be able to assert with a probability of 0.99 that their sample proportion will not be "off" by more than 0.06? What sample size would be required *without* the collateral knowledge that the true proportion is in the neighborhood of 0.60?

17. Suppose we want to estimate what percentage of waitresses working in diners staying open 24 hours will hold their jobs for at least 6 months. How large a random sample will we need to be able to assert with a probability of 0.90 that the error of our estimate (the sample percentage) will be less than 4 per cent? To what figure would this sample size be reduced if we knew that the percentage we want to estimate is less than 25 per cent?

18. Referring to the formulas on page 278, verify that for $\bar{p} = 1/2$ and $\sigma_p^2 = 1/12$ we get $w = \dfrac{n}{n+2}$ and the estimation formula $\dfrac{x+1}{n+2}$.

19. Referring to the production process of the example on page 277, suppose that on a certain day they were able to inspect only 100 transistors and found 3 of them to be defective. Using the collateral information concerning the process given on page 277 and the method of Section 11.2, estimate the true proportion of defective transistors in that day's production.

20. Records of a liberal arts college (collected over many years) show that on the average 76 per cent of all incoming freshmen have I.Q.'s of at least 115. Of course, the percentage varies somewhat from year to year and this variation is measured by a standard deviation of 3 per cent. If a sample check of 25 freshmen entering the college in 1967 showed that only 14 of them have I.Q.'s of at least 115, use the method of Section 11.2 to estimate the true proportion of students with I.Q.'s of at least 115 in that freshman class.

21. The operators of a large chain of gasoline stations in a certain area know that during the month of August the proportion of customers requiring oil as well as gasoline is 0.18. This proportion varies somewhat from station to station, and this variation is measured by a standard deviation of 0.02. If the records of a station (newly opened on August 1) show that among the first 850 customers 194 required oil as well as gasoline, use the method of Section 11.2 to estimate what proportion of the customers of this new station will require oil as well as gasoline at that time of the year. (Assume that the observed data can be looked upon as a random sample.)

11.3 Tests Concerning Proportions

Once the reader understands the fundamental ideas underlying tests of hypotheses, the various tests we shall study in the remainder of this book should not present any conceptual difficulties. The tests we shall take up in this section apply to problems in which we must decide, on the basis of sample data, whether the true value of a proportion (percentage, or probability) equals a given constant p_0. For instance, a manufacturer may want to know whether 0.60 is the correct proportion of housewives who prefer a new unsweetened fruit juice to a sweetened one. Similarly, a doctor may wish to know whether it is true that at least 80 per cent of his patients (having a given disease) will benefit from a new drug, and an efficiency expert employed by a laundry may wish to check whether the probability that a "cleaned" shirt is rejected at final inspection is at most 0.10.

Questions of this kind are usually decided on the basis of a sample proportion or the observed number of "successes" in n trials. In the above examples, the manufacturer would base his decision on the number (or proportion) of housewives preferring the unsweetened juice in a sample of, say, 400; the doctor would base his decision on the number of patients receiving beneficial results from the drug, say, among 250 patients having the given disease; and the efficiency expert might base his decision on the number of shirts rejected, say, in a sample of size 600.

Thus, the sampling distribution with which we shall be concerned is the binomial distribution first studied in Chapter 7. In fact, when n is small, tests concerning a "true" proportion (namely, tests concerning the parameter p of a binomial distribution) are usually based directly on tables of binomial probabilities, such as those referred to in the Bibliography at the end of this chapter. When n is large, however, we generally approximate the binomial distribution with a normal distribution and, as was indicated on page 184, this approximation is satisfactory so long as np and $n(1 - p)$ both exceed 5. Since the mean and the standard deviation of the binomial distribution are given by np and $\sqrt{np(1 - p)}$, respectively, we can base the test of the null hypothesis $p = p_0$ on the statistic

▲ $$z = \frac{x - np_0}{\sqrt{np_0(1 - p_0)}}$$ ▲

having (approximately) the standard normal distribution. The actual test criteria are again the ones shown in Figure 9.8 on page 251: for the one-sided alternative $p < p_0$ we reject the null hypothesis when $z < -z_\alpha$; for the one-sided alternative $p > p_0$ we reject the null hypothesis when $z > z_\alpha$; and for the two-sided alternative $p \neq p_0$ we reject the null hypothesis when $z < -z_{\alpha/2}$ or $z > z_{\alpha/2}$. As before, α is the level of significance, and z_α and $z_{\alpha/2}$ are as defined on page 222.

To illustrate this kind of test, suppose that in the third of the above examples the efficiency expert found 84 rejects in a random sample of 600 shirts, and he now wants to use this information to test the null hypothesis $p = 0.10$ against the alternative $p > 0.10$ at a level of significance of 0.05. Substituting $x = 84$, $n = 600$, and $p_0 = 0.10$ into the above formula for z, he gets

$$z = \frac{84 - 600(0.10)}{\sqrt{600(0.10)(0.90)}} = 3.27$$

and since this exceeds $z_{0.05} = 1.64$, he can conclude that the actual percentage of rejects at final inspection is greater than 10 per cent.

To give an example where it is appropriate to use a two-sided alternative, let us return to the first of the examples on page 283, assuming that the manufacturer wants to know whether 0.60 is the correct proportion of housewives who prefer the new unsweetened juice or whether this figure is *too high or too low*. If 252 of the 400 housewives in the sample actually expressed a preference for the new unsweetened fruit juice while 148 preferred the old sweetened kind, substitution into the formula for z yields

$$z = \frac{252 - 400(0.60)}{\sqrt{400(0.60)(0.40)}} = 1.22$$

Since this value falls between $-z_{0.025} = -1.96$ and $z_{0.025} = 1.96$, the null hypothesis that the true proportion is 0.60 cannot be rejected at $\alpha = 0.05$. Depending on whether a decision one way or the other is required, the manufacturer may reserve judgment or accept 0.60 as the correct proportion.

EXERCISES

1. A national magazine claimed that 55 per cent of all American families received more than one paycheck each week in 1963. Test the hypothesis that this figure still applies today against the alternative that the percentage has increased, if a recent sample survey showed that among 400 families there were 232 with more than one weekly paycheck. Use a level of significance of 0.05.

2. A large TV retailer in San Francisco claims that 80 per cent of all service calls on color TV sets are concerned with the small receiving tube. Test this claim against the alternative $p \neq 0.80$ if a random sample of 120 service calls on color TV sets included 91 which were concerned with the small receiving tube. Use $\alpha = 0.01$.

3. In a speech to the Chamber of Commerce, a city councilman claims that in his city at least 85 per cent of the adult male population is employed. A subsequent sample check taken by a newspaper reporter showed that among 300 adult males polled only 244 were employed. What does this do to the councilman's claim at a level of significance of 0.05?

4. A highway official claims that at least 25 per cent of all cars in the state do not meet requirements concerning brakes, lights, direction signals, etc. Test this claim at a level of significance of 0.01 if among 800 cars stopped at road blocks throughout the state 139 did not meet all these requirements.

5. A college magazine maintains that 70 per cent of all college men expect their dates to furnish their own cigarettes. Test this claim against the alternative $p < 0.70$, if a random sample of 500 college men included 332 who expect their dates to furnish their own cigarettes. Use a level of significance of 0.01.

6. If a sample of 250 toy walkie-talkies contained 27 that did not function properly when they were first assembled by the retailer, test the manufacturer's claim that at most 8 per cent of these toys will require adjustments when first assembled. Use a level of significance of 0.01.

7. A research worker wishes to determine whether a new muscle relaxant will produce beneficial results in a higher proportion of patients suffering from various severe neurological disorders than the 0.85 proportion receiving beneficial results from standard treatment. If in a random sample of 200 patients 177 obtained beneficial results from the new muscle relaxant, how should he interpret this at a level of significance of 0.10?

8. A sample survey showed that 612 of 800 retired persons interviewed preferred to live in apartments rather than in one-family homes. Using a two-sided alternative and a level of significance of 0.05, test the hypothesis that actually 75 per cent of all retired persons have this preference.

9. It has been asserted by a medical research worker that 0.40 is the true proportion of persons belonging to a certain race who have blood type O. Is this claim supported by a study in which 1,000 persons of this race included 429 with type O blood? Use a level of significance of 0.01.

11.4 Differences Between Proportions

There are many problems in which we must decide whether an observed difference between two sample proportions, or percentages, is significant or whether it may reasonably be attributed to chance. For instance, if 66 of 100 high school seniors interviewed in one city say that they want to go on to college, but only 61 of 100 high school seniors interviewed in another city, we may want to decide whether the observed difference of 5 per cent may be attributed to chance or whether it implies that there is an actual difference between the attitudes of the students in the two cities. Similarly, if one manufacturing process shows 28 defective pieces in a sample of size 400 while another process yielded 15 defective pieces in a sample of size 300, it may be of interest to know whether the difference between $28/400 = 0.07$ and $15/300 = 0.05$ may reasonably be attributed to chance.

Questions of this kind are usually decided on the basis of the theory that if x_1 and x_2 are the number of "successes" observed, respectively, in large independent random samples of size n_1 and n_2, and if p_1 and p_2 are the corresponding probabilities for success on an individual trial, then *the sampling distribution of the difference between the two sample proportions,* $x_1/n_1 - x_2/n_2$, *can be approximated closely with a normal distribution having the mean* $p_1 - p_2$ *and the standard deviation*

$$\sqrt{\frac{p\,(1-p\,)}{n_1} + \frac{p_2(1-p_2)}{n_2}}$$

In accordance with the terminology introduced in Chapter 8, we refer to the standard deviation of this sampling distribution as the *standard error of the difference between two proportions.* Discussions of this theory are referred to in the Bibliography at the end of this chapter.

To illustrate what is meant by this sampling distribution, suppose that p_1 is the actual proportion of male voters in Dallas favoring the construction of a new freeway and that p_2 is the corresponding proportion of female voters. If we sent out a large number of interviewers, telling each to interview random samples of n_1 male voters and n_2 female voters in the given city, we would expect that the figures they get for x_1 and x_2 (the number of male and female voters favoring the construction of the new freeway) are not all the same, nor are the values they obtain for the difference between x_1/n_1 and x_2/n_2. If we then constructed a distribution of the differences $x_1/n_1 - x_2/n_2$ obtained by the interviewers, we would get an *experimental sampling distribution of the difference between two proportions.* The sampling distribution referred to above is the corresponding *theoretical sampling distribution.*

This example also serves to illustrate why we stated that the two samples must be *independent*, that they must, so to speak, be selected separately. It stands to reason that we might well get very misleading results if we interviewed married couples, whose political views are apt to be the same.

Using the above theory concerning the sampling distribution of the difference between two proportions, we can now base *large-sample tests* concerning the equality of two population proportions, namely, *large-sample tests* of the null hypothesis $p_1 = p_2$, on the statistic

▲ $$z = \frac{\dfrac{x_1}{n_1} - \dfrac{x_2}{n_2}}{\sqrt{p(1-p)\left(\dfrac{1}{n_1} + \dfrac{1}{n_2}\right)}} \qquad \text{with } p = \frac{x_1 + x_2}{n_1 + n_2}$$ ▲

having approximately the standard normal distribution. We obtained this formula for z by subtracting from the observed difference between the two sample proportions the mean of its sampling distribution (which under the null hypothesis equals $p_1 - p_2 = 0$), and then dividing by the standard deviation with p substituted for p_1 and p_2. It is customary to refer to the expression given for p as a *pooled estimate* of the common value of p_1 and p_2.

Depending on the alternative hypothesis, appropriate tests of the null hypothesis $p_1 = p_2$ are the ones shown in Figure 9.8 on page 251: we reject the null hypothesis for values of z falling into the left-hand tail, the right-hand tail, or both tails of the sampling distribution, depending on whether the alternative hypothesis is, respectively, $p_1 < p_2$, $p_1 > p_2$, or $p_1 \neq p_2$.

To illustrate this kind of test, let us refer to the first example on page 286, where one manufacturing process yielded 28 defective pieces in a random sample of size 400 while another yielded 15 defective pieces in a random sample of size 300. Let us suppose, furthermore, that the null hypothesis $p_1 = p_2$ is to be tested against the two-sided alternative $p_1 \neq p_2$ at the level of significance $\alpha = 0.05$. Substituting $x_1 = 28$, $n_1 = 400$, $x_2 = 15$, and $n_2 = 300$ first into the expression for p and then into the formula for z, we obtain

$$p = \frac{28 + 15}{400 + 300} = 0.061$$

and

$$z = \frac{\frac{28}{400} - \frac{15}{300}}{\sqrt{(0.061)(0.939)\left(\frac{1}{400} + \frac{1}{300}\right)}} = 1.10$$

Since this value falls between $-z_{0.025} = -1.96$ and $z_{0.025} = 1.96$, the null hypothesis cannot be rejected; we cannot conclude that one process is actually better than the other so far as the proportion of defectives is concerned.

The example we have given here is typical of tests concerning the equality of two population proportions. In Exercise 5 on page 291 we shall see how the test can be modified to apply also to tests of the null hypothesis that the difference between the population proportions equals a given constant, that is, the hypothesis $p_1 - p_2 = \delta$, where δ (*delta*) is not necessarily zero. A test which serves to compare more than two sample proportions will be discussed in the next section.

11.5 Differences Among *k* Proportions

In many applications we must decide whether observed differences among more than two sample proportions, or percentages, are significant or whether they can be attributed to chance. For instance, if the park department of a large city plants daffodil bulbs, 400 each of the highest-grade bulb supplied by seed firms A, B, and C, and if 36, 21, and 43 of these turn out inferior, they may want to decide whether the differences can reasonably be attributed to chance. Similarly, if random samples of voters (200 with low incomes, 300 with average incomes, and 100 with high incomes) are asked how they would vote on a certain piece of legislation, it may be of interest to know whether the *actual* proportions of favorable votes are the same for all three groups, when the results are as shown in the following table:

	Voters with Low Incomes	*Voters with Average Incomes*	*Voters with High Incomes*
For the Legislation	116	141	37
Against the Legislation	84	159	63

In other words, it is of interest to know whether the differences among 0.58, 0.47, and 0.37 (the sample proportions of favorable votes obtained for the three income groups) can be attributed to chance.

To illustrate how we handle this kind of problem, let us denote the true proportions of voters favoring the legislation in the three income groups p_1, p_2, and p_3. *Thus, we shall want to test the null hypothesis* $p_1 = p_2 = p_3$ *against the alternative that* p_1, p_2, *and* p_3 *are not all alike.* If the null hypothesis is true, we can combine the three samples and estimate the common proportion of voters favoring the legislation as

$$\frac{116 + 141 + 37}{200 + 300 + 100} = \frac{294}{600} = 0.49$$

With this estimate, we would *expect* $200(0.49) = 98$ votes for the legislation in the first sample, $300(0.49) = 147$ in the second sample, and $100\,(0.49) = 49$ in the third sample. Subtracting these figures from the sizes of the respective samples, we would correspondingly *expect* $200 - 98 = 102$ votes against the legislation in the first sample, $300 - 147 = 153$ in the second sample, and $100 - 49 = 51$ in the third sample. These results are summarized in the following table, where the *expected frequencies* are shown in parentheses below the ones that were actually observed:

	Voters with Low Incomes	*Voters with Average Incomes*	*Voters with High Incomes*
For the Legislation	116 (98)	141 (147)	37 (49)
Against the Legislation	84 (102)	159 (153)	63 (51)

To test the null hypothesis $p_1 = p_2 = p_3$, we shall now compare the frequencies that were actually observed with those we could *expect* if the null hypothesis were true. It stands to reason that the null hypothesis should be accepted if the two sets of frequencies are very much alike; after all, we would then have obtained almost exactly what we could have expected if the null hypothesis were true. On the other hand, if the discrepancies between the two sets of frequencies are large, the observed frequencies do not agree with what we could expect, and this is an indication that the null hypothesis must be false.

Writing the observed frequencies as f's and the expected frequencies as e's, we can put this comparison on a precise basis by using the statistic

▲
$$\chi^2 = \Sigma \frac{(f-e)^2}{e}$$
▲

called "*chi-square.*" Since the notation used in defining this statistic is somewhat abbreviated, let us state in words that χ^2 *is the sum of the quantities obtained by dividing* $(f - e)^2$ *by* e *separately for each "cell" of the table.*

The sampling distribution of this χ^2 statistic can be approximated closely with the *chi-square distribution* introduced first in Chapter 10. In our particular example, the number of degrees of freedom (the parameter of the chi-square distribution) is 2, but in general *when we compare k sample proportions the number of degrees of freedom is k − 1.* If there is a close agreement between the f's and the e's, the differences $f - e$ and, hence, χ^2 will be small; if the agreement is poor, some of the differences $f - e$ and, hence, χ^2 will be large. Consequently, we reject the null hypothesis at the level of significance α *if the value we obtain for the* χ^2 *statistic exceeds* χ^2_α (see also Figure 10.1).

Returning now to our numerical example, we obtain

$$\chi^2 = \frac{(116-98)^2}{98} + \frac{(141-147)^2}{147} + \frac{(37-49)^2}{49} + \frac{(84-102)^2}{102} + \frac{(159-153)^2}{153} + \frac{(63-51)^2}{51}$$
$$= 12.73$$

and since this exceeds 5.991, the value of $\chi^2_{0.05}$ for 2 degrees of freedom (see Table III at the end of the book), the null hypothesis must be rejected. This means that there *is* a difference in attitude concerning the given piece of legislation among the three income groups.

In general, if we want to compare k sample proportions, we first calculate the expected frequencies as we did on page 288. Combining the data, we estimate p as

▲
$$\frac{x_1 + x_2 + \ldots + x_k}{n_1 + n_2 + \ldots + n_k}$$
▲

where the n's are the sizes of the respective samples and the x's are the corresponding numbers of successes. Multiplying the n's by this estimate of p, we obtain the expected frequencies for the first row of the table, and subtracting these values from the totals of the corresponding samples, we obtain the expected frequencies for the second row of the table. (Note that the expected frequency for any one of the cells may also be obtained by multiplying the total of the row to which it belongs by the total of the column to which it belongs, and dividing by the grand total $n_1 + n_2 + \ldots + n_k$.) Next, χ^2 is calculated according to the formula

$$\chi^2 = \Sigma \frac{(f - e)^2}{e}$$

with $(f - e)^2/e$ determined separately for each of the $2k$ cells of the table. Then, we reject the null hypothesis $p_1 = p_2 = \ldots = p_k$ at the level of significance α (against the alternative that these p's are *not all equal*) if the value obtained for χ^2 exceeds χ^2_α for $k - 1$ degrees of freedom.

Since the sampling distribution of this χ^2 statistic is only approximately the chi-square distribution with $k - 1$ degrees of freedom, it is best not to use this test when one or more of the expected frequencies is less than 5. It is also of interest to note that for $k = 2$ the χ^2 statistic of this section actually equals the *square* of the z statistic of Section 11.4 (see Exercises 6 and 7 below); thus, for $k = 2$ the two tests are *equivalent*, although the one of Section 11.4 can be used also when the alternative hypothesis is $p_1 < p_2$ or $p_1 > p_2$.

EXERCISES

1. If 250 castings produced on mold A contained 19 defectives while 300 castings on mold B contained 27 defectives, test the null hypothesis that there is no difference between the true proportions of defectives produced by the two molds. Use the z statistic, a two-sided alternative, and $\alpha = 0.05$.

2. In a true-false test, a test item is *good* if it discriminates between good students and poor students. If a test item was answered correctly by 164 of 200 good students and by 102 of 200 poor students, what can one conclude about its merits? Use an appropriate one-sided alternative and a level of significance of 0.01.

3. The business manager of a college, in trying to decide which of two supposedly identical kinds of soft-drink vending machines to install in the dormitories, tests the machines by dropping 250 coins in each. If the first kind of machine failed to work (that is, neither delivered a drink nor returned the coin) 19 times and the second kind of machine failed to work 8 times, use the z statistic to decide whether this is evidence (at the 0.05 level of significance) that the two machines are not equally good with respect to this kind of failure.

4. To test the effectiveness of a new pain-relieving drug, 80 patients at a clinic are given a pill containing the drug while 80 others are given a placebo. What can one conclude about the effectiveness of the drug if in the first group 56 of the patients felt a beneficial effect while 38 of those who received the placebo felt a beneficial effect? Use an appropriate one-sided alternative and a level of significance of 0.01.

5. If we want to test the null hypothesis that the difference between two population proportions equals some constant δ (*delta*), not necessarily 0, we can use the theory on page 286 and base our decision on the statistic

$$z = \frac{\frac{x_1}{n_1} - \frac{x_2}{n_2} - \delta}{\sqrt{\frac{p_1(1 - p_1)}{n_1} + \frac{p_2(1 - p_2)}{n_2}}}$$

with x_1/n_1 and x_2/n_2 substituted for p_1 and p_2. The sampling distribution of this statistic can be approximated with the standard normal distribution when the samples are sufficiently large.

(a) Referring to Exercise 4, use this theory to test whether the proportion of patients feeling beneficial effects is more than 0.10 higher among those receiving the drug than among those receiving the placebo. Use a one-sided alternative which puts the burden of proof on the drug and $\alpha = 0.05$.

(b) Referring to Exercise 2, use this theory to test whether for the given item the proportion of correct answers is at least 0.20 higher among good students than it is among poor students. Use a level of significance of 0.05.

6. Rework Exercise 1 using the chi-square statistic, and verify that χ^2 equals the square of the value previously obtained for z.

7. Rework Exercise 3 using the chi-square statistic, and verify that χ^2 equals the square of the value previously obtained for z.

8. Referring to the example on page 288 which dealt with daffodil bulbs supplied by three seed firms, test at a level of significance of 0.05 whether the percentage of inferior bulbs is the same for each of the firms.

9. A company's records show that 120 shipments from Vendor A contained 27 that were unsatisfactory for one reason or another, 180 shipments from Vendor B contained 44 that were unsatisfactory, 100 shipments from Vendor C contained 26 that were unsatisfactory, while 200 shipments from Vendor D contained 53 that were unsatisfactory. Use a level of significance of 0.05 to test the null hypothesis that the true probability of receiving an unsatisfactory shipment is the same for each vendor.

10. An opinion research organization wants to determine whether there is any relationship between the quality of an interviewer's work and his score on an introvert-extrovert test of personality. Each interviewer is rated by his superior as being below average, average, or above average in his work and the results are as follows: among the 60 whose work is rated below average there are 28 introverts and 32 extroverts; among the 120 whose work is rated average there are 64 introverts and 56 extroverts; and among the 80 whose work is rated above average there are 37 introverts and 43 extroverts. Using a level of significance of 0.05, what can one conclude from this experiment?

11.6 Contingency Tables

The χ^2 statistic plays an important role in many other tests dealing with *count data*, or *enumeration data*, namely, in problems where information is obtained by counting rather than measuring. The method we shall treat in this section is an extension of the one discussed in the preceding section, and we shall apply it to two distinct kinds of problems. In the first kind of problem we deal with trials permitting *more than two possible outcomes*. For example, in the illustration on page 288 we might have given each person the choice of being for the legislation, against it, or undecided, and we might thus have obtained the following table:

	Voters with Low Incomes	*Voters with Average Incomes*	*Voters with High Incomes*
For the Legislation	96	115	29
Undecided	59	128	43
Against the Legislation	45	57	28

We refer to this kind of table as a 3-by-3 table because it contains 3 rows and 3 columns; more generally, when there are k samples and each trial permits r alternatives, we refer to the resulting table as an *r-by-k table*. Note that as in the examples of Section 11.5, the *column totals* are fixed (they are the sizes of the respective samples) while the row totals are values of random variables (they depend on chance).

In the second kind of problem the column totals as well as the row totals are left to chance. Suppose, for instance, that a management consultant wants to know whether there is any relationship between the sense of humor of a salesman of industrial chemicals and his ability (as measured by his volume of sales). Suppose, furthermore, that he gives 500 salesmen a certain objective test designed to measure sense of humor, and that he obtains the results shown in the following table:

		Sense of Humor		
		Poor	*Average*	*Excellent*
	Low	38	41	29
Volume of Sales	*Average*	72	129	87
	High	17	45	42

This is also a 3-by-3 table, and it is mainly in connection with problems of this kind that r-by-k tables are referred to as *contingency tables.*

Before we illustrate the method of analysis used in problems of either kind, let us first examine what hypotheses we shall want to test. In the first problem, the one dealing with voter reaction to the given piece of legislation, we want to test the null hypothesis that the probabilities of getting a vote for the legislation, a vote against the legislation, or an undecided vote are the same for each income group. In other words, we want to test the null hypothesis that a person's attitude toward the legislation is *independent* of his income. In the second problem we are also concerned with a null hypothesis of *independence:* namely, the null hypothesis that salesmanship and sense of humor are independent.

To illustrate the analysis of an r-by-k table, let us refer to the second example and let us begin by calculating (as in the example of Section 11.5) the *expected cell frequencies.* If the null hypothesis of independence is true, the probability of randomly selecting (from a given population of salesmen of industrial chemicals) a salesman who has a low volume of sales and also a poor sense of humor is given by the *product* of the probability that he has a low volume of sales and the probability that he has a poor sense of humor (see the Special Rule of Multiplication on page 115). Using the totals of the first row and the first column to *estimate* these two probabilities, we obtain 108/500 for the probability that such a salesman has a low volume of sales, and 127/500 for the probability that he has a poor sense of humor. Hence, we estimate the "true" proportion of salesmen of industrial chemicals with low sales volumes *and* a poor sense of humor as $\frac{108}{500}\cdot\frac{127}{500}\cdot$ In a sample of size 500 we would thus expect to find

$$500\cdot\frac{108}{500}\cdot\frac{127}{500} = \frac{108\cdot 127}{500} = 27.4$$

salesmen to fit this description.

Having thus obtained the *expected frequency* for the first cell of the first row of the table, it should be noted that after canceling 500's, we obtained the result by multiplying the total of the first row by the total of the first column and then dividing by the grand total of 500. In general, we can (as on page 290) find the expected frequency for any one of the cells of a contingency table by *multiplying the total of the row to which it belongs by the total of the column to which it belongs and then dividing by the grand total for the whole table.* Using this procedure, we obtain an expected frequency of $\frac{108 \cdot 215}{500} = 46.4$ for the second cell of the first row, and $\frac{288 \cdot 127}{500} = 73.2$ and $\frac{288 \cdot 215}{500} = 123.8$ for the first two cells of the second row. As it can be shown that thesum of the expected frequencies for each row or column must equal the sum of the corresponding observed frequencies, we obtain by subtraction

$$108 - 27.4 - 46.4 = 34.2$$

for the third cell of the first row,

$$288 - 73.2 - 123.8 = 91.0$$

for the third cell of the second row, and

$$127 - 27.4 - 73.2 = 26.4$$

$$215 - 46.4 - 123.8 = 44.8$$

$$158 - 34.2 - 91.0 = 32.8$$

for the three cells of the third row. These results (all rounded to one decimal) are summarized in the following table, where the expected frequencies are shown in parentheses below the corresponding observed cell frequencies:

		Sense of Humor		
		Poor	*Average*	*Excellent*
Volume of Sales	*Low*	38 (27.4)	41 (46.4)	29 (34.2)
	Average	72 (73.2)	129 (123.8)	87 (91.0)
	High	17 (26.4)	45 (44.8)	42 (32.8)

From here on, the work is like that of the preceding section; we let f denote an observed frequency, e an expected frequency, and we calculate the χ^2 statistic according to the formula

$$\chi^2 = \Sigma \frac{(f - e)^2}{e}$$

with $(f - e)^2/e$ calculated separately for each cell of the table. Then *we reject the null hypothesis of independence at the level of significance α if the value obtained for χ^2 exceeds the value of χ^2_α for $(r - 1)(k - 1)$ degrees of freedom*, where r and k are, respectively, the number of rows and the number of columns. In our example the number of degrees of freedom is $(3 - 1)(3 - 1) = 4$, and it should be observed that after we had calculated 4 of the expected frequencies, all the others were obtained by subtraction from the totals of appropriate rows and columns.

Actually calculating χ^2 for our example, we get

$$\chi^2 = \frac{(38 - 27.4)^2}{27.4} + \frac{(41 - 46.4)^2}{46.4} + \frac{(29 - 34.2)^2}{34.2}$$

$$+ \frac{(72 - 73.2)^2}{73.2} + \frac{(129 - 123.8)^2}{123.8} + \frac{(87 - 91.0)^2}{91.0}$$

$$+ \frac{(17 - 26.4)^2}{26.4} + \frac{(45 - 44.8)^2}{44.8} + \frac{(42 - 32.8)^2}{32.8}$$

$$= 11.86$$

and since this exceeds 9.488, the value of $\chi^2_{0.05}$ for 4 degrees of freedom, the null hypothesis must be rejected. We have thus shown that there exists a dependence (or relationship) between salesmanship and sense of humor, at least so far as salesmen of industrial chemicals are concerned.

It is customary in problems of this kind to round the expected cell frequencies to one decimal or to the nearest whole number. Most of the entries of Table III are given to three decimals, but there is seldom any need to carry more than two decimals when calculating χ^2 for an r-by-k table. As we pointed out on page 290, the statistic we are using here has only approximately a chi-square distribution and, hence, it should not be used unless each of the expected frequencies is at least 5. If one or more of the expected frequencies is less than 5, it may nevertheless be possible to use the test by combining some of the cells (and subtracting one degree of freedom for each cell thus eliminated).

11.7 Tests of Goodness of Fit

In this section we shall treat a further application of the χ^2 criterion, in which we compare an observed frequency distribution with a distribution we might expect according to theory or assumptions. To illustrate this method, let us return to the binomial distribution studied in Chapter 7, in particular to the one pertaining to the number of heads obtained in 3 flips of a balanced coin (or when flipping 3 balanced coins). As we saw on page 150, the probabilities of getting 0, 1, 2, or 3 heads are, respectively, 1/8, 3/8, 3/8, and 1/8. Suppose now that we actually flip 3 coins 200 times and that we obtain the results shown in the "observed frequency" column of the following table:

Number of Heads	*Observed Frequency*	*Expected Frequency*
0	18	25
1	63	75
2	84	75
3	35	25

The expected frequencies in the right-hand column were obtained by multiplying each of the corresponding probabilities by 200. [In other words, the number of times we expect 0 heads is $200(1/8) = 25$, the number of times we expect 1 head is $200(3/8) = 75$, and so on.]

As can be seen by inspection, there are some discrepancies between the observed frequencies and those based on the binomial distribution; in fact, there are altogether $0(18) + 1(63) + 2(84) + 3(35) = 336$ heads, which is quite a bit more than the 300 we would expect. To check whether the discrepancies may be attributed to chance, we first determine χ^2 by means of the formula

▲ $$\chi^2 = \Sigma \frac{(f-e)^2}{e}$$ ▲

calculating $(f-e)^2/e$ separately for each class of the distribution. Then, if it turns out that the value we obtain is *too large*, we reject the null hypothesis that the binomial distribution with $n = 3$ and $p = 1/2$ provides the appropriate theory for the given experiment. (Actually, rejection of the null hypothesis would imply that either the coins are not all properly balanced or they were not randomly flipped.)

Substituting the observed and expected frequencies from the above table into the formula for χ^2, we get

$$\chi^2 = \frac{(18-25)^2}{25} + \frac{(63-75)^2}{75} + \frac{(84-75)^2}{75} + \frac{(35-25)^2}{25}$$

$$= 8.96$$

To decide whether this value is large enough to reject the null hypothesis (at the level of significance α), we have only to check whether it exceeds χ^2_α for an appropriate number of degrees of freedom. In general, *the number of degrees of freedom for this kind of test is given by the number of terms* $(f-e)^2/e$

added in obtaining χ^2 minus the number of quantities, obtained from the observed data, that are used in calculating the expected frequencies.

In our numerical example we had 4 terms in the formula for χ^2, and the only quantity needed from the observed data to calculate the expected frequencies was the total frequency 200. Hence the number of degrees of freedom is $4 - 1 = 3$, and for a level of significance of 0.05 Table III yields $\chi^2_{0.05} = 7.815$. Since $\chi^2 = 8.96$ exceeds this value, the null hypothesis must be rejected. This means that the binomial distribution with $n = 3$ and $p = 1/2$ does *not* provide a good fit; either the coins are not all properly balanced or they were not randomly flipped.

The method we have illustrated in this section is used quite generally to test how well distributions we *expect* (on the basis of theory or assumptions) fit, or describe, observed data. In some of the exercises which follow, we shall thus test whether it is reasonable to treat an observed distribution as if it had (at least approximately) the shape of a normal distribution, and we shall also test whether a given set of data fits the pattern of a Piosson distribution.

EXERCISES

1. Analyze the 3-by-3 table on page 292 and decide, at a level of significance of 0.05, whether attitude concerning the given legislation is independent of income.

2. The dean of a large university wants to determine whether there is a connection between academic rank and a faculty member's opinion concerning a proposed curriculum change. Interviewing a sample of 80 instructors, 140 assistant professors, 100 associate professors, and 80 professors, he obtains the results shown in the following table:

	Instructor	*Assistant Professor*	*Associate Professor*	*Professor*
Against	8	19	15	12
Indifferent	40	41	24	16
For	32	80	61	52

Analyze this table and test the null hypothesis that there are no differences of opinion concerning the curriculum change among the four groups. Use a level of significance of 0.05.

3. Reanalyze the table of Exercise 2, leaving out the middle row, that is, considering only those opinions which were either for or against the proposed curriculum change.

4. The following table is based on the career success records and the intelligence ratings of 442 delinquent boys:

		Career Success		
		Doing Well	*Doing Fair*	*Doing Badly*
	Normal or Better	41	12	26
I. Q.	*Border Line*	84	61	48
	Deficient	50	49	61

Analyze this contingency table and decide (at $\alpha = 0.05$) whether there is a relationship between the intelligence of such boys and their career success.

5. Decide on the basis of the information given in the following table whether there is a relationship between a student's ability in mathematics and his interest in statistics (use a level of significance of 0.01):

		Ability in Mathematics		
		Low	*Average*	*High*
	Low	47	34	14
Interest in Statistics	*Average*	41	49	29
	High	16	48	55

6. The following table is based on a study of the relationship between race and blood type in a Near Eastern country:

	Blood Type			
	0	A	B	AB
Race 1	176	148	96	72
Race 2	78	50	45	12
Race 3	15	19	8	7

Use a level of significance of 0.05 to decide whether there is a relationship between race and blood type for the population considered in this study.

7. If the analysis of a contingency table shows that there is a relationship between the two variables under consideration, the *strength* of this relationship may be measured by means of the *contingency coefficient*

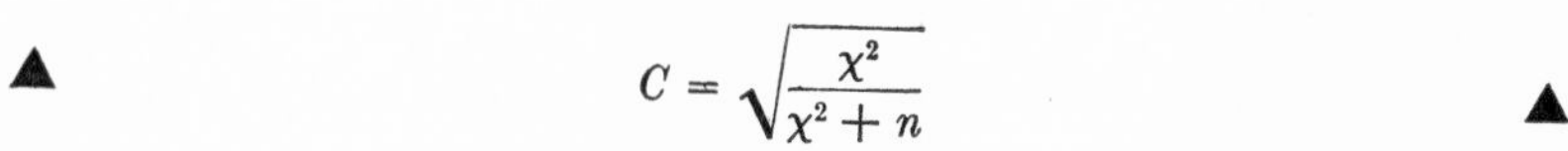

$$C = \sqrt{\frac{\chi^2}{\chi^2 + n}}$$

where n is the total frequency for the entire table. This coefficient assumes values between 0 (corresponding to independence) and a maximum value less than 1, which depends on the number of rows and columns in the table. For example, for a 3-by-3 table the maximum value is 0.816. The larger C is for a given table, the stronger is the dependence between the two variables.

(a) Calculate C for the contingency table of Exercise 4.

(b) Calculate C for the contingency table of Exercise 5.

8. The following is the distribution of the number of females in 160 litters, each consisting of 4 mice:

Number of Females	*Number of Litters*
0	12
1	37
2	55
3	47
4	9

(a) Assuming that there is a fifty-fifty chance for each mouse to be male or female, use the formula for the binomial distribution with $n = 4$ and $p = 1/2$ to show that the corresponding *expected frequencies* for 0, 1, 2, 3, or 4 females in a litter of 4 are, respectively, 10, 40, 60, 40, and 10.

(b) Compare the observed frequencies with the expected frequencies obtained in part (a) by means of an appropriate χ^2 statistic; that is, for the given distribution test the assumptions on which the expected frequencies were based at a level of significance of 0.05.

9. Using any four columns of Table VIII (that is, a total of 200 random digits), construct a table showing how many times each of the digits 0, 1, 2, . . ., and 9 occurred. Compare these observed frequencies with the corresponding expected frequencies (20 in each case, assuming randomness) with the use of an appropriate chi-square statistic. Use a level of significance of 0.01.

10. Referring to Exercise 5 on page 203, test the assumption that the (simulated) die is balanced (at $\alpha = 0.05$).

11. Referring to Exercise 7 on page 203, use an appropriate chi-square statistic to compare the observed frequencies with the corresponding expected frequencies; that is, test for goodness of fit at $\alpha = 0.05$. (*Hint:* Combine adjacent classes, if necessary.)

12. The following is the radiation-count distribution first given on page 13, with the first and last classes relabeled as indicated:

Number of Particles	*Frequency*
9 or less	1
10 – 14	10
15 – 19	37
20 – 24	36
25 – 29	13
30 – 34	2
35 or more	1

As we showed in Chapters 3 and 4, the mean of the original distribution was 20 and its standard deviation was 5.

(a) Given a normal distribution with $\mu = 20$ and $\sigma = 5$, find the area under the curve to the left of 9.5, between 9.5 and 14.5, between 14.5 and 19.5, between 19.5 and 24.5, between 24.5 and 29.5, between 29.5 and 34.5, and to the right of 34.5.

(b) Multiplying by 100 (the total frequency) each of the normal curve areas obtained in part (a), determine the *expected normal curve frequencies* corresponding to the seven classes of the distribution.

(c) Calculate χ^2 for the observed frequencies and the expected frequencies obtained in part (b), and test the null hypothesis that the radiation-count data can be looked upon as a random sample from a normal population. Combine adjacent classes, if necessary, so that none of the expected frequencies is less than 5, and use a level of significance of 0.05. [*Hint:* The number of degrees of freedom for testing the fit of a normal distribution by this method is $k - 3$, where k is the number of terms $(f - e)^2/e$ in the chi-square statistic; does this agree with the rule on page 296?]

13. Use the method of Exercise 12 to test whether it is reasonable to look at the distribution of the 40 means of Figure 8.6 on page 208 as having roughly the shape of a normal distribution. Make use of the fact that the mean of the distribution is 9.4 and its standard deviation is 1.32, and relabel the first and last classes to read, respectively, "less than 7.5" and "11.5 or more." Also, combine adjacent classes, if necessary, so that none of the expected frequencies is less than 5, and use a level of significance of 0.01.

BIBLIOGRAPHY

The most widely used tables of binomial probabilities are

National Bureau of Standards, *Tables of the Binomial Distribution.* Washington, D.C.: U.S. Government Printing Office, 1950.

Romig, H. G., *50–100 Binomial Tables.* New York: John Wiley & Sons, Inc., 1953.

The mathematical theory which underlies the chi-square distribution and its applications is discussed in

Freund, John E., *Mathematical Statistics*. Englewood Cliffs, N.J.: Prentice-Hall, Inc., 1962

and in most other textbooks on mathematical statistics. Theory relating to the distribution of the difference between two proportions is also discussed in this book.

TWELVE
Analysis of Variance

12.1 Differences among *k* Means

Let us now generalize the work of Section 9.8 and consider the problem of deciding whether observed differences among *more than two* means can be attributed to chance, or whether they are indicative of actual differences among the means of the corresponding populations. For example, we may want to decide on the basis of sample data whether there really is a difference in the effectiveness of three methods of teaching computer programming, or we may want to conduct experiments in order to compare the merits of five different kinds of fertilizers. Similarly, we may want to use sample data to compare the mileage yields of different kinds of gasoline. Suppose, for example, that tests are actually performed to compare four kinds of gasoline, and that three test runs with a gallon of each kind of gasoline produced the results (in miles) shown in the following table:

Gasoline 1:	20,	23,	23
Gasoline 2:	17,	20,	20
Gasoline 3:	16,	17,	24
Gasoline 4:	21,	26,	25

The means of these four samples are, respectively, 22, 19, 19, and 24, and we would like to know whether the differences among these figures are significant or whether they can be attributed to chance.

Designating the true average mileages (per gallon) for the four kinds of gasoline μ_1, μ_2, μ_3, and μ_4, we shall want to test the null hypothesis

$$\mu_1 = \mu_2 = \mu_3 = \mu_4$$

against the alternative that μ_1, μ_2, μ_3, and μ_4 are *not all equal*. Informally speaking, small differences among the $\bar{x}$'s may, as always, be attributed to chance, so that if the $\bar{x}$'s are very nearly the same size, this would support the null hypothesis that the population means are all equal. On the other hand, if the differences among the $\bar{x}$'s are large too large, to be reasonably attributed to chance, this would support the alternative hypothesis that the μ's are not all equal. Hence, we need a precise measure of the size of the discrepancies among the $\bar{x}$'s and, correspondingly, a well-defined criterion for testing the null hypothesis concerning the μ's.

An obvious measure of the discrepancies among the $\bar{x}$'s is their variance, and if we calculate it for our example according to the formula on page 62, we obtain

$$s_{\bar{x}}^2 = \frac{(22-21)^2 + (19-21)^2 + (19-21)^2 + (24-21)^2}{4-1}$$

$$= 6$$

Note that we used the subscript $\bar{x}$ to indicate that this quantity measures the variability of the $\bar{x}$'s. As we shall see later, this quantity plays an important role in our ultimate decision whether to accept or reject the null hypothesis concerning the four population means.

Let us now make an assumption which is critical to the method of analysis we shall employ: *it will be assumed that the populations from which the samples were obtained can be approximated closely with normal distributions having the same variance* σ^2. This means that we shall assume that if we tested many gallons of each kind of gasoline, the distribution of the respective mileages for each gasoline would follow the over-all pattern of a normal distribution with the same variance σ^2.

If we combine this assumption with the assumption that the null hypothesis is true, we can now look upon the four samples as samples from *one and the same population.* Making use of the fact that for samples from infinite populations the standard error of the mean is given by $\sigma_{\bar{x}} = \sigma/\sqrt{n}$ (see page 209), we can look upon $s_{\bar{x}}^2$ as an estimate of $\sigma_{\bar{x}}^2 = \sigma^2/n$ and, hence, $n \cdot s_{\bar{x}}^2$ as an estimate of σ^2. Returning to our numerical example, we can thus use $3 \cdot 6 = 18$ as an estimate of the common population variance σ^2.

If σ^2 were known, we could compare $n \cdot s_{\bar{x}}^2$ with σ^2 and reject the null hypothesis if $n \cdot s_{\bar{x}}^2$ were much larger than σ^2. However, in our example (as in most practical problems) σ^2 is unknown and we have no choice but to estimate it on the basis of the given data. Having assumed that the samples all come from populations with the same variance σ^2, we could use each of the sample variances (namely, s_1^2, s_2^2, s_3^2, and s_4^2) as an estimate of σ^2 and, hence, we could also use their mean. Referring again to our numerical example, we shall thus estimate σ^2 by means of the quantity

$$\frac{s_1^2 + s_2^2 + s_3^2 + s_4^2}{4} = \frac{1}{4}\left[\frac{(20-22)^2 + (23-22)^2 + (23-22)^2}{2} + \frac{(17-19)^2 + (20-19)^2 + (20-19)^2}{2} + \frac{(16-19)^2 + (17-19)^2 + (24-19)^2}{2} + \frac{(21-24)^2 + (26-24)^2 + (25-24)^2}{2}\right]$$

$$= 8$$

We now have *two* estimates of σ^2, $n \cdot s_{\bar{x}}^2 = 18$ and $\dfrac{s_1^2 + s_2^2 + s_3^2 + s_4^2}{4} = 8$. Comparing these two estimates, we can now assert that if the first (*which is based on the variation among the means of the samples*) is much larger than the second (*which is based on the variation within the samples*), it is reasonable to reject the null hypothesis. If the null hypothesis is not true, the first estimate is apt to be larger than the second, as it would reflect whatever differences there may exist among the population means as well as chance variation; the second estimate would reflect only chance variation.

To put the comparison of these two estimates of σ^2 on a rigorous basis, we use the statistic

$$\blacktriangle \quad F = \frac{\text{Estimate of } \sigma^2 \text{ based on the variation among the } \bar{x}\text{'s}}{\text{Estimate of } \sigma^2 \text{ based on the variation within the samples}} \quad \blacktriangle$$

appropriately called a *variance ratio*. If the various assumptions made earlier (that the null hypothesis is true and that the samples come from normal populations with equal variances) are true, the sampling distribution of this statistic is the F distribution introduced in Chapter 10. Hence, if the value we get for F exceeds F_α (see page 269 and Figure 10.4), the null hypothesis can be rejected. The necessary values of F_α can be obtained from Table IV for $\alpha = 0.05$ or 0.01; if we compare the means of k samples of size n, the corresponding degrees of freedom are $k - 1$ and $k(n - 1)$. Note that the numerator of the expression for F is an estimate of σ^2 based on $k - 1$ independent deviations from the mean, while the denominator is an estimate of σ^2 based on $k(n - 1)$ independent deviations from the mean, namely, $n - 1$ in each of the k samples.

Returning now to our numerical example, we find that $F_{0.05} = 4.07$ for $k - 1 = 4 - 1 = 3$ and $k(n - 1) = 4(3 - 1) = 8$ degrees of freedom. Since this value is *not* exceeded by

$$F = \frac{18}{8} = 2.25$$

the value of the F statistic for our example, we find that the null hypothesis *cannot be rejected*. Although there are sizeable differences among the means of the four samples, the variations within the samples are also large, and we conclude that the differences among the sample means may well be attributed to chance.

The technique we have just described is the simplest form of a powerful statistical tool called the *analysis of variance*, ANOVA for short. Although we could go ahead and perform F tests for differences among k means without further discussion, it will be instructive to look at the problem from an analysis-of-variance point of view, and we shall do so in the next section.

12.2 One-Way Analysis of Variance

The basic idea of analysis of variance is to express a measure of the total variability of a set of data as a sum of terms, each of which can be attributed to a specific source, or cause, of variation. With reference to the example of the preceding section, two such sources of variation might be (1) actual differences in the effectiveness of the gasolines, and (2) chance, which in problems of this kind is also referred to as the *experimental error*. The measure of the total variation of a set of data we shall use is the *total sum of squares**

$$SS_T = \sum_{i=1}^{k} \sum_{j=1}^{n} (x_{ij} - \bar{x}_{..})^2$$

where x_{ij} is the jth observation of the ith sample ($i = 1, 2, \ldots, k$ and $j = 1, 2, \ldots, n$), and $\bar{x}_{..}$ is the *grand mean*, namely, the mean of all of the nk measurements or observations. Note that if we divided the total sum of squares SS_T by $nk - 1$, we would get the *variance* of the data; hence, the total sum of squares of a set of data is interpreted in much the same way as their sample variance.

Denoting by $\bar{x}_{i.}$ the mean of the ith sample, we can write as follows the formula, or identity, which forms the basis of a *one-way analysis of variance*

$$SS_T = n \cdot \sum_{i=1}^{k} (\bar{x}_{i.} - \bar{x}_{..})^2 + \sum_{i=1}^{k} \sum_{j=1}^{n} (x_{ij} - \bar{x}_{i.})^2$$

If we look closely at the two terms into which the total sum of squares SS_T has been partitioned, we find that the first term is a measure of the variation among the sample means; in fact, if we divide it by $k - 1$ we get the quantity which, on page 303, was denoted $n \cdot s_{\bar{x}}^2$. Similarly, the second term is a measure of the variation within the individual samples, and if we divided this term by $k(n - 1)$ we would get the mean of the variances of the indi-

* The use of double subscripts and double summations is explained briefly in Section 3.6.

vidual samples, namely, the quantity which we put into the denominator of F on page 304.

It is customary to refer to the first term, namely, the quantity which measures the variation *among* the sample means, as the *treatment sum of squares* SS_{Tr}; the second term, which measures the variation *within* the samples, is usually referred to as the *error sum of squares* SS_E. This terminology is explained by the fact that most analysis-of-variance techniques were first developed in connection with agricultural experiments where different fertilizers, for example, were regarded as different *treatments* applied to the soil. The word "error" in "error sum of squares" refers to the *experimental error*, namely, what we referred to in Section 12.1 as *chance.* Although this may sound confusing at first, we shall refer to the four gasolines as four different treatments, and in other experiments we may refer to three different teaching techniques as three different treatments, to five different advertising campaigns as five different treatments, and so on.

Before we go any further, let us verify the identity $SS_T = SS_{Tr} + SS_E$ with reference to the numerical example of Section 12.1. Substituting into the formulas for the various sums of squares we get

$$\begin{aligned} SS_T &= (20-21)^2 + (23-21)^2 + (23-21)^2 + (17-21)^2 \\ &\quad + (20-21)^2 + (20-21)^2 + (16-21)^2 + (17-21)^2 \\ &\quad + (24-21)^2 + (21-21)^2 + (26-21)^2 + (25-21)^2 \\ &= 118 \\ SS_{Tr} &= 3[(22-21)^2 + (19-21)^2 + (19-21)^2 + (24-21)^2] \\ &= 54 \\ SS_E &= (20-22)^2 + (23-22)^2 + (23-22)^2 + (17-19)^2 \\ &\quad + (20-19)^2 + (20-19)^2 + (16-19)^2 + (17-19)^2 \\ &\quad + (24-19)^2 + (21-24)^2 + (26-24)^2 + (25-24)^2 \\ &= 64 \end{aligned}$$

and it follows that

$$SS_{Tr} + SS_E = 54 + 64 = 118 = SS_T$$

To test the null hypothesis $\mu_1 = \mu_2 = \ldots = \mu_k$ against the alternative that these *treatment means* are not all equal, we now proceed as in Section 12.1 and compare SS_{Tr} with SS_E by means of an appropriate F statistic. In practice, it has become the custom to exhibit the necessary work as follows in a so-called *analysis-of-variance table:*

Source of Variation	*Degrees of Freedom*	*Sum of Squares*	*Mean Square*	*F*
Treatment	$k - 1$	SS_{Tr}	$SS_{Tr}/(k-1)$	$\frac{SS_{Tr}/(k-1)}{SS_E/k(n-1)}$
Error	$k(n-1)$	SS_E	$SS_E/k(n-1)$	
Total	$nk - 1$	SS_T		

Here the second column lists the degrees of freedom (the number of independent deviations from the mean on which the respective sums of squares are based), the fourth column lists the *mean squares* which are obtained by dividing the sums of squares by their respective degrees of freedom, and the right-hand column gives the F statistic as the ratio of the two mean squares. Note that the mean squares are the two estimates of σ^2 referred to in Section 12.1, and that the degrees of freedom for the F test are $k - 1$ and $k(n - 1)$, namely, the figures corresponding to treatments and error in the "degrees of freedom" column.

Referring again to the gasoline example, we now get the following analysis-of-variance table:

Source of Variation	*Degrees of Freedom*	*Sum of Squares*	*Mean Square*	*F*
Treatments	3	54	18	2.25
Error	8	64	8	
Total	11	118		

Finally, the test of significance is performed by comparing the value obtained for F with F_α for $k - 1 = 3$ and $k(n - 1) = 8$ degrees of freedom. Since $F = 2.25$ is less than $F_{0.05} = 4.07$ for the given degrees of freedom, we find that (as before) the null hypothesis cannot be rejected.

The numbers used in our illustration were chosen so that the calculations would be very simple. In actual practice, the calculations of the sums of squares can be quite tedious unless we use the following short-cut formulas, where $T_{i.}$ denotes the total of the observations corresponding to the ith treatment (that is, the sum of the values in the ith sample), and $T_{..}$ denotes the *grand total* of all the data:

▲
$$SS_T = \sum_{i=1}^{k} \sum_{j=1}^{n} x_{ij}^2 - \frac{1}{kn} \cdot T_{..}^2$$
▲

▲
$$SS_{Tr} = \frac{1}{n} \cdot \sum_{i=1}^{k} T_{i.}^2 - \frac{1}{kn} \cdot T_{..}^2$$
▲

and by subtraction

▲
$$SS_E = SS_T - SS_{Tr}$$
▲

It will be left to the reader to verify in Exercise 3 below that for the gasoline-mileage example these formulas yield

$$SS_T = 5{,}410 - 5{,}292 = 118$$

$$SS_{Tr} = \frac{1}{3}(66^2 + 57^2 + 57^2 + 72^2) - 5{,}292 = 54$$

and

$$SS_E = 118 - 54 = 64$$

EXERCISES

1. An experiment was conducted to compare three methods of teaching the programming of a certain digital computer. Random samples of size 4 were taken from each of three groups of students taught, respectively, by Method A (straight teaching-machine instruction), Method B (personal instruction and some direct experience working with the computer), and Method C (personal instruction but no work with the computer itself), and the following are the scores obtained by these students on an appropriate achievement test:

Method A: 74, 78, 68, 72
Method B: 93, 83, 89, 87
Method C: 75, 80, 79, 82

(a) Use the method of Section 12.1 and a level of significance of 0.01 to test whether the differences among the three sample means are significant.
(b) Use the short-cut formulas of Section 12.2 to calculate the required sums of squares, construct an analysis-of-variance table, and check the value of the F statistic against that obtained in part (a).

2. Random samples of 5 brands of tires required the following braking distances while going at 30 miles per hour:

Brand A	*Brand B*	*Brand C*	*Brand D*	*Brand E*
27	26	29	25	27
24	31	23	24	27
27	30	28	28	30
26	29	24	23	32

(a) Use the method of Section 12.1 and a level of significance of 0.05 to test whether the differences among the five sample means may be attributed to chance.

(b) Use the short-cut formulas of Section 12.2 to calculate the required sum of squares, construct an analysis-of-variance table, and check the value of the F statistic against that obtained in part (a).

3. Use the short-cut formulas to verify the values of SS_T, SS_{Tr}, and SS_E given on page 308 for the gasoline-mileage example.

4. The following are eight consecutive weeks' earnings (in dollars) of three salesmen employed by a given firm:

Mr. Jones: 143, 182, 159, 166, 202, 175, 168, 190
Mr. Smith: 166, 172, 163, 177, 189, 178, 159, 174
Mr. Green: 155, 191, 167, 185, 179, 163, 172, 188

Using the short-cut formulas to calculate the necessary sums of squares, construct an analysis-of-variance table and test (at $\alpha = 0.05$) whether the differences among the average weekly earnings of these salesmen are significant.

5. Referring to the data on page 51, perform an analysis of variance to test the null hypothesis that on the average the same area is covered by a gallon of each of the three kinds of paint. Use a level of significance of 0.05.

6. The following data show the yields of soybeans (in bushels per acre) planted 2 inches apart on essentially similar plots with the rows 20, 24, 28, and 32 inches apart:

20 in.	*24 in.*	*28 in.*	*32 in.*
20.6	22.3	22.7	20.8
22.5	20.8	20.5	18.0
22.3	20.0	19.1	17.4
22.1	21.3	20.5	18.2
21.7	21.9	20.2	19.3
22.0	20.6	20.8	18.7

Construct an analysis-of-variance table and test (at $\alpha = 0.05$) whether the differences among the four sample means can be attributed to chance.

7. It can be shown that for $k = 2$ the F statistic of Sections 12.1 and 12.2 equals the *square* of the t statistic of Section 9.8 when $n_1 = n_2$. Verify this result by calculating F for the numerical example on page 256 and comparing it with the square of the value obtained for t.

8. The method of Section 12.2 applies only to situations where each sample is of the same size. When the sample sizes are *unequal* and the ith sample contains n_i observations, the computing formulas for the sums of squares become

$$SS_T = \sum_{i=1}^{k} \sum_{j=1}^{n_i} x_{ij}^2 - \frac{1}{N} \cdot T_{..}^2$$

$$SS_{Tr} = \sum_{i=1}^{k} \frac{T_{i.}^2}{n_i} - \frac{1}{N} \cdot T_{..}^2$$

$$SS_E = SS_T - SS_{Tr}$$

where $N = n_1 + n_2 + \ldots + n_k$. The degrees of freedom for the F test, that is, for treatments and error, are $k - 1$ and $N - k$, and the total number of degrees of freedom is $N - 1$.

(a) Use this method (and a level of significance of 0.05) to analyze the following data consisting of scores obtained by random samples of students from four different schools on a standardized achievement test:

School 1: 79, 64, 97, 81, 62, 88, 77, 95, 57, 75
School 2: 87, 98, 99, 65, 83, 89, 99, 77
School 3: 80, 60, 72, 90, 77, 58, 71, 81, 87, 74
School 4: 73, 67, 90, 44, 52, 68

(b) Three groups of rats were given injections of an experimental drug and the following figures are the minutes it took for a reaction to take place:

Group A: 8.6, 10.5, 11.4, 9.4, 9.0, 10.8
Group B: 9.3, 9.6, 8.4, 10.1, 10.2, 7.6, 8.8, 7.6
Group C: 8.5, 9.1, 7.4, 6.9, 9.0, 8.8, 9.2

Analyze this experiment using $\alpha = 0.05$.

12.3 Two-Way Analysis of Variance

When we analyzed the results of the gasoline experiment on page 305, we observed that there were considerable, though not significant, differences among the four sample means. The results were not significant because there were also considerable differences among the values in each of the four samples; these differences, which led to the substitution of a relatively large value into the denominator of F, were attributed to chance, or *experimental error*. Let us now suppose that an interview with the person who conducted the experiment reveals that the first value for each gasoline was obtained with car X (a heavy station wagon), the second value for each gasoline was obtained with car Y (a standard-sized sedan,) while the third value for each gasoline was obtained with car C (a compact model car). *This puts the whole experiment in a completely new light:* rechecking the data we find that the four gasolines averaged 18.5 miles for the station wagon, 21.5 miles for the standard-sized sedan, and 23 miles for the compact car. It follows that *what we referred to as chance variation may well have been caused (at least in part) by the use of different cars.*

Let us now see what part of the total variation of the data can be attributed to the use of different cars. If we let $\bar{x}_{.j}$ stand for the mean of all the values obtained with the jth car, the answer is given by the *block sum of squares*

$$SS_{Bl} = k \cdot \sum_{j=1}^{n} (\bar{x}_{.j} - \bar{x}_{..})^2$$

Note that this formula is very similar to the one for SS_{Tr}; we have only to substitute the means of the columns (the different cars) for those of the different rows (the different gasolines) and correspondingly sum on j instead of i and interchange k and n. We referred to this quantity (which measures the variation among the means corresponding to the three cars) as the *block sum of squares;* indeed, it is customary in analyses of this kind to refer to one classification as *treatments* and the other as *blocks.* Using the language of experimental statistics, we thus refer to the three cars in the experiment as different blocks. Corresponding to the short-cut formula for computing SS_{Tr} we now have analogously

▲ $$SS_{Bl} = \frac{1}{k} \cdot \sum_{j=1}^{n} T_{.j}^2 - \frac{1}{kn} \cdot T_{..}^2$$ ▲

where $T_{.j}$ is the total of the observations in the jth block (in our example, the values obtained for the jth car).

In a *two-way analysis of variance* we compute SS_T and SS_{Tr} according to the formulas on page 308, SS_{Bl} according to the formula of the preceding paragraph, and we then obtain SS_E by subtraction, namely, by making use of the identity

▲ $$SS_T = SS_{Tr} + SS_{Bl} + SS_E$$ ▲

It should be observed that the error sum of squares for a two-way analysis of variance does *not* equal the error sum of squares for a corresponding one-way analysis, even though we denote it with the same symbol. In fact, what we have been doing in this section has been to divide the error sum of squares for the one-way analysis into *two terms:* the block sum of squares and a remainder which consititutes the *new* error sum of squares for the two-way analysis of variance. The following is an *analysis-of-variance table* for a *two-way analysis:*

Source of Variation	*Degrees of Freedom*	*Sum of Squares*	*Mean Square*	*F*
Treatments	$k-1$	SS_{Tr}	$SS_{Tr}/(k-1)$	$\dfrac{SS_{Tr}/(k-1)}{SS_E/(k-1)(n-1)}$
Blocks	$n-1$	SS_{Bl}	$SS_{Bl}/(n-1)$	$\dfrac{SS_{Bl}/(n-1)}{SS_E/(k-1)(n-1)}$
Error	$(k-1)(n-1)$	SS_E	$SS_E/(k-1)(n-1)$	
Total	$nk-1$	SS_T		

The mean squares are again given by the corresponding sums of squares divided by their degrees of freedom, and the two F values are obtained by dividing, respectively, the mean squares for treatments and blocks by the mean square for error. Note also that the degrees of freedom for SS_E can be obtained by subtracting the degrees of freedom for treatments and blocks from the total number of degrees of freedom, namely, from $nk - 1$.

A two-way analysis of variance leads to two tests of significance: the first F statistic serves to test the null hypothesis that the effects of the k treatments are *all equal* (against the alternative that they are *not all equal*) and the second F statistic serves to test the null hypothesis that the effects of the n blocks are *all equal* (against the alternative that they are *not all equal*). The degrees of freedom for the corresponding F tests are $k - 1$ and $(k-1)(n-1)$ for treatments and $n - 1$ and $(k-1)(n-1)$ for blocks.

Returning now to our numerical example, we find that the totals of the mileages obtained for the three cars are 74, 86, and 92, so that

$$SS_{Bl} = \frac{1}{4}(74^2 + 86^2 + 92^2) - 5{,}292$$

$$= 42$$

and, hence, the *new* error sum of squares is

$$SS_E = 118 - 54 - 42 = 22$$

Substituting these values together with the ones obtained for SS_T and SS_{Tr} in Section 12.2, we get the following *analysis-of-variance table:*

Source of Variation	*Degrees of Freedom*	*Sum of Squares*	*Mean Square*	*F*
Treatments	3	54	18	4.90
Blocks	2	42	21	5.72
Error	6	22	3.67	
Total	11	118		

Using a level of significance of 0.05, we find that for 3 and 6 degrees of freedom $F_{0.05} = 4.76$, and that for 2 and 6 degrees of freedom $F_{0.05} = 5.14$. Since the first of these two values is exceeded by $F = 4.90$, we can reject the null hypothesis concerning the treatments; and since the second is exceeded by $F = 5.72$, we can also reject the null hypothesis concerning the blocks. In other words, we conclude that there *is* a difference in the mileage yield of the four gasolines and, as an obvious by-product, that the results will differ depending on whether we use a station wagon, a standard-sized sedan, or a compact car.

An interesting feature of our example is that the *proper* analysis led to significant results, whereas the analysis which failed to account for the use of different cars did not. Of course, which kind of analysis is the proper one in any given situation will have to depend on the way in which the experiment was planned and conducted.

The methods we have described in this chapter are only two examples of an analysis of variance. If an experiment is appropriately designed (or planned) it may be possible to express the total sum of squares as a sum of many terms which can be attributed to various sources of variation—that is, to many different variables and even to the joint effects (*interactions*) of two or more variables which may be of relevance in a given investigation.

EXERCISES

1. The following are the yields of three varieties of wheat (in pounds per plot) obtained with three different kinds of fertilizer:

	Fertilizer 1	*Fertilizer 2*	*Fertilizer 3*
Wheat 1	47.5	33.9	39.7
Wheat 2	41.9	34.4	37.8
Wheat 3	43.6	34.2	38.0

Looking upon the varieties of wheat as treatments and the fertilizers as blocks, perform a two-way analysis of variance. Use a level of significance of 0.05 to test (1) the null hypothesis that there is no difference in the average yield of the three varieties of wheat, and (2) the null hypothesis that there is no difference in the effectiveness of the fertilizers.

2. The following are the number of defective pieces produced by four operators working, in turn, four different machines:

		Operator			
		B_1	B_2	B_3	B_4
Machine	A_1	34	28	33	29
	A_2	30	24	35	22
	A_3	27	20	40	27
	A_4	28	29	29	26

Use a level of significance of 0.05 to test for significant differences among the operators and also for significant differences among the machines.

3. Analyze the data of Exercise 4 on page 309 as a two-way classification, namely, regard the salesmen as "treatments" and weeks as "blocks." Use $\alpha = 0.05$ for each of the tests of significance.

4. Three different, though supposedly equivalent, forms of a standardized test are given to each of six students. The following are their scores:

	Student					
	1	*2*	*3*	*4*	*5*	*6*
Form A	83	72	85	43	78	81
Form B	91	70	88	51	68	87
Form C	85	79	76	49	75	74

Test, at a level of significance of 0.05, whether it is reasonable to treat the three forms as equivalent.

5. An experiment was performed to judge the effect of four different fuels and three different launchers on the range of a certain rocket. The following are the ranges obtained in nautical miles:

	Fuel 1	*Fuel 2*	*Fuel 3*	*Fuel 4*
Launcher 1	54.2	43.7	47.9	59.6
Launcher 2	52.1	40.8	48.0	53.0
Launcher 3	57.3	50.1	47.7	58.9

Analyze this experiment, using a level of significance of 0.01.

BIBLIOGRAPHY

The following are some elementary introductions to analysis of variance.

Guenther, W. C., *Analysis of Variance*. Englewood Cliffs, N.J.: Prentice-Hall, Inc., 1964.

Hicks, C. R., *Fundamental Concepts in the Design of Experiments*. New York: Holt, Rinehart & Winston, Inc., 1964.

Li, C. C., *Introduction to Experimental Statistics*. New York: McGraw-Hill Book Company, 1964.

THIRTEEN
Nonparametric Tests

13.1 Introduction

Most of the tests we have discussed so far required specific assumptions about the population (or populations) from which the samples were obtained. In particular, we often assumed that these populations can be approximated closely with normal distributions. Since there are situations where some, or all, of the required assumptions cannot be met, let us now investigate some methods based on less stringent assumptions; these methods, or at least some of them, have the added advantage that they require fewer computations. The tests we shall discuss in this chapter are referred to as *nonparametric*, because they are not related specifically to the parameters of a given population; they are also called *distribution-free* (although, originally, these two terms were not intended to be synonymous). Such tests have the advantage that they can be used under very general conditions, that they are often easier to understand than the "standard" tests they replace, and that they provide "quick and easy" tests so far as computations are concerned. Unfortunately, they also have some very definite disadvantages; above all, they are often wasteful of information. Specifically, they tend to expose us to greater risks of committing Type II errors than the corresponding "standard" tests. In the remainder of this chapter we shall present a few of the many nonparametric tests which have become popular in recent years.

13.2 The Sign Test

As we pointed out in Section 9.8, the small-sample test for the difference between two means cannot be used unless the populations from which the samples are obtained can be approximated closely with normal distributions with equal variances. If either of these assumptions is not met, we can use instead a nonparametric test called the *sign test*, which is based on the *signs* of observed differences (that is, whether they are positive or negative) instead of their actual magnitudes. The sign test has many important applications; among them, it serves as a convenient alternative to the method described in Exercise 22 on page 260, namely, to the case where two samples are *not independent.*

To illustrate the sign test (as it is used in a problem where two samples are *not independent*), let us consider the following data on the weights (in pounds) of 20 persons before and after they tried a new reducing diet:

	Before	*After*	*Sign of Change*
Mr. A	182	173	−
Mr. B	164	159	−
Mr. C	175	175	
Mr. D	212	199	−
Mr. E	225	219	−
Mr. F	139	142	+
Mr. G	168	162	−
Mr. H	163	157	−
Mr. I	201	188	−
Mr. J	158	155	−
Mr. K	139	132	−
Mr. L	177	173	−
Mr. M	201	194	−
Mr. N	215	218	+
Mr. O	167	161	−
Mr. P	258	233	−
Mr. Q	197	184	−
Mr. R	162	162	
Mr. S	144	147	+
Mr. T	158	150	−

The right-hand column of this table shows whether there was an increase in weight, a decrease in weight, or no change. Counting the signs, we find that there are 15 minus signs, 3 plus signs, and two cases (the 3rd and the 18th) where there was no change at all.

If we ignore the cases where there was no change, the null hypothesis that the reducing diet has no effect whatsoever is equivalent to the null hypothesis that we are as likely to get a minus sign as we are to get a plus. Hence, we test the null hypothesis that the probability of getting a minus sign is $p = 0.50$ against the one-sided alternative $p > 0.50$. We use this one-sided alternative because $p > 0.50$ means here that there is a better than fifty-fifty chance for losing weight; if p were less than 0.50, the diet would be a weight-gaining rather than a reducing diet.

Having expressed the null hypothesis in these terms, we can now use the method of Section 11.3. We have 15 successes in 18 trials, and proceeding as on page 283 we find that for $n = 18$ and $p = 0.50$, the mean and the standard deviation of the corresponding binomial distribution are

$$\mu = 18(0.50) = 9$$

and

$$\sigma = \sqrt{18(0.50)(0.50)} = 2.12$$

Basing the test on the normal curve approximation to the binomial distribution, we get

$$z = \frac{15 - 9}{2.12} = 2.83$$

and since this exceeds $z_{0.05} = 1.64$ (the critical value for a one-sided test with a level of significance of 0.05), we reject the null hypothesis and accept the alternative that *the diet is effective.* When n is very small, it may be preferable to base a test like this on a table of binomial probabilities rather than the normal curve approximation; had we done so in this example, we would have found that the probability of getting 15 or more successes in 18 trials is 0.0038 when $p = 0.50$, and the conclusion would have been the same. Appropriate tables of binomial probabilities are referred to in the Bibliography at the end of Chapter 11.

This example has illustrated one of the many uses of the sign test; several other applications are given in the exercises which follow. Note that because of its extreme simplicity the sign test is sometimes used as a shortcut even though standard techniques are applicable.

EXERCISES

1. The sign test can be used to test the null hypothesis that the mean of a symmetrical population equals μ_0 against a suitable one-sided or two-sided alternative. We replace each sample value exceeding μ_0 by a plus sign, each value less the μ_0 by a minus sign, and then test the null hypothesis $p = 0.50$ on the basis of the number of plus and minus signs obtained in the sample. Use the following sample data on the amounts of money (in dollars) which 40 persons spent in an amusement park, to test the null hypothesis that the average person spends there \$8.50 (against the alternative that this figure is too low):

9.10	7.50	8.25	10.75	12.50	9.65	8.75	7.40	6.25
9.80	5.40	9.25	8.00	8.85	7.60	9.45	10.20	9.45
8.60	10.75	12.60	9.75	6.25	7.45	9.85	10.60	14.35
8.60	9.20	7.95	10.15	9.80	8.75	6.70	8.90	9.80
12.65	10.30	8.30	9.25					

Use a level of significance of 0.05.

2. Suppose we want to use the sample data on page 221 to test the null hypothesis that the given kind of fish has a true mean length of 83.5 mm. Use the method suggested in Exercise 1, a two-sided alternative, and a level of significance of 0.01 to perform a suitable sign test.

3. The quality control department of a large manufacturer obtained the following sample data (in pounds) on the breaking strength of a certain kind of 2-inch cotton ribbon: 145, 162, 170, 148, 155, 157, 151, 148, 163, 168, 140, 157, 160, 159, 154, 162, 148, 159, 137, 159, 162, 171, 153, 158, 160, 144, 159, and 153. Use the method suggested in Exercise 1 and $\alpha = 0.05$ to test the null hypothesis $\mu_0 = 150$ lb against the alternative that this figure is too small.

4. Random samples of fifth graders from two different schools obtained the following scores in an achievement test in mathematics:

School 1: 73, 69, 55, 89, 84, 90, 94, 97, 88, 67, 95, 73, 94, 87, 59, 66, 87, 89, 75, 93, 98, 81, 70, 93, 77

School 2: 86, 71, 42, 53, 68, 71, 97, 91, 85, 63, 59, 48, 85, 60, 60, 85, 34, 60, 72, 75, 31, 72, 60, 65, 73

Randomly match each student from School 1 with a student from School 2, use a plus sign to represent each pair where the student with the higher score belongs to School 1, a minus sign to represent each pair where the student with the higher score belongs to School 2, and perform a sign test of the null hypothesis that there is no difference in the average achievement in mathematics between fifth graders attending these two schools. Use a two-sided alternative, a level of significance of 0.05, and, if necessary, discard pairs with identical scores.

5. The following are the cephalic indices of natives living on two South Pacific islands:

Island P: 72.4, 78.9, 75.4, 74.5, 73.5, 81.1, 77.0, 79.3, 75.4, 72.0, 75.8, 78.2, 74.7, 79.2, 78.6, 75.6

Island Q: 73.6, 77.2, 72.0, 76.8, 75.1, 73.2, 70.5, 71.5, 78.9, 76.3, 72.9, 71.5

Randomly match each measurement from Island Q with one from Island P (thus, omitting some from Island P), use a plus sign to denote each pair where the larger value came from Island P, a minus sign to denote each pair where the larger value came from Island Q, and perform a sign test of the null hypothesis that there is no difference between the average cephalic indices of the inhabitants of the two islands. Use a two-sided alternative and $\alpha = 0.05$.

6. Referring to Exercise 22 on page 260, use a sign test, an appropriate one-sided alternative, and a level of significance of 0.05 to test the claim that on the average Instrument B will give a higher reading than Instrument A.

7. The following are the number of defective pieces produced by two machines on each working day during May, 1965:

	Machine A	*Machine B*		*Machine A*	*Machine B*
May 3	6	8	May 18	5	8
May 4	3	9	May 19	3	6
May 5	5	6	May 20	7	4
May 6	8	8	May 21	5	8
May 7	4	5	May 24	7	7
May 10	8	3	May 25	6	9
May 11	6	7	May 26	4	8
May 12	5	9	May 27	8	4
May 13	2	5	May 28	3	9
May 14	6	10	May 31	1	6
May 17	6	6			

Use a sign test, a two-sided alternative, and $\alpha = 0.01$ to test the null hypothesis that there is no difference in the performance of the two machines so far as the production of defective pieces is concerned.

13.3 Rank-Sum Tests: The Mann-Whitney Test

As we saw in the preceding set of exercises (Exercises 4 and 5), the sign test can be used as an alternative for the *two-sample t test,* namely, for the small-sample test for the difference between two means which we discussed in Section 9.8. Another nonparametric alternative for this kind of test is the *Mann-Whitney test* (also called the *Wilcoxon test* or the *U test*), which is not quite so wasteful of information as the sign test. This test is based on *rank sums,* that is, the combined data are ranked according to size, and the test is based on the sum of the ranks assigned to the observations in either sample.

To illustrate how the Mann-Whitney test is used to decide (on the basis of samples) whether there is a difference between the means of two populations, suppose we want to compare the performance of two groups of students taught French with (Group A) and without (Group B) certain audio equipment. The following are their scores on an appropriate achievement test:

Group A: 77, 86, 43, 72, 95, 79, 93, 71, 54, 90, 61, 69

Group B: 55, 46, 40, 57, 92, 63, 53, 70, 29, 70, 80, 22

The means of these two samples are 74.2 and 56.4, respectively, and the problem is to decide whether their difference is significant. Note that we may well be reluctant to use the standard test of Section 9.8 since the second sample seems to display considerably more variation than the first. (Of course, we could put this to a rigorous test using the F test of Section 10.2.)

To perform the Mann-Whitney test, we first rank the data *jointly* (as if they were one sample) in an increasing (or decreasing) order of magnitude. Using the letters A and B, respectively, to indicate for each value whether it comes from Group A or Group B, we get

22	29	40	43	46	53	54	55	57	61	63	69
B	B	B	A	B	B	A	B	B	A	B	A

70	70	71	72	77	79	80	86	90	92	93	95
B	B	A	A	A	A	B	A	A	B	A	A

Assigning the data *in this order* the ranks 1, 2, 3, . . . , and 24, we find that the values of the first sample (Group A) occupy ranks 4, 7, 10, 12, 15, 16, 17, 18, 20, 21, 23, and 24, while those of the second sample (Group B) occupy ranks 1, 2, 3, 5, 6, 8, 9, 11, 13, 14, 19, and 22. There are no *ties* in this example among values belonging to different samples, but if there were, we would assign each of the tied observations the *mean* of the ranks which they jointly occupy. (Thus, when the fourth and fifth values are identical we assign each the rank $\frac{4+5}{2} = 4.5$, when the ninth, tenth, and eleventh values are identical we assign each the rank $\frac{9+10+11}{3} = 10$, and so on.)

The null hypothesis we shall want to test is that both samples come from identical populations, and it stands to reason that in that case the means of the ranks assigned to the values of the two samples should be more or less the same. The alternative hypothesis is that the populations have unequal means, and if this difference is pronounced, most of the smaller ranks will go to the values of one sample while most of the higher ranks will go to those of the other sample.

Using *rank sums* (rather than the means of the ranks), we shall base the test of this null hypothesis on the statistic

$$U = n_1n_2 + \frac{n_1(n_1+1)}{2} - R_1$$

where n_1 and n_2 are the sizes of the two samples and R_1 is the sum of the ranks assigned to the values of the first sample. (In practice, we find whichever rank sum is most easily obtained, as it is immaterial which sample is referred to as the "first.") In our example we have $n_1 = 12$, $n_2 = 12$, $R_1 = 4+7+10+12+15+16+17+18+20+21+23+24 = 187$, and hence

$$U = 12 \cdot 12 + \frac{12 \cdot 13}{2} - 187 = 35$$

Under the null hypothesis that the $n_1 + n_2$ observations may be regarded as coming from identical populations, or one population, it can be shown that the sampling distribution of U has the mean

▲ $$\mu_U = \frac{n_1 n_2}{2}$$ ▲

and the standard deviation

▲ $$\sigma_U = \sqrt{\frac{n_1 n_2(n_1 + n_2 + 1)}{12}}$$ ▲

Furthermore, if n_1 and n_2 are both greater than 8 (some statisticians prefer that they be both greater than 10), the sampling distribution of U can be approximated closely with a normal distribution. Hence, we reject the null hypothesis (against the alternative that the two population means are *unequal*) if

▲ $$z = \frac{U - \mu_U}{\sigma_U}$$ ▲

is less than $-z_{\alpha/2}$ or exceeds $z_{\alpha/2}$, where α is as always the level of significance. If either n_1 or n_2 is so small that the normal curve approximation cannot be used, the test will have to be based on special tables such as those referred to in the Bibliography at the end of this chapter.

Returning now to our numerical example and substituting $n_1 = 12$ and $n_2 = 12$ into the formulas for μ_U and σ_U, we find that

$$\mu_U = \frac{12 \cdot 12}{2} = 72$$

$$\sigma_U = \sqrt{\frac{12 \cdot 12 \cdot 25}{12}} = 17.3$$

and, hence, that

$$z = \frac{35 - 72}{17.3} = -2.14$$

Since the value of this statistic is less than $-z_{0.025} = -1.96$, we can reject the null hypothesis at a level of significance of 0.05. Note that although there was a large difference between the two sample means, we were barely able to get a significant result with this nonparametric test. As we pointed out earlier, nonparametric tests tend to expose us to greater risks of committing Type II errors; in other words, they generally require rather pronounced differences (departures from the null hypothesis) to yield significant results. The Mann-Whitney test has the important advantage that it requires fewer assumptions than the corresponding "standard" test. In fact, the only assumption needed is that the populations from which we are sampling are continuous, so that the possibility of ties can be ignored in the derivation of the formula for σ_U. There exists a correction for σ_U to account for possible ties, but it is generally negligible unless the number of ties is large. Another advantage of the Mann-Whitney test is that it is very easy to perform; like the sign test, it is thus often used for reasons of simplicity even though "standard" methods could be employed.

An interesting feature of the Mann-Whitney test is that, with a slight modification, it can also be used to test the null hypothesis that two samples come from identical populations against the alternative that the two populations have *unequal dispersions*, namely, that they differ in variability or spread. As before, the values of the two samples are arranged jointly in an increasing (or decreasing) order of magnitude, but now they are ranked *from both ends toward the middle.* We assign Rank 1 to the smallest value, Ranks 2 and 3 to the largest and second largest values, Ranks 4 and 5 to the second and third smallest, Ranks 6 and 7 to the third and fourth largest, and so on. Subsequently, the calculation of U and the performance of the test are the same as before. The only difference is that with this kind of ranking a *small rank sum* tends to indicate that the population from which the sample was obtained has a *greater variation* than the other; its values occupy the more extreme positions. (See Exercises 4 and 5 on page 325.)

13.4 Rank-Sum Tests: The Kruskal-Wallis Test

The Kruskal-Wallis test, also called the H test, is a rank-sum test which is used to test the null hypothesis that k independent samples come from identical populations against the alternative that the means of these populations are not all equal. Thus, it provides a nonparametric alternative for a one-way analysis of variance. As in the Mann-Whitney test, the combined data are ranked according to size; then if R_i is the sum of the ranks assigned to the n_i observations in the ith sample and $n = n_1 + n_2 + \ldots + n_k$, the test is based on the statistic

$$H = \frac{12}{n(n+1)} \sum_{i=1}^{k} \frac{R_i^2}{n_i} - 3(n+1)$$

If the null hypothesis is true and each sample is at least of size 5, the sampling distribution of this statistic can be approximated closely with a chi-square distribution with $k - 1$ degrees of freedom. Consequently, we can reject the null hypothesis at the level of significance α if H exceeds χ^2_α for $k - 1$ degrees of freedom. If the size of one or more samples is too small to use this approximation, the test will have to be based on special tables such as those referred to in the Bibliography at the end of this chapter.

To illustrate the Kruskal-Wallis test, let us refer to part (b) of Exercise 8 on page 310, which dealt with the reaction times of three groups of rats to an experimental drug. These reaction times (in minutes) were:

Group A: 8.6, 10.5, 11.4, 9.4, 9.0, 10.8

Group B: 9.3, 9.6, 8.4, 10.1, 10.2, 7.6, 8.8, 7.6

Group C: 8.5, 9.1, 7.4, 6.9, 9.0 8.8, 9.2

As can easily be verified (see Exercise 9 on page 325), the observations in the first sample are assigned the ranks 7, 10.5, 15, 19, 20, and 21, so that $R_1 =$ 92.5; those in the second sample are assigned the ranks 3, 4, 5, 8.5, 14, 16, 17, and 18, so that $R_2 = 85.5$; and those in the third sample are assigned the ranks 1, 2, 6, 8.5, 10.5, 12, and 13, so that $R_3 = 53.0$. (Observe that tied values are again assigned the mean of the ranks which they jointly occupy.) Substituting these values together with $n_1 = 6$, $n_2 = 8$, and $n_3 = 7$ into the formula for H, we get

$$H = \frac{12}{21 \cdot 22}\left[\frac{92.5^2}{6} + \frac{85.5^2}{8} + \frac{53.0^2}{7}\right] - 3(22) = 5.2$$

and since this is less than 5.991, the value of $\chi^2_{0.05}$ for 2 degrees of freedom, the null hypothesis cannot be rejected. Thus, we can either reserve judgment or conclude that the average reaction times of the three kinds of rats are all equal. Compare this with the result of the one-way analysis of variance performed in Exercise 8 on page 310.

EXERCISES

1. Comparing two kinds of emergency flares, a consumer testing service obtained the following burning times (rounded to the nearest tenth of a minute):

Brand C: 19.4, 21.5, 15.3, 17.4, 16.8, 16.6, 20.3, 22.5, 21.3, 23.4, 19.7, 21.0

Brand D: 16.5, 15.8, 24.7, 10.2, 13.5, 15.9, 15.7, 14.0, 12.1, 17.4, 15.6, 15.8

Use the Mann-Whitney test and a level of significance of 0.05 to check whether it is reasonable to say that there is no difference between the true average burning times of the two kinds of flares.

2. Referring to Exercise 4 on page 319, use the Mann-Whitney test and $\alpha = 0.05$ to test the null hypothesis that there is no difference in the average achievement in mathematics between fifth graders attending the two schools.

3. Referring to Exercise 5 on page 319, use the Mann-Whitney test and a level of significance of 0.05 to test the null hypothesis that the inhabitants of the two islands have the same average cephalic index.

4. The following are the Rockwell hardness numbers obtained for 15 aluminum die castings randomly selected from Lot A, and for 12 castings randomly selected from Lot B:

Lot A: 56, 97, 89, 73, 59, 76, 87, 56, 74, 70, 81, 68, 78, 53, 71

Lot B: 75, 81, 67, 70, 72, 86, 55, 77, 94, 88, 52, 65

(a) Use the Mann-Whitney test and $\alpha = 0.05$ to test the null hypothesis that the two samples come from identical populations against the alternative that the two populations have *unequal means.*

(b) Use the Mann-Whitney test (modified as suggested on page 323) and $\alpha = 0.05$ to test the null hypothesis that the two samples come from identical populations against the alternative that the two populations have *unequal dispersions.*

5. In order to compare two kinds of feed, each kind is fed to ten pigs; the following are their gains in weight (in ounces) after a fixed period of time:

Feed G: 11.0, 10.4, 8.8, 9.2, 8.2, 10.0, 10.0, 10.8, 12.6, 11.2

Feed H: 12.0, 18.2, 8.0, 9.6, 11.8, 8.4, 7.6, 14.0, 6.0, 13.0

(a) Use the Mann-Whitney test and a level of significance of 0.05 to test the null hypothesis that the two samples come from identical populations against the alternative that the two populations have *unequal means.*

(b) Use the Mann-Whitney test (modified as suggested on page 323) and a level of significance of 0.05 to test the null hypothesis that the two samples come from identical populations against the alternative that the two populations have *unequal dispersions.*

6. Apply the Kruskal-Wallis test to the data of Exercise 1 on page 308 and decide whether it is reasonable to say that the three teaching methods are equally good.

7. Apply the Kruskal-Wallis test to the data of Exercise 6 on page 309 and decide whether the null hypothesis concerning the soybean yields can be rejected at $\alpha = 0.05$.

8. Rework part (a) of Exercise 8 on page 310 using the Kruskal-Wallis test as a substitute for the one-way analysis of variance.

9. Verify the ranks and rank sums given as part of the numerical example on page 324.

13.5 Tests of Randomness: Runs

Randomness, as defined in Section 8.1, has served as a basic assumption for all of the tests and estimation procedures we have discussed. Whether this assumption is reasonable in any given situation may be difficult to decide, particularly when we have little or no control over the selection of the data. For instance, if we wanted to predict a car dealer's volume of sales for a given month, we would have no choice but to use sales data from previous years and, perhaps, collateral information about economic conditions in general. None of this information constitutes a random sample in the sense that it was obtained with the use of random numbers or similar schemes. Also, we would have no choice but to rely on whatever records happen to be available if we wanted to make long-range predictions of the weather, if we wanted to estimate the mortality rate of a disease, or if we wanted to study traffic accidents at a dangerous intersection.

Several methods have been developed in recent years which make it possible to judge the randomness of a sample on the basis of the order in which the observations were obtained. We can thus test whether patterns that look suspiciously nonrandom may be attributed to chance and, what is most important, this is done *after the data have been collected.* The technique we shall describe in this section and in Section 13.6 is based on the *theory of runs;* alternate methods are referred to in the Bibliography at the end of this chapter.

A run is a succession of identical letters (or other kinds of symbols) which is followed and preceded by different letters or no letters at all. To illustrate, let us consider the following arrangement of *defective*, d, and *nondefective*, n, pieces produced in the given order by a certain machine

$$\underbrace{n\,n\,n\,n\,n}\,\underbrace{d\,d\,d\,d}\,\underbrace{n\,n\,n\,n\,n\,n\,n\,n\,n\,n}\,\underbrace{d\,d}\,\underbrace{n\,n}\,\underbrace{d\,d\,d\,d}$$

Using braces to combine letters constituting a run, we find that there is first a run of five n's, then a run of four d's, then a run of ten n's, then a run of two d's, then a run of two n's, and finally a run of four d's. In all, there are six runs of varying length.

The total number of runs appearing in an arrangement of this kind is often a good indication of a possible lack of randomness. If there are too few runs, we might suspect a definite grouping or clustering, or perhaps a trend; if there are too many runs, we might suspect some sort of repeated alternating pattern. In our example there seems to be a definite clustering; that is, the defective pieces seem to come in groups. It will have to be seen, however, whether this is significant or whether it may be attributed to chance.

The test we shall use to put this decision on a precise basis utilizes the fact that for arrangements of n_1 letters of one kind and n_2 letters of another kind the sampling distribution of u, the total number of runs, has the mean

$$\mu_u = \frac{2n_1 n_2}{n_1 + n_2} + 1$$

and the standard deviation

$$\sigma_u = \sqrt{\frac{2n_1 n_2(2n_1 n_2 - n_1 - n_2)}{(n_1 + n_2)^2(n_1 + n_2 - 1)}}$$

Furthermore, the sampling distribution of this statistic can be approximated closely with a normal distribution provided that neither n_1 nor n_2 is less than 10; for small values of n_1 and/or n_2 the test will have to be based on special tables such as those referred to in the Bibliography at the end of this chapter. Thus, for sufficiently large values of n_1 and n_2 we base our decision on the statistic

$$z = \frac{u - \mu_u}{\sigma_u}$$

having approximately the standard normal distribution, and we reject the null hypothesis (against the alternative that the arrangement is *nonrandom*) if the value obtained for z is less than $-z_{\alpha/2}$ or exceeds $z_{\alpha/2}$. We would use an appropriate one-tail test if the alternative hypothesis asserted that there is a trend, a definite clustering, or perhaps a repeated cyclic pattern.

Returning now to the numerical example on page 326, the one dealing with the defective and nondefective pieces turned out by the given machine, we find that $n_1 = 17$, $n_2 = 10$, $u = 6$, and hence that

$$\mu_u = \frac{2 \cdot 17 \cdot 10}{17 + 10} + 1 = 13.59$$

$$\sigma_u = \sqrt{\frac{2 \cdot 17 \cdot 10(2 \cdot 17 \cdot 10 - 17 - 10)}{(17 + 10)^2(17 + 10 - 1)}} = 2.37$$

and

$$z = \frac{6 - 13.59}{2.37} = -3.20$$

Since this value is less than $-z_{0.005} = -2.58$, we can reject the null hypothesis of randomness at the level of significance $\alpha = 0.01$. The total number of runs is much smaller than expected and there is a strong indication that the defective pieces appear in clusters or groups; the reason for this will have to be uncovered by an engineer who is familiar with the process.

13.6 Tests of Randomness: Runs Above and Below the Median

The method of the preceding section is not limited to tests of the randomness of series of attributes (such as the d's and n's of our example). Any sample consisting of numerical measurements or observations can be treated similarly by using the letters a and b to denote, respectively, values falling above and below the median of the sample. Numbers equaling the median are omitted. The resulting series of a's and b's can then be tested for randomness on the basis of the total number of runs of a's and b's, namely, the total number of *runs above and below the median*.

To illustrate this technique, let us consider the following data constituting a sample of the speeds (in miles per hour) at which fifty passenger cars were timed passing a certain check-point in the given order: 45, 57, 59, 55, 69, 65, 47, 53, 61, 40, 38, 51, 44, 61, 52, 68, 64, 64, 66, 75, 51, 51, 58, 58, 66, 50, 45, 60, 39, 42, 41, 76, 66, 62, 58, 62, 62, 71, 56, 58, 41, 55, 46, 61, 66, 69, 62, 65, 68, and 72. The median of these speeds is 58.5, and the data can be represented by the following arrangement of a's and b's:

$$b\,b\,a\,b\,a\,a\,b\,b\,a\,b\,b\,b\,b\,a\,b\,a\,a\,a\,a\,a\,b\,b\,b\,b\,a$$
$$b\,b\,a\,b\,b\,b\,a\,a\,a\,b\,a\,a\,b\,b\,b\,b\,b\,a\,a\,a\,a\,a\,a\,a\,a$$

Since $n_1 = 25$, $n_2 = 25$, and $u = 20$, we get

$$\mu_u = \frac{2\cdot25\cdot25}{25+25} + 1 = 26$$

$$\sigma_u = \sqrt{\frac{2\cdot25\cdot25(2\cdot25\cdot25 - 25 - 25)}{25\cdot25\cdot24}} = 10$$

and

$$z = \frac{20-26}{10} = -0.60$$

which falls between $-z_{0.025} = -1.96$ and $z_{0.025} = 1.96$. Hence, the null hypothesis cannot be rejected at a level of significance of 0.05; that is, there is no indication that the sample of speeds is not random.

The method of runs above and below the median is especially useful in detecting trends and cyclic patterns in economic data. If there is a trend, there will be first mostly a's and later mostly b's (or vice versa) and if there is a repeated cyclic pattern there will be a systematic alternation of a's and b's and, probably, too many runs.

EXERCISES

1. Simulate *mentally* 100 flips of a coin by writing down a series of 100 H's and T's (representing *heads* and *tails*). Test for randomness on the basis of the total number of runs using a level of significance of 0.05.

2. Choose any four complete columns of random digits from Table VIII (200 digits in all), represent each even digit by the letter E, each odd digit by the letter O, and test for randomness on the basis of the total number of runs at $\alpha = 0.05$.

3. Use random numbers to simulate an experiment in which 100 voters are asked to choose between Candidate A (represented by the digits 0, 1, 2, 3, 4, and 5) and Candidate B (represented by the digits 6, 7, 8, and 9). Test for randomness at the level of significance $\alpha = 0.05$.

4. The following is the order in which healthy, H, and diseased, D, piñon trees were observed in a survey conducted by the Forestry Service:

$$HHHDHHHHHDDDHHHHHHHHHHHDDDHHHHDDDD$$

   Test for randomness at a level of significance of 0.05.

5. The theory of runs can also be used as a substitute for the Mann-Whitney test: given samples from two populations, we rank the data jointly, write an A below each observation belonging to the first sample, a B below each observation belonging to the second sample, and we can then test the randomness of this arrangement of A's and B's. If there are *too few* runs, this may be indicative of the fact that the samples come from populations with unequal means. Use this method to analyze the data of Exercise 1 on page 324. If necessary, resolve ties by flipping a coin.

6. Use the method of runs above and below the median to test at $\alpha = 0.05$ whether the radioactive-fallout estimates of Exercise 11 on page 24 may be regarded as random. Read off successive rows.

7. The time during working hours in which a machine is not operating owing to failures of one kind or another is called "down time." The following are 50 consecutive down times of a machine (in minutes) which an engineer observed during a certain period of time: 22, 29, 32, 25, 33, 34, 38, 34, 29, 25, 27, 33, 34, 28, 39, 41, 24, 31, 34, 29, 34, 25, 30, 37, 40, 39, 35, 24, 32, 43, 44, 34, 40, 38, 39, 43, 46, 34, 39, 45, 42, 39, 54, 50, 38, 41, 43, 46, 52, 55. Use the method of runs above and below the median and a level of significance of 0.05 to test the null hypothesis of randomness against the alternative that there is a trend.

8. The total numbers of radio-phonographs (in thousands) produced by a company during the years 1942 through 1962 were 100, 120, 145, 151, 119, 108, 142, 150, 159, 143, 122, 138, 124, 112, 110, 122, 143, 152, 125, 117, and 168. Test at a level of significance of 0.05 whether there is a significant trend in these data.

BIBLIOGRAPHY

The nonparametric tests discussed in this chapter and many others are treated in detail in

Siegel, S., *Nonparametric Statistics for the Behavioral Sciences.* New York: McGraw-Hill Book Company, 1956.

Tables needed to perform various nonparametric tests for very small samples are given in the aforementioned book by S. Siegel and, among others, in

Owen, D. B., *Handbook of Statistical Tables.* Reading, Mass.: Addison-Wesley Publishing Co., Inc., 1962.

An extensive list of further tests of randomness may be found in

Walsh, J. E., *Handbook of Nonparametric Statistics,* I. Princeton, N.J.: D. Van Nostrand Co., Inc., 1962.

FOURTEEN
Linear Regression

14.1 Curve Fitting

The main objective of many statistical investigations is to make predictions—that is, to forecast such things as a student's success in college, the growth of an industry, the effectiveness of a new drug, the distance required to stop a car, the ion concentration in a gas, and so on. Although predictions based on statistical information may sometimes agree with the exact values they are intended to predict, this is the exception rather than the rule. It must always be kept in mind that, by their very nature, predictions based on statistical information are at best formulated in terms of probabilities; hence, one must be satisfied if one is right a high percentage of the time or if one's predictions are *on the average* reasonably close.

Whenever possible, scientists strive to express relationship between variables, that is, relationships between quantities that are measured or observed and quantities that are to be predicted, in terms of mathematical equations. This approach has been extremely successful in the physical sciences, where it is known, for instance, that at constant temperature the relationship between the volume (v) and the pressure (p) of a gas is given by the formula

$$v \cdot p = k$$

where k is a numerical constant. Similarly, in biological science it has been discovered that the relationship between the size of a culture of bacteria (y) and the time it has been exposed to certain favorable conditions (x) may be written as

$$y = a \cdot b^x$$

where a and b are numerical constants.

Although the equations of the preceding paragraph referred to examples in physics and biology, they apply equally well to describe relationships in other fields. In economics, for instance, we could let x stand for price, y for demand, and write the equation of a so-called *demand curve* as $x \cdot y = k$; Similarly, the second equation might be used to describe the growth of an industry or phenomena related to the process of learning.

Of the many equations that can be used for purposes of prediction, the simplest and the most widely used is the *linear equation* (in two unknowns) which is of the form

$$y = a + bx$$

where a and b are numerical constants. Once these constants are known (usually, they are determined on the basis of sample data), we can calculate a predicted value of y for any value of x simply by substitution. *Linear equations are important not only because there exist many relationships that are actually of this form, but also because they often provide close approximations*

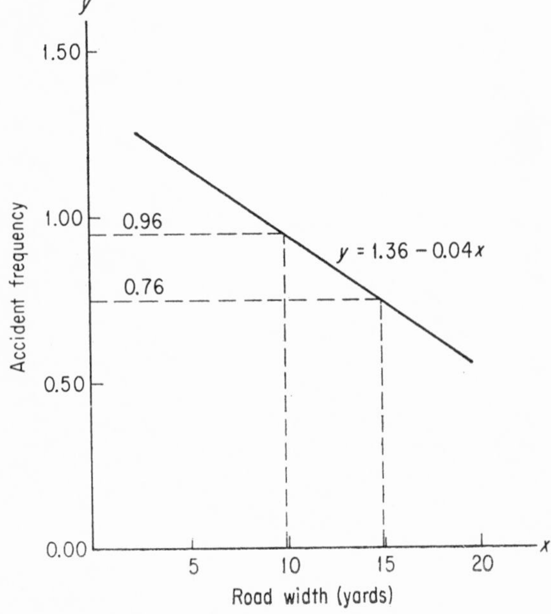

Fig. 14.1 Graph of linear equation.

(at least within a given range of interest) to relationships which would otherwise be difficult to describe in mathematical terms.

The term "linear equation" arises from the fact that, when plotted on ordinary graph paper, all pairs of values of x and y which satisfy an equation of the form $y = a + bx$ will fall on a straight line. To illustrate, let us consider the equation

$$y = 1.36 - 0.04x$$

whose graph is shown in Figure 14.1. In this equation, x stands for road width (in yards) and y stands for the corresponding number of accidents occurring per million vehicle miles; the constants 1.36 and -0.04 were obtained from a study of a state highway department. If the width of a road is 10 yards, the predicted number of accidents per million vehicle miles is $1.36 - 0.04(10) = 0.96$, and by similar substitution, if the width of a road is 15 yards, the predicted number of accidents per million vehicle miles is 0.76. Any pair of values of x and y satisfying the above equation (that is, belonging to the solution set of the equation) constitutes a point (x, y) which falls on the line of Figure 14.1.

In any problem in which predictions are to be based on a mathematical equation we must first decide what kind of curve to fit; that is, we must first decide whether it is to be a straight line, a parabola of the form

$$y = a + bx + cx^2$$

an exponential curve like the one on page 331 (the one concerning the size of a culture of bacteria), or one of many other kinds of curves. This question is sometimes decided for us by the nature of the data, namely, by theory relating the underlying variables, but usually it is decided by direct inspection of the data—we plot the data on ordinary graph paper, sometimes on special logarithmic or log-log graph paper (see Exercises 8 and 9 on pages 342 and 343), and we thus decide upon the kind of curve that will give the best fit. If we are not interested in obtaining a mathematical equation which describes the relationship between the variables, we can indicate the relationship graphically by various means. So-called *moving averages* are thus widely used in connection with economic data (see Exercises 10 and 11 on pages 343 and 344).

14.2 The Method of Least Squares

To illustrate the general procedure used in *fitting* a straight line to data consisting of paired observations of two variables x and y, let us consider the following example: suppose that a laboratory technician has conducted an experiment to determine whatever relationship there may exist between the amount of a certain chemical which will dissolve in 100 cc of water and the temperature of the water; his results are

Temperature (degrees centigrade) x	*Amount of Chemical* (grams) y
10	48
20	60
30	63
40	71
50	72
60	84
70	89
80	90

If we plot the eight points corresponding to the paired temperatures and amounts as in Figure 14.2, it becomes apparent that although the points do not actually fall on a straight line, the over-all pattern of the relationship is

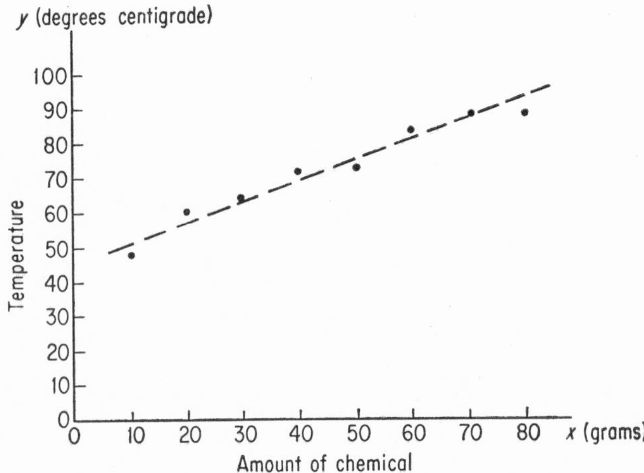

Fig. 14.2 Scattergram of given data.

fairly well described by the dashed line. Consequently, it would seem reasonable to express the relationship between the amount of the chemical which will dissolve in 100 cc of water and the temperature of the water by means of a linear equation; that is, an equation of the form $y = a + bx$.

We now face the problem of finding the equation of the line which in some sense provides the *best fit* to the data and which, it is hoped, will later yield the *best possible predictions*. Logically speaking, there is no limit to the number of straight lines we can draw on a piece of paper; some of these are such obviously poor fits that they can be ruled out immediately, but many others seem to provide a fairly good and close fit.* In order to single out *one* line as the one which "best" fits our data, we will have to state specifically what we mean here by "best"; in other words, we will have to provide a criterion on the basis of which we can decide which line is "best." If all the points actually fell on a straight line there would be no problem, but this is an extreme case we seldom, if ever, encounter in actual practice. In general, we have to be satisfied with lines which have certain desirable (though not perfect) characteristics.

The criterion which, nowadays, is used almost exclusively for defining a "best" fit dates back to the early part of the nineteenth century and the French mathematician Adrien Legendre; it is known as *the criterion* (or *the method*) *of least squares*. As it will be used in this chapter, the least-squares criterion demands that the line which we fit to our data be such that *the sum of the squares of the vertical deviations (distances) from the points to the line is a minimum*. With regard to our numerical example, the method requires that the sum of the squares of the distances represented by the solid line segments of Figure 14.3 be as small as possible. The logic behind this approach may be explained as follows: considering, for example, the case where the water temperature was 60 degrees, we find that the actual amount dissolved

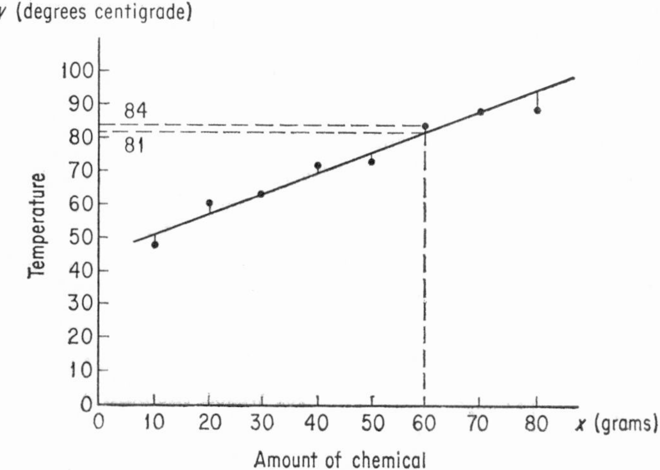

Fig. 14.3 Line fit to given data.

* If the reader has ever had the opportunity to analyze paired data which were plotted as points on a piece of graph paper, he has probably felt the urge to take a ruler, juggle it around, and decide upon a line which, to the eye, presents a fairly good fit. There is no law which says that this cannot be done, but it certainly is not very "scientific." Another argument against *freehand curve fitting* is that it is largely subjective and, hence, there is no direct way of evaluating the "goodness" of subsequent predictions.

was 84 grams. If we read the amount which corresponds to $x = 60$ directly off the line of Figure 14.3, we find that the corresponding "predicted" value is roughly 81 grams, so that the *error* (namely, the difference between the value predicted and the value actually obtained) is $84 - 81 = 3$ grams. There are eight such errors in our example corresponding to the eight temperatures, and the least-squares criterion demands that we minimize the sum of their squares. Observe that we do not minimize the *sum* of the deviations (distances), themselves; some of the differences between the observed y's and the corresponding values read off the line may be positive, others may be negative, so that their sum can be zero even though the errors are *numerically* very large.

As it does not matter which variable is called x and which variable is called y, *we shall agree to reserve y for the variable which is to be predicted in terms of the other*. (If we wanted to predict x in terms of y, we would have to apply the method of least squares differently, minimizing the sum of the squares of the *horizontal deviations* from the line (see Exercise 5 on page 341).

To demonstrate how a *least-squares line* is fitted to a set of paired data, let us consider n pairs of numbers (x_1, y_1), (x_2, y_2), . . ., (x_n, y_n), which might represent the heights and weights of n persons, I.Q.'s and examination grades of n students, measurements of the thrust and speed of n experimental rockets, the number of workers unemployed in two countries in n different years, and so on. Let us suppose, furthermore, that the line which we fit to these data has the equation

$$y' = a + bx$$

where the symbol y' is used to differentiate between observed values of y and the corresponding values calculated by means of the equation of the line. For each given value of x we thus have an observed value y and a calculated value y' obtained by substituting x into $y' = a + bx$.

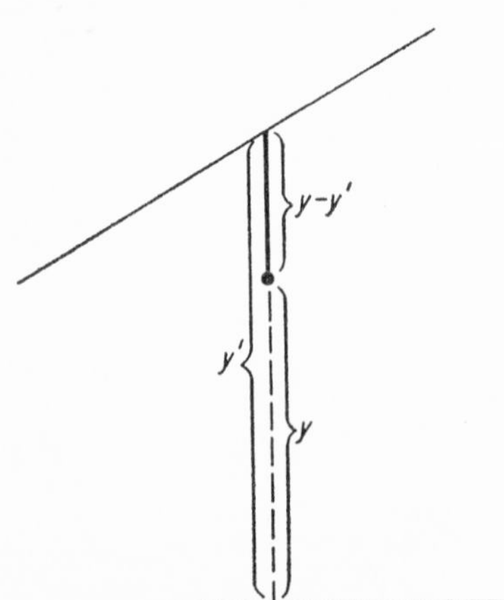

Fig. 14.4 Least squares fit.

Now, the least-squares criterion requires that we find the numerical values of the constants a and b appearing in the equation $y' = a + bx$ for which the sum of squares

$$\Sigma\,(y - y')^2$$

is as small as possible. In other words, we minimize the sum of the squares of the differences between the observed y's and the predicted y's (see Figure 14.4). We shall not go through the actual derivation (which requires calculus or a process called "completing the square"), but simply state the result that

$\Sigma (y - y')^2$ is minimized when a and b are solutions of the two equations

$$\Sigma y = na + b(\Sigma x)$$
$$\Sigma xy = a(\Sigma x) + b(\Sigma x^2)$$

Here n is the number of pairs of observations, Σx and Σy are, respectively, the sums of the given x's and y's, Σx^2 is the sum of the squares of the x's, and Σxy is the sum of the products obtained by multiplying each of the given x's by the corresponding observed value of y. The above equations, whose solution gives the desired least-squares values of a and b, are called the *normal equations*.

Returning now to our numerical example, let us fit a least-squares line to the given data. Copying the first two columns from the table on page 334 and performing the necessary calculations, we get

x	y	x^2	xy
10	48	100	480
20	60	400	1,200
30	63	900	1,890
40	71	1,600	2,840
50	72	2,500	3,600
60	84	3,600	5,040
70	89	4,900	6,230
80	90	6,400	7,200
360	577	20,400	28,480

We thus have $n = 8$, $\Sigma x = 360$, $\Sigma y = 577$, $\Sigma x^2 = 20{,}400$, $\Sigma xy = 28{,}480$, and we shall now have to solve the two normal equations

$$577 = 8a + 360b$$

$$28{,}480 = 360a + 20{,}400b$$

There are several ways in which this system of linear equations can be solved, and the reader may recall from elementary algebra that it is generally done by the *method of elimination* or by the use of *determinants*.

To simplify this work, let us solve the two normal equations symbolically for a and b, so that the solutions can then be obtained by direct substitution. Going through the necessary algebraic steps, we obtain

$$a = \frac{(\Sigma y)(\Sigma x^2) - (\Sigma x)(\Sigma xy)}{n(\Sigma x^2) - (\Sigma x)^2}$$

$$b = \frac{n(\Sigma xy) - (\Sigma x)(\Sigma y)}{n(\Sigma x^2) - (\Sigma x)^2}$$

and for our example we have

$$a = \frac{(577)(20{,}400) - (360)(28{,}480)}{8(20{,}400) - (360)^2} = 45.1$$

$$b = \frac{8(28{,}480) - (360)(577)}{8(20{,}400) - (360)^2} = 0.60$$

To simplify the calculations, we could first calculate b using the above formula, and then substitute the result into the first of the two normal equations to obtain a. Thus, an alternate formula for calculating a is given by

▲ $$a = \frac{\Sigma\, y - b(\Sigma\, x)}{n}$$ ▲

For our illustration this would yield $a = \dfrac{577 - (0.60)360}{8} = 45.1$, which agrees with the result obtained before. A further simplification, which can be used when the x's are *equally spaced*, is given in Exercise 6 on page 342.

We can now write the equation of the least-squares line for our numerical example as

$$y' = 45.1 + (0.60)x$$

and use it to predict, for example, how much of the chemical can be dissolved in 100 cc of water at 35 degrees centigrade. Substituting $x = 35$, we get

$$y' = 45.1 + (0.60)35 = 66.1 \text{ grams}$$

How such a prediction is to be interpreted and how we might judge its "goodness" will be discussed in Section 14.3. Incidentally, the predicted amount could also have been obtained by plotting the line on graph paper and reading off the y which corresponds to $x = 35$. To plot the line, we have only to choose two arbitrary values of x (preferably not too close together), calculate the corresponding values of y', and draw a straight line through the corresponding points.

Although there are many problems in which one variable can be predicted quite accurately in terms of another, it stands to reason that predictions may well be improved if one considers additional relevant information. For instance, we should be able to make better predictions of the demand for pork chops if we consider not only their price but also the price of competing meats. Similarly, we should be able to make better predictions of the attendance at a theater if we consider the quality of the show in addition to the size of the community and, perhaps, its wealth.

Many mathematical formulas can serve to express relationships between more than two variables, but most commonly used in statistics (partly for reasons of simplicity) are linear equations of the form

$$y = b_0 + b_1x_1 + b_2x_2 + b_3x_3 + \ldots + b_kx_k$$

Here y is the variable which is to be predicted, $x_1, x_2, x_3, \ldots,$ and x_k are the k known variables on which predictions are to be based, and $b_0, b_1, b_2, b_3, \ldots,$ and b_k are numerical constants which have to be determined (usually by the method of least squares) on the basis of given data. To give an example, consider the following equation obtained in a study of the demand for beef and veal:

$$y = 3.489 - 0.090x_1 + 0.064x_2 + 0.019x_3$$

where y stands for the total consumption of federally inspected beef and veal in millions of pounds, x_1 stands for the retail price of beef in cents per pound, x_2 stands for the retail price of pork in cents per pound, and x_3 stands for income as measured by a certain payroll index. Once one has obtained an equation like this, one can forecast the total consumption of federally inspected beef and veal on the basis of known (or estimated) values of x_1, x_2, and x_3.

The main problem of obtaining a linear equation in more than two variables which best describes a given set of data is that of finding numerical values for $b_0, b_1, b_2, b_3, \ldots,$ and b_k. This is usually done by the method of least squares; that is, we minimize the sum of squares $\Sigma\,(y - y')^2$, where as before the y's are the observed values and the y''s are the values calculated by means of the linear equation. In principle, the problem of determining the values of $b_0, b_1, b_2, b_3, \ldots,$ and b_k is no different from what we did before; however, the work becomes more tedious because the method of least squares yields as many normal equations as there are unknown constants $b_0, b_1, b_2, b_3, \ldots,$ and b_k. For example, when there are two independent variables x_1 and x_2, and we want to fit a *plane* of the form $y = b_0 + b_1x_1 + b_2x_2$, we must solve the three *normal* equations

$$\begin{aligned}
\Sigma\, y &= n\cdot b_0 + b_1(\Sigma\, x_1) + b_2(\Sigma\, x_2) \\
\Sigma\, x_1y &= b_0(\Sigma\, x_1) + b_1(\Sigma\, x_1^2) + b_2(\Sigma\, x_1x_2) \\
\Sigma\, x_2y &= b_0(\Sigma\, x_2) + b_1(\Sigma\, x_1x_2) + b_2(\Sigma\, x_2^2)
\end{aligned}$$

Here $\Sigma\, x_1y$ is the sum of the products obtained by multiplying each of the given values of x_1 by the corresponding y, $\Sigma\, x_1x_2$ is the sum of the products obtained by multiplying each of the given values of x_1 by the corresponding value of x_2, and so on. We shall not illustrate the solution of such a system of linear equations, but several sets of data (for which they can be solved by the method of elimination or by the use of determinants) are given in Exercises 12 and 13 on page 344.

EXERCISES

1. Various doses of a poison were given to groups of 20 mice and the following results were observed:

Dose in mg x	*Number of Deaths* y
6	1
8	3
10	6
12	5
14	8
16	9
18	14
20	11
22	12
24	16

(a) Use the formulas on page 337 to calculate a and b for the equation of the least-square line which will enable one to predict the number of deaths (per 20 mice) for a given dose of the poison.

(b) Repeat (a) by solving the two normal equations directly and compare the results.

(c) Use the equation obtained in (a) or (b) to predict how many of 20 mice will be killed by a dose of 19 mg of the poison.

2. The following are the grades 15 students obtained in the midterm and final examinations in a freshman course in English:

Midterm Examination x	*Final Examination* y
82	76
73	83
95	89
66	76
84	79
89	73
51	62
82	89
75	77
90	85
60	48
81	69
34	51
49	25
87	74

(a) Fit a least-squares line which will enable one to predict a student's final examination grade on the basis of his midterm examination grade.
(b) Plot the line together with the original data on one diagram.
(c) Predict the final examination grade of a student who scored 82 on the midterm examination by means of the equation obtained in (a) and also by reading it off the line plotted in (b).

3. The following are the elevations and the high temperatures recorded at 12 weather stations in Arizona on Labor Day, 1965:

	Elevation (feet)	*High Temperature* (degrees F)
Buckeye	867	95
Coolidge	1,418	92
Flagstaff	6,905	70
Gila Bend	735	98
Grand Canyon	6,868	71
Parker	420	100
Phoenix	1,092	94
Prescott	5,280	79
Tucson	2,372	88
Wickenburg	2,093	90
Winslow	4,850	86
Yuma	196	96

Fit a least-squares line to these data and use it to estimate the high temperature on that day in Globe, Arizona, elevation 3,541 feet.

4. A manufacturer of photographic equipment has the following data on the total cost (in dollars) of certain custom-made lenses and the number of units produced:

Number of Units	1	2	5	10	15	20
Total Cost	410	476	875	1,230	1,785	2,240

(a) Find a and b for the equation of the least-squares line which will enable the manufacturer to estimate the total cost of such lenses in terms of the size of an order.
(b) Plot the original data as well as the line obtained in (a) on one diagram and read off the estimated (predicted) cost of producing a lot of 8 of these lenses.
(c) Use the equation of the line obtained in (a) to estimate the total cost of producing a lot of 8 of these lenses; compare with the result obtained in (b).

5. Suppose that in Exercise 1 we had been interested in determining what is called the LD-50, namely, the dose which is lethal to 50 per cent of the mice.
(a) Relabel the number of deaths x, the doses y, and obtain a least-squares line which will enable one to estimate the dosage which corresponds to a given number of deaths.

(b) Estimate the LD-50 by substituting $x = 10$ into the equation obtained in part (a).
(c) Show that the estimate of the LD-50 would have been different if we had substituted $y = 10$ into the least-squares equation obtained in Exercise 1, and then solved it for x.

6. When the sum of the x's is zero, the calculation of a and b is greatly simplified; in fact, their formulas become

▲ $$a = \frac{\Sigma y}{n} \quad \text{and} \quad b = \frac{\Sigma xy}{\Sigma x^2}$$ ▲

These formulas can also be used when the x's are *equally spaced*, that is, when the differences between successive values of x are all equal. In that case we use the above formulas after "coding" the x's by assigning them the values $\ldots, -3, -2, -1, 0, 1, 2, 3, \ldots$, when n is *odd*, or the values $\ldots, -5, -3, -1, 1, 3, 5, \ldots$, when n is *even*. Of course, the resulting equation of the least-squares line expresses y in terms of the coded x's, and we have to account for this when using the equation for purposes of prediction. For example, if we are given economic data for the years 1961, 1962, 1963, 1964, and 1965, and these years are coded as $x = -2, -1, 0, 1$, and 2, we must substitute $x = 6$ to obtain a prediction for the year 1969.
(a) The total number of chicken dinners served on Mother's Day 1955 through 1963 by a well-known restaurant in Southern California was 13,641, 14,032, 14,228, 14,645, 14,827, 14,947, 15,238, 15,889, and 16,223. Fit a least-squares line after suitably coding the nine years, and use it to predict how many chicken dinners they can expect to sell on Mother's Day 1968.
(b) The following series shows the total cost (in millions of dollars) of magazine advertising placed for the years 1955 through 1962: 657, 692, 739, 693, 784, 854, 836, and 876. Fit a least-squares line after suitably coding the eight years, and use it to predict the corresponding figure for 1967.

7. Rework Exercise 1, using the kind of coding suggested in Exercise 6.

8. It is common practice to plot points representing paired data on various kinds of graph paper, in order to see whether there are scales for which they might fall close to a straight line. If this is the case when we use *semi-log paper* (with equal subdivisions for x and a logarithmic scale for y), this is an indication that an *exponential curve* will provide a good fit. The equation of such a curve is $y = a \cdot b^x$, or in logarithmic form $\log y = \log a + x(\log b)$, where log stands for logarithm to the base 10. If we apply the method of this section to the x's and the logarithms of the y's, the two normal equations become

▲ $$\begin{aligned} \Sigma \log y &= n(\log a) + (\log b)(\Sigma x) \\ \Sigma x(\log y) &= (\log a)(\Sigma x) + (\log b)(\Sigma x^2) \end{aligned}$$ ▲

and they can be solved for $\log a$ and $\log b$ and, hence, for a and b. Use this method to fit an exponential curve to the following data on the growth of a cactus graft under controlled temperature and other environmental conditions:

Weeks after Grafting x	*Height (inches)* y
1	2.00
2	2.40
3	3.65
4	5.10
5	7.25
6	9.35
7	13.20
8	18.30

(The necessary logarithms may be obtained from Table IX on page 397.) Also use the equation thus obtained to predict the graft's height after 10 weeks.

9. If points representing paired data fall close to a straight line when plotted on *log-log paper* (having logarithmic scales for both x and y), this is an indication that an equation of the form $y = a \cdot x^b$ will provide a good fit. In logarithmic form, the equation of such a *power function* becomes $\log y = \log a + b(\log x)$, and if we apply the method of this section to the logarithms of the x's and the y's, the two normal equations become

▲

$$\Sigma \log y = n(\log a) + b(\Sigma \log x)$$

$$\Sigma (\log x)(\log y) = (\log a)(\Sigma \log x) + b(\Sigma \log^2 x)$$

▲

Here $\Sigma (\log x)(\log y)$ is the sum of the products obtained by multiplying the logarithm of each observed x by the logarithm of the corresponding y, and $\Sigma \log^2 x$ is the sum of the squares of the logarithms of the x's. These two normal equations provide solutions for $\log a$ and b, and, hence, for a and b. Use this method (and Table IX on page 397) to fit a power function to the following data on the unit cost of producing certain electronic components and the number of units produced:

Lot Size x	*Unit Cost* y
50	$108
100	53
250	24
500	9
1,000	5

Note that this kind of relationship will arise when overhead is very large compared to the direct cost of manufacturing the components. Also use the equation thus obtained to estimate the unit cost for a lot of 600 components.

10. In the analysis of economic data we sometimes describe the over-all pattern (relationship) by means of a *moving average* rather than a specific kind of curve. A moving average is obtained by replacing each value in a series of equally spaced data by the *mean* of itself and some of the values directly preceding it and directly following it. For instance, in a *three-year moving average* each annual figure is replaced by the mean of itself and the annual figures corresponding to the two adjacent years. The following figures represent the average monthly production of kerosene (in thousands of barrels) for the years 1930 through 1961: 4,101, 3,537, 3,653, 4,081, 4,488, 4,651, 4,674, 5,442, 5,382, 5,710, 6,157, 6,049, 5,623, 6,023, 6,529, 6,752, 8,699, 9,201, 10,160, 8,513, 9,876, 11,132, 11,025, 10,276, 10,192, 9,761, 10,290, 9,077, 9,167, 9,222, 11,314, and 11,900.

(a) Construct a three-year moving average.

(b) Plot the values of the moving average on a diagram showing also the original data, and connect successive values of the moving average by means of straight lines. (Observe that there are no values of the moving average corresponding to 1930 and 1961.)

11. The following figures represent the average number of bales of cotton (in thousands) consumed per month during the years 1931 through 1962: 454, 418, 518, 452, 471, 592, 618, 492, 614, 671, 882, 953, 889, 808, 762, 819, 796, 758, 656, 804, 836, 765, 777, 711, 755, 747, 696, 678, 748, 726, 710, and 727. Construct a five-year moving average (see Exercise 10) and plot its values on a diagram showing also the original data. Connect successive values of the moving average by means of straight lines.

12. The following are the final examination grades and I.Q.'s of 12 students taking a course in European History, as well as the average number of hours they studied per week:

Final Examination y	*I. Q.* x_1	*Hours Studied* x_2
83	112	9
77	115	6
95	129	14
49	103	4
63	117	8
80	115	12
91	124	10
79	113	9
36	106	5
58	114	7
93	136	8
84	127	3

Fit an equation of the form $y = b_0 + b_1x_1 + b_2x_2$ and use it to predict the final examination grade of a student with an I.Q. of 110, who studies on the average 8 hours per week.

13. The following data were obtained in a study of the effectiveness of a weight-reducing drug:

Weight Loss (pounds) y	*Dosage* (cc) x_1	*Length of Treatment* (months) x_2
9	1.5	3
24	2.5	3
13	1.5	30
94	2.0	11
45	2.0	5
30	2.0	14
30	2.0	3
20	2.0	2
15	2.0	4
16	2.0	1
10	2.0	1
39	2.0	3
15	1.5	2
19	2.0	6
56	3.0	60
45	2.5	12
37	3.0	36
59	5.0	12
26	2.0	24
7	1.5	2
37	3.0	7
34	2.0	18

Fit an equation of the form $y = b_0 + b_1x_1 + b_2x_2$ and use it to predict the weight loss of an individual given a dose of 2.0 cc for 18 months.

14.3 Regression Analysis

Earlier in this chapter, we used a least-squares line to predict that 66.1 grams of a chemical will dissolve in 100 cc of water at 35 degrees centigrade, and in another place we used the equation of a line (presumably a least-squares line fitted to appropriate data) to predict that if a road has a width of 10 yards there will be 0.96 accidents per million vehicle miles. It stands to reason, of course, that if we repeatedly tried to dissolve the chemical at 35 degrees centigrade, we would not always get exactly 66.1 grams; sometimes we would be able to dissolve a little more, sometimes a little less, depending on the purity of the water, the use of different measuring instruments, perhaps, changes in atmospheric pressure and other factors. Similarly, there will not always be exactly 96 accidents for each million cars traveling over a 100-mile stretch of road whose width is 10 yards; sometimes there will be more accidents and sometimes there will be fewer, depending on the weather, the number of police cars used to patrol the road, and numerous other factors. ***This illustrates that predictions based on least-squares equations should not be looked upon as perfect; indeed, to make such predictions meaningful we must interpret them as expectations, namely, as "averages."*** Thus, in the first example we might predict, or estimate, that *on the average* 66.1 grams of the chemical can be dissolved in 100 cc of water at 35 degrees centigrade, and in the second example we might predict, or estimate, that *on the average* there will be 0.96 accidents per million vehicle miles when the road width is 10 yards.

Even if we interpret a prediction based on the equation of a least-squares line as an average, many questions remain. For instance, we might ask:

(a) "How *good* are the values we obtained for the constants a and b in the equation $y = a + bx$? After all, $a = 45.1$ and $b = 0.60$ are only estimates based on samples, and if we repeated the whole experiment we might well get data leading to entirely different values of a and b."

(b) "How *good* an estimate is 66.1 grams of the *true* average amount of the chemical that can be dissolved in 100 cc of water at 35 degrees centigrade?"

(c) "Can we construct limits (two numbers), for which we can assert with a probability of, say, 0.95 that they will contain the amount we would be able to dissolve if we actually went ahead and tried to dissolve the chemical in 100 cc of water at 35 degrees centigrade?"

In order to answer any of these questions, we shall have to make several assumptions: First, we shall assume that the *true mean* of the y's for any given value of x is given by an expression of the form $\alpha + \beta x$; in other words, we assume that the *true means* (of the amount that can be dissolved) fall on the line

$$y = \alpha + \beta x$$

so that we can look upon the values obtained for a and b by the method of least squares as *estimates* of α and β. We usually refer to $y = \alpha + \beta x$ as the (*true*) *regression line* and to α and β as the *regression coefficients;* correspondingly, $y = a + bx$ (with a and b obtained by the method of least squares) is referred to as the *estimated regression line* while a and b are referred to as *estimated regression coefficients.** (If the means of the y's fall on some curve other than a straight line, we refer to it as a *regression curve.*)

To clarify the concept of regression, let us consider Figure 14.5, in which we have drawn the distributions of the y's, the variable to be predicted, for various values of x. Referring again to our two examples, these curves may

* The term *regression,* as it is used here, is due to Francis Galton; he employed it first in connection with a study of the heights of fathers and sons, observing a regression (or turning back) from the heights of sons to the heights of their fathers.

be looked upon as representing the distributions of the amount of the chemical which can be dissolved in 100 cc of water at x_1 degrees, x_2 degrees, x_3 degrees, ..., or distributions of the number of accidents per million vehicle miles at road widths of x_1 yards, x_2 yards, x_3 yards, ... To complete

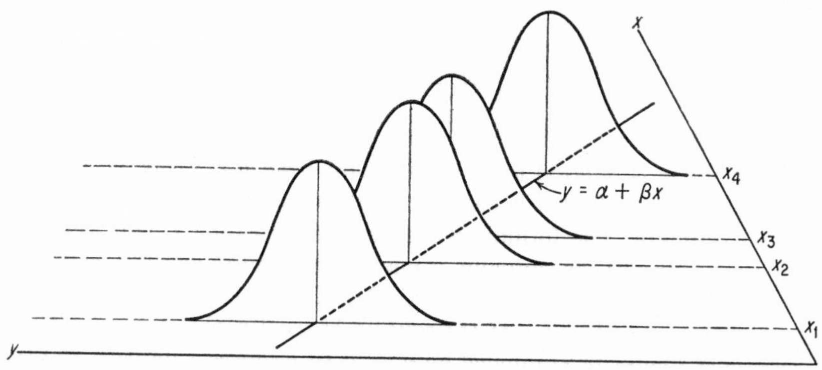

Fig. 14.5 Distributions of the y's for various values of x.

the picture, the reader should be able to visualize similar distributions of the variable to be predicted for various other values of x.

In *linear regression analysis* we assume that the x's are constants, *not* values of random variables, and that for each value of x the variable to be predicted has a certain distribution (as shown in Figure 14.5) whose mean is $\alpha + \beta x$. In *normal regression analysis* we assume, furthermore, that these distributions are all normal curves having the same standard deviation σ. In other words, the distributions pictured in Figure 14.5, as well as those we add mentally, are normal curves having the means $\alpha + \beta x$ and the standard deviation σ. (If the x's are also looked upon as values of random variables, the treatment of the data is referred to as *correlation analysis*, a subject we shall take up in Chapter 15.)

If we make all the assumptions of normal regression analysis, or meet them approximately in practice, questions like the first one on page 346 can be answered by making use of the statistics

$$t = \frac{a - \alpha}{s_e \sqrt{\frac{1}{n} + \frac{n \cdot \bar{x}^2}{n(\Sigma x^2) - (\Sigma x)^2}}}$$

▲ ▲

$$t = \frac{b - \beta}{s_e} \sqrt{\frac{n(\Sigma x^2) - (\Sigma x)^2}{n}}$$

whose sampling distributions are t distributions with $n - 2$ degrees of freedom. Here α and β are the regression coefficients we want to estimate or test, and a and b are the estimated regression coefficients obtained by the method of least squares for a given set of data. Also, n, $\bar{x}$, $\Sigma\, x$, and $\Sigma\, x^2$ are obtained from the data, and s_e is an estimate of σ, the common standard deviation of the normal distributions of Figure 14.5, given by

$$s_e = \sqrt{\frac{\Sigma\, y^2 - a(\Sigma\, y) - b(\Sigma\, xy)}{n - 2}}$$

Customarily, s_e is referred to as the *standard error of estimate*, although it should be observed that it is based on sample data and, therefore, is itself only an estimate. The formula we have given here for s_e is a short-cut computing formula; conceptually, it may be more meaningful to look upon s_e^2 as the sum of the squares of the vertical deviations from the least-squares line (for example, the sum of the squares of the lengths of the solid line segments of Figure 14.3) divided by $n - 2$. In Exercise 1 on page 350 the reader will be asked to verify that the two methods of calculating s_e are, indeed, equivalent.

In most applications β is of more interest than α as it represents the *slope* of the regression line, namely, the change (increase or decrease) in the variable to be predicted which corresponds to an increase of one unit in x. On the other hand, α represents the y-intercept, namely, the value of y which corresponds to $x = 0$. In what follows, we shall discuss the construction of a confidence interval for β and a test concerning α; in Exercises 4, 5, and 6 on pages 350 and 351 the reader will be asked to construct confidence intervals for α and perform tests concerning β.

To construct a confidence interval for β, we have only to substitute the expression for the second t statistic on page 347 into the middle term of $-t_{\alpha/2} < t < t_{\alpha/2}$ and manipulate this double inequality algebraically so that β becomes the middle term. Actually performing these steps, we obtain the confidence limits

$$b \pm \frac{t_{\alpha/2} \cdot s_e}{\sqrt{\dfrac{n(\Sigma\, x^2) - (\Sigma\, x)^2}{n}}}$$

The degree of confidence is $1 - \alpha$ (where α is not to be confused with the symbol used for the other regression coefficient), and $t_{\alpha/2}$ is the entry in Table II corresponding to $n - 2$ degrees of freedom.

To illustrate the actual calculation of such a confidence interval, let us return to the numerical example of Section 14.2. Making use of the results on page 337 to which we now add $\Sigma y^2 = 43{,}175$, we get first of all

$$s_e = \sqrt{\frac{43{,}175 - (45.1)(577) - (0.60)(28{,}480)}{8 - 2}}$$
$$= 3.3$$

If we now substitute this value together with $n = 8$, $\Sigma x = 360$, $\Sigma x^2 = 20{,}400$, and $t_{0.025} = 2.447$ into the formula for the confidence limits, we get

$$0.60 \pm \frac{(2.447)(3.3)}{\sqrt{\frac{8(20{,}400) - (360)^2}{8}}}$$

and hence, the confidence interval

$$0.48 < \beta < 0.72$$

Note that this 0.95 confidence interval applies to the increase in the amount of the chemical (which can be dissolved in 100 cc of water) when the water temperature is increased by 1 degree centigrade.

To illustrate a test concerning the regression coefficient α, let us suppose that it has been claimed that $\alpha = 48.0$ for the given chemical, and that the experiment which we referred to in Section 14.2 was actually designed to check this claim. Suppose, furthermore, that the level of significance is to be 0.05 and that the alternative hypothesis is $\alpha \neq 48.0$. Substituting $n = 8$, $\Sigma x = 360$, $\Sigma x^2 = 20{,}400$, $\bar{x} = 360/8 = 45$, $a = 45.1$, $\alpha = 48.0$, and $s_e = 3.3$ into the formula for the first of the two t statistics on page 347, we get

$$t = \frac{45.1 - 48.0}{3.3\sqrt{\frac{1}{8} + \frac{8(45)^2}{8(20{,}400) - (360)^2}}}$$
$$= -1.1$$

and we have only to compare this value with $-t_{0.025}$ and $t_{0.025}$ for $n - 2 = 6$ degrees of freedom. Since $t = -1.1$ falls between $-t_{0.025} = -2.447$ and $t_{0.025} = 2.447$, the null hypothesis *cannot be rejected;* in other words, the difference between $a = 45.1$ and $\alpha = 48.0$ may reasonably be attributed to chance. Note that if the alternative hypothesis had been $\alpha > 48.0$ we would have rejected the null hypothesis for values of t greater than $t_{0.05}$ (or more generally t_α), and had the alternative hypothesis been $\alpha < 48.0$ we would have rejected the null hypothesis for values of t less than $-t_{0.05}$ (or more generally $-t_\alpha$).

To answer the second and third questions asked on page 346, we use methods which are very similar to the ones just discussed; they are based on two further t statistics which will be given in Exercises 8 and 9 on page 351. The important concept of *limits of prediction* is introduced in the second of these two exercises.

EXERCISES

1. Substitute x = 10, 20, 30, 40, 50, 60, 70, and 80 into $y' = 45.1 + (0.60)x$, the estimated regression equation obtained on page 338, and use these values of y' to calculate $\Sigma\,(y - y')^2$. Compare

$$\sqrt{\frac{\Sigma\,(y - y')^2}{n - 2}}$$

with $s_e = 3.3$, the value obtained for the standard error of estimate on page 349.

2. (a) Referring to Exercise 1 on page 340, construct a 0.95 confidence interval for β.

(b) Referring to Exercise 2 on page 340, construct a 0.99 confidence interval for β.

(c) Referring to Exercise 3 on page 341, construct a 0.99 confidence interval for β.

(d) Referring to Exercise 4 on page 341, construct a 0.95 confidence interval for β.

In each case, state *in words* the significance, or meaning, of the regression coefficient β.

3. (a) Referring to Exercise 1 on page 340, test the null hypothesis $\alpha = -5.0$ against the alternative $\alpha \neq -5.0$ at the level of significance 0.05.

(b) Referring to Exercise 2 on page 340, test the null hypothesis $\alpha = 0$ against the alternative $\alpha > 0$ at the level of significance 0.01.

(c) Referring to Exercise 3 on page 341, test the null hypothesis $\alpha = 105$ against the alternative $\alpha < 105$ at the level of significance 0.05.

4. Substituting the expression for the first of the two t statistics on page 347, into the middle term of $-t_{\alpha/2} < t < t_{\alpha/2}$ one can show that $1 - \alpha$ confidence limits for the regression coefficient α are given by

▲ $$a \pm t_{\alpha/2} \cdot s_e \sqrt{\frac{1}{n} + \frac{n \cdot \bar{x}^2}{n(\Sigma\,x^2) - (\Sigma\,x)^2}}$$ ▲

Referring to the numerical example in the text (dealing with the chemical and water temperature), construct a 0.95 confidence interval for the regression coefficient α. As before, the number of degrees of freedom is $n - 2$.

5. In each of the following, use the confidence-interval formula of Exercise 4:

(a) Referring to Exercise 1 on page 340, construct a 0.95 confidence interval for the regression coefficient α.

(b) Referring to Exercise 3 on page 341, construct a 0.99 confidence interval for the regression coefficient α.

6. In each of the following exercises, base your decision on the value of the second of the two t statistics on page 347:

(a) Referring to Exercise 1 on page 340, test the null hypothesis $\beta = 1$ against the alternative $\beta \neq 1$ at the level of significance 0.05.

(b) Referring to Exercise 3 on page 341, test the null hypothesis $\beta = -0.005$ against the alternative $\beta > -0.005$ at the level of significance 0.01.

7. Referring to the numerical example in the text, test the null hypothesis that when the water temperature is raised one degree, the amount of the chemical which can be dissolved in 100 cc of water is increased by 0.50 gram. Use a two-sided alternative and the level of significance 0.01.

8. To answer the second of the three questions on page 346, we can use the following $1 - \alpha$ confidence limits for $\alpha + \beta x_0$, where x_0 is the value of x for which we want to estimate the mean of the y's:

▲ $$(a + bx_0) \pm t_{\alpha/2} \cdot s_e \sqrt{\frac{1}{n} + \frac{n(x_0 - \bar{x})^2}{n(\Sigma\, x^2) - (\Sigma\, x)^2}}$$ ▲

As before, $t_{\alpha/2}$ is to be obtained from Table II; the number of degrees of freedom is $n - 2$.

(a) Referring to the example in the text, construct a 0.95 confidence interval for the average amount of the chemical which can be dissolved in 100 cc of water at 35 degrees centigrade.

(b) Referring to Exercise 1 on page 340, construct a 0.99 confidence interval for the average number of mice which will be killed when 19 mg of the poison is given to 20 mice.

(c) Referring to Exercise 4 on page 341, construct a 0.95 confidence interval for the average cost of an order of 8 of the given lenses.

9. The third question on page 346 differs from the other two insofar as it does *not* concern an estimate of a population parameter; *instead it pertains to the prediction of a single future observation.* A set of limits for which we can assert (with the probability $1 - \alpha$) that they will contain such an observation are called *limits of prediction;* if the y-value is to be observed when $x = x_0$, appropriate limits of prediction are given by

▲ $$(a + bx_0) \pm t_{\alpha/2} \cdot s_e \sqrt{1 + \frac{1}{n} + \frac{n(x_0 - \bar{x})^2}{n(\Sigma\, x^2) - (\Sigma\, x)^2}}$$ ▲

Again, $t_{\alpha/2}$ must be obtained from Table II and the number of degrees of freedom is $n - 2$.

(a) Referring to the example in the text, construct 0.95 limits of prediction for the amount of the chemical which can be dissolved in 100 cc of water at 35 degrees centigrade.

(b) Referring to Exercise 1 on page 340, construct 0.99 limits of prediction for the number of mice which will be killed when 20 mice are given 19 mg of the poison.

(c) Referring to Exercise 2 on page 340, construct 0.95 limits of prediction for the final examination grade of a student who obtained an 82 on the midterm examination.

BIBLIOGRAPHY

Methods of deciding which kind of curve to fit to a given set of paired data may be found in books on numerical analysis and more advanced texts in statistics. A detailed treatment of problems of regression, including multiple regression, may be found in

Ezekiel, M., and Fox, K. A., *Methods of Correlation and Regression Analysis*, 3rd ed. New York: John Wiley & Sons, Inc., 1959.

FIFTEEN
Correlation

15.1 The Coefficient of Correlation

Now that we have learned how to fit a least-squares line to paired data, let us study a way of describing *how well* such a line actually fits. Since the method of least squares, as we used it in Section 14.2, defines "goodness of fit" in terms of the sum of the squares of the vertical deviations from the line (see Figure 14.3), it would be appropriate to measure this goodness of fit in terms of the quantity $\Sigma\,(y - y')^2$. If the differences between the observed y's and the calculated y''s are *small*, this sum of squares will tend to be *small;* if the differences between the y's and the y''s are *large*, the sum of squares will tend to be large.

Although $\Sigma\,(y - y')^2$ provides an indication of how well a least-squares line fits given data, it has the disadvantage that it depends on the units of y. Suppose that, in a given example, the y's are monthly figures of the wholesale price of bananas; if we change the prices from dollars to cents, this would have the effect of multiplying $\Sigma\,(y - y')^2$ by a factor of *ten thousand.* In order to avoid this difficulty, we do not base our judgment on the magnitude of $\Sigma\,(y - y')^2$ alone, but we compare it with $\Sigma\,(y - \bar{y})^2$. *In words, we compare the sum of the squares of the vertical deviations from the least-squares line with the sum of the squares of the deviations of the y's from their mean.*

To illustrate, consider the two diagrams of Figure 15.1, whose points represent the number of customers who visited a restaurant on 12 consecutive days and the number of steak dinners served on each of these days. The one on the left shows the vertical deviations of the y's from the least-squares line, the one on the right shows the deviations of the y's from their mean, and it is apparent that in this example, *where there seems to be a very close fit,* $\Sigma\,(y - y')^2$ *is much smaller than* $\Sigma\,(y - \bar{y})^2$.

In contrast, let us now consider the two diagrams of Figure 15.2, representing data on personal savings of individuals in the United States and the number of work stoppages in the same years (1940 through 1947). Again, the one on the left shows the vertical deviations of the y's from the least-squares line and the one on the right shows the deviations of the y's from their mean, but this time $\Sigma (y - y')^2$ is just about as large as $\Sigma (y - \bar{y})^2$.

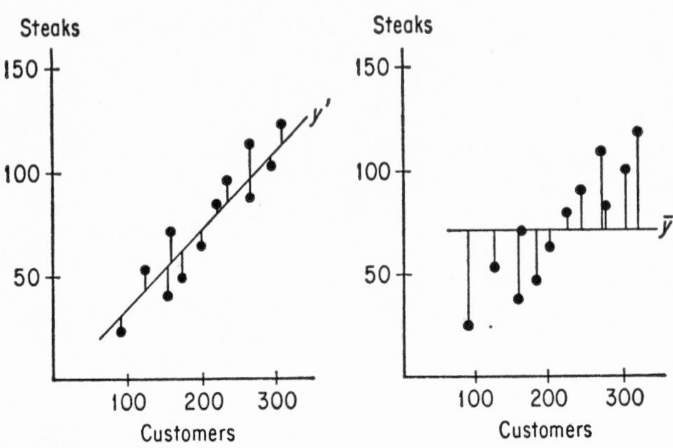

Fig. 15.1 Comparison of $\Sigma (y - y')^2$ and $\Sigma (y - \bar{y})^2$.

Thus, if the fit is good, as in Figure 15.1, $\Sigma (y - y')^2$ is much smaller than $\Sigma (y - \bar{y})^2$, and if the fit is poor, as in Figure 15.2, the two sums of squares are almost the same size.

To put this comparison on a precise basis, we use a statistic called the *coefficient of correlation;* it is given by the formula

$$r = \pm \sqrt{1 - \frac{\Sigma (y - y')^2}{\Sigma (y - \bar{y})^2}}$$

If the fit is *poor*, the ratio of the two sums of squares is close to 1 and r, the

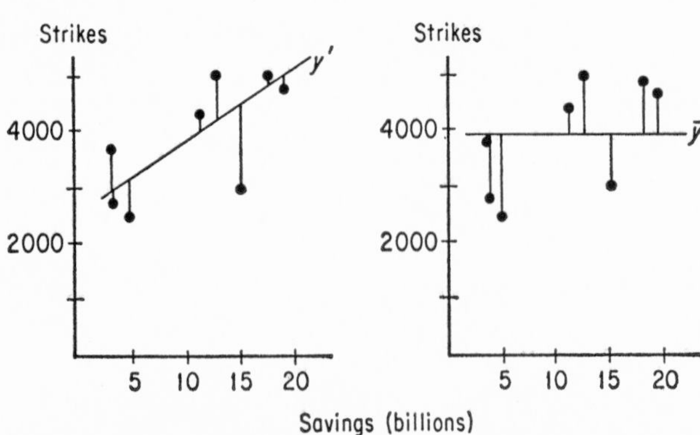

Fig. 15.2 Comparison of $\Sigma (y - y')^2$ and $\Sigma (y - \bar{y})^2$.

coefficient of correlation, is close to 0; if the fit is *good*, the ratio of the two sums of squares is close to 0 and r, the coefficient of correlation, is close to $+1$ or -1. Observe that the ratio of the two sums of squares can never exceed 1; the line was fitted by the method of least squares, and the sum of the squares of the vertical deviations from any other line, even the horizontal line through $\bar{y}$, cannot be less than $\Sigma (y - y')^2$. *Hence, r cannot be less than -1 or greater than $+1$.* The significance of the *sign* of r will be discussed on page 357.

The statistic we have just introduced is, undoubtedly, the most widely used measure of the *strength of the linear relationship between two variables.* It indicates the goodness of the fit of a line fitted by the method of least squares and this, in turn, tells us whether or not it is reasonable to say that there exists a linear relationship (correlation) between x and y. If r is close to 0, the fit is poor and the relationship is very weak or nonexistent; if r is close to $+1$ or -1, the fit is good and this is indicative of a strong linear relationship between x and y. (The coefficient of correlation is sometimes referred to more elaborately as the *Pearson product-moment coefficient of correlation.*)

Although the formula on page 354 serves to *define* the coefficient of correlation, it is seldom, if ever, used in practice. To use it directly, we would first have to find the equation of the least-squares line, calculate each y' by substituting the corresponding value of x, and then determine $\Sigma (y - y')^2$. Alternatively, we could use the formula for s_e, the standard error of estimate, on page 348, since $(n - 2)s_e^2$ equals $\Sigma (y - y')^2$. A good deal of this work can be avoided, however, by using the short-cut computing formula

$$\blacktriangle \qquad r = \frac{n(\Sigma xy) - (\Sigma x)(\Sigma y)}{\sqrt{n(\Sigma x^2) - (\Sigma x)^2}\sqrt{n(\Sigma y^2) - (\Sigma y)^2}} \qquad \blacktriangle$$

Mathematically speaking, the two formulas for r are equivalent, and a derivation of the short-cut formula from the original formula on page 354 is referred to in the Bibliography on page 377. In Exercise 1 on page 361 the reader will be asked to calculate r *both ways* for a given set of data and compare the results; except for errors due to rounding, the two answers should be the same.

Although the short-cut formula may look more formidable than the one which originally defined r, it is easier to use. To find r we have only to calculate the five sums Σx, Σx^2, Σy, Σy^2, Σxy, and substitute them into the formula together with n, the number of pairs of observations.

To illustrate the calculation of r, let us refer again to the numerical example of Section 14.2, where we fitted a least-squares line to data on the amount of a chemical which can be dissolved at various temperatures in 100 cc of water. Having found on page 337 that $n = 8$, $\Sigma x = 360$, $\Sigma x^2 =$

20,400, $\Sigma y = 577$, $\Sigma xy = 28{,}480$, and on page 349 that $\Sigma y^2 = 43{,}175$, we now obtain

$$r = \frac{8(28{,}480) - (360)(577)}{\sqrt{8(20{,}400) - (360)^2}\sqrt{8(43{,}175) - (577)^2}} = 0.98$$

To give another example, let us calculate r as a measure of the "degree of association" between x, the age of a certain make two-door sedan, and y, its price as advertised in a Phoenix newspaper. Writing the original data in the first two columns, we obtain the necessary sums as shown in the following table:

x (years)	y (dollars)	x^2	y^2	xy
4	895	16	801,025	3,580
10	125	100	15,625	1,250
2	1,395	4	1,946,025	2,790
1	1,795	1	3,222,025	1,795
3	1,245	9	1,550,025	3,735
4	695	16	483,025	2,780
24	6,150	146	8,017,750	15,930

(When calculations like these are performed with a desk calculator, the various totals can be accumulated directly without writing down the individual products and squares.) Substituting $n = 6$ and the five sums into the computing formula for r, we get

$$r = \frac{6(15{,}930) - (24)(6{,}150)}{\sqrt{6(146) - (24)^2}\sqrt{6(8{,}017{,}750) - (6{,}150)^2}} = -0.94$$

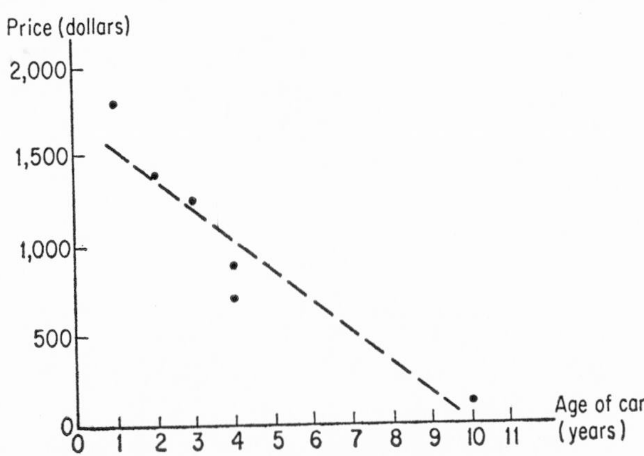

Fig. 15.3 Least squares line with negative slope.

Having obtained a *positive* value of r in the first example and a *negative* value in the second, let us investigate briefly what significance there is attached to the sign of r. If we plot the ages and prices for which we have just calculated r as in Figure 15.3, it can be seen that the least-squares line has a *negative slope* (that is, a *downward slope* going from left to right). This is characteristic of what we call a *negative correlation*—the smaller values of x go with the larger values of y, the larger values of x go with the smaller values of y, and r (as calculated by means of the formula on page 355) is negative. If the line we fit to a set of paired data has a *positive slope* (that is, an *upward slope* going from left to right), r will be positive and we say that there is a *positive correlation.* Thus, we obtained a positive correlation ($r = 0.98$) in our first example, where more and more of the chemical could be dissolved in 100 cc of water when the temperature was increased. *Note that the sign of r is automatically determined if we use the computing formula on page* 355. Geometrically speaking, the idea of a positive correlation and that of a negative correlation are illustrated in Figure 15.4. Incidentally,

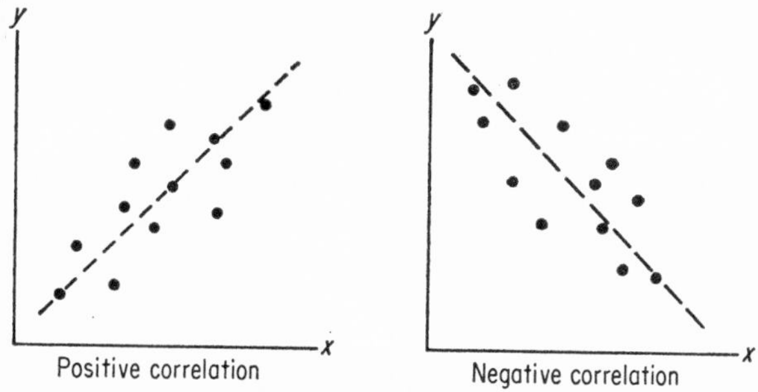

Fig. 15.4 Positive and negative correlation.

when the least-squares line is *horizontal* and $r = 0$, we say that there is *no correlation.*

Since r does not depend on the scales of x and y, its calculation can often be simplified by adding a suitable positive or negative number to each x, to each y, or to both, or by multiplying each x, each y, or both by arbitrary positive constants (see Exercises 5 and 7 on page 363). What numbers to add or subtract and by what numbers to multiply will have to depend on the nature of the data. The important thing to keep in mind is that the purpose of all this is to simplify the arithmetic as much as possible. When dealing with very large sets of data, the calculation of r can also be simplified by first grouping the data into a *two-way table* as is illustrated in Section 15.6, the Technical Note at the end of this chapter. However, grouping does entail some loss of information and there is no real advantage to it if one can use a computer.

15.2 The Interpretation of *r*

We already know how to interpret r when it equals 0, $+1$, or -1; when it is 0, the points are so scattered, the fit of the regression line is so poor, that knowledge of x does not aid in the prediction of y; when it is $+1$ or -1, all the points actually lie on a straight line and it stands to reason that we should be able to make excellent predictions of y by using the equation of the line. Values of r falling between 0 and $+1$ or between 0 and -1 are more difficult to explain; a person who has no knowledge of statistics might easily be led to the *erroneous* idea that a correlation of $r = 0.80$ is "twice as good" as a correlation of $r = 0.40$, or that a correlation of $r = 0.75$ is "three times as good" or "three times as strong" as a correlation of $r = 0.25$.

To explain the significance of intermediate values of r, let us again refer to the numerical example of Section 14.2. It is apparent from the data that there are considerable differences among the amounts of the chemical which can be dissolved in 100 cc of water—they ranged from 48 grams to 90 grams —and it would seem appropriate to investigate *why* such differences exist. An obvious reason is that the water temperature was not always the same, but as we pointed out on page 345, there may also have been differences in the purity of the water, differences in atmospheric pressure, measurements may have been made with different instruments, and so on. Since we are interested primarily in the effects produced by changes in water temperature, let us bunch all of the other factors under the general heading of *chance*, or *experimental error*. Thus, we are interested in determining what portion of the variation of the observed y's (the amounts which were dissolved) can be attributed to differences in water temperature and how much can be attributed to chance.

The total variation of the amounts dissolved may be measured by their *variance*, or without dividing by $n - 1$ by the sum of squares

$$\begin{aligned}\Sigma\,(y - \bar{y})^2 &= \Sigma\,y^2 - \frac{(\Sigma\,y)^2}{n}\\ &= 43{,}175 - \frac{(577)^2}{8}\\ &= 1{,}559\end{aligned}$$

On the other hand, chance variation is measured by the sum of the squares of the vertical deviations from the least-squares line (see discussion on page 336), and using the result on page 349 we have

$$\begin{aligned}\Sigma\,(y - y')^2 &= (n - 2)s_e^2\\ &= 6(3.3)^2\\ &= 65\end{aligned}$$

Thus, 65/1,559 = 0.04 or 4 per cent of the total variation of the y's (the amounts dissolved) can be attributed to chance, and 1 − 0.04 = 0.96 per cent can be attributed to differences in water temperature. Symbolically, we could have written this last percentage as

$$\left[1 - \frac{\Sigma\,(y - y')^2}{\Sigma\,(y - \bar{y})^2}\right]\cdot 100$$

and comparison with the original formula for r shows that we could also have written this as $100 \cdot r^2$. Consequently, *if the coefficient of correlation equals r for a given set of paired data, then $100 \cdot r^2$ per cent of the variation of the y's can be attributed to differences in x, namely, to the relationship with x.* If $r = 0.60$ in a given problem, then 36 per cent of the variation of the y's is accounted for (perhaps caused) by differences in x; similarly, if $r = 0.40$, only 16 per cent of the variation of the y's is accounted for by the relationship with x. In the sense of "percentage of variation accounted for," we can thus say that a correlation of $r = 0.80$ is *four times as strong* as a correlation of $r = 0.40$, and that a correlation of $r = 0.75$ is *nine times as strong* as a correlation of $r = 0.25$. In our example we had $r = 0.98$, and we can say that $100(0.98)^2 = 96$ per cent of the variation of the amounts dissolved can be attributed to differences in water temperature; this agrees with the result obtained before.

In the preceding discussion we did not mention the *sign* of r since this has no bearing on the strength of the relationship. The only distinction between values such as $r = 0.80$ and $r = -0.80$, for example, is that one regression line has an upward slope while the other's slope is downward; this has nothing to do with the goodness of fit or the strength of the relationship between x and y.

As a word of caution let us add that the coefficient of correlation is not only one of the most widely used, but also one of the most widely abused of statistical measures. It is abused in the sense that (1) it is often overlooked that r measures only the strength of *linear* relationships and that (2) it does not necessarily imply a cause-effect relationship.

If r is calculated indiscriminately, for instance, for the data of Figure 15.5, a value of r close to 0 does not imply that the two variables are not related. The dashed curve of Figure 15.5 provides an excellent fit even though the straight line does not. Let us remember, therefore, that r measures only the strength of linear relationships.

The fallacy of interpreting high values of r as implying cause-effect relationships is best explained with a few examples. One such example, which is frequently used as an illustration, is the high positive correlation one obtains for data pertaining to teachers' salaries and the consumption of liquor over the years. This is obviously not a cause-effect relationship; it results from the fact that both variables are effects of a common cause—the over-all standard of living. Another classical example is the strong positive correlation obtained for the number of storks seen nesting in English villages and the number of childbirths recorded in the same communities. We shall leave it to the reader's ingenuity to figure out why there is a strong

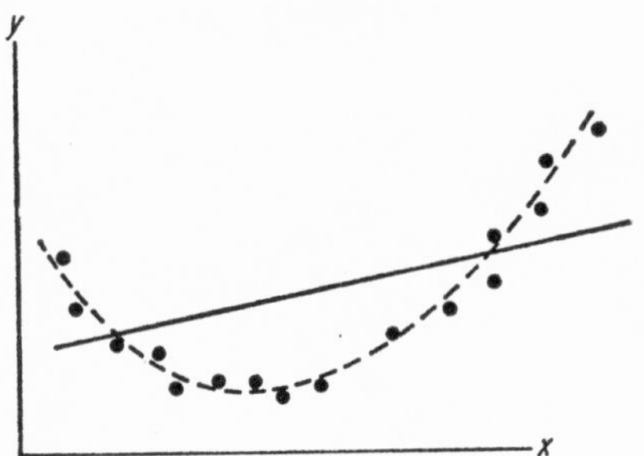

Fig. 15.5 Nonlinear relationship.

positive correlation without there being a cause-effect relationship between storks and babies. These examples serve to illustrate that it is much safer to interpret correlation coefficients as measures of *association* rather than causation. For further information about such *spurious* correlations see the Bibliography at the end of this chapter.

15.3 Correlation Analysis

It is sometimes overlooked that when r is calculated on the basis of sample data, we may get a strong (positive or negative) correlation purely by chance, even though there is actually no relationship whatsoever between the two variables under investigation. To illustrate this point, suppose we take a pair of dice, one red and one green, we roll them five times, and we obtain the following results:

Red Die x	*Green Die* y
4	5
2	2
4	6
2	1
6	4

If we calculate r for these data, we get the surprisingly high value $r = 0.66$, and this raises the question whether anything is wrong with the assumption that there should be no relationship at all. *After all, one die does not know what the other is doing.* In order to answer this question, we shall have to investigate whether this high value of r might be attributed entirely to chance.

When a correlation coefficient is calculated on the basis of sample data, as in the above example, the value we obtain for r is only an *estimate* of a corresponding parameter, the *population correlation coefficient*, which we refer to as ρ(*rho*). To test the null hypothesis of no correlation, namely, the hypothesis that $\rho = 0$, we shall have to make several assumptions about the distribution of the random variables whose values we observe. In *normal correlation analysis* we make the assumptions of *normal regression analysis* (see page 347), except that now the x's are not looked upon as constants but as values of a random variable having itself a normal distribution.*

Since the theory which underlies the sampling distribution of r is considerably beyond the scope of this text, we shall test the null hypothesis of no correlation, namely, the hypothesis $\rho = 0$, with the use of a special table calculated under the assumptions of normal correlation analysis. Table VI on page 391 contains the values of $r_{\alpha/2}$ for $\alpha/2 = 0.025$, 0.010, 0.005, and selected values of n; *we reject the null hypothesis of no correlation at the level of significance α if the value of r calculated for a set of data is less than or equal to $-r_{\alpha/2}$ or greater than or equal to $r_{\alpha/2}$.* If the value we obtain for r falls between $-r_{\alpha/2}$ and $r_{\alpha/2}$, we say that the correlation coefficient (or the correlation) is *not significant.* If n exceeds 92, the largest sample size for which $r_{\alpha/2}$ is given in Table VI, we can use either of the two approximate tests given in Exercises 9 and 10 on page 364.

If we apply this test to the second example of Section 15.1, the one dealing with the ages and prices of certain second-hand cars, we find that $r_{0.005} = 0.917$ for $n = 6$. Since -0.94, the value of r obtained for this example, is less than $-r_{0.005} = -0.917$, the null hypothesis can be rejected at the level of significance 0.01. Obviously, there is a relationship between the ages and the prices of such cars. If we apply this test to the example on page 360 where we rolled a pair of dice, we find that $r_{0.025} = 0.878$ for $n = 5$; since $r = 0.66$ falls between -0.878 and 0.878, we conclude that the correlation is *not significant.* Even though the value of r is fairly large in this example, it can be attributed entirely to chance.

EXERCISES

1. Calculate the coefficient of correlation for the data of Exercise 2 on page 340 using (a) the formula on page 354, and (b) the short-cut computing formula on page 355. Compare the results and also test the null hypothesis of no correlation at the 0.01 level of significance.

* Under these assumptions, it can be shown that $\rho = \frac{\sigma_1}{\sigma_2} \cdot \beta$, which expresses (or defines) the population coefficient ρ in terms of the slope of the regression line $y = \alpha + \beta x$ and σ_1 and σ_2, the standard deviations of the respective normal distributions of the two random variables x and y.

2. The following are the times (in minutes) it took 10 secretaries to complete a certain form in the morning and also in the late afternoon:

Morning	*Afternoon*
7.7	8.5
9.1	9.4
6.5	6.7
8.9	8.3
10.4	11.1
6.6	7.4
8.5	9.0
6.1	6.1
7.9	8.2
14.3	12.1

Calculate r and test the null hypothesis of no correlation at the 0.05 level of significance.

3. As part of a sociological study of the relationship between education and income, a scientist took a sample of 8 cities in a certain geographical region and obtained the following figures from the 1960 Census:

Per cent College Graduate x	*Median Income* y
7.2	\$4,244
6.7	4,915
17.0	7,020
12.5	6,215
6.3	3,816
23.9	7,566
6.0	4,438
10.2	5,387

Calculate r and test its significance at $\alpha = 0.01$.

4. If we actually calculated r for each of the following sets of data, should we be surprised to get $r = 1$ and $r = -1$, respectively? Explain.

(a)

x	y
19	7
25	11

(b)

x	y
13	5
20	2

5. Calculate r for the final examination grades and I.Q.'s (the variables y and x_1) of Exercise 12 on page 344. Repeat the calculations after subtracting 100 from each I.Q. and 74 from each final examination grade. *The results should be identical.* Also test the null hypothesis of no correlation at the 0.05 level of significance.

6. Referring to Exercise 13 on page 344, calculate r for each of the following pairs of variables:
(a) weight loss and dosage;
(b) weight loss and length of treatment;
(c) dosage and length of treatment.
In each case test the null hypothesis of no correlation at the 0.05 level of significance.

7. The following are the average hourly wages paid to production workers in manufacturing industries in the South Atlantic States in 1960 and 1961:

	1960	*1961*
Delaware	$2.31	$2.32
Maryland	2.26	2.34
District of Columbia	2.49	2.55
Virginia	1.77	1.85
West Virginia	2.41	2.48
North Carolina	1.54	1.58
South Carolina	1.57	1.61
Georgia	1.66	1.69
Florida	1.86	1.93

Calculate r after making suitable simplifications in the numbers.

8. State in each case whether one should expect to obtain a positive correlation, a negative correlation, or no correlation:
(a) I.Q.'s of husbands and wives;
(b) golf scores and hours of practice;
(c) a company's dividends and earnings per share;
(d) temperature and inches of snow on the ground at a weather station in the Rocky Mountains;
(e) shirt size and intelligence;
(f) amount of rubber on a tire and the number of miles it has been driven;
(g) pollen count and the sale of anti-allergy drugs.

9. An approximate test of the null hypothesis of no correlation may be obtained by approximating the sampling distribution of r with a normal distribution having the mean 0 and the standard deviation $1/\sqrt{n-1}$. Thus, we reject the null hypothesis of no correlation at the level of significance α if r is less than or equal to $-z_{\alpha/2}/\sqrt{n-1}$ or if it is greater than or equal to $z_{\alpha/2}/\sqrt{n-1}$; as before $z_{\alpha/2}$ equals 1.96 or 2.58 when the level of significance is 0.05 or 0.01, respectively.

(a) Compare the values of $z_{\alpha/2}/\sqrt{n-1}$ with those of $r_{\alpha/2}$ given in Table VI for $\alpha = 0.05$ and $n = 5$, 10, 20, 37, and 82.

(b) What are the (numerically) smallest values of r that are significant at the 0.01 level of significance when n equals, respectively, 100, 400, and 1,000?

(c) In a study of the relationship between the amount of irrigation applied to the soil and the corresponding amount of cotton harvested, an agronomist obtained $r = 0.24$ for $n = 50$ test plots. Use the approximate method explained above to test the null hypothesis of no correlation at the 0.01 level of significance.

10. Inferences concerning correlation coefficients are often based on the so-called *z transformation;* in other words, such inferences are based on the statistic

$$z = \frac{1}{2}\cdot\ln\frac{1+r}{1-r}$$

where ln stands for *natural logarithm,* that is, logarithm to the base e. Making use of the fact that the sampling distribution of z is approximately normal with the mean $\frac{1}{2}\cdot\ln\frac{1+\rho}{1-\rho}$ and the standard deviation $1/\sqrt{n-3}$, we can construct confidence limits for the population correlation coefficient ρ or test hypotheses concerning specific values of ρ. Use this technique to test the null hypothesis $\rho = 0.10$ for a sample of 200 paired observations which yielded $r = 0.18$. [*Hint:* make use of Table IX and the relation $\ln x = (2.303)(\log x)$.]

15.4 Rank Correlation

In Chapter 13 we saw that it is sometimes desirable to replace data by their ranks within samples. Although this will generally entail some loss of information, rank-correlation methods have the advantage that tests of significance require fewer assumptions and that calculations are simplified. To illustrate the calculation of the *rank-correlation coefficient* (often called *Spearman's rank-correlation coefficient*), let us consider the following data, which were obtained in a study designed to measure whatever relationship there may be between a college student's grades in chemistry and in mathematics. The first two columns of the table contain the final examination grades of a sample of students enrolled in both courses:

Chemistry x	*Mathematics* y	*Rank of* x	*Rank of* y	d	d^2
84	69	5	13	−8	64
74	64	11	18	−7	49
48	66	19	15.5	3.5	12.25
54	72	17	9	8	64
72	85	12	6	6	36
71	68	13	14	−1	1
96	87	3	4	−1	1
75	86	10	5	5	25
69	71	14	11	3	9
100	91	1	2	−1	1
23	31	20	20	0	0
58	65	16	17	−1	1
94	89	4	3	1	1
76	71	9	11	−2	4
52	54	18	19	−1	1
61	66	15	15.5	−0.5	0.25
77	78	7.5	8	−0.5	0.25
98	97	2	1	1	1
83	84	6	7	−1	1
77	71	7.5	11	−3.5	12.25
					284.00

In the third column we ranked the x's, giving Rank 1 to the largest value of 100, Rank 2 to 98, Rank 3 to 96, . . ., and Rank 20 to 23; in the fourth column we correspondingly ranked the y's, giving Rank 1 to 97, Rank 2 to 91, Rank 3 to 89, . . ., and Rank 20 to 31. *When there are ties, we assign to each of the tied values the mean of the ranks which they jointly occupy.* Thus, the seventh and eighth highest chemistry grades, which both equal 77, are assigned the rank $\frac{7+8}{2} = 7.5$, and the tenth, eleventh, and twelfth highest mathematics grades, which all equal 71, are assigned the rank $\frac{10+11+12}{3} = 11$.

Proceeding from here, we could calculate r for the two sets of ranks using the computing formula on page 355, but it is generally much simpler to use the formula

$$▲ \qquad r' = 1 - \frac{6(\Sigma\, d^2)}{n(n^2-1)} \qquad ▲$$

which defines the *rank-correlation coefficient.* Here n is the number of pairs of observations and the d's represent the differences between the ranks of the corresponding x's and y's. When there are no ties, r' will actually *equal* the correlation coefficient r calculated for the two sets of ranks; when there are ties, there may be a small (but usually negligible) difference.

Returning to the table on page 365, we find that the d's are given in the fifth column, their squares in the sixth column, and that $\Sigma\, d^2 = 284.00$. Since $n = 20$ in this example, we get

$$r' = 1 - \frac{6(284)}{20(20^2 - 1)} = 0.79$$

It will be left to the reader to verify that if we had calculated r for the two sets of rank we would also have obtained 0.79; had we calculated r for the original (unranked) data, we would have obtained $r = 0.88$.

To test whether a rank correlation is significant, we make use of the fact that, *under the null hypothesis of no correlation*, the sampling distribution of r' has the mean 0 and the standard deviation $\sigma_{r'} = 1/\sqrt{n-1}$. Approximating this sampling distribution with a normal distribution, we thus base the test on the statistic

▲ $$z = \frac{r' - 0}{1/\sqrt{n-1}} = r'\sqrt{n-1}$$ ▲

and *we reject the null hypothesis at the level of significance* α *if* z *is less than or equal to* $-z_{\alpha/2}$ *or greater than or equal to* $z_{\alpha/2}$.* (As before, $z_{\alpha/2}$ is such that the area to its right under the standard normal curve equals $\alpha/2$.) For our example, we get

$$z = 0.79\sqrt{20 - 1} = 3.44$$

and since this exceeds $z_{0.005} = 2.58$, we can say that there is a *significant relationship* between a student's grades in the two subjects (at $\alpha = 0.01$).

15.5 Multiple and Partial Correlation

In the beginning of this chapter we defined the correlation coefficient as a measure of the goodness of the fit of a least-squares line to a set of paired data. If predictions are to be made with a multiple linear regression equation of the form

$$y' = b_0 + b_1x_1 + b_2x_2 + \ldots + b_kx_k$$

(see page 339), we define the *multiple correlation coefficient* by means of the same formula which originally defined r on page 354, namely,

$$\pm\sqrt{1 - \frac{\Sigma\,(y - y')^2}{\Sigma\,(y - \bar{y})^2}}$$

* There exists a correction for $\sigma_{r'}$ that acounts for ties in rank; it is seldom used, however, unless the number of ties is large.

The only difference is that we now calculate the values of y' by means of the *multiple* regression equation instead of the equation $y' = a + bx$.

To illustrate the simplest case, suppose that we are given data on the ages, x_1, heights, x_2, and weights, y, of a number of persons, and that we are interested in obtaining an equation which will enable us to predict weight in terms of age and height by means of an equation of the form $y' = b_0 + b_1x_1 + b_2x_2$. Geometrically speaking, this equation is represented by the *plane* of Figure 15.6. Minimizing the sum of the squares of the

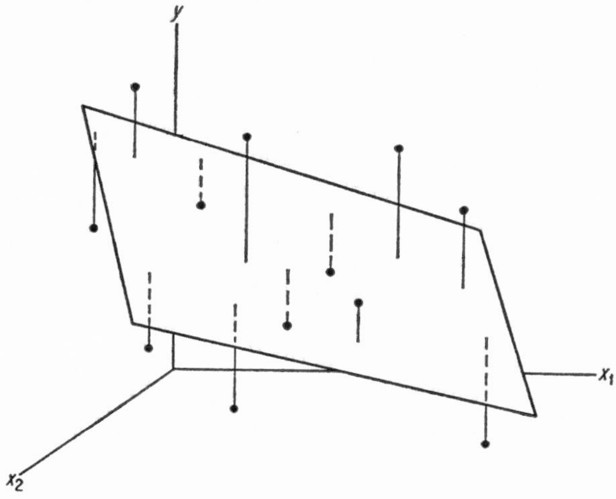

Fig. 15.6 Plane fit to data.

vertical deviations from the plane, we obtain solutions for the regression coefficients b_0, b_1, and b_2; in fact, they are obtained by solving the system of normal equations on page 339. Thus, in this special case the multiple correlation coefficient measures how closely a plane can be fit to a given set of data; in our particular example it measures how well weight can be predicted in terms of age and height.

When we discussed the problem of *correlation and causation*, we showed that a high correlation between two variables can be due entirely to their dependence on a third variable. We illustrated this with the examples of birth registrations and storks, and teachers' salaries and the consumption of liquor. To give another example, let us consider the variables x_1, the weekly amount of hot chocolate sold by a refreshment stand at a summer resort, and x_2, the weekly number of tourists staying at the resort. Let us suppose, also, that on the basis of appropriate data on these variables we obtain a correlation coefficient of $r = -0.30$. This result is surprising;

surely, we would expect higher sales of hot chocolate when there are more tourists and vice versa, and hence a *positive* correlation.

If we investigate this situation more closely, we surmise that the negative correlation of -0.30 may well be accounted for by the fact that sales of hot chocolate as well as the number of tourists staying at the resort are related to a third variable x_3, the average weekly temperature at the resort. If the temperature is high, there will be many tourists, but they will prefer cold drinks to hot chocolate; if the temperature is low, there will be fewer tourists, and they will prefer hot chocolate to cold drinks. Thus, let us suppose that further data yielded a correlation coefficient of $r = -0.70$ for x_1 and x_3 (the sale of hot chocolate and temperature), and a correlation coefficient of $r = 0.80$ for x_2 and x_3 (the number of tourists and temperature). These values seem reasonable since low sales of hot chocolate should go with high temperatures and vice versa, while the number of tourists should be high when the temperature is high, and low when the temperature is low.

To study the *actual* effect of the number of tourists on the sale of hot chocolate, we should investigate the relationship between x_1 and x_2 *when all other factors, primarily temperature, are held fixed.* As it is seldom, if ever, possible to control things to such an extent, it has been found that a statistic called the *partial correlation coefficient* does a fair job of eliminating the effects of other variables. If we write the "ordinary" correlation coefficient for x_1 and x_2 as r_{12}, that for x_1 and x_3 as r_{13}, and that for x_2 and x_3 as r_{23}, the *partial correlation coefficient for x_1 and x_2 with x_3 fixed* is given by

$$\blacktriangle \qquad r_{12.3} = \frac{r_{12} - r_{13} \cdot r_{23}}{\sqrt{1 - r_{13}^2}\sqrt{1 - r_{23}^2}} \qquad \blacktriangle$$

Substituting the numerical values of our example, we get

$$r_{12.3} = \frac{(-0.30) - (-0.70)(0.80)}{\sqrt{1 - (-0.70)^2}\sqrt{1 - (0.80)^2}} = 0.61$$

and this shows that, as we should have expected, there is a *positive* correlation between sales of hot chocolate and the number of tourists visiting the resort *when the temperature is fixed;* that is, when the effect of variations in temperature is eliminated.

We have given this example primarily to illustrate what is meant by *partial correlation;* at the same time the example has also served to emphasize again that "ordinary" correlation coefficients can lead to very misleading conclusions unless they are interpreted with great care.

The formula for $r_{12.3}$ provides a measure of the strength of the correlation between two variables when a third variable is held fixed; however, it can easily be generalized to situations where more than one variable is held fixed. Detailed treatments of multiple and partial correlation, the necessary formulas and computing techniques, are referred to in the Bibliography at the end of this chapter.

EXERCISES

1. Calculate r' for the midterm and final examination grades of Exercise 2 on page 340. Also test the null hypothesis of no correlation at the 0.05 level of significance.

2. Calculate r' for the data of Exercise 3 on page 362 and test for significance at $\alpha = 0.01$.

3. Calculate r' for the data of Exercise 3 on page 341.

4. Calculate r' for the variables x_1 and x_2 (I.Q. and hours studied) of Exercise 12 on page 344. Test for significance at $\alpha = 0.05$.

5. Calculate r' for the data of Exercise 2 on page 362 and test the null hypothesis of no correlation at the 0.05 level of significance.

6. The following are the rankings given by two critics, who were asked to indicate their preferences for 12 television programs appearing on the CBS network:

	Critic A	*Critic B*
Jackie Gleason Show	8	3
Gunsmoke	9	7
Ed Sullivan Show	3	10
Perry Mason	10	2
What's My Line	11	11
Andy Griffith Show	7	12
Red Skelton Show	6	5
Beverly Hillbillies	4	1
Danny Kaye Show	2	8
Dick Van Dyke Show	1	4
Hogan's Heroes	5	6
Gomer Pyle, USMC	12	9

Calculate r' as a measure of the *consistency* (or *inconsistency*) of the two ratings.

7. The following are the ratings of two judges at a beauty contest among representatives of the fourteen Arizona counties:

	Judge X	*Judge Y*
Miss Apache	9	7
Miss Cochise	13	12
Miss Coconino	2	8
Miss Gila	4	2
Miss Graham	10	6
Miss Greenlee	12	11
Miss Maricopa	1	5
Miss Mohave	5	4
Miss Navajo	14	13
Miss Pima	3	1
Miss Pinal	6	3
Miss Santa Cruz	11	9
Miss Yavapai	8	14
Miss Yuma	7	10

Calculate r' as a measure of the *consistency* (or *inconsistency*) of the preferences of the two judges.

8. Use the least-squares equation obtained in Exercise 12 on page 344 to calculate y' for each of the 12 "data points." Then calculate the two sums of squares $\Sigma\,(y - y')^2$ and $\Sigma\,(y - \bar{y})^2$, and substitute into the formula for the multiple correlation coefficient on page 366. Taking the positive square root, compare the result with the "ordinary" correlation coefficient obtained for the I.Q.'s and final examination grades in Exercise 5 on page 363.

9. Referring to the example in the text, calculate the partial correlation coefficient for x_1 and x_3 (sales of hot chocolate and temperature) when x_2 (number of tourists) is held fixed. (*Hint:* Interchange 2 and 3 wherever these numbers appear in the subscripts of the formula for the partial correlation coefficient on page 368.)

10. Use the results of Exercise 6 on page 363 to calculate
(a) the partial correlation coefficient for weight loss and dosage when the length of treatment is held fixed;
(b) the partial correlation coefficient for weight loss and length of treatment when the dosage is held fixed.

15.6 Technical Note (The Calculation of *r* for Grouped Data)

To illustrate the steps required to group paired data and to calculate the coefficient of correlation on the basis of the resulting *two-way frequency table*, let us consider the following data on the scores obtained by 88 cadets firing at a target from a kneeling position, x, and from a standing position, y:

x	y	x	y	x	y	x	y
81	83	81	76	94	86	77	83
93	88	96	81	86	76	97	86
76	78	86	91	91	90	83	78
86	83	91	76	85	87	86	89
99	94	90	81	93	84	98	91
98	87	87	85	83	87	93	82
82	77	90	89	83	81	88	78
92	94	98	91	99	97	90	93
95	94	94	94	90	96	97	92
98	84	75	76	96	86	89	87
91	83	88	88	85	84	88	92
91	98	94	91	96	90	92	81
92	80	93	78	82	79	97	86
96	88	99	89	93	82	84	82
79	77	91	84	89	77	99	83
87	80	89	93	91	85	88	80
98	85	88	81	90	81	90	92
93	87	95	88	94	80	78	75
92	83	87	79	85	76	88	86
84	75	92	88	97	98	81	76
86	82	97	80	89	83	98	87
89	85	87	94	94	88	94	84

The problems we must face when grouping paired data are almost identical with the ones we met in the construction of ordinary frequency distributions. *We must decide how many classes to use for each variable and from where to where each class is to go.* Choosing the *five* classes 75–79, 80–84, 85–89, 90–94, and 95–99 for each of the two kinds of scores, we obtain the following *two-way table:*

		x				
		75 – 79	80 – 84	85 – 89	90 – 94	95 – 99
	75 – 79					
	80 – 84					
y	85 – 89					
	90 – 94					
	95 – 99					

The next step is to tally the data; for instance, $x = 81$ and $y = 83$ goes into the cell belonging to the second row and second column, $x = 93$ and $y = 88$

goes into the cell belonging to the third row and fourth column, and $x = 76$ and $y = 78$ goes into the cell belonging to the first row and first column. After counting the number of checks in each cell, we obtain the following *two-way frequency distribution:*

		x				
		75 – 79	80 – 84	85 – 89	90 – 94	95 – 99
	75 – 79	4	6	5	2	
	80 – 84	1	3	7	12	4
y	85 – 89		1	7	7	9
	90 – 94			4	6	6
	95 – 99				2	2

Graphically, such a two-way distribution may be represented by a *three-dimensional histogram* like the one shown in Figure 15.7. Here the *heights* of the blocks represent the frequencies of the cells on which they stand just as

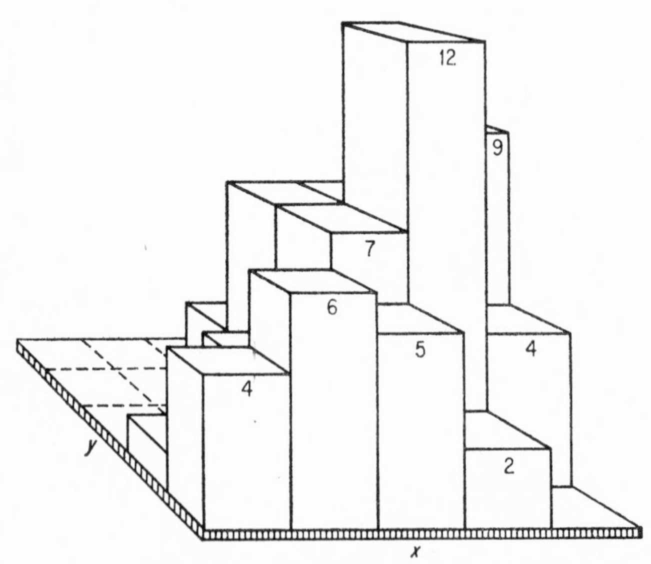

Fig. 15.7 Three-dimensional histogram.

the heights of the rectangles of an ordinary histogram represent the individual class frequencies.

In order to calculate r from a two-way frequency table, we shall have to assume (as in the case of the mean and the standard deviation) that all measurements within a class (cell) are located at the class marks; for instance, we assume that the four "data points" which belong to the first row and the first column of the table are all $x = 77$ and $y = 77$. Similarly, we assume that the 12 "data points" belonging to the second row and fourth column are all $x = 92$ and $y = 82$. If the class intervals of x and y, respectively, are all equal, we can now perform the same kind of *coding* (change of scale) as in Chapters 3 and 4; that is, we can replace the x-scale by a u-scale and the y-scale by a v-scale, numbering successive class marks, . . ., $-3, 2, -1, 0, 1, 2, 3, \ldots$. As before, the choice of the zero of the coded scales is arbitrary, but assigning it in each case to the middle class we get

		u-scale				
		−2	−1	0	1	2
	−2	4	6	5	2	
	−1	1	3	7	12	4
v-scale	0		1	7	7	9
	1			4	6	6
	2				2	2

As we pointed out on page 357, the coefficient of correlation is not affected if we add a constant to all the x's or all the y's or if we multiply all the x's or all the y's by positive constants. *This implies that if we calculate r in terms of the u's and v's, we will get the same result as if we had used the class marks in the original scales.* Thus, substituting u's and v's for the x's and y's in the computing formula for r and allowing for the fact that we are now dealing with grouped data, *the formula for r for grouped data* becomes

▲ $$r = \frac{n(\Sigma\, uvf) - (\Sigma\, uf_u)(\Sigma\, vf_v)}{\sqrt{n(\Sigma\, u^2f_u) - (\Sigma\, uf_u)^2}\,\sqrt{n(\Sigma\, v^2f_v) - (\Sigma\, vf_v)^2}}$$ ▲

The quantities which are needed for the calculation of r for grouped data may be obtained by arranging the calculations as in the following table:

						(1) v	(2) f_v	(3) vf_v	(4) v^2f_v	(5) uvf
	4	6	5	2		−2	17	−34	68	24
	1	3	7	12	4	−1	27	−27	27	−15
		1	7	7	9	0	24	0	0	0
			4	6	6	1	16	16	16	18
				2	2	2	4	8	16	12
(6) u	−2	−1	0	1	2		88	−37	127	39
(7) f_u	5	10	23	29	21	88				
(8) uf_u	−10	−10	0	29	42	51				
(9) u^2f_u	20	10	0	29	84	143				
(10) uvf	18	15	0	−6	12	39				

To simplify the over-all appearance of this table, we put the u- and v-scales at the bottom and at the right-hand side, labeling them row (6) and column (1), respectively. Column (2) contains the frequencies f_v, the number of times each v occurs, and they are obtained by adding the frequencies in the respective rows. Column (3) contains the products vf_v, which are obtained by multiplying the corresponding entries of columns (1) and (2), and column (4) contains the products v^2f_v, which may be obtained by either squaring each entry of column (1) and multiplying by the corresponding entry of column (2) *or* by multiplying the corresponding entries of columns (1) and (3). The numbers shown in rows (7), (8), and (9) are obtained by performing the identical operations on the u's and f_u's.

The totals of columns (2), (3), and (4) provide n, $\Sigma\, vf_v$, and $\Sigma\, v^2f_v$, while the totals of rows (7), (8), and (9) provide n, $\Sigma\, uf_u$, and $\Sigma\, u^2f_u$. To calculate r we still lack $\Sigma\, uvf$, which stands for the sum of the quantities obtained by individually multiplying each cell frequency by the u and the v of the row and column to which it belongs. To simplify these calculations, we shall work on each row separately, first multiplying each cell frequency by the corresponding u and then multiplying the *sum* of these products by the corresponding v. For the *second* row we thus get

$$[1(-2) + 3(-1) + 7(0) + 12(1) + 4(2)](-1) = -15$$

for the *fourth* row we get

$$[4(0) + 6(1) + 6(2)](1) = 18$$

and these are the corresponding entries shown in column (5).

Interchanging the roles of u and v, we can also calculate $\Sigma\, uvf$ by working separately on each column, multiplying each cell frequency by the corresponding v, and then multiplying the *sum* of these products by the corresponding u. For the *fourth* column we would thus get

$$[2(-2) + 12(-1) + 7(0) + 6(1) + 2(2)](1) = -6$$

and this is the corresponding entry shown in row (10). Comparison of the totals of column (5) and row (10) provides a check on the calculations.

If we now substitute the totals of the appropriate rows and columns of the *correlation table* (as such a table is sometimes called) into the formula for r, we finally get

$$r = \frac{88(39) - (51)(-37)}{\sqrt{88(143) - (51)^2}\sqrt{88(127) - (-37)^2}} = 0.54$$

as a measure of the strength of the (linear) relationship between the scores obtained by the cadets while shooting from the two positions.

EXERCISES

1. In a study of the growth of saguaro cacti, an experiment was performed to determine how well the height of such cacti can be estimated from aerial photographs. The following are the heights of 40 saguaros (in inches) estimated from aerial photographs, x, and measured on the ground, y:

x	y	x	y
118	103	163	163
166	160	124	137
141	143	171	173
164	187	165	112
150	111	123	132
127	136	112	92
151	134	142	151
133	121	144	148
122	143	130	117
165	141	135	165
168	149	139	112
109	125	161	121
153	128	170	189
135	101	148	156
158	136	136	158
104	117	174	182
183	121	186	161
173	156	194	153
125	130	181	183
129	84	190	179

Group these data into a two-way table having the classes 100–119, 120–139, 140–159, 160–179, 180–199 for x and the additional class 80–99 for y. Calculate r from this table and test the null hypothesis of no correlation at the 0.05 level of significance.

2. The following are figures on the median income, x (in dollars), of female farm workers and the percentage of farm population, y, in a sample of 30 counties:

x	y	x	y	x	y
957	63	1,295	43	1,263	40
753	83	799	65	758	69
1,087	45	738	40	850	58
923	29	1,958	17	440	74
915	49	672	61	1,388	18
2,048	13	768	51	842	42
1,605	12	1,403	34	424	61
1,219	28	904	58	753	52
746	48	808	49	699	35
890	52	1,219	51	819	50

Group these data into a suitable two-way table and calculate r.

3. Calculate r for the following two-way table representing the heights and weights of 40 athletes:

		Height (inches)				
		60 – 63	64 – 67	68 – 71	72 – 75	76 – 79
Weight (pounds)	120 – 139	1	2	1		
	140 – 159	2	3	2	1	
	160 – 179	2	6	5	2	
	180 – 199		1	4	3	1
	200 – 219			1	2	1

4. Calculate r for the following two-way table representing the annual incomes and expenditures on clothing (both in dollars) of 250 families:

		Amount Spent on Clothing			
		200 – 399	400 – 599	600 – 799	800 – 999
Family Income	3,000 – 4,999	52	19	2	
	5,000 – 6,999	27	43	14	1
	7,000 – 8,999	12	29	16	5
	9,000 – 10,999	2	18	6	4

BIBLIOGRAPHY

A derivation of the computing formula for r may be found in many more advanced texts, for example, in

Richardson, C. H., *An Introduction to Statistical Analysis*. New York: Harcourt, Brace & World, Inc., 1944, Chap. 8.

A detailed treatment of multiple and partial correlation, theory as well as applications, is given in

Ezekiel, M., and Fox, K. A., *Methods of Correlation and Regression Analysis*, 3rd ed. New York: John Wiley & Sons, Inc., 1959.

Various kinds of spurious correlations are discussed in

Johnson, P. O., and Jackson, R. W., *Introduction to Statistical Methods*. Englewood Cliffs, N.J.: Prentice-Hall, Inc., 1953,

and a more theoretical treatment is given in

Simon, H. A., "Spurious Correlation: A Causal Interpretation," *Journal of the American Statistical Association*, Vol. 49 (1954), No. 267.

Statistical Tables

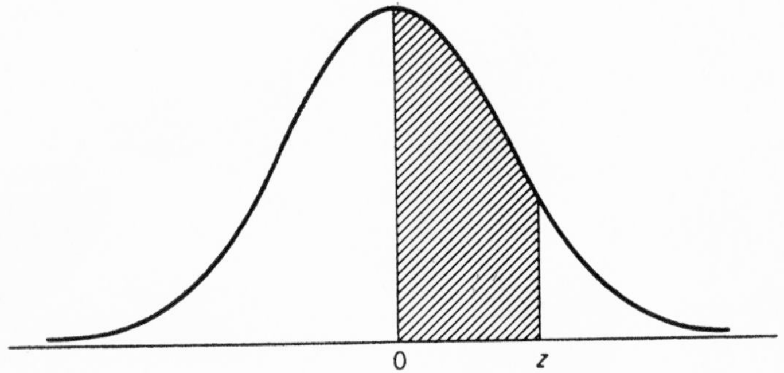

The entries in Table I are the probabilities that a random variable having the standard normal distribution assumes a value between 0 and z; they are given by the area under the curve shaded in the figure shown above.

Table I

THE STANDARD NORMAL DISTRIBUTION

z	.00	.01	.02	.03	.04	.05	.06	.07	.08	.09
0.0	.0000	.0040	.0080	.0120	.0160	.0199	.0239	.0279	.0319	.0359
0.1	.0398	.0438	.0478	.0517	.0557	.0596	.0636	.0675	.0714	.0753
0.2	.0793	.0832	.0871	.0910	.0948	.0987	.1026	.1064	.1103	.1141
0.3	.1179	.1217	.1255	.1293	.1331	.1368	.1406	.1443	.1480	.1517
0.4	.1554	.1591	.1628	.1664	.1700	.1736	.1772	.1808	.1844	.1879
0.5	.1915	.1950	.1985	.2019	.2054	.2088	.2123	.2157	.2190	.2224
0.6	.2257	.2291	.2324	.2357	.2389	.2422	.2454	.2486	.2517	.2549
0.7	.2580	.2611	.2642	.2673	.2704	.2734	.2764	.2794	.2823	.2852
0.8	.2881	.2910	.2939	.2967	.2995	.3023	.3051	.3078	.3106	.3133
0.9	.3159	.3186	.3212	.3238	.3264	.3289	.3315	.3340	.3365	.3389
1.0	.3413	.3438	.3461	.3485	.3508	.3531	.3554	.3577	.3599	.3621
1.1	.3643	.3665	.3686	.3708	.3729	.3749	.3770	.3790	.3810	.3830
1.2	.3849	.3869	.3888	.3907	.3925	.3944	.3962	.3980	.3997	.4015
1.3	.4032	.4049	.4066	.4082	.4099	.4115	.4131	.4147	.4162	.4177
1.4	.4192	.4207	.4222	.4236	.4251	.4265	.4279	.4292	.4306	.4319
1.5	.4332	.4345	.4357	.4370	.4382	.4394	.4406	.4418	.4429	.4441
1.6	.4452	.4463	.4474	.4484	.4495	.4505	.4515	.4525	.4535	.4545
1.7	.4554	.4564	.4573	.4582	.4591	.4599	.4608	.4616	.4625	.4633
1.8	.4641	.4649	.4656	.4664	.4671	.4678	.4686	.4693	.4699	.4706
1.9	.4713	.4719	.4726	.4732	.4738	.4744	.4750	.4756	.4761	.4767
2.0	.4772	.4778	.4783	.4788	.4793	.4798	.4803	.4808	.4812	.4817
2.1	.4821	.4826	.4830	.4834	.4838	.4842	.4846	.4850	.4854	.4857
2.2	.4861	.4864	.4868	.4871	.4875	.4878	.4881	.4884	.4887	.4890
2.3	.4893	.4896	.4898	.4901	.4904	.4906	.4909	.4911	.4913	.4916
2.4	.4918	.4920	.4922	.4925	.4927	.4929	.4931	.4932	.4934	.4936
2.5	.4938	.4940	.4941	.4943	.4945	.4946	.4948	.4949	.4951	.4952
2.6	.4953	.4955	.4956	.4957	.4959	.4960	.4961	.4962	.4963	.4964
2.7	.4965	.4966	.4967	.4968	.4969	.4970	.4971	.4972	.4973	.4974
2.8	.4974	.4975	.4976	.4977	.4977	.4978	.4979	.4979	.4980	.4981
2.9	.4981	.4982	.4982	.4983	.4984	.4984	.4985	.4985	.4986	.4986
3.0	.4987	.4987	.4987	.4988	.4988	.4989	.4989	.4989	.4990	.4990

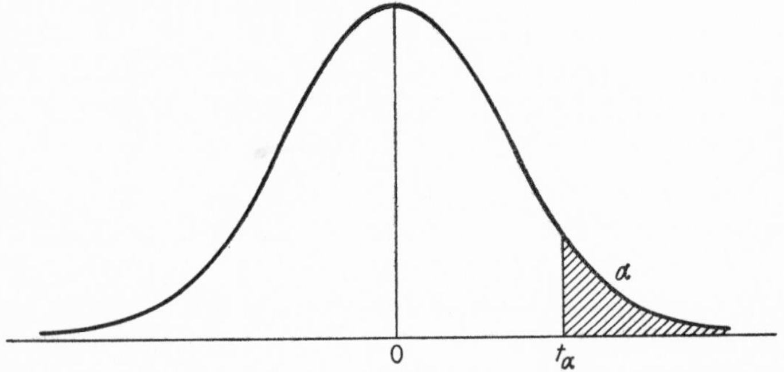

The entries in Table II are values for which the area to their right under the t distribution with given degrees of freedom (the area shaded in the figure shown above) is equal to α.

Table II

THE t DISTRIBUTION (VALUES OF t_α)*

d.f.	$t_{.100}$	$t_{.050}$	$t_{.025}$	$t_{.010}$	$t_{.005}$	*d.f.*
1	3.078	6.314	12.706	31.821	63.657	1
2	1.886	2.920	4.303	6.965	9.925	2
3	1.638	2.353	3.182	4.541	5.841	3
4	1.533	2.132	2.776	3.747	4.604	4
5	1.476	2.015	2.571	3.365	4.032	5
6	1.440	1.943	2.447	3.143	3.707	6
7	1.415	1.895	2.365	2.998	3.499	7
8	1.397	1.860	2.306	2.896	3.355	8
9	1.383	1.833	2.262	2.821	3.250	9
10	1.372	1.812	2.228	2.764	3.169	10
11	1.363	1.796	2.201	2.718	3.106	11
12	1.356	1.782	2.179	2.681	3.055	12
13	1.350	1.771	2.160	2.650	3.012	13
14	1.345	1.761	2.145	2.624	2.977	14
15	1.341	1.753	2.131	2.602	2.947	15
16	1.337	1.746	2.120	2.583	2.921	16
17	1.333	1.740	2.110	2.567	2.898	17
18	1.330	1.734	2.101	2.552	2.878	18
19	1.328	1.729	2.093	2.539	2.861	19
20	1.325	1.725	2.086	2.528	2.845	20
21	1.323	1.721	2.080	2.518	2.831	21
22	1.321	1.717	2.074	2.508	2.819	22
23	1.319	1.714	2.069	2.500	2.807	23
24	1.318	1.711	2.064	2.492	2.797	24
25	1.316	1.708	2.060	2.485	2.787	25
26	1.315	1.706	2.056	2.479	2.779	26
27	1.314	1.703	2.052	2.473	2.771	27
28	1.313	1.701	2.048	2.467	2.763	28
29	1.311	1.699	2.045	2.462	2.756	29
inf.	1.282	1.645	1.960	2.326	2.576	inf.

*This table is abridged from Table IV of R. A. Fisher, *Statistical Methods for Research Workers*, published by Oliver and Boyd, Ltd., Edinburgh, by permission of the author's literary executor and publiphers.

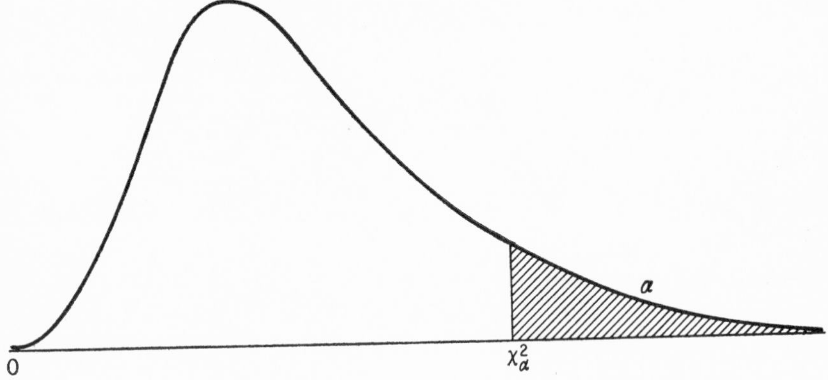

The entries in Table III are values for which the area to their right under the chi-square distribution with given degrees of freedom (the area shaded in the figure shown above) is equal to α.

Table III

THE CHI-SQUARE DISTRIBUTION (VALUES OF χ^2_α)*

d.f.	$\chi^2_{.995}$	$\chi^2_{.99}$	$\chi^2_{.975}$	$\chi^2_{.95}$	$\chi^2_{.05}$	$\chi^2_{.025}$	$\chi^2_{.01}$	$\chi^2_{.005}$	d.f.
1	.0000393	.000157	.000982	.00393	3.841	5.024	6.635	7.879	1
2	.0100	.0201	.0506	.103	5.991	7.378	9.210	10.597	2
3	.0717	.115	.216	.352	7.815	9.348	11.345	12.838	3
4	.207	.297	.484	.711	9.488	11.143	13.277	14.860	4
5	.412	.554	.831	1.145	11.070	12.832	15.086	16.750	5
6	.676	.872	1.237	1.635	12.592	14.449	16.812	18.548	6
7	.989	1.239	1.690	2.167	14.067	16.013	18.475	20.278	7
8	1.344	1.646	2.180	2.733	15.507	17.535	20.090	21.955	8
9	1.735	2.088	2.700	3.325	16.919	19.023	21.666	23.589	9
10	2.156	2.558	3.247	3.940	18.307	20.483	23.209	25.188	10
11	2.603	3.053	3.816	4.575	19.675	21.920	24.725	26.757	11
12	3.074	3.571	4.404	5.226	21.026	23.337	26.217	28.300	12
13	3.565	4.107	5.009	5.892	22.362	24.736	27.688	29.819	13
14	4.075	4.660	5.629	6.571	23.685	26.119	29.141	31.319	14
15	4.601	5.229	6.262	7.261	24.996	27.488	30.578	32.801	15
16	5.142	5.812	6.908	7.962	26.296	28.845	32.000	34.267	16
17	5.697	6.408	7.564	8.672	27.587	30.191	33.409	35.718	17
18	6.265	7.015	8.231	9.390	28.869	31.526	34.805	37.156	18
19	6.844	7.633	8.907	10.117	30.144	32.852	36.191	38.582	19
20	7.434	8.260	9.591	10.851	31.410	34.170	37.566	39.997	20
21	8.034	8.897	10.283	11.591	32.671	35.479	38.932	41.401	21
22	8.643	9.542	10.982	12.338	33.924	36.781	40.289	42.796	22
23	9.260	10.196	11.689	13.091	35.172	38.076	41.638	44.181	23
24	9.886	10.856	12.401	13.848	36.415	39.364	42.980	45.558	24
25	10.520	11.524	13.120	14.611	37.652	40.646	44.314	46.928	25
26	11.160	12.198	13.844	15.379	38.885	41.923	45.642	48.290	26
27	11.808	12.879	14.573	16.151	40.113	43.194	46.963	49.645	27
28	12.461	13.565	15.308	16.928	41.337	44.461	48.278	50.993	28
29	13.121	14.256	16.047	17.708	42.557	45.722	49.588	52.336	29
30	13.787	14.953	16.791	18.493	43.773	46.979	50.892	53.672	30

* This table is based on Table 8 of *Biometrika Tables for Statisticians, Volume I*, by permission of the *Biometrika* trustees.

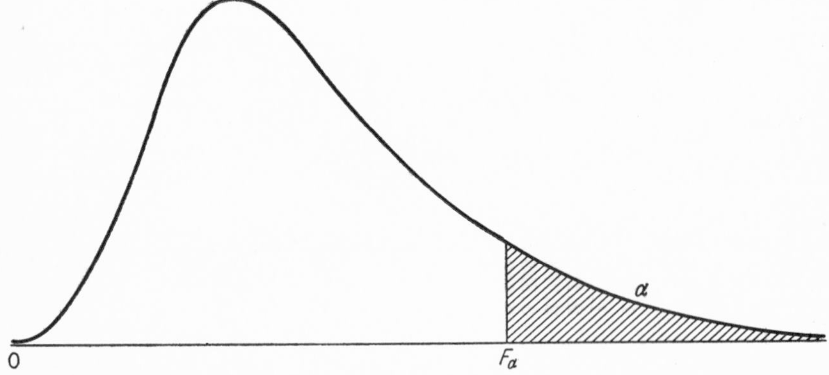

The entries in Tables IVa and IVb are values for which the area to their right under the F distribution with given degrees of freedom (the area shaded in the figure shown above) is equal to α.

Table IVa

THE F DISTRIBUTION (VALUES OF $F_{.05}$)*

Degrees of freedom for numerator

Degrees of freedom for numerator	1	2	3	4	5	6	7	8	9	10	12	15	20	24	30	40	60	120	∞
1	161	200	216	225	230	234	237	239	241	242	244	246	248	249	250	251	252	253	254
2	18.5	19.0	19.2	19.2	19.3	19.3	19.4	19.4	19.4	19.4	19.4	19.4	19.4	19.5	19.5	19.5	19.5	19.5	19.5
3	10.1	9.55	9.28	9.12	9.01	8.94	8.89	8.85	8.81	8.79	8.74	8.70	8.66	8.64	8.62	8.59	8.57	8.55	8.53
4	7.71	6.94	6.59	6.39	6.26	6.16	6.09	6.04	6.00	5.96	5.91	5.86	5.80	5.77	5.75	5.72	5.69	5.66	5.63
5	6.61	5.79	5.41	5.19	5.05	4.95	4.88	4.82	4.77	4.74	4.68	4.62	4.56	4.53	4.50	4.46	4.43	4.40	4.37
6	5.99	5.14	4.76	4.53	4.39	4.28	4.21	4.15	4.10	4.06	4.00	3.94	3.87	3.84	3.81	3.77	3.74	3.70	3.67
7	5.59	4.74	4.35	4.12	3.97	3.87	3.79	3.73	3.68	3.64	3.57	3.51	3.44	3.41	3.38	3.34	3.30	3.27	3.23
8	5.32	4.46	4.07	3.84	3.69	3.58	3.50	3.44	3.39	3.35	3.28	3.22	3.15	3.12	3.08	3.04	3.01	2.97	2.93
9	5.12	4.26	3.86	3.63	3.48	3.37	3.29	3.23	3.18	3.14	3.07	3.01	2.94	2.90	2.86	2.83	2.79	2.75	2.71
10	4.96	4.10	3.71	3.48	3.33	3.22	3.14	3.07	3.02	2.98	2.91	2.85	2.77	2.74	2.70	2.66	2.62	2.58	2.54
11	4.84	3.98	3.59	3.36	3.20	3.09	3.01	2.95	2.90	2.85	2.79	2.72	2.65	2.61	2.57	2.53	2.49	2.45	2.40
12	4.75	3.89	3.49	3.26	3.11	3.00	2.91	2.85	2.80	2.75	2.69	2.62	2.54	2.51	2.47	2.43	2.38	2.34	2.30
13	4.67	3.81	3.41	3.18	3.03	2.92	2.83	2.77	2.71	2.67	2.60	2.53	2.46	2.42	2.38	2.34	2.30	2.25	2.21
14	4.60	3.74	3.34	3.11	2.96	2.85	2.76	2.70	2.65	2.60	2.53	2.46	2.39	2.35	2.31	2.27	2.22	2.18	2.13
15	4.54	3.68	3.29	3.06	2.90	2.79	2.71	2.64	2.59	2.54	2.48	2.40	2.33	2.29	2.25	2.20	2.16	2.11	2.07
16	4.49	3.63	3.24	3.01	2.85	2.74	2.66	2.59	2.54	2.49	2.42	2.35	2.28	2.24	2.19	2.15	2.11	2.06	2.01
17	4.45	3.59	3.20	2.96	2.81	2.70	2.61	2.55	2.49	2.45	2.38	2.31	2.23	2.19	2.15	2.10	2.06	2.01	1.96
18	4.41	3.55	3.16	2.93	2.77	2.66	2.58	2.51	2.46	2.41	2.34	2.27	2.19	2.15	2.11	2.06	2.02	1.97	1.92
19	4.38	3.52	3.13	2.90	2.74	2.63	2.54	2.48	2.42	2.38	2.31	2.23	2.16	2.11	2.07	2.03	1.98	1.93	1.88
20	4.35	3.49	3.10	2.87	2.71	2.60	2.51	2.45	2.39	2.35	2.28	2.20	2.12	2.08	2.04	1.99	1.95	1.90	1.84
21	4.32	3.47	3.07	2.84	2.68	2.57	2.49	2.42	2.37	2.32	2.25	2.18	2.10	2.05	2.01	1.96	1.92	1.87	1.81
22	4.30	3.44	3.05	2.82	2.66	2.55	2.46	2.40	2.34	2.30	2.23	2.15	2.07	2.03	1.98	1.94	1.89	1.84	1.78
23	4.28	3.42	3.03	2.80	2.64	2.53	2.44	2.37	2.32	2.27	2.20	2.13	2.05	2.01	1.96	1.91	1.86	1.81	1.76
24	4.26	3.40	3.01	2.78	2.62	2.51	2.42	2.36	2.30	2.25	2.18	2.11	2.03	1.98	1.94	1.89	1.84	1.79	1.73
25	4.24	3.39	2.99	2.76	2.60	2.49	2.40	2.34	2.28	2.24	2.16	2.09	2.01	1.96	1.92	1.87	1.82	1.77	1.71
30	4.17	3.32	2.92	2.69	2.53	2.42	2.33	2.27	2.21	2.16	2.09	2.01	1.93	1.89	1.84	1.79	1.74	1.68	1.62
40	4.08	3.23	2.84	2.61	2.45	2.34	2.25	2.18	2.12	2.08	2.00	1.92	1.84	1.79	1.74	1.69	1.64	1.58	1.51
60	4.00	3.15	2.76	2.53	2.37	2.25	2.17	2.10	2.04	1.99	1.92	1.84	1.75	1.70	1.65	1.59	1.53	1.47	1.39
120	3.92	3.07	2.68	2.45	2.29	2.18	2.09	2.02	1.96	1.91	1.83	1.75	1.66	1.61	1.55	1.50	1.43	1.35	1.25
∞	3.84	3.00	2.60	2.37	2.21	2.10	2.01	1.94	1.88	1.83	1.75	1.67	1.57	1.52	1.46	1.39	1.32	1.22	1.00

*This table is reproduced from M. Merrington and C. M. Thompson, "Tables of percentage points of the inverted beta (F) distribution," *Biometrika*, vol. 33 (1943), by permission of the *Biometrika* trustees.

Table IVb

THE F DISTRIBUTION (VALUES OF $F_{.01}$)*

Degrees of freedom for numerator

Degrees of freedom for numerator	1	2	3	4	5	6	7	8	9	10	12	15	20	24	30	40	60	120	∞
1	4,052	5,000	5,403	5,625	5,764	5,859	5,928	5,982	6,023	6,056	6,106	6,157	6,209	6,235	6,261	6,287	6,313	6,339	6,366
2	98.5	99.0	99.2	99.2	99.3	99.3	99.4	99.4	99.4	99.4	99.4	99.4	99.4	99.5	99.5	99.5	99.5	99.5	99.5
3	34.1	30.8	29.5	28.7	28.2	27.9	27.7	27.5	27.3	27.2	27.1	26.9	26.7	26.6	26.5	26.4	26.3	26.2	26.1
4	21.2	18.0	16.7	16.0	15.5	15.2	15.0	14.8	14.7	14.5	14.4	14.2	14.0	13.9	13.8	13.7	13.7	13.6	13.5
5	16.3	13.3	12.1	11.4	11.0	10.7	10.5	10.3	10.2	10.1	9.89	9.72	9.55	9.47	9.38	9.29	9.20	9.11	9.02
6	13.7	10.9	9.78	9.15	8.75	8.47	8.26	8.10	7.98	7.87	7.72	7.56	7.40	7.31	7.23	7.14	7.06	6.97	6.88
7	12.2	9.55	8.45	7.85	7.46	7.19	6.99	6.84	6.72	6.62	6.47	6.31	6.16	6.07	5.99	5.91	5.82	5.74	5.65
8	11.3	8.65	7.59	7.01	6.63	6.37	6.18	6.03	5.91	5.81	5.67	5.52	5.36	5.28	5.20	5.12	5.03	4.95	4.86
9	10.6	8.02	6.99	6.42	6.06	5.80	5.61	5.47	5.35	5.26	5.11	4.96	4.81	4.73	4.65	4.57	4.48	4.40	4.31
10	10.0	7.56	6.55	5.99	5.64	5.39	5.20	5.06	4.94	4.85	4.71	4.56	4.41	4.33	4.25	4.17	4.08	4.00	3.91
11	9.65	7.21	6.22	5.67	5.32	5.07	4.89	4.74	4.63	4.54	4.40	4.25	4.10	4.02	3.94	3.86	3.78	3.69	3.60
12	9.33	6.93	5.95	5.41	5.06	4.82	4.64	4.50	4.39	4.30	4.16	4.01	3.86	3.78	3.70	3.62	3.54	3.45	3.36
13	9.07	6.70	5.74	5.21	4.86	4.62	4.44	4.30	4.19	4.10	3.96	3.82	3.66	3.59	3.51	3.43	3.34	3.25	3.17
14	8.86	6.51	5.56	5.04	4.70	4.46	4.28	4.14	4.03	3.94	3.80	3.66	3.51	3.43	3.35	3.27	3.18	3.09	3.00
15	8.68	6.36	5.42	4.89	4.56	4.32	4.14	4.00	3.89	3.80	3.67	3.52	3.37	3.29	3.21	3.13	3.05	2.96	2.87
16	8.53	6.23	5.29	4.77	4.44	4.20	4.03	3.89	3.78	3.69	3.55	3.41	3.26	3.18	3.10	3.02	2.93	2.84	2.75
17	8.40	6.11	5.19	4.67	4.34	4.10	3.93	3.79	3.68	3.59	3.46	3.31	3.16	3.08	3.00	2.92	2.83	2.75	2.65
18	8.29	6.01	5.09	4.58	4.25	4.01	3.84	3.71	3.60	3.51	3.37	3.23	3.08	3.00	2.92	2.84	2.75	2.66	2.57
19	8.19	5.93	5.01	4.50	4.17	3.94	3.77	3.63	3.52	3.43	3.30	3.15	3.00	2.92	2.84	2.76	2.67	2.58	2.49
20	8.10	5.85	4.94	4.43	4.10	3.87	3.70	3.56	3.46	3.37	3.23	3.09	2.94	2.86	2.78	2.69	2.61	2.52	2.42
21	8.02	5.78	4.87	4.37	4.04	3.81	3.64	3.51	3.40	3.31	3.17	3.03	2.88	2.80	2.72	2.64	2.55	2.46	2.36
22	7.95	5.72	4.82	4.31	3.99	3.76	3.59	3.45	3.35	3.26	3.12	2.98	2.83	2.75	2.67	2.58	2.50	2.40	2.31
23	7.88	5.66	4.76	4.26	3.94	3.71	3.54	3.41	3.30	3.21	3.07	2.93	2.78	2.70	2.62	2.54	2.45	2.35	2.26
24	7.82	5.61	4.72	4.22	3.90	3.67	3.50	3.36	3.26	3.17	3.03	2.89	2.74	2.66	2.58	2.49	2.40	2.31	2.21
25	7.77	5.57	4.68	4.18	3.86	3.63	3.46	3.32	3.22	3.13	2.99	2.85	2.70	2.62	2.53	2.45	2.36	2.27	2.17
30	7.56	5.39	4.51	4.02	3.70	3.47	3.30	3.17	3.07	2.98	2.84	2.70	2.55	2.47	2.39	2.30	2.21	2.11	2.01
40	7.31	5.18	4.31	3.83	3.51	3.29	3.12	2.99	2.89	2.80	2.66	2.52	2.37	2.29	2.20	2.11	2.02	1.92	1.80
60	7.08	4.98	4.13	3.65	3.34	3.12	2.95	2.82	2.72	2.63	2.50	2.35	2.20	2.12	2.03	1.94	1.84	1.73	1.60
120	6.85	4.79	3.95	3.48	3.17	2.96	2.79	2.66	2.56	2.47	2.34	2.19	2.03	1.95	1.86	1.76	1.66	1.53	1.38
∞	6.63	4.61	3.78	3.32	3.02	2.80	2.64	2.51	2.41	2.32	2.18	2.04	1.88	1.79	1.70	1.59	1.47	1.32	1.00

*This table is reproduced from M. Merrington and C. M. Thompson, "Tables of percentage points of the inverted beta (F) distribution," *Biometrika*, vol. 33 (1943), by permission of the *Biometrika* trustees.

Table Va

0.95 CONFIDENCE INTERVALS FOR PROPORTIONS*

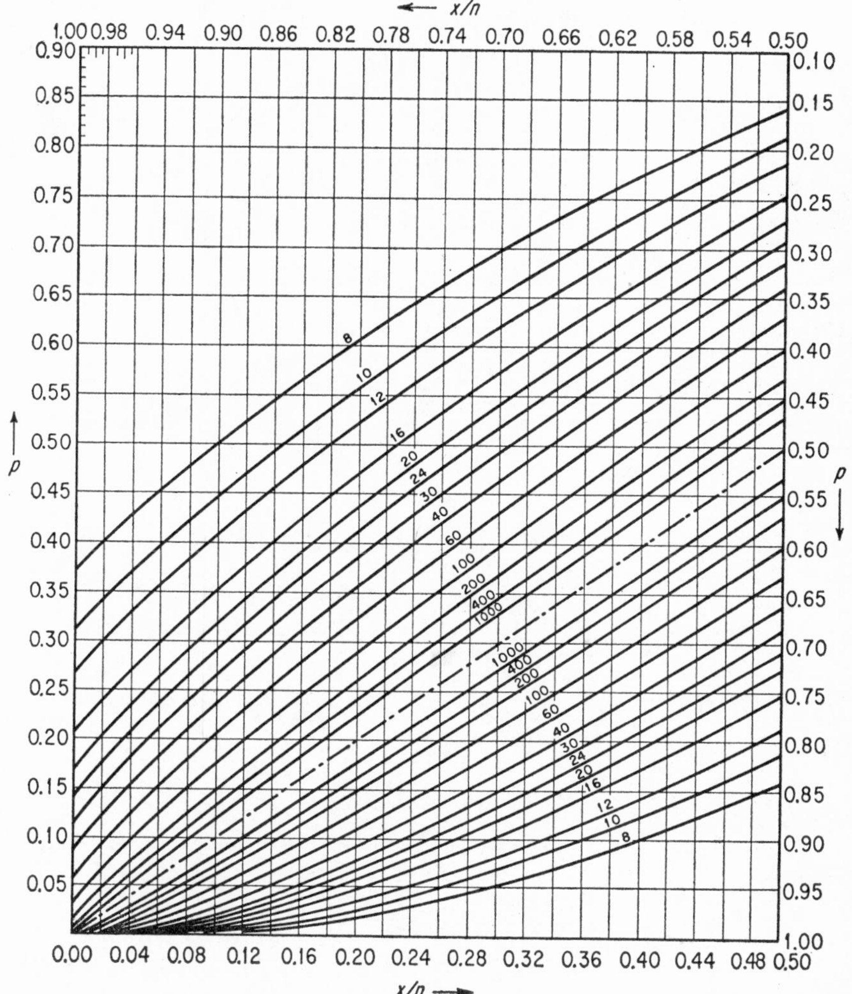

* This table is reproduced from Table 41 of the *Biometrika Tables for Statisticians*, Vol. I (New York: Cambridge University Press, 1954) by permission of the *Biometrika* trustees.

Table Vb

0.99 CONFIDENCE INTERVALS FOR PROPORTIONS*

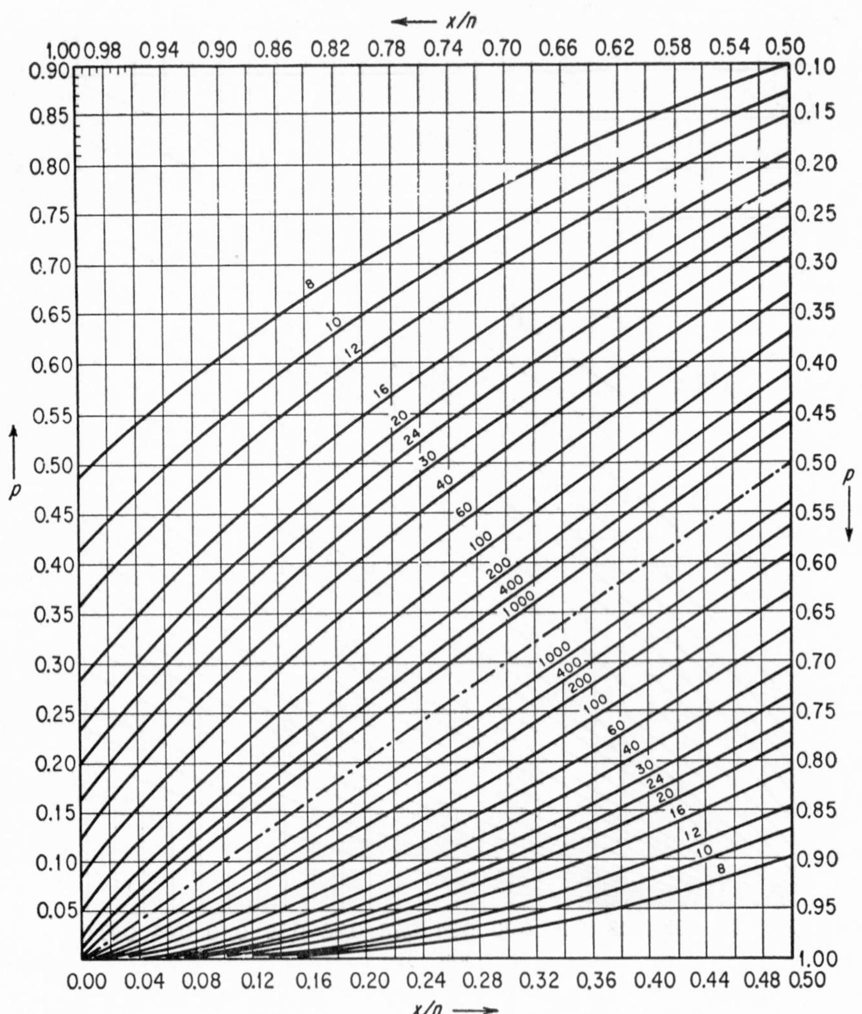

* This table is reproduced from Table 41 of the *Biometrika Tables for Statisticians*, Vol. I. (New York: Cambridge University Press, 1954) by permission of the *Biometrika* trustees.

Table VI

CRITICAL VALUES OF r

n	$r_{.025}$	$r_{.010}$	$r_{.005}$	n	$r_{.025}$	$r_{.010}$	$r_{.005}$
3	0.997			18	0.468	0.543	0.590
4	0.950	0.990	0.999	19	0.456	0.529	0.575
5	0.878	0.934	0.959	20	0.444	0.516	0.561
6	0.811	0.882	0.917	21	0.433	0.503	0.549
7	0.754	0.833	0.875	22	0.423	0.492	0.537
8	0.707	0.789	0.834	27	0.381	0.445	0.487
9	0.666	0.750	0.798	32	0.349	0.409	0.449
10	0.632	0.715	0.765	37	0.325	0.381	0.418
11	0.602	0.685	0.735	42	0.304	0.358	0.393
12	0.576	0.658	0.708	47	0.288	0.338	0.372
13	0.553	0.634	0.684	52	0.273	0.322	0.354
14	0.532	0.612	0.661	62	0.250	0.295	0.325
15	0.514	0.592	0.641	72	0.232	0.274	0.302
16	0.497	0.574	0.623	82	0.217	0.256	0.283
17	0.482	0.558	0.606	92	0.205	0.242	0.267

* This table is abridged from Table VI of R. A. Fisher and F. Yates, *Statistical Tables for Biological, Agricultural, and Medical Research,* published by Oliver and Boyd, Ltd , Edinburgh, by permission of the author's literary executor and publishers.

Table VII

BINOMIAL COEFFICIENTS

n	$\binom{n}{0}$	$\binom{n}{1}$	$\binom{n}{2}$	$\binom{n}{3}$	$\binom{n}{4}$	$\binom{n}{5}$	$\binom{n}{6}$	$\binom{n}{7}$	$\binom{n}{8}$	$\binom{n}{9}$	$\binom{n}{10}$
0	1										
1	1	1									
2	1	2	1								
3	1	3	3	1							
4	1	4	6	4	1						
5	1	5	10	10	5	1					
6	1	6	15	20	15	6	1				
7	1	7	21	35	35	21	7	1			
8	1	8	28	56	70	56	28	8	1		
9	1	9	36	84	126	126	84	36	9	1	
10	1	10	45	120	210	252	210	120	45	10	1
11	1	11	55	165	330	462	462	330	165	55	11
12	1	12	66	220	495	792	924	792	495	220	66
13	1	13	78	286	715	1287	1716	1716	1287	715	286
14	1	14	91	364	1001	2002	3003	3432	3003	2002	1001
15	1	15	105	455	1365	3003	5005	6435	6435	5005	3003
16	1	16	120	560	1820	4368	8008	11440	12870	11440	8008
17	1	17	136	680	2380	6188	12376	19448	24310	24310	19448
18	1	18	153	816	3060	8568	18564	31824	43758	48620	43758
19	1	19	171	969	3876	11628	27132	50388	75582	92378	92378
20	1	20	190	1140	4845	15504	38760	77520	125970	167960	184756

For $k > 10$ it may be necessary to make use of the identity $\binom{n}{k} = \binom{n}{n-k}$.

Table VIII

RANDOM NUMBERS*

04433	80674	24520	18222	10610	05794	37515
60298	47829	72648	37414	75755	04717	29899
67884	59651	67533	68123	17730	95862	08034
89512	32155	51906	61662	64130	16688	37275
32653	01895	12506	88535	36553	23757	34209
95913	15405	13772	76638	48423	25018	99041
55864	21694	13122	44115	01601	50541	00147
35334	49810	91601	40617	72876	33967	73830
57729	32196	76487	11622	96297	24160	09903
86648	13697	63677	70119	94739	25875	38829
30574	47609	07967	32422	76791	39725	53711
81307	43694	83580	79974	45929	85113	72268
02410	54905	79007	54939	21410	86980	91772
18969	75274	52233	62319	08598	09066	95288
87863	82384	66860	62297	80198	19347	73234
68397	71708	15438	62311	72844	60203	46412
28529	54447	58729	10854	99058	18260	38765
44285	06372	15867	70418	57012	72122	36634
86299	83430	33571	23309	57040	29285	67870
84842	68668	90894	61658	15001	94055	36308
56970	83609	52098	04184	54967	72938	56834
83125	71257	60490	44369	66130	72936	69848
55503	52423	02464	26141	68779	66388	75242
47019	76273	33203	29608	54553	25971	69573
84828	32592	79526	29554	84580	37859	28504
68921	08141	79227	05748	51276	57143	31926
36458	96045	30424	98420	72925	40729	22337
95752	59445	36847	87729	81679	59126	59437
26768	47323	58454	56958	20575	76746	49878
42613	37056	43636	58085	06766	60227	96414
95457	30566	65482	25596	02678	54592	63607
95276	17894	63564	95958	39750	64379	46059
66954	52324	64776	92345	95110	59448	77249
17457	18481	14113	62462	02798	54977	48349
03704	36872	83214	59337	01695	60666	97410
21538	86497	33210	60337	27976	70661	08250
57178	67619	98310	70348	11317	71623	55510
31048	97558	94953	55866	96283	46620	52087
69799	55380	16498	80733	96422	58078	99643
90595	61867	59231	17772	67831	33317	00520
33570	04981	98939	78784	09977	29398	93896
15340	93460	57477	13898	48431	72936	78160
64079	42483	36512	56186	99098	48850	72527
63491	05546	67118	62063	74958	20946	28147
92003	63868	41034	28260	79708	00770	88643
52360	46658	66511	04172	73085	11795	52594
74622	12142	68355	65635	21828	39539	18988
04157	50079	61343	64315	70836	82857	35335
86003	60070	66241	32836	27573	11479	94114
41268	80187	20351	09636	84668	42486	71303

* Based on parts of *Table of 105,000 Random Decimal Digits*, Interstate Commerce Commission, Bureau of Transport Economics and Statistics, Washington, D.C.

Table VIII

RANDOM NUMBERS (*Continued*)

48611	62866	33963	14045	79451	04934	45576
78812	03509	78673	73181	29973	18664	04555
19472	63971	37271	31445	49019	49405	46925
51266	11569	08697	91120	64156	40365	74297
55806	96275	26130	47949	14877	69594	83041
77527	81360	18180	97421	55541	90275	18213
77680	58788	33016	61173	93049	04694	43534
15404	96554	88265	34537	38526	67924	40474
14045	22917	60718	66487	46346	30949	03173
68376	43918	77653	04127	69930	43283	35766
93385	13421	67957	20384	58731	53396	59723
09858	52104	32014	53115	03727	98624	84616
93307	34116	49516	42148	57740	31198	70336
04794	01534	92058	03157	91758	80611	45357
86265	49096	97021	92582	61422	75890	86442
65943	79232	45702	67055	39024	57383	44424
90038	94209	04055	27393	61517	23002	96560
97283	95943	78363	36498	40662	94188	18202
21913	72958	75637	99936	58715	07943	23748
41161	37341	81838	19389	80336	46346	91895
23777	98392	31417	98547	92058	02277	50315
59973	08144	61070	73094	27059	69181	55623
82690	74099	77885	23813	10054	11900	44653
83854	24715	48866	65745	31131	47636	45137
61980	34997	41825	11623	07320	15003	56774
99915	45821	97702	87125	44488	77613	56823
48293	86847	43186	42951	37804	85129	28993
33225	31280	41232	34750	91097	60752	69783
06846	32828	24425	30249	78801	26977	92074
32671	45587	79620	84831	38156	74211	82752
82096	21913	75544	55228	89796	05694	91552
51666	10433	10945	55306	78562	89630	41230
54044	67942	24145	42294	27427	84875	37022
66738	60184	75679	38120	17640	36242	99357
55064	17427	89180	74018	44865	53197	74810
69599	60264	84549	78007	88450	06488	72274
64756	87759	92354	78694	63638	80939	98644
80817	74533	68407	55862	32476	19326	95558
39847	96884	84657	33697	39578	90197	80532
90401	41700	95510	61166	33757	23279	85523
78227	90110	81378	96659	37008	04050	04228
87240	52716	87697	79433	16336	52862	69149
08486	10951	26832	39763	02485	71688	90936
39338	32169	03713	93510	61244	73774	01245
21188	01850	69689	49426	49128	14660	14143
13287	82531	04388	64693	11934	35051	68576
53609	04001	19648	14053	49623	10840	31915
87900	36194	31567	53506	34304	39910	79630
81641	00496	36058	75899	46620	70024	88753
19512	50277	71508	20116	79520	06269	74173

Table VIII

RANDOM NUMBERS (*Continued*)

24418	23508	91507	76455	54941	72711	39406
57404	73678	08272	62941	02349	71389	45605
77644	98489	86268	73652	98210	44546	27174
68366	65614	01443	07607	11826	91326	29664
64472	72294	95432	53555	96810	17100	35066
88205	37913	98633	81009	81060	33449	68055
98455	78685	71250	10329	56135	80647	51404
48977	36794	56054	59243	57361	65304	93258
93077	72941	92779	23581	24548	56415	61927
84533	26564	91583	83411	66504	02036	02922
11338	12903	14514	27585	45068	05520	56321
23853	68500	92274	87026	99717	01542	72990
94096	74920	25822	98026	05394	61840	83089
83160	82362	09350	98536	38155	42661	02363
97425	47335	69709	01386	74319	04318	99387
83951	11954	24317	20345	18134	90062	10761
93085	35203	05740	03206	92012	42710	34650
33762	83193	58045	89880	78101	44392	53767
49665	85397	85137	30496	23469	42846	94810
37541	82627	80051	72521	35342	56119	97190
22145	85304	35348	82854	55846	18076	12415
27153	08662	61078	52433	22184	33998	87436
00301	49425	66682	25442	83668	66236	79655
43815	43272	73778	63469	50083	70696	13558
14689	86482	74157	46012	97765	27552	49617
16680	55936	82453	19532	49988	13176	94219
86938	60429	01137	86168	78257	86249	46134
33944	29219	73161	46061	30946	22210	79302
16045	67736	18608	18198	19468	76358	69203
37044	52523	25627	63107	30806	80857	84383
61471	45322	35340	35132	42163	69332	98851
47422	21296	16785	66393	39249	51463	95963
24133	39719	14484	58613	88717	29289	77360
67253	67064	10748	16006	16767	57345	42285
62382	76941	01635	35829	77516	98468	51686
98011	16503	09201	03523	87192	66483	55649
37366	24386	20654	85117	74078	64120	04643
73587	83993	54176	05221	94119	20108	78101
33583	68291	50547	96085	62180	27453	18567
02878	33223	39199	49536	56199	05993	71201
91498	41673	17195	33175	04994	09879	70337
91127	19815	30219	55591	21725	43827	78862
12997	55013	18662	81724	24305	37661	18956
96098	13651	15393	69995	14762	69734	89150
97627	17837	10472	18983	28387	99781	52977
40064	47981	31484	76603	54088	91095	00010
16239	68743	71374	55863	22672	91609	51514
58354	24913	20435	30965	17453	65623	93058
52567	65085	60220	84641	18273	49604	47418
06236	29052	91392	07551	83532	68130	56970

Table VIII

RANDOM NUMBERS (*Continued*)

94620	27963	96478	21559	19246	88097	44926
60947	60775	73181	43264	56895	04232	59604
27499	53523	63110	57106	20865	91683	80688
01603	23156	89223	43429	95353	44662	59433
00815	01552	06392	31437	70385	45863	75971
83844	90942	74857	52419	68723	47830	63010
06626	10042	93629	37609	57215	08409	81906
56760	63348	24949	11859	29793	37457	59377
64416	29934	00755	09418	14230	62887	92683
63569	17906	38076	32135	19096	96970	75917
22693	35089	72994	04252	23791	60249	83010
43413	59744	01275	71326	91382	45114	20245
09224	78530	50566	49965	04851	18280	14039
67625	34683	03142	74733	63558	09665	22610
86874	12549	98699	54952	91579	26023	81076
54548	49505	62515	63903	13193	33905	66936
73236	66167	49728	03581	40699	10396	81827
15220	66319	13543	14071	59148	95154	72852
16151	08029	36954	03891	38313	34016	18671
43635	84249	88984	80993	55431	90793	62603
30193	42776	85611	57635	51362	79907	77364
37430	45246	11400	20986	43996	73122	88474
88312	93047	12088	86937	70794	01041	74867
98995	58159	04700	90443	13168	31553	67891
51734	20849	70198	67906	00880	82899	66065
88698	41755	56216	66852	17748	04963	54859
51865	09836	73966	65711	41699	11732	17173
40300	08852	27528	84648	79589	95295	72895
02760	28625	70476	76410	32988	10194	94917
78450	26245	91763	73117	33047	03577	62599
50252	56911	62693	73817	98693	18728	94741
07929	66728	47761	81472	44806	15592	71357
09030	39605	87507	85446	51257	89555	75520
56670	88445	85799	76200	21795	38894	58070
48140	13583	94911	13318	64741	64336	95103
36764	86132	12463	28385	94242	32063	45233
14351	71381	28133	68269	65145	28152	39087
81276	00835	63835	87174	42446	08882	27067
55524	86088	00069	59254	24654	77371	26409
78852	65889	32719	13758	23937	90740	16866
11861	69032	51915	23510	32050	52052	24004
67699	01009	07050	73324	06732	27510	33761
50064	39500	17450	18030	63124	48061	59412
93126	17700	94400	76075	08317	27324	72723
01657	92602	41043	05686	15650	29970	95877
13800	76690	75133	60456	28491	03845	11507
98135	42870	48578	29036	69876	86563	61729
08313	99293	00990	13595	77457	79969	11339
90974	83965	62732	85161	54330	22406	86253
33273	61993	88407	69399	17301	70975	99129

Table IX

LOGARITHMS

N	0	1	2	3	4	5	6	7	8	9
10	0000	0043	0086	0128	0170	0212	0253	0294	0334	0374
11	0414	0453	0492	0531	0569	0607	0645	0682	0719	0755
12	0792	0828	0864	0899	0934	0969	1004	1038	1072	1106
13	1139	1173	1206	1239	1271	1303	1335	1367	1399	1430
14	1461	1492	1523	1553	1584	1614	1644	1673	1703	1732
15	1761	1790	1818	1847	1875	1903	1931	1959	1987	2014
16	2041	2068	2095	2122	2148	2175	2201	2227	2253	2279
17	2304	2330	2355	2380	2405	2430	2455	2480	2504	2529
18	2553	2577	2601	2625	2648	2672	2695	2718	2742	2765
19	2788	2810	2833	2856	2878	2900	2923	2945	2967	2989
20	3010	3032	3054	3075	3096	3118	3139	3160	3181	3201
21	3222	3243	3263	3284	3304	3324	3345	3365	3385	3404
22	3424	3444	3464	3483	3502	3522	3541	3560	3579	3598
23	3617	3636	3655	3674	3692	3711	3729	3747	3766	3784
24	3802	3820	3838	3856	3874	3892	3909	3927	3945	3962
25	3979	3997	4014	4031	4048	4065	4082	4099	4116	4133
26	4150	4166	4183	4200	4216	4232	4249	4265	4281	4298
27	4314	4330	4346	4362	4378	4393	4409	4425	4440	4456
28	4472	4487	4502	4518	4533	4548	4564	4579	4594	4609
29	4624	4639	4654	4669	4683	4698	4713	4728	4742	4757
30	4771	4786	4800	4814	4829	4843	4857	4871	4886	4900
31	4914	4928	4942	4955	4969	4983	4997	5011	5024	5038
32	5051	5065	5079	5092	5105	5119	5132	5145	5159	5172
33	5185	5198	5211	5224	5237	5250	5263	5276	5289	5302
34	5315	5328	5340	5353	5366	5378	5391	5403	5416	5428
35	5441	5453	5465	5478	5490	5502	5514	5527	5539	5551
36	5563	5575	5587	5599	5611	5623	5635	5647	5658	5670
37	5682	5694	5705	5717	5729	5740	5752	5763	5775	5786
38	5798	5809	5821	5832	5843	5855	5866	5877	5888	5899
39	5911	5922	5933	5944	5955	5966	5977	5988	5999	6010
40	6021	6031	6042	6053	6064	6075	6085	6096	6107	6117
41	6128	6138	6149	6160	6170	6180	6191	6201	6212	6222
42	6232	6243	6253	6263	6274	6284	6294	6304	6314	6325
43	6335	6345	6355	6365	6375	6385	6395	6405	6415	6425
44	6435	6444	6454	6464	6474	6484	6493	6503	6513	6522
45	6532	6542	6551	6561	6571	6580	6590	6599	6609	6618
46	6628	6637	6646	6656	6665	6675	6684	6693	6702	6712
47	6721	6730	6739	6749	6758	6767	6776	6785	6794	6803
48	6812	6821	6830	6839	6848	6857	6866	6875	6884	6893
49	6902	6911	6920	6928	6937	6946	6955	6964	6972	6981
50	6990	6998	7007	7016	7024	7033	7042	7050	7059	7067
51	7076	7084	7093	7101	7110	7118	7126	7135	7143	7152
52	7160	7168	7177	7185	7193	7202	7210	7218	7226	7235
53	7243	7251	7259	7267	7275	7284	7292	7300	7308	7316
54	7324	7332	7340	7348	7356	7364	7372	7380	7388	7396

Table IX

LOGARITHMS (*Continued*)

N	0	1	2	3	4	5	6	7	8	9
55	7404	7412	7419	7427	7435	7443	7451	7459	7466	7474
56	7482	7490	7497	7505	7513	7520	7528	7536	7543	7551
57	7559	7566	7574	7582	7589	7597	7604	7612	7619	7627
58	7634	7642	7649	7657	7664	7672	7679	7686	7694	7701
59	7709	7716	7723	7731	7738	7745	7752	7760	7767	7774
60	7782	7789	7796	7803	7810	7818	7825	7832	7839	7846
61	7853	7860	7868	7875	7882	7889	7896	7903	7910	7917
62	7924	7931	7938	7945	7952	7959	7966	7973	7980	7987
63	7993	8000	8007	8014	8021	8028	8035	8041	8048	8055
64	8062	8069	8075	8082	8089	8096	8102	8109	8116	8122
65	8129	8136	8142	8149	8156	8162	8169	8176	8182	8189
66	8195	8202	8209	8215	8222	8228	8235	8241	8248	8254
67	8261	8267	8274	8280	8287	8293	8299	8306	8312	8319
68	8325	8331	8338	8344	8351	8357	8363	8370	8376	8382
69	8388	8395	8401	8407	8414	8420	8426	8432	8439	8445
70	8451	8457	8463	8470	8476	8482	8488	8494	8500	8506
71	8513	8519	8525	8531	8537	8543	8549	8555	8561	8567
72	8573	8579	8585	8591	8597	8603	8609	8615	8621	8627
73	8633	8639	8645	8651	8657	8663	8669	8675	8681	8686
74	8692	8698	8704	8710	8716	8722	8727	8733	8739	8745
75	8751	8756	8762	8768	8774	8779	8785	8791	8797	8802
76	8808	8814	8820	8825	8831	8837	8842	8848	8854	8859
77	8865	8871	8876	8882	8887	8893	8899	8904	8910	8915
78	8921	8927	8932	8938	8943	8949	8954	8960	8965	8971
79	8976	8982	8987	8993	8998	9004	9009	9015	9020	9025
80	9031	9036	9042	9047	9053	9058	9063	9069	9074	9079
81	9085	9090	9096	9101	9106	9112	9117	9122	9128	9133
82	9138	9143	9149	9154	9159	9165	9170	9175	9180	9186
83	9191	9196	9201	9206	9212	9217	9222	9227	9232	9238
84	9243	9248	9253	9258	9263	9269	9274	9279	9284	9289
85	9294	9299	9304	9309	9315	9320	9325	9330	9335	9340
86	9345	9350	9355	9360	9365	9370	9375	9380	9385	9390
87	9395	9400	9405	9410	9415	9420	9425	9430	9435	9440
88	9445	9450	9455	9460	9465	9469	9474	9479	9484	9489
89	9494	9499	9504	9509	9513	9518	9523	9528	9533	9538
90	9542	9547	9552	9557	9562	9566	9571	9576	9581	9586
91	9590	9595	9600	9605	9609	9614	9619	9624	9628	9633
92	9638	9643	9647	9652	9657	9661	9666	9671	9675	9680
93	9685	9689	9694	9699	9703	9708	9713	9717	9722	9727
94	9731	9736	9741	9745	9750	9754	9759	9763	9768	9773
95	9777	9782	9786	9791	9795	9800	9805	9809	9814	9818
96	9823	9827	9832	9836	9841	9845	9850	9854	9859	9863
97	9868	9872	9877	9881	9886	9890	9894	9899	9903	9908
98	9912	9917	9921	9926	9930	9934	9939	9943	9948	9952
99	9956	9961	9965	9969	9974	9978	9983	9987	9991	9996

Table X

VALUES OF e^{-x}

x	e^{-x}	x	e^{-x}	x	e^{-x}	x	e^{-x}
0.0	1.000	2.5	0.082	5.0	0.0067	7.5	0.00055
0.1	0.905	2.6	0.074	5.1	0.0061	7.6	0.00050
0.2	0.819	2.7	0.067	5.2	0.0055	7.7	0.00045
0.3	0.741	2.8	0.061	5.3	0.0050	7.8	0.00041
0.4	0.670	2.9	0.055	5.4	0.0045	7.9	0.00037
0.5	0.607	3.0	0.050	5.5	0.0041	8.0	0.00034
0.6	0.549	3.1	0.045	5.6	0.0037	8.1	0.00030
0.7	0.497	3.2	0.041	5.7	0.0033	8.2	0.00028
0.8	0.449	3.3	0.037	5.8	0.0030	8.3	0.00025
0.9	0.407	3.4	0.033	5.9	0.0027	8.4	0.00023
1.0	0.368	3.5	0.030	6.0	0.0025	8.5	0.00020
1.1	0.333	3.6	0.027	6.1	0.0022	8.6	0.00018
1.2	0.301	3.7	0.025	6.2	0.0020	8.7	0.00017
1.3	0.273	3.8	0.022	6.3	0.0018	8.8	0.00015
1.4	0.247	3.9	0.020	6.4	0.0017	8.9	0.00014
1.5	0.223	4.0	0.018	6.5	0.0015	9.0	0.00012
1.6	0.202	4.1	0.017	6.6	0.0014	9.1	0.00011
1.7	0.183	4.2	0.015	6.7	0.0012	9.2	0.00010
1.8	0.165	4.3	0.014	6.8	0.0011	9.3	0.00009
1.9	0.150	4.4	0.012	6.9	0.0010	9.4	0.00008
2.0	0.135	4.5	0.011	7.0	0.0009	9.5	0.00008
2.1	0.122	4.6	0.010	7.1	0.0008	9.6	0.00007
2.2	0.111	4.7	0.009	7.2	0.0007	9.7	0.00006
2.3	0.100	4.8	0.008	7.3	0.0007	9.8	0.00006
2.4	0.091	4.9	0.007	7.4	0.0006	9.9	0.00005

Table XI

SQUARES AND SQUARE ROOTS

n	n^2	$\sqrt{n}$	$\sqrt{10n}$
1.00	1.0000	1.000000	3.162278
1.01	1.0201	1.004988	3.178050
1.02	1.0404	1.009950	3.193744
1.03	1.0609	1.014889	3.209361
1.04	1.0816	1.019804	3.224903
1.05	1.1025	1.024695	3.240370
1.06	1.1236	1.029563	3.255764
1.07	1.1449	1.034408	3.271085
1.08	1.1664	1.039230	3.286335
1.09	1.1881	1.044031	3.301515
1.10	1.2100	1.048809	3.316625
1.11	1.2321	1.053565	3.331666
1.12	1.2544	1.058301	3.346640
1.13	1.2769	1.063015	3.361547
1.14	1.2996	1.067708	3.376389
1.15	1.3225	1.072381	3.391165
1.16	1.3456	1.077033	3.405877
1.17	1.3689	1.081665	3.420526
1.18	1.3924	1.086278	3.435113
1.19	1.4161	1.090871	3.449638
1.20	1.4400	1.095445	3.464102
1.21	1.4641	1.100000	3.478505
1.22	1.4884	1.104536	3.492850
1.23	1.5129	1.109054	3.507136
1.24	1.5376	1.113553	3.521363
1.25	1.5625	1.118034	3.535534
1.26	1.5876	1.122497	3.549648
1.27	1.6129	1.126943	3.563706
1.28	1.6384	1.131371	3.577709
1.29	1.6641	1.135782	3.591657
1.30	1.6900	1.140175	3.605551
1.31	1.7161	1.144552	3.619392
1.32	1.7424	1.148913	3.633180
1.33	1.7689	1.153256	3.646917
1.34	1.7956	1.157584	3.660601
1.35	1.8255	1.161895	3.674235
1.36	1.8496	1.166190	3.687818
1.37	1.8769	1.170470	3.701351
1.38	1.9044	1.174734	3.714835
1.39	1.9321	1.178983	3.728270
1.40	1.9600	1.183216	3.741657
1.41	1.9881	1.187434	3.754997
1.42	2.0164	1.191638	3.768289
1.43	2.0449	1.195826	3.781534
1.44	2.0736	1.200000	3.794733
1.45	2.1025	1.204159	3.807887
1.46	2.1316	1.208305	3.820995
1.47	2.1609	1.212436	3.834058
1.48	2.1904	1.216553	3.847077
1.49	2.2201	1.220656	3.860052

n	n^2	$\sqrt{n}$	$\sqrt{10n}$
1.50	2.2500	1.224745	3.872983
1.51	2.2801	1.228821	3.885872
1.52	2.3104	1.232883	3.898718
1.53	2.3409	1.236932	3.911521
1.54	2.3716	1.240967	3.924283
1.55	2.4025	1.244990	3.937004
1.56	2.4336	1.249000	3.949684
1.57	2.4649	1.252996	3.962323
1.58	2.4964	1.256981	3.974921
1.59	2.5281	1.260952	3.987480
1.60	2.5600	1.264911	4.000000
1.61	2.5921	1.268858	4.012481
1.62	2.6244	1.272792	4.024922
1.63	2.6569	1.276715	4.037326
1.64	2.6896	1.280625	4.049691
1.65	2.7225	1.284523	4.062019
1.66	2.7556	1.288410	4.074310
1.67	2.7889	1.292285	4.086563
1.68	2.8224	1.296148	4.098780
1.69	2.8561	1.300000	4.110961
1.70	2.8900	1.303840	4.123106
1.71	2.9241	1.307670	4.135215
1.72	2.9584	1.311488	4.147288
1.73	2.9929	1.315295	4.159327
1.74	3.0276	1.319091	4.171331
1.75	3.0625	1.322876	4.183300
1.76	3.0976	1.326650	4.195235
1.77	3.1329	1.330413	4.207137
1.78	3.1684	1.334166	4.219005
1.79	3.2041	1.337909	4.230839
1.80	3.2400	1.341641	4.242641
1.81	3.2761	1.345362	4.254409
1.82	3.3124	1.349074	4.266146
1.83	3.3489	1.352775	4.277850
1.84	3.3856	1.356466	4.289522
1.85	3.4225	1.360147	4.301163
1.86	3.4596	1.363818	4.312772
1.87	3.4969	1.367479	4.324350
1.88	3.5344	1.371131	4.335897
1.89	3.5721	1.374773	4.347413
1.90	3.6100	1.378405	4.358899
1.91	3.6481	1.382027	4.370355
1.92	3.6864	1.385641	4.381780
1.93	3.7249	1.389244	4.393177
1.94	3.7636	1.392839	4.404543
1.95	3.8025	1.396424	4.415880
1.96	3.8416	1.400000	4.427189
1.97	3.8809	1.403567	4.438468
1.98	3.9204	1.407125	4.449719
1.99	3.9601	1.410674	4.460942

Table XI

SQUARES AND SQUARE ROOTS (*Continued*)

n	n^2	$\sqrt{n}$	$\sqrt{10n}$
2.00	4.0000	1.414214	4.472136
2.01	4.0401	1.417745	4.483302
2.02	4.0804	1.421267	4.494441
2.03	4.1209	1.424781	4.505552
2.04	4.1616	1.428286	4.516636
2.05	4.2025	1.431782	4.527693
2.06	4.2436	1.435270	4.538722
2.07	4.2849	1.438749	4.549725
2.08	4.3264	1.442221	4.560702
2.09	4.3681	1.445683	4.571652
2.10	4.4100	1.449138	4.582576
2.11	4.4521	1.452584	4.593474
2.12	4.4944	1.456022	4.604346
2.13	4.5369	1.459452	4.615192
2.14	4.5796	1.462874	4.626013
2.15	4.6225	1.466288	4.636809
2.16	4.6656	1.469694	4.647580
2.17	4.7089	1.473092	4.658326
2.18	4.7524	1.476482	4.669047
2.19	4.7961	1.479865	4.679744
2.20	4.8400	1.483240	4.690416
2.21	4.8841	1.486607	4.701064
2.22	4.9284	1.489966	4.711688
2.23	4.9729	1.493318	4.722288
2.24	5.0176	1.496663	4.732864
2.25	5.0625	1.500000	4.743416
2.26	5.1076	1.503330	4.753946
2.27	5.1529	1.506652	4.764452
2.28	5.1984	1.509967	4.774935
2.29	5.2441	1.513275	4.785394
2.30	5.2900	1.516575	4.795832
2.31	5.3361	1.519868	4.806246
2.32	5.3824	1.523155	4.816638
2.33	5.4289	1.526434	4.827007
2.34	5.4756	1.529706	4.837355
2.35	5.5225	1.532971	4.847680
2.36	5.5696	1.536229	4.857983
2.37	5.6169	1.539480	4.868265
2.38	5.6644	1.542725	4.878524
2.39	5.7121	1.545962	4.888763
2.40	5.7600	1.549193	4.898979
2.41	5.8081	1.552417	4.909175
2.42	5.8564	1.555635	4.919350
2.43	5.9049	1.558846	4.929503
2.44	5.9536	1.562050	4.939636
2.45	6.0025	1.565248	4.949747
2.46	6.0516	1.568439	4.959839
2.47	6.1009	1.571623	4.969909
2.48	6.1504	1.574802	4.979960
2.49	6.2001	1.577973	4.989990
2.50	6.2500	1.581139	5.000000
2.51	6.3001	1.584298	5.009990
2.52	6.3504	1.587451	5.019960
2.53	6.4009	1.590597	5.029911
2.54	6.4516	1.593738	5.039841
2.55	6.5025	1.596872	5.049752
2.56	6.5536	1.600000	5.059644
2.57	6.6049	1.603122	5.069517
2.58	6.6564	1.606238	5.079370
2.59	6.7081	1.609348	5.089204
2.60	6.7600	1.612452	5.099020
2.61	6.8121	1.615549	5.108816
2.62	6.8644	1.618641	5.118594
2.63	6.9169	1.621727	5.128353
2.64	6.9696	1.624808	5.138093
2.65	7.0225	1.627882	5.147815
2.66	7.0756	1.630951	5.157519
2.67	7.1289	1.634013	5.167204
2.68	7.1824	1.637071	5.176872
2.69	7.2361	1.640122	5.186521
2.70	7.2900	1.643168	5.196152
2.71	7.3441	1.646208	5.205766
2.72	7.3984	1.649242	5.215362
2.73	7.4529	1.652271	5.224940
2.74	7.5076	1.655295	5.234501
2.75	7.5625	1.658312	5.244044
2.76	7.6176	1.661325	5.253570
2.77	7.6729	1.664332	5.263079
2.78	7.7284	1.667333	5.272571
2.79	7.7841	1.670329	5.282045
2.80	7.8400	1.673320	5.291503
2.81	7.8961	1.676305	5.300943
2.82	7.9524	1.679286	5.310367
2.83	8.0089	1.682260	5.319774
2.84	8.0656	1.685230	5.329165
2.85	8.1225	1.688194	5.338539
2.86	8.1796	1.691153	5.347897
2.87	8.2369	1.694107	5.357238
2.88	8.2944	1.697056	5.366563
2.89	8.3521	1.700000	5.375872
2.90	8.4100	1.702939	5.385165
2.91	8.4681	1.705872	5.394442
2.92	8.5264	1.708801	5.403702
2.93	8.5849	1.711724	5.412947
2.94	8.6436	1.714643	5.422177
2.95	8.7025	1.717556	5.431390
2.96	8.7616	1.720465	5.440588
2.97	8.8209	1.723369	5.449771
2.98	8.8804	1.726268	5.458938
2.99	8.9401	1.729162	5.468089

Table XI

SQUARES AND SQUARE ROOTS (*Continued*)

n	n^2	$\sqrt{n}$	$\sqrt{10n}$	n	n^2	$\sqrt{n}$	$\sqrt{10n}$
3.00	9.0000	1.732051	5.477226	3.50	12.2500	1.870829	5.916080
3.01	9.0601	1.734935	5.486347	3.51	12.3201	1.873499	5.924525
3.02	9.1204	1.737815	5.495453	3.52	12.3904	1.876166	5.932959
3.03	9.1809	1.740690	5.504544	3.53	12.4609	1.878829	5.941380
3.04	9.2416	1.743560	5.513620	3.54	12.5316	1.881489	5.949790
3.05	9.3025	1.746425	5.522681	3.55	12.6025	1.884144	5.958188
3.06	9.3636	1.749286	5.531727	3.56	12.6736	1.886796	5.966574
3.07	9.4249	1.752142	5.540758	3.57	12.7449	1.889444	5.974948
3.08	9.4864	1.754993	5.549775	3.58	12.8164	1.892089	5.983310
3.09	9.5481	1.757840	5.558777	3.59	12.8881	1.894730	5.991661
3.10	9.6100	1.760682	5.567764	3.60	12.9600	1.897367	6.000000
3.11	9.6721	1.763519	5.576737	3.61	13.0321	1.900000	6.008328
3.12	9.7344	1.766352	5.585696	3.62	13.1044	1.902630	6.016644
3.13	9.7969	1.769181	5.594640	3.63	13.1769	1.905256	6.024948
3.14	9.8596	1.772005	5.603570	3.64	13.2496	1.907878	6.033241
3.15	9.9225	1.774824	5.612486	3.65	13.3225	1.910497	6.041523
3.16	9.9856	1.777639	5.621388	3.66	13.3956	1.913113	6.049793
3.17	10.0489	1.780449	5.630275	3.67	13.4689	1.915724	6.058052
3.18	10.1124	1.783255	5.639149	3.68	13.5424	1.918333	6.066300
3.19	10.1761	1.786057	5.648008	3.69	13.6161	1.920937	6.074537
3.20	10.2400	1.788854	5.656854	3.70	13.6900	1.923538	6.082763
3.21	10.3041	1.791647	5.665686	3.71	13.7641	1.926136	6.090977
3.22	10.3684	1.794436	5.674504	3.72	13.8384	1.928730	6.099180
3.23	10.4329	1.797220	5.683309	3.73	13.9129	1.931321	6.107373
3.24	10.4976	1.800000	5.692100	3.74	13.9876	1.933908	6.115554
3.25	10.5625	1.802776	5.700877	3.75	14.0625	1.936492	6.123724
3.26	10.6276	1.805547	5.709641	3.76	14.1376	1.939072	6.131884
3.27	10.6929	1.808314	5.718391	3.77	14.2129	1.941649	6.140033
3.28	10.7584	1.811077	5.727128	3.78	14.2884	1.944222	6.148170
3.29	10.8241	1.813836	5.735852	3.79	14.3641	1.946792	6.156298
3.30	10.8900	1.816590	5.744563	3.80	14.4400	1.949359	6.164414
3.31	10.9561	1.819341	5.753260	3.81	14.5161	1.951922	6.172520
3.32	11.0224	1.822087	5.761944	3.82	14.5924	1.954483	6.180615
3.33	11.0889	1.824829	5.770615	3.83	14.6689	1.957039	6.188699
3.34	11.1556	1.827567	5.779273	3.84	14.7456	1.959592	6.196773
3.35	11.2225	1.830301	5.787918	3.85	14.8225	1.962142	6.204837
3.36	11.2896	1.833030	5.796551	3.86	14.8996	1.964688	6.212890
3.37	11.3569	1.835756	5.805170	3.87	14.9769	1.967232	6.220932
3.38	11.4244	1.838478	5.813777	3.88	15.0544	1.969772	6.228965
3.39	11.4921	1.841195	5.822371	3.89	15.1321	1.972308	6.236986
3.40	11.5600	1.843909	5.830952	3.90	15.2100	1.974842	6.244998
3.41	11.6281	1.846619	5.839521	3.91	15.2881	1.977372	6.252999
3.42	11.6964	1.849324	5.848077	3.92	15.3664	1.979899	5.260990
3.43	11.7649	1.852026	5.856620	3.93	15.4449	1.982423	6.268971
3.44	11.8336	1.854724	5.865151	3.94	15.5236	1.984943	6.276942
3.45	11.9025	1.857418	5.873670	3.95	15.6025	1.987461	6.284903
3.46	11.9716	1.860108	5.882176	3.96	15.6816	1.989975	6.292853
3.47	12.0409	1.862794	5.890671	3.97	15.7609	1.992486	6.300794
3.48	12.1104	1.865476	5.899152	3.98	15.8404	1.994994	6.308724
3.49	12.1801	1.868154	5.907622	3.99	15.9201	1.997498	6.316645

Table XI

SQUARES AND SQUARE ROOTS (*Continued*)

n	n^2	$\sqrt{n}$	$\sqrt{10n}$
4.00	16.0000	2.000000	6.324555
4.01	16.0801	2.002498	6.332456
4.02	16.1604	2.004994	6.340347
4.03	16.2409	2.007486	6.348228
4.04	16.3216	2.009975	6.356099
4.05	16.4025	2.012461	6.363961
4.06	16.4836	2.014944	6.371813
4.07	16.5649	2.017424	6.379655
4.08	16.6464	2.019901	6.387488
4.09	16.7281	2.022375	6.395311
4.10	16.8100	2.024846	6.403124
4.11	16.8921	20.27313	6.410928
4.12	16.9744	2.029778	6.418723
4.13	17.0569	2.032240	6.426508
4.14	17.1396	2.034699	6.434283
4.15	17.2225	2.037155	6.442049
4.16	17.3056	2.039608	6.449806
4.17	17.3889	2.042058	6.457554
4.18	17.4724	2.044505	6.465292
4.19	17.5561	2.046949	6.473021
4.20	17.6400	2.049390	6.480741
4.21	17.7241	2.051828	6.488451
4.22	17.8084	2.054264	6.496153
4.23	17.8929	2.056696	6.503845
4.24	17.9776	2.059126	6.511528
4.25	18.0625	2.061553	6.519202
4.26	18.1476	2.063977	6.526868
4.27	18.2329	2.066398	6.534524
4.28	18.3184	2.068816	6.542171
4.29	18.4041	2.071232	6.549809
4.30	18.4900	2.073644	6.557439
4.31	18.5761	2.076054	6.565059
4.32	18.6624	2.078461	6.572671
4.33	18.7489	2.080865	6.580274
4.34	18.8356	2.083267	6.587868
4.35	18.9225	2.085665	6.595453
4.36	19.0096	2.088061	6.603030
4.37	19.0969	2.090454	6.610598
4.38	19.1844	2.092845	6.618157
4.39	19.2721	2.095233	6.625708
4.40	19.3600	2.097618	6.633250
4.41	19.4481	2.100000	6.640783
4.42	19.5364	2.102380	6.648308
4.43	19.6249	2.104757	6.655825
4.44	19.7136	2.107131	6.663332
4.45	19.8025	2.109502	6.670832
4.46	19.8916	2.111871	6.678323
4.47	19.9809	2.114237	6.685806
4.48	20.0704	2.116601	6.693280
4.49	20.1601	2.118962	6.700746

n	n^2	$\sqrt{n}$	$\sqrt{10n}$
4.50	20.2500	2.121320	6.708204
4.51	20.3401	2.123676	6.715653
4.52	20.4304	2.126029	6.723095
4.53	20.5209	2.128380	6.730527
4.54	20.6116	2.130728	6.737952
4.55	20.7025	2.133073	6.745369
4.56	20.7936	2.135416	6.752777
4.57	20.8849	2.137756	6.760178
4.58	20.9764	2.140093	6.767570
4.59	21.0681	2.142429	6.774954
4.60	21.1600	2.144761	6.782330
4.61	21.2521	2.147091	6.789698
4.62	21.3444	2.149419	6.797058
4.63	21.4369	2.151743	6.804410
4.64	21.5296	2.154066	6.811755
4.65	21.6225	2.156386	6.819091
4.66	21.7156	2.158703	6.826419
4.67	21.8089	2.161018	6.833740
4.68	21.9024	2.163331	6.841053
4.69	21.9961	2.165641	6.848357
4.70	22.0900	2.167948	6.855655
4.71	22.1841	2.170253	6.862944
4.72	22.2784	2.172556	6.870226
4.73	22.3729	2.174856	6.877500
4.74	22.4676	2.177154	6.884766
4.75	22.5625	2.179449	6.892024
4.76	22.6576	2.181742	6.899275
4.77	22.7529	2.184033	6.906519
4.78	22.8484	2.186321	6.913754
4.79	22.9441	2.188607	6.920983
4.80	23.0400	2.190890	6.928203
4.81	23.1361	2.193171	6.935416
4.82	23.2324	2.195450	6.942622
4.83	23.3289	2.197726	6.949820
4.84	23.4256	2.200000	6.957011
4.85	23.5225	2.202272	6.964194
4.86	23.6196	2.204541	6.971370
4.87	23.7169	2.206808	6.978539
4.88	23.8144	2.209072	6.985700
4.89	23.9121	2.211334	6.992853
4.90	24.0100	2.213594	7.000000
4.91	24.1081	2.215852	7.007139
4.92	24.2064	2.218107	7.014271
4.93	24.3049	2.220360	7.021396
4.94	24.4036	2.222611	7.028513
4.95	24.5025	2.224860	7.035624
4.96	24.6016	2.227106	7.042727
4.97	24.7009	2.229350	7.049823
4.98	24.8004	2.231591	7.056912
4.99	24.9001	2.233831	7.063993

Table XI

SQUARES AND SQUARE ROOTS (*Continued*)

n	n^2	$\sqrt{n}$	$\sqrt{10n}$
5.00	25.0000	2.236068	7.071068
5.01	25.1001	2.238303	7.078135
5.02	25.2004	2.240536	7.085196
5.03	25.3009	2.242766	7.092249
5.04	25.4016	2.244994	7.099296
5.05	25.5025	2.247221	7.106335
5.06	25.6036	2.249444	7.113368
5.07	25.7049	2.251666	7.120393
5.08	25.8064	2.253886	7.127412
5.09	25.9081	2.256103	7.134424
5.10	26.0100	2.258318	7.141428
5.11	26.1121	2.260531	7.148426
5.12	26.2144	2.262742	7.155418
5.13	26.3169	2.264950	7.162402
5.14	26.4196	2.267157	7.169379
5.15	26.5225	2.269361	7.176350
5.16	26.6256	2.271563	7.183314
5.17	26.7289	2.273763	7.190271
5.18	26.8324	2.275961	7.197222
5.19	26.9361	2.278157	7.204165
5.20	27.0400	2.280351	7.211103
5.21	27.1441	2.282542	7.218033
5.22	27.2484	2.284732	7.224957
5.23	27.3529	2.286919	7.231874
5.24	27.4576	2.289105	7.238784
5.25	27.5625	2.291288	7.245688
5.26	27.6676	2.293469	7.252586
5.27	27.7729	2.295648	7.259477
5.28	27.8784	2.297825	7.266361
5.29	27.9841	2.300000	7.273239
5.30	28.0900	2.302173	7.280110
5.31	28.1961	2.304344	7.286975
5.32	28.3024	2.306513	7.293833
5.33	28.4089	2.308679	7.300685
5.34	28.5156	2.310844	7.307530
5.35	28.6225	2.313007	7.314369
5.36	28.7296	2.315167	7.321202
5.37	28.8369	2.317326	7.328028
5.38	28.9444	2.319483	7.334848
5.39	29.0521	2.321637	7.341662
5.40	29.1600	2.323790	7.348469
5.41	29.2681	2.325941	7.355270
5.42	29.3764	2.328089	7.362065
5.43	29.4849	2.330236	7.368853
5.44	29.5936	2.332381	7.357636
5.45	29.7025	2.334524	7.382412
5.46	29.8116	2.336664	7.389181
5.47	29.9209	2.338803	7.395945
5.48	30.0304	2.340940	7.402702
5.49	30.1401	2.343075	7.409453

n	n^2	$\sqrt{n}$	$\sqrt{10n}$
5.50	30.2500	2.345208	7.416198
5.51	30.3601	2.347339	7.422937
5.52	30.4704	2.349468	7.429670
5.53	30.5809	2.351595	7.436397
5.54	30.6916	2.353720	7.443118
5.55	30.8025	2.355844	7.449832
5.56	30.9136	2.357965	7.456541
5.57	31.0249	2.360085	7.463243
5.58	31.1364	2.362202	7.469940
5.59	31.2481	2.364318	7.476630
5.60	31.3600	2.366432	7.483315
5.61	31.4721	2.368544	7.489993
5.62	31.5844	2.370654	7.496666
5.63	31.6969	2.372762	7.503333
5.64	31.8096	2.374868	7.509993
5.65	31.9225	2.376973	7.516648
5.66	32.0356	2.379075	7.523297
5.67	32.1489	2.381176	7.529940
5.68	32.2624	2.383275	7.536577
5.69	32.3761	2.385372	7.543209
5.70	32.4900	2.387467	7.549834
5.71	32.6041	2.389561	7.556454
5.72	32.7184	2.391652	7.563068
5.73	32.8329	2.393742	7.569676
5.74	32.9476	2.395830	7.576279
5.75	33.0625	2.397916	7.582875
5.76	33.1776	2.400000	7.589466
5.77	33.2929	2.402082	7.596052
5.78	33.4084	2.404163	7.602631
5.79	33.5241	2.406242	7.609205
5.80	33.6400	2.408319	7.615773
5.81	33.7561	2.410394	7.622336
5.82	33.8724	2.412468	7.628892
5.83	33.9889	2.414539	7.635444
5.84	34.1056	2.416609	7.641989
5.85	34.2225	2.418677	7.648529
5.86	34.3396	2.420744	7.655064
5.87	34.4569	2.422808	7.661593
5.88	34.5744	2.424871	7.668116
5.89	34.6921	2.426932	7.674634
5.90	34.8100	2.428992	7.681146
5.91	34.9281	2.431049	7.687652
5.92	35.0464	2.433105	7.694154
5.93	35.1649	2.435159	7.700649
5.94	35.2836	2.437212	7.707140
5.95	35.4025	2.439262	7.713624
5.96	35.5216	2.441311	7.720104
5.97	35.6409	2.443358	7.726578
5.98	35.7604	2.445404	7.733046
5.99	35.8801	2.447448	7.739509

Table XI

SQUARES AND SQUARE ROOTS (*Continued*)

n	n^2	$\sqrt{n}$	$\sqrt{10n}$	n	n^2	$\sqrt{n}$	$\sqrt{10n}$
6.00	36.0000	2.449490	7.745967	6.50	42.2500	2.549510	8.062258
6.01	36.1201	2.451530	7.752419	6.51	42.3801	2.551470	8.068457
6.02	36.2404	2.453569	7.758866	6.52	42.5104	2.553429	8.074652
6.03	36.3609	2.455606	7.765307	6.53	42.6409	2.555386	8.080842
6.04	36.4816	2.457641	7.771744	6.54	42.7716	2.557342	8.087027
6.05	36.6025	2.459675	7.778175	6.55	42.9025	2.559297	8.093207
6.06	36.7236	2.461707	7.784600	6.56	43.0336	2.561250	8.099383
6.07	36.8449	2.463737	7.791020	6.57	43.1649	2.563201	8.105554
6.08	36.9664	2.465766	7.797435	6.58	43.2964	2.565151	8.111720
6.09	37.0881	2.467793	7.803845	6.59	43.4281	2.567100	8.117881
6.10	37.2100	2.469818	7.810250	6.60	43.5600	2.569047	8.124038
6.11	37.3321	2.471841	7.816649	6.61	43.6921	2.570992	8.130191
6.12	37.4544	2.473863	7.823043	6.62	43.8244	2.572936	8.136338
6.13	37.5769	2.475884	7.829432	6.63	43.9569	2.574879	8.142481
6.14	37.6996	2.477902	7.835815	6.64	44.0896	2.576820	8.148620
6.15	37.8225	2.479919	7.842194	6.65	44.2225	2.578759	8.154753
6.16	37.9456	2.481935	7.848567	6.66	44.3556	2.580698	8.160882
6.17	38.0689	2.483948	7.854935	6.67	44.4889	2.582634	8.167007
6.18	38.1924	2.485961	7.861298	6.68	44.6224	2.584570	8.173127
6.19	38.3161	2.487971	7.867655	6.69	44.7561	2.586503	8.179242
6.20	38.4400	2.489980	7.874008	6.70	44.8900	2.588436	8.185353
6.21	38.5641	2.491987	7.880355	6.71	45.0241	2.590367	8.191459
6.22	38.6884	2.493993	7.886698	6.72	45.1584	2.592296	8.197561
6.23	38.8129	2.495997	7.893035	6.73	45.2929	2.594224	8.203658
6.24	38.9376	2.497999	7.899367	6.74	45.4276	2.596151	8.209750
6.25	39.0625	2.500000	7.905694	6.75	45.5625	2.598076	8.215838
6.26	39.1876	2.501999	7.912016	6.76	45.6976	2.600000	8.221922
6.27	39.3129	2.503997	7.918333	6.77	45.8329	2.601922	8.228001
6.28	39.4384	2.505993	7.924645	6.78	45.9684	2.603843	8.234076
6.29	39.5641	2.507987	7.930952	6.79	46.1041	2.605763	8.240146
6.30	39.6900	2.509980	7.937254	6.80	46.2400	2.607681	8.246211
6.31	39.8161	2.511971	7.943551	6.81	46.3761	2.609598	8.242272
6.32	39.9424	2.513961	7.949843	6.82	46.5124	2.611513	8.258329
6.33	40.0689	2.515949	7.956130	6.83	46.6489	2.613427	8.264381
6.34	40.1956	2.517936	7.962412	6.84	46.7856	2.615339	8.270429
6.35	40.3225	2.519921	7.968689	6.85	46.9225	2.617250	8.276473
6.36	40.4496	2.521904	7.974961	6.86	47 0596	2 619160	8.282512
6.37	40.5769	2.523886	7.981228	6.87	47.1969	2.621068	8.288546
6.38	40.7044	2.525866	7.987490	6.88	47.3344	2.622975	8.294577
6.39	40.8321	2.527845	7.993748	6.89	47.4721	2.624881	8.300602
6.40	40.9600	2.529822	8.000000	6.90	47.6100	2.626785	8.306624
6.41	41.0881	2.531798	8.006248	6.91	47.7481	2.628688	8.312641
6.42	41.2164	2.533772	8.012490	6.92	47.8864	2.630589	8.318654
6.43	41.3449	2.535744	8.018728	6.93	48.0249	2.632489	8.324662
6.44	41.4736	2.537716	8.024961	6.94	48.1636	2.634388	8.330666
6.45	41.6025	2.539685	8.031189	6.95	48.3025	2.636285	8.336666
6.46	41.7316	2.541653	8.037413	6.96	48.4416	2.638181	8.342661
6.47	41.8609	2.543619	8.043631	6.97	48.5809	2.640076	8.348653
6.48	41.9904	2.545584	8.049845	6.98	48.7204	2.641969	8.354639
6.49	42.1201	2.547548	8.056054	6.99	48.8601	2.643861	8.360622

Table XI

SQUARES AND SQUARE ROOTS (*Continued*)

n	n^2	$\sqrt{n}$	$\sqrt{10n}$	n	n^2	$\sqrt{n}$	$\sqrt{10n}$
7.00	49.0000	2.645751	8.366600	7.50	56.2500	2.738613	8.660254
7.01	49.1401	2.647640	8.372574	7.51	56.4001	2.740438	8.660026
7.02	49.2804	2.649528	8.378544	7.52	56.5504	2.742262	8.671793
7.03	49.4209	2.651415	8.384510	7.53	56.7009	2.744085	8.677557
7.04	49.5616	2.653300	8.390471	7.54	56.8516	2.745906	8.683317
7.05	49.7025	2.655184	8.396428	7.55	57.0025	2.747726	8.689074
7.06	49.8436	2.657066	8.402381	7.56	57.1536	2.749545	8.694826
7.07	49.9849	2.658947	8.408329	7.57	57.3049	2.751363	8.700575
7.08	50.1264	2.660827	8.414274	7.58	57.4564	2.753180	8.706320
7.09	50.2681	2.662705	8.420214	7.59	57.6081	2.754995	8.712061
7.10	50.4100	2.664583	8.426150	7.60	57.7600	2.756810	8.717798
7.11	50.5521	2.666458	8.432082	7.61	57.9121	2.758623	8.723531
7.12	50.6944	2.668333	8.438009	7.62	58.0644	2.760435	8.729261
7.13	50.8369	2.670206	8.443933	7.63	58.2169	2.762245	8.734987
7.14	50.9796	2.672078	8.449852	7.64	58.3696	2.764055	8.740709
7.15	51.1225	2.673948	8.455767	7.65	58.5225	2.765863	8.746428
7.16	51.2656	2.675818	8.461678	7.66	58.6756	2.767671	8.752143
7.17	51.4089	2.677686	8.467585	7.67	58.8289	2.769476	8.757854
7.18	51.5524	2.679552	8.473488	7.68	58.9824	2.771281	8.763561
7.19	51.6961	2.681418	8.479387	7.69	59.1361	2.773085	8.769265
7.20	51.8400	2.683282	8.485281	7.70	59.2900	2.774887	8.774964
7.21	51.9841	2.685144	8.491172	7.71	59.4441	2.776689	8.780661
7.22	52.1284	2.687006	8.497058	7.72	59.5984	2.778489	8.786353
7.23	52.2729	2.688866	8.502941	7.73	59.7529	2.780288	8.792042
7.24	52.4176	2.690725	8.508819	7.74	59.9076	2.782086	8.797727
7.25	52.5625	2.692582	8.514693	7.75	60.0625	2.783882	8.803408
7.26	52.7076	2.694439	8.520563	7.76	60.2176	2.785678	8.809086
7.27	52.8529	2.696294	8.526429	7.77	60.3729	2.787472	8.814760
7.28	52.9984	2.698148	8.532292	7.78	60.5284	2.789265	8.820431
7.29	53.1441	2.700000	8.538150	7.79	60.6841	2.791057	8.826098
7.30	53.2900	2.701851	8.544004	7.80	60.8400	2.792848	8.831761
7.31	53.4361	2.703701	8.549854	7.81	60.9961	2.794638	8.837420
7.32	53.5824	2.705550	8.555700	7.82	61.1524	2.796426	8.843076
7.33	53.7289	2.707397	8.561542	7.83	61.3089	2.798214	8.848729
7.34	53.8756	2.709243	8.567380	7.84	61.4656	2.800000	8.854377
7.35	54.0225	2.711088	8.573214	7.85	61.6225	2.801785	8.860023
7.36	54.1696	2.712932	8.579044	7.86	61.7796	2.803569	8.865664
7.37	54.3169	2.714774	8.584870	7.87	61.9369	2.805352	8.871302
7.38	54.4644	2.716616	8.590693	7.88	62.0944	2.807134	8.876936
7.39	54.6121	2.718455	8.596511	7.89	62.2521	2.808914	8.882567
7.40	54.7600	2.720294	8.602325	7.90	62.4100	2.810694	8.888194
7.41	54.9081	2.722132	8.608136	7.91	62.5681	2.812472	8.893818
7.42	55.0564	2.723968	8.613942	7.92	62.7264	2.814249	8.899438
7.43	55.2049	2.725803	8.619745	7.93	62.8849	2.816026	8.905055
7.44	55.3536	2.727636	8.625543	7.94	63.0436	2.817801	8.910668
7.45	55.5025	2.729469	8.631338	7.95	63.2025	2.819574	8.916277
7.46	55.6516	2.731300	8.637129	7.96	63.3616	2.821347	8.921883
7.47	55.8009	2.733130	8.642916	7.97	63.5209	2.823119	8.927486
7.48	55.9504	2.734959	8.648699	7.98	63.6804	2.824889	8.933085
7.49	56.1001	2.736786	8.654479	7.99	63.8401	2.826659	8.938680

Table XI

SQUARES AND SQUARE ROOTS (*Continued*)

n	n^2	$\sqrt{n}$	$\sqrt{10n}$
8.00	64.0000	2.828427	8.944272
8.01	64.1601	2.830194	8.949860
8.02	64.3204	2.831960	8.955445
8.03	64.4809	2.833725	8.961027
8.04	64.6416	2.835489	8.966605
8.05	64.8025	2.837252	8.972179
8.06	64.9636	2.839014	8.977750
8.07	65.1249	2.840775	8.983318
8.08	65.2864	2.842534	8.988882
8.09	65.4481	2.844293	8.994443
8.10	65.6100	2.846050	9.000000
8.11	65.7721	2.847806	9.005554
8.12	65.9344	2.849561	9.011104
8.13	66.0969	2.851315	9.016651
8.14	66.2596	2.853069	9.022195
8.15	66.4225	2.854820	9.027735
8.16	66.5856	2.856571	9.033272
8.17	66.7489	2.858321	9.038805
8.18	66.9124	2.860070	9.044335
8.19	67.0761	2.861818	9.049862
8.20	67.2400	2.863564	9.055385
8.21	67.4041	2.865310	9.060905
8.22	67.5684	2.867054	9.066422
8.23	67.7329	2.868798	9.071935
8.24	67.8976	2.870540	9.077445
8.25	68.0625	2.872281	9.082951
8.26	68.2276	2.874022	9.088454
8.27	68.3929	2.875761	9.093954
8.28	68.5584	2.877499	9.099451
8.29	68.7241	2.879236	9.104944
8.30	68.8900	2.880972	9.110434
8.31	69.0561	2.882707	9.115920
8.32	69.2224	2.884441	9.121403
8.33	69.3889	2.886174	9.126883
8.34	69.5556	2.887906	9.132360
8.35	69.7225	2.889637	9.137833
8.36	69.8896	2.891366	9.143304
8.37	7.00569	2.893095	9.148770
8.38	70.2244	2.894823	9.154234
8.39	70.3921	2.896550	9.159694
8.40	70.5600	2.898275	9.165151
8.41	70.7281	2.900000	9.170605
8.42	70.8964	2.901724	9.176056
8.43	71.0649	2.903446	9.181503
8.44	71.2336	2.905168	9.186947
8.45	71.4025	2.906888	9.192388
8.46	71.5716	2.908608	9.197826
8.47	71.7409	2.910326	9.203260
8.48	71.9104	2.912044	9.208692
8.49	72.0801	2.913760	9.214120
8.50	72.2500	2.915476	9.219544
8.51	72.4201	2.917190	9.224966
8.52	72.5904	2.918904	9.230385
8.53	72.7609	2.920616	9.235800
8.54	72.9316	2.922328	9.241212
8.55	73.1025	2.924038	9.246621
8.56	73.2736	2.925748	9.252027
8.57	73.4449	2.927456	9.257429
8.58	73.6164	2.929164	9.262829
8.59	73.7881	2.930870	9.268225
8.60	73.9600	2.932576	9.273618
8.61	74.1321	2.934280	9.279009
8.62	74.3044	2.935984	9.284396
8.63	74.4769	2.937686	9.289779
8.64	74.6496	2.939388	9.295160
8.65	74.8225	2.941088	9.300538
8.66	74.9956	2.942788	9.305912
8.67	75.1689	2.944486	9.311283
8.68	75.3424	2.946184	9.316652
8.69	75.5161	2.947881	9.322017
8.70	75.6900	2.949576	9.327379
8.71	75.8641	2.951271	9.332738
8.72	76.0384	2.952965	9.338094
8.73	76.2129	2.954657	9.343447
8.74	76.3876	2.956349	9.348797
8.75	76.5625	2.958040	9.354143
8.76	76.7376	2.959730	9.359487
8.77	76.9129	2.961419	9.364828
8.78	77.0884	2.963106	9.370165
8.79	77.2641	2.964793	9.375500
8.80	77.4400	2.966479	9.380832
8.81	77.6161	2.968164	9.386160
8.82	77.7924	2.969848	9.391486
8.83	77.9689	2.971532	9.396808
8.84	78.1456	2.973214	9.402127
8.85	78.3225	2.974895	9.407444
8.86	78.4996	2.976575	9.412757
8.87	78.6769	2.978255	9.418068
8.88	78.8544	2.979933	9.423375
8.89	79.0321	2.981610	9.428680
8.90	79.2100	2.983287	9.433981
8.91	79.3881	2.984962	9.439280
8.92	79.5664	2.986637	9.444575
8.93	79.7449	2.988311	9.449868
8.94	79.9236	2.989983	9.455157
8.95	80.1025	2.991655	9.460444
8.96	80.2816	2.993326	9.465728
8.97	80.4609	2.994996	9.471008
8.98	80.6404	2.996665	9.476286
8.99	80.8201	2.998333	9.481561

Table XI

SQUARES AND SQUARE ROOTS (*Continued*)

n	n^2	$\sqrt{n}$	$\sqrt{10n}$	n	n^2	$\sqrt{n}$	$\sqrt{10n}$
9.00	81.0000	3.000000	9.486833	9.50	90.2500	3.082207	9.746794
9.01	81.1801	3.001666	9.492102	9.51	90.4401	3.083829	9.751923
9.02	81.3604	3.003331	9.497368	9.52	90.6304	3.085450	9.757049
9.03	81.5409	3.004996	9.502631	9.53	90.8209	3.087070	9.762172
9.04	81.7216	3.006659	9.507891	9.54	91.0116	3.088689	9.767292
9.05	81.9025	3.008322	9.513149	9.55	91.2025	3.090307	9.772410
9.06	82.0836	3.009983	9.518403	9.56	91.3936	3.091925	9.777525
9.07	82.2649	3.011644	9.523655	9.57	91.5849	3.093542	9.782638
9.08	82.4464	3.013304	9.528903	9.58	91.7764	3.095158	9.787747
9.09	82.6281	3.014963	9.534149	9.59	91.9681	3.096773	9.792855
9.10	82.8100	3.016621	9.539392	9.60	92.1600	3.098387	9.797959
9.11	82.9921	3.018278	9.544632	9.61	92.3521	3.100000	9.803061
9.12	83.1744	3.019934	9.549869	9.62	92.5444	3.101612	9.808160
9.13	83.3569	3.021589	9.555103	9.63	92.7369	3.103224	9.813256
9.14	83.5396	3.023243	9.560335	9.64	92.9296	3.104835	9.818350
9.15	83.7225	3.024897	9.565563	9.65	93.1225	3.106445	9.823441
9.16	83.9056	3.026549	9.570789	9.66	93.3156	3.108054	9.828530
9.17	84.0889	3.028201	9.576012	9.67	93.5089	3.109662	9.833616
9.18	84.2724	3.029851	9.581232	9.68	93.7024	3.111270	9.838699
9.19	84.4561	3.031501	9.586449	9.69	93.8961	3.112876	9.843780
9.20	84.6400	3.033150	9.591663	9.70	94.0900	3.114482	9.848858
9.21	84.8241	3.034798	9.596874	9.71	94.2841	3.116087	9.853933
9.22	85.0084	3.036445	9.602083	9.72	94.4784	3.117691	9.859006
9.23	85.1929	3.038092	9.607289	9.73	94.6729	3.119295	9.864076
9.24	85.3776	3.039737	9.612492	9.74	94.8676	3.120897	9.869144
9.25	85.5625	3.041381	9.617692	9.75	95.0625	3.122499	9.874209
9.26	85.7476	3.043025	9.622889	9.76	95.2576	3.124100	9.879271
9.27	85.9329	3.044667	9.628084	9.77	95.4529	3.125700	9.884331
9.28	86.1184	3.046309	9.633276	9.78	95.6484	3.127299	9.889388
9.29	86.3041	3.047950	9.638465	9.79	95.8441	3.128898	9.894443
9.30	86.4900	3.049590	9.643651	9.80	96.0400	3.130495	9.899495
9.31	86.6761	3.051229	9.648834	9.81	96.2361	3.132092	9.904544
9.32	86.8624	3.052868	9.654015	9.82	96.4324	3.133688	9.909591
9.33	87.0489	3.054505	9.659193	9.83	96.6289	3.135283	9.914636
9.34	87.2356	3.056141	9.664368	9.84	96.8256	3.136877	9.919677
9.35	87.4225	3.057777	9.669540	9.85	97.0225	3.138471	9.924717
9.36	87.6096	3.059412	9.674709	9.86	97.2196	3.140064	9.929753
9.37	87.7969	3.061046	9.679876	9.87	97.4169	3.141656	9.934787
9.38	87.9844	3.062679	9.685040	9.88	97.6144	3.143247	9.939819
9.39	88.1721	3.064311	9.690201	9.89	97.8121	3.144837	9.944848
9.40	88.3600	3.065942	9.695360	9.90	98.0100	3.146427	9.949874
9.41	88.5481	3.067572	9.700515	9.91	98.2081	3.148015	9.954898
9.42	88.7364	3.069202	9.705668	9.92	98.4064	3.149603	9.959920
9.43	88.9249	3.070831	9.710819	9.93	98.6049	3.151190	9.964939
9.44	89.1136	3.072458	9.715966	9.94	98.8036	3.152777	9.969955
9.45	89.3025	3.074085	9.721111	9.95	99.0025	3.154362	9.974969
9.46	89.4916	3.075711	9.726253	9.96	99.2016	3.155947	9.979980
9.47	89.6809	3.077337	9.731393	9.97	99.4009	3.157531	9.984989
9.48	89.8704	3.078961	9.736529	9.98	99.6004	3.159114	9.989995
9.49	90.0601	3.080584	9.741663	9.99	99.8001	3.160696	9.994999

Answers to Odd-Numbered Exercises

Page 22

1. (a) yes, 52 times; (b) no; (c) no; (d) yes, 52 times.

5. 50.00–74.99, 75.00–99.99, 100.00–124.99, 125.00–149.99.

7. The class boundaries are 9.5, 13.5, 17.5, 21.5, 25.5, 29.5, 33.5; the class marks are 11.5, 15.5, 19.5, 23.5, 27.5, 31.5; the class interval is 4.

9. (a) The class frequencies are 5, 18, 27, 22, 6, 1, 1; (b) the cumulative frequencies are 0, 5, 23, 50, 72, 78, 79, 80.

11. (a) The class frequencies are 1, 3, 11, 11, 18, 20, 14, 10, 8, 4, 2; (b) the cumulative frequencies are 1, 4, 15, 26, 44, 64, 78, 88, 96, 100, 102.

15. (a) The frequencies are 28, 4, 6, 4, 0, 1, 2, 1, 0, 1, 14; (b) the class boundaries are 0, 5, 15, 25, 35, 45, 55, 65, 75, 85, 95, 100.

Page 39

5. (a) 420; (b) 420.

7. For arrivals 74,491.83, for departures 73,885.50.

9. 7.966.

11. Let the readings be 9°, −11°, −10°, 4°, 18°, −10°, in which case the mean is 0°.

15. (a) 49; (b) 48.9.

17. 6.08.

19. 98.7.

21. 110.6 as compared to 101.6.

23. (b) 81.6.

25. 4 per cent.

27. 23.47 cents.

29. $2.99.

31. (a) 82.0; (b) 82.4; (c) 91.2.

Page 52

1. 43.7, 44, and 44. **3.** 65.5. **5.** (a) 46; (b) 155.

7. 99.5 and 126.75; median is preferable.

11. (a) 5.62, 8.86, and 7.24; (b) 4.28 and 9.95; (c) 6.02 and 8.50.

13. 5.30, 3.90, and 6.84.

15. (a) $P_9 = 59.5$, stock 60 steaks; (b) $Q_1 = 43.9$, stock 84 steaks.

17. (a) 5.8; (b) 5.88.

19. 19 and 20 each occur 9 times; mid-range is 22.5.

21. $8.00. **23.** Jungle Cruise.

Page 56

1. (a) $x_1 + x_2 + x_3 + x_4$;
(b) $x_1^2 + x_2^2 + x_3^2$;
(c) $(x_1 + y_1) + (x_2 + y_2) + (x_3 + y_3) + (x_4 + y_4) + (x_5 + y_5)$;
(d) $(x_1 + 4) + (x_2 + 4) + (x_3 + 4) + (x_4 + 4) + (x_5 + 4)$;
(e) $x_1y_1 + x_2y_2 + x_3y_3 + x_4y_4 + x_5y_5 + x_6y_6 + x_7y_7 + x_8y_8$;
(f) $x_1f_1 + x_2f_2 + x_3f_3 + x_4f_4$.

3. 8 and 68.

5. $\sum_{i=1}^{n} (x_i - \bar{x}) = \sum_{i=1}^{n} x_i - \sum_{i=1}^{n} \bar{x} = \sum_{i=1}^{n} x_i - n\cdot\bar{x} = n\cdot\bar{x} - n\cdot\bar{x} = 0.$

7. $\bar{x} = \frac{\Sigma\, x_i f_i}{n} = \frac{\Sigma\, (cu_i + x_0)f_i}{n} = \frac{c(\Sigma\, u_i f_i) + x_0(\Sigma\, f_i)}{n} = \frac{c(\Sigma\, u_i f_i)}{n} + \frac{x_0 \cdot n}{n}$

$= c\cdot\bar{u} + x_0.$

9. (a) 30; (b) 30.

Page 70

1. 35 degrees. **3.** 8.6. **5.** 3.33.

7. (a) 10.0; (b) 10.0; (c) 10.0. **9.** 3.98.

11. $\sigma = 2.37$.

13. $s^2 = 0.32$ for the means, and $s^2 = 1.38$ for the medians.

15. (a) 5.89; (b) 5.89; (c) 4.33. **21.** 624 students.

23. Sell Stock B; it is relatively furthest above its average price.

25. Dr. A is relatively most expensive.

27. 25.1 per cent.

29. 20.1 per cent.

31. 2.92, 2.68, and 2.93 per cent.

33. (a) yes; (b) yes; (c) no; (d) yes; (e) no.

Page 76

1. 0.03.

3. 0.32.

5. $\alpha_4 = 3.2$ and $\alpha_4 = 2.6$.

Page 93

3. There are 36 ways of making sales on Monday, Tuesday, and Wednesday.

5. 60.

7. (a) 12; (b) 6; (c) 3.

9. 378.

11. 180 ways; 45 ways and 12 ways.

13. (a) (2, 2), (2, 1), (1, 1), (1, 2);
(b) (1, 1), (2, 2), (3, 3), (4, 4), (5, 5), (6, 6);
(c) (1, 1), (1, 2), (1, 3), (1, 4), (1, 5), (1, 6), (2, 1), (3, 1), (4, 1), (5, 1), (6, 1);
(d) (1, 1), (1, 2), (2, 1), (6, 6).

15. (a) (0, 4), (0, 3), (0, 2), (0, 1), (0, 0), (1, 0), (2, 0), (3, 0), (4, 0) (5, 0);
(b) (1, 1), (2, 0), (0, 2), (0, 4), (1, 3), (2, 2), (3, 1), (4, 0), (2, 4), (3, 3), (4, 2), (5, 1);
(c) (0, 0), (1, 1), (2, 2), (3, 3), (4, 4);
(d) (0, 4), (0, 3), (0, 2), (0, 1), (0, 0), (1, 0), (2, 0), (3, 0), (4, 0), (5, 0), (1, 1), (1, 3), (2, 2), (3, 1), (2, 4), (3, 3), (4, 2), (5, 1);
(e) (0, 4), (0, 2), (2, 0), (4, 0);
(f) (1, 1), (2, 0), (0, 2), (0, 4), (1, 3), (2, 2), (3, 1), (4, 0), (2, 4), (3, 3), (4, 2), (5, 1), (0, 0), (4, 4);
(g) (0, 4), (0, 3), (0, 2), (0, 1), (0, 0), (1, 0), (2, 0), (3, 0), (4, 0), (5, 0), (1, 1), (2, 2), (3, 3), (4, 4);
(h) (0, 4), (0, 3), (0, 2), (0, 1), (1, 0), (2, 0), (3, 0), (4, 0), (5, 0);
(i) (2, 1), (2, 3), (1, 2), (1, 4), (3, 2), (3, 4), (4, 1), (4, 3), (4, 4), (5, 2), (5, 3), (5, 4).

17. (a) (3, 2), (4, 1);
(b) (1, 1), (2, 2), (3, 3);
(c) (2, 1), (2, 2), (3, 1), (3, 2), (3, 3), (4, 1), (4, 2), (4, 3);
(d) (2, 1), (3, 1), (3, 2), (4, 1), (4, 2), (4, 3);
(e) (3, 2), (4, 1), (2, 1), (3, 1), (4, 2), (4, 3);
(f) none;
(g) (2, 1), (3, 1), (3, 2), (4, 1), (4, 2), (4, 3);
(h) (2, 1), (3, 1), (3, 2), (4, 1), (4, 2), (4, 3).

23. 27 students.

Page 104

1. (a) The probability of no drop in barometric pressure; (b) the probability of a rise in temperature; (c) the probability of a drop in barometric pressure and also a rise in temperature; (d) the probability of a drop in barometric pressure or no rise in temperature; (e) the probability of neither a drop in barometric pressure nor a rise in temperature.

3. The proportion of heads has increased from 0.30 to 0.36, which is entirely in accordance with the law of large numbers.

5. (a) 0.75; (b) 0.40; (c) 0.85; (d) 0; (e) 1; (f) 0.15.

7. (a) To his advantage; (b) fair; (c) to his disadvantage.

9. Part (c) would be fair, and part (a) would be to his greatest advantage.

11. (a) The probability is greater than or equal to 1/5; (b) the probability is less than 1/5.

13. His probability that he will get seasick is greater than or equal to 1/10.

15. (a) $P(A \cup A') = P(S) = 1$; hence, $P(A) + P(A') = 1$, and since $P(A') \geqslant 0$, it follows that $P(A) \leqslant 1$; (b) $P(S \cup \varnothing) = P(S) + P(\varnothing) = 1 + P(\varnothing)$; since $S \cup \varnothing = S$, $P(S \cup \varnothing) = P(S) = 1$ and, hence, $1 + P(\varnothing) = 1$ and $P(\varnothing) = 0$.

Page 109

1. The claims of the first and third economists cannot be correct; for the first the sum of the probabilities is less than 1, and for the third the sum of the probabilities is greater than 1.

3. (a) not permissible, the sum of the probabilities exceeds 1; (b) permissible; (c) not permissible, one of the probabilities is negative; (d) permissible.

5. (a) 0.81; (b) 0.81; (c) 0.64.

7. (a) 0.51; (b) 0.51; (c) 0.72.

9. (a) 1/5; (b) 7/10; (c) 9/10; (d) 9/10; (e) 1/5; (f) 9/10; (g) 0; (h) 1/10.

11. (a) 2/5; (b) 13/50; (c) 11/50; (d) 2/25.

13. (a) 1/6; (b) 2/3; (c) 5/36; (d) 2/9.

15. (a) 0.37; (b) 0.72; (c) 0.80; (d) 0.52; (e) 0.83; (f) 0.20.

17. (a) 0.42; (b) 0.92.

Page 119

1. (a) The probability that a person discharged from the armed forces who returns to his home town will get married within a year; (b) the probability that a person discharged from the armed forces who does not return to his home town will immediately find work; (c) the probability that a person discharged from the armed services who immediately finds work will get married within a year; (d) the probability that a person discharged from the armed services who returns to his home town will immediately find work and get married within a year; (e) the probability that a person discharged from the armed services who returns to his home town and finds work immediately will get married within a year; (f) the probability that a person discharged from the armed services who does not return to his home town will neither get married within a year nor immediately find work.

3. (a) The probability that there will be a drop in barometric pressure, given that there is a rise in temperature; (b) the probability that there will be a rise in temperature, given that there is a drop in barometric pressure; (c) the probability that there will be a rise in temperature, given that there is no drop in barometric pressure; (d) the probability that there will be no drop in barometric pressure, given that there is no rise in temperature.

5. (a) 0; (b) 0.90; (c) 0; (d) 0; (e) 0.60; (f) 1.

7. (a) 2/3; (b) 51/180; (c) 53/120; (d) 9/40; (e) 11/40; (f) 53/86; (g) 27/80; (h) 33/40; (i) 53/80.

9. (a) 3/10; (b) 5/9; (c) 3/7; (d) 11/25.

11. 2/9.

13. (a) 66/190; (b) 15/190; (c) 36/95; (d) 6/95.

15. (a) 0.40; (b) 0.40; (c) 0.50; (d) 0.50.

17. *a*, *c*, and *f*.

19. 0.0063.

21. (a) 13/24; (b) 9/13.

23. 0.705.

25. (a) 0.31; (b) 0.18.

27. 3/4.

29. (a) 0.15; (b) 0.35.

Page 128

1. \$0.60.

3. \$5.00.

5. \$13,200.

7. Not worthwhile, expectation is \$0.43.

9. $5\frac{13}{16}$ games and $\frac{5}{8}$ games.

11. 2.62 persons.

13. Value exceeds \$50.00.

15. His probability is 0.20.

17. 0.128.

19. In either case, the mathematical expectation is \$5.00 if one decides between "red" and "white" by flipping a coin. These fifty-fifty odds for making the right choice cannot be improved even if one knows that the box contains 50 red marbles and 50 white marbles.

Page 140

1. (a) He should sell now; (b) he should not sell now; (d) he should sell now.

3. (a) Hotel A; (b) Hotel B.

5. (a) 2,000 boxes; (b) 3,000 boxes.

7. Buy Batch 2.

9. (a) Strategies I and 2, value is 6; (b) strategies II and 1, value is 8; (c) strategies I and 1, value is -1; (d) strategies I and 2, value is 2.

11. (a) There is a saddle point corresponding to strategies III and 2, the value is 0; (b) there are saddle points corresponding to strategies II and 3, IV and 3, II and 4, and IV and 4; the value is 4.

13. (a) 5/11 and 6/11; (b) 4/11 and 7/11; (c) 13/11.

15. (b) Player A should assign his two strategies probabilities of 2/3 and 1/3. Player B should assign his three strategies probabilities of 2/3, 1/3, and 0; the value is 12.

19. The country should randomize the choice of its strategies with probabilities of 1/6 and 5/6; the enemy should randomize with probabilities of 5/6 and 1/6: the value is $1,033,333.

21. 1/2 and 1/2.

23. Prepare 3,000 boxes.

25. Randomize the choice with probabilities of 3/10 and 7/10.

Page 148

1. No cakes at all.

3. 16.5, the mid-range.

5. (a) 17, the mode; (b) 18, the median; (c) 19, the mean; (d) 20, the mid-range.

Page 156

1. (b) 2/5; (c) 4/5.

3. 720 ways.

5. (a) 120; (b) 720.

7. (c) 1, 6, 15, 20, 15, 6, 1.

9. 56.

11. 158,918,760.

13. (a) 420; (b) 3,326,400.

17. (a) 0.146; (b) 0.056; (c) 0.0035.

19. 0.237.

21. The probability of this happening is 0.006; he should be surprised.

23. 0.2352.

25. (a) 0.491; (b) 0.193; (c) 0.049.

27. 0.274.

29. (a) 0.140; (b) 0.093; (c) 0.045.

31. The probability that Mr. Butler is right becomes 0.21; the probability that Mr. Daniels is right becomes 0.79.

33. 0.13, 0.30, and 0.57.

35. 0.69 and 0.31.

37. (a) Accept $p = 0.02$; (b) 0.07, 0.36, and 0.57; (c) accept $p = 0.03$.

Page 167

1. $3\frac{2}{3}$.

5. (a) $\mu = 450$ and $\sigma = 15$; (b) $\mu = 125$ and $\sigma = 10$; (c) $\mu = 120$ and $\sigma = \sqrt{48}$; (d) $\mu = 20$ and $\sigma = \sqrt{15}$.

7. $\mu = 1.196$ and $\sigma^2 = 1.184$.

9. The probability is less than 0.16.

11. The probability is less than 0.15; actual value of the probability is 0.007.

Page 178

1. (a) 0.259, 0.449, and 0.074; (b) 0.551 and 0.099; (c) 0.223.

3. (a) 1.14; (b) 0.54; (c) -0.24; (d) -2.43; (e) 1.38.

5. (a) 1.28; (b) 1.64; (c) 1.96; (d) 2.05; (e) 2.33; (f) 2.58.

7. $\sigma = 10$.

Page 186

1. (a) 0.009; (b) 0.337; (c) 0.799.

3. 33 per cent or about 1,320.

5. 0.0918 and 0.0062.

7. (a) 0.06; (b) 0.06.

9. 0.0228.

11. 0.008.

13. 0.30.

15. 0.1635.

Page 196

1. (a) 10; (b) 190; (c) 1,225.

3. *abc, abd, abe, acd, ace, ade, bcd, bce, bde, cde*. The probability is 3/5 for each element.

5. 1 and 2, 1 and 3, 1 and 4, 1 and 5, 1 and 6, 1 and 7, 1 and 8, 2 and 3, 2 and 4, 2 and 5, 2 and 6, 2 and 7, 2 and 8, 3 and 4, 3 and 5, 3 and 6, 3 and 7, 3 and 8, 4 and 5, 4 and 6, 4 and 7, 4 and 8, 5 and 6, 5 and 7, 5 and 8, 6 and 7, 6 and 8, 7 and 8; each element is contained in 7 of the 28 samples; the odds are 3 to 1 *against it*.

9. (a) Not all voters have telephones; there are apt to be fewer telephones among those having lower incomes; (b) longer logs have a better chance of being included in a sample than shorter logs; (c) there are apt to be fewer replies from those who are relatively unsuccessful; (d) people are likely to say yes even if they don't; (e) there is apt to be confusion since Frigidaire is often used as a generic term for refrigerators in general; (f) certain names are more common among persons belonging to particular groups.

11. (a) 115 and 125, 115 and 135, 115 and 185, 115 and 195, 115 and 205, 125 and 135, 125 and 185, 125 and 195, 125 and 205, 135 and 185, 135 and 195, 135 and 205, 185 and 195, 185 and 205, 195 and 205; the means are 120, 125, 150, 155, 160, 130, 155, 160, 165, 160, 165, 170, 190, 195, 200;
(b) 115 and 185, 115 and 195, 115 and 205, 125 and 185, 125 and 195, 125 and 205, 135 and 185, 135 and 195, 135 and 205; the means are 150, 155, 160, 155, 160, 165, 160, 165, 170;
(c) 115 and 125, 115 and 135, 125 and 135, 185 and 195, 185 and 205, 195 and 205; the means are 120, 125, 130, 190, 195, 200.

Page 213

1. (b) 0 and 2, 0 and 4, 0 and 6, 0 and 8, 0 and 10, 2 and 4, 2 and 6, 2 and 8, 2 and 10, 4 and 6, 4 and 8, 4 and 10, 6 and 8, 6 and 10, 8 and 10; the means are 1, 2, 3, 4, 5, 3, 4, 5, 6, 5, 6, 7, 7, 8, 9;
(c) the probabilities for 1, 2, 3, 4, 5, 6, 7, 8, and 9 are, respectively, 1/15, 1/15, 2/15, 2/15, 3/15, 2/15, 2/15, 1/15, 1/15;
(d) $\mu_{\bar{x}} = 5$ and $\sigma_{\bar{x}} = \sqrt{14/3}$.

5. The means are 9.6, 9.0, 9.3, 9.4, 9.6, 10.8, 10.7, 10.2, 10.7, 9.8, 9.3, 9.6, 7.5, 10.3, 8.7, 9.4, 7.1, 9.5, 9.3, 9.9; the mean is 9.485 and the standard deviation is 0.92.

7. 1.67; fairly close to the "experimental" value of 1.55.

9. (a) It is reduced to 1/2 of what it was; (b) it is reduced to 1/3 of what it was; (c) it is reduced to 1/10 of what it was.

11. 0.84; there is a fifty-fifty chance that the mean of a random sample of size 100 taken from this population will differ from the population mean by less than 0.84.

15. (a) The probability is at least 0.36; (b) the probability is 0.7888.

17. 0.0918.

Page 233

1. The error is less than 0.0608 gm. **3.** $41{,}941 < \mu < 43{,}059$.

5. (a) The error is less than 0.039 seconds; (b) $11.70 < \mu < 11.80$.

7. 0.978. **9.** $n = 62$. **11.** $n = 130$.

13. The error is less than \$0.86.

17. $7.8 < \mu < 16.2$.

19. The error is less than 1.39 gallons.

21. (a) $61.8 < \mu < 75.2$; (b) the error is less than 8.5 minutes.

23. $\$235.35 < \mu < \$260.03$.

25. (a) 0.43; (b) 0.60; (c) \$1,495.76; (d) \$1,476.20; (e) differences are relatively small.

27. (a) 738; (b) 715; (c) 720.

29. (a) We can assert that μ lies between \$1,158 and \$1,796; (b) the distributor can assert that μ lies between 705.9 and 734.1; (c) the professor can assert that μ lies between 63.0 and 67.6.

Page 248

1. Type II error; Type I error.

3. Type I error; Type II error.

5. (a) Commercial is not effective; (b) commercial is effective.

7. (a) 0.1164; (b) 0.01, 0.09, 0.35, 0.72, 0.72, 0.35, 0.09, 0.01.

11. (a) $\mu_2 > \mu_1$, and buy new machine only if this alternative can be accepted; (b) $\mu_2 < \mu_1$, and buy new machine unless this alternative can be accepted.

Page 257

1. $z = -3.37$; reject the police chief's claim.

3. $z = 6.77$; reject the null hypothesis $\mu = \$108.65$.

5. $z = -1.83$; the hypothesis $\mu = 10$ seconds cannot be rejected.

7. $z = 1.69$; no adjustment required.

9. $t = 2.92$; reject the claim.

11. $t = -2.09$; the null hypothesis $\mu = 2{,}500$ cannot be rejected.

13. $t = -1.17$; this supports the claim.

15. $z = 2.94$; difference is significant.

17. Null hypothesis $\mu_1 - \mu_2 = 2.5$ hours; alternative hypothesis $\mu_1 - \mu_2 < 2.5$ hours; $z = -0.24$ and the null hypothesis cannot be rejected.

19. $t = 1.87$; difference is not significant.

21. $t = -2.80$; no, difference is significant.

23. $t = -2.65$; cannot reject the null hypothesis, that is, evidence is not sufficient to prove diet effective.

Page 265

1. $3.1 < \sigma < 8.2$. **3.** $0.30 < \sigma < 0.92$.

5. (a) $2.19 < \sigma < 3.90$; (b) $2.19 < \sigma < 3.87$.

7. $0.568 < \sigma < 0.682$. **9.** 17.3.

Page 270

1. $\chi^2 = 26.0$; reject the null hypothesis.

3. $\chi^2 = 5.26$; the null hypothesis $\sigma = 7.5$ cannot be rejected.

5. $z = 0.7$; null hypothesis cannot be rejected.

7. $F = 2.59$; assumption is reasonable.

Page 279

1. $0.18 < p < 0.26$. **3.** $0.51 < p < 0.85$.

5. (a) $0.62 < p < 0.68$; (b) the error is less than 0.030.

7. (a) $0.54 < p < 0.66$; (b) $0.545 < p < 0.655$.

9. (a) $0.48 < p < 0.58$; (b) $0.481 < p < 0.579$.

11. (a) $0.182 < p < 0.263$; (b) $0.12 < p < 0.42$.

13. $n = 601$ (rounded up). **15.** $n = 457$ (rounded up).

17. $n = 421$ (rounded up) and $n = 316$ (rounded up).

19. 0.115. **21.** 0.214.

Page 284

1. $z = 1.21$; cannot reject the null hypothesis that the figure still applies.

3. $z = -1.78$; accept the alternative hypothesis that $p < 0.85$.

5. $z = -1.76$; cannot reject the claim.

7. $z = 1.39$; the muscle relaxant is effective.

9. $z = 1.87$; null hypothesis cannot be rejected.

Page 290

1. $z = -0.59$; cannot reject the null hypothesis.

3. $z = 2.18$; reject the null hypothesis that the machines are equally good.

5. (a) $z = 1.65$; proportion is more than 0.10 higher; (b) $z = 2.47$; proportion is at least 0.20 higher.

7. $\chi^2 = 4.738$, $z^2 = 4.75$.

9. $\chi^2 = 0.722$; cannot reject the null hypothesis that the probability is the same for each vendor.

Page 297

1. $\chi^2 = 15.45$; reject null hypothesis of independence.

3. $\chi^2 = 0.04$; no significant differences of opinion.

5. $\chi^2 = 42.45$; there is a relationship.

7. (a) 0.17; (b) 0.34.

13. $\chi^2 = 0.29$; excellent fit.

Page 308

1. (a) $F = \dfrac{228}{130/9} = 15.8$; reject the null hypothesis;

(b)

Source of Variation	*Degrees of Freedom*	*Sum of Squares*	*Mean Square*	*F*
Treatments	2	456	228	15.8
Error	9	130	130/9	
Total	11	586		

5.

Source of Variation	*Degrees of Freedom*	*Sum of Squares*	*Mean Square*	*F*
Treatments	2	173	86.5	0.41
Error	12	2,522	210	
Total	14	2,695		

Cannot reject the null hypothesis.

7. $F = 3.38$, which equals t^2.

Page 313

1.

Source of Variation	*Degrees of Freedom*	*Sum of Squares*	*Mean Square*	*F*
Treatments	2	8.9	4.45	1.79
Blocks	2	156.2	78.1	31.5
Error	4	9.9	2.48	
Total	8	175.0		

Differences among the varieties of wheat are not significant; differences among the fertilizers are significant.

3.

Source of Variation	*Degrees of Freedom*	*Sum of Squares*	*Mean Square*	*F*
Treatments	2	32	16	0.18
Blocks	7	2,922	417.4	4.64
Error	14	1,260	90	
Total	23	4,214		

Differences among treatments (salesmen) are not significant; differences among blocks (weeks) are significant.

5.

Source of Variation	*Degrees of Freedom*	*Sum of Squares*	*Mean Square*	*F*
Treatments	2	50.84	25.42	4.43
Blocks	3	293.69	97.90	17.06
Error	6	34.47	5.74	
Total	11	379.00		

Differences among launchers are not significant; differences among fuels are significant.

Page 318

1. $z = 2.53$; reject the null hypothesis.

3. $z = 2.64$; reject the null hypothesis.

7. $z = 2.83$; reject the null hypothesis.

Page 324

1. $z = 2.92$; it is not reasonable.

3. $z - 2.0$; reject the null hypothesis.

5. (a) $z = -0.15$; null hypothesis cannot be rejected; (b) $z = 2.88$; reject the null hypothesis.

7. $H = 11.96$; differences are significant.

Page 329

5. $z = -2.5$; reject the null hypothesis; that is, the population means are not equal.

7. $z = -4.01$; the arrangement is not random.

Page 340

1. (a) $a = -2.91$ and $b = 0.76$; (b) $b = 0.76$ and $a = -2.90$; (c) 11.54.

3. $y' = 98.9 - 0.0039x$; 85.1°.

5. (a) $y' = 4.86 + 1.19x$; (b) 16.8; (c) 17.0.

9. $\log y = 3.8118 - 1.04(\log x)$ or $y = 6480x^{-1.04}$; \$8.37.

11. The values for the years 1933 through 1960 are 462.6, 490.2, 530.2, 525.0, 557.4, 597.4, 655.4, 722.4, 801.8, 840.6, 858.8, 846.2, 814.8, 788.6, 758.2, 766.6, 770.0, 763.8, 767.6, 778.6, 768.8, 751.0, 737.2, 717.4, 724.8, 719.0, 711.6, 717.8.

13. $y = 1.460 + 11.696x_1 + 0.289x_2$; 30 pounds.

Page 350

1. 3.0; difference is due to rounding.

3. (a) $t = 1.48$; cannot reject null hypothesis; (b) $t = 1.11$; cannot reject null hypothesis; (c) $t = -3.39$; reject the null hypothesis.

5. (a) $-6.17 < \alpha < 0.35$; (b) $93.2 < \alpha < 104.6$.

7. $t = 1.96$; null hypothesis cannot be rejected.

9. (a) 57.5 – 74.7; (b) 5.80 – 17.28; (c) 51.3 – 102.9 or 51.3 – 100 if maximum grade is 100.

Page 361

1. 0.77; significant.

3. 0.95; significant.

5. 0.79; significant.

7. 0.999.

9. (a) 0.98, 0.65, 0.45, 0.33, 0.22, compared to 0.878, 0.632, 0.444, 0.325, 0.217; (b) 0.26, 0.13, and 0.08; (c) correlation is not significant.

Page 369

1. 0.68; significant.

3. −0.98.

5. 0.94; significant.

7. 0.69.

9. −0.80.

Page 375

1. 0.63.

3. 0.56.

Index